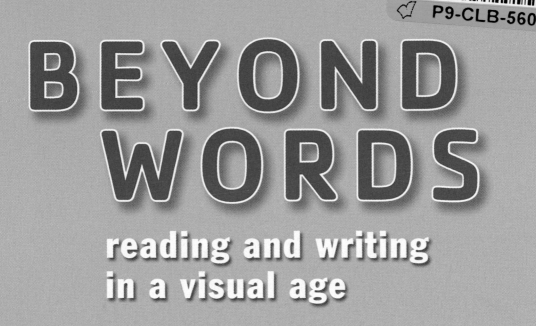

BEYOND WORDS

reading and writing in a visual age

John Ruszkiewicz
University of Texas at Austin

Daniel Anderson
University of North Carolina at Chapel Hill

Christy Friend
University of South Carolina

PEARSON
Longman

New York Boston San Francisco
London Toronto Sydney Tokyo Singapore Madrid
Mexico City Munich Paris Cape Town Hong Kong Montreal

Senior Acquisitions Editor: Lynn M. Huddon
Development Editor: Michael S. Greer
Senior Marketing Manager: Alexandra Rivas-Smith
Senior Supplements Editor: Donna Campion
Media Supplements Editor: Jenna Egan
Production Manager: Ellen MacElree
Project Coordination and Electronic Page Makeup: Nesbitt Graphics
Text Design: Original concepts by Elliot Kreloff. Final design by GGS Book Services, Inc.
Cover Design Manager: Wendy Ann Fredericks
Cover Designer: Dorling Kindersley
Cover Art: Top to bottom from left to right. *First row*: Milton Glaser, Designer; Scala/Art
Resource; and Marc Riboud/Magnum Photos *Second row:* Photofest; Rick Friedman/
Corbis; and Steve McCurry/Magnum Photos *Third row:* SSPL/The Image Works;
AP/Wide World Photos; and Grant Wood, American Gothic, 1930, Oil on beaver board,
Friends of American Art Collection, 1930.934, Photograph by Bob Hashimoto,
Reproduction, The Art Institute of Chicago *Fourth row:* Mark Ulriksen/The New Yorker;
Jon Foster; and Coles Hairston
Photo Researcher: Photosearch Inc.
Manufacturing Manager: Mary Fischer
Printer and Binder: Courier Kendallville
Cover Printer: Coral Graphic Services

For permission to use copyrighted material, grateful acknowledgment is made to the
copyright holders on page 599, which is hereby made part of this copyright page.

Library of Congress Cataloging-in-Publication Data on file with the Library of Congress.

Please visit our website at http://www.ablongman.com/beyondwords

ISBN 0-321-27601-9

1 2 3 4 5 6 7 8 9 10—CRK—08 07 06 05

Contents

CHAPTER **3**
Picturing Ourselves:
Writing to Express Identities 74

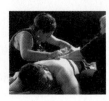

INTERLUDE **1**
Henriata Nicholas 154

Uhi Ta Moko: Designs Carved in Skin

CHAPTER **4**

Seeing Places: Writing to Describe Landscapes and Environments 160

CONTENTS

INTERLUDE **2**
Milton Glaser 240

A Conversation about Designing Restaurants

v

CHAPTER 6
Mapping Ideas:
Writing to Inform and Explain 330

INTERLUDE 4
Robin Williams and John Tollett 418

Evaluating a Web Site

INTERLUDE **5**
Kurtis Harris 510
Crime Scene Photography

CHAPTER **8**
Debating Culture: Writing to Advocate and Persuade 516

Preface

The eye of man hath not heard, the ear of man hath not seen, man's hand is not able to taste, his tongue to conceive, nor his heart to report, what my dream was.

—BOTTOM
Shakespeare's *Midsummers Night's Dream*

Shakespeare's comic character Nick Bottom is transformed into a donkey and then shares a potion-induced love affair with the Queen of Fairies before awakening to recognize that the world can be strange and hard to comprehend. For many of us, awakening to the latest transformations in communication and technology can seem equally disorienting. Others just take it for granted that their telephones can send pictures or text messages. The reality is, we're often working at the edges of media and communication that are rooted in the past but also transforming knowledge in the present. We're now connected to electronic pulses that blossom into words, sounds, and images and then morph into messages that are simultaneously new and familiar. In this environment, the ways we read and write and what we consider to be "texts" inevitably shift and take on new meanings.

We wrote *Beyond Words* in large part to respond to the challenges raised by these transformations in communication and composition, challenges that call for both students and instructors to develop instincts for understanding media of all sorts. The book presents a rich array of visual and verbal texts that invite writers to respond in familiar and innovative ways—including six full chapters of material carefully introduced and set into challenging thematic contexts. But *Beyond Words* does much more.

Readings and Organization

What distinguishes *Beyond Words* is the powerful way it connects new kinds of media to a familiar sequence of assignments that writing teachers can adapt easily to their existing course goals and designs. If they offer thematic courses, they'll find powerful and timely topics in every chapter. If they structure their courses rhetorically, they'll find a logical sequence of assignments in the book, from personal writing to public argument. The readings and visual texts in the six core chapters provide a sturdy framework for many kinds of writing courses:

The readings and assignments in Chapter 3, "Picturing Ourselves," for example, examine identity and portraiture across a wide range of cultures and traditions. Students might respond to these materials with biographies, arguments concerning identity or society, photo essays, collages, or other types of compositions. The texts in the chapter and the responses to them might be presented to students as examples of expressive writing–but they do not have to be.

We've taken a similar approach with subsequent chapters, encouraging instructors to explore the materials in different ways and to follow different sequences, depending on their pedagogical preferences. An instructor interested in themes of culture and identity might emphasize Chapters 3 through 5, which focus on people, their environments, and their stories. An instructor more invested in political and social themes might prefer the issues related to technology, design, and cultural memory explored in Chapters 6 through 8.

And of course, an instructor hoping to expose students to a variety of rhetorical situations can find in the overall sequence of chapters many works, examples, and assignments, ranging from expressive images to argumentative texts. We believe that the coherent framework of the book, built around thematic concerns and a flexible sequence of writing activities, will help students engage a variety of texts, allowing them to say, "Wow, let me think. . . ." rather than "Whoa, what do I do with this?"

We want students to be surprised and challenged by the range of materials in *Beyond Words*. We include essays in numerous traditional nonfiction genres: personal reflections, manifestos, columns, op-ed pieces, news stories, technical analyses, reviews, and arguments. We also offer fiction of several kinds, including poems and selections from novels. But we have added many examples of texts less common in collections for writing courses: photographs, photo essays, Web sites, Web essays, magazine covers, song lyrics, montages, film stills, print ads and TV commercials, cartoons, graphic novels, maps, MRIs, bumper stickers, and much more. If we've done our job well, students will come away from *Beyond Words* appreciating exactly what the title means.

Pedagogical Innovation

Beyond Words breaks new ground, too, by being an anthology that offers all the support most students will require to move from reading to writing. That's no small claim. The varied and sometimes eye-catching selections throughout the anthology certainly invite students to think about a wide range of topics and issues. But the tougher challenge is moving them to respond to the selections powerfully or to create texts of their own. Tip boxes, checklists, or exercises alone won't do it—though *Beyond Words* offers such features. What's required is a strategy for instruction built deep into the structure of the book that provides students with the concepts, tools, and examples they need to compose successfully. Not surprisingly, that instruction begins with an innovative pair of opening chapters that frame the book's pedagogical strategy.

CHAPTER 1 **Paying Attention: Reading Texts** Using commonsense questions as a guide and a series of lively examples, this chapter provides students with a method for reading texts of all kinds. The questions introduce many important rhetorical concepts without weighing students down with unfamiliar terminology or jargon:

- **What do you see?**
- **What is it about?**
- **To what does it relate?**
- **How is it composed?**
- **What details matter?**

The responses to these questions are equally fresh and provocative. The chapter encourages students to approach texts with both their eyes and their minds open. They'll quickly discover that the five questions generate many possible and valid answers, some of them even contradictory. And that's the point—to move readers beyond their initial gut responses to texts toward more nuanced and complex appreciations. Just as important, the strategies introduced here provide a framework for the introductory sections in each anthology chapter (Chapters 3–8), offering a consistent framework for analysis.

CHAPTER 2 **Getting Attention: Composing Texts** What Chapter 1 does for reading, Chapter 2 does for writing, setting out a series of questions that will guide all the major writing assignments and projects in the book:

- **What's it to you?**
- **What do you want to say about it?**

- Who will listen?
- What do you need to know?
- How will you do it?
- How well does it work?

In addition to giving students a supportive heuristic for composing in many different media (writing foremost), the chapter makes it clear that students have a responsibility to engage with a world growing ever more complex.

The anthology chapters (3–8) build upon these opening chapters, using the ideas and strategies they introduce to lead students through texts many will find unfamiliar and challenging. These chapters have their own pedagogical sequence.

- **Signature images selected to provoke response.** Each chapter begins with a thought-provoking pair of images. For example, a bare-chested Eminem and a Renaissance courtier vie for attention on the opening pages of Chapter 3 on identity, while a Hummer H2 and contrasting Toyota Prius open Chapter 7 on design. The images are followed by a thought-provoking analysis, a model for the kind of reading the chapter itself will encourage from students.

- **Detailed guides to reading.** Having seen and read about a provocative text, students are given detailed advice about reading related texts, both verbal and visual. That advice comes in the answers to the questions first posed in Chapter 1, now varied slightly to fit the theme of the chapter and illustrated by numerous examples so that students are encouraged to think about portraits (or narratives, or maps, or arguments) in fertile ways. Students considering issues of identity while reading Chapter 3, for example, will immediately encounter images by Walker Evans and Dorothea Lange, a poem by Billy Collins, and even some very bad ID photos. Because the basic questions repeat in each chapter, they become a tool for reading that students can use long after they're finished with *Beyond Words*. This section also leads, naturally, into the anthology selections within the chapter.

- **Clustered selections.** The readings and media texts in the anthology chapters are arranged thematically, giving instructors more options for teaching. The clusters provide students with multiple perspectives on a given topic, making for more nuanced responses. In Chapter 8, on argument, for example, are clusters on three broad subjects: of "Rocking the Vote," "Pushing the Hot Buttons," and "Making Our Place in History."

- **Innovative Assignments and Projects.** Each anthology chapter ends with two fully developed assignments or projects that can become the focal point for instruction throughout the chapter. These assignments are explained fully, drawing on the questions first introduced in Chapter 2 as a guide to composing. Students will see the familiar terms and know how to get started. Unlike books that offer scant instruction for helping students move beyond analysis of new media, we offer significant opportunities for students to practice writing and to compose a variety of texts. Our approach is to cover a number of options, ranging from familiar print essays to essays incorporating and discussing images to innovative multimedia projects. The assignments are always based on realistic assessments of what a college student might manage in a few weeks: an identity collage, a research essay, a multimedia profile, a rhetorical analysis, a visual argument, and so on. Students working with new ideas and media need to see examples of the projects they are being asked to create and *Beyond Words* provides such examples in each chapter as part of all the major writing assignments. The samples vary from traditional essays to multimedia projects. They also demonstrate a range of sophistication and media savvy.

Special Features

Even at a glance, *Beyond Words* looks like a different kind of anthology, visually rich and layered with features consistent with its emphasis on media, art, technology, and letters. And that impression is accurate. Students and instructors alike will be surprised by what they find between its covers. Here are some highlights.

- **An extraordinary design consistent with the aims of the book.** *Beyond Words* had to look good, and it does. Its four-color design accommodates its wide range of features, texts, and images and encourages students to browse. Yet it is clean and uncluttered, enabling users to find what they need quickly and to know where they are in any chapter.

- **Interludes that showcase people engaged in multimedia activities and projects.** Inserted between most of the chapters in *Beyond Words*, the Interludes take readers into the worlds of tattoo artist Henriata Nicholas, crime scene photographer Kurtis Harris, graphic designer Milton Glaser, children's author Maira Kalman, Web designer Robin Williams, and snowboard and surf photographer Jon Foster. These richly illustrated sections take readers to primary sources, people who live in worlds where images and texts work together every day.

- **Innovative exercises to prompt careful reading and appealing writing.** Can exercises be special? They have to be in an anthology that deals with so vast an array of texts and media. *Beyond Words* attaches a sequence of prompts to most major texts and images, even introductory material.

Attentive reading is the aim of numerous **Consider** exercises; **Compose** exercises ask for written responses to the text at hand; **Challenge** exercises ask students to stretch themselves a bit, to go beyond an individual text or reading or to look at a reading from a different perspective. The exercise choices are tailored to individual selections: When an item doesn't suggest a Challenge prompt, for example, none is offered.

- **Writing Tip boxes.** Writing Tip boxes complement the writing instruction built deep into the structure of *Beyond Words*. These remarkably detailed guides offer writers help precisely when and where they need it. For example, when an exercise asks students to consider composing a proposal, a Writing Tip box gives them specific advice about choice of topic, organization, and language.

- **FYI boxes.** In addition, numerous FYI boxes provide important or unexpected bits of information about authors or images in the anthology, adding one more layer of interest.

We hope students find the materials in *Beyond Words* relevant to their lives, and we want them to develop and defend their own responses to the texts they engage. We want them to capitalize on their technological instincts but also to understand them and critique them powerfully. We want them to cultivate a sense of history and connection without losing the thrill of living in revolutionary times. And we want to give teachers a tool for connecting their courses in writing or rhetoric to environments their students will find both exciting and challenging.

Supplements

Our **Companion Website**, www.ablongman.com/beyondwords, prompts students to continue thinking critically about the works and ideas covered in *Beyond Words*. Tutorials on reading visual and verbal texts, composing texts, researching and documenting visual sources, and using images in documents provide guided practice in these skills, keyed to the book's core questions on reading and composing texts. Integrated Web icons connect featured verbal and visual texts in the book with additional contexts, writing prompts, and online resources on the site. Activities and assignments, additional student work, and related composing and design projects are included on the site for each chapter and of all our interludes. Our Web site also includes resources for instructors, including links and resources on visual literacy, writing with and about images, reading checklists and other handouts, and information on how to use *Beyond Words* in conjunction with the WPA outcomes statement.

MyCompLab provides multimedia resources for students and teachers on one easy-to-use site. On this site, students will find guided assistance through each step of the writing process including activities that prompt students to respond to videos, images, Web sites, and conventional texts; *Exchange*, Longman's online peer-review program; the "Avoiding Plagiarism" tutorial; diagnostic grammar tests and more than 3500 practice exercises; and *Research Navigator*™, research paper guide with *AutoCite* bibliography maker program and searchable databases of credible academic sources; and access to Longman's English Tutor Center. Tour the site at **www.mycomplab.com**.

Written by Christy Friend and Lee Bauknight, the **Instructor's Resource Manual** provides teachers with clear and concise strategies for using *Beyond Words*. in a variety of courses. The IRM outlines practical classroom approaches to help teachers prepare their students to read, analyze, and write about visual and verbal texts in several genres. To this end, the manual includes sample course syllabi as well as specific teaching ideas, reading and writing exercises and prompts, and lists of additional resources for each chapter of *Beyond Words*.

Acknowledgments

Obviously, a book as wide-ranging as *Beyond Words* required the talents and assistance of many people. The book simply would not exist without the determination of our editor, Lynn Huddon, who had a spirited vision for this project, extraordinary standards for its execution, and the skill to assemble a team that truly enjoyed working together. The book also owes much to the encouragement, creativity, and expertise of our development editor, Michael Greer.

The design and production of *Beyond Words* reflects the creative energy of a talented team, including Rubin Pfeffer, Janet Lanphier, Ellen MacElree, Kathy Smith, Jerilyn Bockorick, and Laura Coaty. We're grateful to Lee Bauknight for providing invaluable ideas and editorial help, especially in Chapter 4. We also appreciate the skill and pedagogical expertise with which he prepared the instructor's manual for *Beyond Words*. Brian Wellborn and Kyle Shelton helped out with research in the early stages of development. We thank Russell Cobb and Brooke Rollins for their contributions to the Companion Website. We are grateful to Melissa Meeks for her contributions to the "Mapping a Project Visually" assignment at the end of Chapter 6.

We are indebted to our colleagues who reviewed the manuscript for their generous and useful insights: Barclay Barrios, Rutgers University; Amy Braziller, Red Rocks Community College; Mike Chaser, University of Iowa;

Ron Christiansen, Salt Lake Community College; Keith Comer, Idaho State University; Karen Culver, University of Miami; Patricia M. Garcia, Our Lady of the Lake University; Judith Gardner, University of Texas, San Antonio; Bruce Henderson, Fullerton College; Ellen Hendrix, Georgia Southern University; Brooke Hessler, Oklahoma City University; Charlie Hill, University of Wisconsin, Oshkosh; Van Hillard, Duke University; Bryan Hull, Portland Community College; Edward Joyce, Suffolk County Community College; Kate Maurer, University of Minnesota–Duluth; Joan Faber McAlister, University of Iowa; Gloria McMillan, Pima Community College; Tamara Miles, Orangeburg-Calhoun Technical College; Hildy Miller, Portland State University; Michael Neal, Clemson University; Stephanie Paterson, California State University Stanislaus; Dara Perales, Mira Costa College; Beverly Reed, Stephen F. Austin State University; Thomas Rickert, Purdue University; Patricia Roby, University of Wisconsin, Washington County; Sara Safdie, Bellevue Community College; Sherry Suisman, San Francisco State University; Deborah Coxwell Teague, Florida State University; Lou Thompson, Texas Women's University; Monica Parrish Trent, Montgomery College; Mark Tursi, University of Denver; Greta Vollmer, Sonoma State University; Eve Wiederhold, University of North Carolina at Greensboro; and Xiaoye You, Purdue University.

Finally, we are indebted to a number of thoughtful students who took part in an early focus group that offered sound criticism and imaginative suggestions that helped to make this a more useful and student-friendly book: Thomas Bourque, Liz Brancato, Ana Rebelo, Mikki Burzon, Ben Dauksewicz, Grant Henderson, Josh Rudnick and Kristie Surfus from Boston University; and Greg Van Ermen from the University of Massachusetts, Boston. Special thanks to Matthew Parfitt, of Boston University, for locating students for the focus group.

John Ruszkiewicz   **Daniel Anderson**   **Christy Friend**

PRELUDE

t's easy to feel overwhelmed by technology these days, even by things that improve our lives and extend our capabilities. A little like the hero of *Spider-Man 2* in the grip of Doc Ock's tentacles, we might sometimes wish for a few more arms to wrestle with the complications introduced into our lives by computers and the digital revolution.

Of course, many of us now take cell phones for granted, converse with friends via instant messages, find most of the information we need on the Internet, and look forward to buying favorite films on DVD. If you're younger, downloading music is probably second nature to you, as is sending digital photographs via e-mail. It's likely, too, that you've always played video games and have no idea what carbon paper is.

But being immersed in new media is not the same as understanding all its messages or dealing with its demands. For centuries, people were considered literate if they could just read and write. That's still the case. But reading and composing mean much more than they used to.

For instance, we now assume that communication should be instantaneous and available everywhere. Libraries remain crucial storehouses of knowledge, but we expect most basic information, especially journal articles and newspaper stories, to be available online. We want instant weather reports (complete with Doppler radar scans, which we've all learned to interpret), inning-by-inning baseball box scores, and click-to-view video coverage of news events. To satisfy these expectations, more and more public places—from coffee

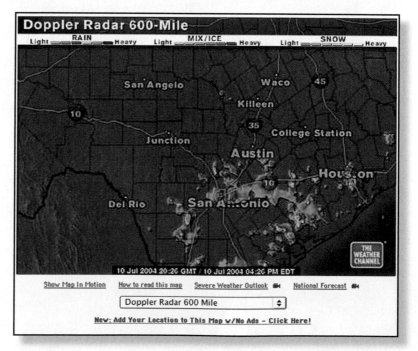

Source: weather.com®. Courtesy of The Weather Channel.

UNDERSTANDING HOW WE READ AND WRITE TODAY

shops to highway rest stops—are going wireless, allowing Web and e-mail access to anyone with a laptop or suitable Wi-Fi gadget.

For good or ill, the microchip has changed the way many of us interact with the world. We may feel occasionally battered by e-mail, but we depend on its immediate transmission of news and information. The Web often fails us, but it has trained us to appreciate the connections between words and images. And computers, complex and still prone to infuriating crashes, have spurred our creativity and extended both our capabilities and our potential audiences.

This book acknowledges such changes. It challenges you to explore an expanded notion of literacy, one that pushes you to consider reading and composing in more than words alone. Why? Because you already live in an environment that assumes you *are* literate in this way, that you know about Web design, white space, fonts, hypertext, design language, MP3s, jpgs, video games, and much more. If a bit overwhelming, it's an invigorating world—just like Spider-Man's New York.

But not everything is different. The past continues to influence the present, and what a great loss it would be if that weren't the case—if the only "texts" you encountered were digital and online. And so we try in *Beyond Words* to show you how and where the more traditional forms of reading, writing, and rhetoric intersect with the novel sorts of "texts" you'll encounter and create every day. You don't have to choose between old and new. You can enjoy both, creating a challenging new reality of your own.

Understanding How We Read and Write Today

One marker of the new literacy is the ease with which people are expected to shift between and among media. Once again, for good or ill, the boundaries have largely disappeared between knowledge, art, news, and commerce.

Consider how complicated the phenomenon of launching a movie has become. It usually starts now with a Web site for the forthcoming film, requiring Flash plug-ins to experience the cast photos, interviews, interactive games, chat rooms, screen savers, and contests tied to the launch of the product. The site will also give you access to the film's trailers—noisy, fast-paced teasers often more entertaining than the film itself—which will play in movie houses months before the epic itself opens. As the movie premiere nears, the lead actors drop in on news/talk programs to show clips, and their action figures appear in stores and fast-food outlets. (The producers of *Spider-Man 2* even tried to put Spider-Man artwork on the bases at professional baseball games.) As the film opens its run in theaters, critics review it in print, on the radio, and on

TV ("Two thumbs up!"). Whether a success or a bomb in its initial release, the film will reappear a few months later on video and DVD, with the DVD version including enhancements—possibly a director's cut—and lots of extras, including outtakes, stills, and even artwork that influenced the production, as in the case of *Master and Commander*. The film might spawn a sequel or two, a book, a music CD, a TV series, a video game, a board game, maybe even a Broadway musical. How many media is that? And, naturally, many films have their origins in other vehicles—novels, plays, musicals, comic books, TV series, historical events, news events, paintings, and amusement park rides.

Even something as "simple" as a Web page can be a multimedia event. A single screen of CNN.com, for example, features not only headlines, news, and photographs but also links to audio and video files. It may also include ads that move and change and innumerable paths to more pages and still more visual and aural kicks. The screen might look like a mess to someone accustomed to the sober front pages of the print-version *Wall Street Journal* or *New York Times*. But most Web users probably find it lively, inviting, and highly readable.

Why? Because they've gotten used to managing their own computer screens, layered with applications. Consider for a moment just a few of the media you might navigate as you develop a paper on, say, the phenomenon of fan films (discussed in more detail in Chapter 2). Does the following scenario sound implausible? Probably not.

1. You've been browsing some digital photographs you took recently when you decide it's time to return to work.

2. You begin reading an article you downloaded several weeks earlier from the online version of *The Weekly Standard*. The feature by M. E. Russell titled "The Fan Film Strikes Back" discusses what fan films are and who makes them.

3. You open a Word® file to take notes on Russell's article.

4. Since it's getting late and everyone else in the wireless study area has departed, you decide to listen to an online radio station.

5. You had also better check your schedule, sent to your computer via your Palm Pilot.

UNDERSTANDING HOW WE READ AND WRITE TODAY

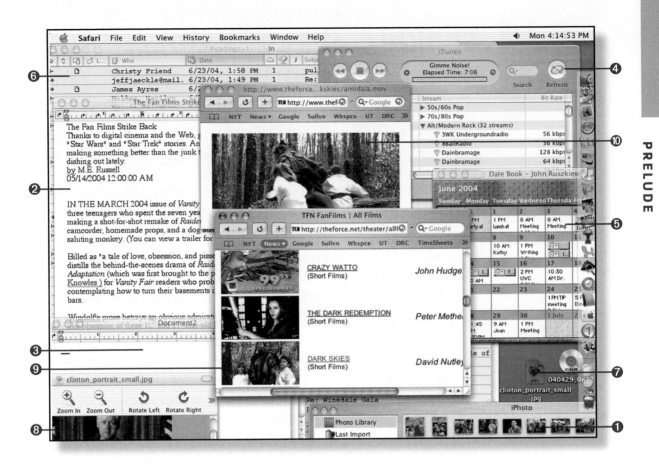

6. In the background, your e-mail is running. A friend suggests that you check out an image of former President Clinton, a parody of a portrait newly hung in the White House.

7. You download the item and click to open it.

8. Clinton is in his boxers. You return to the Russell article and find a reference to Fanfilms.com.

9. You open your browser and examine the site, pulling up a list of fan films. You click on one called *Dark Skies*.

10. The film *Dark Skies* opens in Quicktime®.

All this takes just a few minutes. Working in such environments, you're as much a conductor or juggler as a writer. You've adapted to the unprecedented speed and fluidity of media and know, almost intuitively, how to move from reading an article to taking notes to responding to e-mails to checking a calendar to watching a film clip, and on and on. The process isn't so much linear as simultaneous; its very ease conceals its remarkable power. You are in fact *managing* technologies that have profoundly altered almost every aspect of our lives, from the personal to the political. And we're just beginning to learn how to use them.

Looking at the History of Words and Images

If visual and technical complexity strikes you as uniquely modern, however, think again. We didn't invent multimedia in the past decade, nor are we the first generation to live with texts and images. Perhaps the ancient Egyptians led the way. Thousands of years before the Greeks built the Parthenon (432 BCE) or the Romans their Coliseum (75 CE), the Egyptians were ornamenting their sculptures, buildings, and books with images and hieroglyphics. This glossing of physical objects was routine: Almost no wall went undecorated.

Ideas and images met on papyrus too. A page from the *Book of the Dead*, for instance, is as visually rich as any modern text, even if it lacks electronic hype. Such mergers of text and images are also a feature of Japanese painting and art.

The ancient Greeks and Romans, too, shuttled easily between media. The Greeks, of course, invented principles of rhetoric still influential today and created public spaces for both oratory and theater. The Romans, who imitated and extended the Greek's accomplishments in language, were also great builders. Although we think of the edifices and sculptures of this period as stark constructs of white marble (like our government buildings in Washington, D.C., designed to echo classical models), in fact, the Romans relished color—lost to us after centuries of wear and tear. Their statues, too, imitated life down to the pigments of the skin, and Roman interiors were elaborately (if not always skillfully) decorated with images drawn from life and religion. And when the emperor Trajan decided to memorialize his conquests in the early second century CE, he did so on a

Page from the *Book of the Dead* (1040-945 BCE)

6

100-foot column on which the story of his conquests winds around the column in an ascending spiral, even if no one could see the ending once the column was erected. (According to art historian Paul Johnson, citizens in Rome could learn more about Trajan's victories at a nearby library, a very modern multimedia touch.)

Centuries later, during an era inappropriately dubbed the Dark Ages, monks in Northumbria (northern England) produced what may be Western culture's most beautiful book, the Lindisfarne Gospels (715–720 CE). The monks who illuminated the gospels were doing more than adding pictures to biblical stories. Their rich designs embodied complex theological concepts and mysteries, and deepened the experience of reading the scriptures.

The European Middle Ages also produced a multimedia experience perhaps never quite equaled: the Gothic cathedral. The largely illiterate population knew how to "read" the Bible stories on the elaborately sculpted

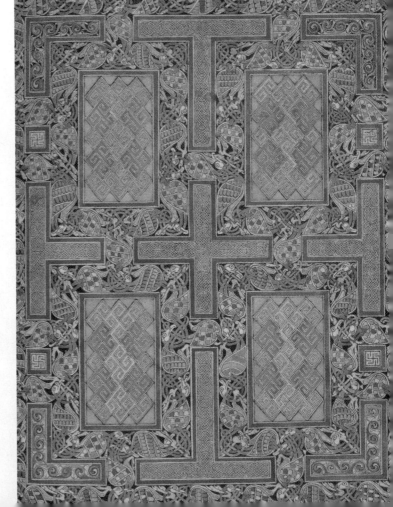

A page from the Lindisfarne Gospels (715–720 CE)

facades and stained-glass windows of the cathedrals. Inside, the faithful could hear a Mass, which, on the greatest feast days, might incorporate appeals to every sense:

- music and bells for the ears
- candles, decorated altars, and processions of clerics in colorful robes for the eyes
- incense for the olfactory sense
- readings and sermons for the mind and heart

Such spectacles earned the ire of Reformation theologians, many of whom objected strongly to the presence of statues, images, music, and art in churches. Such reformers joined a long list of "iconoclasts" over the ages suspicious enough of the power of the visual to forbid or even destroy "graven images"—one of the latest being the Taliban in Afghanistan, who in 2001 demolished centuries-old statues of Buddha carved into a mountainside.

Statue of Buddha before and after destruction by the Taliban in Afghanistan (2001)

> TV will never be a serious competitor for radio because people must sit and keep their eyes glued on a screen; the average American family hasn't time for it.
>
> — *NEW YORK TIMES*, 1939

Over the centuries, too, media themselves have mutated and developed—and thinkers such as Marshall McLuhan (1911–1980) have argued that such shifts have far-reaching consequences, even changing how we think and relate to one another.

The story of writing and printing alone could fill several volumes, as texts migrated from papyrus and scrolls to early handwritten books on vellum to Gutenberg's printing press to personal computers. Writing instruments, too, shaped culture, beginning perhaps with the stylus used to inscribe clay tablets. The Romans really did carve some of their laws in stone, though they used wax for less enduring communications. Pencils, quill pens, fountain pens, ballpoints, and felt-tips are part of the culture of composition, as is the manual and then electric typewriter, the telegraph and fax, the computer, and the word processor.

And each medium of expression and communication—sculpture, painting, architecture, landscaping, photography, film, graphic design—has its own equally complex history, usually tied inextricably to other arts. Today, all these stories and streams of influence come together when, as the heirs of great traditions refreshed by new technologies, you read and compose.

A Guided Tour of *Beyond Words*

Our title *Beyond Words* tells you that we intend to look at literacy in its many forms. And we'll do so by presenting items drawn from many media. But words remain at the heart of the enterprise, the medium that enables us to talk about all the rest. Although we may appreciate paintings and architecture, music and photography, maps and posters, our best and deepest way of sharing what we know about them remains language. So this anthology is a collection of images and readings that explore the many shapes literacy takes today. We hope you will respond to these texts and pictures with words and images of your own. Today, potentially, everyone's a printer, publisher, cartoonist, editor, and designer. Everyone's a would-be sports reporter, artist, journalist, filmmaker, or musician. And, of course, everyone's a writer.

Given the vast scope of our subject—and we genuinely hope you'll be surprised by the diversity of material you'll find in *Beyond Words*—we needed a structure that would be both familiar and roomy, one that would accommodate an exciting variety of images and readings but still lead you through a thoughtful succession of texts and assignments, whether you read the book in sequence or just browse.

THE FRAMEWORK OF COMMUNICATION

We begin with a rhetorical pyramid to remind you that any act of communication involves relationships (always changing) among an **author** or creator (in our version, *you*), a **subject** matter, an **audience**, and a **medium** of communication. We've positioned this structure within a globe because all communication occurs within a tangle of social, political, and cultural environments—which together make up our world. And if this weren't a book, we'd set our pyramid and globe spinning together to suggest the dynamic relationships among all these elements.

The first two chapters of *Beyond Words* present the general issues you'll face in encountering texts. In particular, we offer series of open-ended questions to help you when reading and responding to texts of all varieties. The subsequent chapters then direct you to the corners of the pyramid, focusing on reasons for composing, and shifting

- From **personal** texts that focus on individuals and their environments—Chapters 3 and 4
- To **analytical** chapters that look at the way the world can be presented in words, images, and other media—Chapters 5 and 6
- To **persuasive** and **argumentative** images and readings, designed to move audiences to action—Chapters 7 and 8.

If you read through the chapters sequentially, you'll sense this movement from *individual* to *public*, from the *personal* to the *political*. But our chapters, we admit, have porous borders because texts themselves doggedly resist classifications and boundaries. (And that's a good thing.) For example, you might be moved by an oddly composed self-portrait—a painting, perhaps, or a photograph or collage. Doing a little research and analysis, you learn about the cultural environment that evoked the image and the political impact it had in its era. You realize that the portrait might, in fact, be a kind of visual argument—and you are ready to make that case in your own words. In encountering that text as first a reader and then a writer, you'll have covered a lot of ground and jumped more than a few fences yourself.

What of **medium**, the fourth point of our pyramid? Media, too, can cross boundaries and serve different purposes, sometimes even drawing attention to themselves—for instance, when a movie is about the process of making a movie. Because of this variation, especially among electronic texts, we didn't want to limit any chapter to a single medium of communication. But we have framed each chapter around a focal point that invites questions about media. Again, the general movement is from personal to political, from portraits of individuals to arguments about public monuments.

WHAT'S IN EACH CHAPTER?

CHAPTER 1 **"Paying Attention"** might be alternatively titled "Critical Reading" except that it encourages you to look at media *in addition to* the printed word. Exactly how might you react critically to a photograph, film, or controversial new building, learning enough about it in the process to respond intelligently? Chapter 1 provides a series of questions that guide you through the process and give structure to Chapters 3 through 8:

- What do you see?
- What is it about?
- To what does it relate?
- How is it composed?
- What details matter?

Allusions in the chapter range from *The Towering Inferno* to Shakespeare, which is about as broad as ranges get. You'll also be introduced (briefly) to the architecture of Frank Gehry and to an Elizabethan sonnet, which, we swear, you will enjoy.

11

CHAPTER 2 "**Getting Attention**" offers detailed advice for composing texts on your own. Coordinated with the major assignments in *Beyond Words*, the chapter outlines the process of composing by posing a series of questions about an assignment and the response you will make to it:

- What's it to you?
- What do you want to say about it?
- Who will listen?
- What do you need to know?
- How will you do it?
- How well does it work?

In addition, the chapter will introduce you to the phenomenon of "fan films" and examine the strengths and weaknesses of various media, including speech, printed words, video, and photography.

CHAPTER 3 "**Picturing Ourselves**" looks at how people present themselves and others in portraits, paintings, photographs, and words. If you've ever been photographed or tattooed, there's something in "Picturing Ourselves" to which you'll relate. The chapter invites you to create portraits of your own, trying various media.

CHAPTER 4 "**Seeing Places**" explores the way environments locate and define who we are. It shows that the places where we live are not mere backdrops to our activities but an essential part of them. The chapter ranges widely, looking at the world of skateboarders in *Dogtown and Z Boys* as well as the final landscape painted by van Gogh. And it spends considerable time in American suburbia examining the values implied in the huge homes and sprawling neighborhoods we build there.

CHAPTER 5 "**Moving Pictures**" examines how to read and create pictures that tell stories. It opens with a detailed look at a painting for which the artist has supplied a narrative, explaining the details we see in it. But are we oblig-

ated to accept that interpretation, or can we construct a story of our own? Sometimes we are encouraged to exercise our imaginations. In other cases, narratives aim to present a kind of reality—they document the realities of war or homelessness or tell tales about the times in which we live. This chapter looks at the broad ambitions of narratives and the details that can make them memorable.

CHAPTER 6 "**Mapping Ideas**" presents the various ways we use media—words, shapes, forms, lines, images—to depict reality, to make it easier

for us to grasp. It explores how we create metaphorical spaces that help us navigate the world, from maps of the continents to maps of our own bodies. It invites a critique of the way metaphors can constrain our view of the world and encourages the creation of new sorts of maps.

CHAPTER 7 "**Exploring Design**" turns an analytical eye on design. The Toyota Prius and Hummer H2 are the poster children for the chapter, two vehicles that use their very different design languages to define their markets and attract buyers. The chapter also considers what makes iPods so cool, what holiday lights tell us about our outlook on life, and what tennis shoes mean politically. In short, the chapter explores how designs and designers labor to steer our values and desires. Understanding such strategies, you are ready to critique such efforts and, when appropriate, resist them.

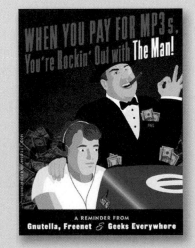

CHAPTER 8 "**Debating Culture**" takes a detailed look at the many ways arguments get made, both verbally and visually. The chapter begins by examining two very different advertisements designed to influence young people who use the Internet to illegally download music and movies. You'll examine, among other issues, whether and how scare tactics, factual evidence, humor, and other elements work to persuade an audience. Then the chapter explores other controversies, from "get out the vote" efforts to fast-food marketing campaigns. It concludes by examining arguments about the monuments we build to mark our history and honor our heroes. Naturally, the chapter invites you to join the fray, making arguments of your own.

WHEN YOU PAY FOR MP3s, You're Rockin' Out with The Man!

A REMINDER FROM
Gnutella, Freenet & Geeks Everywhere

GETTING AN INSIDER'S VIEW

Cementing the package are six provocative items we call **Interludes**, serving as bridges between our chapters. We have asked people from a wide range of creative professions to talk in these interludes about their work as writers, designers, graphic artists, tattoo artists, and more. In themselves, the interludes offer a rousing rationale for *Beyond Words*, embodying the diverse kinds of literacy that have become a part of our world. We showcase real lives and work, from high-tech to no-tech, to give a human face to composing. In this company, you'll find

Henriata Nicholas, a Maori *ta moko* tattoo artist from New Zealand discussing the history of *ta moko* and the process itself (it can take place over several months)

Milton Glaser, an influential graphics designer, describing the design of a famous restaurant in New York and the process by which a magical space was visualized and built

Maira Kalman, a noted writer and illustrator of children's books, talking about her work on *Fireboat*, a children's story written to explain the events of 9/11

Robin Williams and John Tollett, noted authors and Web designers, explaining the features that distinguish an effective Web site from a poorly designed one

Kurtis Harris, a retired New York police detective and crime scene photographer, describing the process crime scene investigators use to record and analyze evidence through crime scene photography

Jon Foster, the publisher and creative director of *Snowboard Journal*, writing about the challenges a photographer faces in creating powerful images of surfers and snowboarders

As you can see, our intention in *Beyond Words* is to offer you a systematic way of thinking about and responding to texts that shape the new realities of our time. We want you to learn to appreciate the introspection of the portrait painter, the architect's sense of space, the steady gaze of the mapmaker, the cunning of the advertiser, the grace of the designer, the passion of the activist. No book can cover every motive for composing or explore every intriguing theme. But we hope you'll find much in *Beyond Words* that expands the way you think about literacy and writing, about images and art, indeed, about all media. But most of all, we hope it encourages you to write.

PAYING ATTENTION

reading texts

Pere Borrell del Caso, *Escaping Criticism* (1874)

Introduction

Just moving from a classroom to your dorm or apartment, you encounter so many appeals and messages that you may notice none of them—not the posters on the classroom walls, EXIT signs above doors, headlines in the campus paper, logos on T-shirts, shouts from activists on the mall, banners strung over the street, traffic signs all down your route, music in your ears, billboards for Scion, Red Bull, Aveda, and on and on.

To gain attention, a message practically has to jump out at you, a little like the youth in a painting by Pere Borrell del Caso featured a few years ago in an exhibit at the National Gallery of Art called "Deceptions and Illusions: Five Centuries of Trompe l'Oeil Painting." The French term *trompe l'œil*, which means "fools the eye," refers to an enduring style of painting in which artists create images so true-to-life that they blur the line between reality and illusion.

Borrell's painting certainly makes you take notice. But why, exactly? For one thing, we expect subjects to stay inside their frames. This wide-eyed boy is climbing into our world, and he seems as astounded by the situation as we are. But wait a minute. Is that frame *around* the painting or a part of it? And where is the youngster coming from—and heading to? Is he a hooligan up to no good or a would-be cherub escaping yet another fresco? Some questions may be answered by knowing that Borrell named this 1874 painting *Escaping Criticism*. Yet that title seems too calculated for this likable piece, which probably wins your attention by cleverly thumbing its nose at conventions and provoking all sorts of questions.

Images like *Escaping Criticism* call out for interpretation, but even less visually striking images and texts invite us to look more closely. Don't wait until messages start jumping out of their frames to grab your attention. Take initiative as a reader, writer, and *maker* of texts.

What's in This Chapter?

Media clutter has grown to the point that an honest message intelligently conveyed might not get noticed. While no one can blame you for playing it cool in the face of media overload, you might miss much that really matters if you don't actively seek out and respond to what's special, beautiful, sacred, awesome, or weighty in the world.

This chapter provides questions for reading and exploring texts *to make you a more perceptive and active reader.* We discuss each question briefly and then follow up with examples and exercises that draw from a range of media. Throughout this book, we define *text* very broadly to include *anything deliberately fashioned by human beings to convey an idea, a message, or even a feeling.* By our definition, then, a forest isn't a text, but a photograph of one could be. A city in itself might be too vast and random to be a coherent text, but it contains many messages worth reading and writing about. Movies, paintings, posters, murals, songs, symphonies, sculptures, advertisements, bumper stickers, T-shirts, video games, and e-mail messages are all texts. Most important for our purposes, words and images are texts that carry messages and make meaning. We read and explore these texts by looking at them closely, and by seeing how they connect to and illuminate other texts.

Reading
Texts

The world is full of texts that challenge you to read them carefully—great books, movies, and TV productions, splendid pieces of music, thought-provoking buildings, and important political documents, to name but a few. But there are texts, too, whose creators would probably prefer that you not look too closely: They may have things to conceal in their message or their craft. They depend on your not showing enough interest to search them for meaning. Just a few questions can open these texts up.

What do you see?

What is it about?

To what does it relate?

How is it composed?

What details matter?

Reading Texts:
A Tutorial
www.ablongman.com/beyondwords01

What do you see?

If someone handed you a slide rule today to figure out your taxes or do the calculations for a math test, you might feel confused and disoriented. What is this contraption, with its tiny numbers and parallel scales? What's it for? How does it operate? The moving ruler and clear plastic slides might tempt you to experiment with it, but you'd need plenty of assistance before you'd know how to read this unfamiliar text, which was common in American high schools prior to the invention of the pocket calculator.

A feeling of disorientation (or wonder) is actually a good place to begin your encounter with any new text—verbal, visual, aural, tactile. An intriguing text should attract your attention and provoke questions.

- What do you focus on in the work? Your reading begins with a spark of interest. Can you identify what caused it—what the **focal point** of the work might be?

- What kind of work is it? When we meet a dog, most of us immediately try to identify its breed or mix in order to appreciate its looks, temperament, and characteristics. We do the same with texts we encounter, substituting **genre** for *breed*. Genres are expressed through conventions—the features and structures that make them what they are.

- How does this work differ from others like it? Works routinely bend **conventions** and cross boundaries. That's what makes many contemporary texts so intriguing and provoking. They have been reinvented by the infusion of electronic technologies.

- What is the work's **medium**? Different media convey different kinds of information and make different kinds of demands.

FIND FOCAL POINTS Writers, artists, designers, architects, and even musicians know how important it is to focus their work. To be a good reader, you need to notice how they do it. If you've ever written a paper with a thesis statement or a paragraph with a topic sentence, you are familiar with one simple device for focusing with words: a sentence or two that clearly announce what the writer intends to discuss.

But there are dozens of other techniques for focusing attention. On a printed page, a big headline, an underscored heading, boldfaced or italic type, or a four-color photo might entice your eye. In a photograph, an artist might use light and shadow to seduce your gaze, whereas a painter might align objects to create a subtle focal point, moving you almost subconsciously in a specific direction. On a Web page, you might first encounter a striking graphic or a tempting menu of options to engage your attention.

So you can easily begin your encounters with texts by noting where you look first and then asking *why*. But be prepared, too, to be puzzled or deliberately thrown off balance. Many texts will resist your efforts to understand them at a glance, to pluck out the heart of their mysteries.

IDENTIFY THE GENRE After you've first encountered a text, you'll likely ask—consciously or not—what it resembles or into what genres it fits. A genre is simply a category we use to name and identify a text with consistent and familiar features. Without much effort, you could enumerate the features of the letter; you could also explain the differences between subgenres such as the business letter and the personal letter. And you could likely identify many other types of letters, each with distinctive features or missions: job application letters, letters to the editor, "Dear John" letters, and so on.

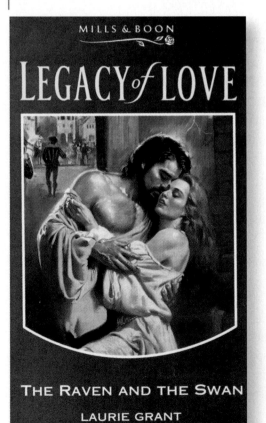

Cover art for a series romance novel

Genres can seem relatively stable, but their boundaries are rarely fixed. For instance, you likely know what a novel is: Let's say it's *a prose tale told at some length involving characters whose lives engage you*. When you pick up a novel and consider reading it, you'll likely study the dust jacket, perhaps looking for the signals that will slot it into a favored category or subgenre—mystery, romance, historical fiction, cyberpunk novel. But some novels will resist categorization or tell their stories in unanticipated ways or media.

EXAMINE CONVENTIONS Once you've identified the genre or subgenre of a text, you then know how to read some of its features: In a romance novel, you'll expect to find a tale of passionate lovers set in exotic locales. And because you have these generic expectations, you can also appreciate when a writer or artist defies or parodies conventions.

The fun starts when texts start bending conventions and forming new ones. Not infrequently, new genres borrow

Still from an early silent film

their wardrobes from older ones. Very old movies, for instance, sometimes look like stage plays because that's how early filmmakers imagined stories should be told visually. Pioneer screenwriters also drew upon novels and plays for their scripts, again using well-established conventions to help invent new ones. Today, creators of video games sometimes take their inspiration from movies— and, amazingly, vice versa. Indeed, the electronic revolution of the past few decades has spawned many fresh ways of sharing words and images, some of which have quickly evolved conventions of their own. E-mail, for example, might be categorized as a subgenre of the letter, and carries forward conventions like senders and recipients, but adds new ones like emoticons.

So in encountering a text, old or new, you want to ask questions about what the thing *is*. You may have to do some research to find out. In a museum, you'll find signs and guidebooks to help you appreciate artifacts you may not recognize. Libraries are full of reference tools that can introduce you to everything from epic poems to classic movies. But for many texts and objects, you may have to define genres on the fly, thinking critically about their shape, asking yourself what they resemble and how they work.

CONSIDER THE MEDIUM Like early filmmakers, you'll probably transfer what you already know about existing genres to any new medium you encounter. That multifunction cell phone is, after all, just a very smart communication device that can remember your schedule, take photos, download instant messages and e-mail, and keep tabs on stock prices. But somewhere in a mix like this, something may change and suddenly you're handling ideas in a novel way. What had been a cell phone evolves into an environment for new genres of texts. That's certainly what happened to the computer, which started out as a very smart calculator. Now silicon brains power all sorts of "new media."

As a result, you're probably more aware of media now than ever before, and it's important not to take these media for granted, thinking, for instance, that reading words on a page is the same experience as reading words on a screen. Media deliver messages to us in different ways at different speeds, and we process and experience those messages differently.

For example, you've probably encountered Shakespeare's *Romeo and Juliet* on the page, on stage, and on film. What changes? Almost everything. Each medium makes its own demands on your imagination and your senses. Read the play, and you create most of the work in your head. Watch it from a front-row theater seat, and you might duck when the swords start clashing. See it on DVD, and Leonardo DiCaprio becomes the default Romeo in your mind.

Or consider how differently you experience a news event if you learn of it via a magazine, a newspaper, a nightly news program, a twenty-four-hour news channel, or a Web site or blog. The medium shapes the message, or at least a good part of it.

EXAMPLES Mention the word *poem*, and you have some idea what to expect of this genre: words artfully chosen and arranged to convey some powerful idea or feeling. You may love poetry or run away from the stuff. But when you encounter a poem, it might help to know something about the many subgenres into which it might fall: There are *epics, lyrics, odes, acrostics,* and *haiku,* to name just a very few. One type you probably recognize is the sonnet—by tradition, *a love poem in fourteen lines with a specific pattern of rhyme.* With a little research, you could discover many things about the sonnet subgenre that add to your appreciation of such poems: for instance, that they often use fairly conventional imagery (like ruby lips and cherry cheeks) and that they often come in sequences that tell the story of a man's pursuit of an ideal woman. Recognizing these conventions helps when you meet a famous work such as Shakespeare's "Sonnet 130," (1609), a poem addressed to a mysterious "dark lady," who may or may not have played a role in the poet's life.

My mistress' eyes are nothing like the sun;
Coral is far more red than her lips' red;
If snow be white, why then her breasts are dun;
If hairs be wires, black wires grow on her head.

I have seen roses damask'd, red and white,
But no such roses see I in her cheeks;
And in some perfumes is there more delight
Than in the breath that from my mistress reeks.

I love to hear her speak, yet well I know
That music hath a far more pleasing sound.
I grant I never saw a goddess go;
My mistress, when she walks, treads on the ground.

And yet, by heaven, I think my love as rare
As any she belied with false compare.

Many later poets have also employed the sonnet form, but they have moved
it in new directions. Their poems are not always about romantic love, don't
always run for just fourteen lines, or may not rhyme conventionally. But they
do claim the brevity, concentration, and intricacy of the original genre. Here,
in the third poem of a sequence called "Clearances," is Nobel laureate Seamus
Heaney (b. 1939) using the sonnet form to memorialize his mother. The work
appears in the collection *The Haw Lantern* (1987).

When all the others were away at Mass
I was all hers as we peeled potatoes.
They broke the silence, let fall one by one
Like solder weeping off the soldering iron:
Cold comforts set between us, things to share
Gleaming in a bucket of clean water.
And again let fall. Little pleasant splashes
From each other's work would bring us to our senses.

So while the parish priest at her bedside
Went hammer and tongs at the prayers for the dying
And some were responding and some crying
I remembered her head bent towards my head,
Her breath in mine, our fluent dipping knives—
Never closer the whole rest of our lives.

Heaney, an Irish poet, uses simple images, occasional rhymes, and irregular rhythms to present a moment when the memory of a much-loved woman eases the pain of her loss.

■ ■ ■

Sometimes you notice the sheer novelty of a text or design before all else. You see something you don't expect and so you look again and again. That's part of the charm of Borrell's *Escaping Criticism*, and it certainly contributes to both the fame and the appeal of architect Frank Gehry's most famous buildings, which have a style of their own. Their sweeping facades, crooked walls, and *Alice in Wonderland* corridors challenge architectural conventions in ways people find entertaining or absurd. Either way, people pay attention. But then they probably begin thinking about them in terms of their genres too. After all, even a Gehry building has to serve a particular purpose—as a concert hall, a campus building, a museum. What should buildings of this type do? And how well does the Gehry version meet those expectations? These are questions critics have addressed and are the same sort of questions you should ask once you've decided what something is.

Stata Center, MIT

Disney Concert Hall

Jan Vermeer, *Woman Holding a Balance* (1664)

CONSIDER

1. Take a moment to study Vermeer's *Woman Holding a Balance* (above). Its title probably tells you what to notice first in the painting, the woman's delicate fingers holding a balance in the very center of the work. But what else in the painting moves you to look there? What devices does the artist employ to direct your attention to that spot? Consider elements such as light, shadow, gestures, and other objects in the painting.

2. The grille is what you probably notice first on this publicity shot for the 2005 Chrysler 300C (right). What elements in the photograph lead you to focus on the grille, the largest design element on most cars and trucks? What message or messages might the manufacturer be sending potential buyers through this image? Could you transform the message into words? Give it a try.

3. Make a list of the different kinds of writing you do in a single day. Don't include academic types of writing only. List all your uses of words, whether on paper or screen. Any surprises in your list?

4. Find a page of TV listings, and create a list of genres into which the programs on that page fit. Then briefly try to define several of the genres by identifying their purpose and enumerating their conventions. For example, *The O'Reilly Factor* might be placed in the news/talk or news/opinion genre, in which hosts with political axes to grind debate hot-button political issues with figures in the news.

5. Identify a text that you have experienced in at least two different media: book and film, stage play and film, film and TV version, TV and newspaper, magazine and newspaper, original painting and reproduction, digital photo and print photo. As best you can, explain and then analyze the differences you experienced between the works.

"Coming up in your rearview mirror, it [the Chrysler 300C] looks meaner than Dick Cheney in a duck blind with a hangover and a cold. It would make a great cop car. It is so dope."

—JAMIE KITTMAN
"All American?"
Automobile, June 2004

25

What is it about?

Books, articles, movies, images, and even ads have to do more than just gain your attention. They have to hold it, and they can do that by offering a subject worth your attention, one that gets you thinking.

IDENTIFY THE SUBJECT The subject matter of a text can be signaled in an almost infinite number of ways. A topic may be simply and clearly announced—as is the case in reference works, textbooks, and research reports. Titles, too, can define subject matter—though they can also be mysterious, deliberately elusive, or provocative. Consider how Borrell's painting at the beginning of this chapter is limited by its title *Escaping Criticism*. Now imagine how the work would change if its title were *Playing Hooky*.

Often the subject matter of a text has to be inferred or interpreted. A book or film may just seem to tell a story. What is the subject matter of the *Lord of the Rings* trilogy? In some ways, it's the story of a Hobbit with a mission to destroy a sinister ring. But on other levels, it may be a reiteration of the heroic myths of Western culture or a retelling of the Second World War or yet another unfurling of a good-versus-evil saga. The effort to understand the subject matter of a

Front pages from the September 12, 2001 editions of the *San Francisco Examiner*, *Arizona Republic*, and *Hartford Courant* newspapers

complex text is one of the pleasures of reading. Great works tempt us to return to them often to discover new, different, and sometimes contradictory meanings.

Of course, you need to be able to explain *how* you found those meanings in a text. A text should provide evidence for the interpretations you offer.

UNDERSTAND THE PURPOSE As is probably clear, the treatment of a subject is almost always connected to the purpose of a work. A given text may serve any number of purposes. It may evoke personal reflection, like a family portrait or photograph. It may arouse memories, like an urban cityscape or a rural scene. It may be quietly decorative, like a piece of sculpture on a lawn, or robustly informative and pushy, like a traffic sign. A text may try to seduce you, change you, persuade you, or move you to action. And it may do several things at once or different things at different times: A figure such as Uncle Sam may incite good humor at a Fourth of July parade and patriotic fervor on a recruitment poster.

Texts shouldn't always make you suspicious. But you should read them carefully to see what they are telling you and for what purpose.

EXAMPLES On the day following September 11, 2001, it's unlikely that readers of American newspapers were trying to learn what had happened the day before. More probably, they were already looking for reactions to the terrorist attack on New York City and Washington, D.C., with assessments of its consequences. The *San Francisco Examiner* signals its subject matter and purpose by three all-cap headings: SPECIAL EDITION, BASTARDS! and A CHANGED AMERICA. The cover photograph provides all the evidence necessary to explain those headings. Related photos have the same impact in the *Arizona Republic* and the *Hartford Courant* and similar relationships to their headlines.

But the subject matter of a front page may not be the same when borders are crossed. Compare the reactions in Albuquerque, New Mexico, and Calgary, British Columbia, to the death of U.S. President Ronald Reagan at a moment when the Canadian city had a team playing for the Stanley Cup.

■ ■ ■

Front pages from the June 6, 2004 editions of the *Albuquerque Journal* and the *Calgary Sun*

"Building 20's greatness was its absence of architecture. In a building so lacking in character, it was impossible to establish academic or social hierarchies. Everyone was equal, and science was democratic, creative, and free-wheeling. You could perform improbable experiments or bang holes in walls or roofs to connect up new equipment, because nobody cared what happened to Building 20. The result, say scientists, was the most productive building of its size in American history."

—ROBERT CAMPBELL AND PETER VANDERWARKER
"Building for Science," *New York Times*, April 18, 2004

Building 20, MIT

Sometimes the purpose of a text isn't immediately visible. On the campus of the Massachusetts Institute of Technology, architect Frank Gehry was asked to replace Building 20 with a new structure—what would become the Ray and Maria Stata Center for Computer, Information, and Intelligence Sciences. To an outsider, MIT sacrificed an undistinguished heap for a world-class new structure. But as always, there's more here than meets the eye, as Robert Campbell and Peter Vanderwarker explain above.

CONSIDER

1. Working in a group, imagine some thoughtful alternative titles for Pere Borrell's *Escaping Criticism* (left). How do your new titles change the subject matter of the piece or the way viewers might encounter it?

2. We're accustomed to seeing titles on papers, books, paintings, and poems. But where else do you find titles or "subject lines" that help you understand what a text might be about? Describe several of these items and how they function. Be open-minded, considering a wide variety of media.

3. The advertisements in glossy magazines are obviously designed to persuade you to buy products. But do some of them have aims that move beyond the purely commercial? Find and examine several such "soft-sell" ads that either make their sales pitches indirectly or seem to champion a worthy social cause. Do you find such strategies appealing or offensive? Are they effective? What might such advertisements *really* be selling? Explain.

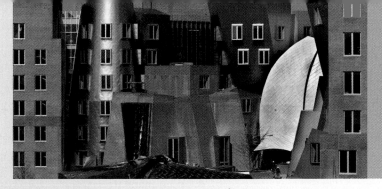

"The Stata Center . . . is the opposite. It tries to do with architecture what Building 20 did by not having any. The architect is the world's currently most famous, Frank Gehry, whose Walt Disney Concert Hall in Los Angeles opened last fall to general acclaim. At Stata, Gehry's playful shapes create a partylike atmosphere. And his architectural swoops and collisions make for a building that will always look as if it's still under construction. The building is a metaphor for the cutting-edge innovation that will occur, it is hoped, in its labs, offices, and classrooms."

—ROBERT CAMPBELL AND PETER VANDERWARKER
"Building for Science," *New York Times*, April 18, 2004

Stata Center, MIT

To what does it relate?

Every book, article, painting, sculpture, cartoon, photograph—you name it—exists within a context. Several, in fact. Context is nothing more or less than the *who, what, where, when,* and *why* that surround every word, image, or artifact. We read every text wanting to know how it meshes with the world, both now and in the past (if it has a past yet).

CONSIDER CONTEXTS We probably notice context most when we're missing some part of it. Works that are anonymous or not reliably dated leave us guessing about their origins and wanting to know more. But centuries don't have to pass to erase a text's neighborhood. So much stuff gets lost or displaced in our daily lives that there is even a periodical—*Found Magazine,* from Ann Arbor,

on the winter sidewalk sat half a photograph—i looked around but i couldn't find the other half anywhere. on the back i can make out the partial word "acova (19)" and beneath that "Greece"

what sort of emotions made the owner tear it in half? and what was in the other half of the picture?

—NIKOLAUS MAACK
Found Magazine

Greece Gone Wrong, found by Nikolaus Maack, Ottawa, Ontario, Canada

Michigan, with a Web site at FoundMagazine.com—for people eager to share displaced objects they discover in odd places, from garbage cans to crowded attics.

In presenting such fragments of people's pasts, *Found* raises just the sorts of questions you should consider when encountering a text unfamiliar to you:

- Who made it?
- When was it composed?
- To what does it respond?
- What trends, fashions, or attitudes does it represent?
- Who was or is the audience for the text?
- How did people respond to it initially?

Editorial cartoon by
Stephen Breen (1998)

In some ways, uncovering the context of a text breathes new life into it. This renewal makes an important point about context: *It always changes.* But context isn't only a matter of discovering in what year the original *Shrek* was released or how popular *Rubber Soul* was when it debuted or why Dorothea Lange photographed migrant workers during the Great Depression. Sometimes you also have to connect a work to current events or popular culture to understand it. Editorial cartoons in newspapers demonstrate this principle about as well as any item. Stephen Breen of the *Asbury Park* (N.J.) *Press* won a Pulitzer Prize in 1998 for cartooning, but one of his award-winning submissions would already be puzzling to people who don't know or recall that then President Bill Clinton was criticized for using White House social events to raise funds for his campaign. Breen's imaginative presidential seal—with its coffee cup, telephone, dollar signs, and "Show me the money" motto—would now have to be explained to many readers, though it made perfect sense in 1998.

EXPLORE PERSONAL ASSOCIATIONS You may bring your own highly personal associations to reading and responding to texts. Writers and artists may stimulate your imagination, but they cannot control it. Nor can they anticipate the layers of history and memory that any individual or group brings to the world. By birth, education, and experience, we all come to texts differently, find different things in them, and react in unique ways. These personal connections are so important that they shape many of the responses you bring to a work. A Chicana may identify more powerfully with a work by

Poster for *The Towering Inferno* (1979)

Sandra Cisneros than an Italian American, who might in turn have plenty to say about *The Sopranos*, much of it critical. And so on down the line through a full roster of religious, ethnic, gender, cultural, and even physical differences. The key here is *differences*. The contexts we bring to texts personally aren't a matter of right and wrong; they are crucially distinct ways of seeing.

EXAMPLES To many Americans, the images from the attack on the World Trade Center in 2001 seemed unreal—more like something from a Hollywood disaster film such as *Independence Day* (1996), *Armageddon* (1998), or, most eerily, *The Towering Inferno* (1979). A look at the film poster explains why people might have made such a connection.

Contexts can be quite personal, based on one's own experiences and knowledge. A building like Frank Gehry's Stata Center at MIT is just the sort to generate all sorts of odd associations. This sophisticated structure probably strikes many as oddly childlike or playful, like buildings they remember from picture books or science fiction tales. Film buffs may have a startling different take on the Stata Center. It may remind them of *The Cabinet of Dr.*

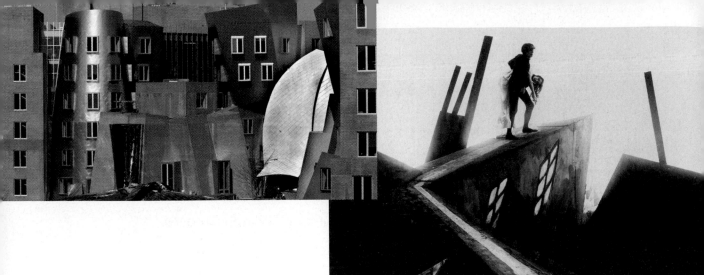

Still from *The Cabinet of Dr. Caligari* (1919)

Caligari, a classic movie from the silent era whose sets featured memorably distorted buildings and streets. These expressionistic sets have been interpreted as the manifestation of a lead character's madness or as a criticism of the German government. For Gehry, however, the peculiar geometry seems to express new architectural possibilities. Still, the connection offers tantalizing possibilities for a response to Gehry's architecture.

CONSIDER

1. Examine an editorial cartoon in a newspaper today. What is the context for the item? What kinds of knowledge does a reader need to get the cartoonist's point? How well informed does the cartoonist assume the reader is? How well would the item work a decade from today?

2. Go to theonion.com, and pick a story at least a few paragraphs long. Then list all the cultural connections you would need to recognize in order to understand it fully. You might want to work on this assignment with a group since one person may not catch all the allusions. How funny will the story be a year from now, five years from now, a century from now? Will it even be comprehensible?

3. Find a personal object in your closet, attic, or elsewhere, that has not aged well—it might be a piece of clothing, an ugly radio, a picture of an old pet or car, a graduation present, or a souvenir. As well as you can, explain how the object is connected to you through memories and associations. What might you want other people to know about the object if it showed up in *Found* magazine?

4. Pick a film released prior to 1975, and do as much research as you can to describe the world into which it premiered and the way it is regarded now. Choose a film that has some standing today. For example, what attracted audiences to *The Wizard of Oz* in 1939? What struck them as new or different? What other films debuted that year? Did producers of the film anticipate that *The Wizard of Oz* would become a classic? How is the film regarded now?

How is it composed?

Many kids go through a phase when they take things apart. Even if the results are sometimes catastrophic, the impulse is a good one. Seeing how the pieces of a clock, VCR, or talking doll fit together can give a hands-on feel for the way the object actually works.

TAKE THE TEXT APART You usually can't disassemble texts you read quite the same way, but to understand them, you'll want to develop a similar sense for how their parts work together. You'll quickly discover that composition is a complex activity differing widely from medium to medium. Yet certain strategies for reading structure and organization apply widely.

Look for elements that give **unity** to a text. A work that is unified seems to develop a dominant idea, theme, or feeling. That doesn't mean that a work expresses only one notion but that its elements seem coherent or stay on message.

Look for **sequences** that link events or different parts of a text. For example, a story may be organized by a plot that explains what happened first, what happened second, and so on. Even when flashbacks or reminiscences (techniques especially common in movies) interrupt such tales, you can still usually assemble a coherent sequence. Many other kinds of works use numbers or progressions to keep things in order, from timelines and sonnet sequences to slide shows and movies on DVD. Even chapters and other divisions in books are numbered to give order to a work.

Look to the way a whole is divided into **parts**. Many texts are organized by some principle of division that helps us see relationships. Sometimes that division is quite simple—just a breakdown of an idea or object into separable items, like the tracks on a CD or rows in a garden. But texts can also be organized by more thoughtful principles based on a rigorous classification of ideas, images, or even colors and shapes.

Look for **patterns** that organize a text. Repetitions of any kind stick in our minds and help us read texts. Consider the power of **repetition** and **rhythm** in music—and how easily you can distinguish between the verses of a song and its chorus. You'll find patterns, large and small, in written texts too that help orga-

33

nize them. Any work written to a formula, from a biology lab report to a screenplay for a movie, is following a pattern that readers are trained to recognize. And, naturally, patterns play an enormous role in organizing visual texts. The facades of buildings, for instance, typically present us with many patterns, subtly varied to keep us interested. Look for both: pattern and variation.

Look for **arrangement** and **balance**. The physical layout of elements in a text can be an important structural feature. In an image such as a photograph, a single dominant figure front and center has a different impact than two figures who are balanced, positioned off center, or counterbalanced by other elements. Your eye moves in different ways in encountering and reacting to such arrangements. As a result some texts seem static; others feel more dynamic.

Clockwise from top left:
Photo with a single figure balanced front and center
Photo with two figures in motion, off center
Photo with two figures, balanced and centered

> "The real meaning of form is made clearer by its opposite."
>
> —JAN TSCHICHOLD
> *The New Typography*

Michelangelo da Caravaggio, *David and Goliath* (c. 1600)

Look for **contrasts** that organize information by focusing attention. Contrast is what makes black text on a white page stand out. Many texts are organized on the same principle: that we see things more clearly when they stand next to their opposites. That is as true of ideas as of colors and shapes. Contrast guides many kinds of works, from traditional comparison-and-contrast essays and pro-and-con arguments to visual and aural pieces of all sorts. The painter Caravaggio, for example, invented dramatic lighting effects to shape complex and graphic scenes of unusual power. Photographers, too, particularly those working in black and white, use patterns of light and dark to structure their work and make us more aware of patterns.

Look for a **hierarchy** in texts. Some things are more important than others, and texts use various devices to signal what is of greater and lesser importance: size, color, highlighting, positioning, placement, length, and so on. All of these cues help guide you through a text. For instance, the size and style of headings and subheadings in books may mark the difference between chapter titles and subheads at various levels of importance.

UNDERSTAND HOW THE PARTS WORK TOGETHER Consider also how the elements of a text work together to achieve an effect. If it helps, think about how you yourself "compose" a photograph on vacation, getting your friends (one tall, one short) in just the right relationship to the mountain behind them and the tree in front of them. You move in, move out, try different camera angles, and maybe frame the shot with a convenient overhanging limb. Thanks to digital photography, you may be able to judge the results immediately. Perhaps you've nailed the shot. More likely, you may have to recompose it to better capture your sense of the moment. Composition can be a matter of trial and error and of juggling many different concerns, elements, and techniques.

Photo with grid lines showing the "rule of thirds"

For example, some photographers organize their shots using what they call the "rule of thirds." Employing this principle, photographers avoid centering the most important elements in a photograph. Instead, they position them roughly at the points where imaginary lines, both horizontal and vertical, divide an image into thirds. (In the photo, note that the head of the king is exactly at one of those intersections.) The rule is not hard and fast. Sometimes an image requires more balance or symmetry. But the eye seems to respond well to structures that promote complex or intriguing relationships, as the rule of thirds does.

Clarity is another important element in composition. In successful graphs, charts, and tables, for example, various elements must mesh to make numbers and their relationships easy to read and interpret. Note how "Population Growth" achieves such clarity through its simple composition. Red bars rising above a zero line indicate growth in population; dark blue bars descending from the same line show population decline. Alternating vertical columns of light blue and gray separate the names of the ten countries studied, while horizontal white lines map out the levels of growth or decline. Thanks to this simple, highly patterned structure, a reader can tell immediately which countries will grow in population over the next fifty years (and by how much) and which will decline. Conventions like those used in bar graphs have evolved over the years and they have to be learned. Most readers are familiar with them today—as they are with line graphs (useful for tracking changes over time or showing trends) and pie charts (effective devices for displaying part-to-whole distributions).

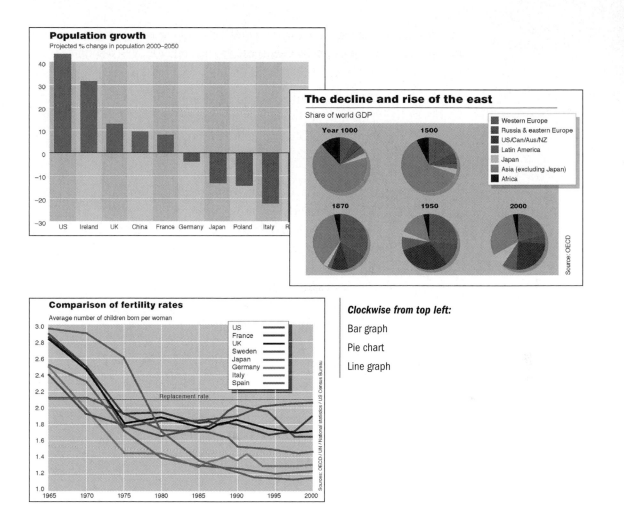

Clockwise from top left:

Bar graph

Pie chart

Line graph

EXAMPLES Why do sonnets remain such a popular form of poetry? One reason is certainly their challenging structure, which seems simple but demands great skill from poets. A typical sonnet runs only fourteen lines, long enough to develop a clever thought without belaboring it (or exhausting the patience of readers). Sonnets also entertain readers with prescribed rhyme schemes that challenge the ingenuity of poets. But there's yet another structural demand: The poem must execute a turn in its thinking at just the right moment. In the Petrarchan or Italian sonnet, that shift usually occurs after line eight; in the Shakespearean or English sonnet, the turn occurs in the couplet that follows the twelfth line.

And somehow, as a poet jumps these technical hurdles, the poem must still sound easy, passionate, natural, and sincere. A reader aware of what the poet is accomplishing almost wants to applaud as the requirements are met. In a tour de force, Shakespeare even went so far as to weave the complex architecture of the sonnet into his play *Romeo and Juliet*. When the tragic young lovers meet for the first time, for example, they speak to each other in, yes, a sonnet:

ROMEO: (1) If I profane with my unworthiest hand
(2) This holy shrine, the gentle fine is this:
(3) My lips, two blushing pilgrims, ready stand
(4) To smooth that rough touch with a tender kiss.

JULIET: (5) Good pilgrim, you do wrong your hand too much,
(6) Which mannerly devotion shows in this;
(7) For saints have hands that pilgrims' hands do touch,
(8) And palm to palm is holy palmers' kiss.

ROMEO: (9) Have not saints lips, and holy palmers too?

JULIET: (10) Ay, pilgrim, lips that they must use in prayer.

ROMEO: (11) O, then, dear saint, let lips do what hands do;
(12) They pray, grant thou, lest faith turn to despair.

JULIET: (13) Saints do not move, though grant for prayers' sake.

ROMEO: (14) Then move not, while my prayer's effect I take.

■ ■ ■

Texts that challenge your expectations may be the hardest to read. Because you don't recognize the patterns or structures according to which they are composed, you may tend to dismiss them or even ridicule them—until they start to look more familiar because you've begun to understand them. (Of course, you can still dislike them, but perhaps more knowledgeably.) Frank Gehry's buildings challenge almost every popular convention of architecture. Their dizzying facades, curved surfaces, and seemingly random shapes make them look, some would argue, more heaped than composed. Yet they are designed to open up possibilities for both the people who use the buildings and those who design other works in Gehry's wake. Gehry's work wouldn't be possible without computers figuring out how to bend materials into the odd shapes he envisions. But now that machines give architects this new freedom, why not use it? Why shouldn't buildings entertain us? Gehry dares us to welcome new shapes into our lives.

"The Stata [Center at MIT] is always going to look unfinished. It also looks as if it's about to collapse. Columns tilt at scary angles. Walls teeter, swerve, and collide in random curves and angles. Materials change wherever you look: brick, mirror-surface steel, brushed aluminum, brightly colored paint, corrugated metal. Everything looks improvised, as if thrown up at the last moment. That's the point. The Stata's appearance is a metaphor for the freedom, daring, and creativity of the research that's supposed to occur inside it."

—ROBERT CAMPBELL
"Dizzying Heights," *Boston Globe*,
April 25, 2004

Stata Center, MIT

CONSIDER

1. In writing courses, you've probably been introduced to patterns and structures such as description, narration, process analysis, classification, comparison and contrast, and analogy. Try to apply two of the patterns you recognize or recall to a medium other than writing. For instance, a process analysis explains how something is done. In what other media might you expect to see explanations of how to do or create something?

2. Look for photographs in magazines or online—or perhaps some you have taken yourself—that seem to violate the rule of thirds. Would the photographs have been more dynamic if they followed the guideline? Why or why not? Try to explain when it might feel right to center a subject.

What details matter?

Books, articles, movies, photographs, buildings, and even ads—especially ads—must do more than just gain your attention. They have to hold it. If you've ever picked up a supermarket tabloid, you probably know what happens when the details of a story don't live up to a sensational headline.

Successful texts get you thinking beyond their first impressions by offering up rich details. You may not notice these details initially because they are deliberately secondary—like the separate stones that make up an arch. But remove one stone and watch what happens. In written texts, it's often the details that provide support for a claim or make a story plausible. In visual texts, the details enrich or complicate our initial experience and encourage us to look again and again. In music, the backbeat may be what defines a song and makes it memorable or tuneful.

LOOK CLOSELY Because of the sheer variety of texts, it's hard to provide general directions for paying attention to details beyond the obvious: Read, look, and listen carefully. Still, some habits might be useful in appreciating the details in a text.

- Don't trust first impressions. They may very well be wrong or misleading, especially when something you are reading is truly new or moves contrary to your expectations.

- Assume that more may be going on than you suspect. Read any text imaginatively and creatively. Take for granted that someone has paid careful attention while creating it and that all its elements serve a purpose. In particular, look for connections between the primary aim, theme, or thesis of the work and all the supporting details.

- Approach every text, especially a familiar or conventional one, as if you were encountering it for the first time. Sometimes we stop paying attention when the terrain we are covering seems familiar—like driving the same road every day.

- Examine how the graphic details contribute to a work. Study the lighting technique used by the photographer, the brushstrokes of a painter, the similes and metaphors of a writer, and so on. Learn as much as you can about any texts you encounter often.

- Think about what the text has excluded or left out. Pay attention to the framing or cropping of an image, the topics not covered in an article or newspaper, the people whose names or faces aren't represented in a work. These omissions may prove to be more than a matter of detail.

EXAMINE THE POINT OF VIEW For example, **perspective**—the illusion of depth in paintings—is a detail you may not notice the first time you look at a work of art. Yet perspective contributes significantly to your experience. Artists can decide whether their subjects will imitate life in three dimensions or whether flattening or distorting these items better serves their ends. Similarly, **point of view**—what a photographer calls the "camera angle"—can give shape to a composition and highlight specific themes. Illustrator and painter Mark Ulriksen manipulates both perspective and point of view in his images of our canine friends. These elements in his paintings encourage us to see our relationships with dogs in new ways.

Mark Ulriksen, *Little Dog* (2000): Close up, low angle

Mark Ulriksen, *Puppy Love* (2001): Distant, high angle

Bill Greene, Boston College graduation (2004)

What actually ends up in an image is an important detail too, one that's easy to overlook because what we see can seem like the whole story, complete in itself. Notice how photographer Bill Greene crops his photo of the audience at the 2004 graduation at Boston College to provide a selective view of the event, which featured speaker Tim Russert. It's doubtful that all the students were quite so bored by the NBC commentator's commencement address, but the shot leaves that impression—one that irritated officials at the school. But consider how much less interesting the image would be if we saw more of the graduates.

Of course, any photograph can be cropped for deliberate effect, a process now much easier for an amateur using a digital camera to manage. Your subject doesn't even have to fit within a traditional frame. It may be more powerful if parts get clipped off.

In fact, digital photography now makes it possible to alter photographs in ways only dictators could do formerly, eliminating inconvenient people with a click of the mouse.

Photograph before and after digital cropping

NOTICE WHAT'S MISSING What may be even more difficult to notice than cropping or framing is what's not in a text to begin with. The *Wall Street Journal* has one of the most distinctive and traditional designs of any major newspaper. But it may take a moment or more for you to realize that something very familiar is missing from its pages—photographs. The absence of photographs reflects the philosophy of the paper and its focus on hard news. But the *Journal* is not without images. In fact, since 1979 it has used a unique form of illustration called "hedcuts," portraits built from dots and lines designed to complement rather than overwhelm the surrounding print. Based on photographs but drawn by artists, hedcuts have become one of the enduring pleasures of American journalism, at least among readers who don't miss the photographs. It's a detail that adds to the experience of reading the newspaper.

EXAMPLES Can the details ever be more important than the focal point of a text? Yes, it happens all the time, especially in material that deals with statistics and factual information. Consider the bar graph tracking population growth over the next fifty years. The focal point may be the title, but most readers would linger there only a moment before moving on to the fascinating numbers. (Did you imagine that the United States would grow faster than China?) The chart was created by Hamish McRae using statistics provided by the United Nations.

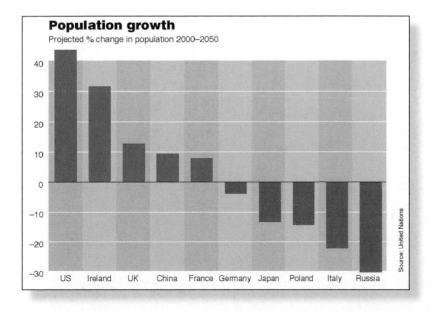

Population growth
Projected % change in population 2000–2050

Source: United Nations

US Ireland UK China France Germany Japan Poland Italy Russia

It goes without saying, then, that the details of a text may tease us into thinking more deeply about what it is doing. Borrell's *Escaping Criticism* obviously leaves a great deal concealed and unsaid, encouraging us to discover its meanings on our own. The boy leaps into our world from a dark background, only a hint of light around his left elbow. We see no buildings, landscapes, or companions. We have no idea who the boy is either or what he does. His feet are sunburnt brown and either muscled or chubby; his chest is pale and white, perhaps from too much school or modeling. Given the title of the work, perhaps he is supposed to represent the spirit of art or creativity, young and vital before the critics get to him. And of course, we have no way of knowing where he is heading except that he's stepping into our world, blurring the line between reality and illusion.

■ ■ ■

Some poems seem almost entirely about the details: They ask us to pay attention to what is right in front of us. Consider the spare but specific images in this deceptively simple poem.

William Carlos Williams

The Red Wheelbarrow
(1923)

so much depends
upon

a red wheel
barrow

glazed with rain
water

beside the white
chickens

Notice how the arrangement of the lines compels you to examine each word carefully and to think about its meaning and placement. This is poetry in which every detail matters. It may lack the complex structure of a Shakespearean sonnet or the wealth of allusion in one of Seamus Heaney's poems. But it makes its point just as memorably.

■ ■ ■

While a stunning piece of architecture can be fun to look at, its details will determine how livable it will be. Frank Gehry's Stata Center Building at MIT makes a visual statement from every angle, but its odd shapes, complex surfaces, and open corridors contribute to goals set by MIT administrators, who wanted a building that encouraged community and collaboration. So the building juxtaposes classrooms, laboratories, offices, and corridors (called "student streets") in ways that ease movement and communication. Even the building materials, ranging from brick to stainless steel, challenge expectations and entertain the eye with unexpected shapes and surfaces. The Stata Center is not a building that can be taken in at a glance or navigated confidently. But its distinctive features have earned names such as Nose, Helmet, and Kiva that steer visitors in the right direction. The endless details make the building more than the sum of its parts.

"The street is lined with colorful walls and with benches and niches for conversation, some alongside giant blackboards and bulletin boards. Curving staircases climb above the street at both ends, and catwalks above it give access to upper-level areas. The building's interior doesn't inspire awe the way a cathedral might, but its angled planes and unexpected curves are likely to delight anyone walking among them. So will hanging walls that seem to defy gravity, or at least logic, and occasional glimpses of odd, high towers that would look right at home in a Dr. Seuss book."

—LAWRENCE BIEMILLER
"MIT Splices Whimsy into Its Architectural DNA,"
Chronicle of Higher Education, May 7, 2004

Stata Center, MIT

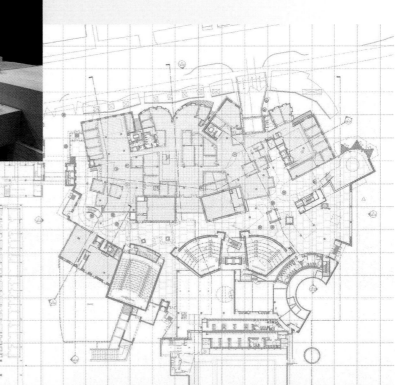

Floor plan of the Stata Center

1. Describe how the varying perspectives and points of view in the two Ulriksen dog paintings dictate your response to them. Do the titles of the paintings on page 41 make a difference as well?

2. A surprising number of people have never paid much attention to the details of the story told in the first verse of the national anthem of the United States of America:

   > Oh, say can you see, by the dawn's early light,
   > What so proudly we hailed at the twilight's last gleaming?
   > Whose broad stripes and bright stars, through the perilous fight,
   > O'er the ramparts we watched, were so gallantly streaming?
   > And the rockets' red glare, the bombs bursting in air,
   > Gave proof through the night that our flag was still there.
   > O say, does that star-spangled banner yet wave
   > O'er the land of the free and the home of the brave?

   Study the verse and, in a paragraph, summarize precisely what is happening in the song. Who might be speaking? When did the action begin? What do we know by the end of the verse? If you *are* brave, summarize the story told in the complete anthem—all four verses. You can find the other three verses easily on the Web.

3. Borrell's *Escaping Criticism* is a detail woven throughout this chapter. Review the chapter to see how often and where it is mentioned. What is the effect of this repetition on your reading? How does the image contribute to your overall impression of the chapter? Do you find it an important element or a distracting detail?

4. If you have access to digital photographs and software by which to crop and manipulate images, choose a single photograph you have taken and rework it several ways. Then present those images to your classmates, explaining how manipulating the details might change the purpose of the photograph. Here, for example, is a color photograph of vultures on a suburban chimney, cropped and manipulated to create first a more sinister and then a more abstract image, using nothing fancier than an image editing application.

CHAPTER 2

GETTING ATTENTION

composing texts

Poster for *Dark Skies*, a *Star Wars* fan film by David Nutley

Introduction

Have you seen a movie recently that you liked a lot? How did you respond? Did you recommend it to your friends, hoping they'd share your enthusiasm? Buy it when it came out on DVD? Review it for your college paper or local arts journal? Sensible reactions all.

A tutorial from David Nutley's *Star Wars* fan film site.

But did you ever consider creating your own version of the film? You could borrow a digital video camera, persuade a few friends to play Neo or Amidala, or Spider-Man, rework the original story to suit the local scenery, and start shooting your prequel, sequel, or reimagined epic. Sound weird? Yet a surprising number of people have been doing exactly that for years, creating a phenomenon called "fan films."

Invented well before digital video recorders became both cheap and sophisticated and computers enabled amateurs to create special effects, these short amateur productions usually mimic the themes and styles of action films such as *Star Wars*, *Star Trek*, and *The Matrix*. Some fan films poke fun at the works they imitate, but more often they pay homage to the originals, reinvigorating and reinventing them. A few fan films go on to become cult objects on their own, downloaded by eager viewers from Web sites (try googling "fan films"). The site for David Nutley's $17^1/_2$-minute fan film *Dark Skies* promises a sequel and even includes tutorials to help others make technically sophisticated *Star Wars* clones. What was initially a geekish response to movies has in effect become a new subgenre, blurring all sorts of lines and conventions. Fan films even get reviewed.

"The fan-filmmaker can't profit from his work, because he's usually already stretching the notion of fair use to the limits. This is a critical point: A fan film may occasionally make fun, but it's a different animal from satire. Unlike, say, a *Saturday Night Live* sketch, most fan films have some narrative meat on their bones."

—M. E. RUSSELL
"The Fan Films Strike Back," *Weekly Standard*, May 14, 2004

Though you may never make a fan film, you'll respond to texts of all kinds with varying degrees of concern and passion. Many of your responses will be in writing, though it will be writing that more and more often merges with images or other media. Sometimes you'll reflect on what you've seen and read, and your responses will be conventional–you'll report, analyze, and evaluate. In other cases, you will, like the creators of fan films, use your own deep knowledge of texts and genres (see Chapter 1) to strike out in new directions, challenging others with the power of your imagination. You'll discover that you have a remarkable number of choices today when you compose. That's both the opportunity and challenge of writing.

What's in This Chapter?

Just as Chapter 1 provided questions to guide the process of reading texts, here we offer questions designed to help you to compose texts of your own. Our assumption is that in most cases, you will be using these questions to compose responses to images, readings, and writing assignments throughout this book. But the guidelines here aren't narrow or specialized; rather, they walk you through elements that shape every message and aspect of communication: *subject, purpose, audience, content, medium,* and *process.*

Composing
Texts

We usually write or compose because something pushes us to do it. We want to express ourselves, learn more about our environment, tell a story, explain something, analyze something, or argue something. Very often the urge to compose is sparked by someone else's work. A photograph of our great-grandmother makes us think about our own heritage and identity. A documentary opens our eyes to social conditions we'd ignored for a long time. An editorial makes us angry enough to write a letter to the editor. The following questions should help you assess your options and opportunities for responding in such situations.

What's it to you?

What do you want to say about it?

Who will listen?

What do you need to know?

How will you do it?

How well does it work?

**Composing Texts:
A Tutorial**
www.ablongman.com/beyondwords02

What's it to you?

It's easy to be excited when an assignment, topic, or text appeals to you personally. Consider the instant messages you write to friends to bring them up to speed on your life or the latest episode of *The O.C.* You don't worry about your incentive for writing. You just do it because you've got an inclination to communicate.

Such enthusiasm for composing can't be manufactured, but it can be cultivated. The advice we offer in Chapter 1 is in part designed to make you push back against the words and images pummeling you every day. When you read any text critically and attentively, chances are you will find something in it that sparks a critical impulse. *Critical* here is not a negative term. It means seeing something with eyes wide open. Such a gaze prepares you to write with intelligence and grip.

But first, you need to understand to whom you are responding and who the *you* actually is in your project—tall orders both.

UNDERSTAND YOUR RELATIONSHIP TO YOUR SUBJECT

Who or what created the work to which you're responding will have a huge impact on what you do with it. For instance, you likely know how to respond to messages from close acquaintances, people you may love, hate, admire, fear, trust, or disbelieve. You recognize instinctively when to counter a roommate's political rants or respond directly to an e-mail from an angry parent. You also sense when to remain silent. That's because you've developed relationships with people over time.

You may have a different sense of closeness to authors, reporters, columnists, cartoonists, artists, bloggers, and the like, whom you know chiefly through their work or reputations. It's not unusual to be passionate about such figures, especially when their work becomes part of your regular routine. You might write directly and vociferously to a Sean Hannity or an Alan Colmes just because you see them nightly on cable news and know enough about their lives and politics to feel invested in responding to them. (Of course, their relationship to you would be very different; you're just an anonymous member of a sizeable viewing audience.)

But attach even an unfamiliar name to a text, and a conversation begins. And thanks to Web search engines, you can find information about any author today, famous or not, living or dead, and learn more about his or her work. Such knowledge can give you additional motives for responding to texts of all sorts, whether a textbook chapter or the editorial cartoon spanning three columns in today's paper.

Look more closely at that same newspaper page and you'll likely find a strong opinion piece *without* a signature, the daily editorial offered up not by a person but by the newspaper itself *as an institution*. And anonymous and unsigned texts can be found almost anywhere you look. Who is the author of that possibly sexist jeans ad you passed on a building wall? The poster is surely the responsibility of the company selling the clothes, but you suspect an ad agency bears some responsibility for it too and, maybe, the owner of the building itself. And, who might be responsible for snapping the photograph of the Indian woman in traditional dress walking by the poster? These images may provoke a strong reaction because they are working hard to influence you. What are they up to? Chances are, these people want something from you.

To put it another way, your investment in a text or a project may be related to its investment in you as a reader, critic, citizen, or consumer. The more you come to know about the author or authors of a text, the more likely you will be motivated to respond intelligently.

But who are *you* exactly? In some situations, you will be that private individual who smiles obediently when a friend aims a camera in your direction at a party. Given the right opportunity, you might be goaded into sharing your life story in a letter, diary, or journal or film, explaining your experiences, beliefs, and values. But you are also a person who carries others with you—those who share your gender, religion, race, sexual orientation, or dozens of other commonalities. When you read a history book, you read it as yourself and, perhaps, also as an African American and a woman, wondering why you don't find more of yourself in the story. You listen to a comedian poking fun at lawyers and squirm a little because you want to be one. You find yourself gearing up to write an op-ed piece for your college paper because it published yet another photograph meant to demean fraternities—and you're Greek. What does a subject or an assignment mean to you? In many ways, that will depend on which *you* is touched or energized by a project and how much passion, knowledge, expertise, and interest you can bring to it.

A casual snapshot may conceal as much as it reveals.

In all people I see myself, none more and not one a barley-corn less,
And the good or bad I say of myself I say of them.

I know I am solid and sound,
To me the converging objects of the universe perpetually flow,
All are written to me, and I must get what the writing means.

—WALT WHITMAN,
from "Song of Myself" (1891)

1. List a number of people whose work you know well enough that you would feel comfortable conversing with them about serious issues if you met them in an airport lounge. (Leave out figures in the sports or entertainment industries.) Why would knowledge about their lives or work give you this confidence? Which persons on your list do you believe might be as willing to speak with you?

2. Check out the front page of your local newspaper or the online version of a national newspaper, and find the name of one person mentioned in a story whom you don't recognize or don't know much about but who has some public standing. (In other words, don't look for the name of a random accident victim or a campus celebrity.) Do a Google search on that name, and see what turns up. Does the information you discover change your appreciation for the original story?

3. Look for an advertisement or public service announcement for one product that piggybacks on another—for example, a fast-food promotion on a cereal box or a missing-child label on a milk carton. Briefly discuss the relationship between the items. Who is trying to get you to respond and why? How is the appeal enhanced or changed by its relationship with another product, sponsor, or institution?

4. What aspects of *you* make you identify with others when cultural or political issues are raised? Does that *you* change in more casual situations, on a Friday night at the movies, for example? Why or why not? How many *you*s are there?

COMPOSE

5. Have you ever responded as deeply and personally to an author, book, movie, TV show, or other text as the *auteurs* of fan films do to *Star Wars* and *Star Trek*? In a page or two, describe what such a fascination (or obsession) has led you or someone you know to do in response. What have you created, cataloged, or collected? With whom have you shared your interest?

What do you want to say about it?

Thinking about your subject can help you formulate and refine a topic for your writing projects. You've probably been advised to work with subjects you know well, and that's fine advice in many cases. We all like to write to our strengths. But you may also be assigned a subject or you may wish to explore something new. A major reason for engaging with other texts is to expand what you know and to extend your reach as a thinker—to push yourself to comprehend perspectives different from your own and to learn from or challenge them. As you consider subjects for writing, allow this impulse to explore to help you identify specific topics.

Dorothea Lange, *Migrant Mother* (1936)

CONSIDER YOUR PURPOSE You can also think about your purpose and about the best kind of writing to meet your needs. You can engage a rich text in a variety of ways, each of which can help you express what you have to say. In this book we organize some of these ways of writing using the following categories: self-expression, description, narration, explanation and reporting, analysis, and argument. Consider how you might choose among these modes of writing to respond to a photograph such as Dorothea Lange's famous *Migrant Mother* (1936)—which we discuss in more detail in Chapter 3.

- You could **express** your personal reactions to *Migrant Mother* as a human portrait, explaining what you see in it and how its depiction of hard times and human endurance touches your life. Or you could try to create a portrait that captures similar concerns using a digital camera.

- You could **describe** the scene that Dorothea Lange presents in the image and explore the harsh environments in which this and other of her Depression-era photographs were taken for the Farm Security Administration (FSA). Or you could locate the image within an older tradition of "Madonna and child" portraits and explore similarities and differences.

- You could **narrate** the cultural history that explains *Migrant Mother,* placing it in the context of similar works, such as the film version of John Steinbeck's *The Grapes of Wrath* (1940).

- You could **explain** the technical aspects of Lange's craft as a photographer, reporting information about her career, techniques, and her body of work.

- You could **analyze** the enduring impact that photographs by Lange and others of the Depression era have had on viewers both in the United States and worldwide.

- You could **argue** that artists do or do not have a responsibility to address social concerns in their work.

Excerpt from a student paper that discusses Lange's *Migrant Mother* in the context of other images of the Great Depression.

Ditched, Stalled and Stranded San Joaquin Valley California 1935, by Dorothea Lange

We can see that Lange's work participates primarily in context of suffering and displacement by considering connections between her FSA images and other important representations of Depression era life. Consider for instance, the similarities between Lange's *Ditched, Stalled, and Stranded San Joaquin Valley* (California 1935) and the stories of exodus represented by John Steinbeck's *The Grapes of Wrath*. The connection between Lange's work and Steinbeck's novel is strong enough that it was noted by the creators of the 1940 film version of *The Grapes of Wrath*. It is almost as if the filmmakers translated Lange's subject to celluloid, highlighting in the process the themes of human endurance in the face of depression that permeate Lange's photographs.

Film Still from *The Grapes of Wrath* (1940)

CONSIDER

1. Choose a film that you've seen recently, preferably one that got you thinking, and explore what you might do with it as the subject of a paper, running through the same six categories: *express, describe, narrate, explain, analyze, argue.* If you prefer, do this assignment with a provocative editorial cartoon or an attention-getting advertisement or series of ads.

2. First, identify a subject you know a lot about, one that others even identify with you. Then, from your position of expertise, explain what you'd like to know more about within that subject. What aspect would you happily explore on your own, given the time and the opportunity?

As you decide what to say and how best to say it, consider some techniques for generating topic ideas: *listing, brainstorming, free writing, idea mapping, outlining*, and so on. Choose the techniques best suited to your subject. And don't ignore spending productive hours in a library or exploring ideas with others.

Who will listen?

Big corporations conduct demographic studies to pinpoint the age, sex, income level, hobbies, and inclinations of potential consumers. Of course, audiences are far more complicated and unpredictable than researchers would like, and your job as a writer will not likely involve selling a product. But still, you should invest a good deal of your energy in evaluating the characteristics of those you wish to engage.

IDENTIFY YOUR AUDIENCE Although you need to keep your own purpose in sharp focus, you can't afford to ignore your audience. Who is likely to respond to the writing you are doing or the project you are developing? An instructor? Colleagues in a class? Friends and family? Members of a student organization? A community of readers? You must consider your obligations to them and what you hope to accomplish with your work.

Consider how tough it can be to decide what a teacher wants. Often assignments provide plenty of guidance about what your instructor expects, from the nature of the topic to acceptable formats for the project. Attention to expectations of this kind is one way of signaling your respect for an audience. An instructor with integrity hopes you'll be excited by a project; he or she wants you to learn from the experience and to gain control over the composing process. It often helps to think of audiences as people drawn to your work by a common interest.

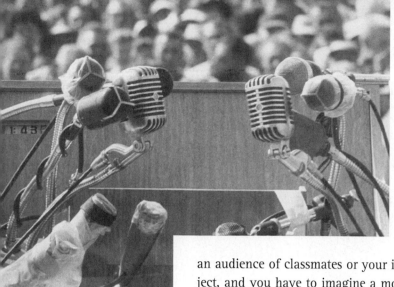

What kind of audiences might be reached through Web projects and other media?

Learn to recognize and work with the parameters of your writing task even as you put your own personal stamp on the process.

And you should probably think about multiple audiences too, especially when your project is in a medium that increases your potential reach. A research paper might demand that you address an audience of classmates or your instructor. Turn that paper into a Web project, and you have to imagine a more complex audience, larger and far more diverse. The same might be true with photographs or videos you create, paintings you exhibit, or multimedia projects on which you collaborate.

Sometimes you'll design a project to reach specific audiences while excluding others. Political speeches or ads designed to activate the base—that is, stir up core supporters for a candidate or party—deliberately make fewer concessions to independent voters or members of the opposing party. They offer red meat to those already committed to a position. Web logs (blogs) cater to very specific audiences too. You find blogs for everyone from political junkies to cat fanciers. Evaluating the specific make-up of an audience can help you identify its needs.

On a basic level, audiences may need background information, definitions of technical terms, and points of reference to enter your project. Considering audience needs can help you fine-tune such material. Provide too little background information, and readers will be confused; give too much, and you will lose their attention. Similarly, audiences have specific needs related to what you have to say and how you intend to say it. Readers of paper documents need organization, logical headings, appropriate formatting, and so on. Web readers might require descriptive language for hyperlinks, thumbnail images that conserve bandwidth, or standardized navigation options. Especially with projects that use new media, you may need to pay attention to the requirements of audiences with disabilities. On the Web, for instance, your material can be accessible to the blind if you pay proper attention to the arrangement of information on your pages and to the careful tagging of visual items. To learn about accessibility issues, simply search the phrase "Web accessibility" on the Internet.

On another level, audiences often share communal needs or standards for communicating. You can tap into these conventions by choosing the right vocabulary, using the expected conventions, or making allusions to familiar texts, authors, or themes. For instance, when you learn to write a research paper in correct CSE or APA form, you are signaling to a select group of schol-

COMPOSING TEXTS

ars that you have the qualifications necessary to join their club. You have to demonstrate that expertise before they'll take your work seriously.

Finally, sometimes what your audience needs is the media equivalent of a good kick in the pants. You want people to wake up and pay attention to what you have to say. Even when you've created something important, you can't safely assume that audiences will notice it just because you've put it out there. As we noted in Chapter 1, texts are always competing for attention, so your work needs presence. Sometimes you can achieve that power through language alone; sometimes an image can be worth the proverbial thousand words. Or maybe you need to combine media, amplifying your words with images, animating them with cartoons, or making them a part of a Web presentation, poster, or collage. Do whatever works.

What strategies does this student Web project use to draw attention to the obesity problem?

Critics and scholars are evangelists, plucking the public by the sleeve, saying "Look at this," or "Listen to this," or "See how this works."

—HELEN VENDLER
"The Ocean, the Bird, and the Scholar," Jefferson Lecture, 2004

1. Pick up several magazines and examine them carefully to identify what signals they send aimed at specific needs of potential readers. Try to look at a range of periodicals, from mass-market monthlies such as *Reader's Digest* and *Rolling Stone* to enthusiast's magazines such as *Hooked on Crochet!* and *Popular Woodworking*. Why, for example, do many men push away from *Cosmo* while women roll their eyes at *Maxim*? Can you recognize signals concerning the gender, income, class, age, or other characteristics of its intended readers?

2. Find a text in your local or campus environment, and consider how you might make it accessible or comprehensible to someone who does not experience it the way you do. How might you make a large bronze statue accessible to someone who is not sighted? How might you help a sighted person appreciate a Braille text? Can you imagine sharing an opera or rock concert with someone who is hearing-impaired?

COMPOSE

3. Find an instruction manual for a product you own, and write a paragraph analyzing how well it serves its potential readers. What efforts does it make to explain steps for using the product effectively or safely? Does the manual assume that the user is reasonably intelligent, technically sophisticated, or an idiot? How well, if at all, does the manual deal with the problem of readers with different levels of experience with the product? How much of the manual is genuinely aimed at the buyer of the product, and how much is written for product liability lawyers eager to sue?

What do you need to know?

Among your responsibilities to an audience is knowing what you're talking about. Gut reactions are fine when it comes to deciding to tackle a project or offer an opinion. But you quickly want to move beyond that basic level of response.

GATHER INFORMATION ABOUT YOUR SUBJECT For instance, you may think that *The Lord of the Rings* is the finest film trilogy ever made. But to make that argument in a paper or on a Web site, what would you have to do? For one thing, you'd have to look over the field of other credible film trilogies. Off the top of your head, you might come up with the three *Jurassic Park* movies, and the original set of *Star Wars* films, Spielberg's *Raiders of the Lost Ark* series, and of course the *Godfather* trilogy, of which the first two films earned Best Picture Oscars. But "off the top of your head" wouldn't be good enough. To support as sweeping a claim as you started with, you'd need to develop some expertise with your subject. You might do some digging in film his-

A family views the Vietnam Veterans Memorial in Washington, D.C.

tory, where you'd discover that some of the world's most distinguished filmmakers have made trilogies, including Ingmar Bergman, Hiroshi Inagaki, and Michelangelo Antonioni. Things just got complicated. Your sweeping claim obligates you to track down and watch films you may never have heard of. And then you need to weigh them by some reasonable criteria against *The Lord of the Rings*. Can you do it? Sure. Will it be easy? No one ever said it would be. Could you modify your claim to make the task more manageable? That would be a sensible option: *The Lord of the Rings* might very well be the *best English-language action-adventure film trilogy of modern times*.

Learning what you need to know about a subject should be more than just work: research of this sort makes life interesting. Think about a time—perhaps you were younger—when sightseeing was a pain. The Little Big Horn was just a rolling hillside miles from anything else in Montana, or that long black wall in Washington, D.C., was one of a dozen monuments your parents dragged you by on a rainy afternoon. At the time, you may not have recognized the significance of what you'd experienced—or, more accurately, you may not have had enough experience or information to appreciate it at the time. You don't want to make the same mistake when responding to texts or assignments, dismissing them because you are uninformed or uninterested.

Research is in many ways much easier to do today than ever before, thanks to the power of digitized information. You can find a little bit about almost anything on the Web and a great deal about many contemporary subjects—especially political and social topics.

The Web is also a splendid tool for generating ideas. Imagine for a moment that you encounter an amazing image by a photographer you don't know. So you spend half a minute searching for more about her on the Web, using Google or Yahoo or Ask Jeeves. Following up those leads, you learn about other works she has produced and galleries where she has exhibited. One of those galleries has an online catalog that links to artists who do similar work. Before you know it, you've been introduced to a style of photography you didn't even know existed, one you might want to write about or imitate.

Develop your skills as a researcher.
Resources for finding and evaluating visual sources
www.ablongman.com/beyondwords03

But the Web is also just a preliminary tool of research. You need to push beyond it, using all of the research sources available to you, from the online resources of your campus library to a physical tour of the reference room in a library and a discussion with a reference librarian. Learn to evaluate and use materials online, but don't forget to make physical contact with the resources of a library, a museum, or a special collection of any kind. Our Web site can help you develop your skills as a researcher.

Remember, too, that people can be valuable resources for your projects. You can learn a lot from serious discussions with experts who can lead you to reputable sources or valuable research techniques. They've got a wealth of experience and will probably be glad to share it, just as you should do in the future. Again, the Web can help jump start the process. You might want to explore the discussions archived at the Google Groups pages where you can tap into many of the conversations of experts. You can also find a number of discussions taking place in Web forums and on e-mail discussion lists by conducting Internet searches.

With many projects today, you'll need to develop technical skills for gathering information, for using technology, or for managing various media.

For instance, you may be asked to do fieldwork or to do a survey in response to some texts. Chances are that such assignments will help you learn more about techniques of observation. Or you'll be given specific directions in guiding you to do informal fieldwork.

USE TECHNOLOGY Learning to use technology also requires some investment. Many people prefer fiddling with devices until they've mastered the basic skills, using various help menus or options to fine-tune their knowledge. Yet there's much to be said for reading a manual and locating people who can offer guidance to help you prepare to do work with technology.

You might check whether a support center on campus offers tutorials or find out how to reach people who can help you out. The best help may come from classmates or acquaintances. Don't be afraid to ask for help or to explore new technology. One of the hardest habits to break is the tendency to use only the most familiar tools, never exploring what's new until the older technology disappears.

But mastering unfamiliar ways of communicating involves far more than just getting equipment to work—as you know if you've ever sat through a highly polished but deadly dull PowerPoint presentation. You need to learn how to manage the rhetoric of any medium you choose, whether you are creating photographs, videos, brochures, posters, or research papers. Each medium and genre has its expectations, which you can learn best by observing and studying successful models. What makes them work? How are they constructed? How do they reach their audience? What techniques do they employ?

DOCUMENT YOUR SOURCES Finally, in gathering information for any project, you must respect intellectual property concerns and understand the conventions for documenting information. Working with written texts, you probably know your responsibilities to keep track of your sources, document your use of ideas or words borrowed from others, use quotation marks around word-for-word borrowings, and provide a list of sources used in your project. You probably have a handbook that explains the conventions of various systems of documentation—Modern Language Association (MLA), American Psychological Association (APA), *The Chicago Manual of Style* (CMS), Council of Science Editors (CSE), and perhaps some others—one of which you should use in any paper or project requiring formal documentation. (Your instructor will tell you which style to follow.)

But you also need to give proper credit to any photographers, filmmakers, musicians, or other artists you borrow from, especially when those items might appear in a publicly displayed work. A photograph or a film must be documented as carefully as a journal or newspaper article—though that credit might be handled differently, with a credit line, for example, rather than a footnote. Handbooks now explain how to document many nontraditional sources. Remember, too, that readers may want to know some background information about the images you use, especially the name of the artist responsible for the image and the date when it was produced, simply to give them some context for reading it. Help them out with a caption or note.

1. From the following list, choose a person or subject about which you'd like to know more. Then spend an hour in the library and some time online learning more about the topic—enough for you to make a brief in-class oral presentation. Keep track of your sources of information, and identify those that proved to be most helpful, comparing what you found in the library to online resources.

- Georgia O'Keeffe (painter)
- iPod
- Marshall McLuhan (media theorist)
- *Dogtown and Z Boys* (2001, film)
- Jonathan Ives (designer)
- Dorothea Lange (photographer)
- Art Deco movement
- Gordon Parks Sr. (photographer)

- Edward Curtis (photographer)
- Hybrid gas-electric cars
- The Glass House (1939, Philip Johnson building)
- Al Jourgenson (musician)
- Hiroshi Inagaki (filmmaker)
- *The Sixth Sense* (1999, film)

2. In a current writer's handbook that covers MLA and APA documentation, review the standards for documenting online and nonprint works (films, plays, cartoons). How do the systems differ in their treatment of these items? How are they alike?

How will you do it?

To convey ideas, you'll use some physical means of transmission, a *medium*. Speech is one medium with many variants; printed words are another. There are also numerous forms of visual and aural communication—oil paintings, watercolors, pencil drawings, film photography, digital photography, film, video, DVDs, Web sites, presentation software, CDs, vinyl records, radio, MP3s, and on and on. The vast array of media possibilities provides many options for responding to texts or ideas. Following are just a few major ones, some of which we focus on in subsequent chapters.

CHOOSE WHICH MEDIA YOU WILL USE

THE SPOKEN WORD remains a powerful medium because it involves direct human contact. Words can be delivered with whatever tone, volume, and pace a speaker chooses and at whatever length and with accompanying body language and gestures (though these movements might be invisible if the words are delivered via radio, yet another medium). In a live performance, a speaker receives immediate feedback from the audience that can range from appreciative to disgruntled to bored. In many presentations speakers will incorporate visuals or other aids (perhaps using PowerPoint slides) to help engage their audience. Conversation is an even more active form of the spoken

"I cannot help feeling, Phaedrus, that writing is unfortunately like painting; for the creations of the painter have the attitude of life, and yet if you ask them a question they preserve a solemn silence. And the same may be said of speeches. You would imagine that they had intelligence, but if you want to know anything and put a question to one of them, the speaker always gives one unvarying answer. And when they have been once written down they are tumbled about anywhere among those who may or may not understand them, and know not to whom they should reply, to whom not: and, if they are maltreated or abused, they have no parent to protect them; and they cannot protect or defend themselves."

—SOCRATES AS DEPICTED BY PLATO
in *Phaedrus* (360 BCE), translated by Benjamin Jowett

word, with participants learning from the give-and-take of dialogue. Unless recorded, however, speech evaporates into memory. In cultures that do not value memory, spoken words and testimony are considered less reliable than written documents and "hard evidence."

WRITTEN WORDS allow for the precise expression of complex ideas. Thoughts can be set down in endless detail, complete with supporting evidence and meticulous qualifications. Words can also record and inspire subtle human feelings and emotions. On paper, words transmit ideas in a convenient form that endures for millennia under ideal conditions. However, words are a relatively static medium, less conducive than speech to the interplay of ideas—except, perhaps, in some electronic forums. Printed words are also, as Plato noted, mute and unvarying and the enemies of memory. They can also be clumsy devices for describing physical objects or conveying proportion, perspective, or spatial relationships.

THE FINE ARTS in general—drawing, painting, sculpture, dance, and so on—provide various media for human expression. Appealing to the senses as well as the imagination, they encourage interpretation and provoke commentary. These arts tend to be tactile—objects or activities with a physical dimension or quality. Some, like oil paintings or pieces of sculpture, are permanent; others, like a dance or a musical production, exist in the moment of performance. Most of these works can be transmitted in some form, especially the performing arts. But many lose their impact when they are reproduced: The original work in oil, stone, or wood, represents the ultimate expression of the artist's achievement. Copies are not the same.

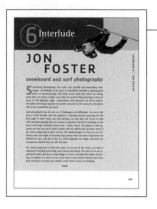

THE GRAPHIC ARTS are often servants to other media—for example, when a designer chooses fonts, colors, and elements for a book or designs clip art for use on Web pages or brochures. Yet, increasingly, the design elements of texts are becoming part of the message—as when a spreadsheet program makes it possible to turn numbers into graphs, tables, and charts or when digital technologies encourage authors to weave images into their compositions. Writers make more and more design decisions as graphic elements become part of their communication. This is clearly the case for software such as PowerPoint which asks writers to use charts, graphs, and design elements to deliver lectures, sales reports, and education.

PHOTOGRAPHY is an essential medium for transmitting static images via film or, increasingly, digital media. Photographs provide a relatively accurate means of recording aspects of the physical world using equipment available to most anyone, including rank amateurs. Photographers can produce work that is scientific, personal, or commercial, preserving on film everything from cellular structures and news events to crime scenes and vacation memories. Yet they also reach into the realms of high art. By its nature, photography is a static medium, and its images are open to interpretation, sometimes requiring words to explain them or give them context.

FILMS or movies are an ideal medium for capturing and embodying movement and action. Like still photography, film can provide a record of important events, activities, and processes; yet it is also (or simultaneously) an artistic medium, one that can tell stories, shape opinions, and provide entertainment. Film can be cut and spliced to manage the flow of images, ideas, and time; each shot also provides opportunities for artistic (or other) manipulation. So film can convey ideas powerfully and serve as a medium for documenting events. But films can also distort, falsify, or create "reality." Film also represents a medium that integrates other media—for instance, audio plays a key role in the composition of a film and the performances of actors account for a good deal of the film's message.

VIDEO shares many of the qualities of film. Like film, video can capture and edit movement. But the images in a video medium are stored and reproduced on a screen electronically rather than through the projection of light. (Of course, many movies originally shot on film have been transferred to video formats, such as VHS, DVD, and now HDTV.) Images shot with video cameras have a different quality than works captured on film—video feels more immediate and "realistic" than film but also cruder, colder, and less sharp. These differences are obvious enough to affect the response of audiences, although the distinctions between digital video and film are rapidly breaking down.

THE WORLD WIDE WEB is an important new medium, just one of many spawned by the computer and digital revolutions of the past two or three decades. Although it uses many media—including the printed word, sound, and video—it does not just combine them. Rather, the Web is a true network that provides an endless selection of links that bring media together. The Web can convey up-to-date information and entertainment in stunningly original and interactive ways; yet it can also be distressingly confusing. Long texts are hard to read on the screen, and the Web still has to prove its ability to archive materials over time. Yet it is remarkable that the same medium that offers to download pop music and provides moment-by-moment updates of stock prices can also reach deeply into library and museum collections. We still haven't fathomed all the dimensions of this medium.

MULTIMEDIA is a catchall term for any combination of media. As we point out in Chapter 1, such combinations are nothing new. Images and words have worked together since at least the time of the Egyptian Pharaohs. Digital technologies now enable almost anyone to integrate words, images, and sounds into texts. These hybrid media can create environments nicely adapted to specific subject situations: the online version of the *New York Times* provides not only words and pictures but also audio and video files and slide shows of news events, depending on the story covered. The downside of multimedia is that the technology can easily swamp the content, drawing attention to itself.

As recently as a decade ago, your choice of medium for responding to texts or assignments would have been limited to what was really a choice among genres, most of which involved language: You could compose a lab report, research paper, essay, book review, journal entry, and so on. Yet even then, texts like these might have included visual components. Illustrations and visuals have always played a crucial role in the sciences—take biology, for example, where drawings of plants, animals, and living structures were essential to fieldwork. In business, too—in fact, in any discipline that deals with numbers and statistics—knowing how to produce graphs, charts, and tables was required. Style books for MLA and APA documentation have long had rules for handling both figures and illustrations in research papers. Even personal journals and diaries were often illustrated with photographs or hand drawings.

It's just that now it's become much more routine to compose visually simply because technology makes it easier for nonexperts to do professional-looking work.

DECIDE WHAT TO DO The enhanced options you have for composing mean that you have more choices to make about media. But you will also make countless other decisions as you figure out how to compose responses to the texts you encounter everyday. Above all, return to the concerns spelled out at the beginning of this chapter. What is your purpose? Who is your audience? What do you know, and what do you have to say?

And you are likely to have to make choices about new forms of media. Should you use visuals in a conventional printed text when images aren't required? When do you add them? The simple answer would seem to be when they enhance the words or can convey information that words don't handle well. Your verbal description of a brown adobe church in New Mexico might never quite do justice to the structure the way a simple photograph would—though a picture isn't always superior to words in this regard. In many technical fields, a simple line drawing, chart, table, or other figure might be essential to conveying information. But sometimes words and pictures working together might prove a useful combination. The popular online site Mapquest.com, for example, offers both written directions and a map to users seeking information on how to get from one place to another.

Your decisions should begin, then, with what works best in a particular situation for a specific audience, understanding that this can mean many things. In some cases, the ability to convey information is paramount; in others,

How might a verbal description of this New Mexico church differ from this photograph?

what counts may be creating texts with emotional power or even physical beauty. A simple memo or even an e-mail might do an efficient job announcing a wedding, but wedding invitations don't look like memos or arrive via the Web—at least not yet. Guests planning to attend a wedding, sometimes at considerable cost, still expect the embossed letters, creamy parchment, and formal script of typical invitations. Rhetorical decisions of this sort, in which you respond to the realities of a situation, will dictate how you go about composing your project.

Similarly, you have to assess your own skills before you select a medium and begin composing. Making a Web site for an academic assignment may seem cooler than writing a conventional paper and less work. But those are both inadequate grounds upon which to create a project. Almost certainly, for a novice, building a competent Web site will consume more time than composing an essay. A decision to build a Web site should be based on reasons connected to your subject and purpose—for example, if the material is better served by the linked environment provided by the Web or the project has a service-learning component that needs the wider audience an online project will provide.

1. Plato observes that "oratory is the art of enchanting the soul." Apply this formula to compose definitions of several other media, especially modern ones. For example, "PowerPoint is the art of making important ideas seem trivial" or "Writing e-mail is the verbal equivalent of dropping in uninvited." Compare your aphorism with those composed by others in the class. Then choose one of your observations, and defend it in a paragraph.

2. Choose one of the nine categories of media just discussed (*spoken word, printed word, film*, and so on), and annotate the description with additional examples that either illustrate or undercut the claims made. For example, you have grown up with video, thanks to TV productions, videotapes, and camcorders. Is it true that "images shot with video cameras have a different quality than works captured on film"? Or that "video feels more immediate and 'realistic' than film"? What evidence would you use to confirm these claims or make others think twice about them?

3. Reflect on your usual composing process. How do you generally begin a writing project? Do you normally weigh concerns of purpose and audience? What are your strengths and weaknesses when it comes to composing? Write a paragraph in which you describe your typical writing process and sketch out possible adjustments that you might try in your next project.

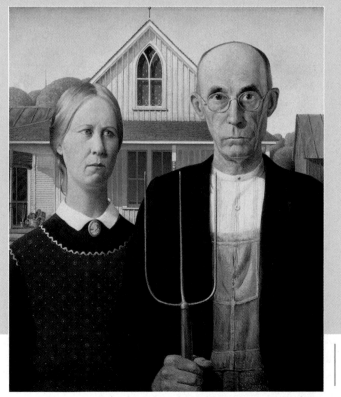

4. Write a brief proposal explaining how you would take a text already famous in one genre and move it to another. Filmmakers have been doing this for decades, taking novels, plays, or even comic books and turning them into movies. Argue the value of doing the same with some other text, but try to be imaginative in your migration from medium to medium. For example, could you turn Grant Wood's well-known painting *American Gothic* into a TV sitcom? What would be the rationale for doing that? What would be the theme for your *American Gothic* series? Who would the supporting characters be—in addition to the couple in the painting—and who would play them? Or how about turning a political show such as *Hardball* or *The O'Reilly Factor* into a video game? Again, what would be the challenge? How would players score? What would be the interface? And for any such shift of medium, what would be the point of the transformation?

Grant Wood, *American Gothic,* 1930, Friends of American Art Collection, 1930.934. Reproduction, The Art Institute of Chicago.

How well does it work?

No matter what your task, whether it is as different as creating a photo essay, analyzing a print advertisement, or designing a Web site to encourage voter registration, your choice of a subject, audience, and medium will guide your process of composing. No "one size fits all" formula works when you are responding to texts or assignments.

But certain choices have to be made and possibly revised. As we've suggested earlier in this chapter, at some point in any creative or composing process, you will decide

- What your subject or content will be
- What spin you'll give your material to meet your purpose
- What audiences you'll want to reach (or ignore)
- What you'll cover or exclude
- What medium or genre will work to organize the material

You will make such choices, consciously or not. Consciously is better.

You also probably understand already that the whole business of composing is messy, involving false starts, dead ends, uncooperative tools, unpredictable audiences, and so on. But composing also moves ahead by moments of illumination, triumph, and satisfaction, as you find yourself connecting with ideas and audiences.

EVALUATE AND REVISE YOUR WORK For all of your projects, you should improve your work by deliberately revising after reflection. All this means is that you need to test your project at various stages, using your own judgment or drawing on that of knowledgeable colleagues, friends, or even potential members of your audience. Before you revise, it helps to get some distance between yourself and the project. Put a paper aside for a few days, and you are far more likely to detect false assumptions, inadequate evidence, gaps in its coverage, windy paragraphs, or problems in mechanics and usage when you read through it again.

The same is true of projects in other media. Here a second or third opinion may encourage you to pull back a bit when you use images for their own sake or insist on imbedding an audio file on a page just because you've recently learned that skill. You might excuse a little graininess in a photograph you took because you really like the subject. A more experienced photographer might bring you down to earth or suggest how you might tinker with the image to take advantage of its roughness.

You can actually assess the effectiveness of some projects at the draft stage. Show a brochure you are creating to a test group, and ask members if they understand its point or can find essential information easily. Review a Web page you have created to see if it travels well from Mac to PC platforms. Ask someone who hasn't seen Martin Scorsese's *The Aviator* to judge how well your review explains the film.

Obviously, when you share your work with others, you automatically gain multiple perspectives. That's a great advantage, especially when you can make appropriate use of team members' differing talents. But even the best collaborative reviews will be of little use if you and your peers don't provide searching feedback. Look for deeper-level problems when you begin evaluat-

Film still from *The Aviator* (2004)

ing someone's work. Don't nitpick or personalize your criticisms. And take the concerns of readers to heart, thinking through their questions or suggestions to spur you toward meaningful revisions.

One final bit of advice: Spend some time sweating the details. With a paper, that means checking facts and proofreading. On a Web project, test all the links. In a slide show, be certain the images are in the right order and have the correct captions. Make sure everything is spelled right in any work. Details that seem insignificant to you may well damage your project in the eyes of readers or viewers accustomed to quality work.

COMPOSE

Fan films are mostly amateur efforts, but some are nicely plotted or show imaginative use of special effects. Do a Web search of "fan films" to locate some works you might review, and examine several. Then respond to one as if you have been asked by the director to look at a rough cut and suggest improvements. Summarize your recommendations in a short but specific document. Begin by affirming what works: Explain what you would not change. Next, make comments about the film as a whole: Does the story work? Is the narrative coherent? Are the characters appropriately motivated and cast? Is the pacing right? How about the lighting, the setting, the costumes? Then offer specific suggestions about production details that might be improved or corrected. Are there any obvious slips?

CHAPTER 3

PICTURING OURSELVES

writing to express identities

Titian, *Portrait of a Man in a Red Cap* (1516)

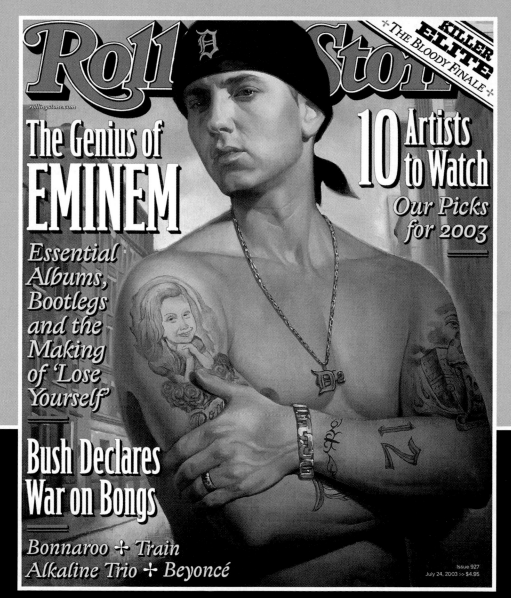

Roberto Parada, *Eminem* (*Rolling Stone,* July 24, 2003)

What do the two portraits tell us about these young men? What might you infer about their backgrounds, occupations, personalities, and daily lives?

In what ways do the portraits suggest that not much has changed since 1516?

Introduction

The two portraits that open this chapter have a lot in common, even though they were composed nearly five centuries apart. They both show guys with attitude. No one knows the identity of the man in the red cap in the portrait by the Italian artist Titian (c. 1477–1576), but you probably recognize Eminem staring out from the cover of *Rolling Stone*.

The subjects are both young, drawn from the waist up, wearing caps, and facing to the right, heads cocked to offer good profiles. They both look smug, Eminem even pouting a little. In Titian's painting, expensive clothing suggests the youth had money and maybe influence (notice how the use of lighting emphasizes the frilled collar and fur stole). Similarly, the tattoos, jewelry, and do-rag tell us something about Eminem in Roberto Parada's painting.

You can develop interpretations from these details. Even if you've never seen Titian's painting before, you may wonder about the significance of the sword in the young man's hand. Does it represent a transition from adolescence to manhood? The beginning of an adventurous life? In the portrait of Eminem, you may notice that both his do-rag and chain sport a stylized letter D—the logo representing the Detroit Tigers baseball team. Here you may begin to look outside the frame of the image and ask, what connection exists between Eminem and the city of Detroit?

Details like these, whether they're presented in a visual image, an essay, or another kind of portrait, are worth paying attention to precisely because they reflect who people are. Our identities are shaped by kinship, friends, celebrities, communities, histories, occupations, and many other complex aspects of society. At the same time, identity is closely related to our bodies and to the experiences that make us unique. Because portraits capture the essence of people, we can recognize in them both the reflections of a larger social context and the particular individuals they portray.

Of course, paintings are only one type of portrait. Family snapshots, wedding portraits, baby pictures, yearbook stills (ugh!), and driver's license or ID pictures also tell us a great deal about people. Further, portraits don't come only as pictures. Your grandparents probably reminisce about people they once knew, maybe in more detail than you'd like. Or you follow a National Public Radio oral history series on the lives of famous blues musicians. Or you record your daily thoughts in a journal. Or you take out a personal ad and describe yourself with a few choice details: *SWM, fun-loving, easygoing, likes dogs, seeks SWF same*. Portraits, all.

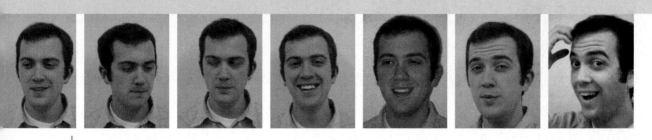

Snapshots of Trevor Rosen by John Ruszkiewicz

What's in This Chapter?

In this chapter, you'll find many different kinds of portraits. Some are paintings and photographs of individuals—famous and otherwise—whom we hope you will find intriguing. Some of the images, like Dorothea Lange's famous portrait *Migrant Mother* (page 87), are iconic—they have come to symbolize a particular era or social movement. Other portraits cross boundaries between media.

We explore how images reflect the complex relationships between individuals and society. We consider how people are defined by their culture, race, ethnicity, nationality, gender, profession, peer group, class, politics, habits, and more. Images also reveal how identity changes—we may be many people in a single day and different people for varying audiences. This chapter examines as well the relationships between identity and bodies. To appreciate how concepts of self and character are evolving, we look at subjects ranging from the revival of tattooing to hairstyles, from classic portraits of Native Americans to gritty photos of homeless teens.

Reading
Portraits

When a portrait attracts you—makes you really look at it—something about its composition has touched you. People sometimes resist or even resent the effort to discover just how such an effect, whether in words, images, or even music, has been achieved. They resist interpretation because it seems so subjective or ruins the experience, sucking out all the magic.

But knowing how to read an image doesn't destroy it. You may find that a portrait grows in richness and character when you know what elements to look for. They aren't especially complex, as our checklist (first introduced in Chapter 1) shows. Because we live in a world of images, you've developed most of these habits already. You just need to make them more conscious, both as you respond to portraits and as you create them.

What do you see?

What is it about?

To what does it relate?

How is it composed?

What details matter?

What do you see?

When you encounter any portrait, what you see is partly a function of its **physical medium**—the materials the artist has used to create it. Vincent van Gogh's 1884 self-portrait, for instance, is an *oil-on-board painting,* using oil paint on a wood surface. Van Gogh (1853–1890) was able to manipulate aspects like color, texture, and value (the amount of paint used) to create an image that expresses his identity. Notice the rough brushstrokes and the pale, shiny colors he used to paint the face. Why would an artist create such an unflattering image of himself? you may wonder. What qualities was he trying to convey—ill health, psychological unrest, an unhappy career? Perhaps all three, you may conclude—especially if you know something about van Gogh's well-documented struggle with mental illness.

> **Explore this van Gogh self-portrait in depth.**
> www.ablongman.com/beyondwords04

You can also think about a portrait in terms of its **genre**, the general category of images or texts into which it fits. Every genre has its own particular *conventions*—typical patterns of conveying meaning—related to its purpose and its intended audience. Portrait photography often deemphasizes the background of an image, for example. Think of the plain gray backdrops used for yearbook or driver's license photos: The intent is to bring out the personality of the subject by focusing our sole attention on the person.

You should also consider the **medium of transmission** for the portrait—how the work reaches its audience. A painting like van Gogh's self-portrait might be seen in a museum, with a handful of people viewing it in a setting that emphasizes its status as an art object. Other portraits are displayed on billboards, framed on walls, reproduced in magazines, shared on the Web, and so on. Each medium of transmission shapes both how the image is composed and how viewers interpret it. Of course, portraits take many forms other than images. Essays, letters, shared playlists, Web pages, and instant messages are examples of the ways we use

Vincent van Gogh, *Self-Portrait* (1884)

different media and genres to express our identity. And even work done in a single medium may draw on a range of senses and experiences. Consider how in the descriptive passage below, writer N. Scott Momaday (b. 1934) conjures up not only visual images of his Kiowa grandmother but also her sounds and movements.

From The Way to Rainy Mountain

N. Scott Momaday
(1969)

Now that I can have her only in memory, I see my grandmother in the several postures that were peculiar to her: standing at the wood stove on a winter morning and turning meat in a great iron skillet; sitting at the south window, bent above her beadwork, and afterwards, when her vision failed, looking down for a long time into the fold of her hands; going out upon a cane, very slowly as she did when the weight of age came upon her; praying. I remember her most often at prayer. She made long, rambling prayers out of suffering and hope, having seen many things. I was never sure I had the right to hear, so exclusive were they of all mere custom and company. The last time I saw her she prayed standing by the side of the bed at night, naked to the waist, the light of the kerosene lamp moving upon her dark skin. Her long black hair, always drawn and braided in the day, lay upon her shoulders and against her breasts like a shawl. I do not speak Kiowa, and never understood her prayers, but there was something inherently sad in the sound, some merest hesitation upon the syllables of sorrow. She began in the high and descending pitch, exhausting her breath to silence, then again and again—and always the same intensity of effort, of something that is, and is not, like urgency in the human voice. Transported so in the dancing light among the shadows of her room, she seemed beyond the reach of time.

FYI N. Scott Momaday's book *The Way to Rainy Mountain* includes illustrations by his father Al Momaday, a painter.

CONSIDER

1. In what ways does the medium affect the message in van Gogh's self-portrait? Look at the relationship between the subject and the background. Examine the details of the face. What impression do you have of van Gogh after examining this portrait—what kind of person do you see? How can these aspects of the painting be discussed in terms of the oil paint and board materials?

2. Reread Momaday's description of his grandmother. Which details do you find most compelling? Do you think this description could be captured in a picture? Why or why not?

COMPOSE

3. Imagine that you've been asked to craft a self-portrait. What physical medium or media would you choose and why? What aspects of your identity would you want to emphasize in your portrait, and how do you think this particular medium would help you to do that? Write a paragraph explaining your choice.

What is it about?

Portraits almost always focus our attention on people. But before the shutter snaps or the paint hits the canvas, the artist has made a decision about the **subject** of the image. Why choose this person above all others? That question may have as many answers as there are portraits, driven by the rhetorical issues of purpose and audience explored in Chapter 2.

Sometimes a portrait captures a subject intended to represent the ordinary or the typical. Robert Rehm and his family, for example, were chosen as subjects for a 1951 portrait of the "average American family." Taken in Levittown, New York (one of America's first suburbs), this photo was accompanied by the following caption. "Robert Rehm, who fits the census bureau's description of the 'average American,' takes a walk with his family through his suburban community. Mr. Rehm fits the 'average American' classification to a 'T.' He's a semi-skilled

The "average American family," Levittown, New York (1951)

worker, has a wife and two children and an average income of around $3,000, owns a refrigerator, radio, and telephone, and is still paying on his home."

At other times, artists create portraits that capture the unique qualities of celebrities or other remarkable individuals—or they may focus on an otherwise ordinary individual who encapsulates a larger event or issue. You may not recognize either of the women shown here, but you can probably surmise that they represented very different things to the artists whose images have immortalized them. The first is a celebrity portrait of Greta Garbo, a film star whose glamour and air of mystery fascinated fans around the globe. The woman in the second image became an anonymous emblem of the worldwide economic depression that began with the 1929 stock market crash. Both the portraits seem remarkably simple, yet each is, in its own way, haunting and profound, capturing far more than just a face.

Edward Steichen, *Greta Garbo* (1928)
Photo by Edward Steichen, courtesy International Museum of Photography and Film, George Eastman House. Reprinted with permission of Joanna T. Steichen.

Walker Evans, *Hale County, Alabama* (1936)

1. What is your first reaction to the subjects depicted in the "average American family" photograph on page 81? What elements do you notice first and why? What details in this portrait mark these individuals as ordinary, unremarkable, "average"? Why do you think the photographer chose these subjects?

2. What do you think made Garbo a potent subject for photographer Edward Steichen? How does the image capture aspects of her profession and character?

3. What does the title of Walker Evans's photo suggest about his subject's identity? About Evans's purpose?

4. What kind of subject would you choose today to represent "average Americans"? How would you create such a portrait? Write a brief description of what your photograph would include and how it would look.

5. What problems from our own time might a photographer embody through a single powerful portrait? Can you imagine one human face capturing a smoldering issue of class, race, gender, religion, or war? Describe a photograph you might take, or borrow a digital camera and take such a photograph.

The **focal points** in a portrait also give us clues about how to interpret it. We tend to see or think about things one at a time. So painters, photographers, and writers use many devices to manage our attention, making sure we see approximately what they intend. Writers use devices of language—similes, metaphors, analogies—to focus our attention; photographers and painters achieve comparable effects by playing with light and shadows or manipulating images in various ways.

Naturally, we can read a portrait in many different ways. But notice where photographer Harry Benson draws our eyes in the photo on page 84 taken after boxer Muhammad Ali's 1964 bout with world champion Sonny Liston. Reflecting the glare of the spotlights against the dark background of the ring, and shot from a low angle, the champion's hand—raised in victory—simply dominates the image. It is clearly the story here, as it must be, given Ali's victory and subsequent career. But perhaps the hand seems precarious too, isolated, like the man himself, his eyes averted from the camera. So we might read the rest of the portrait in terms of that hand, noticing the way the light also highlights the boxer's shoulders, chest, and arm.

Harry Benson, *Jubilant Clay*
(1964)

Another focal point that deserves attention is the *gaze* of the subject of a portrait. When the subject looks directly at viewers, we are placed in the position of the artist and get a sense of the rapport the artist may have with that person. When the subject looks at an object within the painting, that object is emphasized. When the subject looks away, the gaze brings the viewer and the subject together as they consider an imaginary focal point outside the frame of the picture.

CONSIDER

1. Harry Benson's photo of Muhammad Ali may have several focal points. In addition to the boxer's hand, what other focal points can you identify? How do different focal points change your impression of Ali or the story this image might have to tell about him? Where is Ali's gaze directed in this photo? Why?

COMPOSE

2. Write a two- or three-paragraph description of someone you know well, organizing your observations around one focal point—one characteristic, activity, or trait that reveals something about the person's identity.

To what does it relate?

Portraits capture their subjects in a single moment, but they also suggest connections to larger contexts and issues. One way to read a portrait is to ask how it corresponds to events and experiences in the artist's or subject's life, to his or her **biographical context**. By choosing to depict himself at three stages of life, for example, Albrecht Dürer (1471–1526) created a sequence of revealing self-portraits. You can ask what these paintings might tell you about the changes in Dürer's life, even if you know little about his biography or times.

Self-portraits by **Albrecht Dürer** at ages 22, 26, and 28

CONSIDER

1. What specific differences can you see in Dürer's three paintings? What elements stay more or less the same? What do these similarities and changes suggest about his circumstances, his career, and his identity?

2. Compare Dürer's paintings to a sequence of formal portraits you have had taken, such as school photographs, yearbook or graduation pictures, or wedding portraits. How well do these portraits capture you? How much control did you have over the images?

COMPOSE

3. Write three paragraphs, each describing yourself at a different age or period in your life. Imagine that these paragraphs could become part of a family album or perhaps the narrative portion of a video.

Dorothea Lange, *Drought refugees from Oklahoma camping by the roadside, Blythe, California* (1936)

When we write or create visual images, we often also try to say something about our world, taking up an issue of importance and persuading others to pay attention—we respond, in other words, to the **social** or **historical contexts** that surround the people we see in portraits. The images crafted by photographers enlisted by the government-run Farm Security Administration (FSA) during the 1930s, for example, are responses to specific historical events. At the height of the Great Depression in the 1930s, overwhelming numbers of farmers and their families lost their livelihood, devastated by the collapse of the economy, the dust bowl, and the advent of mechanized agriculture. The FSA enlisted photographers like Walker Evans and Dorothea Lange to capture images that would persuade other government officials and the general public of the significance of the problems and the need to provide support for these displaced families. These photographers intended their images to influence policy and bring about tangible social change. Examine Dorothea Lange's photo of the drought refugees. How is the historical context reflected in the choice of subjects and the composition of the image?

CONSIDER

1. Look closely at Lange's photograph above. What can you infer about the identities and circumstances of the family members it depicts? Who is the focal point of the portrait, in your opinion? How do you know?

COMPOSE

2. Do you think that the political agenda that inspired Lange's photograph enriches or detracts from the artistic qualities of the image? Write two or three paragraphs explaining and justifying your opinion.

CHALLENGE

3. Can you think of artists and writers today whose work reflects their social or political commitments? What do you think of these artists' work?

How is it composed?

We are comfortable with the idea that houses, highways, and even research papers have structures. But it may be harder to appreciate such a framework operating within a portrait. But it is there, even in a simple head shot or character sketch in words. You have to take the time to see the parts and their relationship to the whole.

Arrangement and **structure** derive from the relationships among the figures or objects in a portrait, as well as the gestures and poses depicted. When you examine the structure of an image, first consider how the image is framed. What occupies the center of the frame? Is the frame divided into sections in any significant way? Do objects create interesting lines of sight across the frame? How are elements within the image spaced and organized?

A photograph such as *Migrant Mother* by Dorothea Lange (1895–1965) gains some of its considerable power from its structure. On one level, the structure

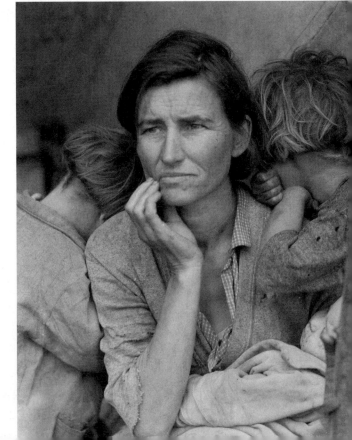

Dorothea Lange, *Migrant Mother* (1936)

reveals itself in the placement of the figures within the frame of the image. Vertically, the face of the mother occupies the top third of the image. Photographers often try to divide an image into thirds as a way of structuring its composition. Moving the focal point away from the center adds interest and shifts our attitude toward the image.

The composition of such an image rarely happens by accident; it's the result of careful preparation, skill, and selection. Lange took numerous photos of most of her subjects, as the series of shots shown on page 88 illustrates. She would shoot from different angles, adjust the framing of the image, or allow her subjects to shift positions or go about their tasks until the right moment came along. She took the time to get to know the people she photographed, developing a rapport that she believed allowed her to understand something about their experiences and to accurately portray their lives.

You can find patterns in other kinds of portraits, too. Consider how the theme of the following poem by Billy Collins (b. 1941) creates an intriguing and, given its subject, inevitable two-part structure. "Embrace" turns on the line "From the front is another story." The title of the poem provides the haunting connection between the parts and comments on the whole.

FYI Billy Collins explores relationships between words and images in other poems, including "The Brooklyn Museum of Art" and "Introduction to Poetry." A professor at Lehman College, City University of New York, Collins served as poet laureate of the United States from 2001–2003.

Dorothea Lange, *Migrant Mother* sequence (1936)

Billy Collins

Embrace
(1988)

You know the parlor trick.
Wrap your arms around your own body
and from the back it looks like
someone is embracing you,
her hands grasping your shirt,
her fingernails teasing your neck.
From the front is another story.
You never looked so alone,
your crossed elbows and screwy grin.
You could be waiting for a tailor
to fit you for a straitjacket,
one that would hold you really tight.

Learn more about Billy Collins and his poetry.
www.ablongman.com/beyondwords05

1. Look again at the series of alternative shots Dorothea Lange took of the subjects depicted in *Migrant Mother* on page 88. Choose one of these and analyze its structure. How do framing, arrangement, gestures, and poses create a particular impression of the family? Do you think the photograph you've choosen to analyze is more or less effective than *Migrant Mother*? Why or why not?

2. Borrow a digital camera and a willing friend, and turn "Embrace" into a photograph. Would it be enough to show one side of the person? Which side might you show? Could two images better capture the essence of the poem? If you don't have access to a camera, explain in a paragraph how you might structure a shot that would capture the point you think Collins is making.

What details matter?

"God is in the details," architect Ludwig Mies van der Rohe once observed. That's one good reason to read any portrait with the assumption that all the elements in it contribute something to your understanding of the subject. Sometimes these details become clearer once you understand the context or purpose for the image. Sometimes they will remain mysterious and for that reason intriguing. And sometimes they turn out to be just pointless. But you can't know until you've given them appropriate attention.

The February 2004 issue of *Wired* (shown on page 90), for instance, featured a startling cover that told many stories. Every detail is worth examining, from the modification of the masthead to suit the theme to the rich, contrasting colors. It offers an image of a beautiful young Indian woman, with a hand covering the lower half of her face. On the hand, written in henna, are lines of computer code. The caption below the image reads: "The New Face of the Silicon Age" and below that, a tagline explains, "Tech jobs are fleeing to India faster than ever. You got a problem with that?" Consider all that the cover designer might be suggesting on this complex page.

Knowing some key **principles of design**—principles such as *emphasis, contrast, balance, proportion*, and *unity*—can help you interpret the details in a portrait. In *Black and White* (shown on page 91), for instance, Man Ray uses lighting techniques to experiment with contrast and balance. See how the shadow beneath the face of the woman is achieved with top lighting, creating bright highlights on the chin, cheek, and forehead, which contrast with the shadows below. Consider, too, how a secondary source of light casts a shadow to the right of the mask. The effect establishes a sense of balance that aligns the mask with the human face.

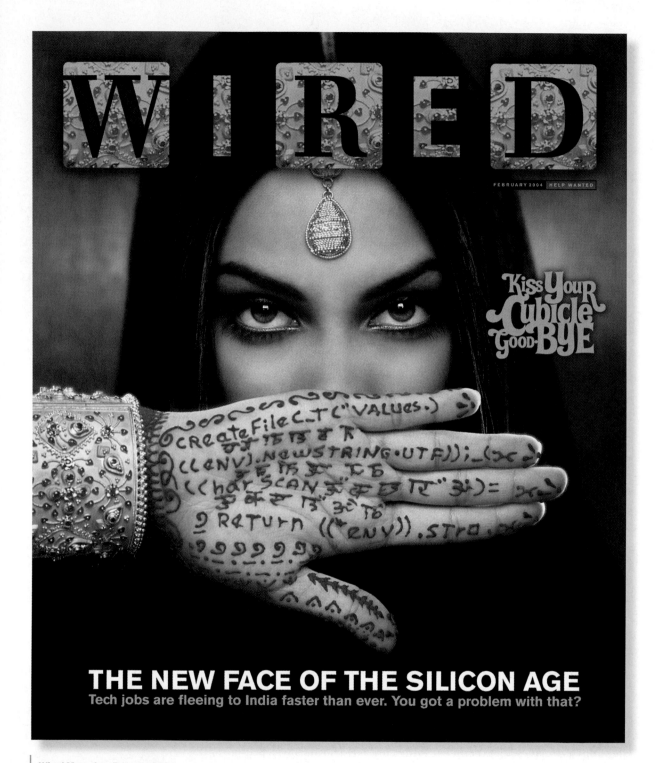

Wired **Magazine,** February 2004
Ian White / Wired, Conde Nast Publications, Inc.

Man Ray, *Black and White* (*Noire et Blanche*) (1926)

CONSIDER

1. Think about the messages the *Wired* cover sends, and then describe another way the editors might have handled the issue raised in this cover using a different human image.

2. Identify one or two design elements that you think are used effectively in the *Wired* cover, and write a paragraph explaining why you think so.

3. Do you think you would experience *Black and White* differently if the photograph were in color? Explain.

COMPOSE

4. Details count in written portraits, too. Try writing a paragraph that conveys all the information captured in the *Wired* cover. Which version—your paragraph or the cover—do you find more effective? Why?

American Icons

What makes you who you are? And how do you see others? There are surely no easy formulas. But it's not uncommon for portraits to explore certain common themes, such as the groups we belong to as a result of our nationality, upbringing, or education; the race or ethnicity we are born into; the religion we inherit or choose; or the gender we inhabit.

However, we base shared identities not only on our own inside groups but also in relation to others who remain outside them. We may arbitrarily associate characteristics with another group as a way of strengthening our own group identity—perhaps construing its members as exotic, savage, or primitive.

The following selections invite you to explore how identities are expressed and celebrated in representations of two groups fundamental to our national identity: cowboys and American Indians. As many historians have pointed out, the history of the United States is often told as a "frontier myth" of a nation created by adventurous white settlers who pushed westward to conquer a wilderness and the Native Americans who inhabited it. And so it is not surprising that the two major antagonists in this story, the frontier cowboy and the American Indian, have become key icons in our national mythology, idealized and nostalgic figures who may have little in common with the real individuals who make up these groups today.

Visualizing Native Americans

When you think of Native Americans, what images come to mind? And where did these images come from—movies, history books, cartoons? If they don't come from personal experience, chances are that your impressions may be influenced by turn-of-the-twentieth-century representations of American Indians like those created by Edward Curtis (1868–1952) and Gertrude Käsebier (1852–1934). Both photographers recognized that many native traditions were disappearing or changing and wanted to document what remained. Curtis spent nearly thirty years traversing the American West with his camera and primitive recording equipment, accumulating forty thousand images of eighty tribal groups. Käsebier, a popular New York portrait photographer, took many studio portraits of Native Americans. Both artists' portraits are now considered classics.

Yet as impressive as Curtis's and Käsebier's photographs are, they necessarily reflect both artists' position as cultural outsiders—observers looking in. And, as the subsequent images and readings in this chapter illustrate, Native American artists and writers like Hulleah Tsinhnahjinnie, Richard Ray Whitman, Luci Tapahonso, and Sherman Alexie have their own stories—sometimes quite different stories—to tell.

Edward Curtis, *A Navaho* (c. 1904) (above). *White Duck* (c. 1908) (above right). **Gertrude Käsebier,** *Zitkala-Sa* (1898) (right).

1. What do you notice about Curtis's and Käsebier's choices of subject, focal point, arrangement, design elements, or details? What might these details suggest about how Curtis and Käsebier perceived their subject's cultures?

2. Partly because of the technical limitations of his equipment, Curtis sometimes staged images—posing the subjects and adding or removing items in order to focus on the details that he believed to be most culturally authentic. Does knowing this fact affect how you see his portraits? Does it affect your sense of how "real" his representations might be?

I Hated Tonto (Still Do)

FYI

Sherman Alexie, winner of a PEN/Hemingway Award for Best First Book in 1992, has written prolifically about his experiences growing up on a Spokane Indian reservation in Washington. His work uses several different genres, including poetry, short stories, novels, film, and stand-up comedy.

Sherman Alexie

(1998)

I was a little Spokane Indian boy who read every book and saw every movie about Indians, no matter how terrible. I'd read those historical romance novels about the stereotypical Indian warrior ravaging the virginal white schoolteacher.

I can still see the cover art.

The handsome, blue-eyed warrior (the Indians in romance novels are always blue-eyed because half-breeds are somehow sexier than full-blooded Indians) would be nuzzling (the Indians in romance novels are always performing acts that are described in animalistic terms) the impossibly pale neck of a white woman as she reared her head back in primitive ecstasy (the Indians in romance novels always inspire white women to commit acts of primitive ecstasy).

Of course, after reading such novels, I imagined myself to be a blue-eyed warrior nuzzling the necks of various random, primitive, and ecstatic white women.

And I just as often imagined myself to be a cinematic Indian, splattered with Day-Glo Hollywood war paint as I rode off into yet another battle against the latest actor to portray Gen. George Armstrong Custer.

But I never, not once, imagined myself to be Tonto.

I hated Tonto then and I hate him now.

However, despite my hatred of Tonto, I loved movies about Indians, loved them beyond all reasoning and saw no fault with any of them.

I loved John Ford's *The Searchers*.

I rooted for John Wayne as he searched for his niece for years and years. I rooted for John Wayne even though I knew he was going to kill his niece because she had been "soiled" by the Indians. Hell, I rooted for John Wayne because I understood why he wanted to kill his niece.

I hated those savage Indians just as much as John Wayne did.

■ ■ ■

I mean, jeez, they had kidnapped Natalie Wood, transcendent white beauty who certainly didn't deserve to be nuzzled, nibbled, or nipped by some Indian warrior, especially an Indian warrior who only spoke in monosyllables and whose every movement was accompanied by ominous music.

■ ■ ■

In the movies, Indians are always accompanied by ominous music. And I've seen so many Indian movies that I feel like I'm constantly accompanied by ominous music. I always feel that something bad is about to happen.

I am always aware of how my whole life is shaped by my hatred of Tonto. Whenever I think of Tonto, I hear ominous music.

Clayton Moore as the Lone Ranger and Jay Silverheels as Tonto in the TV series *The Lone Ranger*, which ran from 1949 to 1957.

I walk into shopping malls or family restaurants, as the ominous music drops a few octaves, and imagine that I am Billy Jack, the half-breed Indian and Vietnam vet turned flower-power pacifist (now there's a combination) who loses his temper now and again, takes off his shoes (while his opponents patiently wait for him to do so), and then kicks the red out of the necks of a few dozen racist white extras.

You have to remember Billy Jack, right?

Every Indian remembers Billy Jack. I mean, back in the day, Indians worshiped Billy Jack.

Whenever a new Billy Jack movie opened in Spokane, my entire tribe would climb into two or three vans like so many circus clowns and drive to the East Trent Drive-In for a long evening of greasy popcorn, flat soda pop, fossilized licorice rope, and interracial violence.

We Indians cheered as Billy Jack fought for us, for every single Indian.

Of course, we conveniently ignored the fact that Tom Laughlin, the actor who played Billy Jack, was definitely not Indian.

After all, such luminary white actors as Charles Bronson, Chuck Connors, Burt Reynolds, Burt Lancaster, Sal Mineo, Anthony Quinn, and Charlton Heston had already portrayed Indians, so who were we to argue?

I mean, Tom Laughlin did have a nice tan and he spoke in monosyllables and wore cowboy boots and a jean jacket just like Indians. And he did have a Cherokee grandmother or grandfather or butcher, so he was Indian by proximity, and that was good enough in 1972, when disco music was about to rear its ugly head and bell-bottom pants were just beginning to change the shape of our legs.

When it came to the movies, Indians had learned to be happy with less.

We didn't mind that cinematic Indians never had jobs.

We didn't mind that cinematic Indians were deadly serious.

We didn't mind that cinematic Indians were rarely played by Indian actors.

We made up excuses.

"Well, that Tom Laughlin may not be Indian, but he sure should be."

"Well, that movie wasn't so good, but Sal Mineo looked sort of like Uncle Stubby when he was still living out on the reservation."

"Well, I hear Burt Reynolds is a little bit Cherokee. Look at his cheekbones. He's got them Indian cheekbones."

"Well, it's better than nothing."

Yes, that became our battle cry.

"Sometimes, it's a good day to die. Sometimes, it's better than nothing."

We Indians became so numb to the possibility of dissent, so accepting of our own lowered expectations, that we canonized a film like *Powwow Highway*.

When it was first released, I loved *Powwow Highway*. I cried when I first saw it in the theater, then cried again when I stayed and watched it again a second time.

I mean, I loved that movie. I memorized whole passages of dialogue. But recently, I watched the film for the first time in many years and cringed in shame and embarrassment with every stereotypical scene.

I cringed when Philbert Bono climbed to the top of a sacred mountain and left a Hershey chocolate bar as an offering.

I cringed when Philbert and Buddy Red Bow waded into a stream and sang Indian songs to the moon.

I cringed when Buddy had a vision of himself as an Indian warrior throwing a tomahawk through the window of a police cruiser.

I mean, I don't know a single Indian who would leave a chocolate bar as an offering. I don't know any Indians who have ever climbed to the top of any mountain. I don't know any Indians who wade into streams and sing to the moon. I don't know of any Indians who imagine themselves to be Indian warriors.

■ ■ ■

Wait —

I was wrong. I know of at least one Indian boy who always imagined himself to be a cinematic Indian warrior.

Me.

I watched the movies and saw the kind of Indian I was supposed to be.

A cinematic Indian is supposed to climb mountains.

I am afraid of heights.

A cinematic Indian is supposed to wade into streams and sing songs.

I don't know how to swim.

A cinematic Indian is supposed to be a warrior.

I haven't been in a fistfight since sixth grade and she beat the crap out of me.

I mean, I knew I could never be as brave, as strong, as wise a visionary, as white as the Indians in the movies.

I was just one little Indian boy who hated Tonto because Tonto was the only cinematic Indian who looked like me.

It Has Always Been This Way

Luci Tapahonso
(1993)

FYI Acclaimed Navajo poet Luci Tapahonso is a professor of English at the University of Arizona. Many of her poems incorporate vocabulary and syntactic patterns of the Navajo language Diné.

Being born is not the beginning.
Life begins months before the time of birth.

Inside the mother, the baby floats in warm fluid,
and she is careful not to go near noisy or evil places.
She will not cut meat or take part in the killing of food.
Navajo babies were always protected in these ways.

The baby is born and cries out loud,
and the mother murmurs and nurtures the baby.
A pinch of pollen on the baby's tongue
for strong lungs and steady growth.
The belly button dries and falls off.
It is buried near the house so the child
will always return home and help the mother.
It has been this way for centuries among us.

Much care is taken to shape the baby's head well
and to talk and sing to the baby softly in the right way.
It has been this way for centuries among us.

The baby laughs aloud and it is celebrated with rock salt,
lots of food, and relatives laughing.
Everyone passes the baby around.
This is so the child will always be generous,
will always be surrounded by happiness,
and will always be surrounded by lots of relatives.
It has been this way for centuries among us.

The child starts school and leaves with a pinch of pollen
on top of her head and on her tongue.
This is done so the child will think clearly,
listen quietly, and learn well away from home.
The child leaves home with prayers and good thoughts.
It has been this way for centuries among us.

This is how we were raised.
We were raised with care and attention
because it has always been this way.
It has worked well for centuries.

You are here.
Your parents are here.
Your relatives are here.
We are all here together.
It is all this: the care, the prayers, songs,
and our own lives as Navajos we carry with us all the time.
It has been this way for centuries among us.
It has been this way for centuries among us.

Richard Ray Whitman, *Man's Best Friend* (2003)

Hulleah J. Tsinhnahjinnie, *Damn!* (1998)

CONSIDER

1. Alexie draws a distinction between the "cinematic Indians" he saw at the movies and the Native Americans who lived in his community. What differences does he identify? What do you think he means when he says that the "cinematic Indians" were the "Indians we were supposed to be"?

2. Reread Luci Tapahonso's "It Has Always Been This Way." According to the speaker, how does the Navajo child acquire a cultural identity? Compare and contrast this notion of identity with the one developed in Alexie's essay.

3. Compare and contrast the image by Hulleah J. Tsinhnahjinnie with Whitman's *Man's Best Friend*. What can you say about their choice of subjects and focal points? What do these choices suggest about their views of Native American culture and life?

CHALLENGE

4. How do you think others view some of the groups that you belong to? Think about a group that contributes to your identity: a nationality, a religion, a profession, a lifestyle. Has your group been depicted in television, films, or other popular media? If so, how accurate do you think these representations are? Can you imagine an outsider capturing your group adequately in words or images? Can you point to someone who has done so?

"The American West did attract me, I'm sure, because of both the space that affords solitude and the independence of a lot of the individuals out there. Also, to a degree, there's the dedication some of those individuals have for doing things right—even if it might be a simple thing as branding a calf or riding a horse well, but doing it right."

—WILLIAM ALBERT ALLARD
commenting on the photos in his book *Vanishing Breed*, which included *Henry Gray*

William Albert Allard,
Henry Gray, Arizona, 1972

Visualizing Cowboys

When we think of the American West, we often envision a cowboy galloping in to save the day when trouble comes to town, and then riding off into the sunset. First popularized in late-nineteenth-century "Wild West" shows and glamorized in decades of movies, country ballads, and even cigarette advertisements, the image of the cowboy became a widespread symbol of male independence and strength. Cowboys, these images tell us, are our link to simpler times, when good guys and bad guys were distinguishable and when men were strong-minded and principled.

Of course, more than a century later, we recognize that this cowboy ideal left out a lot. Good guys and bad guys aren't always easy to tell apart; "right" and "wrong" can mean different things in different situations, and a shootout is rarely the most effective way of solving conflicts. Perhaps most important, the popular image of the cowboy is implicitly white and male—it obscures the roles that women, people of color, and other marginalized groups have played in our history and culture.

The images and texts that follow give you a glimpse of some modern-day cowboys, a group whose membership is rapidly shrinking as urban and suburban development encroaches on ranchland across the West. As you read, ask yourself, is the cowboy myth still relevant to most Americans' sense of identity, or has it become obsolete?

Coles Hairston, *6666 Ranch in Texas* (1999)

CONSIDER

1. What can you say about the presence of the mirror in Allard's portrait of Henry Gray? Why do you think he included it in the photograph? What does its presence say about Gray's life and identity?

2. How would you describe the subject of Coles Hairston's photograph? Is it fair to call it a portrait? Why or why not? How would you characterize the individuals in the photograph?

3. Raised on a working ranch, Hairston has an affinity for the rhythms of cowboy life, whereas Allard documents this culture as an outsider. Compare and contrast the focal points, structure, and details shown in the images. Do you see any differences between the two photographers' depictions?

Mammas Don't Let Your Babies Grow Up to Be Cowboys

Ed Bruce and Patsy Bruce

(As Adapted and Performed by Willie Nelson with Waylon Jennings)

(1975)

Mammas don't let your babies grow up to be cowboys
Don't let 'em pick guitars and drive them old trucks
Make 'em be doctors and lawyers and such
Mammas don't let your babies grow up to be cowboys
They'll never stay home and they're always alone
Even with someone they love

Cowboys ain't easy to love and they're hard to hold
And they'd rather give you a song than diamonds or gold
Lonestar belt buckles and old faded Levi's
Each night begins a new day
And if you don't understand him he won't die young
He'll probably just ride away.

Mammas don't let your babies grow up to be cowboys
Don't let 'em pick guitars and drive them old trucks
Make 'em be doctors and lawyers and such
Mammas don't let your babies grow up to be cowboys
They'll never stay home and they're always alone
Even with someone they love.

Cowboys like smoky old pool rooms and cool mountain mornings
Little warm puppies and children and girls of the night
And them that don't know him won't like him
And them that do sometimes won't know how to take him
He ain't wrong, he's just different
But his pride won't let him do things to make you think he's right.

Mammas don't let your babies grow up to be cowboys
Don't let 'em pick guitars and drive them old trucks
Make 'em be doctors and lawyers and such
Mammas don't let your babies grow up to be cowboys
They'll never stay home and they're always alone
Even with someone they love.

Bernard Williams, *Sergeant Buffalo* (1997)

"Hollywood and many history writers are mighty guilty of misrepresenting the story. I got pretty angry when I began to read about black cowboys. One out of every three or four cowboys was either black or Mexican. We've been fed this image of the white cowboy, and I'm out to retake some visual territory with these paintings. My cowboys are symbols of the untold and whitewashed history of colored people who are part of the American story."

—BERNARD WILLIAMS

Explore the relationships between country music and images of the American cowboy.
www.ablongman.com/beyondwords06

CONSIDER

1. What do you think the songwriters mean when they advise mothers against raising their children to be cowboys? What do these lyrics suggest about the rewards and drawbacks of cowboy life? Do you think the advice in the song is serious? Why or why not?

2. Analyze the composition and design elements used in the painting *Sergeant Buffalo*. What can you say about how Williams uses his medium to convey a political and historical argument? Do you think the painting is effective in conveying that argument? Explain.

COMPOSE

3. In the library or on the Internet, research how cowboys have been portrayed in the popular media during the past fifty years. Write a short essay describing the patterns you see, incorporating specific images and examples that illustrate those patterns.

4. Imagine that you've been commissioned to create a portrait that accurately documents and preserves for future generations a group that you belong to. What medium would you choose? What would the portrait include? Write a paragraph describing the portrait you would create (or actually create the portrait).

Struggling for Self-Expression

The readings and images in this section spotlight two groups of young people struggling to claim and express an individual identity in the face of powerful social pressures. Susan Bordo's article dramatizes the myriad ways in which media images affect young women's body image, while the work of Alison Stateman and Jim Goldberg focuses on homeless teens and young adults.

Just Pictures?
The Power of Body Images

To many Americans, the body represents a paradox. Advertisers bombard us with images of impossibly thin models that drive young people to anorexia and other eating disorders, and yet for the first time in our national history, the majority of American adults are seriously overweight. (Perhaps Benjamin Franklin was right when he suggested that our national bird should be the turkey, but he probably didn't mean with stuffing and gravy.)

FYI Susan Bordo teaches philosophy at the University of Kentucky. Her book *Unbearable Weight* was named a Notable Book of 1993 by the *New York Times* and nominated for a Pulitzer Prize. It was among the first scholarly books to draw connections between images of the body and eating disorders.

Zoe Leonard, detail from the exhibit *Mouth Open, Teeth Showing* (2000)

The Empire of Images in Our World of Bodies

Susan Bordo
(2003)

In our Sunday news. With our morning coffee. On the bus, in the airport, at the checkout line. It may be a 5 a.m. addiction to the glittering promises of the infomercial: the latest in fat-dissolving pills, miracle hair restoration, makeup secrets of the stars. Or a glancing relationship while waiting at the dentist, trying to distract ourselves from the impending root canal. A teen magazine: tips on how to dress, how to wear your hair, how to make him want you. The endless commercials and advertisements that we believe we pay no attention to.

Constant, everywhere, no big deal. Like water in a goldfish bowl, barely noticed by its inhabitants. Or noticed, but dismissed: "eye candy" —a harmless indulgence. They go down so easily, in and out, digested and forgotten.

Just pictures.

Or perhaps, more accurately, perceptual pedagogy: "How to Interpret Your Body 101." It's become a global requirement; eventually, everyone must enroll. Fiji is just one example. Until television was introduced in 1995, the islands had no reported cases of eating disorders. In 1998, three years after programs from the United States and Britain began broadcasting there, 62 percent of the girls surveyed reported dieting. The anthropologist Anne Becker was surprised by the change; she had thought that Fijian aesthetics, which favor voluptuous bodies, would "withstand" the influence of media images. Becker hadn't yet understood that we live in an empire of images and that there are no protective borders.

I am not protected either. I was carded until I was 35. Even when I was 45, people were shocked to learn my age. Young men flirted with me even when I was 50. Having hated my appearance as a child—freckles, Jewish nose, bushy red hair—I was surprised to find myself fairly pleased with it as an adult. Then, suddenly, it all changed. Women at the makeup counter no longer compliment me on my skin. Men don't catch my eye with playful promise in theirs.

I'm 56. The magazines tell me that at this age, a woman can still be beautiful. But they don't mean me. They mean Cher, Goldie, Faye, Candace. Women whose jowls have disappeared as they've aged, whose eyes have become less droopy, lips grown plumper, foreheads smoother with the passing years. They mean Susan Sarandon, who looked older in 1991's *Thelma and Louise* than she does in her movies today. "Aging beautifully" used to mean wearing one's years with style, confidence, and vitality. Today, it means not appearing to age at all. And—like breasts that defy gravity—it's becoming a new bodily norm.

In my 1993 book *Unbearable Weight,* I described the postmodern body, increasingly fed on "fantasies of rearranging, transforming, and correcting, limitless improvement and change, defying the historicity, the mortality, and, indeed, the very materiality of the body. In place of that materiality, we now have cultural plastic."

When I wrote those words, the most recent statistics, from 1989, listed 681,000 surgical procedures performed. In 2001, 8.5 million procedures were performed. They are cheaper than ever, safer than ever, and increasingly used not for correcting major defects but for "contouring" the face and body. Plastic surgeons seem to have no ethical problem with this. "I'm not here to play philosopher king," said Dr. Randal Haworth in a *Vogue* interview. "I don't have a problem with women who already look good who want to look perfect." Perfect. When did "perfection" become applicable to a human body? The word suggests a Platonic form of timeless beauty—appropriate for marble, perhaps, but not for living flesh.

Greta Van Susteren: former CNN legal analyst, 47 years old. When she had a face-lift, it was a real escalation in the stakes for ordinary women. She had a signature style: no bullshit, a down-to-earth lack of pretense. (During the O.J. trial, she was the only white reporter many black Americans trusted.) Always stylishly dressed and coiffed, she wasn't really pretty. No one could argue that her career was built on her looks. Perhaps quite the opposite. She sent out a subversive message: Brains and personality still count, even on television.

When Greta had her face lifted, another source of inspiration and hope bit the dust. The story was on the cover of *People*, and folks tuned in to her new show on Fox just to see the change—which was significant. But at least she was open about it. The beauties rarely admit they've had "work." Or if they do, it's vague, nonspecific, minimizing of the extent. Cher: "If I'd had as much plastic surgery as people say, there'd be another whole person left over!" OK, so how much have you had? The interviewers accept the silences and evasions. They even embellish the lie. How many interviews have you read that began: "She came into the restaurant looking at least 20 years younger than she is, fresh and relaxed, without a speck of makeup."

This collusion, this myth, that Cher or Goldie or Faye Dunaway, unaltered, is what 50-something looks like today has altered my face, however—without benefit of surgery. By comparison with theirs, it has become much older than it is.

My expression now appears more serious, too (just what a feminist needs), thanks to the widespread use of Botox. "It's now rare in certain social circles to see a woman over the age of 35 with the ability to look angry," a *New York Times* reporter observed recently. That has frustrated some film directors, like Baz Luhrmann, who directed *Moulin Rouge*. "Their faces can't really move properly," Luhrmann complained. Last week I saw a sign in the beauty parlor where I get my hair cut. "Botox Party! Sign Up!" So my 56-year-old forehead will now be judged against my neighbor's, not just Goldie's, Cher's, and Faye's. On television, a commercial describes the product (which really is a toxin, a dilution of botulism) as "Botox cosmetic." No different from mascara and blush, it's just stuck in with a needle, and it makes your forehead numb.

To add insult to injury, the rhetoric of feminism has been adopted to help advance and justify the industries in anti-aging and body-alteration. Facelifts, implants, and liposuction are advertised as empowerment, "taking charge" of one's life. "I'm doing it for me" goes the mantra of the talk shows. "Defy your age!" says Melanie Griffith, for Revlon. We're making a revolution, girls. Step right up and get your injections.

Am I immune? Of course not. My bathroom shelves are cluttered with the ridiculously expensive age-defying lotions and potions that beckon to me at the Lancôme and Dior counters. I want my lines, bags, and sags to disappear, and so do the women who can only afford to buy their alphahydroxies at Kmart. There's a limit, though, to what fruit acids can do. As surgeons develop ever more extensive and fine-tuned procedures to correct gravity and erase history from the faces of their patients, the difference between the cosmetically altered and the rest of us grows more and more dramatic.

"The rest of us" includes not only those who resist or are afraid of surgery but the many people who cannot afford basic health care, let alone aesthetic tinkering. As celebrity faces become increasingly more surreal in their wide-eyed, ever-bright agelessness, as *Time* and *Newsweek* (and *Discover* and *Psychology Today*) proclaim that we can now all "stay young forever," the poor continue to sag and wrinkle and lose their teeth. But in the empire of images, where even people in the news for stock scandals or producing septuplets are given instant digital dental work for magazine covers, that is a well-guarded secret. The celebrity testimonials, the advertisements, the beauty columns, all participate in the fiction that the required time, money, and technologies are available to all.

I've been lecturing about media images, eating problems, and our culture of body "enhancement" for nearly 20 years now. Undergraduates frequently make up a large share of my audiences, and they are the ones most likely to "get it." My generation (and older) still refers to "airbrushing." Many still believe it is possible to "just turn off the television." They are scornful, disdainful, sure of their own immunity to the world I talk about. No one really believes the ads, do they? Don't we all know those are just images, designed to sell products? Scholars in the audience may trot out theory about cultural resistance and "agency." Men may insist that they love fleshy women.

Fifteen years ago, I felt very alone when my own generation said these things; it seemed that they were living in a different world from the one I was tracking and that there was little hope of bridging the gap. Now, I simply catch the eyes of the 20-year-olds in the audience. They know. They understand that you can be as cynical as you want about the ads—and many of them are—and still feel powerless to resist their messages. They are aware that virtually every advertisement, every magazine cover, has been digitally modified and that very little of what they see is "real." That doesn't stop them from hating their own bodies for failing to live up to computer-generated standards. They know, no matter what their parents, teachers, and clergy are telling them, that "inner beauty" is a big laugh in this culture. If they come from communities that traditionally have celebrated voluptuous bodies and within which food represents love, safety, and home, they may feel isolation and guilt over the widening gap between the values they've grown up with and those tugging at them now.

In the world in which our children are growing up, there is a size zero, and it's a status symbol. The chronic dieters have been at it since they were 8 and 9 years old. They know all about eating disorders; being preached to about the dangers turns them right off. Their world is one in which anorexics swap starvation-diet tips on the Internet, participate in group fasts, offer advice on how to hide your "ana" from family members, and share inspirational photos of emaciated models. But full-blown anorexia has never been the norm among teenage girls; the real epidemic is among the girls with seemingly healthy eating habits, seemingly healthy bodies, who vomit or work their butts off as a regular form of anti-fat maintenance. These girls not only look "normal" but consider themselves normal. The new criterion circulating among teenage girls: If you get rid of it through exercise rather than purging or laxatives, you don't have a problem. Theirs is a world in which groups of dorm girls will plow voraciously through pizzas, chewing and then spitting out each mouthful. Do they have a disorder? Of course not—look, they're eating pizza.

Generations raised in the empire of images are both vulnerable and savvy. They snort when magazines periodically proclaim (about once every six months, the same frequency with which they run cover stories about "starving stars") that in the "new" Hollywood one can be "sexy at any size." They are literati, connoisseurs of the images; they pay close attention to the pounds coming and going—on J. Lo, Reese, Thora, Christina Aguilera, Beyoncé. They know that Kate Winslet, whom the director James Cameron called "Kate Weighs-a-lot" on the set of *Titanic,* was described by the tabloids as "packing on," "ballooning to," "swelling to," "shooting up to," "tipping the scales at" a "walloping," "staggering" weight—of 135 pounds. That slender Courtney Thorne-Smith, who played Calista Flockhart's friend and rival on *Ally McBeal,* quit the show because she could no longer keep up with the pressure to remain as thin as the series's creator, David E. Kelley, wanted them to be. That Missy Elliot and Queen Latifah are not on diets just for reasons of health.

I track the culture of young girls today with particular concern, because I'm a mother now. My 4-year-old daughter is a superb athlete with supreme confidence in her body, who prides herself on being able to do anything the boys can do—and better. When I see young girls being diminished and harassed by the culture it feels even more personal to me now. I'm grateful that there's a new generation of female athletes to inspire and support girls like my daughter, Cassie. That our icons are no longer just tiny gymnasts, but powerful soccer, softball, and tennis players, broad-shouldered track stars—Mia Hamm, Sarah Walden, Serena Williams, Marion Jones. During a recent visit to a high school, I saw how the eyes of a 14-year-old athlete shone as she talked about what Marion Jones means to her, and that fills me with hope.

But then, I accidentally tune in to the Maury Povich show, and my heart is torn in two. The topic of the day is "back-to-girl" makeovers. One by one, five beautiful 12-, 13-, and 14-year-old "tomboys" (as Maury called them) are "brought back to their feminine side" (Maury again) through a fashion makeover. We first see them in sweatshirts and caps, insisting that they are as strong as any boy, that they want to dress for comfort, that they're tired of being badgered to look like girls. Why, then, are they submitting to this one-time, on-air transformation? To please their moms. And indeed, as each one is brought back on stage, in full makeup and glamour outfit, hair swinging (and, in the case of the black girls, straightened), striking vampy supermodel "power" poses, their mothers sob as if they had just learned their daughters' cancers were in remission. The moms are so overwhelmed they don't need more, but Maury is clearly bent on complete conversion: "Do you know how pretty you are?" "Look how gorgeous you look!" "Are you going to dress like this more often?" Most of the girls, unsurprisingly, say yes. It's been a frontal assault, there's no room for escape.

As jaded as I am, this Maury show really got to me. I wanted to fold each girl in my arms and get her out of there. Of course, what I really fear is that I won't be able to protect Cassie from the same assault. It's happening already. I watch public-television kids' shows with her and can rarely find fault with the gender-neutral world they portray. We go to Disney movies and see resourceful, spirited heroines. Some of them, like the Hawaiian girls in *Lilo and Stitch*, even have thick legs and solid bodies. But then, on the way home from the movies, we stop at McDonald's for a Happy Meal, and, despite the fact that Cassie insists she's a boy and wants the boy's toy—a hot-wheels car—she is given a box containing a mini-Barbie.

Illustrating the box is Barbie's room, and my daughter is given the challenging task of finding all the matching pairs of shoes on the floor.

Later that day, I open a Pottery Barn catalog, browsing for ideas for Cassie's room. The designated boy's room is in primary colors, the bedspread dotted with balls, bats, catching mitts. The caption reads: "I play so many sports that it's hard to pick my favorites." Sounds like my daughter. On the opposite page, the girls' room is pictured, a pastel planetary design. The caption reads: "I like stars because they are shiny." That, too, sounds like my daughter. But Pottery Barn doesn't think a child can inhabit both worlds. If its catalogs were as segregated and stereotyped racially as they are by gender, people would boycott.

I rent a video—*Jimmy Neutron, Boy Genius*—for Cassie. It's marketed as a kids' movie, and the movie is OK for the most part. But then we get to the music video that follows the movie, unaccompanied by any warnings. A group I've never heard of sings a song called "Kids in America." Two of the girls are 13, two are 15, and one is 16—their ages are emblazoned across the screen as each makes her appearance. They are in full vixen attire, with professionally undulating bodies and professionally made-up, come-hither eyes.

Why are we told their ages, I wonder? Are we supposed to be amazed at the illusion of womanhood created by their performance? Or is their youth supposed to make it all right to show this to little kids, a way of saying, "It's only make-believe, only a dress-up game"? It wasn't so long ago that people were outraged by news clips of JonBenet Ramsey performing in children's beauty pageants. In 2002, toddler versions of Britney Spears were walking the streets on Halloween night. Can it really be that we now think dressing our daughters up like tiny prostitutes is cute? That's what the psychologist Sharon Lamb, author of *The Secret Lives of Girls*, thinks. She advises mothers to chill out if their 9-year-old girls "play lovely little games in high heels, strip teasing, flouncing, and jutting their chests out," to relax if their 11-year-olds go out with "thick blue eye shadow, spaghetti straps and bra straps intertwined, long and leggy with short black dresses." They are "silly and adorable, sexy and marvelous all at once," she tells us, as they "celebrate their objectification," "playing out male fantasies . . . but without risk."

Without risk? I have nothing against girls playing dress-up. But flouncing is one thing; strip teasing is another. Thick blue eye shadow in mommy's bathroom is fine; an 11-year-old's night on the town is not. Reading those words "without risk," I want to remind Sharon Lamb that 22 to 29 percent of all rapes against girls occur when they are 11 and younger. We might like to think that those rapes are the work of deranged madmen, so disconnected from reality as to be oblivious to the culture around them. Or that all we need to do to protect our daughters is simply teach them not to take candy from or go into cars with strangers. The reality, however, is that young girls are much more likely to be raped by friends and family members than by strangers and

that very few men, whether strangers or acquaintances, are unaffected by a visual culture of nymphets prancing before their eyes, exuding a sexual knowledge and experience that preteens don't really have. Feminists used to call this "rape culture." We never hear that phrase anymore.

Still, progressive forces are not entirely asleep in the empire of images. I think of *YM* teen magazine, for example. After conducting a survey that revealed that 86 percent of its young readers were dissatisfied with the way their bodies looked, *YM* openly declared war on eating disorders and body-image problems, instituting an editorial policy against the publishing of diet pieces and deliberately seeking out full-size models—without identifying them as such—for all its fashion spreads. A colleague suggested that this resistance to the hegemony of the fat-free body may have something to do with the fact that the editors are young enough to have studied feminism and cultural studies while they got their B.A.'s in English and journalism.

Most progressive developments in the media, of course, are driven by market considerations rather than social conscience. So, for example, the fact that 49 million women are size 12 or more is clearly the motive behind new, flesh-normalizing campaigns created by "Just My Size" and Lane Bryant. Ad campaigns for these lines of clothing proudly show off zaftig bodies in sexy underwear and, unlike older marketing to "plus size" women, refuse to use that term, insisting (accurately) that what has been called plus size is in fact average. It's a great strategy for making profits, but a species of resistance nonetheless. "I won't allow myself to be invisible anymore," these ads proclaim, on our behalf. "But I won't be made visible as a cultural oddity or a joke, either, because I'm not. I'm the norm."

The amorality of consumer capitalism, in its restless search for new markets and new ways to generate and feed desire, has also created a world of racial representations that are far more diverse now than when I wrote *Unbearable Weight*. This is another issue that has acquired special meaning for me, because my daughter is biracial, and I am acutely aware of the world that she sees and what it is telling her about herself. Leafing through current magazines, noting the variety of skin tones, noses, mouths depicted there, I'm glad, for the moment, that Cassie is growing up today rather than in the '70s, when Cheryl Tiegs ruled. It's always possible, of course, to find things that are still "wrong" with these representations; racist codes and aesthetics die hard. The Jezebels and geishas are still with us; and, although black male models and toddlers are allowed to have locks and "naturals," straight hair—straighter nowadays than I ever thought it was possible for anyone's hair to be—seems almost mandatory for young black women.

It's easy, too, to be cynical. Today's fashionable diversity is brought to us, after all, by the same people who brought us the hegemony of the blue-eyed blonde and who've made wrinkles and cellulite into diseases. It's easy to dismiss fashion's current love affair with full lips and biracial children as a shameless attempt to exploit ethnic markets while providing ethnic chic for white beauty tourists. Having a child, however, has given me another perspective, as I try to imagine how the models look through her eyes. Cassie knows nothing about the motives of the people who've produced the images. At her age, she can only take them at face value. And at face value, they present a world that includes and celebrates her, as the world that I grew up in did not include and celebrate me. For all my anger, cynicism, and frustration with our empire of images, I cannot help but be grateful for that.

And sometimes, surveying the plastic, digitalized world of bodies that are the norm now, I am convinced that our present state of enchantment is just a moment away from revulsion, or perhaps simply boredom. I see a 20-something woman dancing at a local outdoor swing party, her tummy softly protruding over the thick leather belt of her low-rider jeans. Not taut, not toned, not artfully camouflaged like some unsightly deformity, but proudly, sensuously displayed, reminding me of Madonna in the days before she became the sinewy dominatrix. Is it possible that we are beginning to rebel against the manufactured look of celebrity bodies, beginning to be repelled by their armored perfection?

Such hopeful moments, I have to admit, are fleeting. Usually, I feel horrified. I am sharply aware that expressing my horror openly nowadays invites being thought of as a preachy prude, a relic of an outmoded feminism. At talks to young audiences, I try to lighten my touch, celebrate the positive, make sure that my criticisms of our culture are not confused with being anti-beauty, anti-fitness, or anti-sex. But I also know that when parents and teachers become fully one with the culture, children are abandoned to it. I don't tell them to love their bodies or turn off the television—useless admonitions today, and ones I cannot obey myself—but I do try to disrupt, if only temporarily, their everyday immersion in the culture. For just an hour or so, I won't let it pass itself off simply as "normalcy."

The lights go down, the slides go up. For just a moment, we confront how bizarre, how impossible, how contradictory the images are. We laugh together over Oprah's head digitally grafted to another woman's body, at the ad for breast implants in which the breasts stick straight up in the air. We gasp together as the before and after photos of Jennifer Lopez are placed side by side. We cheer for Marion Jones's shoulders, boo the fact that WNBA Barbie is just the same old Barbie, but with a basketball in her hand. For just a moment, we are in charge of the impact the faked images of "perfect" bodies have on us.

We look at them together and share —just for a moment —outrage.

Explore this essay in depth.
www.ablongman.com/beyondwords07

COMPOSE

1. According to Bordo, we are routinely bombarded by so many idealized images of the human body that we may not even notice when or how they distort our sense of self. Make a list of where and when you encounter such images during a specific period of time (an hour, an afternoon, a day). Then use your evidence to evaluate Bordo's claim.

2. Bordo, as a feminist, is concerned primarily with the way images shape the body images of young women and girls. Are boys and young men similarly bombarded by unhealthy images? How do the popular media portray young men? Are 12- and 13-year-old boys, for example, sexualized in the ways Bordo claims young girls are? Or are boys stereotyped in different ways? In a mixed group, discuss your findings and their implications.

CONSIDER

3. Why do people—particularly young women—admire or emulate bodies they know have been improved by surgery, impossible exercise regimens, photographic enhancement, or other feints? Why do we refuse to buy the claim that "one can be 'sexy at any size'"? In a brief essay, explore possible explanations for this phenomenon, perhaps focusing on the people and communities you know best.

4. "The Empire of Images in Our World of Bodies" ends with some hope that younger women, while still influenced by media images, are beginning to read them more critically and hence resist them. Read Bordo's concluding paragraphs in context with the *Rolling Stone* covers that appear later in this chapter (pages 142–143). Do they suggest any changes in the way younger people—one of the target audiences of *Rolling Stone*—think about beauty, physical perfection, and gender stereotypes? Which covers reinforce potentially hurtful stereotypes, and which undermine them? Offer your thoughts in a few detailed paragraphs.

Living on the Street

For many teens from homes with broken marriages or abusive parents, a life on the street seems to offer a better option. Struggles with parental authority or with drugs or alcohol may lead them away from home. Others may be drawn by a sense of adventure or a desire to escape the unexciting inevitability represented by staying in school, getting a job, and joining the system.

None of these explanations answers every question about teen homelessness. Indeed, the more we examine the issue, the more we realize that simple solutions are not likely to present themselves. Instead, we can open our eyes to the lives of teens on the street as a way of beginning to understand their concerns.

FYI Alison Stateman is an award-winning writer whose work has appeared in the *New York Times* and the *Washington Post.* As a former resident of NYC's East Village, she observed urban nomads' migration patterns firsthand, as they'd come and settle in each summer, sometimes right outside her front door. She wanted to explore their lives of perpetual motion and the often-angry responses their mere presence provoked among some of the neighborhood's residents.

Postcards from the Edge

Alison Stateman
(2003)

It's one of those bone-numbing rainy days, the kind that gets under your fleece and rain gear, rendering all attempts at warmth futile. Julie, 26, is in a mood as foul as the weekend weather.

"This is ridiculous," she said, her words punctuated with four-letter invectives. "You would think that people would be more willing to help out, but it's not like that."

"Actually," she added, gesturing toward her plastic cup, clearly disappointed with its thin layer of coins, "on nicer days I make more money."

Strangers are both intrigued and repelled by this slight, black-clad figure, a pilled skullcap low on her forehead, who is slumped against a wall adorned with graffiti. Black dirt is caked under her fingernails and nestled in the crevices of her open palms.

A patch of sidewalk near the corner of 14th Street and University Place is Julie's regular spot to beg for spare change, to "spange," as she and her friends put it. This is where Julie spends most of her days, along with

Whiskey, her tawny shepherd–pit bull mix, and Samantha, a pretty, 20-year-old brunette. Samantha, who goes by Sam and is from upstate New York, is dressed in baggy combat pants ripped at the crotch, and, like her companion, refuses to give her last name.

Along with "Dumpster diving"—scrounging for garbage outside restaurants—Julie and Sam meet their needs for food and shelter by using signs that advertise their plight. Sometimes Sam carries a sign that reads, "Trying to Get Home to My Mother's House." Julie's current sign, which is illustrated with paw prints, reads: "Homeless, Hungry and Broke. We are trying to get off the street tonight. Need @ $30 for a place to sleep. Please help. Thank you!!" The amount requested is her share of the approximately $65 that she and Sam will need to rent a cheap room for the night.

If they come up short, they will sleep on a side street, under scaffolding or an awning. Julie used to stay in squats on the Lower East Side, but more often than not, it's a cold, concrete bed for her.

For the last decade Julie has been part of a little-known segment of homeless youth often called urban nomads. Year in and year out they travel to a few select North American cities, living on little or no money on the fringes of a society they have grown disillusioned with or, like Julie, actively despise.

Like birds, they migrate according to the weather, spending the winter in the warmer parts of the South and West—San Francisco, New Orleans and Austin are favorites—before returning north as the weather grows milder. Manhattan is a prime destination, even though the life, never easy, is likely to get harder, given impending budget cuts that would affect the city's social services.

According to statistics provided by the Partnership for the Homeless, an advocacy group, an estimated 19,000 homeless and runaway youths live in New York's shelters or on its streets.

"New York is a place where people come for all reasons," said City Councilman Alan J. Gerson, who sponsored a conference at Pace University two weeks ago to explore the growing problem of homeless youth in the city. "That's the history of New York. So if a person is homeless on our streets, they are our problem and our imperative."

BASIC BLACK, AND TATTOOS

Urban nomads like Julie are a population that social scientists have only recently begun to study. Chief among those who focus on this group is Don

C. Des Jarlais, research director at the Baron Edmond de Rothschild Chemical Dependency Institute at Beth Israel Medical Center. The center has just issued preliminary findings from its Urban Nomad Study, now in its third year.

For the purposes of the study, urban nomads are defined as youths who have traveled to at least five different cities or towns in the past three years and at least three within the past year. After interviewing several hundred people who fit these criteria, the researchers are getting a feel for who they are, though hard statistics are elusive.

"We haven't really attempted to get a good estimate of the numbers, but I'd say it's probably in the thousands," said Dr. Des Jarlais. He estimates that nationally there may be 5,000 to 10,000 urban nomads, 1,000 of whom pass through New York each year.

Dr. Des Jarlais discovered urban nomads during an earlier study of drug users on the Lower East Side. "I was curious how they managed, how they survive," he said. "And the subtext was, 'Could I do that?'"

"This is a challenging lifestyle," he added. "But it's not as if they have totally given up on their lives."

Dr. Des Jarlais says that while urban nomads sometimes exaggerate or dramatize their pasts, they tend not to make up stories. Their parents are often ambivalent about their children leaving. "Some parents were probably very upset that they left, and some were probably very happy to see them go." Seventy to 80 percent of urban nomads said they stayed in touch with their parents, usually their mothers, but, he said, "when we asked, 'Could you go back home?' only 50 percent said they could."

While urban nomads and the city's traditional homeless youth often share a history of physical or sexual abuse, the two groups differ in many respects. Typically, New York's population of runaways and homeless youths is heavily minority and includes both girls and boys. By contrast, urban nomads tend to be white and largely male, with backgrounds that are typically working-class and occasionally middle-class. Many are children from homes where a parent's remarriage has produced family conflicts. Others are simply bored.

"In general, their home situations are not good, but it is not like they are in dire danger or anything like that," Dr. Des Jarlais said. "They are sort of not getting along well at home and they want to do something different, so they leave."

Unlike most of New York's runaways, who often pursue the dual street-survival occupations of drug-dealing and prostitution and hang out in places like Times Square, urban nomads tend to shun prostitution and heavy drug use and are drawn to the East Village and the Lower East Side.

The East Village holds a particular attraction because of its history of social and political unrest, its squatter tradition and its punk roots, typified by landmarks like CBGB's on the Bowery. The usual attire of combat or work clothes or basic black, set off by multiple piercings and tattoos, also mirrors the punk and working-man sympathies of the typical urban nomad.

But looking different can backfire. "From the moment they get into town, they're targeted by police because of the way they look," said John Welch, program director of Safe Horizon's Streetwork Project on the Lower East Side, a group that serves several hundred urban nomads each year. "They're more visible." As a result, they are often ticketed for minor offenses, like panhandling.

DRUG-FREE, BURNED OUT

Passers-by will tell Julie she doesn't need money if she has enough cash to pay for her tattoos and all that silver. In fact, she often wears long-sleeve shirts to hide her extensive network of tattoos, and she readily explains that she got them for free from friends who were budding tattoo artists and practiced on her.

It may, however, be the choice of artwork that makes people pause. A pentagram and a black skull with twisted horns are imprinted on her neck, and her hands and left upper arm are decorated with the phrases "Godless" and "What Life?"

"It's a scare tactic," she said. "I'm not in any way a holy person, but I'm also not satanic. It kind of reflects how I feel inside about people and life and the world and stuff. I'm not a happy, colorful, optimistic person, so a lot of my tattoos interpret the way I feel about everything."

Julie's physical condition also startles. Her front teeth, which arch out slightly, are yellowed, and she is rail-thin even for her petite frame. Julie hasn't been to a doctor or dentist in more than 10 years. However, she can recite the dates on which Whiskey was vaccinated and spayed and carries the paperwork to prove it in her army-green pack.

In fact, Whiskey seems to be the only being she doesn't seem to dislike, herself included. At one point, she grasped Whiskey's face and wept. "I love this dog, man," she said as Whiskey licked her tears before she could wipe them away.

Dogs play a big part in the urban nomad culture, providing their street-bound owners with companionship and protection. "A lot of people say, 'Oh, why don't you stay in a shelter?'" Julie said, mimicking their concerned tone. "Well, obviously it's because I have a dog. 'Well, why don't you give the dog away?' I love my dog. I'm not going to give my dog away so I can stay in a shelter. I'd rather sleep in the street."

Almost everyone who passes her stares. Some people grimace in disgust; a few cross the street. When a woman starts to take a picture of Julie, the action pushes her over the edge. "Can you not do that, please?" Julie asks.

"People think of us as some kind of New York landmark," she said later, her pale blue eyes glowering. "It's amusing to them. I am amusing to them. 'Oh, look at that, honey,'" she said in the mocking tone she adopts when impersonating strangers. "'That little creep with the dog begging for money.'"

Indeed, many passers-by are drawn less by her than by her pet, who this day rests a weary head upon Julie's thigh and shivers despite the red sweater wrapped tightly around her. Several people who drop change in Julie's cup announce, "This is for the dog."

This angers Julie. "They think I'm going to use it for drugs," she explained. She admits that she used heroin for four years, but said she has been drug-free since 2001.

Although Julie says she has been coming to the city every year since she was 17, making cross-country excursions to San Francisco and Portland when she can prevail on Sam to watch Whiskey, she is hard pressed to explain exactly why she is here.

"First of all, I'm kind of preoccupied with my financial situation," she said, "and No. 2, five or six years ago I might be able to speak really clearly about how I feel about things, but now I'm just so exhausted with having to explain myself all the time. Maybe it's just because I've had so much time to think, because I'm just sitting around thinking, that it's just like my brain is just burned out.

"I've become this kind of totally miserable, hateful person because I have to look at all these people every single day," she added. "But I put myself here, so I can't really blame anybody else. I guess I could have done things a little differently when I was younger, but I don't know."

Julie says she ran away from her home in New Hampshire at the age of 15. Asked why she left, she responds with an obscenity about her parents. According to her account of her early years, she spent time in a children's home and a year at Keene State College in New Hampshire before flunking out and hitting the road with like-minded friends.

She says she misses her father, who just turned 60 and used to work in computers. But the few times she has reached out to her parents, she said, by phone or through visits, she has been rejected. According to Julie, they are still angry at her for running away.

After so many years on the street, Julie doesn't seem to know what to make of generosity or choice. When a sailor in town for Fleet Week approached and peeled off a $5 bill, she asked awkwardly if he were really a sailor. Later on, when asked what she'd like for dinner, she had to think for several minutes, not wanting to blow a rare opportunity to choose her food. She opted for Taco Bell.

Despite evidence to the contrary, Julie doesn't think of herself as homeless.

"Homeless people to me are people who push around shopping carts and push strollers and they just sit around," she said. "Lazy and crazy is what I say."

The next day she's not so sure. "Once you do this for a while," she said, "it gets kind of exhausting and it's hard not to give in to those things that will make your life a little bit easier, such as getting a job and settling down and having security blankets and a nice place to live."

Could she ever lead that kind of life? "I hope so," she replied morosely, "because I don't want to be pushing a shopping cart around when I'm 50. If I make it to 50."

Dr. Des Jarlais has found that urban nomads seldom reach that age. "We've found almost nobody over 30," he said. "Some of them tend to move into conventional society and some of them, of course, develop health problems and die." Few find their way into organized programs, in part because programs that meet their needs are scarce.

THE "GRAPES OF WRATH" ROUTE

Urban nomad culture is built upon a patchwork of traditions that reflect its anti-establishment bent. Hopping freight trains, a practice that harkens back to the hobo of the Depression, is a favored mode of transportation. Many urban nomads find work sporadically as house painters or migrant laborers in the tradition chronicled in John Steinbeck's *Grapes of Wrath*.

Shane, 26, a soft-spoken friend of Julie's who travels to Maine each August to harvest the state's famed blueberries, matches the template perfectly.

Unlike Julie, who is all explosive energy, Shane is mellowness personified. Though coated in grime from the top of his once-beige Dewar's baseball cap to the tips of his work boots, though his backpacks emit the musky odor of too many nights spent sleeping in the rain and soot, he manages to maintain an air of dignity.

Even his choice of tattoos belies a gentler nature, from the character from his favorite comic book, *The Realm of Chaos*, etched on his forearm to the heart and scroll adorned with the names of his two former dogs, Sasha and Blue, on his bicep. Perhaps because of the shave he just finagled in a restroom at Kmart on Astor Place, his angular face, punctuated by a strawberry-blond goatee, looks surprisingly youthful.

Shane, who is stationed across the street from Julie, is biding his time in the city before moving on to his next odd job.

"I follow the harvest," he said. "I do blueberries in Maine, then I do beets. I go down to Virginia and do apples. I go up to Alaska and work in the canneries. I don't like to stay in one place for too long. I love traveling. I don't like the whole 9-to-5 thing. I like to go to work for a couple of weeks, a couple of months at a time, and save up for whatever gear I need and go on to the next place."

Shane said he has a regular winter gig painting houses in Townsend, Wash., a job that provides a steady income and a trailer for shelter. Like the majority of older urban nomads, he eventually tired of the city circuit and began opting for odd jobs that took him to smaller towns; by contrast, younger nomads are usually drawn to the glitz that bigger urban environments offer.

Shane says he likes his life. But even if he wanted to get a conventional job, doing so without a permanent address would be nearly impossible.

"Some people tell you to get a job," he said. "They don't understand that I'd love to have a job, but it's kind of hard when you're homeless to walk into a place when you don't have an address or anything. To get a place to live, you have to have a job, but then again to get a job, you have to have a place to live where you can wake up every day to go to work. That's why I do the harvests. You can camp right there and go to work."

Shane, who said he was born and raised in Washington State, was not always the self-described laid-back person he presents himself as today. A decade ago, he was a rebellious, hard-partying teenager, with a tough Navy man as a stepfather. At one point, his mother gave him an ultimatum: Follow the house rules or get out.

"I was doing a lot of drinking, so I wasn't listening to my mother, so I ended up getting kicked out when I was 16, so I've been on my own since then," he said. "She told me if I couldn't follow her rules and my stepfather's rules, then I wasn't welcome to live there. And being the know-it-all that I was as a teenager, I just left."

He first came to New York at 17, drawn by a sense that this was his true place. His real father, who had left his mother around the time Shane was born, was originally from the city, and though Shane has never met his father, the city has not disappointed.

"When I was young, I used to picture New York a lot and see movies about it," he said from his curbside vantage point, surrounded by skeletons of umbrellas, abandoned cigarettes and clouds of bus exhaust. "I guess I just always wanted to see it.

"It was just like I thought it would be," he added. "It's just beautiful. The old brownstones and old buildings. It's such an old city and has such history. I like it here."

Shane recently earned his high school equivalency diploma and spends time in the main reading room of the New York Public Library, writing in his journal and reading books like *Last Exit to Brooklyn*.

His mother, a former teacher, is retired and lives with his stepfather in Spain. He calls and writes her regularly, and he gets her mail sent care of Streetwork's Lower East Side center. "Me and mom are really close," he said. "I talk to her a lot."

Reaching into a torn Duane Reade bag, he pulled out photographs of his mother's Chihuahua, dressed in a sweater, and a postcard she had sent him from Portugal. Does his mother worry about him? "I think she used to because I used to be into a lot of drugs," he said. "But she knows I've grown out of that."

CONSIDER

1. How do urban nomads compare to your preconceptions of homeless teens? Is it fair to say they choose to be homeless? Why or why not?

2. What are your thoughts about the lifestyle of urban nomads? Are there elements that appeal to you? What does their lifestyle say about more conventional ways of living?

3. Would you say the urban nomad is a contemporary problem? If so, how might you explain the development of the problem? If not, how would you relate current urban nomads to earlier times?

Images from *Raised by Wolves*

Jim Goldberg
(1995)

Raised by Wolves collects a series of photographs of street youth that Jim Goldberg has taken over the years. He follows several youth in the book, providing a number of images that detail the progression of their lives on the street. He also includes snippets from notebooks, maps, and detailed accounts of conversations that tell the stories of these homeless teens. Here are two images from that book, with Goldberg's captions.

USA. Hollywood, California. 1990. *Kato, Hollywood Boulevard.* Photo by Jim Goldberg with handwritten caption by Kato.

It's Not Like you CAN go Home And WAtch TV

USA. Hollywood, California. 1988. *Dave Panhandling.* Photographer Jim Goldberg adds the following note: "Tweeky Dave panhandles next to Marilyn Monroe's star on Hollywood Boulevard, beside a McDonald's. Dave weighs less than 100 pounds due to living on the street and being a junkie. He also claims this is because he has leukemia."

CONSIDER

1. How important are Goldberg's captions to your reading of his images? Without the explanations of the photographs, would their message be as strong?

2. What kinds of emotional responses do Goldberg's photographs evoke? How do you think Goldberg expects his viewers and readers to respond? Does he expect to prompt viewers to action?

COMPOSE

3. How would you compare the stories told by Goldberg's images from *Raised by Wolves* with the images evoked by the urban nomad stories in Alison Stateman's "Postcards from the Edge"? In a two- or three-page paper, compare the ways these works help us understand teen homelessness.

View more photos from *Raised by Wolves* and other works by Jim Goldberg.
www.ablongman.com/beyondwords08

Fashioning Identities

The texts and images in the following section examine some of the different ways people modify their bodies as an expression of identity—how they decorate it, eroticize it, abuse it, and even use it to make judgments about others. Is the body just a container for identity, or is it the defining architecture?

Tattoo You

Not all that long ago, tattoos might be found on the bodies of sailors, working-class stiffs, and—discreetly—members of fraternal organizations. You didn't expect respectable professionals to display them, especially if they were women. But given the long history of body art, that reluctance to decorate our limbs and other body parts may have been the aberration. Tattoos are back, giving people in many walks of life more options for self-expression or, in the opinion of some, self-mutilation. Josie Appleton, writing for spiked.com, a London-based Web journal, takes a critical look at the rationales people offer for their body modification and raises some provocative objections.

FYI Josie Appleton writes about politics and culture for spiked.com, an online journal based in London. She is author of *Museums for 'The People'?*, and has contributed to publications including the *Spectator* and *BBC History Magazine*.

The Body Piercing Project

Josie Appleton
(2003)

The opening of a tattoo and piercing section in the up-market London store Selfridges shows that body modification has lost its last trace of taboo.

"Metal Morphosis," nestled in the thick of the ladies' clothing section, is a world away from the backstreets of Soho—where the company has its other branch. Teenagers, middle-aged women, men in suits and young guys in jeans flock to peer at the rows of tastefully displayed rings and leaf through the tattoo brochures.

Tattooist Greg said that he had seen a "broad variety" of people: "everything from the girl who turned 18 to the two Philippino cousins who just turned 40." The piercer, Barry, said that a number of "Sloanies" come for piercings (the most expensive navel bar retails at £3000, and there is a broad selection that would set you back several hundred pounds). A handful of women have even asked to be tattooed with the label of their favourite bottle of wine.[1]

This is not just affecting London high-streets. According to current estimates, between 10 and 25 percent of American adolescents have some kind of piercing or tattoo.[2] And their mothers are taking it up, too—in the late 1990s, the fastest growing demographic group seeking tattoo services in America was middle-class suburban women.[3]

But while tattoos have been taken up by university students and ladies who lunch, more traditional wearers of tattoos—sailors, soldiers, bikers, gangs—find themselves increasingly censured.

In June 2003, the police rejected an applicant because his tattoos were deemed to have an "implication of racism, sexism or religious prejudice."[4] The U.S. Navy has banned "tattoos/body art/brands that are excessive, obscene, sexually explicit or advocate or symbolize sex, gender, racial, religious, ethnic or national origin discrimination" and "symbols denoting any gang affiliation, supremacist or extremist groups, or drug use."[5]

New-style tattoos are a very different ball-game to their frowned-upon forebears. While the tattoos of football supporters, sailors and gang-members tend to be symbols of camaraderie or group affiliation, the Selfridges brigade are seeking something much more individual.

For some, tattoos and piercing are a matter of personal taste or fashion. "It's purely aesthetic decoration," said 37-year-old Sarah, waiting to get her navel pierced at Metal Morphosis. The erosion of moral censure on tattooing, and the increasing hygiene of tattoo parlors, has meant that body modification has become a fashion option for a much wider group of people.

For others, tattooing seems to go more than skin-deep. Tattoo artist Greg thinks that many of those getting tattoos today are looking for "self-empowerment"—tattoos, he says, are about establishing an "identity for the self." As a permanent mark on your body that you choose for yourself, a tattoo is "something no one will ever be able to take away from you," that allows you to say *this is mine.*"

Seventeen-year-old Laura said that she got her piercings done because she "wanted to make a statement." When she turned 18, she planned to have "XXX" tattooed on the base of her spine, symbolising her pledge not to drink, smoke or take drugs. "It's not to prove anything to anyone else," she said; "it's a pact with myself completely."

Sue said that she had her navel pierced on her fortieth birthday to mark a turning point in her life. Another young man planned to have his girlfriend's name, and the dates when they met, tattooed on his arm "to show her that I love her"—and to remind himself of this moment. "The tattoo will be there forever. Whether or not I feel that in the future, I will remember that I felt it at the time, that I felt strong enough to have the tattoo."

The tattoos of bikers, sailors and gang-members would be a kind of social symbol that would establish them as having a particular occupation or belonging to a particular cultural subgroup. By contrast, Laura's "XXX" symbol is a sign to herself of how she has chosen to live her life; Sue pierced her navel to mark her transition to middle-age. These are not symbols that could be interpreted by anyone else. Even the man who wanted to get tattooed with his girlfriend's name had a modern, personal twist to his tale: the tattoo was less a pact to stay with her forever than to remind himself of his feelings at this point.

Much new-style body modification is just another way to look good. But the trend also presents a more profound, and worrying, shift: the growing crisis in personal identity.

In his book *Modernity and Self-Identity* (1991), sociologist Anthony Giddens argues that it is the erosion of important sources of identity that helps to explain the growing focus on the body.[6] Body modification began to really take off and move into the mainstream in the late 1980s and early 1990s. At around this time, personal and community relationships that previously helped to provide people with an enduring sense of self could no longer be depended upon. The main ideological frameworks that provided a system to understand the world and the individual's place in it, such as class, religion, or the work ethic, began to erode.

These changes have left individuals at sea, trying to establish their own sense of who they are. In their piercing or tattooing, people are trying to construct a "narrative of self" on the last thing that remains solid and tangible: their physical bodies. While much about social experience is uncertain and insecure, the body at least retains a permanence and reliability. Making marks upon their bodies is an attempt by people to build a lasting story of who they are.

Many—including, to an extent, Giddens—celebrate modification as a liberating and creative act. "If you want to and it makes you feel good, you should do it," Greg tells me. Web sites such as the Body Modification Ezine (BMEzine)[7] are full of readers' stories about how their piercing has completely changed their life. One piercer said that getting a piercing "helped me know who I am." Another said that they felt "more complete . . . a better, more rounded and fuller person."[8] Others even talk about unlocking their soul, or finally discovering that "I AM."

But what these stories actually show is less the virtues of body piercing than the desperation of individuals' attempts to find a foothold for themselves. There is a notable contrast between the superlatives about discovering identity and Being and the ultimately banal act of sticking a piece of metal through your flesh.

Piercings and tattoos are used to plot out significant life moments, helping to lend a sense of continuity to experience. A first date, the birth of a child, moving house: each event can be marked out on the body, like the notches of time on a stick. One woman said that her piercings helped to give her memory, to "stop me forgetting who I am." They work as a "diary" that "no one can take off you."[9]

This springs from the fact that there is a great deal of confusion about the stages of life today. Old turning points that marked adulthood—job, marriage, house, kids—have both stopped being compulsory and lost much of their significance. It is more difficult to see life in terms of a narrative, as a plot with key moments of transition and an overall aim. Piercings and tattoos are used to highlight formative experiences and link them together.

Some also claim that body modification helps them to feel "comfortable in my own skin" or proud of parts of their body of which they were previously ashamed. The whole process of piercing—which involves caring for the wound and paying special attention to bodily processes—is given great significance. By modifying a body part, some argue that you are taking possession of it, making it truly yours. The nipple piercings have really changed my relationship to my breasts," one woman said.[10]

This is trying to resolve a sense of self-estrangement—the feeling of detachment from experiences, the feeling that your life doesn't really belong to you. One young woman says how she uses piercing: "[It's been] done at times when I felt like I needed to ground myself. Sometimes I feel like I'm not in my body—then it's time."[11]

But piercing is trying to deal with the problem at the most primitive and brutal level—in the manner of "I hurt, therefore I am." The experience of pain becomes one of the few authentic experiences. It also tries to resolve the crisis in individual identity in relation to my breasts or my navel, rather than in relation to other people or anything more meaningful in the world.

Many claims are made as to the transformative and creative potential of body modification. One girl, who had just had her tongue pierced, writes: "I've always been kind of quiet in school and very predictable. . . . I wanted to think of myself as original and creative, so I decided I wanted something pierced. . . . Now people don't think of me as shy and predictable, they respect me and the person I've become and call me crazily spontaneous."[12]

Others say they use modification to help master traumatic events. Transforming the body is seen as helping to re-establish a sense of self-control in the face of disrupting or degrading experiences. One woman carved out a Sagittarius symbol on her thigh to commemorate a lover who died. "It was my way of coming to terms with the grief I felt," she said. "It enabled me to always have him with me and to let him go."[13]

Steve McCurry, Tattooed man in Los Angeles (1991)

Here the body being modified is a way of trying to effect change in people's lives. It is the way to express creativity, find a challenge, or put themselves through the hoops. "I was ecstatic. I did it!," writes one contributor to BMEzine. Instead of a life project, this is a "body project." In the absence of obvious social outlets for creativity, the individual turns back on himself and to the transformation of his own flesh.

Body piercing expresses the crisis of social identity—but it actually also makes it worse, too. Focusing on claiming control over my body amounts to making a declaration of independence from everybody else.

People with hidden piercings comment on how pleased they were they had something private. One says: "I get so happy just walking along and knowing that I have a secret that no one else could ever guess!" Another said that they now had "something that people could not judge me for, and something that I could hide." Another said that her piercing made her realize that "what other people say or think doesn't matter. The only thing that mattered at that moment was that I was happy with this piercing; I felt beautiful and comfortable in my own skin. . . . They remind me that I'm beautiful to who it matters . . . **me**."[14]

Body modification encourages a turn away from trying to build personal identity through relationships with others and instead tries to resolve problems in relation to one's own body. When things are getting rough, or when somebody wants to change their lives, the answer could be a new piercing or a new tattoo. There is even an underlying element of self-hatred here, as individuals try to deal with their problems by doing violence to themselves. As 17-year-old Laura told me: "You push yourself to do more and more. . . . You want it to hurt."

This means that the biggest questions—of existence, self-identity, life progression, creativity—are being tackled with the flimsiest of solutions. A mark on the skin or a piercing through the tongue cannot genuinely resolve grief, increase creativity, or give a solid grounding to self-identity. For this reason, body modification can become an endless, unfulfilling quest, as one piercing only fuels a desire for another. All the contributions to BMEzine start by saying how much their life has been changed—but then promptly go on to plan their next series of piercings. "Piercing can be addictive!" they warn cheerily.

Body modification should be put back in the fashion box. As a way of improving personal appearance, piercing and tattooing are no better or worse than clothes, makeup or hair gel. It is when body modification is loaded with existential significance that the problems start.

Notes

1. "Ladies who lunch get a tattoo for starters," *London Times*, 18 June 2003.
2. "Body piercing, tattooing, self-esteem, and body investment in adolescent girls," *Adolescence*, Fall 2002.
3. *The Changing Status of Tattoo Art*, by Hoag Levins.
4. "Police reject tattooed applicant," BBC News, 16 June 2003.
5. "Navy draws a line on some forms of body piercing, ornamentation, tattoos," *Stars and Stripes*, European edition, 29 January 2003.
6. *Modernity and Self-Identity: Self and Society in the Late Modern Age*, by Anthony Giddens, 1991.
7. Body Modification Ezine, www.bmezine.com.
8. Quoted in *Body Modification*, ed. by Mike Featherstone, 2000.
9. Quoted in *Body Modification*.
10. Quoted in *The Body Aesthetic*, ed. by Tobin A Siebers, 2000.
11. *Body Piercing in the West: A Sociological Inquiry*, by Susan Holtham.
12. "My beautiful piercing," on BMEzine.
13. *The Customized Body*, by Ted Polhemus and Housk Randall, 2000.
14. All from BMEzine.

On December 3, 1999, a fire in Worcester started with a candle in an abandoned warehouse. It ended with temperatures above 3,000 degrees and the men of the Worcester fire department in a fight for their lives. From left: Kevin Reando, Rich Roy, Gary Williams, Dave Halvorsen, Steve "Yeah" Connole, and Robert A. Johnson in the station house; the tattoos on their shoulders are inscribed with the date of the fire as well as slogans such as "last alarm," "WFD," and "Box 1438." Photo by Bruce Davidson.

Steve McCurry, Ramlila pageant participant (1993)

1. Early in "The Body Piercing Project," Appleton distinguishes tattoos that affirm group identities (among bikers, sailors, gangs) and fashionable tattoos that are supposed to be expressions of individuality. Do you accept this distinction? Does it apply to you or people you know with tattoos or piercings?

2. The people Appleton cites offer a full list of reasons for modifying their bodies to heighten their sense of identity or commitment. Which of their reasons, if any, do you find most convincing?

3. Examine the photos of tattoos on pages 128–130. Do these images reinforce Appleton's characterizations of people who practice body modification, or do the pictures suggest a different story? Explain your position.

4. In most respects, "The Body Piercing Project" is an example of a causal analysis, a type of argument that attempts to explain a phenomenon—in this case, the growing popularity of body modifications. Try your hand at writing a similar analysis relating to another current fad that might really be about issues of group or personal identity. Topics might include anything from clothing fads to trends in gaming, sports, personal Web sites or blogs, or anything that people you know use to express an aspect of their identity.

Doing Hair

If you've ever gotten a really bad haircut, you surely appreciate the role your hair plays in building your self-confidence and your sense of personal style. But you might not often think about the ways in which your hair connects you to larger cultural, racial, political, and even religious traditions. The following images and readings explore how these different aspects of identity converge in hairstyles.

Dreads: It Must Be like the Mating of Lions

Alice Walker
(1997)

It has been over ten years since I last combed my hair. When I mention this, friends and family are sometimes scandalized. I am amused by their reactions. During the same ten years they've poured gallons of possibly carcino-

FYI A distinguished novelist, poet, essayist and activist, Alice Walker won the Pulitzer Prize for *The Color Purple* (1982) and has most recently published *Absolute Trust in the Goodness of the Earth* (2003), a book of poems.

genic "relaxer" chemicals on themselves, and their once proud, interestingly crinkled or kinky hair has been forced to lie flat as a slab over a grave. But I understand this, having for many years done the same thing to myself.

Bob Marley is the person who taught me to trust the Universe enough to respect my hair. I don't even have to close my eyes to see him dancing his shamanic dance onstage as he sang his "redemption songs" and consistently poured out his heart to us. If anyone ever truly loved us, it was Bob Marley, and much of that affirmation came out of the way he felt about himself. I remember the first time I saw pictures of Marley and of that other amazing rebel, Peter Tosh. I couldn't imagine those black ropes on their heads were hair. And then, because the songs they were singing meant the ropes had to be hair, natural hair to which nothing was added, not even brushing, I realized they had managed to bring, or to reintroduce, a healthful new look, and way, to the world. I wondered what such hair felt like, smelled like. What a person dreamed about at night, with hair like that spread across the pillow. And, even more intriguing, what would it be like to make love to someone with hair on your head like that, and to be made love to by someone with hair on his or her head like that? It must be like the mating of lions, I thought. Aroused.

Bob Marley, photographed by Denis O'Regan

It wasn't until the filming of *The Color Purple* in 1985 that I got to explore someone's dreads. By then I had started "baby dreads" of my own, from tiny plaits, and had only blind faith that they'd grow eventually into proper locks. It was during a scene in which Sofia's sisters are packing up her things, as she prepares to leave her trying-to-be-abusive husband, Harpo. All Sofia's "sisters" were large, good-looking local women ("location" was Monroe, North Carolina), and one of them was explaining why she had to wear a cap in the scene instead of the more acceptable-to-the-period head-rag or straw hat. "I have too much hair," she said. Besides, back then (the 1920s) nobody would have been wearing dreads. Saying this, she swept off her roomy cap, and a cascade of vigorous locks fell way down her back. From a downtrodden, hardworking Southern Black woman she was transformed into a free, Amazonian goddess. I laughed in wonder at the transformation, my fingers instantly seeking her hair.

I then asked the question I would find so exasperating myself in years to come: "How do you wash it?"

She became very serious, as if about to divulge a major secret: "Well," she said, "I use something called shampoo, that you can buy at places like supermarkets and health food stores. I get into something called a shower, wet my hair, and rub this stuff all over it. I stand under the water and I scrub and scrub, working up a mighty lather. Then I rinse." She smiled suddenly, and I realized how ridiculous my question was. Through the years I would find myself responding to people exactly as she had, delighting in their belated recognition that I am joking with them.

The texture of her hair was somehow both firm and soft, springy; with the clear, fresh scent of almonds. It was warm black, and sunlight was caught in each kink and crinkle, so that up close there was a lot of purple and blue. I could feel how, miraculously, each lock wove itself into a flat or rounded pattern shortly after it left her scalp—a machine could not have done it with more precision—so that the "matting" I has assumed was characteristic of dreadlocks could more accurately be described as "knitting." How many Black people had any idea that, left pretty much to itself, our hair would do this? I wondered. Not very many, I was sure. I had certainly been among the uninformed. It was one of those moments that was so satisfying, when I felt my faith in my desire to be natural so well deserved, that it is not an exaggeration to say there is a way in which I was made happy forever. After all, if this major mystery could be discovered right on top of one's head, I thought, what other wonders might not be experienced in the Universe's exuberant, inexhaustible store?

"Mainstream trendsetters in Tokyo pay thousands of yen to have their poker-straight strands literally drilled into dreads. Hair is coated in a chemical concoction, then grouped into thick sections which are attached one at a time to a toothed, rotating apparatus that twists the 'insta-lock' up to its roots. Each freshly coiled section is clipped in place and left to dry. In extreme cases, glue is added to help the hair clump. The average price for this procedure is $500."

—FRANCESCO MASTALIA AND
ALFONSE PAGANO,
Dreads

Woman with dreadlocks, from *Dreads* by Francesco Mastalia and Alfonse Pagano

CONSIDER

1. What do you know about dreadlocks? Do some research in the library or on the Internet to find out more about the origins and meanings associated with this hairstyle. Where did dreads originate? When did they start to become popular in the United States? What can you discover about Peter Tosh and Bob Marley, whom Alice Walker credits with introducing her to dreadlocks?

2. What descriptive words and metaphors does Walker use to describe dreadlocks? Why do you think she devotes such a large part of the essay to these details? How did reading Walker's description influence your perceptions of the style?

COMPOSE

3. Given that dreads are associated with particular cultural and religious traditions, some have contended that it's inappropriate for people to wear the style simply as a fashion statement. What do you think? Write a paragraph that responds to this argument.

FYI

Henry Louis Gates Jr., chair of the Department of Afro-American Studies at Harvard University, has written a number of scholarly and popular books, among them his memoir *Colored People*, from which "In the Kitchen" is excerpted.

In the Kitchen

Henry Louis Gates Jr.
(1994)

We always had a gas stove in the kitchen, in our house in Piedmont, West Virginia, where I grew up. Never electric, though using electric became fashionable in Piedmont in the sixties, like using Crest toothpaste rather than Colgate, or watching Huntley and Brinkley rather than Walter Cronkite. But not us: gas, Colgate, and good ole Walter Cronkite, come what may. We used gas partly out of loyalty to Big Mom, Mama's Mama, because she was mostly blind and still loved to cook, and could feel her way more easily with gas than with electric. But the most important thing about our gas-equipped kitchen was that Mama used to do hair there. The "hot comb" was a fine-toothed iron instrument with a long wooden handle and a pair of iron curlers that opened and closed like scissors. Mama would put it in the gas fire until it glowed. You could smell those prongs heating up.

I liked that smell. Not the smell so much, I guess, as what the smell meant for the shape of my day. There was an intimate warmth in the women's tones as they talked with my Mama, doing their hair. I knew what the women had been through to get their hair ready to be "done," because I would watch Mama do it to herself. How that kink could be transformed through grease and fire into that magnificent head of wavy hair was a miracle to me, and still is.

Mama would wash her hair over the sink, a towel wrapped around her shoulders, wearing just her slip and her white bra. (We had no shower—just a galvanized tub that we stored in the kitchen—until we moved down Rat Tail Road into Doc Wolverton's house, in 1954.) After she dried it, she would grease her scalp thoroughly with blue Bergamot hair grease, which came in a short, fat jar with a picture of a beautiful colored lady on it. It's important to grease your scalp real good, my Mama would explain, to keep from burning yourself. Of course, her hair would return to its natural kink almost as soon as the hot water and shampoo hit it. To me, it was another miracle how hair so "straight" would so quickly become kinky again the second it even approached some water.

My Mama had only a few "clients" whose heads she "did"—did, I think, because she enjoyed it, rather than for the few pennies it brought in. They would sit on one of our red plastic kitchen chairs, the kind with the shiny metal legs, and brace themselves for the process. Mama would stroke that red-hot iron—which by this time had been in the gas fire for half an hour or more—slowly but firmly through their hair, from scalp to strand's end. It made a scorching, crinkly sound, the hot iron did, as it burned its way through kink, leaving in its wake straight strands of hair, standing long and tall but drooping over at the ends, their shape like the top of a heavy willow tree. Slowly, steadily, Mama's hands would transform a round mound of Odetta kink into a darkened swamp of everglades. The Bergamot made the hair shiny; the heat of the hot iron gave it a brownish-red cast. Once all the hair was as straight as God allows kink to get, Mama would take the well-heated curling iron and twirl the straightened strands into more or less loosely wrapped curls. She claimed that she owed her skill as a hairdresser to the strength in her wrists, and as she worked her little finger would poke out, the way it did when she sipped tea. Mama was a southpaw, and wrote upside down and backward to produce the cleanest, roundest letters you've ever seen.

The "kitchen" she would all but remove from sight with a handheld pair of shears, bought just for this purpose. Now, the kitchen was the room in which we were sitting—the room where Mama did hair and washed clothes, and where we all took a bath in that galvanized tub. But the word has another meaning, and the kitchen that I'm speaking of is the very kinky bit of hair at the back of your head, where your neck meets your shirt collar. If there was ever a part of our African past that resisted assimilation, it was the kitchen. No matter how hot the iron, no matter how powerful the chemical, no matter how stringent the mashed-potatoes-and-lye formula of a man's "process," neither God nor woman nor Sammy Davis, Jr., could straighten the kitchen. The kitchen was permanent, irredeemable, irresistible kink. Unassimilably African. No matter what you did, no matter how hard you tried, you couldn't de-kink a person's kitchen. So you trimmed it off as best you could.

When hair had begun to "turn," as they'd say—to return to its natural kinky glory—it was the kitchen that turned first (the kitchen around the back, and nappy edges at the temples). When the kitchen started creeping up the back of the neck, it was time to get your hair done again.

■ ■ ■

Sometimes, after dark, a man would come to have his hair done. It was Mr. Charlie Carroll. He was very light-complected and had a ruddy nose—it made me think of Edmund Gwenn, who played Kris Kringle in "Miracle on 34th Street." At first, Mama did him after my brother, Rocky, and I had gone to sleep. It was only later that we found out that he had come to our house so Mama could iron his hair—not with a hot comb or a curling iron but with our very own Proctor-Silex steam iron. For some reason I never understood, Mr. Charlie would conceal his Frederick Douglass–like mane under a big white Stetson hat. I never saw him take it off except when he came to our house, at night, to have his hair pressed. (Later, Daddy would tell us about Mr. Charlie's most prized piece of knowledge, something that the man would only confide after his hair had been pressed, as a token of intimacy. "Not many people know this," he'd say, in a tone of circumspection, "but George Washington was Abraham Lincoln's daddy." Nodding solemnly, he'd add the clincher: "A white man told me." Though he was in dead earnest, this became a humorous refrain around our house—"a white man told me"—which we used to punctuate especially preposterous assertions.)

My mother examined my daughters' kitchens whenever we went home to visit, in the early eighties. It became a game between us. I had told her not to do it, because I didn't like the politics it suggested—the notion of "good" and "bad" hair. "Good" hair was "straight," "bad" hair kinky. Even in the late sixties, at the height of Black Power, almost nobody could bring themselves to say "bad" for good and "good" for bad. People still said that hair like white people's hair was "good," even if they encapsulated it in a disclaimer, like "what we used to call 'good.'"

Maggie would be seated in her high chair, throwing food this way and that, and Mama would be cooing about how cute it all was, how I used to do just like Maggie was doing, and wondering whether her flinging her food with her left hand meant that she was going to be left-handed like Mama. When my daughter was just about covered with Chef Boyardee Spaghetti-O's, Mama would seize the opportunity: wiping her clean, she would tilt Maggie's head to one side and reach down the back of her neck. Sometimes Mama would even rub a curl between her fingers, just to make sure that her bifocals had not deceived her. Then she'd sigh with satisfaction and relief: No kink . . . . yet. Mama! I'd shout, pretending to be angry. Every once in a while, if no one was looking, I'd peek, too.

I say "yet" because most black babies are born with soft, silken hair. But after a few months it begins to turn, as inevitably as do the seasons or the leaves on a tree. People once thought baby oil would stop it. They were wrong.

Mary Wilson of the Motown soul-pop group Diana Ross and the Supremes (1968)

Everybody I knew as a child wanted to have good hair. You could be as ugly as homemade sin dipped in misery and still be thought attractive if you had good hair. "Jesus moss," the girls at Camp Lee, Virginia, had called Daddy's naturally "good" hair during the war. I know that he played that thick head of hair for all it was worth, too.

My own hair was "not a bad grade," as barbers would tell me when they cut it for the first time. It was like a doctor reporting the results of the first full physical he has given you. Like "You're in good shape" or "Blood pressure's kind of high—better cut down on salt."

I spent most of my childhood and adolescence messing with my hair. I definitely wanted straight hair. Like Pop's. When I was about three, I tried to stick a wad of Bazooka bubble gum to that straight hair of his. I suppose what fixed that memory for me is the spanking I got for doing so: he turned me upside down, holding me by my feet, the better to paddle my behind. Little *nigger*, he had shouted, walloping away. I started to laugh about it two days later, when my behind stopped hurting.

When black people say "straight," of course, they don't usually mean literally straight—they're not describing hair like, say, Peggy Lipton's (she was the white girl on "The Mod Squad"), or like Mary's of Peter, Paul & Mary fame; black people call that "stringy" hair. No, "straight" just means not kinky, no matter what contours the curl may take. I would have done *anything* to have straight hair—and I used to try everything, short of getting a process.

Of the wide variety of techniques and methods I came to master in the challenging prestidigitation of the follicle, almost all had two things in common: a heavy grease and the application of pressure. It's not an accident that some of the biggest black-owned companies in the fifties and sixties made hair products. And I tried them all, in search of that certain silken touch, the one that would leave neither the hand nor the pillow sullied by grease.

I always wondered what Frederick Douglass put on *his* hair, or what Phillis Wheatley put on hers. Or why Wheatley has that rag on her head in the little engraving in the frontispiece of her book. One thing is for sure: you can bet that when Phillis Wheatley went to England and saw the Countess of Huntingdon she did not stop by the Queen's coiffeur on her way there. So many black people still get their hair straightened that it's a wonder we don't have a national holiday for Madame C. J. Walker, the woman who invented the process of straightening kinky hair. Call it Jheri-Kurled or call it "relaxed," it's still fried hair.

I used all the greases, from sea-blue Bergamot and creamy vanilla Duke (in its clear jar with the orange-white-and-green label) to the godfather of grease, the formidable Murray's. Now, Murray's was some *serious* grease. Whereas Bergamot was like oily jello, and Duke was viscous and sickly sweet, Murray's was light brown and *hard*. Hard as lard and twice as greasy, Daddy used to say. Murray's came in an orange can with a press-on top. It was so hard that some people would put a match to the can, just to soften the stuff and make it more manageable. Then, in the late sixties, when Afros came into style, I used Afro Sheen. From Murray's to Duke to Afro Sheen: that was my progression in black consciousness.

We used to put hot towels or washrags over our Murray-coated heads, in order to melt the wax into the scalp and the follicles. Unfortunately, the wax also had the habit of running down your neck, ears, and forehead. Not to mention your pillowcase. Another problem was that if you put two palmfuls of Murray's on your head your hair turned white. (Duke did the same thing.) The challenge was to get rid of that white color. Because if you got rid of the white stuff you had a magnificent head of wavy hair. That was the beauty of it: Murray's was so hard that it froze your hair into the wavy style you brushed it into. It looked really good if you wore a part. A lot of guys had parts *cut* into their hair by a barber, either with the clippers or with a straight-edge razor. Especially if you had kinky hair—then you'd generally wear a short razor cut, or what we called a Quo Vadis.

We tried to be as innovative as possible. Everyone knew about using a stocking cap, because your father or your uncle wore one whenever something really big was about to happen, whether sacred or secular: a funeral or a dance, a wedding or a trip in which you confronted official white people. Any time you were trying to look really sharp, you wore a stocking cap in preparation. And if the event was really a big one, you made a new cap. You asked your mother for a pair of her hose, and cut it with scissors about six inches or so from the open end—the end with the elastic that goes up to the top of the thigh. Then you knotted the cut end, and it became a beehive-shaped hat, with an elastic band that you pulled down low on your forehead and down around your neck in the back. To work well, the cap had to fit tightly and snugly, like a press. And it had to fit that tightly because it was a press: it pressed your hair with the force of the hose's elastic. If you greased your hair down real good, and left the stocking cap on long enough, *voilà*: you got a head of pressed-

Diana Ross (1968)

against-the-scalp waves. (You also got a ring around your forehead when you woke up, but it went away.) And then you could enjoy your concrete do. Swore we were bad, too, with all that grease and those flat heads. My brother and I would brush it out a bit in the mornings, so that it looked—well, "natural." Grown men still wear stocking caps—especially older men, who generally keep their stocking caps in their top drawers, along with their cufflinks and their see-through silk socks, their "Maverick" ties, their silk handkerchiefs, and whatever else they prize the most.

A Murrayed-down stocking cap was the respectable version of the process, which, by contrast, was most definitely not a cool thing to have unless you were an entertainer by trade. Zeke and Keith and Poochie and a few other stars of the high-school basketball team all used to get a process once or twice a year. It was expensive, and you had to go somewhere like Pittsburgh or D.C. or Uniontown—somewhere where there were enough colored people to support a trade. The guys would disappear, then reappear a day or two later, strutting like peacocks, their hair burned slightly red from the lye base. They'd also wear "rags"—cloths or handkerchiefs—around their heads when they slept or played basketball. Do-rags, they were called. But the result was straight hair, with just a hint of wave. No curl. Do-it-yourselfers took their chances at home with a concoction of mashed potatoes and lye.

Nat "King" Cole

The most famous process of all, however, outside of the process Malcolm X describes in his "Autobiography," and maybe the process of Sammy Davis, Jr., was Nat King Cole's process. Nat King Cole had patent-leather hair. That man's got the finest process money can buy, or so Daddy said the night we saw Cole's TV show on NBC. It was November 5, 1956. I remember the date because everyone came to our house to watch it and to celebrate one of Daddy's buddies' birthdays. Yeah, Uncle Joe chimed in, they can do shit to his hair that the average Negro can't even *think* about—secret shit.

Nat King Cole was *clean*. I've had an ongoing argument with a Nigerian friend about Nat King Cole for twenty years now. Not about whether he could sing—any fool knows that he could—but about whether or not he was a handkerchief head for wearing that patent-leather process.

Sammy Davis, Jr.'s process was the one I detested. It didn't look good on him. Worse still, he liked to have a fried strand dangling down the middle of his forehead, so he could shake it out from the crown when he sang. But Nat King Cole's hair was a thing unto itself, a beautifully sculpted work of art that he and he alone had the right to wear. The only difference between a process and a stocking cap, really, was taste; but Nat King Cole, unlike, say, Michael Jackson, looked *good* in his. His head looked like Valentino's head in the twenties, and some say it was Valentino the process was imitating. But Nat King Cole wore a process because it suited his face, his demeanor, his name, his style. He was as clean as he wanted to be.

I had forgotten all about that patent-leather look until one day in 1971, when I was sitting in an Arab restaurant on the island of Zanzibar surrounded by men in fezzes and white caftans, trying to learn how to eat curried goat and rice with the fingers of my right hand and feeling two million miles from home. All of a sudden, an old transistor radio sitting on top of a china cupboard stopped blaring out its Swahili music and started playing "Fly Me to the Moon," by Nat King Cole. The restaurant's din was not affected at all, but in my mind's eye I saw it: the King's magnificent sleek black tiara. I managed, barely, to blink back the tears.

CONSIDER

1. What meanings are associated with the "kitchen" in Gates's essay? What is the effect of the ambiguity he creates with these multiple associations?

2. Walker and Gates both describe the transformative effects of their discoveries about hair. Upon discovering dreads, Walker writes that "there is a way in which I was made happy forever," while Gates says, "From Murray's to Duke to Afro Sheen: that was my progression in black consciousness." What do you think these comments mean?

On the Cover of
Rolling Stone: Photo Montage

December 25, 2003

January 22, 2004

February 5, 2004

February 19, 2004

March 4, 2004

March 18, 2004

April 1, 2004

April 29, 2004

May 13, 2004

May 27, 2004

June 10, 2004

July 8, 2004

August 19, 2004

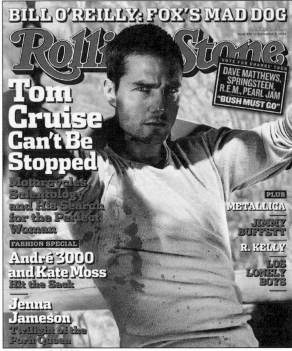
September 2, 2004

September 16, 2004

October 14, 2004

October 28, 2004

November 11, 2004

November 25, 2004

December 30, 2004

Assignments and Projects

Project 1

Composing an Identity Collage

This chapter has explored some of the many ways in which people communicate who they are. This project will shift the focus to you: Do you like to read? Watch TV? Listen to music? Chat online? What do you like to watch, hear, read, or talk about? And how do your interests and choices reflect your identity?

For this project, create a collage that combines words and images to express an aspect of your identity. Your collage should include at least four visual images of any kind—family photos, drawings, illustrations from books or magazines, images downloaded from the Web, and so on. It should also incorporate at least one word, but no more than one sentence, of text. Depending on your instructor's preference, you should either (1) turn in a hard copy of your collage or (2) post your collage on the Web. (Ask your instructor for details.)

The questions for composing introduced in Chapter 2 can help you begin to develop ideas, gather materials, and draft your collage:

WHAT'S IT TO YOU?

- On one level, your **investment** in this project is obvious—everyone feels a strong investment in himself or herself, and so a project focused on personal identity has a certain intrinsic appeal. However, some student writers feel ambivalent about discussing autobiographical material in a course assignment, especially if their work will be shared with classmates. It's normal to feel a bit awkward about self-revelation; in fact, it's a sign that you're thinking about your audience, a skill central to good writing. As long as you approach personal writing assignments with common sense (don't reveal embarrassing or damaging information) and civility (treat your classmates' work with respect), you should welcome the opportunity to improve both your writing and your self-understanding.

WHAT DO YOU WANT TO SAY?

■ Have a good idea of the main themes or **focal points** you want to concentrate on before you begin to collect images—without a focus, a multimedia project can become unmanageable. How can you discover these key points? Many composition instructors recommend freewriting, an idea-generating exercise especially useful for personal and expressive writing.

WHO WILL LISTEN?

■ Your life is made up of experiences, memories, feelings, and ideas that only you fully understand. To communicate your identity to an **audience**, you'll need to make these individual references understandable and public. As you choose and combine elements for your collage, ask yourself: Will readers know what this means? What connections can I expect my audience to make on their own? What connections will I need to make more explicit?

WHAT DO YOU NEED TO KNOW?

■ You can find images for your collage just about anywhere. Check your home or dorm room for family snapshots, drawings, or other images that have personal meanings. Using Google or another online search engine, enter several keywords related to major themes you want to explore in your collage. Browse the pages your search has generated, looking especially for images that suggest interesting connections. Remember to save citation information for any outside sources.

HOW WILL YOU DO IT?

■ Collage is a nonlinear **genre**—it allows both writer and reader to create multiple networks of connections, unlike a printed essay, which moves in one direction from beginning to end. This feature of the genre means that its structure and arrangement are both more flexible and more complicated than the print genres. You may also find it useful to look at several examples of collage, like those on the Web site of the International Museum of Collage Assemblage and Construction (collagemuseum.com). Consider drafting your project using a program like Adobe Photoshop, which allows you to layer images and text within a document.

HOW WELL DOES IT WORK?

■ Once you've drafted your collage, review it with a critical eye, assessing how successfully you've met the rhetorical challenges outlined in the five previous questions. If possible, ask a classmate or friend to view your collage and summarize its message—the person's response may pinpoint needed **revisions**.

STUDENT SAMPLE

Peter Anderson "Identity Collage"

This collage represents my interests and experiences. The picture of me running represents my favorite sport, cross country. I also like to travel, especially in the West. I have three cats, and I love cars. These pictures tell everyone something about me.

Project 2

Researching and Profiling a Person

This assignment asks you to create a researched portrait of a well-known artist, focused on explaining how his or her work responds to particular social issues. For example, when you encountered the photo *Migrant Mother* on page 87, perhaps you were curious about how it fit into photographer Dorothea Lange's larger body of work: Did she take other photographs related to the Great Depression? Do her photographs share common themes or design choices? What events in her life motivated her to document such scenes? What was the contribution of her work to public awareness of poverty? These are exactly the sorts of questions that can be asked about any artist's work—and they're the kinds of questions your project will address.

Depending on your instructor's preference, your profile may take the form either of a three- to five-page MLA-style essay or a multimedia exploration. (Ask your instructor for details.) Whichever form your project takes, it should strive to include at least two images or examples of your subject's work.

Here are some resources you may find helpful as you begin this project: First, take a look at Billy Smith's paper (pages 149–153), which was produced in response to this assignment. For information about conducting research on a topic and citing and documenting sources, consult Chapter 2, pages 60–63.

WHAT'S IT TO YOU?

- You'll feel more invested in this project if you choose an artist whose work you're genuinely curious about. Perhaps you want to figure out why a local hip-hop artist has written so many songs about police brutality. If you're interested in the **subject**, you'll enjoy researching his or her work, and readers will pick up on your enthusiasm.

  But what if I'm not interested in any artists? you may ask. What if I don't know anything about art at all? If that's the case, start with an issue that interests you—censorship, child labor, or sports drugs, for example—and do a keyword search to find out which artists' work has dealt with that issue. You'll be surprised at how many intriguing possibilities you find.

WHAT DO YOU WANT TO SAY?

- As you begin your research, keep the **purpose** of this project in mind: Can you find enough information about the artist to create a substantive portrait? Can you identify works that address social issues? Can you discern a pattern in the artist's reaction to those issues? Your answers to these questions will help you focus your project.

WHO WILL LISTEN?

- Though you want your profile to be rich and substantive, it shouldn't be an exhaustive catalog of your subject's every accomplishment—don't overwhelm readers. Instead, organize your profile around one or two interesting **focal points**. Ask yourself: What key points or works will you emphasize? How will you draw readers' attention to these focal points? What nonessential information can you condense or leave out?

WHAT DO YOU NEED TO KNOW?

- Because your project will make claims about the relationship between the artist's work and its social or political context, readers will expect to see plenty of **supporting evidence**. Begin your **research** with *primary sources*—your subject's work and letters, commentary, or interviews. Although you can find samples of many artists' work online, you can often find a larger and higher-quality selection of images at a library or an art museum. *Secondary sources* such as biographies, encyclopedia entries, and commentary by art historians or critics, can help you begin to identify patterns in the artist's work. As with any research project, accurately cite and document all outside sources you use, including images you scan or download.

HOW WILL YOU DO IT?

- Think carefully about whether and how you can use images or other **media** to present your points effectively. For example, a series of thumbnail images might illustrate an artist's experimental approaches to lighting more efficiently than a long explanation in prose, but names and dates are better conveyed in words.

  Because your project will synthesize and present a lot of information, **structure** and **arrangement** are especially important: Will you organize your research chronologically? Thematically? Alphabetically by the title of particular works? Any of these patterns might work, depending on your subject and audience.

HOW WELL DOES IT WORK?

- Once you've completed a draft, review it with a critical eye, using the five questions we've just discussed to guide your evaluation. If possible, have a classmate or friend review the draft as well. Ask the person to point out items that are unclear and to suggest **revisions**.

STUDENT SAMPLE

Billy Smith, "Gordon Parks: Using Photographs to Spark Social Change"

While reading this paper, you can view the photographs Smith analyzes by visiting http:www.masters-of-photography.com/P/parks.html

Smith 1

Billy Smith

Professor Strong

Composition 101

23 June 2005

Gordon Parks: Using Photographs
to Spark Social Change

In America, it is quite possible to live in a cocoon, oblivious to the world around you. Confined living situations and close-knit social structures can prevent an individual from ever experiencing a reality outside of his or her own. Through an artistic medium such as photography, though, one can get a glimpse of a world far removed. Gordon Parks, photographer, artist, and writer, was a liaison between those Americans in one world and their fellow citizens who subsisted in a completely different one. Parks's work as an artist during the 1940s, '50s, and '60s revealed a population suffering from poverty, prejudice, and racism. Through his illustrative portrayals of Americans bearing the burdens of hardship, Parks opened the eyes of policymakers and voters alike and helped to jump start a movement for improved social conditions.

Gordon Parks, an African American, was born in Fort Scott, Kansas, in 1912. Working at jobs ranging from dining car waiter to semiprofessional basketball player, Parks got his big break in 1942 when he began taking photographs for the Farm Security Administration. The move that brought him into the national spotlight, though, was his addition later that year to the staff of <u>Life</u> magazine. Parks would eventually find success as a novelist and poet, a musical composer, and a film director-producer

(<u>Shaft</u>, <u>The Learning Tree</u>). However, it was during his tenure taking photographs for <u>Life</u> that Parks was really able to display his talent as an artist while simultaneously expanding cultural awareness of social ills.

From a historical standpoint, Gordon Parks found himself in a volatile period in American history. At the start of his professional career, the nation was consumed by World War II. After the war, much of the nation was enjoying the peace and prosperity of the 1950s. Parks, however, was examining the people who weren't reveling in postwar glory. Parks sought out the laborers, the underpaid, underfed, underhoused, and underrepresented. As the 1960s approached, the nation began to quiver with the tension of the civil rights movement. People like Malcolm X and Martin Luther King Jr. were constantly in the spotlight. Parks chose to exploit the abundance of prolific artistic material not so much to further his professional career. Rather, he also used his medium to portray the conflicts and struggles in American society during his lifetime, to tell the stories of people who were barely surviving in the boiler rooms and alleyways of America and of those whose faces were as recognizable as the flag itself.

Post–World War II America was a fascinating time to be shooting pictures. Before and during the war, most journalists focused on relaying news-related topics. Photographs were supplements to factual information, often grave war-related matters, to be printed in a news magazine or newspaper. After the war, though, people were less concerned with affairs of life or death and had the leisure time to become interested in their fellow Americans. Thus was born the human interest story. By highlighting a particular person or group, journalists could play on familiar and desirable themes such as heroics, love, hate, suffering, and triumph. <u>Life</u> magazine was a significant member of this new guard of personal journalism. As a staff member of <u>Life</u>, Parks was trained in this new photographic style, and much of his work reflected this concentration on the human condition. At the time, it was important for photographers to distinguish their work along certain themes. Parks, not surprisingly, found his artistic passion in portraying social situations through American people, especially African Americans.

Possibly Parks's most memorable contribution to the artistic community was his piece titled American Gothic. The image depicts a woman named Ella Watson, armed with a mop and a broom, staring directly at the camera with a large American flag in the background. Watson, a person Parks came to know through a colleague, had struggled through life while trying to support her children and grandchildren on a meager salary. The photograph conveys Watson's intensity and strength, and the viewer can see the suffering and determination in the woman's eyes. The shot mirrors a classic American painting by the same name, a choice Parks made in an effort to heighten the drama of the piece. With the flag behind her, Watson stands as a symbol of an America that is so foreign to the upper classes, an America that does not embrace all of its children.

Growing up as a black man in a ferociously segregated world, Parks's artwork served as an avenue for his feelings about race relations and the social circumstances of many blacks in America. Parks himself worked hard to overcome the barriers to his own success and ended up being financially comfortable. However, he focused a substantial part of his work on those African Americans who had not been so lucky, who were struggling just to make it to the next day. Such examples would be his pieces Muslim Schoolchildren (1963) and Family in Birmingham, Alabama (1956). Parks was torn by the poor conditions in which these people found themselves, but he also wrestled with how best he could help them. "I see some kid up there who cannot appreciate the distance that I have come. He is still poor. He's still cold. He's still hungry, and he's still being discriminated against" (Harris 64). Parks used his powers as a photographer to demonstrate the hardships of these people.

The "interest" in the human interest story was not limited to just those who were barely surviving. Parks also portrayed prominent figures in society, often African American, as another way to fight racial segregation and the poor conditions of many blacks at the time. For example, people like Louis Armstrong, Muhammad Ali, Malcolm X, and Pastor Ledbetter of Chicago were all successful black Americans. Parks wanted to use the fame of these people, as well as his own prominent status, to inspire younger African Americans to not settle for a poor start in life. As Parks was once quoted concerning his own accomplishments in a segregated world, "I could not be hampered by racism and what racism does to people. I refused to accept it. I ignored it. I walked around it" (Harris 69). Parks hoped that his tenacity and drive would be an example for other young people to not use race as a crutch but to work harder to overcome it.

From high atop the mountain of wealth and comfort, it is difficult to see those who toil at the mountain's base. Gordon Parks made it his life's work to bridge that gap, to capture a moment in time on film and then display that moment to the rest of the nation, who undoubtedly weren't there to see it first hand. Being fortunate enough to publish in a well-read magazine like <u>Life</u>, Parks had access to an audience that was vast and varied, and his messages could be poignant and insightful. Though he was able to open the eyes of many Americans to the troubles of their compatriots, Parks was constantly torn by the idea that he could not do more. "Disillusionment sinks in when in the end you must leave the inhabitants of these places to their own fate, and that was always the case" (Bush 87). Ultimately, Gordon Parks felt that his role in advancing social change was to simply take the photographs. If he could bring to the attention of those with political power the nation's bruised and beaten, tired and hungry, abused and mistreated, perhaps the powerful could take the necessary initiatives to assist these people. And if Parks could bring to the attention of the poor and forgotten those figures who had risen from similar standing, despite racism and elitism, to take their own place at the top of the mountain, perhaps the poor would never give up hope of making it in America.

Works Consulted

Bush, Martin H. <u>The Photographs of Gordon Parks</u>. Wichita: Wichita State
    UP, 1983.

"Gordon Parks" <u>Masters of Photography</u>. 2004. 10 June 2005
    <http://www.masters-of-photography.com/P/parks/parks.html>.

Harris, Mark Edward. <u>Faces of the Twentieth Century: Master
    Photographers and Their Work</u>. New York: Abbeville, 1998.

Parks, Gordon. <u>Half Past Autumn</u>. Boston: Bullfinch, 1997.

Tausk, Peter. <u>Photography in the 20th Century.</u> London: Focal, 1980.

Additional Student Work
www.ablongman.com/beyondwords09

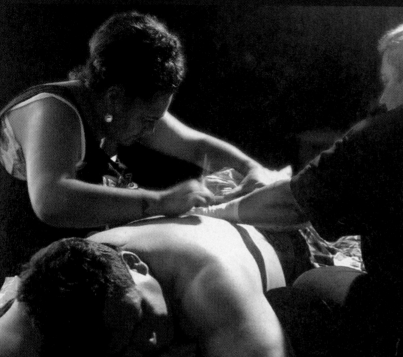

▲ *Uhi Moko* takes place on the floor (*papa whenua*), to be close to the heartbeat of *Papatuanuku* (Mother Earth), and to provide a more relaxing way to work. (above)

▼ *Uhi*, traditional tools used to *Ta Moko*. (below)

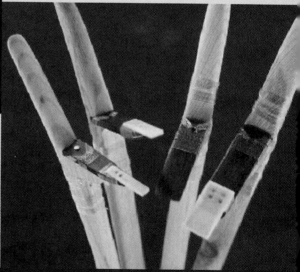

HENRIATA NICHOLAS

WITH DR. NGAHUIA TE AWEKOTUKU

Uhi Ta Moko – designs carved in skin

I am *Wahine Maori* (Maori woman), an artist, designer, and practitioner of *Uhi Ta Moko*. What is exciting about my art form is that my client is the canvas and the visual interpretation of the final design. The design becomes a living, breathing, ever-changing and growing medium that not only communicates its own meaning but also shares intimate insights into the process of application. The canvas itself speaks of the pain endured, and it reflects on the personal and public reactions to the work.

I work with *Uhi*. These are the traditional tools I use to *Ta Moko*, or mark the skin. *Ta Moko* is the process, and the end result is called *Moko*, a stunning visual effect of traditional design elements on the body. The design represents a personal statement of one's culture, *mana*, identity, genealogy, and accomplishments.

CARVING THE SKIN

From the South Pacific and Polynesia and northward into Indo-China, the art of skin adornment using pigment has long been widely practiced. The word *tattoo* itself is a mispronunciation of the Tahitian word *Tatau*. The fundamentals of the art form that were taken back to England, Europe, and the Americas on the bodies of gentlemen and sailors alike led to a new, Westernized tradition of body adornment.

What makes Maori *Ta Moko* distinctive among other Pacific cultures are the ornately curvilinear, raised textural markings achieved by *Uhi*. The *Uhi* that I use are best described as two tools that work in harmony with one another. One tool (made from hardwood) is held in the palm of a hand; attached to one end is a bone blade with serrated edges dipped into ink—this is held over the particular body part to be marked. The second tool (also made from hardwood) is somewhat thicker but comfortable to hold in the other hand; it strikes the first tool, thus pushing the inked blade into the skin. The tapping sound resonates as a harmonic, soothing *waiata* (song).

OUR HISTORY

Although techniques varied throughout the Pacific, marking the skin continued to be part of normal life for Polynesians until the 1800s when, due to colonization and missionary influence, the art form was largely disconnected from natural traditional practices and in some instances was lost forever. This was due, in most part, to missionaries claiming that natural tribal and clan rituals and art forms were "evil" and "ungodly." Some tribes, for reasons of economic survival, replaced their natural beliefs with New World religions.

Te Rangi Kaihoro was a Maori visionary that led the way back for Maori to once again wear the markings of their ancestors. A *Tohunga Kai Whakairo* (master carver), he gave Maori a choice to be marked by their own, with something more meaningful than a design from a tattoo parlor wall. This sparked huge interest in other artists to learn one of our natural rituals and art forms and take up the tattoo gun.

TA MOKO VERSUS *KIRITUHI*

Today we live in a global society full of technology that brings people closer together, where information is shared and identifiers within a culture can be easily duplicated and mass-produced. For this reason, there is a certain degree of unwillingness to share the intimate details of indigenous rituals and processes. *Ta Moko* is one process that Maori consider to be sacred. This is for a number of reasons: during the process, blood is spilled, making the process sacred; certain prayers are recited, and the patterns that are formed and placed on the body are *whakapapa* (ancestral). All these things are considered to hold the spirituality of the practitioner, the client, and their subtribes. This information is not to be shared willingly or without respect. Therefore, Maori see *Ta Moko* and *Moko* as something to be shared among Maori only.

What is *Kirituhi*? *Ta Moko* has had a huge impact on tattoo in the modern world—so much so that non-Maori want to share in its immediacy, spiritual

The first drawing of the *Paetuara* shows the first pattern of his *Puhoro*. The *Puhoro* design area for the lower body consists of the lower back, buttocks, and stomach, extending around the belly button down to the knees. Occasionally, a design may continue to the ankles and feet.

relevance, and cultural integrity and are willing to travel to New Zealand and pay to be part of this modern ritual. Some Maori practitioners that work globally on Maori and non-Maori coined the term *Kirituhi* to create a difference between what is placed on Maori skin as opposed to non-Maori skin. They describe *Kirituhi* as a skin tattoo that is void of *whakapapa* and cultural meaning. The only part of the process that is cultural is the Maori practitioner who performs the task. If you consider only the design aspects of both processes, the differences are not easily seen. *Ta Moko* and *Kirituhi* are actually similar in function and form. What sets *Kirituhi* apart from *Ta Moko* is in the substance of the discussion the practitioner has with the non-Maori client.

From the point of view of a designer and practitioner of *Uhi Ta Moko*, cultural integrity is of paramount importance when working within the realms of *Moko* or any other art form. If I use the same process to create the design and to achieve markings on the skin, and the markings on the skin hold within them the same structure, style, and form; if the same amount of time, effort, discussion, and relationship-building have taken place between the client and me, then why should I relabel my work and call it something different because the color and texture of the canvas has changed? This is a hot topic of debate among *Ta Moko* practitioners and among Maori who see their traditional ritual turning into a commodity easily purchased over the Internet. They see their lifestyle choice to become wearers of their *whakapapa* and achievements as exciting and invigorating. They also see it as a huge undertaking, with the current wave of negative opinion rife in some parts of New Zealand. They grab hold of their natural right with a passion and view non-Maori wearing *Moko* or *Kirituhi* as a blunt blade tearing at the very fibers of Maoridom.

THE PROCESS AND OUTCOMES

There are all sorts of things to think about when first designing patterns. The most important is the relationship between the artist and the skin. Patterns look good when beautifully rendered with pen and paper or even digitally manipulated on a computer. This fails to impress when your flat piece of paper, wrapped, for example, around your client's arm, defies application and a certain muscle group changes the design from a lovely symbolic lizard into a twisted, barely recognizable worm! Nonetheless, getting to know your medium or canvas is a high priority, and so is the person to whom it belongs. Therein is the beginning of a journey the client and practitioner must take together. The connection that bonds them to each other is the *kaupapa* (the

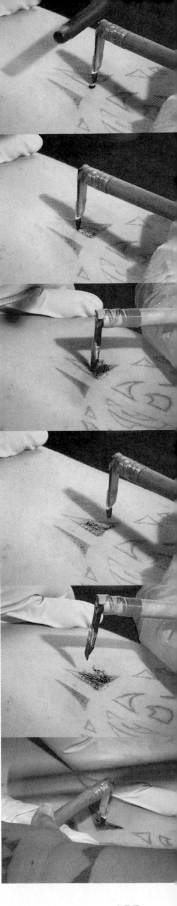

The first taps begin to fill in the *Paetuara*. Two *Uhi* (tools) work in harmony. As one hardwood tool strikes the other, the inked bone blade is pushed into the skin. The tapping sound resonates as a harmonic, soothing song.

story behind the *Moko*), and the relationship will be nurtured on the openness and honesty of the information shared.

Spirituality plays an important part within the journey for both the client and me. Our culture is based essentially on the connection we have with one another, the environment, all living things, the universe, our ancestor connections, and the creator of all things. Because the process deals with the spilling of blood, the whole experience is enveloped by *tapu*–sacredness. So it becomes my job to make sure that the client, the stretcher (who pulls the client's skin tight), myself, and anyone attending are safe and everything is protected and honored with absolute respect and humility.

My first discussion with clients begins with their life journey. We engage in conversations about their genealogy, specific landmarks, historical events, and *Kaitiaki* (spiritual guides) that have brought them to this place, at this time, to think about marking their skin. This is where I find out what their why is. When information like this is shared, there is also a certain amount of trust that is shared between us--the client not only trusts that the chisels will leave good marks but also that delicate personal information will remain private. Making each *Moko* distinctive and unique to that person and each pattern formed or design template created from the original conversation has a specific *kaupapa*. Therefore, the *Moko* belongs to the client not only in bodily terms but also in intellectual property terms, and any photographs or visual representation of the particular *Moko* are owned outright by the client. What I negotiate are the terms in which I can reference the process of application and the final product.

EXAMPLES OF WORK

One of the most exciting design areas, besides the face, is the lower body area. It covers a wide range of muscular formations and therefore poses a technical and process-of-application challenge. The area consists of the lower back, buttocks, and front and back thighs, and it sometimes covers the stomach around the belly button and down into the genital area. The whole design area can continue down to the ankles and feet, but in most cases it stops just above the knee. The design pattern for this area is called *Puhoro*.

This group of patterning depicts speed, swiftness, agility, and strength. Some individual design areas, like the patterns on the lower legs, can be compared to the way water laps and curls against a moving canoe when gliding through it. Individual design areas within the *Puhoro* pertain to nature and spirituality and describe the way in which man interacts within it. For example, the *koru* pattern depicts the spiral form of the closed fern frond and describes the beginnings of a journey or idea and talks about the changes and growth it endures while it unfolds.

Three details from the design shown on the next page. In *Moko*, the skin is the positive and the ink is the negative. The most distinctive quality is the way the negative interplays with the positive.

There are two unique things to remember when designing *Moko*. Each individual pattern field should interact with each other, flowing and ebbing and adding to the overall design (The photo below shows eight different pattern fields that work into one complete half of the whole design). The most distinctive quality of *Moko* is the way the negative interplays with the positive. The skin is the positive and the ink is the negative—therefore, the ink inserted into the skin is accentuating the pattern to be shown, which is the skin (The details on page 164 show individual pattern fields of the same *Puhoro*).

The *Puhoro* being shown is completely achieved by *Uhi,* and the whole process has spanned five months and has included many conversations, issues, and changes to the final goal.

For additional writing projects related to this Interlude see
www.ablongman.com/beyondwords10

CHALLENGE

1. Nicholas observes that to talk publicly about the "intimate details" of indigenous traditions such as *Uhi Ta Moko* makes it easier for outsiders to copy and mass produce these art forms. Can you think of other art forms or rituals once limited to a particular culture that have become widely popular or commercialized? What risks and benefits result from this kind of popularization? Do some preliminary research and write a short essay exploring your thoughts on this issue.

2. This Interlude is a **profile essay**—it uses words and images to create a portrait of Nicholas focused on her work. Using this Interlude as a model, write your own profile essay, focusing on an individual you know whose job, hobby, or other activity is central to his or her identity. If possible, interview your subject, observe him or her at work, and/or take photographs, so that you'll have plenty of concrete and visual detail to incorporate into your essay.

The spiral form of the closed fern frond is echoed in the *koru* pattern. This shape often suggests the beginning of a journey or idea. Growth and change are represented in its unfolding. (above left)

In this design, eight different pattern fields interact with each other, flowing and ebbing and adding to the overall design. This photo represents one complete half of the overall design. (above right)

CHAPTER 4

SEEING PLACES

writing to describe landscapes and environments

David Hockney, *A Bigger Splash* (1967)

Still from *Dogtown and Z-Boys* (2001)

Which of these two images most closely matches your own experiences and associations with swimming pools? Why? Which specific details in the image seem familiar?

Do you have associations or experiences with pools that aren't represented here? If so, what are they?

Introduction

I t's hard to imagine a space more symbolic of the American dream than the swimming pool. For many of us, pools are part of the landscape of growing up: As toddlers, we splash in backyard wading pools; as children, we brave the high diving board at summer camp; in high school, we rent movies like *Spring Break Beach Party* and spend vacations working on the perfect tan. Pools are part of our cultural landscape, too. Owning a private pool is a universally recognized sign of financial success, and glamorous poolside shots are staples of the celebrity profiles that appear in popular magazines.

It's not surprising, then, that swimming pools have been pictured in many different ways. Consider the two images that open this chapter. Both depict suburban swimming pools built during the 1960s and 1970s in California—but there the similarities end.

The pool in David Hockney's painting *A Bigger Splash* evokes an affluent, leisure-oriented lifestyle often associated with California. Rendered in sunny blues, yellows, and pinks, the scene is composed of even surfaces and straight lines. There are no human figures to disturb the peaceful scene—only the white trace of the swimmer's splash. We can almost imagine ourselves stepping through the frame and jumping into the water.

In contrast, the pool in the still from director Stacy Peralta's skateboarding documentary *Dogtown and Z-Boys* is neither restful nor inviting. Here the elegant image of the suburban pool is turned literally upside down. The pool itself is no longer the focal point; instead, it serves as a backdrop for the acrobatic maneuvers of 1970s skateboarding icon Tony Alva. Nor is this pool a well-tended paradise: It has been drained of water, the diving board is pockmarked with rust, and the surrounding lawn is overgrown. Alva, too, uses the pool in a radically different way. Rather than slipping smoothly into the space, as Hockney's imagined swimmer does, Alva defies gravity, hovering above the rim at a 90-degree angle to the ground, poised in the split second before hurtling downward. We're tempted to step backwards to avoid what seems like an inevitable crash.

What should we make of these two very different swimming pools? Why pay so much attention to describing two scenes that, if we walked past them tomorrow, we might not even notice? It's because everyday places—shopping malls, fast-food restaurants, classrooms, parks, and yes, even swimming pools—shape our lives. They define where and how we work, play, eat, do business, express ourselves, and communicate. When artists create images of places, they capture something of these identities. And so do you when you make sense of the places you encounter in your reading, your composing, and your daily life.

What's in This Chapter?

In this chapter, you'll see images of many different places. Some are
paintings and photographs depicting natural landscapes; others showcase the built spaces of city and suburban environments. Others—such
as William Eggleston's photographs of Memphis—focus on sites where
wild and cultivated environments come together. These images present
a range of purposes and points of view. Some, like Alice Attie's photographs of Harlem, preserve moments in our history or document unfamiliar cultures. Still others, such as the Web sites advertising Jamaica,
use places to promote particular attitudes.

Yet as our discussion of swimming pools suggests, places don't exist
only in pictures. We also experience them directly, meaning that such
environments and the ways we interact with them can affect what we do
and how we think. So throughout the chapter, we also discuss the structure and design of places like homes, parks, and restaurants. We'll even
revisit *Dogtown and Z-Boys* as we consider how skateboarders and other
groups find unexpected uses for older environments. We'll challenge you
to engage in on-site observation and description of such places and to
interpret them using many of the same strategies you'd use to explore a
photo or an essay. All of these examples, we hope, will encourage you to
think about relationships between places and people that you might apply in your reading and composing.

Reading Landscapes and Environments

I t's easy to ignore places or to regard them simply as neutral backdrops for what we do. Certainly many of the surroundings we experience seem so ordinary that it's difficult to imagine them as meaningful: How does one analyze a barren stretch of interstate? Or a convenience store that looks exactly like every other 7-Eleven in town?

Cultural meanings and patterns *are* easier to spot when they appear in spectacular landscapes—Las Vegas's neon skyline clearly says something about American attitudes toward money, and the 1,776-foot-high Freedom Tower in New York City will dramatically embody patriotic ideals. Yet the same habits of observation that enable you to spot these patterns can also help you find meanings in less obvious places. When you see a landscape image or examine a particular space, ask yourself the following questions:

What do you see?

What is it about?

To what does it relate?

How is it composed?

What details matter?

David Muench, *Grand Canyon*

What do you see?

When you encounter a place or an image of one, first ask, "Where am I?" and "What sort of place is this?" Knowing some terminology that artists, urban planners, and other professionals use to talk about spaces will help you draw some useful distinctions.

Airstream trailer at the Grand Canyon

Natural environments exist apart from human civilization. In their purest form, they incorporate nothing man-made—they are composed of the terrain, climate, geological formations, and animal and plant life. Artistic depictions of the natural world, such as landscapes and seascapes, have long encouraged viewers to reflect on the power and beauty of untouched nature and to consider the place of human beings in the larger world.

Consider, for example, two landscape photographs. The Grand Canyon landscape above, photographed by David Muench—with its delicate colors and dramatic patterns of sunlight and shadow—creates a breathtaking scene. Muench says that his photo celebrates the "mystical forces of nature that shape all our destinies" and expresses his "commitment to preserve our wild lands . . . to improve and maintain a balance between economy and ecology."

Now consider a photograph showing a human presence in the landscape. The photograph of the Airstream trailer above, for instance, features majestic rock formations similar to those in Muench's image, but the adjoining highway, complete with travel trailer and gawking tourists, is just as prominent. What sort of landscape is this? you might ask. A nature scene, a highway scene, or something in between? And in fact, even natural landmarks as seemingly untouched as the Grand Canyon are continually influenced by the park administrators who monitor the placement of roads and trails, manage tourist activities and trash pickup, and implement conservation plans.

So when you encounter either a natural environment or an image depicting one, pay attention: What natural features are present? What makes the place unique, powerful, beautiful, or worth noticing? What relationship does this place have to human activities and structures? And from what vantage point are you looking at this place?

In contrast to natural environments, **built environments** and spaces are partly or wholly made by human beings. Whether these spaces have been casually crafted (such as a children's treehouse or a small roadside produce stand) or formally designed by a professional city planner, architect, or landscape engineer (such as a museum or park), all serve specific functions and reflect the choices of the people who imagined them. Consider the Milwaukee Museum of

The Milwaukee Museum of Art

READING LANDSCAPES AND ENVIRONMENTS

Art, shown on the previous page. Its design, which incorporates large indoor galleries, clearly serves the practical function of housing the city's art collections. Yet its unusual shape and construction suggest additional purposes. The much-photographed "wings" on the roof, designed to move continually with the breezes in one of the nation's windiest cities, express both the architect's aesthetic vision and the city's commitment to the arts. Not incidentally, the spectacular roof makes the museum a splendid tourist attraction.

Large, impressive public buildings aren't the only built spaces worth analyzing, though. Smaller, more ordinary places like laundromats and barbershops also serve important functions and influence the people who use them every day. Melissa Ann Pinney draws our attention to one such space in her photo of a diaper-changing room at Walt Disney World in Orlando, Florida.

Pinney's photo might lead us to ask several questions: Where are the children's fathers? Why aren't they helping? Why aren't these spaces larger and designed to make this sort of work physically less awkward? Why is the space

"Although I have always been drawn to what is hidden, especially concerning women's experiences, I couldn't say for certain that I would have recognized the secluded diaper-changing scene at Disney World as a possible subject until my daughter, Emma, was born. . . . These photographs . . . are an expression of my interests in feminine identity and the specific qualities of light and place."

—MELISSA ANN PINNEY

Melissa Ann Pinney, *Disney World, Orlando, Florida* (1998)

so dark and institutional-looking (and at the Magic Kingdom, no less)? What do these features say about parenting and gender in our culture? Finally, does Pinney's point of view affect how we react to this scene? Might another photographer's rendition show us a different changing room?

When you analyze a built space or an image of one, then, keep a few key questions in mind: What function does the space serve? Of what materials is it constructed, and how is it arranged? How does its design affect the way in which people use it? And from what vantage point are you looking at the space?

What is it about?

We don't often think about it, but places and representations of them are usually constructed with a purpose. A travel writer, for instance, may describe a locale in order to encourage tourists to visit. A university might locate parking on its outskirts and incorporate walking paths in order to foster a pedestrian-friendly atmosphere.

You can find clues to the purpose of a place by identifying its **focal points**: What do you notice first? What takes center stage? Where are the most important objects and activities? Consider artist-writer Alice Attie's documentary photo series *Harlem in Transition*. In this series, Attie directs viewers' attention to Harlem storefronts, highlighting the contrasts between small, locally owned businesses—often boarded up or on the verge of going under—and the gleaming corporate chain stores now moving into this New York City area. The stark differences suggest Attie's purpose: to document this older neighborhood culture before it vanishes entirely.

Alice Attie, photographs from the series
Harlem in Transition (2000)

1. Take another look at Attie's photographs (see previous page). What specific details of architecture, signage, décor, or other elements seem to characterize the chain storefronts versus the locally owned business? What social, cultural, or economic factors do you think might contribute to these different styles?

2. Why do you think Attie includes a human figure in the photos of the Starbucks and Disney Store franchises? Write a few sentences explaining what you think the man in the suit and the girl on the bicycle add to the images.

3. Harlem is a neighborhood with a rich heritage. Do some research in the library or on the Internet to learn about the history and culture of the area, and then look again at Attie's photographs. Write a paragraph discussing how these images fit into your overall impression of the place.

4. If you were asked to create a documentary to preserve a place you know well, what place would you choose? Why? Write a paragraph or two explaining what you would include in your documentary and why.

5. In her introduction to *Harlem in Transition*, Attie writes, "This transitional moment in Harlem has larger implications for a world in which small communities are being increasingly forced to confront global economic power." What do you think she means by this statement? Can you think of other communities and areas in the world that are facing similar transitions?

To what does it relate?

Images of places (and places themselves) never exist in isolation. Knowing something about an artist's experiences and his or her thoughts about a particular place—the **biographical context**—can help you better understand its meanings. For example, if you glance at the painting shown on the next page, you might simply see a field lush with nearly ripe wheat and populated by a flock of birds. The scene might suggest any number of associations.

Now consider that many scholars believe that this was the last canvas Postimpressionist painter Vincent van Gogh completed before committing suicide, shooting himself in a field similar to the one pictured here. As theorist John Berger observes in his book *Ways of Seeing*, this fact irrevocably changes what you see: Perhaps the vivid colors and rough brushwork begin to take on an ominous quality. Perhaps the crows—carrion-eating birds—now

Vincent van Gogh, *Wheat Field with Crows* (1890)

look predatory or foreboding. The landscape may seem less peaceful and more desolate. The scene is no longer quite the same.

Of course, no single biographical detail, even such a dramatic one, can fully determine the meaning of this or any image. Your response might change again upon learning that van Gogh included crows in several other paintings and that in at least one of his letters he referred to the birds as friendly presences. The contexts within which we interpret places and images of them are complicated and constantly evolving.

Historical and **social contexts** add other dimensions of meaning. For instance, van Gogh and other artists during the late nineteenth century worked at a time when industrialism was rapidly altering rural life across Europe, displacing workers who had made the land their livelihood and blurring the line between city and country. Several of van Gogh's early paintings depict the poverty and backbreaking labor endured by rural workers. So in examining *Wheat Field with Crows*, you might investigate how this landscape compares with other rural scenes painted during the era or with commentary on rural issues appearing elsewhere. Your research might lead you to speculate that the swirling skies in this painting—a common feature in van Gogh's landscapes—reflect the rapid changes in rural life.

Van Gogh's troubled portraits of rural landscapes can also be read in the context of earlier and later art that engages similar issues. Dorothea Lange, whose photographs you'll see in several chapters in this text, explores such issues in a different era and medium by documenting the struggles faced by rural Americans during the Great Depression. Today, you'll see similar themes played out in the images and texts created by proponents of organic farming and farmworker advocacy groups objecting to corporate farming operations.

Finally, place images can take on different meanings depending on the **physical context** in which they appear. Look at the mural in the photograph below, a rendition of van Gogh's famous painting *Starry Night*, painted by middle-school art students on the back wall of a neighborhood grocery store in South Carolina. How does the irregular brick surface, punctuated with plumbing pipes, affect what you see? What about the surrounding landscape, complete with trash cans, telephone wires, and traffic? Or the fact that children created the image as a community project and as part of their education in the arts? Your response to the mural is likely quite different from the reaction you would have to seeing van Gogh's original painting, specially lit and positioned on a museum wall.

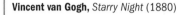

Vincent van Gogh, *Starry Night* (1880)

Brad Station, Children's mural, Columbia, South Carolina (2004)

1. Which bits of contextual information most strongly affect your interpretation of the van Gogh images (see pages 171 and 172)? Why?

2. What would you say to someone who argued that the *Starry Night* mural isn't "real art"? Would you agree or disagree? What reasons would you give to support your position?

3. On the Web, do a keyword search on "van Gogh" and list some of the different media and contexts in which this painter's work has been reproduced—for example, as posters, T-shirts, and wallpaper. Write a paragraph or two discussing how you think the meaning of the images might vary across these different contexts.

4. Choose an image of a place that you especially like and do research in the library or on the Internet to discover what you can about the biographical, social, and historical contexts in which the image was created. Write two or three paragraphs summarizing your findings and then a paragraph commenting on whether and how this information changes your response to the image.

How is it composed?

How we experience a place depends a great deal on how it is structured and arranged, either by artists representing places or by designers giving shape to built environments. In traditional landscape painting and photography, artists frequently use one-point perspective—a way of representing space in which everything recedes to a single horizon point. Images structured in this way emphasize what's placed in the **foreground** of the image, the area nearest to the viewer and farthest from the **horizon line**. Items located in the **background**, near or at the horizon, are deemphasized. The scene depicting Ulysses Grant's Tomb in New York City exemplifies this pattern. In the foreground, we see the well-populated and carefully manicured grounds surrounding the landmark, which is located in the center of the image, set back but still in the foreground. The area behind the tomb recedes into the distance, obscuring all that might distract from the artist's subject.

Lithograph of the tomb of Ulysses S. Grant

173

| **Susan Meiselas,** *Soldiers Search Bus Passengers along the Northern Highway* (1981)

Writers and artists also use **point of view** to create angles from which we can see the image or the design. Where are we asked to "stand" or to look? In this striking photograph from her book *El Salvador*, photojournalist Susan Meiselas depicts bus passengers lined up by soldiers for a search. The camera is positioned above the passengers, at a slight angle, rather than at eye level as a typical news shot might be. But even more unexpected is the way the high angle of the sun interacts with the point of view in the photo. The camera angle and stark shadows cast on the wall invite us to infer much of what is taking place as the soldiers conduct their searches.

The structural technique of **framing** also contributes to the composition of an image. Is the image divided into sections? If so, what occupies each section? How are elements within the image spaced in relation to each other?

Marc Riboud's *A Street in Old Beijing*, shown on the next page, reveals a bustling scene outside a government-run art business, which Riboud photographed through a nearby shop window. The frames of the window break the image into six smaller sections, each of which can be read as an individual scene. The top left-hand section, for example, encloses the gilded sign above the business, which reads, "Prosperity." The people captured in the bottom frames emerge as individuals busy with their lives, not equally aware of being photographed. According to critic Ian Jeffrey, Riboud's framing device in this photograph emphasizes his view that "individuality in China survived the persistence of [Communist] ideology, and showed itself in the kind of glances and small transactions carried out here."

174   **READING LANDSCAPES AND ENVIRONMENTS**

Marc Riboud, *A Street in Old Beijing* (1965)

CONSIDER

1. In your opinion, how effective is the point of view Meiselas adopts in her photo of the bus passengers (see previous page)? Think of two or three alternative points of view she might have chosen, and write a few sentences discussing how each might suggest a different interpretation of the scene.

2. Imagine what Riboud's photo (above) would look like without the window frames. How might you experience the place differently? Might you be inclined to group the people in different ways? If so, how?

3. Find and examine several picture postcards of tourist sites in your city or state, paying special attention to what's in the background and foreground of each image. Do you see any patterns? What tends to be emphasized and deemphasized?

COMPOSE

4. Take photographs of your bedroom or another familiar place from five or six different angles. Write a paragraph discussing how each angle creates a different impression. Which image is your favorite? Why?

5. Find a snapshot from a family vacation, school field trip, or other excursion, and use photo editing software (for a digital photo), scissors, or a black marker to frame the image differently. Then write a paragraph analyzing how the changes affect the way viewers would interpret the scene.

Stephen Shore, *El Paso Street, El Paso, Texas* (1975)

What details matter?

Sometimes the smallest details make a big difference in the impact of an image or the design of a space. Would a Coca-Cola taste the same, if we drank it out of a yellow can? Would you patronize a fancy restaurant lit by fluorescent lights and staffed by waiters in polyester smocks and hairnets? Look for key details when you consider places, whether they are rendered in environments, images, or words.

For instance, if you glance quickly at Stephen Shore's streetscape of El Paso, two details will likely catch your eye: the **human figure** and the **colors**. That lone person staring at the scene from the foreground of the image establishes the point of view and reminds us that we're looking at a constructed image, not a "real" place. At the same time, the sunny pastels of the buildings give a nostalgic, fifties-style feel to the shot, despite the fact that the photo was taken in the mid-1970s. Imagine the same scene photographed in plain black and white, without the human figure, and you'll get a sense of how important these two details are.

The first thing you might notice about Gueorgui Pinkhassov's *Tokyo*, on the other hand, is the unusual pattern of the **light**, which filters through window blinds and covers the space and its inhabitants with a dappled pattern. But there are other details in the image as well. What can be said about the **layout** of the central hallway or the human figures in the image? The figures seem confined by the space and unlikely to encounter each other.

Of course, artists and designers use many other kinds of details—for example, the presence or location of objects or the facial expressions of human figures in an image—to create particular impressions of a place. And thus you'll need to look closely at each space you encounter to discern the little things that create a specific atmosphere. Does the effect come from color? Lighting? The placement of key objects or human figures? Lines? Or you might discover entirely different patterns. The important thing is to read critically—to pay attention.

Additional practice reading landscapes and environments
www.ablongman.com/beyondwords11

CONSIDER

1. Besides the use of a human figure and of color, what other significant details do you notice in Shore's portrait of El Paso (see previous page)? What do these details add to your understanding of the image?

2. Think about a place you visit regularly—a coffeehouse, a basketball court, or your calculus classroom, for instance. What particular details, in your opinion, combine to create its particular atmosphere? If those details changed, how would people experience the place differently?

COMPOSE

3. Carefully reexamine Pinkhassov's photo (above), and then compose a short narrative that accounts for what's going on in the image. Use specific details from the photograph in your narrative.

4. Choose a place image you find interesting, and write a few paragraphs analyzing the artist's use of color, lighting, lines, human figures, and significant objects.

Places We Live

Suburbia: American Dream or "Geography of Nowhere"?

If you ask a dozen people to name the place that holds the most memories and emotional associations, you'll likely get a single response: "Home." For many Americans, "home" means a single-family house with a lawn and a garage in a residential neighborhood filled with similar houses—in other words, a suburb.

But what you may not know is that the suburban house became the typical home in this country only within the past fifty years—and that in much of the rest of the world, "home" more commonly refers to urban apartments, single-family farms, or small villages. As Robert Fishman explains in his book *Bourgeois Utopias,* in the years immediately following World War II, economic, industrial, and governmental initiatives converged so that "for the first time in any society, the single-family detached house was brought within the economic grasp of the majority of households"—working-class and middle-class alike.

But fifty years into this transformation, scholars are calling attention to effects that developers and the homeowners who flocked to their developments didn't anticipate. James Kunstler, for example, complains that the suburbanization of American cities has decentralized jobs and housing, weakened community identity and civic involvement, and increased both pollution and consumption—a state of affairs he calls a "geography of nowhere."

No matter where you grew up, you should be able to see, in the images and readings that follow, evidence of this complicated legacy of suburbanization. As you read and study this material, think about how you visualize "home" and what you—and others—do with the space in which you live.

Page from a 1950s Sears catalog advertising "The Dover," a prefabricated house designed for first-time home buyers.

THE DOVER ▴ ▴
▴ SIX ROOMS, BATH AND LAVATORY

THERE is a certain warmth and "hominess" about a wooden house—a readiness to receive the stamp of its owner's personality and an ability to adapt itself to its environment. It answers the needs of well-to-do or modest builder and holds its own in town or country.

The Dover is an Americanized English type Colonial story and a half cottage with a convenient floor plan. The massive chimney helps to "tie in" the front gable and the cowled roof lines help to give a compact appearance. The exterior walls are planned for clear bevel siding but will look equally attractive if shingles are used. In either case, we suggest light colors of paint or stain, in contrast to dark shutters, chimney and weathered roof.

The shutters on the front windows are batten type, to match the batten type circle head front door.

Our home building service will furnish every detail to help you have a home as attractive as the Dover. We guarantee quality and quantity, and our ready cut system of construction conserves your building dollars.

MODERN HOME
No. 3262
ALREADY CUT AND FITTED

SECOND FLOOR PLAN

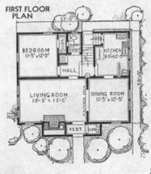

FIRST FLOOR PLAN

THE FLOOR PLANS

From the terrace, the front door opens into a vestibule which has a large coat closet for outer wraps. Handy for your guests. The living room and dining room extend across the entire front of the house and are connected with a plaster arch, also used from living room to vestibule and hall. Plenty of windows assure bright cheerful rooms and a pleasant outlook.

Most every family can use a first floor bedroom—if not for the family, a guest likes a little privacy from the Master bedrooms. Many have converted this room into a combination library and den and still have a "spare" bedroom available by putting a "rollaway" bed in the closet. Note that the semi-open stairs also open into the kitchen—a step-saving convenience. The kitchen will accommodate cabinets quoted in options. The second floor contains two large bedrooms and the bath is above the average size. Linen storage and good closets. Fill out blank for complete delivered price.

Sears, Roebuck and Co.

641 ▶ Page 33 ◀

CONSIDER

1. Examine the floor plan for "The Dover," a prefabricated home advertised to first-time buyers by Sears, Roebuck during the early 1950s, and speculate: What sort of buyer would have considered this a "dream house"? How does this house's size and layout compare to the places you've lived? Is this a house you'd aspire to buy? Why or why not?

2. Think about the focal points and the point of view in the photo of the home buyers. What draws your attention: The couple? The car? The houses? What do you think the photographer wants you to focus on? Why?

3. Drawing on your experience and on the text and images shown on the preceding page, put together an ad—including a floor plan—for the kind of single-family living space you think would appeal to a wide range of today's consumers. Focus on the space itself and on the neighborhood or development where it will be located.

4. On the Web or in a newspaper, browse through some advertisements for new housing developments and compare them to the ad for "The Dover." What differences and similarities do you see? Write a paragraph or two summarizing your findings.

5. Without consulting a dictionary, write a one-paragraph definition of *suburbanite*.

CHALLENGE

6. Do an informal survey of students on your campus, asking this question: "Does your family live in the suburbs?" As people respond, pay attention to any positive or negative implications in their answers. After completing your survey and considering the results, revisit your definition of *suburbanite*, and revise it as necessary.

1950s family room from *Life* magazine

William Eggleston, *Memphis* (c. 1972)

Artists and photographers over the years have been fascinated by images of suburban life. Here are some scenes that depict suburban scenes and mores, including a still from the 1998 film *Pleasantville*, which portrayed a black-and-white suburb sitcom world that gradually blossomed into a richer and more colorful version of life.

"We're really happy. Our kids are healthy, we eat good food, and we have a nice home." From Bill Owens, *Suburbia* (1973)

Still from *Pleasantville* (1998)

1. Examine the depictions of suburban family life from the 1950s to the 1970s on the previous page. (Released in 1998, *Pleasantville* depicts a 1950s suburb.) Which images seem the most positive, and which seem ambivalent or negative? In which of these places would you most like to live? Why?

2. In compiling *Suburbia*, Bill Owens asked the families he photographed to comment on the pictures and then used their words as captions. What does the caption of "We're really happy" reveal about the couple in the photograph on page 181? Do you think the caption is an effective one? Why or why not?

3. Look closely at the placement of people in the photographs. Which arrangement do you find most effective? Most interesting? Why? Which is least interesting? Which seems most natural or authentic? Which seems least natural?

4. Think about the use of color film versus black and white in these images and about why the photographers made the choices they did. If you had to illustrate an essay on the American suburb, would you choose color or black-and-white film? Why do you think *Pleasantville* uses both black and white and color?

COMPOSE

5. Examine the photos for clues to the different eras they represent. Make a list of the clues you find for each image, and then explain how these details affect the photos and how you react to them.

6. Imagine that you work at *Life,* the renowned picture magazine, and have been asked to add captions to any two of the photos. Compose captions that you think would be appropriate. Then compose new captions for the two photos appropriate for one of the following placements: a history textbook on America in the twentieth century, a 1950s advertisement for life insurance, a modern-day humorous greeting card (you choose the occasion), or a current Web site for an organization critical of Americans' materialism.

Exurbia: The New Suburban Frontier

If you live in a suburban neighborhood today, chances are that it doesn't much resemble the original tract home developments of the fifties, with row after row of nearly identical homes. As economic and technological developments drive new-home construction ever farther away from urban centers, the character of new suburban communities is rapidly changing. The texts and images here explore some of these newest developments, areas often referred to as "edge cities" or "exurbia."

FYI

Cathleeen McGuigan is Senior Editor for the Arts and serves as the architecture critic for *Newsweek* magazine. Her articles on film and visual culture have also appeared in the *New York Times Magazine*, *Harper's*, and *Rolling Stone*.

The McMansion Next Door: Why the American House Needs a Makeover

Cathleen McGuigan
(2003)

Design is everywhere, right? Your toothbrush, your running shoes, your cool-looking couch, your latte machine, your laptop. OK, no one would mistake Indiana for Italy, but you can finally buy good design almost anywhere, from the mall to the Internet. But there's one big-ticket item in this country that is virtually untouched by the hand of a good designer: your house.

Most new off-the-rack houses aren't so much designed as themed: Mediterranean, French country, faux Tudor, neo-Colonial. These houses may offer—on the high end—every option money can buy, from a media room to a separate shower for the dog. But the market actually gives consumers little true choice: the developer house, in most price ranges, is amazingly similar from coast to coast, across different climate zones and topographies.

If you ripped off the roofs—and the turrets and gables and fake widow's walks—or peered into the windows—double-hung, round, Palladian, picture (often in the same house!)—you'd find essentially the same thing: a vast foyer with chandelier; formal living and dining rooms (rarely used); open-plan kitchen/ family room; master suite

and bedrooms; many bathrooms; at least a three-car garage. It makes me wonder whatever happened to the modern house, and why the core idea of modernism—that through mass production, ordinary people could afford the best design—never caught on when it came to houses.

Le Corbusier called the house "a machine for living in"—which meant, notes New York architect Deborah Gans, that the house is a tool people control, not the other way round.

The brilliance of the modern house was in the flexible spaces that flowed one to the next, and in the simplicity and toughness of the materials. Postwar America saw a few great experiments, most famously in L.A.'s Case Study Houses in the late 1940s and '50s. Occasionally, a visionary developer, such as Joseph Eichler in California, used good modern architects to design his subdivisions. Today they're high-priced collectibles.

Modernist houses, custom-designed for an elite clientele, are still built, of course. But when I recently asked Barbara Neski, who, with her husband, Julian, designed such houses in the 1960s and beyond, why modern never went mainstream, she replied, "What happens when you ask a child to draw a house?" You get a box with a triangle on top. A little gabled house still says "home."

Yet the cozy warmth of that iconic image doesn't explain the market for neotraditional houses today. Not all these houses are ugly and shoddy: though most are badly proportioned pastiches of different styles, some are built with attention to detail and materials. But, as the epithet *McMansion* suggests, they're just too big—for their lots, for their neighborhoods and for the number of people who actually live in them. And why do they keep getting bigger, when families are getting smaller? In 1970, the average new single-family house was 1,400 square feet; today it's 2,300.

The housing industry says that we want bigger and bigger houses. But I think they're not taking credit for their marketing skills. Last year's annual report for Pulte Homes, one of the nation's biggest builders, contains an astonishing fact: if you adjust for inflation, houses of the same size and comparable features are the same price today as they were in the 1970s. That means that if business is going to grow, the industry has to sell more product—not just more houses but more square footage. It's like the junk-food-marketing genius who figured out that people wouldn't go back for seconds but they'd pay more upfront to get, say, the 32-ounce Big Gulp.

This year, Pulte predicts, the number of houses built will be only slightly higher than last year's. "More and more of the same might not sound particularly exciting, but it is," the report says. "That's because houses . . . will continue to get bigger and better, ensuring that real inflation-adjusted spending on residential construction will continue to rise." Bully for them—and for the folks in the real-estate and financing industries who base value on size not quality.

But finally some people are saying "Enough already." Sarah Susanka, a Minnesota architect, started a mini-movement with her best-selling 1998 book, *The Not So Big House*. Susanka argues that a good architect understands the importance of human scale. Under the dome of St. Peter's, you're meant to feel awe. But if your bedroom's the size of a barn, how cozy can you get?

The eco-conscious hate big houses, too, with the energy cost of heating and cooling all those big empty rooms. And now that McMansions not only are the staple of new suburbs but are invading older, leafy neighborhoods, built in place of tear-downs and overpowering the smaller vintage houses nearby, communities from Greenwich, Conn., to Miami Beach are beginning to take action.

Some middle-class people who care about design have opted out of the new-house market. They'll remodel an old house, one with an honest patina of history that all the money in the world can't reproduce. And some architects are hatching low-cost plans for the mainstream market. Prefab is hot right now: designs that use factory-built modules are assembled on-site. It's much cheaper than conventional construction, and if it's done well, it can look great—and modern.

"We have this concept about design and mass culture in America, with Target, Banana Republic, Design Within Reach," says Joseph Tanney of Resolution: 4 Architecture, which won a *Dwell* magazine competition to design a cool house in North Carolina for only $80 a square foot (a custom house would be $200 to $400 per). The house is prefab, and the firm has half a dozen more in the works. Seattle architect James Cutler (who designed Bill Gates's Xanadu) is working with Lindal Cedar Homes, a national builder, to adapt a wood-and-glass modernist house for modular construction.

"I think there's a return to an interest in modernism," says New York architect Deborah Berke, "and I would call it warm modernism, not sleek minimalism." She argues that a younger generation, steeped in a love of cool design and loft living and ready for a first house, isn't going to buy a mini-McMansion. "That's where the industry is not reading the social signs yet."

As more people get into design—even starting with a toothbrush—the more they'll want their houses to reflect what they value. Flat roof? Peaked roof? It doesn't really matter: the best design reflects who we are and the time in which we live. Who knows what our grandchildren might come up with if someone hands them a crayon and says "Draw a house"?

FYI David Brooks is a columnist for the *New York Times.* His latest book, *On Paradise Drive: How We Live Now (and Always Have) in the Future Tense,* from which this essay is adapted, was published in 2004 by Simon & Schuster.

Our Sprawling, Supersize Utopia

David Brooks
(2004)

We're living in the age of the great dispersal. Americans continue to move from the Northeast and Midwest to the South and West. But the truly historic migration is from the inner suburbs to the outer suburbs, to the suburbs of suburbia. From New Hampshire down to Georgia, across Texas to Arizona and up through California, you now have the booming ex-urban sprawls that have broken free of the gravitational pull of the cities and now float in a new space far beyond them. For example, the population of metropolitan Pittsburgh has declined by 8 percent since 1980, but as people spread out, the amount of developed land in the Pittsburgh area increased by nearly 43 percent. The population of Atlanta increased by 22,000 during the 90's, but the expanding suburbs grew by 2.1 million.

The geography of work has been turned upside down. Jobs used to be concentrated in downtowns. But the suburbs now account for more rental office space than the cities in most of the major metro areas of the country except Chicago and New York. In the Bay Area in California, suburban Santa Clara County alone has five times as many of the region's larger public companies as San Francisco. Ninety percent of the office space built in America by the end of the 1990's was built in suburbia, much of it in far-flung office parks stretched along the interstates.

These new spaces are huge and hugely attractive to millions of people. Mesa, Ariz., a suburb of Phoenix, now has a larger population than Minneapolis, St. Louis, or Cincinnati. It's as if Zeus came down and started plopping vast developments in the middle of farmland and the desert overnight. Boom! A master planned community. Boom! A big-box mall. Boom! A rec center and 4,000 soccer fields. The food courts come and the people follow. How many times in American history have 300,000-person communities materialized practically out of nothing?

In these new, exploding suburbs, the geography, the very landscape of life, is new and unparalleled. In the first place, there are no centers, no recognizable borders to shape a sense of geographic identity. Throughout human history, most people have lived around some definable place—a tribal ring, an oasis, a river junction, a port, a town square. But in exurbia, each individual has his or her own polycentric nodes—the school, the church, and the office park. Life is different in ways big and small. When the New Jersey Devils won the Stanley Cup, they had their victory parade in a parking lot; no downtown street is central to the team's fans. Robert Lang, a demographer at Virginia Tech, compares these new sprawling exurbs to the dark matter in the universe: stuff that is very hard to define but somehow accounts for more mass than all the planets, stars, and moons put together.

We are having a hard time understanding the cultural implications of this new landscape because when it comes to suburbia, our imaginations are motionless. Many of us still live with the suburban stereotypes laid down by the first wave of suburban critics—that the suburbs are dull, white-bread kind of places where Ozzie and Harriet families go to raise their kids. But there are no people so conformist as those who fault the supposed conformity of the suburbs. They regurgitate the same critiques decade after decade, regardless of the suburban reality flowering around them.

The reality is that modern suburbia is merely the latest iteration of the American dream. Far from being dull, artificial, and spiritually vacuous, today's suburbs are the products of the same religious longings and the same deep tensions that produced the American identity from the start. The complex faith of Jonathan Edwards, the propelling ambition of Benjamin Franklin, the dark, meritocratic fatalism of Lincoln—all these inheritances have shaped the outer suburbs.

At the same time the suburbs were sprawling, they were getting more complicated and more interesting, and they were going quietly berserk. When you move through suburbia—from the old inner-ring suburbs out through the most distant exurbs—you see the most unexpected things: lesbian dentists, Iranian McMansions, Korean megachurches, outlaw-biker subdevelopments, Orthodox shtetls with Hasidic families walking past strip malls on their way to shul. When you actually live in suburbia, you see that radically different cultural zones are emerging, usually within a few miles of one another and in places that are as architecturally interesting as a piece of aluminum siding. That's because in the age of the great dispersal, it becomes much easier to search out and congregate with people who are basically like yourself. People are less tied down to a factory, a mine or a harbor. They have more choice over which sort of neighborhood to live in. Society becomes more segmented, and everything that was once hierarchical turns granular.

You don't have to travel very far in America to see radically different sorts of people, most of whom know very little about the communities and subcultures just down the highway. For example, if you are driving across the northern band of the country—especially in Vermont, Massachusetts, Wisconsin or Oregon—you are likely to stumble across a crunchy suburb. These are places with meat-free food co-ops, pottery galleries, sandal shops (because people with progressive politics have a strange penchant for toe exhibitionism). Not many people in these places know much about the for-profit sector of the economy, but they do build wonderful all-wood playgrounds for their kids, who tend to have names like Milo and Mandela. You know you're in a crunchy suburb because you see the anti-lawns, which declare just how fervently crunchy suburbanites reject the soul-destroying standards of conventional success. Anti-lawns look like regular lawns with eating disorders. Some are bare patches of dirt, others are scraggly spreads of ragged, weedlike vegetation, the horticultural version of a grunge rocker's face.

Then a few miles away, you might find yourself in an entirely different cultural zone, in an upscale suburban town center packed with restaurants— one of those communities that perform the neat trick of being clearly suburban while still making it nearly impossible to park. The people here tend to be lawyers, doctors, and professors, and they drive around in Volvos, Audis and Saabs because it is socially acceptable to buy a luxury car as long as it comes from a country hostile to U.S. foreign policy.

Here you can find your Trader Joe's grocery stores, where all the cashiers look as if they are on loan from Amnesty International and all the snack food is especially designed for kids who come home from school screaming, "Mom, I want a snack that will prevent colorectal cancer!" Here you've got newly renovated Arts and Crafts seven-bedroom homes whose owners have developed views on beveled granite; no dinner party in this clique has gone all the way to dessert without a conversational phase on the merits and demerits of Corian countertops. Bathroom tile is their cocaine: instead of white powder, they blow their life savings on handcrafted Italian wall covering from Waterworks.

You travel a few miles from these upscale enclaves, and suddenly you're in yet another cultural milieu. You're in one of the suburban light-industry zones, and you start noting small Asian groceries offering live tilapia fish and premade bibimbap dishes. You see Indian video rental outlets with movies straight from Bollywood. You notice a Japanese bookstore, newspaper boxes offering the *Korea Central Daily News* and hair salons offering DynaSky phone cards to Peru.

One out of every nine people in America was born in a foreign country. Immigrants used to settle in cities and then migrate out, but now many head straight for suburbia, so today you see little Taiwanese girls in the figure skating clinics, Ukrainian boys learning to pitch and hints of cholo culture spreading across Nevada. People here develop their own customs and patterns that grow up largely unnoticed by the general culture. You go to a scraggly playing field on a Saturday morning, and there is a crowd of Nigerians playing soccer. You show up the next day, and it is all Mexicans kicking a ball around. No lifestyle magazine is geared to the people who live in these immigrant-heavy wholesale warehouse zones.

You drive farther out, and suddenly you're lost in the shapeless, mostly middle-class expanse of exurbia. (The inner-ring suburbs tend to have tremendous income inequality.) Those who live out here are very likely living in the cultural shadow of golf. It's not so much the game of golf that influences manners and morals; it's the Zenlike golf ideal. The perfect human being, defined by golf, is competitive and success-oriented, yet calm and neat while casually dressed. Everything he owns looks as if it is made of titanium, from his driver to his BlackBerry to his wife's Wonderbra. He has achieved mastery over the great dragons: hurry, anxiety and disorder.

His DVD collection is organized, as is his walk-in closet. His car is clean and vacuumed. His frequently dialed numbers are programmed into his phone, and his rate plan is well tailored to his needs. His casual slacks are well pressed, and he is so calm and together that next to him, Dick Cheney looks bipolar. The new suburbs appeal to him because everything is fresh and neat. The philosopher George Santayana once suggested that Americans don't solve problems; we just leave them behind. The exurbanite has left behind that exorbitant mortgage, that long commute, all those weird people who watch "My Daughter Is a Slut" on daytime TV talk shows. He has come to be surrounded by regular, friendly people who do not scoff at his daughter's competitive cheerleading obsession and whose wardrobes are as Lands' End–dependent as his is.

Exurban places have one ideal that soars above all others: ample parking. You can drive diagonally across acres of empty parking spaces on your way from Bed, Bath & Beyond to Linens 'n Things. These parking lots are so big that you could recreate the Battle of Gettysburg in the middle and nobody would notice at the stores on either end. Off on one side, partly obscured by the curvature of the earth, you will see a sneaker warehouse big enough to qualify for membership in the United Nations, and then at the other end there will be a Home Depot. Still, shoppers measure their suburban manliness by how close they can park to the Best Buy. So if a normal healthy

American sees a family about to pull out of one of those treasured close-in spots just next to the maternity ones, he will put on his blinker and wait for the departing family to load up its minivan and apparently read a few chapters of "Ulysses" before it finally pulls out and lets him slide in.

You look out across this landscape, with its sprawling diversity of suburban types, and sometimes you can't help considering the possibility that we Americans may not be the most profound people on earth. You look out across the suburban landscape that is the essence of modern America, and you see the culture of Slurp & Gulps, McDonald's, Disney, breast enlargements and "The Bachelor." You see a country that gave us Prozac and Viagra, paper party hats, pinball machines, commercial jingles, expensive orthodontia, and Monster Truck rallies. You see a trashy consumer culture that has perfected parade floats, corporate-sponsorship deals, low-slung jeans, and frosted Cocoa Puffs; a culture that finds its quintessential means of self-expression through bumper stickers ("Rehab Is for Quitters").

Indeed, over the past half century, there has been an endless flow of novels, movies, anti-sprawl tracts, essays and pop songs all lamenting the shallow conformity of suburban life. If you scan these documents all at once, or even if, like the average person, you absorb them over the course of a lifetime, you find their depictions congeal into the same sorry scene. Suburban America as a comfortable but somewhat vacuous realm of unreality: consumerist, wasteful, complacent, materialistic, and self-absorbed.

Disneyfied Americans, in this view, have become too concerned with small and vulgar pleasures, pointless one-upmanship. Their lives are distracted by a buzz of trivial images, by relentless hurry instead of contemplation, information rather than wisdom and a profusion of unsatisfying lifestyle choices. Modern suburban Americans, it is argued, rarely sink to the level of depravity—they are too tepid for that—but they don't achieve the highest virtues or the most demanding excellences.

These criticisms don't get suburbia right. They don't get America right. The criticisms tend to come enshrouded in predictions of decline or cultural catastrophe. Yet somehow imperial decline never comes, and the social catastrophe never materializes. American standards of living surpassed those in Europe around 1740. For more than 260 years, in other words, Americans have been rich, money-mad, vulgar, materialistic and complacent people. And yet somehow America became and continues to be the most powerful nation on earth and the most productive. Religion flourishes. Universities flourish. Crime rates drop, teen pregnancy declines, teen-suicide rates fall, along with divorce rates. Despite all the problems that plague this country, social healing takes place. If we're so great, can we really be that shallow?

Nor do the standard critiques of suburbia really solve the mystery of motivation—the inability of many Americans to sit still, even when they sincerely want to simplify their lives. Americans are the hardest-working people on earth. The average American works 350 hours a year—nearly 10 weeks—more than the average Western European. Americans switch jobs more frequently than people from other nations. The average job tenure in the U.S. is 6.8 years, compared with more than a decade in France, Germany and Japan. What propels Americans to live so feverishly, even against their own self-interest? What energy source accounts for all this?

Finally, the critiques don't explain the dispersion. They don't explain why so many millions of Americans throw themselves into the unknown every year. In 2002, about 14.2 percent of Americans relocated. Compare that with the 4 percent of Dutch and Germans and the 8 percent of Britons who move in a typical year. According to one survey, only slightly more than a quarter of American teenagers expect to live in their hometowns as adults.

What sort of longing causes people to pick up and head out for the horizon? Why do people uproot their families from California, New York, Ohio and elsewhere and move into new developments in Arizona or Nevada or North Carolina, imagining their kids at high schools that haven't even been built yet, picturing themselves with new friends they haven't yet met, fantasizing about touch-football games on lawns that haven't been seeded? Millions of people every year leap out into the void, heading out to communities that don't exist, to office parks that are not yet finished, to places where everything is new. This mysterious longing is the root of the great dispersal.

To grasp that longing, you have to take seriously the central cliché of American life: the American dream. Albert Einstein once said that imagination is more important than knowledge, and when you actually look at modern mainstream America, you see what a huge role fantasy plays even in the seemingly dullest areas of life. The suburbs themselves are conservative utopias, where people go because they imagine orderly and perfect lives can be led there. This is the nation of Hollywood, Las Vegas, professional wrestling, Elvis impersonators, *Penthouse* letters, computer gamers, grown men in LeBron James basketball jerseys, faith healers, and the whole range of ampersand magazines (*Town & Country, Food & Wine*) that display perfect parties, perfect homes, perfect vacations, and perfect lives. This is the land of Rainforest Cafe theme restaurants, Ralph Lauren WASP-fantasy fashions, Civil War re-enactors, gated communities with names like Sherwood Forest and vehicles with names like Yukon, Durango, Expedition and Mustang, as if their accountant-owners were going to chase down some cattle rustlers on the way to the Piggly Wiggly. This is the land in which people dream of the most Walter Mitty-esque personal transformations as a result of the low-carb diet, cosmetic surgery, or their move to the Sun Belt.

Americans—seemingly bland, ordinary Americans—often have a remarkably tenuous grip on reality. Under the seeming superficiality of suburban American life, there is an imaginative fire that animates Americans and propels us to work so hard, move so much and leap so wantonly.

Ralph Waldo Emerson once wrote that those who "complain of the flatness of American life have no perception of its destiny. They are not Americans." They don't see that "here is man in the garden of Eden; here, the Genesis and the Exodus." And here, he concluded fervently, will come the final Revelation. Emerson was expressing the eschatological longing that is the essence of the American identity: the assumption that some culminating happiness is possible here, that history can be brought to a close here.

The historian Sacvan Bercovitch has observed that the United States is the example par excellence of a nation formed by collective fantasy. Despite all the claims that American culture is materialist and pragmatic, what is striking about this country is how material things are shot through with enchantment.

America, after all, was born in a frenzy of imagination. For the first European settlers and for all the subsequent immigrants, the new continent begs to be fantasized about. The early settlers were aware of and almost oppressed by the obvious potential of the land. They saw the possibility of plenty everywhere, yet at the start they lived in harsh conditions. Their lives took on a slingshot shape—they had to pull back in order to someday shoot forward. Through the temporary hardships they dwelt imaginatively in the grandeur that would inevitably mark their future.

This future-minded mentality deepened decade after decade, century after century. Each time the early settlers pushed West, they found what was to them virgin land, and they perceived it as paradise. Fantasy about the future lured them. Guides who led and sometimes exploited the 19th-century pioneers were shocked by how little the trekkers often knew about the surroundings they had thrown themselves into, or what would be involved in their new lives. As so often happens in American history, as happens every day in the newly sprawling areas, people leapt before they really looked.

"Suburbia is becoming the most important single market in the country. It is the suburbanite who starts the mass fashions—for children, . . . dungarees, vodka martinis, outdoor barbecues, functional furniture, [and] picture windows. . . . All suburbs are not alike, but they are more alike than they are different."

—WILLIAM H. WHYTE
The Organization Man (1956)

Americans found themselves drawn to places where the possibilities seemed boundless and where there was no history. Francis Parkman, the great 19th-century historian, wrote of his youthful self, "His thoughts were always in the forest, whose features possessed his waking and sleeping dreams, filling him with vague cravings impossible to satisfy."

Our minds are still with Parkman's in the forest. Our imagination still tricks us into undertaking grand projects—starting a business, writing a book, raising a family, moving to a new place—by enchanting us with visions of future joys. When these tasks turn out to be more difficult than we dreamed, the necessary exertions bring out new skills and abilities and make us better than we planned on being.

And so we see the distinctive American mentality, which explains the westward crossing as much as the suburban sprawl and the frenzied dot-com-style enthusiasms. It is the Paradise Spell: the tendency to see the present from the vantage point of the future. It starts with imagination—the ability to fantasize about what some imminent happiness will look like. Then the future-minded person leaps rashly toward that gauzy image. He or she is subtly more attached to the glorious future than to the temporary and unsatisfactory present. Time isn't pushed from the remembered past to the felt present to the mysterious future. It is pulled by the golden future from the unsatisfactory present and away from the dim past.

Born in abundance, inspired by opportunity, nurtured in imagination, spiritualized by a sense of God's blessing and call and realized in ordinary life day by day, this Paradise Spell is the controlling ideology of national life. Just out of reach, just beyond the next ridge, just in the farther-out suburb or with the next entrepreneurial scheme, just with the next diet plan or credit card purchase, the next true love or political hero, the next summer home or all-terrain vehicle, the next meditation schools, the right moral revival, the right beer and the right set of buddies; just with the next technology or after the next shopping spree—there is this spot you can get to where all tensions will melt, all time pressures will be relieved and happiness can be realized.

This Paradise Spell is at the root of our tendency to work so hard, consume so feverishly, to move so much. It inspires our illimitable faith in education, our frequent born-again experiences. It explains why, alone among developed nations, we have shaped our welfare system to encourage opportunity at the expense of support and security; and why, more than people in comparable nations, we wreck our families and move on. It is the call that makes us heedless of the past, disrespectful toward traditions, short on contemplation, wasteful in our use of the things around us, impious toward restraints, but consumed by hope, driven ineluctably to improve, fervently optimistic, relentlessly aspiring, spiritually alert, and, in this period of human history, the irresistible and discombobulating locomotive of the world.

1. Examine the photo on page 183 that accompanies Cathleen McGuigan's essay on design. Do you see anything wrong with this house? What do you think of McGuigan's contention that the American house needs a makeover?

2. How does Brooks define "The Paradise Spell"? Do you agree with his explanation of why Americans are so mobile?

3. Can you identify any "cultural zones," as David Brooks describes them, where you live?

4. Using the resources of your campus library or the Web, explore the history and cultural impact of Levittown, Pennsylvania, a planned community built after World War II to provide single-family homes for returning GIs and their new families. Summarize your findings in a brief report, illustrated if possible.

COMPOSE

5. Write a letter to one of the photographers or writers featured on pages 180–194 in which you take issue with his or her representation of suburbia.

6. David Brooks writes that "throughout human history, most people have lived around some definable place." Write a paragraph in which you describe the geographic center of your hometown.

CHALLENGE

7. Cathleen McGuigan writes that "the best design reflects who we are and the time in which we live." Using words and images, design a home that reflects who you are and the time in which you live.

Subverting Suburbia: The Radical Landscape of Skateboarding

While places affect us, they don't control us. And just as they influence us, we in turn shape them. The readings and images that follow introduce you to the Z-Boys, a group of skateboarders in the 1970s who refused to be contained by the run-down suburban neighborhoods where they lived. The radical and sometimes dangerous or illegal use they made of empty swimming pools, drainage ditches, and parking lots sparked a renaissance in skateboarding—and paved the way for new thinking about how city parks and sports facilities should be designed.

"Two hundred years of American technology has unwittingly created a massive cement playground of unlimited potential. But it was the minds of 11-year-olds that could see that potential."

—CRAIG STECYK
Skateboarder magazine

Still from *Dogtown and Z-Boys* (2001)

"Skaters by their very nature are urban guerrillas. The skater makes everyday use of the useless artifacts of the technological burden. The skating urban anarchist employs [structures] in a thousand ways that the original architects could never dream of."

—CRAIG STECYK
Skateboarder magazine

CONSIDER

1. Examine the places depicted in the three photos—two empty swimming pools and a graffiti-covered alleyway. What do you think Stecyk means when he says that skaters "make everyday use of the useless artifacts of the technological burden"? Where do you see evidence of this phenomenon in the photos?

2. Which photo do you find most interesting, surprising, or powerful? What elements of structure, arrangement, or design do you think contribute to this effect?

3. All of these photos appeared in skateboarding magazines. What purposes do you think "action" photos serve in such publications?

197

You Go Blindfolded:
An Interview with Stacy Peralta

FYI

Cynthia Fuchs is associate professor of English and cultural studies at George Mason University, as well as a regular film, media, and book reviewer for the *Philadelphia Citypaper*, *popmatters.com* and *reelimagesmagazine.com*.

Director of *Dogtown and Z-Boys*

Cynthia Fuchs
(2002)

Stacy Peralta, winner of the 2001 Sundance Film Festival Director's Award, wears a sweatshirt and sneakers. He's tossed his backpack against the wall of this awkwardly large hotel conference room. Peralta's used to appropriating spaces not designed for him, being a former Z-Boy. That is, a member of Los Angeles's Zephyr Skate Team, legendary during the 1970s and setting the stage for today's skateboard culture and industry (as in Tony Hawk's video games, the X Games, etc.). At a time long before anyone even thought about building a skate park, the Z-Boys made the sidewalks, swimming pools, and schoolyards of Southern California their own.

Peralta has made a documentary, *Dogtown and Z-Boys.* Narrated by Sean Penn and comprised of Craig Stecyk and Glen E. Friedman's video footage and photos, as well as interviews and a slamming soundtrack (including Hendrix, Zep, Iggy, and Neil Young), the film traces the impacts of a unique convergence of factors: the low-income environment, the kids' "latchkey" existence, the invention of the urethane wheel, and the emergence of vert skateboarding. Structured around the diverging stories of two skaters—the brilliantly athletic Tony Alva and the ethereal Jay Adams—*Z-Boys* recovers and reflects a particular countercultural moment.

CYNTHIA FUCHS: Even aside from its subcultural subject matter, *Dogtown and Z-Boys* might inspire young filmmakers.

STACY PERALTA: It does show that filmmaking is accessible to young people. That's what my skateboarding videos were all about. I found out so many years later that they empowered kids to pick up cameras and do it themselves. We made the film *Dogtown and Z-Boys* look the way it does not only because it reflects the subject matter, but I have a case to make against this age of production value. Everything we see is so well produced that it doesn't even look like reality. And it all looks the same—commercials and episodic TV and motion pictures—they're all lit so perfectly that it doesn't look like any world that I know of. It removes us from that process.

■ ■ ■

CF: The film raises this question of "authenticity," about what it means to sell out, while getting the word out.

SP: I can tell you this much. There's no selling out in this film. I hardly made any money on it. I don't own the film, and in order to support myself to be able to make it, I had to take two directing jobs, one for a series on Bravo, *Influences*, which is basically not a creative thing. We made the film in 6 months, and for those 6 months, I was probably paid for 2 months of work. But hey, this was a cause, had to do it. Since I was one of the guys, I knew many of the people who had footage, and was able to bargain for poverty wages. We spent probably $40,000 on footage that could have cost over $100,000.

■ ■ ■

CF: But you can see how young people, perhaps especially, are anxious about the future.

SP: Absolutely. I heard this when I was growing up, becoming what I'm trying to become: "You've gotta be confident. You've gotta go in the room and fill the room with your energy." I'm sorry, but I'll never be able to do that. What I've learned is, you don't need confidence. What you need is ideas and the ability to get up and move forward. You need drive. You only get confidence by doing what you do. You don't get it before. You get it by having the experiences of falling down and getting back up. I'm sure there are people that do wake up bursting with confidence, but that person's not me.

CF: Skating is literal about that.

SP: It is. People ask me, "You didn't wear pads back then. How did you survive?" We survived because we learned how to fall. We grew up in the age of clay wheels, which were like rocks, and if you didn't learn to fall properly, you couldn't proceed. We wanted the film to be a reflection of that, the imperfect and subversive nature of skateboarding. So we broke it up and put the burn marks and the leader. And if someone would get too longwinded, we'd just speed up to the next part of the film. We didn't want to hide it, to make it pretty.

CF: It's refreshing, since the popular standard for documentaries now, at least those using still photos, is to zoom in slowly, with fiddle music in the background.

SP: [*laughs*] We went into the matte camera stage, where there's lights and a table and the camera, and off to the side, a guy who programs the computer to smooth out all those moves. I said, "I don't want you to program anything, just use the joysticks and do it freehand." And we wanted to shoot as many different angles as possible and as many speed-ups as possible, so Paul could have as many opportunities as possible when he edited. It made it fun. We didn't make this film for anyone in particular, as long as we liked it.

CF: And now that you're traveling with it, what are you seeing in audiences?

SP: When you make a film like this, you always have in mind that you can't lose the core audience, or your film gets bad-mouthed. That's the one thing we tried to keep our ears attuned to. What's been a surprise is how many non-skating people have looked at this as a cultural phenomenon, like, "Wow, we knew this was in America, we've seen Tony Hawk, but we didn't know why."

CF: So it's recovering a history.

SP: Yes. And really, it's the kids who really have no idea. When Tony Hawk saw this, he goes, "I've been involved in skateboarding my whole life, and while I knew about this, I didn't really know the depth, or why it happened." This is a distinct American phenomenon, with no European influences. You can trace it back to Hawaii and surfing. It's so American.

CF: To that end, your crew was fairly diverse, even given that you were mostly "latchkey" kids of a certain class, and that Jay and you and others were so *blond.*

SP: Right. There was Jeff [Ho], Peggy Oki, Shogo Kubo, Tony [Alva], who's Mexican American. We had a black surfer on our team. Now this is very normal; back then it was very abnormal. When we would leave our area and go skateboarding anywhere else, it was all blond, blue-eyed kids. Today when you look at skateboarding, it has become very multicultural and very "urban." The kids that are doing it today would have been kids 20 years ago, who were in gangs and didn't like skateboarders. It's left its surfing roots completely and become inner city. Which I think is fantastic: skateboarding's one of the few sports you can do where you can leave the designated areas and do it anywhere. Every skateboarding kid wants to taste that illicit thrill of doing it where he's not supposed to do it, to try different aspects of his talent on terrain that wasn't built for him. And he can potentially make a name for himself by developing a trick someplace that doesn't belong to him. That's what's going to keep skateboarding subversive. Even though they're building skateboarding parks, kids are always going to sneak into pools or skateboard on railings in front of buildings where there's security guards. It's just part of the process.

CF: How self-conscious were you all, at the time, that you were being "subversive," in whatever ways?

SP: It was more of a thing where we were living in the shadow of the '60s when skateboarding had come and gone so quickly, and so we were skateboarding when there wasn't such a thing as it anymore. We were used to being kicked out of everywhere we went. Everywhere. Skateboarding: doing it is almost like being part of a virus. Viruses come in, occupy the body as if it's their own, use the resources of the body to replenish and remake themselves, and then leave. Skateboarding's the same way. You see an empty pool: this belongs to you. You use it as long as you can and then you leave. We never thought we were doing anything that was interesting, except to ourselves. It's hard to think it's going to turn into something else when everyone is telling you that what you're doing is wrong—"This is wrong. Leave." Our parents didn't understand it because there was no context to understand it. They looked at us and thought, "You'll outgrow this." It had the respectability of a yo-yo. Or a hula-hoop. They didn't realize that what we were doing was physically demanding, took a lot of pre-thought. And they didn't see the beauty in it. It was developed very clandestinely.

■ ■ ■

CF: Can you talk about how Dogtown, the place, affected the art and culture of skateboarding?

SP: Dogtown is basically West Los Angeles, where all of Los Angeles points at the beach. Like we say in the film, the end of Route 66. It's very rare for a coastal area to be low-income. Now if you look at it, it's Beverly Hills at the Beach, it's all money. At the time, Hughes Aircraft and Douglas had aircraft factories near there, so there were a lot of assembly line workers and rent-controlled apartments. It's just a beautiful slice of rundown coastline. And right where we surfed on the beach, there's a building that today is now a five-star hotel and in the '40s was a hotel and beach club where movie stars would go. But when we were there, it was a place called Synanon, a place for very serious drug rehab. But the low-income surroundings allowed people to grow, [and] there were a lot of artists there, like Jeff.

And because of the layout of Los Angeles—it's a very hilly area—you had this concentration of schoolyards that had these asphalt waves that you couldn't find anywhere else, in that abundance. Plus, Los Angeles is the swimming pool capital of the world. And not just swimming pools, but movie star pools, with the big sensuous bowls. So we had so many things going for us. People ask, would the X Games be where they are today if it wasn't for you guys? My answer is yes, because it would have happened eventually, somewhere else.

The 16,000-square-foot Youth Activities Center Skate Park in Santa Clara, California is considered to be a model of modern public skate park design.

But we had everything going for us at the start. We had the terrain, the urethane wheel, *and* the weather—the drought. As we call it in the film, it was a "disharmonic convergence," because no one else wanted it to happen. But even that favored us.

■ ■ ■

CF: How does "style"—anti-establishment but also welcoming such mainstream elements as this premiere gauntlet—shape the culture?

SP: Today, we live in an age of extremism. Kids today are like stuntmen, going as big as you possibly can. But back then, your body form, the carriage of your body, was an identification marker for who you were. It was like an anatomical hangtag. If you looked good, everyone wanted to watch you. It was that as well as being aggressive. How to look the best you could, at the most critical moment. And that took years to get there. The guys who faked it, you could see right through them. It was beautiful to watch. I'd see Tony Alva or Jay Adams and be inspired. I'd go my next run and tuck down more, and feel it.

When you get into a critical moment, you can feel it. We were all pushing each other, in that regard. If you could carve a pool, and in a critical moment, just kind of tilt your back a little, wow! It's like a matador. The audience goes insane. They might not be able to do it, but they can feel it. I don't want to get too crazy with the metaphors here, but if you have a room full of pianos and hit the E key on one, the E keys on all those pianos will hum. It's the same thing. When you hit something true in one human being, it hums through everyone. We would do that to each other. Some guy would do it, and boom, we were all vibrating to it, thinking, I've got to keep the session going.

CF: Did you talk a lot about it, at the time?

SP: We did talk about what was possible, and we argued about it a lot. For instance, we would do what was called backside kick-turns, where your back is to the wall. We didn't think it was physically possible to do a frontside kick-turn. And I told Bob Biniak, "I know it's possible, and I know you can do it." I stood on the top of the pool and I egged him on until he did it. That was a huge turning point for us.

CF: You knew Bob could do that kick-turn. How aware were you of each other's differences and abilities?

SP: That was something that I think was specific to me. This is one of the reasons I think I succeeded with my own team. I had an ability to look at other people and see they could do things, without an ego attachment to it, like, if he does that, he'll be better than me. For me, I found the whole process fascinating. I found myself at contests, coaching the other guys. I don't know where that came from. It was an innate thing that I just did, and it came in handy later, as a coach and a filmmaker too. Especially for a documentary: you have to be able to walk in and say, "What's the story here?"

FYI Stacy Peralta also wrote the script for *Lords of Dogtown*, a 2005 feature film based on the exploits of the Z-Boys in 1970s Venice, California.

CONSIDER

1. According to Peralta, why did he decide not to make a traditional documentary film about the history of skateboarding, one featuring "still photos with fiddle music in the background" (a veiled reference to filmmaker Ken Burns's *Civil War* series developed for PBS)?

2. Peralta uses several metaphors—a virus, a room full of pianos humming—to describe skateboarding. If you've done a lot of skateboarding, discuss whether or not you think these images capture the flavor of the sport. If you haven't, which of the metaphors do you find most suggestive or interesting?

3. Peralta argues that the "disharmonic convergence" of geographic and cultural realities in 1970s Dogtown ("basically West Los Angeles") made possible the skateboarding renaissance that *Dogtown and Z-Boys* chronicles. Do you think that the sport would have evolved differently if this renaissance had happened someplace else—Miami, for example, or Iowa City? Boston, El Paso, East Saint Louis, or Tupelo? Explain.

COMPOSE

4. Skateboarders aren't the only ones who make creative use of traditional spaces. For example, maybe you've transformed your parents' garage into a rehearsal studio for your blues band or used the roof of your apartment building as an ice rink after a winter storm. Think of a situation in which you've used a place in an unexpected or oppositional way, and write a few paragraphs describing the experience. What features of the place inspired you to use it in a new way? What did you hope to accomplish? How did others react?

Places We Go

The preceding images and readings looked at how the spaces we call "home" shape our identities. But places that are "not home" often occupy an equally important space in our imaginations. When we travel, we become the outsider in various locales, and images of these unfamiliar spaces play to our hopes, our desires—and sometimes our fears.

Images of places we visit typically fall into two categories: representations that draw us to these places (through travel brochures, advertisements, and the like) and representations that help us remember them (such as postcards, snapshots, or home videos). Though the images in the first category are usually more generic and those in the second more personal, both kinds share an important feature: Their purpose is to show the places we visit in the best possible light.

But we don't live in a picture postcard world. Because portraits of places—visual and written—are created from particular perspectives, in particular contexts, and with particular purposes in mind, they are always incomplete.

The text and images that follow offer varied glimpses of Jamaica, an archetypal tourist destination. As you study the words and pictures, think about the purpose of each text, what message it sends, and what it leaves out.

Greetings from Jamaica

Search for "Jamaica" on the Internet, and you'll be inundated with Web sites, most of them selling the Caribbean island as a breathtaking tourist destination. "In Jamaica," the Jamaican Tourism Board says, "you'll discover new worlds, and familiar ones too, lots to learn about, and even more to love." Commercial travel sites call the island a "vacation paradise," "a kaleidoscope of beauty," and "the most precious jewel in the Caribbean." If you sort your search results carefully, however, you'll find other representations. According to the Christian aid organization Food for the Poor, for example: "The colorful images of Jamaica presented in travel brochures don't tell the whole story. As in most countries, beautiful, affluent places do exist. But in many other areas of Jamaica, poverty is the norm." Which of the words and images that follow captures the "real" Jamaica? None of them, perhaps. Or maybe all of them taken together.

Here are some visual and verbal portraits of the island created by the tourist industry.

"Greetings from Jamaica." This vintage postcard presenting 1950s tourists with an image of a lush, tropical paradise populated by picturesque local inhabitants.

Vintage postcard of Jamaica

"The true Garden of Eden." The Sandals.com Web site contains the following description: "Sandals is a collection of 11 of the most romantic beachfront resorts on earth, created exclusively for couples in love, in Jamaica, St. Lucia, Antigua and The Bahamas. Discover the Caribbean's most luxurious beachfront rooms and oceanview suites. Enjoy an astounding array of land and watersports, including unlimited golf and scuba diving."

"Create your own paradise each day." Half Moon Resorts' Web page lures visitors with this verbal landscape: "Welcome to Half Moon, Montego Bay. A transformation begins when guests enter through the ornately carved wrought iron gates that frame the exclusive Half Moon resort community. A warm island greeting bids you into the sprawling open-air lobby filled with colorful artwork, tropical plants, gracious furnishings and expansive views of the Caribbean Sea and inspires a sense of calm and relaxation. . . . Time is yours while staying at Half Moon. Do nothing or take advantage of all that the resort has to offer. Let each sunrise dictate what the day will bring."

Resort hotel in Jamaica

1. What kinds of places are depicted in these tourist-oriented portraits of Jamaica? How do design elements in the photographs—such as lighting, color, framing, and point of view—shape your impression of the landscape?

2. What do you notice about the people and activities depicted in these portraits? What do these patterns tell you about prospective vacationers' expectations and associations with this region?

3. Have you ever visited or worked at a tourist resort? How did your experience of the place match or differ from advertisements for the resort?

4. How does viewing the tourism images with those from Food for the Poor affect your thinking about Jamaica? Which images seem more powerful to you? Why?

5. Why do you think Food for the Poor chose to use black-and-white photographs (see below) on its Web site? What other differences do you see in the two groups of images? How do these design differences create different impressions of the place?

Now consider this portrait of the island presented on the web site of Food for the Poor, a nonprofit agency dedicated to eliminating hunger worldwide.

"Desperate and frustrated." From www.foodforthepoor.org: "Jamaica's economy has been in decline since 1974, when the energy-deficient country was hit hard by a rise in fuel costs. In addition, a worldwide recession reduced foreign demand for Jamaican products. Jamaica's economy has also been hurt by its limited agricultural base. . . . Housing has become another problem for Jamaica's urban poor. When people move to Kingston in search of work, it's often difficult for them to find jobs. Some become homeless, while others are forced to accept low-paying jobs. To afford food and other necessities, they move into abandoned properties. Some become squatters, building shacks of cardboard, wood, and rusted tin on land owned by others."

Images from www.foodforthepoor.org

COMPOSE

6. Imagine that you've been hired to create a tourism brochure for your hometown or campus. Take several photographs that capture places, activities, and associations you think would appeal to prospective visitors, and compose an appropriate caption for each photo.

7. Now take some photographs of the same locale that you would *not* include in a tourism brochure, and caption them as well. If you are working with a group, set up an exhibit of the contrasting or at least quite different photographs of the same locales.

FYI

A native of Jamaica, Margaret Cezair-Thompson writes and teaches English at Wellesley College near Boston. In the essay that follows, she alludes to "the violence in Jamaica in the '70s," a theme that pervades her widely acclaimed debut novel, *The True History of Paradise* (1999). According to the *Sunday Business Post* of Ireland, the novel "is based partly on her own experiences: the daughter of the Jamaican security minister, Cezair-Thompson left her home country in her twenties to study in New York. While there, she heard on the radio that her father had been assassinated. It wasn't actually him—'it was one of his deputy ministers, but for 24 hours I thought he had been killed.'" "Geography Lessons" appeared in the *Washington Post Magazine* in December 1999.

Geography Lessons

Margaret Cezair-Thompson
(1999)

Aunt Justine was nobody's favorite aunt. She had a quick temper and a harsh voice. Her husband, Uncle Nev, took her bad moods in stride, but her daughter used to come to our house to get away from her. Strangely enough, whenever my mother had to leave me somewhere for the day, I would ask to go to Aunt Justine's.

Like most houses in Jamaica, hers had a large, cool tile veranda. Several tiles were broken and they formed little ridges and valleys; it was a terrain I knew well. I would play on the veranda while Aunt Justine chain-smoked and worked at her easel, painting landscapes from memory. There were a lot of books in her house. Uncle Nev was a geography teacher, so along with my aunt's mystery and romance novels, there were atlases and geography textbooks, and these in particular enthralled me. Words like *tundra* appealed to me, and I would imagine myself living in extreme climates, in an igloo or a nomad's tent. When Uncle Nev was there, he quizzed me on things like the largest river in the world. He would sit on the veranda in khaki shorts and draw continents on a grapefruit. Then he would slice the grapefruit in half and offer me a hemisphere.

Every Christmas the whole family gathered at Aunt Justine's. What I remember most is playing outside in the warm sun and hearing the grown-ups' veranda talk and veranda laughter. There were three Christmas drinks: sorrel, made from the acidic red petals of a kind of hibiscus and spiced with ginger; Aunt Justine's famous egg punch, made with rum; and pimento dram, a chilled brandy made from pimento (allspice) berries. There were a lot of us, so we ate buffet-style on the veranda: roast suckling pig, ham, "rice-an'-peas," baked plantain, pureed boiled green bananas. Dessert was Jamaican Christmas pudding, a dark, moist fruitcake that had been soaking in rum and brandy for months.

When air conditioners first came to the island, Uncle Leo, whose company installed them in the big hotels, conspired with Uncle Nev to air-condition Aunt Justine's living room in time for Christmas. It was to be a surprise. Everybody except Aunt Justine knew and had an opinion: Some looked forward to the novelty of a cool Christmas, others said they didn't want to spend Christmas shut up inside the house shivering. Uncle Nev reasoned: "Those who want a white Christmas can sit in the living room, and those who want a red Christmas can sit on the veranda." By "red Christmas" he meant the poinsettias that grew in people's gardens and turned blood-red in December.

Christmas Day was burning hot, but I put on my sweater even before I reached Aunt Justine's. My sister asked if it was going to snow. I said no, but it would be cold, like real Christmas. In those days, Jamaican children were educated as though they lived in England. At school we painted snowmen and holly on our Christmas cards. The cards, the carols and Charles Dickens all gave me the impression that Christmas in Jamaica was counterfeit. As for our "red Christmas," though I looked forward to the changing poinsettia leaves, I thought it a paltry substitute for winter.

When we got to Aunt Justine's, the doors were wide open and Uncle Nev was on the veranda in his shorts.

"Wha' 'appen, Nev? No air conditioner?"

"Man, Justine say' no food goin' cook today if we bring cold weather into her house."

I went back for Christmas 1997. I had lived most of my adult life in the United States, and the violence in Jamaica in the '70s had alienated me. As I was driving from the airport, familiar sights reassured me: the noisy commerce of cart men, roadside higglers and crowded buses. The island seemed more lush and beautiful than ever; the violence of men had not denuded the landscape.

My parents and siblings were abroad. There was no family home to return to. I went to Aunt Justine's house even though I knew it had been sold. No one had prepared me for the hotel parking lot that had replaced it. It had been the most stable feature of my childhood.

Uncle Nev had died, and Aunt Justine lived in a tiny apartment without even a balcony. She had given most of her furniture and books to her daughter, Phyllis, but the walls were crowded with her unframed landscapes. Arthritic fingers now prevented her from painting, and she was almost blind. She spent her days "listening" to the TV, mostly American talk shows.

Phyllis continued her mother's Christmas Day tradition. Her veranda, like most in Kingston, had been enclosed, barricaded in iron grillwork. We sat in the living room, about a dozen of us. The country relatives no longer came to Kingston because of carjackings. There was no egg punch or pimento dram, but my cousin made sorrel spiked with rum. Her teenage sons sat in the TV room watching American football, and that seemed a sacrilege; soccer is football. Looking around, I thought we could have been a group of Jamaicans celebrating a Christmas anywhere.

There had been a number of particularly gruesome killings, and everyone was agreeing that the "dons," drug lords, were now running the country. Someone said, "Is de politicians' fault, man, dem sell off de country."

Things had not gotten much better; I wished I had not come "home." I got up and wandered around the house like a ghost looking for old things among the new.

I found what I was looking for, its cover worn but intact: *World Geography for Primary Schools*, Vol. I. I asked Phyllis if I could have it. She said yes, it had outlived its usefulness; geography was now an optional subject in the schools. I realized that this was true not only in Jamaica but most places. Like Latin, the language of geography was dead. Words that had captivated me as a child—*steppe, antipodes*—seemed anachronistic, at best poetic. Uncle Nev and his lessons, Aunt Justine's house, the changes in Jamaica, and in myself. I went out to the veranda carrying the book as if it alone contained my many-sided grief.

Aunt Justine was by herself out there, smoking. Before I had the chance to sit and talk with her, other guests began trickling out, bringing rum and their animated discussion of politics and crime. Phyllis brought out dessert. There was praise for the pudding, and then there was talk about whether Jamaica was becoming a less religious country.

"No, man, Jamaicans still love to go to church."

"Which church? Ganja church?"

Everyone laughed, then someone told a preacher joke, then someone else told another. The jokes became more raunchy, the laughter more raucous.

They were not mourners, but revelers. The book on my lap made me feel like a moody schoolgirl. My cousin had specially prepared some of my favorite Jamaican foods. And there was Aunt Justine, arthritic, blind and all! On the stereo Nat King Cole was singing, "Chestnuts roasting on an open fire . . ." and through the grillwork I could see my cousin's garden full of red poinsettias. I was 18 degrees north of the equator, and it was really Christmas.

**Explore "Geography Lessons"
in depth**
www.ablongman.com/beyondwords12

SHOWING AND TELLING IN DESCRIPTIVE WRITING

No matter what you write, it will be more appealing to your audience if you include specific details rather than page after page of generalities. This is especially true when you write about places: When you take readers to a specific locale, you become their guide. They can see, hear, taste, smell, and feel only what you set before them. And if you omit these kinds of details, their trip to the place will be flat and less than memorable.

If you haven't already, you'll probably soon hear a teacher talk about the difference, in writing, between showing and telling. The most common scenario goes something like this: Telling—simply writing *about* something ("it was 95 degrees in the shade")—is not as effective as showing—letting readers share an experience with you ("I felt my skin melting as I stood in the afternoon heat"). *Telling* isn't always a bad technique, however. Often, for reasons of pacing, priority, and space, telling works well—readers can't experience everything. Consider this example from Margaret Cezair-Thompson's essay "Geography Lessons" (pages 207–210):

> I went back for Christmas 1997. I had lived most of my adult life in the United States, and the violence in Jamaica in the '70s had alienated me. As I was driving from the airport, familiar sights reassured me: the noisy commerce of cart men, roadside higglers and crowded buses. The island seemed more lush and beautiful than ever; the violence of men had not denuded the landscape.

Although her trip from the airport is important, it isn't the central point of her essay, so Cezair-Thompson tells readers what she wants them to know in a few sentences. Showing all of this might have taken a few pages. Notice, however, that even in her telling, Cezair-Thompson appeals to readers' senses by using such words as *noisy* and *lush*.

And that's the point: The best descriptive writing combines showing *and* telling, using strong verbs, evocative adjectives and adverbs (in small doses), and lots of sensory details.

As you undertake your writing assignments, keep the following in mind to bring people and places to life:

- Think about the details. If you're writing about a place, list the critical details that make that place what it is, that set it off from other places.
- Group your list by sense (sight, sound, taste, smell, touch). How many of the details are visual? Probably most of them, since we rely most heavily on what we can see when describing places. Try to think of details that appeal to the other senses as well.
- Decide which of these details you want to show and which you want to tell. These choices will depend on your purpose, the amount of space you have, and in some cases your audience.
- Incorporate details into your draft.

Damien Marley performing at the Roots, Rock, Reggae Tour in Vienna, Virginia

The Pulse of Jamaica

Reggae is just one of many kinds of folk music popular in Jamaica, but it is certainly the best known in the rest of the world. Like blues in the southern United States, reggae has its roots in Africa and was developed and popularized by black artists. The appeal of reggae, however, crosses racial, national, and class lines.

Although reggae's popularity is in large part based in its pulsating, infectious rhythms, the lyrics, too, have a broad appeal. Reggae songs—whether about love and peace, violence and suffering, anger and rebellion, or spiritual uplift and overcoming—are often songs rooted in Jamaica itself and thus present a strong sense of place. Consider, for example, the lyrics to "My Island," by Burning Spear.

My Island

Burning Spear
(1997)

You live on my island
And you own all my rights
I want you to know
Give me what is mine
You live on my island
And you own all my rights
I want you to know
Give me what is mine

Is this another Christopher Columbus
Is this another old pirate game
Is this another Christopher Columbus
Is this another old pirate game

If this is a war, a musical war
I want you to know, I decided to fight
Come in my soldiers
Come and let us fight
Come and let us fight
Fight for our right
Come in my soldiers
Come and let us fight
Come and let us fight
Fight for our right
I and I yading in the footstep, the footstep of the Kings Highway
I and I yading in the footstep, the footstep of the Kings Highway
I want you to know
Give me what is mine

You live on my island
And you own all my rights
I want you to know
Give me what is mine

So you think you come again to trick us
So you think you come again to fool us
So you think you come again to trick us

FYI Burning Spear is a living legend of Reggae music who has been recording since 1969. He grew up in the parish of St. Ann's, Jamaica, the same area that produced Bob Marley and the Wailers.

So you think you come again to fool us
Long, long, long, long, long time ago
My old great grandfather father, usually work in this plantation
Long, long, long, long, long time ago
My old great grandfather father, usually work in this plantation
Water carrier / Food server

So you think you come again to trick us
So you think you come again to fool us
So you think you come again to trick us
So you think you come again to fool us

You live on my island
And you own all my rights
I want you to know
Give me what is mine
If this is a war, a musical war
I want you to know, I decided to fight
Come in my soldiers
Come and let us fight
Come and let us fight
Fight for our right
I and I yading in the footstep, the footstep of the Kings Highway
I and I yading in the footstep, the footstep of the Kings Highway

You live on my island
And you own all my rights
I want you to know
Give me what is mine
You live on my island
And you own all my rights
I want you to know
Give me what is mine
Remember you live on my island

**Learn more about Burning Spear
and Reggae music.**
www.ablongman.com/beyondwords13

CONSIDER

1. Notice the structure of Cezair-Thompson's essay. Why do you think she uses Christmas as a focal point for her remembrances? How does this choice affect the portrait she creates?

2. Compare the language used in "Geography Lesson" and "My Island." Notice the moments when the authors incorporate vocabulary and phrases from Jamaican dialect—such as "I and I," "Jah," "yading," and "ganja"—into their work. How do these words and phrases affect your response to the texts? How do they affect your impression of Jamaica? How might the portraits be different if they had been written solely in academic English or only in dialect?

3. Based on their words, what do you think Cezair-Thompson and Burning Spear would say about the Web site depictions that open the discussion of Jamaica? Which, if any, do you think they would see as the most "complete" or "accurate"? Point to specific passages in the essays and the song lyrics to support your opinion.

COMPOSE

4. Each text discussed here—the Web sites, the essays, and the song lyrics—has a purpose. Write a paragraph or two in which you describe what you see as the purpose of each and assess whether the words and images are effective in that context.

5. Conduct research in the library or on the Internet to learn something about the history, cultures, and politics of Jamaica. Write a few paragraphs reporting your findings; then comment on whether and how this information changes your response to the images and readings in this chapter.

CHALLENGE

6. Reexamine the materials in this section. Given all the facets of Jamaica you've seen, can you imagine any possible consequences for a place where extreme affluence and poverty exist so closely?

7. Where in your state—or in another state or country you've visited—might these kinds of extremes be found in the same proximity? Using that more familiar location from which to draw your examples, write a paper in which you explore the ways affluence and poverty intersect and what may follow, politically and socially, from such contact.

Places We Miss

We often use stories to make sense of the world, and we use them to remember. Many of the stories we tell, in fact, are born of nostalgia: Because we miss something (or someone), we talk about it and tell a story to try to bring some part of it back, if for only a moment.

These nostalgic stories—and the ways they are told—vary as much as the tellers themselves. But what many have in common is a strong sense of place (the root of *nostalgia* is the Greek *nostos*, "return home"). In a recent online discussion thread, under the title "Disappearing Places" (www.photo.net) photographer Marc Williams laments the passing of many of the places that made his childhood neighborhood unique. He concludes by asking, "Do you have something that you could post here on this subject? No critiques please, but a few remembrances, or even current things on the endangered list."

This section begins with Williams's initial Internet posting and some responses, as well as an essay in which another writer mourns the loss of a special childhood place. It concludes with two views of a legendary U.S. roadway, Route 66, which has faded in the years since the development of the interstate highway system.

Williams writes:

> I just discovered [an] Allied Moving box with hundreds of neg[ative]s that had been missing for years. In it was part of a project I had undertaken to record the things of my life that were disappearing (ironic, that the negs disappeared also).

> In the neighborhood where I grew up, before mega-malls, multiplex grocery stores and "bedroom only" zoning laws, there were neighborhood candy stores, barber shops, tiny markets, women's salons and soda fountains. Often the owners lived up above the store. In some places, these still exist, but in many others they are fast disappearing. In their place are the ubiquitous Condo, Colonial and other assorted Characterless Crap.

> It really promoted a sense of neighborhood. [In my opinion], it is a good thing to chronicle the disappearing aspects of our lives. Like I wish I had a picture of all my brothers and sisters in our PJs on top of my father's Pontiac station wagon at the now rare Drive-in Theater.

Marc A. Williams, *Neighborhood Café, Cleveland*

In his posting on the same Internet site, Ralph Barker writes that "small towns in the Southwest . . . boomed during the heyday of the fabled Route 66 in the 1950s—a time when family auto touring and 'road trips' were 'the' vacation. The bright paint that once attracted customers has long since faded, and now just peels." Morgan Foehl, in response, writes, "Ralph's shot reminded me of this image of another Route 66 casualty I snapped in New Mexico. It makes me wish there were still a way to drive across the U.S. and be able to pull right off the highway into little places like this owned by locals. Here's to the Interstates . . ."

Ralph Barker, untitled (2002)

Morgan Foehl, *Route 66, New Mexico* (2002)

CONSIDER

1. Can a single image capture the essence of a place? Can a hundred images? A thousand? Explain your answer.

2. What is the effect of leaving people out of the photographs on pages 217–218? How is the decision to focus solely on the place tied to the photographers' purpose? Can you think of contexts in which a photographer might effectively include people to tell the story of a "disappearing place"?

COMPOSE

3. Over the past several years, numerous "urban exploration" sites have sprung up on the Internet. As a group called Infiltration (www.infiltration.org) puts it, these sites are about "going places you're not supposed to go"—abandoned malls, shopping centers, factories, mills, even disaster sites. Visit one of these Web sites, and analyze the portraits of the vanishing places that are presented. For example, you might think about what it is that "urban explorers" see in these places that is worthy of their attention and documentation.

My Ghost Town: A Vanishing Personal History

Jenny Attiyeh
(2001)

FYI Jenny Attiyeh has been reporting on politics, the arts, and culture since 1987. She is currently a freelance reporter based in Boston, writing regularly for newspapers including the *Christian Science Monitor* and the *Boston Globe*.

GRAFTON, Utah—My grandfather liked to dare me to walk to the cemetery at night, up the mud road from our house, past the orchards, the looming cows, past the tumble-down barn into the open, empty fields. From there I could almost see the mounds rising against the bluff. Grampa urged me on. Early settlers were buried here in unmarked graves, and nearby lay the headstone of a young boy, killed by Indians. As I turned and headed rapidly for home, I could hear Grampa chuckling in the dark.

It was Grampa who had brought us to Grafton, this ghost town on the edge of Zion National Park. He was born and raised in Utah, and wanted us to take part, to learn to love it as he did. So we camped out in an old adobe brick house, without running water or electricity, on a few acres of land my parents had bought. I was a little girl in diapers when we first came here for long holidays, driving from Los Angeles in a tattered VW Bug. The town—a handful of abandoned buildings, apple trees, lizards and the Virgin River, carving too close to the bank—became mine.

Happiness for me was waking up from a nap to eat watermelon by the irrigation ditch that ran in front of our house. At least that's how it seems when I look at the photograph—my eyes are still sleepy, my white shirt a makeshift napkin, fingerprinted with a mixture of juice and red Utah dust. At night we slept on cots, with an applewood fire spitting out cinders onto our canvas sleeping bags. In the mornings, frost lined the windows, and it was so cold I was afraid to get out of bed.

But that was 30 years ago. Today, Grafton as I knew it is dying. There are no windows left in the old brick house, and the walls are scarred with graffiti. On the mantelpiece it reads, "Albert Loves Rhonda for Eternity and Mike." Deep cracks in the walls have encouraged passers-by to help themselves to the fired bricks. And down by the river, another empty house gapes, its front porch torn off by vandals. With its supports removed, the second story wall collapsed soon after, exposing adobe bricks to the melting rain.

We'd heard the rumors, of course. Grafton was falling apart, but we were far away. Now, we've finally come back to see what's left of our land.

I had no idea it was so beautiful. As a child, I had taken the place for granted—the still warmth of the afternoons, the slow brown river, the red sandstone cliffs poking into the sky. Down the road, I looked for the Indian chief my grandfather had drawn on the blackboard of the schoolhouse, but he was long gone.

As I stood and watched, a dozen teenagers climbed into the open face of a deserted house nearby, up the broken staircase to the second floor. They were laughing and shoving each other—giggling at the poetry sprayed on the plaster walls. I felt like a tight-faced schoolmarm, injured and entitled, and I told them to get down. "Can't you guys read the sign?" They did not answer, and moved off.

It became clear to me that I really didn't want to share this town with anyone—I just wanted to be left alone, to piece together the past. But my claims on Grafton were as nothing compared to those who came before me. Built by Mormons in 1859, the settlement was doomed from the start. Frequent flooding of the Virgin River washed away the crops and destroyed irrigation ditches, making life close to impossible. At one point, the entire town was relocated upstream, but to no avail. By the 1930s, Grafton had turned into a ghost town, gathering beer bottles and tumbleweeds.

I realize now that I, too, have abandoned Grafton—to the trash, the vandals, the deterioration. Perhaps I can make amends. Sheepishly, I begin to clean up. My father and I pick up loose boards from a collapsed shed and put them in a pile. A rusty nail grazes my palm. We make slow progress, but as the debris grows higher, I feel vaguely comforted.

Soon, the town will be busy with the sounds of restoration. In the past few years, a group of local townspeople and grassroots environmentalists has banded together to preserve what's left of Grafton. They plan to stabilize the old buildings and keep a close watch on the place to cut down on vandalism. There's already a shiny red gate blocking access to the adobe church, and a spanking-new sign explaining what is to come.

Grafton is soon to become a place of public purpose. But when I consider the pamphlets to be distributed at the information booth, I am sick at the thought—for Grafton is no longer mine. It has been appropriated.

For my part, I like Grafton best the way it used to be, but it is too late for that now. Already, too many tourists, drawn by the guidebooks, come to gawk at the town, leaving behind their lunch wrappers. I want the Grafton of my childhood, serene and apart. A place where I could commune with cows and watch the stinging red ants build their hills in the dirt. I would have liked my own daughter to play here someday, lost in daydreams.

It is almost dusk now, and the crickets buzz softly in the grass. As I stretch out on the front porch, I hear my parents' voices inside, low and reassuring. The red mountains fade to brown in the dying light. Gawkers pass by, making tracks in the dirt road. They call out, "No Trespassing!" and drive on by.

"We own the place," I tell them. But they probably don't believe me. And, in some way, it really isn't true. Slowly the dust resettles, and the crickets start up again. Slightly panicked, I look around at my old haunts. I'd like the sun to set quietly on Grafton, and its ghosts. At the cemetery up the road, there is no more room.

CONSIDER

1. Reread "My Ghost Town: A Vanishing Personal History," paying special attention to the specific details Attiyeh uses to describe Grafton. Which details are most effective in helping you "see" the town? Which particular words and phrases do you find most powerful?

2. Why do you think Attiyeh is annoyed when she encounters teenagers exploring the old schoolhouse? How, in her opinion, is their interest in Grafton different from hers? Do you agree that there's a difference? Why or why not?

COMPOSE

3. Make a list of ten places that are or have been important in your life. Then list the events, experiences, and emotions you associate with each place. Have any of these "disappeared" from your life? If so, how? If not, why not?

CHALLENGE

4. Nostalgia is a powerful feeling, one that shows up in nearly every aspect of our lives and influences fashion, art, architecture, film, and product design. More often than not, nostalgia is considered harmless. But might this relentless yearning for times past create problems for an individual or even a society? (For example, some Russians living now in a freer and less stable society long for the stability of the more repressive Communist era.) Study manifestations of nostalgia in a specific group or segment of society, and then write a serious paper evaluating the very human inclination to cherish things long gone.

5. Write an essay eulogizing a place from your childhood that no longer exists.

From The Grapes of Wrath

John Steinbeck
(1939)

CHAPTER 12

Highway 66 is the main migrant road. 66—the long concrete path across the country, waving gently up and down on the map, from the Mississippi to Bakersfield—over the red lands and the gray lands, twisting up into the mountains, crossing the divide and down into the bright and terrible desert, and across the desert to the mountains again, and into the rich California valleys.

66 is the path of a people in flight, refugees from dust and shrinking land, from the thunder of tractors and shrinking ownership, from the desert's slow northward invasion, from the twisting winds that howl up out of Texas, from the floods that bring no richness to the land and steal what little richness is there. From all of these the people are in flight, and they come into 66 from the tributary side roads, from the wagon tracks and the rutted country roads. 66 is the mother road, the road of flight.

Clarksville and Ozark and Van Buren and Fort Smith on 64, and there's an end of Arkansas. And all the roads into Oklahoma City, 66 down from Tulsa, 270 up from McAlester. 81 from Wichita Falls south, from Enid north. Edmond, McLoud, Purcell. 66 out of Oklahoma City; El Reno and Clinton, going west on 66. Hydro, Elk City, and Texola; and there's an end to Oklahoma. 66 across the Panhandle of Texas. Shamrock and McLean, Conway and Amarillo, the yellow. Wildorado and Vega and Boise, and there's an end of Texas. Tucumcari and Santa Rosa and into the New

Mexican mountains to Albuquerque, where the road comes down from Santa Fe. Then down the gorged Rio Grande to Las Lunas and west again on 66 to Gallup, and there's the border of New Mexico.

And now the high mountains. Holbrook and Winslow and Flagstaff in the high mountains of Arizona. Then the great plateau rolling like a ground swell. Ashfork and Kingman and stone mountains again, where water must be hauled and sold. Then out of the broken sun-rotted mountains of Arizona to the Colorado, with green reeds on its banks, and that's the end of Arizona. There's California just over the river, and a pretty town to start it. Needles, on the river. But the river is a stranger in this place. Up from Needles and over a burned range, and there's the desert. And 66 goes on over the terrible desert, where the distance shimmers and the black center mountains hang unbearably in the distance. At last there's Barstow, and more desert until at last the mountains rise up again, the good mountains, and 66 winds through them. Then suddenly a pass, and below the beautiful valley, below orchards and vineyards and little houses, and in the distance a city. And, oh, my God, it's over.

The people in flight streamed out on 66, sometimes a single car, sometimes a little caravan. All day they rolled slowly along the road, and at night they stopped near water. In the day ancient leaky radiators sent up columns of steam, loose connecting rods hammered and pounded. And the men driving the trucks and the overloaded cars listened apprehensively. How far between towns? It is a terror between towns. If something breaks—well, if something breaks we camp right here while Jim walks to town and gets a part and walks back and—how much food we got?

Listen to the motor. Listen to the wheels. Listen with your ears and with your hands on the steering wheel; listen with the palm of your hand on the gearshift lever; listen with your feet on the floor boards. Listen to the pounding old jalopy with all your senses, for a change of tone, a variation of rhythm may mean—a week here? That rattle—that's tappets. Don't hurt a bit. Tappets can rattle till Jesus comes again without no harm. But that thudding as the car moves along—can't hear that—just kind of feel it. Maybe oil isn't gettin' someplace. Maybe a bearin's startin' to go. Jesus, if it's a bearing, what'll we do? Money's goin' fast. And why's the son-of-a-bitch heat up so hot today? This ain't no climb. Le's look. God Almighty, the fan belt's gone! Here, make a belt outa this little piece a rope. Le's see how long—there. I'll splice the ends. Now take her slow—slow, till we can get to a town. That rope belt won't last long.

'F we can on'y get to California where the oranges grow before this here ol' jug blows up. 'F we on'y can.

And the tires—two layers of fabric worn through. On'y a four-ply tire. Might get a hundred miles more outa her if we don't hit a rock an' blow her. Which'll we take—a hunderd, maybe, miles, or maybe spoil the tubes? Which? A hunderd miles. Well, that's somepin you got to think about. We got tube patches. Maybe when she goes she'll only spring a leak. How about makin' a boot? Might get five hunderd more miles. Le's go on till she blows.

We got to get a tire, but, Jesus, they want a lot for a ol' tire. They look a fella over. They know he got to go on. They know he can't wait. And the price goes up.

Take it or leave it. I ain't in business for my health. I'm here a-sellin' tires. I ain't givin' 'em away. I can't help what happens to you. I got to think what happens to me.

How far's the nex' town?

I seen forty-two cars a you fellas go by yesterday. Where you all come from? Where all of you goin'?

Well, California's a big state.

It ain't that big. The whole United States ain't that big. It ain't that big. It ain't big enough. There ain't room enough for you an' me, for your kind an' my kind, for rich and poor together all in one country, for thieves and honest men. For hunger and fat. Whyn't you go back where you come from?

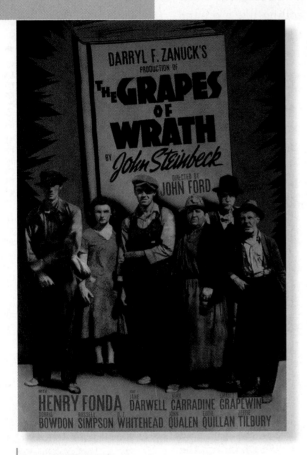

Poster for the 1940 film based on *The Grapes of Wrath*, directed by John Ford

This is a free country. Fella can go where he wants.

That's what *you* think! Ever hear of the border patrol on the California line? Police from Los Angeles—stopped you bastards, turned you back. Says, if you can't buy no real estate we don't want you. Says, got a driver's license'? Le's see it. Tore it up. Says you can't come in without no driver's license.

It's a free country.

Well, try to get some freedom to do. Fella says you're jus' as free as you got jack to pay for it.

In California they got high wages. I got a han'bill here tells about it.

Baloney! I seen folks comin' back. Somebody's kiddin' you. You want that tire or don't ya'?

Got to take it, but, Jesus, mister, it cuts into our money! We ain't got much left.

Well, I ain't no charity. Take her along.

Got to, I guess. Let's look her over. Open her up, look a' the casing—you son-of-a-bitch, you said the casing was good. She's broke damn near through.

The hell she is. Well—by George! How come I didn' see that?

You did see it, you son-of-a-bitch. You wanta charge us four bucks for a busted casing. I'd like to take a sock at you.

Now keep your shirt on! I didn' see it, I tell you. Here—tell ya what I'll do. I'll give ya this one for three-fifty.

You'll take a flying jump at the moon! We'll try to make the nex' town.

Think we can make it on that tire? Got to. I'll go on the rim before I'd give that son-of-a-bitch a dime.

What do ya think a guy in business is? Like he says, he ain't in it for his health. That's what business is. What'd you think it was? Fella's got—See that sign 'longside the road there? Service Club. Luncheon Tuesday, Colmado Hotel? Welcome, brother. That's a Service Club. Fella had a story. Went to one of them meetings an' told the story to all them business men. Says, when I was a kid my ol' man give me a haltered heifer an' says take her down an' git her serviced. An the fella says, I done it, an' ever' time since then when I hear a business man talkin' about service, I wonder who's gettin' screwed. Fella in business got to lie an cheat, but he calls it somepin else. That's what's impor-tant. You go steal that tire an' you're a thief, but he tried to steal your four dollars for a busted tire. They call that sound business.

Danny in the back seat wants a cup a water. Have to wait. Got no water here.

Listen—that the rear end? Can't tell.

Sound telegraphs through the frame. There goes a gasket. Got to go on. Listen to her whistle. Find a nice place to camp an' I'll jerk the head off. But, God Almighty, the food's gettin' low, the money's gettin' low. When we can't buy no more gas—what then?

Danny in the back seat wants a cup a water. Little fella's thirsty.

Listen to that gasket whistle. Chee-rist! There she went. Blowed tube an' casing all to hell. Have to fix her. Save that casing to make boots; cut 'em out an' stick 'em inside a weak place.

Cars pulled up beside the road, engine heads off, tires mended. Cars limping along 66 like wounded things, panting and struggling. Too hot, loose connections, loose bearings, rattling bodies.

Danny wants a cup a water.

People in flight along 66. And the concrete road shone like a mirror under the sun, and in the distance the heat made it seem that there were pools of water in the road.

Danny wants a cup a water.

He'll have to wait, poor little fella. He's hot. Nex' service station. *Service* station, like the fella says.

Two hundred and fifty thousand people over the road. Fifty thousand old cars—wounded, steaming. Wrecks along the road, abandoned. Well, what happened to them? What happened to the folks in that car? Did they walk? Where are they? Where does the courage come from? Where does the terrible faith come from?

And here's a story you can hardly believe, but it's true, and it's funny and it's beautiful. There was a family of twelve and they were forced off the land. They had no car. They built a trailer out of junk and loaded it with their possessions. They pulled it to the side of 66 and waited. And pretty soon a sedan picked them up. Five of them rode in the sedan and seven on the trailer, and a dog on the trailer. They got to California in two jumps. The man who pulled them fed them. And that's true. But how can such courage be, and such faith in their own species? Very few things would teach such faith.

The people in flight from the terror behind—strange things happen to them, some bitterly cruel and some so beautiful that the faith is refired forever.

Route 66

Bobby Troup
(1946)

Well if you ever plan to motor west
Just take my way that's the highway that's the best
Get your kicks on Route 66

Well it winds from Chicago to L.A.
More than 2000 miles all the way
Get your kicks on Route 66

Well goes from St. Louie down to Missouri
Oklahoma City looks oh so pretty
You'll see Amarillo and Gallup, New Mexico
Flagstaff, Arizona, don't forget Winona
Kingman, Barstow, San Bernadino

Would you get hip to this kindly tip
And go take that California trip
Get your kicks on Route 66

Well goes from St. Louie down to Missouri
Oklahoma city looks oh so pretty
You'll see Amarillo and Gallup, New Mexico
Flagstaff, Arizona, don't forget Winona
Kingman, Barstow, San Bernadino

Would you get hip to this kindly tip
And go take that California trip
Get your kicks on Route 66

Explore the history and lore of Route 66.
www.ablongman.com/beyondwords14

CONSIDER

1. What is the effect of Steinbeck's use of so many place names in his description of Highway 66 and the people traveling on it? Are you familiar with any of them? Does this matter?

2. What do the lyrics of Troup's 1946 song suggest had changed about Route 66 and the country since Steinbeck wrote in the 1930s?

COMPOSE

3. Compose a piece about a road you routinely travel. It can be in the form of a short paper, a song lyric, a poem, or a photo essay.

CHALLENGE

4. Nearly seventy years after the Dust Bowl migration, thousands of people desperate for a new life are still trying to get to California, though they are traveling north. Using your library or the Internet, research the flow of immigrants from Mexico and the conditions they endure to try to enter America. How are these people different from those who traveled Route 66 to California in the 1930s? How are they the same?

Assignments and Projects

Project 1

Analyzing a Representation of a Place

The images of Jamaica you've encountered in this chapter illustrate that describing a place, whether in words or in images, is always a rhetorical process: What a writer or artist "sees" in a place reflects his or her particular context and point of view. For this project, find a textual or visual representation of a place you know well, and then compose a three- to five-page essay analyzing this representation. Think about the kind of portrait the text or image creates; how it uses words, images, or design elements to convey an impression; and how well it reflects your own sense of what the place is like. For example, you might compare a brochure advertising dormitories at your campus to your own experience living there or evaluate a Web site advertising the restaurant where you waited tables last summer. Or perhaps you recently visited the city where your favorite television show is set. Whatever place you choose, your task is to examine the representation in light of your own experience there.

Before you begin, take a look at "'Still More Monkeys than People': Costa Verde's Rhetorical Paradise" on pages 231–235 to see how student writer Beth Murff approached this task. Consider also the questions for composition first presented in Chapter 2.

WHAT'S IT TO YOU?

- Choose as your **subject** a place that you have strong feelings about, either positive or negative. If you don't care about a place, you probably won't be sufficiently motivated to sift through various representations of that locale to produce an interesting rhetorical analysis.

WHAT DO YOU WANT TO SAY ABOUT IT?

- The **purpose** of your essay will be to help readers understand the representation of a place. You'll need to critically examine the depiction(s) you've selected and bring your own experiences into the discussion to explore the rhetorical dimensions of the representation.

WHO WILL LISTEN?

■ Readers will find your analysis most engaging if they learn something new or unexpected from it. Look for a text that reveals an unusual point of view or that conflicts in interesting ways with your own experiences and might generate a response from your readers. An essay explaining that "this postcard view of the Springlake Amusement Park is completely accurate" doesn't give your **audience** much to think about. But an analysis that helps readers think about the role of amusement parks in contemporary culture will have a broader appeal.

WHAT DO YOU NEED TO KNOW?

■ Once you've chosen the text or image you'll analyze, look closely to determine what qualities of the place it emphasizes. Begin by identifying the qualities of the representation that will become part of the **content** of your essay: What objects or structures are *foregrounded* in the text or image? What is *de-emphasized* or left out? What *point of view* does the text or image invite you to adopt? If people are part of the text or image, who are they and what are they doing? What *emotional associations* does the text or image evoke?

As you begin to identify patterns in the text or image, look for *specific examples*—key words, phrases, images, design elements, or other items—that illustrate those patterns.

Finally, you'll need to inventory your *personal experiences* and memories. Start by freewriting your own description of the place—writing nonstop for five minutes or so on your subject to generate ideas. Then compare your description, point by point, to the patterns you see in the text or image you've analyzed.

HOW WILL YOU DO IT?

■ When you think about the **purpose** of your project, keep in mind that a *rhetorical analysis* of any text—whether it's visual, print, or multimedia—has two main components: First you describe *what* the text does; then you explain *how* it does it. Suppose you're analyzing an informational booklet about the retirement facility where your grandparents live. You will need to describe for your readers the booklet's depiction of the facility ("The booklet emphasizes the homelike atmosphere of Forest Hills Village"); then you will need to show *how* the booklet creates this depiction, pointing to specific words, phrases, or images ("The photos of individual rooms and apartments feature upholstered couches, bookcases, and other typical home furnishings.

Although hospital beds, wheelchairs, and other medical equipment are part of the services offered, these institutional items are never pictured.")

Once you've developed your description and analysis, decide how this material will fit into a larger **structure** or **arrangement**. Since the assignment for your project asks you to analyze and compare, consider a *comparison-and-contrast pattern* (see the Writing Tip below).

Because this is an essay assignment, your primary **medium** will be words. However, if you're analyzing a visual representation of a place, you may decide to include that image or portions of the image to support your analysis, as Beth Murff does in "Still More Monkeys than People." Remember to discuss, cite, and document appropriately any outside text or images that appear in your paper.

HOW WELL DOES IT WORK?

■ Even skilled writers often make **revisions** to an analytical essay after doing a first draft. Review your draft carefully, and if possible, have a classmate or friend review it and offer feedback. Don't hesitate to return to the text or image you're analyzing to check your arguments or to find additional supporting examples. Before you turn in the paper, proofread the text and check the formatting.

> **Tutorial:**
> **Using images in documents**
> www.ablongman.com/beyondwords15

writingTIP

COMPARING AND CONTRASTING

Throughout college and your professional career, you'll likely be asked to make comparisons between two (or more) items and to compose a report, evaluation, or analysis. Here's one effective way to structure a comparison-and-contrast analysis, based on the assignment in Project 1. This model can be adapted for other types of projects as well.

1. Introduce readers to the place and to the image you'll analyze; provide a purpose statement or thesis forecasting your major points
2. Describe the representation you're examining (What does it say about the place?)
3. Analyze the representation you're examining with supporting examples (How does it create that impression?)
4. Compare ways in which the representation is similar to your own experience in the place
5. Contrast ways in which the representation differs from your experiences in the place
6. Summarize your key points and help readers to see their significance.

Of course, this model is only one possibility—arrange your essay to best suit the points you want to make, and consult your instructor or a writing handbook for additional options.

STUDENT PROJECT

Beth Murff, "Still More Monkeys than People":
Costa Verde's Rhetorical Paradise

Murff 1

Beth Murff

Professor Gordon

Composition 103

29 May 2004

"Still More Monkeys than People":
Costa Verde's Rhetorical Paradise

You're going to Costa Rica. What do you want to see while you're there? White sand beaches. The ocean. Palm trees. You want to lounge by the pool with a refreshing drink in hand. You want to see the sights--you know, all that rain forest stuff. The first thing is to find a place to stay. You surf onto the Web site for the Costa Verde Hotel. "Still More Monkeys than People," it says. Monkeys? There are monkeys in Costa Rica! You definitely must see the monkeys. You scroll down to a panoramic ocean view above jungle treetops from a swimming pool sundeck. . . . How do you make reservations?

The Costa Verde is just one of an increasing number of resorts catering to eco-tourists. In this paper, I investigate how the alluring advertisement of this hotel appears to the viewer and how it differs from the reality of the tourists' experience, drawing on materials from the hotel's Web site and experiences from my own one-week stay at the hotel. Do luxury and sensitivity to the local environment really go hand in hand?

It is important to understand why Costa Rica is such an optimal eco-tourist destination. Although the country is made up of only 19,730 square miles and represents a mere 0.03 percent of the landmass of the earth, it is considered "one of the most biologically diverse countries of the world" (Dunlap 83). In fact, about 4 percent of the world's flora and fauna can be found in Costa Rica. Twenty-five percent of the country is protected by national parks, and there are over one hundred private reserves (Dunlop 84). This richness of wildlife lured over one million visitors in 1999 alone, to "visit the birthplace of the term eco-tourism," according to the Costa Rican Tourism Institute (Dunlop 10).

Costa Rica also has its share of environmental problems. Forest cover has decreased from 70 percent to only 23 percent since the 1950s. Even national parks are not free from the dangers of deforestation, because 20 percent of nationally protected areas are still privately owned (Dunlap 100). The Costa Verde Hotel, in fact, is one of the owners of the Manuel Antonio National Park, in which it is located. Manuel Antonio Park covers 1,687 acres of the Pacific coast of Costa Rica, a humid tropical forest zone known for its wildlife and beaches--especially the Central American squirrel monkey, or mono titi (Dunlop 102). Since the monkeys "do not recognize [the] man-made boundaries of the park, they roam freely through the forest, into areas developed for tourism, even onto hotel grounds" (Sheck 168). The Costa Verde is one such hotel whose grounds are traversed daily and nightly by troops of monkeys and other animals. The small hotel is American-owned but locally run, and tourists travel here mostly during Costa Rica's dry season, from December to April.

The first thing one sees on the Costa Verde Web site is the hotel's logo and slogan. The logo is in big green letters, with squirrel monkeys perched on various letters. Underneath it is the slogan "Still More Monkeys than People." There is a site map directly to the left, and

beneath it is a panoramic view of the ocean, seen over lush green tree-tops from a deck beside a blue swimming pool. A brief description of the hotel's amenities is just to the left of an indoor shot of one of the hotel's rooms. Below this are more pool shots and an aerial view pointing to a dense forest, indicating where the hotel is apparently located. Subpages include "Rates," "Rooms," "Houses/Bungalows," "Testimonials," "Our Monkeys," "National Park," "Map," "Q&A," "Weddings," "Restaurants," "Attractions," and "Photo Gallery."

All of these subpages feature several photographs of beaches, pools, and hotel rooms; there are also recurring mentions of monkeys and other wildlife. But there is little actual wildlife pictured other than plants. Only the "Our Monkeys" subpage has several copyrighted photos of squirrel monkeys and an accompanying article from <u>Smithsonian</u> magazine. The remainder of the photos on the site consists mainly of deserted beaches and amiable-looking people in bars and restaurants.

The key words used in the Costa Verde Web site are "monkeys," "view," and "observe." The absence of animals in the photos is a recurring visual element. All of these patterns are significant in terms of frequency. Words frequently used in conjunction with "monkeys" are "foliage," "trees," and "birds." These words suggest that the author of the site views monkeys very much as part of the local environment. The frequent use of the word "monkeys" creates an expectation that there will be many monkeys readily visible but the site presents them as something to be viewed from a distance, as one might view a tree.

The focus on the view is seen even more in the frequent uses of the word "observe," which is used repeatedly to describe what the visitor will do at Costa Verde, such as observing "monkeys," "iguanas," "sloths," "birds," "dolphins," "animals," "plants," and "stones." In the case of the park, the visitor is invited to "observe" rather than remove anything from the grounds. The visitor will be able to sit back and observe nature from a comfortable distance.

Most of the monkeys and sloths that do appear on the Web site are cartoon images rather than actual photos. Perhaps a reason for this is to maintain the professional and civilized demeanor of the hotel. Tourists value comfort, convenience, and luxury, and these are the aspects of the hotel that the Web site portrays.

In summary, the reader is led to believe that a vacation at the Costa Verde Hotel will be full of exotic natural beauty--observed as the "good view" from the window and balcony. The visitor will be able to "see the sights," to experience the wilderness right from his or her air-conditioned hotel room, and feel warm and fuzzy for appreciating nature.

This, however, is not what the visitor experiences at the Costa Verde. The first room we were given had no view at all of the jungle or the ocean. We decided to accept it until we were awakened the next day by children's squeals heard through the wall. After complaining, we moved to a different building closer to the beach. The view was spectacu-lar. The staff at the hotel was friendly--yet there was something unprofes-sional about the place.

The free-roaming monkeys, sloths, and iguanas also gave Costa Verde a much more wild feeling than we expected from the Web site. Walking down a road or sidewalk, I would frequently encounter an iguana in my path. Sitting on my balcony in the evening, I would be startled as a monkey jumped off the roof into the tree not ten feet away. Chatting, we would find a sloth hanging in a shrub behind the pool bar. I did not just "observe" wildlife at Costa Verde--I encountered it at every turn. These experiences did not take place on organized tours and outings; they took place at unpredictable moments.

The culture of Manuel Antonio was also inseparable from the vacation experience. The beach was public, and because of this interaction, the native residents are very present to the visitors. The pristine view of the rain forest is not lessened by the presence of locals, but rather it is the presence of tourists that intrudes on the local culture and ecosystem. For example, one of the biggest dangers to the animals is the power lines that run the length of the tourist beach strip. Even the report's Website admits that electrocution is a common cause of death for its monkeys (Sheck 169).

Is eco-tourism really as eco-friendly as the tourism industry would have you believe? Is the average tourist aware that there may be environmental implications to his or her visit? We have observed how the Costa Verde uses rhetoric on its Web site to convey a certain idea of the place to the viewer. Visitors who have viewed this page may come to Costa Verde with the idea that they will simply be observing nature from a comfortable distance, not interacting with it and thus not disrupting or harming it. They may assume that tourist luxuries and unspoiled wilderness can exist in the same space, without one affecting the other. However, the reality is that man and nature are not separate entities--we must learn to coexist not only in our own backyards and cities but also all over the world.

Works Cited

Costa Verde Hotel Web site. May 20, 2004 <http://www.hotelcostaverde.com/index.htm>.

Dunlop, Fiona. <u>Fodor's Exploring Costa Rica</u>. New York: Fodor's, 2001.

Sheck, Ree Strange. <u>Costa Rica: A Natural Destination</u>. Santa Fe: Muir, 1990.

Project 2

Observing and Analyzing a Public Space

Many of the writers and artists featured in this chapter are fascinated with documenting how the physical characteristics of places influence (and are influenced by) the people who inhabit them. For this project, you'll engage in a similar process of observation. You'll visit a public place, then write a three- to five-page paper that carefully describes and analyzes it in order to identify the connections among the physical space, the people in it, and the activities that go on there. The questions for composing can help you begin developing ideas, collecting material, and writing your draft:

WHAT'S IT TO YOU?

■ Begin by selecting your **subject**—the place you'll visit and describe. Your site can be a building; a small cluster of related buildings, like a strip mall; a portion of a building, such as the lobby of your apartment complex; or an open area such as a park, graffiti wall, or cemetery. Whatever your focus, keep the following points in mind:

Choose a space that interests you and that's not too familiar. If you know a place well, it can be difficult to achieve the *critical distance* that you'll need to observe it with an analytical eye.

Check the *accessibility* of your site. Is it nearby and open to the public? A state prison, hard-hat construction site, or a monastery, no matter how intriguing, probably won't allow easy access, for example.

Reflect on *ethical considerations*. Will the presence of an observer alarm or embarrass people using the space? A lone male observer sitting in a parking garage after dark would almost certainly startle women en route to their cars. Also avoid sites where you're likely to intrude on private conversations or activities—as you might in the locker room at a fitness center.

WHAT DO YOU WANT TO SAY ABOUT IT?

■ While it's important that you provide detailed descriptions of the place you've selected, details alone aren't enough. A key part of your **purpose** is to *analyze* what these details say about the relationship between the physical features of the space and the people and activities you observe there. You'll need to look for interesting *patterns* and *connections* in the information you've collected and use these to focus your discussion:

What catches your eye? Does this space look similar to or different from places that serve similar functions?

Who is here? What are they wearing, doing, and saying? Do they appear comfortable, excited, impatient, tired? Who is not here, and why? Is the space designed to interest particular groups?

How do people use this space? Where do they sit, stand, or gather? What is a "normal" activity here? How can you tell?

How do people interact in this space? Who talks to whom? Who seems to be in charge? How can you tell?

Do you see anything that surprises you? Does anyone use the space in an unexpected way?

WHO WILL LISTEN?

- It's likely that the **audience** for your paper won't have visited your site, so you'll need to describe it thoroughly and vividly (see the Writing Tip on page 211) and to provide specific examples to illustrate the patterns you see. Strive to engage your readers by bringing the sights, sounds, and activities of the place to life, and then by helping your audience see the significance of these details.

WHAT DO YOU NEED TO KNOW?

- Although you'll gather most of the **content** for this project through direct observation, you may first need to do some **background research**: Who owns this space? When was it built, and has it been renovated or changed since that time? Has the space ever been used for something other than its current purpose? Find the answers to these questions by asking owners or employees, consulting local historical societies, checking the archives of local newspapers, or conducting research in the library or online.

  You'll need to spend plenty of time systematically recording what you see. Social scientists use the term **field observation** to refer to this process of collecting information. You'll find guidelines to get you started in the Writing Tip on page 238.

HOW WILL YOU DO IT?

- Think about the **structure** or **arrangement** of your paper in two parts. First you'll introduce readers to your site, providing relevant background information and a thorough *description* of it based on your field observation. Then you'll conclude with *analysis*, drawing readers' attention to one or more ways in which the physical layout of the place seems to influence the ways in which people use or inhabit it. As with all analytical writing, you'll need to provide *supporting examples* and details to illustrate the major points you make in your analysis.

Considerations of **style**—the choices you make about word selection and tone—are especially important in descriptive writing. Concrete details and precise, vivid language will give readers a clear sense of the place and enhance your credibility by showing that you know your subject well. See the Writing Tip on page 211 for more details.

Finally, although the primary **medium** for this project is words, keep in mind that drawings, maps, diagrams, or photographs can introduce readers to your site and provide powerful evidence to support your analysis. Remember that any visual materials you didn't create yourself must be appropriately cited and documented.

HOW WELL DOES IT WORK?

- Start your paper early enough so that you'll have time to return to the site if needed to check facts or fill gaps in your observations. Once you've completed a draft, review it or have a classmate or friend do so, suggesting areas for **revision** and **editing**.

writing TIP

FIELD OBSERVATION

For anthropologists and other social scientists, field observation is a research technique conducted according to well-established, formal methods. As a non-specialist, you won't adhere to such strict conventions in this project. But by following a series of steps similar to those used by social scientists, you can build a detailed and thorough description of a place.

- **Preview your site and make a plan.** Plan at least two visits when you can observe without distractions for at least one hour. Decide in advance what times you'll go, where you'll sit, and how you'll record your observations. Try observing at different times of day and on different days of the week to get a sense of whether activities vary.
- **Draw a map of the space,** showing the location of key structures, surfaces, paths, objects, and other permanent features.
- **Take careful field notes.** Buy a notebook expressly for this purpose, and begin your notes describing each visit on a separate page marked with the date and time. Look carefully at the space and what goes on there, and take as many notes as possible. Decide in advance how you'll organize your field notes. Many researchers use a two-column format, writing factual observations in the left-hand column and personal interpretations and comments in the right-hand column.
- **Review your notes as soon as possible** after the observation session, filling in details, words, or other items that you've left out.
- **Analyze your notes** after a few hours or days have passed, looking for interesting patterns or unexpected findings.

Repeat your field observation process each time you visit the site. And as you analyze each set of notes, look for commonalities and differences from one session to the next.

STUDENT PROJECT

Jeni Byars, "The Rhetoric of Animals in Captivity in South Carolina: The Riverbanks Zoo in Columbia, South Carolina"

In this excerpt from the paper she composed in response to the assignment for Project 2, writer Jeni Byars uses details from several field observation sessions to create a rich portrait of the penguin exhibit at the Riverbanks Zoo:

Byars 4

The penguin exhibit is indoors, with wooden floors and rocks to sit on. Older children and adults mostly sat on the rocks, and the younger kids ran around, walked, and climbed on the exhibit. There is a nook within the wall of the exhibit, a concave glass window that is perfectly child-sized and well-occupied. Sounds of splashing water and seagulls and the smell of fish pervade the atmosphere. A dark brown net draped on a dark purple wall frames an information poster. There is a daily feeding show in this exhibit as well, but the animals are not trained or asked to perform. They provide an interesting, natural show. One stood with his wings puffed up and seemed to be airing himself out. Another penguin rested on his belly and perked upright when humans with food came into the exhibit. The Rock Hopper variety are the only ones that enter the water feet first (the rest dive, head first).

The penguins are first fed in the water and then hand fed, especially the ones in nesting holes (in the wall). Each is given a multivitamin every day, and each has a foot identification band. The floor in the exhibit is made of intercore, in order to protect the birds from "bumblefoot," or callous-like abrasions. The air and water temperature behind the glass is 50 degrees (F), and a painted cloudy and blue sky tapers into the distance on the walls behind the birds. This exhibit illustrates some advantages for animals living in captivity. Their life expectancy rises from 20-25 years (in the wild) to 40 years. They also receive aid when sick, even as much as surgery, if necessary (one was going to have surgery soon for cataracts).

Additional Student Work and the full text of Jeni Byars' paper
www.ablongman.com/beyondwords16

FYI Milton Glaser was educated at the Cooper Union art school in New York and, via a Fulbright Scholarship, the Academy of Fine Arts in Bologna, Italy. His artwork has been featured in exhibits worldwide, including one-man shows at both the Centre Georges Pompidou in Paris and the Museum of Modern Art in New York. His work is in the permanent collections of many museums. Glaser also is a renowned graphic and architectural designer with a body of work ranging from the iconic I♥NY logo to complete graphic and decorative programs for the restaurants in the World Trade Center in New York.

②Interlude

MILTON GLASER

a conversation about designing restaurants

You have worked in so many media. How does restaurant design fit in?

I love to design restaurants—they deal with many elements of form that I'm interested in, including light. I'm very interested in the effect of light on color, in space issues that don't exist on a flat surface. I'm very interested in the fact that you can create, through the use of space, light, and color, a place where people are transformed emotionally. I love the social effect of restaurants—the fact that for a brief moment, you feel better there than elsewhere. Listen to the conversation, the laughter; look at the physiognomies: People seem more sophisticated, more knowledgeable, more elegant—in the right restaurant, you feel enlarged.

What do you think makes people feel good in a space?

We know that people respond naturally to beauty—a mysterious concept that is very difficult to define. There is a kind of satisfaction that comes from beauty, a kind of closure. You experience beauty, and you like it. You feel that you are better for it. This has to do with a sense of form, and the appropriateness of the relationships of forms, like picking the right word, not a general word, but one that seems to be specifically intended for that use in a sentence. The same thing is true about form. There is a sense of inevitability about form, where you say, "Yes, that's exactly the way it should be." As a designer, that's what you aspire to achieve. It means that the systems are perceived as being complete. The same is also true in music. You hear a line of

Mozart, for example, and you realize that the line couldn't be any different. It has to be that way. That line, for that instrument: inevitable. So there is this aspect of inevitability or appropriateness or beauty. We sort of rummage around that a little bit because it's so hard to objectify. But you know a space is working when people feel that they're in the right place.

Achieving this is not easy. You have to do studies. You have to do models. You really have to think things out. You do get to a methodology that works for you, and you begin to anticipate some of the issues, but it's always more complex than you think. You have got to be very adaptable.

What role would you say development plays in design?

Development is extremely important. You've got to keep hacking away at it. And the more complex the problem, the more development there has to be. One thing that has happened that has really damaged the development process is the computer's ability to represent ideas quickly and easily and in a finished way. Writers have told me that when they type something on the computer, it looks so great, they don't want to fuss around with it. They don't want to revisit it—even though it's easy to do—because it already looks "produced." The incentive to modify and change things that occurs when they have a scrawling page of notes and words all over the place doesn't exist when they are working on a computer.

The same thing is true of doing visual work on the computer. It looks already complete, and the middle part—you have an idea, you have development, and you have finish—the middle part gets shrunk because it's already finished as far as you can see. But in the iterative process, you have an idea, you put it down; it's not quite right, so you modify it and change it. There is a sort of fuzzy quality to sketching something when you're not quite sure what it is, but the act of doing it leads you somewhere. There are no sketches in the computer. As soon as you do it, you're finished. You have to make choices from the beginning— this typeface, this color—with the result that it gets clear too soon. As a result, the emphasis shifts from development to getting to the final product, which has become about surface, texture, and appearance. It's as though the skin is great, but the muscularity to support it isn't there because the thinking isn't developed. The thoughtfulness that has to occur while you're struggling with something to change it to its most effective form doesn't get called into play.

What were you hoping to achieve with the Trattoria dell'Arte?

For the Trattoria dell'Arte, one of my objectives was to clearly separate the experience of the spaces. It is a big restaurant, and hard to control experientially, so I wanted there to be a difference between one part of the restaurant and the other. This was partially to accommodate people's different feelings at different times and also to create the sense that the different experiences would justify a return visit. So it was an aesthetic idea as well as a marketing idea as well as a formal idea. All of those considerations came together in the decision to divide the spaces using color strongly, so that as customers move from place to place, they could have a different kind of experience, which would let them be more flexible in where they wanted to sit and what kind of experience they wanted to have.

Incidentally, I learned this from designing supermarkets. The most important thing about designing supermarkets is to change the experience as the person walks through the supermarket. The relentless thing about supermarkets that causes fatigue is the uniformity of the lighting and the experience of space. People get tired when there's no variation. And the same is true of restaurants, especially restaurants the size of Trattoria. You want to make the experience varied enough so people can have different kinds of experiences every time they go.

Do you have any regrets about Trattoria?

Generally speaking, I think this was a very successful job, and I guess what validates it is the fact that it has been so durable and successful for so long. One of the things you're concerned with when you do a restaurant is not to make it trendy. A trendy restaurant, basically, is a doomed restaurant. It means that it's great this year, it's hot this year, but next year, it isn't going to be. The trendy people will have gone elsewhere. So you have to design a restaurant so that the signals are durable. So that people come in and the satisfaction doesn't evaporate, and it doesn't look as though it's "this year's" restaurant. It has to have a kind of spine that makes people feel it's permanent in some way, even though it also has to have excitement and freshness and all the other things.

Exterior   When I was approached to design an Italian restaurant across the street from Carnegie Hall in New York City, I thought of doing an homage to the time I spent in Italy in the early fifties, studying at the Academy of Fine Arts in Bologna. For whatever reason, I thought of putting a large nose in the window (essential to our sense of taste) and calling the place "Il Naso" (The Nose). The owner, a cautious man, was concerned that his Jewish customers might be offended because it sounded too much like "The Nazi." He suggested "Trattoria Dell'Arte," less provocative and safer. In any event, the giant nose remained.

The bar The restaurant consists of a series of spaces, each with a clearly defined spirit. One enters into an informal, low-ceilinged bar area distinguished by a large painting of famous Italian noses in history, by Teresa Fasolino.

Italian sushi bar The floor in the bar is enlivened by a series of tile "throw rugs." At the end of the bar room, we designed an Italian sushi bar with the idea of serving single diners and those in a hurry in an effective and pleasant way. The plaster cast above the banquets to the right of the sushi bar is one of several that form a decorative theme throughout the restaurant. They are enlarged versions of the plaster casts we worked from at the academy to develop our drawing skills. When the restaurant opened, the references to art school were entirely misunderstood by the restaurant critics, who perceived them as some sort of perverse misogynist expression.

Central room The central, high-ceilinged yellow room is based on the studios at the academy, with paintings of human anatomy by Elliot Levine stacked against the wall and a simulated skylight. I wanted the feeling of the room to be expansive. People like to be in an energized space, and they like the idea of the expansive color, light, and high ceiling of this room. Where there is generosity in a space, people get a lift. It is a very different feeling from what is produced by a low ceiling and a darker, more subdued color. Not necessarily a better feeling, but different.

Green room Adjacent to the studio is a more protected, less noisy green room that encourages quieter dining. The color is very strong, and theoretically, if I saw it, I'd say it probably wouldn't work. It seems to be OK, though. Part of it may be just because there is so much yellow adjacent to it in the central room. One of the things that's tough about color and visualizing color is that it is totally susceptible to how much of it there is. This is why, when you see a small color swatch on a wall, it bears no relationship to what it's really going to look like. In addition, lighting conditions totally change the meaning of a color: it can look great under certain light and horrible under others. So the amount of space, the proximity of other colors, the lighting conditions, the atmosphere, the height of the ceilings—all these things have a tremendous impact, and nobody knows anything about it. People will tell you things about saturation in generalities. But the reality is, as anybody who has painted a room knows, it can look great in the can and horrible on the wall. In all design things, you discover, context is everything.

For additional writing projects related to this Interlude see
www.ablongman.com/beyondwords17

CHALLENGE

1. Glaser's purpose is to design places that make people feel good. What are the elements of design that accomplish this goal? What about a place—a restaurant, an apartment, a mall, a retail store—contributes to making people feel good? Based on Glaser's discussion of restaurant design, write an essay that develops a set of criteria for evaluating the design of a place, and then applies these criteria to a specific place that you think is especially well designed.

2. How would you summarize Glaser's opinion of computers as design tools? What, according to his comments here, are the benefits and drawbacks of computer-assisted design? Try an experiment in which you do two versions of a design for a place, one created entirely as freehand sketches on paper, and one entirely on a computer. You might want to create a design for a restaurant, or you could try something different, like an apartment makeover or even an imaginary world for a videogame level. Explore the differences between the two versions and write an analytical essay to present your findings about how computer design tools affect the creative process.

5

MOVING PICTURES

writing to tell stories

Howard Pyle, *Dead Men Tell No Tales* (1899, Oil on Canvas, Kelly Collection of American Illustration)

My picture may be explained as follows
The captain of the pirate vessel and the
first mate called upon three of the crew and
together they have carried a chest of treasures
up among the sand hills on the Atlantic Coast....
The mate shot two of the men as they stood
together resting from their toil....The third
victim started to run, but the captain...
knocked him over with a clean and well
directed shot. As the situation now stands
the mate has no load in either of his pistols
and the captain has one pistol which is yet
loaded. I do not know what happened after
I drew my picture.
—Howard Pyle

Howard Pyle, letter to Mrs. Merton McDonald, describing *Dead Men Tell No Tales*

How important is Pyle's explanation to your understanding of what's going on in *Dead Men Tell No Tales*? Would the painting be more or less compelling without the text alongside it?

How would you tell the story of *Dead Men Tell No Tales*? What would you say about the figure of the captain? What other beginnings or endings can you imagine to the story?

Introduction

I f, as they say, every picture tells a story, why does Howard Pyle bother explaining what happens in *Dead Men Tell No Tales*? Isn't it clear that the captain and the first mate have shot the men dead in the sand? Why do we need to know more? The truth is that recognizing and interpreting the stories told by pictures often requires more than a glance. In fact, Pyle's words help us see just how necessary it is to consider details and weigh alternative possibilities as we read an image.

Pyle explains in his letter that "the third victim started to run" and that the captain tracked his movements, shot, and killed him. We can infer these movements from the footprints in the sand: One set leads to the dead figure in the distance and the other to the captain on the left. We might also analyze the cross atop the mound of sand. What does the fallen shovel signify? When and how was the mound dug? We construct the story by studying these details and developing possible explanations.

When we ask, "*What has happened here*?" we are exploring aspects of narrative. We often associate narrative with fictional texts—novels, plays, poems, and short stories. Yet historical and factual subjects often also take narrative shapes. Think of the stories we find in the news. Photojournalists create images that capture moments in time, instants that might be considered episodes in a larger story. As with Pyle's painting, we can analyze the details in these narratives to consider what takes place before and after that moment.

FYI The beginning of the twentieth century saw an explosion of adventure stories published in serials such as the *Saturday Evening Post* or *Harper's*. The publishing industry recruited numerous artists to create illustrations to accompany stories like *Treasure Island*. Howard Pyle (1853–1911) was among the first and best known of these serial illustrators. His method was to paint a canvas that would then be translated into an etching that could be used by the publishers. He founded the Brandywine school of illustration in 1900, where he trained a number of young painters in the art of illustration.

INTRODUCTION

What's in This Chapter?

In this chapter, we look further at how words and images relate events and tell stories. We begin by examining some texts that describe factual events. Historical images create shared representations of people, places, and events from the past. News images or reports create records that can be quickly distributed, allowing audiences to visualize events almost in real time. Documentary images dramatize social concerns such as child labor and war.

We'll also invite you to look at photographs, stories, and essays that discuss *how* words and images tell stories. For example, we will explore the work of war photographers like Alexander Gardner and essayists who write about images of war, including Susan Sontag. Finally, we will examine how images are used to tell fictional stories in film and graphic novels.

Still from *Girl with a Pearl Earring* (2003)

Reading
Stories

Reading a narrative requires us to examine and interpret details and to think about how they connect information and events. A story pays careful attention to plot, to the sequencing of events. Plot has a corollary in the composition of an image. We can look at the placement of objects, the locations and gestures of figures, foreground and background elements, and the framing of images to better understand what is taking place and what is significant.

Narratives teach us that stories have a beginning, a middle, and an end. Often we think that images present a moment frozen in time, a middle that has no past or future. In fact, every image derives from countless decisions made prior to the clicking of the shutter or the brush of paint on the canvas. Further, images project their messages forward into time, often with deliberate effects in mind. As we examine the ways that words and images tell stories, we can think about these possibilities and consider how they affect our understanding.

As you interpret and respond to the stories told by photographs, drawings, essays, and movie screens, keep in mind the general strategies for analyzing texts outlined in Chapter 1.

What do you see?

What is it about?

To what does it relate?

How is it composed?

What details matter?

What do you see?

When we think of images, we often group them into handy categories—**genres** like portraits, landscapes, advertisements, news photos, and so on. We use similar groupings to understand stories—mystery, science fiction, romance, or adventure. Contemporary narratives, however, expand these categories to include photo essays, slide shows, radio essays, and even music and film. We won't cover all of these categories here, but we will look at some of the ways current methods of communication require us to think beyond simple stories when we consider narrative.

Carole Naggar, from "A Fax for Henri" (2004), a photo essay dedicated to the memory of photographer Henri Cartier-Bresson (1908–2004)

Agitated Buddhist, you probably did not last inside your glass-fronted casket. Elfish spirit you already inhabit the narrow passage between lightning and cloud, rain and sun; you already are within the places, the people, the objects that you photographed and drew ceaselessly, in the mystery of their skin, their sprigs, their pulp. You already live in the boughs of the chestnut trees swayed by Ile de France's breeze; in a ray of gray light over gray slate; on the scissor of legs reflected in a puddle; in the ruins of war; the sleeping, exhausted bodies in a train, these other bodies in ecstasy; you reside in the wrinkles of the writers, musicians and painters you loved, in the perfect gesture of a dancer. In Paris, New York, London. In Africa, India, China. Here? Here. Elsewhere? Elsewhere.

Last year you commented of certain visitors:" They came to touch the hunchback' s hump before he croaks". You, a hunchback? It is true that your life was touched by a great good fortune. But you released time and again its obstructed source, and fanned it like a flame. Against the world and the people, you sharpened your curiosity and wonder like a flint.

We have reached half-life. These last few years, the spiritual landscape that has nourished our beginnings is fading fast. After you, the profession of looking has become more than deserted: it has shrunk, like a shirt too often scrubbed in the boiling waters of commerce.

Consider the growing popularity of Internet slide shows and photo essays. These compositions bring images and text together to tell a story. Unlike texts composed in a single medium, these new genres give writers an opportunity to comment on an image by composing captions that distill its essential qualities or that introduce background information.

These compositions also open up new opportunities for arrangement and sequencing. Their writers must decide not only what to include in the essay, but also in what order to place images and explanatory text. (Find out how to compose your own photo essays and see the work of other students at the end of this chapter and on our Web site.)

Radio essays and slide shows with audio add another level of complication to contemporary forms of narration. Many slide shows include commentary from artists or photographers about the images they have created—often in the form of voice-overs. Items like reports on public radio stations bring together familiar elements of essays—background research, interviews with experts, explanations that describe key issues for listeners—and combine them all into a radio stream offering a story in audio.

The National Public Radio Web site brings oral narrative into a new medium through the technology of streaming audio.

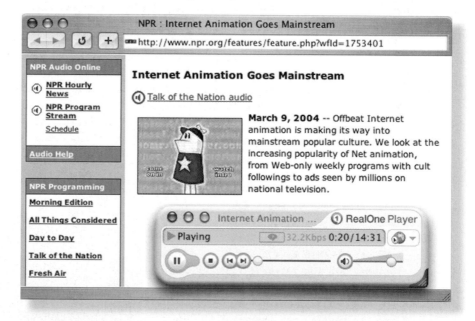

As you interact with audio narratives or photo essays, consider how they both replicate and revise earlier forms of storytelling. Radio essays, for instance, bring forward many traditional elements of oral narrative. At the same time, careful editing selects which parts of the story get told—much of what gets said ends up in the recycling bin. With slide shows and photo essays, you can also consider the decisions made to tell the story—which images are included and why? How are they sequenced? How do they relate to explanatory text?

CONSIDER

CONSIDER

1. How would you respond to someone who argued that photo essays simplify issues and events by reducing explanations to just the short segments of text that ordinarily accompany images? Support your answer after exploring several photo essays in museums, magazines, or online. You can usually find slide shows on current topics at the *New York Times* and *USA Today* Web sites (www.nytimes.com, www.usatoday.com).

2. Do you associate radio programs with delivering information or telling stories? What resources does radio have to enhance the experience of hearing either news or narratives? Before answering, explore the National Public Radio Web site (www.npr.org).

COMPOSE

3. Writing clear and concise captions for a photo essay is challenging. The words must support the images and provide necessary information without overexplaining them. Find several images related to a recent event or trend, and try your hand at writing captions that would help readers understand the significance of the photographs and their relationship to one another.

What is it about?

The core of any story is its plot: You need to understand what's happening. When you encounter an image, the first questions to ask are, "Who's here?" "Who is doing what?" and "Who gets to tell the story?" We can examine the **figures**—the people present in the image itself—as well as the individual or groups who produced it. The figures in an image serve as characters that help tell a story. And as with any message, we can locate the **speaker**, or producer of the image, leading us to considerations of purpose and evaluations of the ethos of the speaker. (For more on ethos, see pages 528–529; for tips on gaining readers' trust, see page 256.)

Determining the speaker behind an image is not always simple. For example, it's easy to miss the tiny print at the end of the "Got Milk?" ad (see page 254) that tells us its sponsor: The National Association of Dairy Farmers. Similarly, we might not recognize the ad's spokesman, world-champion BMX bicyclist Dave Mirra. However, we can still consider both the producer of the image and the figure the image represents as we uncover the story the image is telling. How would you describe Mirra, the lone human figure? What adjectives would you choose to characterize him? What does his pose—standing shirtless and milk-mustached with a bike in one hand, a half-full bottle of milk in the other—suggest about the message offered by the ad?

Miracle maker.

They call me Miracle Boy. Not for my gold medals, but because I've survived double back flips, getting hit by a car, and the mega ramp. What makes me so indestructible? Milk. It helps prevent broken bones. So you can concentrate on breaking records.

got milk?

DAVE MIRRA ©2004 AMERICA'S DAIRY FARMERS AND MILK PROCESSORS

Advertisement created by America's Dairy Farmers and Processors, 2004.

Sometimes we need to investigate the artist or creator behind the image we wish to study. Examining the couple in this photograph by Martin Parr encourages us to refer to Parr's other work to figure out what story he might be trying to convey here. A few minutes of research would reveal that Parr has produced collections with titles like *Bored Couples* and often celebrates average people in everyday situations. We recognize this kind of celebration in the image itself.

Martin Parr, from *Bored Couples* (1993)

More photos by Martin Parr and other images of "ordinary people"
www.ablongman.com/beyondwords18

As important as the speaker or figures in a narrative are the actions they present. When we think of **action** happening in pictures, we generally have movies or television in mind. However, even still images express movement.

The photo of a man running on the platform at Amsterdam Railway Station demonstrates some of the ways action can be represented in an image. The man running is obviously in motion as the shutter snaps (look at his right foot in midair). We can see in his hand gesture a sense of urgency—he is trying to wave someone

Vince Paolo Gerace, *Man Running on the Platform at Amsterdam Railway Station*

down. But there are other kinds of action in the image as well. What about the man holding the little girl? Are they waiting for someone on the train? If so, an implied action is about to take place when their companion enters the frame after stepping off the train.

The *structure* of the image also suggests movement. The train, obviously, conveys a sense of motion. But look also at the logo on the side: its stylized arrows, pointing forward and backward, suggest action. The concrete edge of the platform and the bright yellow bands across the railcar contribute to the sense of horizontal movement.

The *lines* that structure an image also help us visualize movement. Lines may link two objects in a cause-and-effect connection. They may suggest an action in progress, as in Harold Edgerton's high-speed photograph of a bullet passing through a playing card. Can you imagine the trajectory of the bullet and see the trace of its movement in the image?

Harold Edgerton,
High-speed stroboscopic
photo

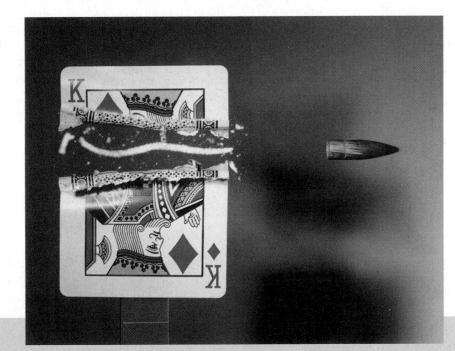

CONSIDER

1. In the photo of the man running on the railway platform, would you say the line created by the handle on the child's tricycle conveys motion? Why or why not?

2. How important are the figures to understanding the actions in *Man Running on the Platform at Amsterdam Railway Station*? If the image consisted only of the railcar and the platform, would it still convey a sense of movement? Explain your answer.

CHALLENGE

3. Locate a photograph that you find interesting and consider all of the ways it expresses movement. What role does the lighting play? What is the relationship between straight and curved lines? How do the foreground and the background create a sense of motion? Write a detailed analysis of how the action in the image contributes to the photograph's message.

To what does it relate?

We often begin thinking about stories by considering their settings. In fictional stories, the setting establishes the atmosphere in which the action takes place. In documentary stories, the setting provides information about the contexts in which an event occurs.

Consider Lewis Hine's photograph of a girl in a cotton mill. We can begin analyzing the image by exploring the **visual setting**. We see innumerable spools of thread mounted in a long line down the length of a mechanical loom housed in a cavernous warehouse. Bare bulbs hang from the ceiling. What mood does the photographer create in showing us this setting? What do these surroundings tell us about the young girl's working environment?

We should also extend our analysis beyond the frame of the image to the **social and historical contexts** in which it originated. *Girl Worker* was taken in 1908, the year Hine began working for the National Child Labor Committee, a nonprofit organization established in 1904 to put an end to child labor. Although thousands of child labor laws, both federal and local, were on the books at the time, most were never enforced. Acceptance of working children was pervasive—rural communities accepted child labor in agriculture, and urban child labor was seen as an economic opportunity for immigrants and poor families. Read within this context, we can see that Hine is telling a much different story.

Lewis Hine, *Girl Worker in a Cotton Mill* (1908)

When images ask us to consider their contexts, they also demand that we examine how our **contemporary context** relates to the historical times and places they document. Obviously, child labor in the United States is no longer a large-scale problem. However, some estimates put the number of child laborers worldwide at over 250 million. We can recognize in efforts to document the abuses of sweatshops and the problems with child labor in agriculture the same need to inform the public about a real problem that might otherwise be ignored.

Images of child labor
www.ablongman.com/beyondwords19

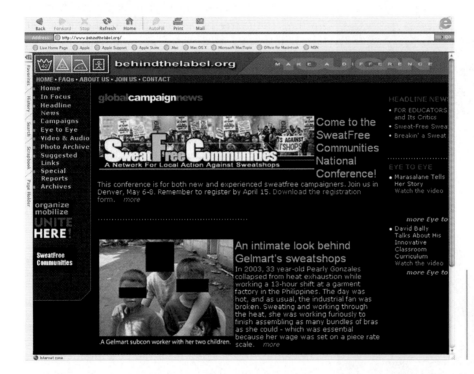

Home page for *behindthelabel.org*, a Web site documenting child labor and related human rights violations in the global clothing industry.

CONSIDER

1. How does knowing the historical and social context of Hine's photograph affect your understanding of the story the photograph tells? Support your answer with specific details from the image.

2. Analyze the setting of the image in the "behind the label" Web page. What can you say about the atmosphere and historical or social contexts evoked by the image?

COMPOSE

3. Browse through the links to images depicting child labor on the *Beyond Words* Web site. Select one image and write a paragraph explaining what its setting reveals about the historical context.

How is it composed?

The arrangement of objects and figures in an image determines in part how images tell their stories. Stories are rarely spontaneous—they are the products of skill and careful planning. Look closely at this set of images taken outside of an arraignment hearing for Michael Jackson. What can you say about how his body functions as an element within the structure of the images?

In the first image, Jackson occupies the left third of the photo, his hands together in applause. A group of fans in the tree in the right third of the image balance Jackson's figure. This **arrangement**, in which Jackson and the group of fans are similarly prominent, presents the singer as a participant caught up in the excitement of the media event. The second image uses the space of the frame quite differently. Jackson occupies the center, and the perspective of the image is cantered up. His raised hand extends the low-angle shot in a gesture of victory. The third image deemphasizes the fans, filling the image with the black-clad figures of Jackson and the man with the video camera.

Smaller objects in the images also speak to issues of arrangement and structure. In the second image, the cameras held aloft by fans are emphasized in the low-angle perspective of the shot—these cameras, like the one snapping the picture, suggest that Jackson is the focal point for fan attention. The third image contains the video camera and the umbrella. In terms of structure and arrangement, the presence of the umbrella is significant. It occupies as much space as either figure, creating an impressive angular shape that draws our attention.

These objects carry symbolic meanings as well. Looking closely, we can also see an insignia on Jackson's jacket—the insignia is the coat of arms for a British military regiment with the motto "Nothing worthwhile is achieved without hard work." The umbrella may function as a symbol for shelter or protection; it also resonates with the black color scheme in all three images of Jackson.

CONSIDER

1. Take a position on whether the Michael Jackson photos on page 260 are authentic or staged. What elements of the images would you cite to support your position?

2. Interpret the significance of the armbands worn by Jackson and his fans in the first and second images. How do they contribute to the story of Jackson's arraignment?

COMPOSE

3. Write one or two paragraphs that analyze how the color black functions in the Jackson images. Would you say the correspondence between the black umbrella and the black clothing of Jackson and his entourage is intentional or accidental? How does black create unity within the images? How do the black objects relate to other elements in the images?

As we read images, we naturally move back and forth between these kinds of symbolic considerations of objects and figures and thinking related to their placement in the structure of the image.

PARAGRAPH ORGANIZATION

writing **TIP**

Thinking about the ways images are arranged can lead us to reflect on how we organize the main elements in a paper—the paragraphs. Each paragraph presents an important component of the overall message. We can look at these main ideas much as we would the objects and figures that make up an image. You are already probably familiar with outlines, which present a linear picture of the components in a paper. You may also have been asked to make a cognitive map or web demonstrating the main ideas in a paper. Both outlining and mapping, however, usually take place before a paper is composed.

As an alternative to these strategies, try creating a visual representation of your paper's organization after you have completed a first draft. Read through the paper, and note in the margin the key idea for each paragraph—if you have trouble recognizing the main idea, you need to tighten the paragraph's focus. Once you have a list of main ideas, experiment with reorganizing them: Arrange ideas in a new sequence. Write some ideas larger than others to show their relative significance. Place ideas in relation to one another horizontally or visually. When you have mapped out an optimal structure for your paper, go back and revise its organization.

What details matter?

As the preceding section points out, even the smallest objects and **design elements** in the composition of an image affect the story it tells. We can touch on only a few ways that films can tell stories here, so we encourage you to look additional insights as you examine the details of the movie and television images you encounter.

For example, film frames can be read using most of the strategies for examining the details in any image—we can look at aspects like *framing*, *arrangement*, and *lighting* to describe and interpret what we see. How, for instance, would you say lighting and framing work in this film still from *The Girl with the Pearl Earring* (2003)? Do differences in lighting shape your response to the two characters?

We can also look at camera distance and angles when thinking about images from films. Shots can range from extreme long shots to extreme close-ups, the distance determining how much of the image fills the frame.

Camera angles also reveal something about the point of view represented in a film. What effect would you say the camera angle in this image from *Gladiator* (2000) has on the figure? Does he appear vulnerable or invincible? Why? The complete picture created by elements like arrangement, framing, and camera angles is often called the *mise-en-scène* of the film image. This French term literally means "putting into the scene" and includes every aspect of the image within the frame of the film.

Stills from *American Beauty* (1999)

You should also pay attention to **editing** when you examine films. In films, stories are told by weaving together a number of shots to create a scene. A shot represents the moment the camera begins rolling to the moment it stops—one take of the camera. Shots may be continuous, tracking subjects within a scene and moving from one figure to another, or they may be discrete, individual takes that are then sequenced together in editing. The two frames above from the film *American Beauty* (1999) demonstrate two distinct shots that are edited together as part of a scene in which Lester Burnham (Kevin Spacey) discovers that his wife Carolyn (Annette Bening) is having an affair and she learns that he is secretly serving fast food. In this scene, the camera angles allow us to view the perspectives of both Lester and Carolyn as they confront one another.

Examine the role of editing and narration in film.
www.ablongman.com/beyondwords20

CONSIDER

1. Do you think it does justice to the medium of film to break movies down into frames and study them as images? What potential drawbacks can you think of? What benefits?

2. Most films involve multiple people working together to create images—lighting technicians, directors, camera operators, actors. Can you think of other images that are created collaboratively?

3. Most films strive to achieve continuity in their editing—that is, they present an arrangement of shots, scenes, and transitions that feels natural and seamless. How conscious are you of editing techniques when you view movies or television? How might we apply the storytelling techniques of films to our other compositions?

COMPOSE

4. Think about the film term *mise-en-scène*. The term applies to technical elements such as framing, arrangement, lighting, and camera angles, but also to the general atmosphere created on a film frame. *Mise-en-scène* considers the details as parts of a whole and offers descriptions of the overall look and feel of the image. Select two or more images from this chapter, and evaluate them in terms of *mise-en-scène*.

Spreading the News:
Stories of War

Some of the most compelling news stories told through pictures record the lives of soldiers and civilians transformed by the conflicts that seem to define every generation. These stories of war depict not only the atrocities of battle and the destruction wrought by military conflict but also the complex relationships among soldiers, civilians, and reporters.

The Civil War photographs at right by Alexander Gardner do more than represent the aftermath of a terrible chapter in American history. They raise continuing questions about the objectivity and purposes of the individuals who record history. Take *The Sharpshooter's Home.* When it first appeared in a collection of war photographs published by Gardner, it included an elaborate caption describing how the sharpshooter had fired at Union soldiers from behind the rock wall before suffering a wound from a shell ricocheting off the rock formations.

Historians, however, have pieced together a different story. They identified the same soldier in photographs taken below the hill. They also studied the sharpshooter's rifle and concluded that it was likely a prop employed by Gardner in most of his shots. The body of the soldier is most likely that of an infantryman. Gardner and his assistants had carried the body behind the wall, posed it, and taken the picture.

At the time of the Civil War, portrait artists and professional photographers rushed to the battlefield to record the war using the new medium of the photograph. The public was hungry for news and magazines such as *Harper's* that included images became especially popular. Given this climate, it may be that the manipulations behind the photographs can be interpreted as necessary changes to make the events more compelling. At the same time, the newness of the medium meant that questions about the accuracy of representations of events had yet to be explored.

Civil War photographs also reveal the influential role of technologies on images and reporting. Early photographs required technicians to mix chemicals and pour them over glass plates. Plates were heavy and required a portable darkroom for development. The technical difficulties made it impossible for photographers to capture events as they happened. Instead, photographers would arrive after the battle, often taking their time to arrange bodies or otherwise compose images they felt would convey a sense of the conflict.

Alexander Gardner, *Dead Confederate Sharpshooter in "the devil's den"* (1863)

Alexander Gardner, *The Sharpshooter's Home* (1863)

CONSIDER

1. How important are photographs to our understanding of historical conflicts as distant in time from us as the American Civil War (1861–1865)? Given the technological limits of early photography, how confident should we be of their accuracy?

2. Is it possible to represent war fairly in photographs taken after the fact or restaged to enhance their impact? Examine arguments on several sides of the issue.

3. How do you think war photography today relates to that of the Civil War era? What new impediments do battlefield photographers and camera operators face today now that their equipment is more sophisticated, rugged, and mobile?

Contemporary war photography raises additional questions about the representation of war. Advances in technology provide the means for capturing and disseminating images with startling detail and speed. Still, the concerns about how best to represent the atrocities of war persist, as argued in the following article by David Carr and essay by Susan Sontag.

FYI

David Carr reports on media for the *New York Times*. Prior to joining the *Times*, Carr wrote commentary and criticism about the media for *Inside.com*.

Telling War's Deadly Story at Just Enough Distance

David Carr
(April 7, 2003)

In the darkness of a conference room at *Time* magazine last Friday, a war of terrible and beautiful images unfurled on a screen: the steely-eyed marine taking aim, the awe-struck Iraqi pointing to bombers in the sky, the bloodied head of a dead Iraqi with an American soldier standing tall in the background.

The last image was an appalling but vivid representation of American dominance in a very violent week. But Stephen J. Koepp, deputy managing editor of *Time*, dismissed the photograph as a candidate for the issue to be published today. "You want a little picture with your blood," Mr. Koepp said. The photo and editorial staff assembled in the half-light murmured in agreement.

Large numbers of Iraqi soldiers have been killed, according to the Pentagon, and more than 2,000 Iraqi civilians, the government of Saddam Hussein said, many of them in the last week. But when James Kelly, the managing editor of *Time*, lays out the 20 pages of photos intended to anchor the magazine's coverage of the war, there were pictures of soldiers, battles and rubble, but no corpses.

The squeamishness about the carnage that is war's chief byproduct is not restricted to *Time* magazine. During an era when popular culture is filled with depictions of violence and death, and the combination of technology and battlefield access for reporters has put the public in the middle of a shooting war, the images that many Americans are seeing are remarkably bloodless. The heroic narrative is shaped in part by what editors and producers view as a need to maintain standards and not offend their audience. But some cultural critics say that the relatively softened imagery has more to do with a political need to celebrate victory without dwelling on its price. If this is war, they ask, where is the gore?

"War is about dead people, not gorgeous-looking soldiers," said Susan Sontag, author of *Regarding the Pain of Others*. She suggested, "Being a spectator of calamities taking place in another country is a quintessentially modern experience."

It does not get any more modern than a correspondent in the midst of a firefight with a satellite phone and a live visual feed to a 24-hour news channel. But the leap in technology comes with a trade-off in visual clarity. The resolution of the video images is low enough and absent in detail that the war appears scary and chaotic, but rarely bloody.

The real-time field reports are a long march from the work of Matthew Brady, the Civil War photographer whose pictures showed the dead, Americans all, stacked like cordwood. There, too, technology was destiny. Mr. Brady's cumbersome photographic process put a premium on the stillness of the subjects, and no subjects are more patient than the dead. But as photography evolved toward lightweight cameras and higher-speed films, the dead became less visible.

The images of the victims of American wars past—the villagers of My Lai, the charred head of an Iraqi soldier from the Persian Gulf War—created significant controversy when they were published. Some editors and photographers say war photography is edited with a heavier hand because of its ability not just to offend the viewer, but to implicate him or her as well.

"The distinction with war photography is that we have willed that person dead," said Harold Evans, author of *Pictures on a Page*, adding, "We have willed it by sending the soldier there to do that dirty work for us."

Mr. Evans was a vocal defender of publication of the picture of the Iraqi soldier immolated in his vehicle, which created an outcry when it appeared in the *Observer* of London. Daniel Okrent, then managing editor of a weekly version of *Life*, declined to publish the picture.

"It was too horrible, but then I remember thinking, how can it be too horrible to depict war?" Mr. Okrent said. "I don't know if we did the right thing."

Scott Peterson, *US Marines Evacuate Medical Cases from Fallujah,* 17 November 2004

Mr. Kelly of *Time* is in the midst of wondering about similar things. As a way to communicate the costs of the war, he chose a photograph of an Iraqi boy being tended to by his aunt who had been severely burned in a firefight near Baghdad, in addition to losing both his arms and his family.

"You don't want to give the reader a sanitized war, but there has to be some judgment and taste," he said.

Ms. Sontag wondered whom such standards actually protect. "The friends I have all over the world are seeing horrifying images of what is happening when those bombs drop," she said. "I am always suspicious when institutions talk about good taste. Taste belongs to individuals."

John Gaps III, photography director of the *Des Moines Register,* agreed to a point. "Any time you start applying the word *taste* to war, you minimize and trivialize what is happening on the battlefield," said Mr. Gaps, a former Associated Press combat photographer.

Arab news executives said their Western counterparts were misleading viewers and readers by showing a war without death and pain.

"What happens in Iraq is not covered honestly on CNN, BBC," an Al-Jazeera news executive said in a telephone interview from Doha, Qatar. "We don't see any of those killed by the American forces." It also explains, he said, why the rest of the world feels so differently about this war than most Americans do.

Network news executives gave various reasons for their limited tolerance of gore compared with their Arab colleagues. For one, they said, there are more

Arab reporters roving around the towns and villages of the country on their own, while many Western journalists travel with military units that fight and move on. "I don't think people have been walking around body-littered fields," said Jim Murphy, executive producer of the *CBS Evening News*.

Steve Capus, executive producer of the *NBC Nightly News*, said his program is able to communicate the reality of war without reveling in death or injury. "You watch some Arab coverage and you get a sense that there is a bloodbath at the hands of the U.S. military," he said. "That is not my take on it."

Ted Koppel, the anchor of *Nightline*, who is traveling with the Third Infantry Division in Iraq, said the conflict might seem bloodless to viewers at home because it sometimes even seems sanitized to troops who rely on long-range weapons.

"This war is fought in many respects at arm's length," Mr. Koppel said. "The damage is done, people are killed, but without the people who do the killing seeing very much of the consequences until hours or days later, when they advance."

By then, he said, Iraqis have often removed their dead soldiers' bodies. *Nightline* has focused its cameras on bombing victims more than perhaps any other American news program. One recent night, the program focused on civilians mistakenly hit by fire from the Third Infantry Division. One man's chest was bloody, and the camera did not shy away. Another man's left eye was gouged; it showed that, too.

"The fact that people get killed in a war is precisely what people need to be reminded of," Mr. Koppel said.

Ephemeral American standards—no one seems to know where the line is, yet very few transgress it—seem consistent for still and motion photography. The objective, said Howell Raines, executive editor of the *New York Times*, is "to try to capture the true nature of an event, whether it's a disaster like the World Trade Center or a war, but also to do so with restraint and an avoidance of the gratuitous use of images simply for shock value."

Sometimes the shock value of particularly gruesome imagery can have a practical effect. The last time Saddam Hussein was backed into a corner by the United States—in 1991—broadcast reports showed the "highway of death," seeming to indicate an assault on fleeing Iraqis that had turned into mass killing. By some accounts, the administration's fear of the negative publicity led top United States officials to declare a cease-fire without a move first to capture Baghdad or to destroy Republican Guard units. Saddam Hussein lived to fight another day.

John Szarkowski, former director of photography at the Museum of Modern Art and author of several books on photography, said that the scarcity of truly horrific images of war preserves their power when they eventually appear.

"I don't think that editors should feel an obligation to print every bloody picture that comes in," he said. "After a while, people get inured to the suffering in the photograph, and that is not good for anyone. In that sense, each successive image has less impact than the one that came before it."

FYI

Susan Sontag, an essayist, novelist, theater director, and activist who died in 2005, had an abiding interest in photography and culture. Her 1978 book *On Photography* is often cited as groundbreaking in its analysis of the role of photographs in the media and society. She applied a background in literature to critique photographs in terms of both their status as art objects and forces that shape belief and culture. In *Regarding the Pain of Others*, from which this essay is taken, she updates her position on the power of images to change the ways we think about violence. The excerpt reprinted here reflects Sontag's thinking about images and war, although it was written before the War in Iraq began.

From Regarding the Pain of Others

Susan Sontag
(2003)

In June 1938 Virginia Woolf published *Three Guineas,* her brave, unwelcomed reflections on the roots of war. Written during the preceding two years, while she and most of her intimates and fellow writers were rapt by the advancing fascist insurrection in Spain, the book was couched as the very tardy reply to a letter from an eminent lawyer in London who had asked, "How in your opinion are we to prevent war?" Woolf begins by observing tartly that a truthful dialogue between them may not be possible. For though they belong to the same class, "the educated class," a vast gulf separates them: the lawyer is a man and she is a woman. Men make war. Men (most men) like war, since for men there is "some glory, some necessity, some satisfaction in fighting" that women (most women) do not feel or enjoy. What does an educated—read: privileged, well-off—woman like her know of war? Can her recoil from its allure be like his? Let us test this "difficulty of communication," Woolf proposes, by looking together at images of war. The images are some of the photographs the beleaguered Spanish government has been sending out twice a week; she footnotes: "Written in the winter of 1936–37." Let's see, Woolf writes, "whether when we look at the same photographs we feel the same things." She continues:

> This morning's collection contains the photograph of what might be a man's body, or a woman's; it is so mutilated that it might, on the other hand, be the body of a pig. But those certainly are dead children, and that undoubtedly is the section of a house. A bomb has torn open the side; there is still a bird-cage hanging in what was presumably the sitting room. . . .

The quickest, driest way to convey the inner commotion caused by these photographs is by noting that one can't always make out the subject, so thorough is the ruin of flesh and stone they depict. And from there Woolf speeds to her conclusion. We do have the same responses, "however different the education, the traditions behind us," she says to the lawyer. Her evidence: both "we"—here women are the "we"—and you might well respond in the same words.

> You, Sir, call them "horror and disgust." We also call them horror and disgust. . . . War, you say, is an abomination; a barbarity; war must be stopped at whatever cost. And we echo your words. War is an abomination; a barbarity; war must be stopped.

Who believes today that war can be abolished? No one, not even pacifists. We hope only (so far in vain) to stop genocide and to bring to justice those who commit gross violations of the laws of war (for there are laws of war, to which combatants should be held), and to be able to stop specific wars by imposing negotiated alternatives to armed conflict. It may be hard to credit the desperate resolve produced by the aftershock of the First World War, when the realization of the ruin Europe had brought on itself took hold. Condemning war as such did not seem so futile or irrelevant in the wake of the paper fantasies of the Kellogg-Briand Pact of 1928, in which fifteen leading nations, including the United States, France, Great Britain, Germany, Italy, and Japan, solemnly renounced war as an instrument of national policy; even Freud and Einstein were drawn into the debate with a public exchange of letters in 1932 titled "Why War?" Woolf's *Three Guineas,* appearing toward the close of nearly two decades of plangent denunciations of war, offered the originality (which made this the least well received of all her books) of focusing on what was regarded as too obvious or inapposite to be mentioned, much less brooded over: that war is a man's game—that the killing machine has a gender, and it is male. Nevertheless, the temerity of

Woolf's version of "Why War?" does not make her revulsion against war any less conventional in its rhetoric, in its summations, rich in repeated phrases. And photographs of the victims of war are themselves a species of rhetoric. They reiterate. They simplify. They agitate. They create the illusion of consensus.

Invoking this hypothetical shared experience ("we are seeing with you the same dead bodies, the same ruined houses"), Woolf professes to believe that the shock of such pictures cannot fail to unite people of good will. Does it? To be sure, Woolf and the unnamed addressee of this book-length letter are not any two people. Although they are separated by the age-old affinities of feeling and practice of their respective sexes, as Woolf has reminded him, the lawyer is hardly a standard-issue bellicose male. His antiwar opinions are no more in doubt than are hers. After all, his question was not, What are your thoughts about preventing war? It was, How in your opinion are we to prevent war?

It is this "we" that Woolf challenges at the start of her book: she refuses to allow her interlocutor to take a "we" for granted. But into this "we," after the pages devoted to the feminist point, she then subsides. No "we" should be taken for granted when the subject is looking at other people's pain.

Who are the "we" at whom such shock-pictures are aimed? That "we" would include not just the sympathizers of a smallish nation or a stateless people fighting for its life, but—a far larger constituency—those only nominally concerned about some nasty war taking place in another country. The photographs are a means of making "real" (or "more real") matters that the privileged and the merely safe might prefer to ignore.

"Here then on the table before us are photographs," Woolf writes of the thought experiment she is proposing to the reader as well as to the spectral lawyer, who is eminent enough, as she mentions, to have K.C., King's Counsel, after his name and may or may not be a real person. Imagine then a spread of loose photographs extracted from an envelope that arrived in the morning post. They show the mangled bodies of adults and children. They show how war evacuates, shatters, breaks apart, levels the built world. "A bomb has torn open the side," Woolf writes of the house in one of the pictures. To be sure, a cityscape is not made of flesh. Still, sheared-off buildings are almost as eloquent as bodies in the street. (Kabul, Sarajevo, East Mostar, Grozny, sixteen acres of lower Manhattan after September 11, 2001, the refugee camp in Jenin. . . .) Look, the photographs say, *this* is what it's like. This is what war does. And *that*, that is what it does, too. War tears, rends. War rips open, eviscerates. War scorches. War dismembers. War ruins.

Not to be pained by these pictures, not to recoil from them, not to strive to abolish what causes this havoc, this carnage—these, for Woolf, would be the

Running for Cover,
January 1942

reactions of a moral monster. And, she is saying, we are not monsters, we are members of the educated class. Our failure is one of imagination, of empathy: we have failed to hold this reality in mind.

But is it true that these photographs, documenting the slaughter of non-combatants rather than the clash of armies, could only stimulate the repudiation of war? Surely they could also foster greater militancy on behalf of the Republic. Isn't this what they were meant to do? The agreement between Woolf and the lawyer seems entirely presumptive, with the grisly photographs confirming an opinion already held in common. Had the question been, How can we best contribute to the defense of the Spanish Republic against the forces of militarist and clerical fascism? the photographs might instead have reinforced their belief in the justness of that struggle.

The pictures Woolf has conjured up do not in fact show what war, war as such, does. They show a particular way of waging war, a way at that time routinely described as "barbaric," in which civilians are the target. General Franco was using the same tactics of bombardment, massacre, torture, and the killing and mutilation of prisoners that he had perfected as a commanding officer in Morocco in the 1920s. Then, more acceptably to ruling powers, his victims had been Spain's colonial subjects, darker-hued and infidels to boot; now his victims were compatriots. To read in the pictures, as Woolf does, only what confirms a general abhorrence of war is to stand back from an engagement with Spain as a country with a history. It is to dismiss politics.

For Woolf, as for many antiwar polemicists, war is generic, and the images she describes are of anonymous, generic victims. The pictures sent out by the government in Madrid seem, improbably, not to have been labeled. (Or perhaps Woolf is simply assuming that a photograph should speak for itself.) But the case against war does not rely on information about who and

George Strock, *Dead US Soldiers on the Beach at Buna, New Guinea* (1943)

when and where; the arbitrariness of the relentless slaughter is evidence enough. To those who are sure that right is on one side, oppression and injustice on the other, and that the fighting must go on, what matters is precisely who is killed and by whom. To an Israeli Jew, a photograph of a child torn apart in the attack on the Sbarro pizzeria in downtown Jerusalem is first of all a photograph of a Jewish child killed by a Palestinian suicide-bomber. To a Palestinian, a photograph of a child torn apart by a tank round in Gaza is first of all a photograph of a Palestinian child killed by Israeli ordnance. To the militant, identity is everything. And all photographs wait to be explained or falsified by their captions. During the fighting between Serbs and Croats at the beginning of the recent Balkan wars, the same photographs of children killed in the shelling of a village were passed around at both Serb and Croat propaganda briefings. Alter the caption, and the children's deaths could be used and reused.

Images of dead civilians and smashed houses may serve to quicken hatred of the foe, as did the hourly reruns by Al-Jazeera, the Arab satellite television network based in Qatar, of the destruction in the Jenin refugee camp in April 2002. Incendiary as that footage was to the many who watch Al-Jazeera throughout the world, it did not tell them anything about the Israeli army they were not already primed to believe. In contrast, images offering evidence that contradicts cherished pieties are invariably dismissed as having been staged for the camera. To photographic corroboration of the atrocities committed by one's own side, the standard response is that the pictures are a fabrication, that no such atrocity ever took place, those were bodies the other side had brought in trucks from the city morgue and placed about the street, or that, yes, it happened and it was the other side who did it, to themselves. Thus the chief of propaganda for Franco's Nationalist rebellion maintained that it was the Basques who had destroyed their own ancient town and former capital, Guernica, on April 26, 1937, by placing dynamite in the sewers (in a later version, by dropping bombs manufactured in Basque territory) in order to inspire indignation abroad and reinforce the Republican resistance. And thus a majority of Serbs living in Serbia or abroad maintained right to the end of the Serb siege of Sarajevo, and even after, that the Bosnians themselves perpetrated the horrific "breadline massacre" in May 1992 and "market massacre" in February 1994, lobbing large-caliber shells into the center of their capital or planting mines in order to create some exceptionally gruesome sights for the foreign journalists' cameras and rally more international support for the Bosnian side.

Photographs of mutilated bodies certainly can be used the way Woolf does, to vivify the condemnation of war, and may bring home, for a spell, a portion of its reality to those who have no experience of war at all. However, someone who accepts that in the world as currently divided war can become inevitable, and even just, might reply that the photographs supply no evidence, none at all, for renouncing war—except to those for whom the notions of valor and sacrifice have been emptied of meaning and credibility. The destructiveness of war—short of total destruction, which is not war but suicide—is not in itself an argument against waging war unless one thinks (as few people actually do think) that violence is always unjustifiable, that force is always and in all circumstances wrong—wrong because, as Simone Weil affirms in her sublime essay on war, "The Iliad, or The Poem of Force" (1940), violence turns anybody subjected to it into a thing. No, retort those who in a given situation see no alternative to armed struggle, violence can exalt someone subjected to it into a martyr or a hero. In fact, there are many uses of the innumerable opportunities a modern life supplies for regarding—at a distance, through the medium of photography—other people's pain. Photographs of an atrocity may give rise to opposing responses. A call for peace. A cry for revenge. Or simply the bemused awareness, continually restocked by photographic information, that terrible things happen. Who can forget the three color pictures by Tyler Hicks that the *New York Times* ran across the upper half of the first page of its daily section devoted to America's new war, "A Nation Challenged," on November 13, 2001? The triptych depicted the fate of a wounded Taliban soldier in uniform who had been found in a ditch by Northern Alliance soldiers advancing toward Kabul. First panel: being dragged on his back by two of his captors—one has grabbed an arm, the other a leg—along a rocky road. Second panel (the camera is very near): surrounded, gazing up in terror as he is being pulled to his feet. Third panel: at the moment of death, supine with arms outstretched and knees bent, naked and bloodied from the waist down, being finished off by the military mob that has gathered to butcher him. An ample reservoir of stoicism is needed to get through the great newspaper of record each morning, given the likelihood of seeing photographs that could make you cry. And the pity and disgust that pictures like Hicks's inspire should not distract you from asking what pictures, whose cruelties, whose deaths are *not* being shown.

For a long time some people believed that if the horror could be made vivid enough, most people would finally take in the outrageousness, the insanity of war.

Fourteen years before Woolf published *Three Guineas*—in 1924, on the tenth anniversary of the national mobilization in Germany for the First World War—the conscientious objector Ernst Friedrich published his *Krieg dem Kriege! (War Against War!)*. This is photography as shock therapy: an album of more than one hundred and eighty photographs mostly drawn from German military and medical archives, many of which were deemed unpublishable by government censors while the war was on. The book starts with pictures of toy soldiers, toy cannons, and other delights of male children everywhere, and concludes with pictures taken in military cemeteries. Between the toys and the graves, the reader has an excruciating photo-tour of four years of ruin, slaughter, and degradation: pages of wrecked and plundered churches and castles, obliterated villages, ravaged forests, torpedoed passenger steamers, shattered vehicles, hanged conscientious objectors, half-naked prostitutes in military brothels, soldiers in death agonies after a poison-gas attack, skeletal Armenian children. Almost all the sequences in *War Against War!* are difficult to look at, notably the pictures of dead soldiers belonging to the various armies putrefying in heaps on fields and roads and in the front-line trenches. But surely the most unbearable pages in this book, the whole of which was designed to horrify and demoralize, are in the section titled "The Face of War," twenty-four close-ups of soldiers with huge facial wounds. And Friedrich did not make the mistake of supposing that heartrending, stomach-turning pictures would simply speak for themselves. Each photograph has an impassioned caption in four languages (German, French, Dutch, and English), and the wickedness of militarist ideology is excoriated and mocked on every page. Immediately denounced by the government and by veterans' and other patriotic organizations—in some cities the police raided bookstores, and lawsuits were brought against the public display of the photographs—Friedrich's declaration of war against war was acclaimed by left-wing writers, artists, and intellectuals, as well as by the constituencies of the numerous antiwar leagues, who predicted that the book would have a decisive influence on public opinion. By 1930, *War Against War!* had gone through ten editions in Germany and been translated into many languages.

In 1938, the year of Woolf's *Three Guineas,* the great French director Abel Gance featured in close-up some of the mostly hidden population of hideously disfigured excombatants—*les gueules cassées* ("the broken mugs") they were nicknamed in French at the climax of his new *J'accuse.* (Gance had made an earlier, primitive version of his incomparable antiwar film, with the same hallowed title, in 1918.) As in the final section of Friedrich's book, Gance's film ends in a new military cemetery, not just to remind us of how many millions of young men were sacrificed to militarism and ineptitude between 1914 and 1918 in the war cheered on as "the war to end all wars," but to advance the sacred judgment these dead would surely bring against Europe's politicians and generals could they know that, twenty years later, another war was imminent. "*Morts de Verdun, levez-vous!*" (Rise, dead of Verdun!), cries the deranged veteran who is the protagonist of the film, and he repeats his summons in German and in English: "Your sacrifices were in vain!" And the vast mortuary plain disgorges its multitudes, an army of shambling ghosts in rotted uniforms with mutilated faces, who rise from their graves and set out in all directions, causing mass panic among the populace already mobilized for a new pan-European war. "Fill your eyes with this horror! It is the only thing that can stop you!" the madman cries to the fleeing multitudes of the living, who reward him with a martyr's death, after which he joins his dead comrades: a sea of impassive ghosts overrunning the cowering future combatants and victims of *la guerre de demain.* War beaten back by apocalypse.

And the following year the war came.

Explore Sontag's essay in depth.
www.ablongman.com/beyondwords21

CONSIDER

1. What standards should the media use in choosing images of war for public broadcast? When—if ever—might it be acceptable to "sanitize" images of war in newspapers or TV broadcasts?

2. Has the public become desensitized to images of war and violence now that newspapers, television news, and the Web bring combat and terror incidents directly into the home? What would we gain in sensitivity—if anything—by restricting the graphic images?

3. What point does Susan Sontag make about men, women, and war? Do you agree? Why or why not?

COMPOSE

4. The embedding of journalists and photographers with coalition combat troops during the 2003 war between the United States and Iraq was controversial. The public received battlefield reports and films of combat almost instantly. Some analysts argue that the objectivity and independence of the journalists were compromised by the close relationships they developed with coalition troops and the restrictions placed on them by the need to conceal troop movements, numbers, and strategies. Use library and Web resources to explore the issues raised by embedded coverage of the Iraq war, and write a paper evaluating the strategy from the point of view of the public. Did it help citizens understand the war better?

Film Stories of the Twentieth Century

Step into any video store, and where do you find most people? The new releases section, of course. We've come to expect the latest and greatest visual effects. We flock to the current blockbuster and anticipate trailers telling us what to expect next. Ironically, though, movies represent a form of narrative that relies on a strong connection with films that have come before, often decades earlier, that established the techniques and motifs we take for granted in the steady stream of the latest releases to DVD.

Most films pick up on traditions that we may never recognize without a sense of what has come before—we might suppose a film like *The Godfather* (1972) broke new ground with its realistic portrayal of mafia violence (which it did), but we will better understand that portrayal and the achievement of the film when we consider how it modifies earlier films from the gangster genre, such as *White Heat* (1949).

Some older films seem almost comic in their sentiments and crude in their production, but they offer a window through which we view earlier cultural moments. They also often reflect the state of the art of filmmaking and story-

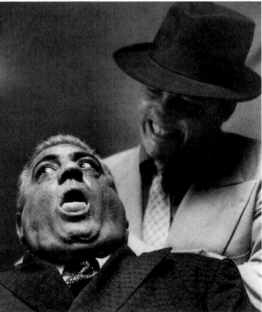

Still from *The Godfather* (1972)

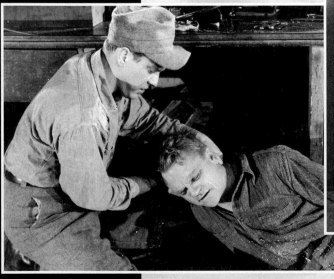

Still from *White Heat* (1949)

telling of the past—Alfred Hitchcock's films may pale next to recent thrillers, but at their time they changed the way people viewed movies and kept viewers on the edge of their seats. Some films continue to influence current movies and speak to us with voices from the past.

Casablanca

If you have never seen *Casablanca*, you may or may not recognize the many famous lines spawned by the film—"Here's looking at you, kid," "We'll always have Paris"—but you will no doubt be able to pick up on the chemistry between Humphrey Bogart and Ingrid Bergman that has established the film as one of the most poignant romance movies ever made. You will also quickly pick up on the film's historical context. The Nazi threat that hovers in the background and eventually determines the outcome of the film deliberately appeals to *Casablanca's* audience of 1942 America. The film reveals the emotional intensity and sadness of thwarted love, the intrigue of wartime danger, and the unique character of a time and place from the past.

Left: Paul Henreid, Ingrid Bergman, and Humphrey Bogart in *Casablanca* (1942) directed by Michael Curtiz. *Below:* Claude Reins, Paul Henreid, and Ingrid Bergman in *Casablanca.*

CONSIDER

View *Casablanca;* then respond to the following questions.

1. Decide whether you could best interpret the film in terms of its romantic story or its historical context. How would you explain your choice?

2. Do you think still images from *Casablanca* capture the relationships between the characters? What about the images most clearly demonstrates their state of mind?

3. From which points of view is the story told? How does the film demonstrate aspects of its characters and tell its story?

North by Northwest

Alfred Hitchcock may be the name most often associated with mystery and suspense. In part this connection stems from the incredible breadth of his career—he started making films in 1926 and was working on his final film at the time of his death in 1976. Films like *The Birds*, *Psycho*, *Rear Window*, and *Vertigo* demonstrate the innovations and narrative experiments Hitchcock undertook. By pushing the boundaries for effects and plot development, Hitchcock introduced elements of intrigue and realistic terror into movies that continue to dominate the offerings of studios even today.

North by Northwest exemplifies the filmmaking invention and themes of suspense that are hallmark Hitchcock. From the famous car chase, crop-dusting, and cliff-hanging scenes to the motif of the innocent man wrongfully accused, the film represents a storytelling classic that many filmmakers have followed and elaborated on.

Cary Grant, pursued by a crop-duster in *North by Northwest* (1959), directed by Alfred Hitchcock

Eva Marie Saint and Cary Grant in *North by Northwest* (1959)

CONSIDER

View *North by Northwest;* then respond to the following questions.

1. The crop-dusting scene from *North by Northwest* is one of the best known in film. What makes chase scenes so appealing to filmgoers? Based on elements of suspense like chases and cliff-hangers, how would you compare films to other forms of storytelling such as novels or plays?

2. How would concepts like arrangement or motion help you interpret the images from *North by Northwest*?

3. How aware of filmmaking techniques are you when you watch movies? How aware should you be? Discuss these questions in a group, drawing on recent films you have seen or classics from the past. Is a technique that draws attention to itself—the amazing slow motion shots in the *Matrix* trilogy, for example—distracting or riveting (or both)? At what point does a technique become a cliché?

CHALLENGE

4. View one or two Hitchcock films in addition to *North by Northwest,* and then think through all of the films you have seen that present echoes of the themes and scenes found in them. How do spy movies relate to Hitchcock's work? What about action or suspense films? Slasher movies? Choose one or two later movies, and write a paper exploring how they emulate and extend the earlier films.

Do the Right Thing

As Amy Taubin notes, *Do the Right Thing* does not always make it to the top of critics' lists of favorites, but the 1989 film stands out for alluding to historical events as it prompts us to ask how we might respond to problems with race relations in the world. The film also marks the emergence of director Spike Lee as a force in Hollywood filmmaking. The film uses music and a plot that encapsulates the events of a single day to home in on concerns of race and violence.

Fear of a Black Cinema

Amy Taubin
(2002)

FYI Amy Taubin has been a film critic for the *Village Voice* since 1987 and is contributing editor of *Sight and Sound*. In addition to writing about film, Taubin has also acted on stage and in film. She has appeared in avant-garde films, among them Michael Snow's *Wavelength* and Andy Warhol's *Couch* and *The Thirteen Most Beautiful Women*.

Top-ten lists: fun to read, painful to write. Always sucker myself into doing them on the grounds it would be cowardly not to. It's not the fear that colleagues and readers will mock my choices that makes the task so fraught with anxiety. ("They're all gonna laugh at you," as Carrie's mother warned her; and shouldn't it give me pause that *Carrie* gets shut out year after year from my list and everyone else's?) No, it's being limited to ten—the eternal frustrating ten. Ten might have been reasonable 50 years ago when cinema had been around for only half a century and few critics had access to film cultures other than those of the U.S., Western Europe and occasionally the Soviet Union. But even those early lists were possible only with the tacit agreement to exclude entire categories of cinema—no avant-garde films, perhaps a token documentary, and, of course, forget about the tawdry glories of exploitation.

Now, however, with the vast increase in production and with films from virtually every country on the globe available in specialized theaters, ten is out of the question. This time around, shall I bump Chantal Akerman's *Jeanne Dielman 23, quai du Commerce, 1080 Bruxelles*, a formally stringent harbinger of a feminist cinema that is still slow in coming, in order to accommodate Zacharias Kunuk's *The Fast Runner* (*Atanarjuat*), the first-ever Inuit theatrical feature, which employs digital video, the medium of the future, to record a myth of origins set in a primal white-on-white landscape far stranger and more ravishing than that of *Star Wars*? Completed in 2001, the first year of the new millennium, *The Fast Runner* suggests that cinema has not lost its capacity for radical renewal. But alas, the list is filled, and so I rationalize the omission with a new rule—no films that have not stood the test of time for at least 25 years—which I impulsively break with the last-minute addition of David Cronenberg's as yet unreleased *Spider*. What can I say? Cronenberg's ingenious deployment of first-person narrative in a medium that's characteristically resistant to subjectivity seems a greater—and more perverse—achievement than Kunuk's epic action-adventure. (Since list-making is a perverse endeavor, perversity has the advantage.) My other even more bizarre rules: I categorically exclude silent cinema except for its last stand in Dziga Vertov's *The Man with a Movie Camera*, comedy (thus slighting pleasure at its most direct) and any film not produced in Europe or North America (thus reinforcing a hegemony I claim to despise). It's a contortionist's nightmare, which could be solved by increasing the number to a plausible 25.

In which case, Spike Lee's *Do the Right Thing* is guaranteed a place. How could it not be, since it established Lee as the most dedicated resistance fighter to infiltrate the Hollywood system—the film-maker who put the fraught and disavowed issues of race and racism at the center of his films and refused to be ghettoized for doing so? Released in 1989, *Do the Right Thing* was Lee's third feature and the first to deal with the relationships between black characters (the residents of a single block in the Brooklyn neighborhood of [Bedford-Stuyvesant]) and white characters (the owner of the local pizzeria and his two sons, and the police).

Made after eight years of Reaganism had rolled back the gains of the Civil Rights movement and during the summer that the first George Bush was making his bid for the presidency with the help of the blatantly racist Willie Horton ads, *Do the Right Thing* was directly inspired by a series of incidents of racial violence and police brutality. There was Eleanor Bumpers, a very large, very likely psychotic black woman who was shot to death when she waved a knife at cops who'd come to arrest her. The cops claimed they acted in self-defense, but considering that the first bullet tore off Bumpers' hand, it was hard to understand why they felt obliged to keep firing. There was also Michael Stewart, a graffiti artist who was arrested for defacing subway

Still from *Do the Right Thing* (1989), directed by Spike Lee

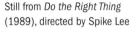

property and strangled to death in a police chokehold. (The cops maintained he had a heart attack.)

At the climax of *Do the Right Thing* one of the neighborhood teenagers is similarly strangled while struggling with police. His death precipitates a riot that ends with the pizzeria burnt to the ground. To say the film struck a nerve would be an understatement. Lee was attacked for inciting black youth to riot in the streets, for sabotaging the upcoming mayoral campaign of David Dinkins, the African-American opponent of 12-year incumbent Ed Koch, and for single-handedly turning back the clock to the fiery racial confrontations of the 1960s. It was not only members of the white establishment press who were outraged; Lee caught heat from black intellectuals including conservative black writer Stanley Crouch, who accused him of "proto-fascism." The racism inherent in the attacks on *Do the Right Thing* is evidenced in the fact that most of the critics were more horrified by the destruction of white-owned property than by the death of the black teenager, which was almost never mentioned. As Lee has frequently noted, none of the critics who attacked him apologized when Dinkins, indeed, defeated Koch and New York did not go up in flames. It was, rather, South Central L.A. which, a few years later, was burnt and looted; the cause, however, was not a movie but the acquittal of the cops in the Rodney King case. And, of course, police brutality continues unabated (witness the killing of Amadou Diallo and the torture of Abner Louima at the hands of the NYPD).

The noise surrounding *Do the Right Thing* propelled Lee on to the covers of *Time, Newsweek* and various other mainstream media showcases (a neither unwelcome nor, one imagines, entirely unstrategized development), but it also obscured the brilliance of the film itself: its bold, ingenious formal hybridity, its unforced emotional range from exuberance to despair, the way its individual images and actions are packed with contradictory meanings. The setting is a single 24-hour day—the hottest day of the summer—on a single street in one of Brooklyn's poor, black neighborhoods. The title sequence—Rosie Perez dancing to Public Enemy's "Fight the Power"—encapsulates the theatrical style and confrontational strategy of the whole. Perez is part prize-fighter and part hootchy-kootchy dancer, but even when she's bumping and grinding, she's too fierce and self-contained to be read as a seductress. The dance is more political than sexual provocation, as if Lee were baiting the feminist critics, who dismissed his first feature *She's Gotta Have It* (1986) as male fantasy, to have another go at him.

In a series of fast-cut vignettes we're introduced to the residents of the block. Mister Señor Love Daddy (Samuel L. Jackson), the local-radio DJ, watches over the neighborhood like an angelic referee as he spins records and issues advice. The narrative is framed between his morning wake-up call and his final admonition to "register to vote." The film has more than its share of caustic observers. Da Mayor (Ossie Davis), an elderly drunk, stumbles up and down the street and romantically yearns for Mother-Sister (Ruby Dee), perpetually glaring down at him from her upper-floor window. At the end of the block, just past the Korean-owned grocery store and the Italian-owned pizzeria, sit three beer-bellied middle-aged men whose sole purpose in life is to provide a running commentary on their own bodily functions and everyone else's problems, particularly those of their busier, although not necessarily more purposeful, neighbors. There's a trio of young men with fragile, stunted identities—Buggin' Out (Giancarlo Esposito), Smiley (Roger Guenveur Smith) and Radio Raheem (Bill Nunn), the designated martyr who looks as menacing as NBA player Patrick Ewing in the post but clings to his outsized boom-box as his only hedge against invisibility. Their inchoate anger and frustrated desire for agency eventually focuses, with tragic consequences, on Sal (Danny Aiello), the paternalistic proprietor of the pizzeria, and his two sons (John Turturro and Richard Edson).

"Always do the right thing," says Da Mayor, buttonholing Mookie (Spike Lee), who's on his way to deliver a pizza and can't believe Da Mayor has interrupted him mid-stride with such an obvious piece of advice. "Mookie does not have heroic stature" was Wim Wenders' lame explanation of why the Cannes jury decided to award the Palme d'Or to Steven Soderbergh's *sex, lies, and videotape* rather than to *Do the Right Thing* (as if James Spader's impotent video freak

John Turturro, Danny Aiello, and Richard Edson in a still from *Do the Right Thing* (1989)

did). There are no heroes in *Do the Right Thing*, but Mookie and Sal are more realist constructions than the film's other characters, who are so markedly one-dimensional they seem to have been lifted from a medieval morality play. The passive-aggressive Mookie has two women in his life—his beautiful, introspective sister Jackie (Joie Lee) and his girlfriend Tina, who's even more pugilistic in her speech than in her dancing. (She's the woman in the opening sequence.) But it's Mookie's father-son relationship with Sal, complicated by race and economic dependence, that becomes intolerable for him. When Mookie, in a rage at Sal for being instrumental in Radio Raheem's death, hurls a garbage can through the pizzeria's plate-glass facade, thus precipitating the riot, it's an act of liberation and destruction—over-determined all around.

But it's also a futile act, since it has no political context. Anyone who thinks this film could inspire violence is seeing their own paranoia and not what's on screen. Watching Mookie sitting shellshocked on the curb as the pizzeria burns, and Smiley tip-toeing through the embers to paste his fetishised Xeroxed image of Malcolm X and Martin Luther King on the skeleton of the wall which Sal had dedicated to curling stock photos of Italian-American celebrities, one feels overwhelmingly sadness—that the moment of a political movement with visionary, charismatic leaders and an organized strategy to "fight the power" is past and nothing has replaced it. Lee says he's been asked many times—although never by an African-American—if Mookie did the right thing. The more interesting question is, where does he go from here? On the depressing morning after, Mookie and Sal forge an uneasy truce based on their mutual knowledge that they'll never see each other again. Sal asks Mookie what he's going to do, and Mookie, who was introduced counting his cash, answers as he walks away, "Get paid." Even as one finds relief in the open ending, one has to wonder if Mookie is going to follow the path of Spike Lee, who may have final cut on his films, but also has learned to make strategic accommodations to the "powers that be." Or will he choose a more vampiristic form of black entrepreneurship? In Lee's *Clockers* (1995) Delroy Lindo's neighborhood drug honcho Rodney, when asked why he sells crack to kids, answers, just as flatly as Mookie, "to get paid."

Part hip-hop musical, *Do the Right Thing* has deeper roots in the agit-prop theater of the 1930s and 1940s. "Fight the Power" is the film's anthem, but the soundtrack is dominated by William J. E. Lee's orchestral jazz score, its harmonies, rhythms and textures echoing the stage-musical scores of Marc Blitzstein and Aaron Copland. Lee may have fond memories of the film version of *Bye Bye Birdie* (1963), but *Do the Right Thing* is a lot closer to Blitzstein's *The Cradle Will Rock*, the 1938 musical about organized labor that Orson Welles directed on Broadway. And it's Welles' combination of theatrical showmanship and cinematic confidence that Lee seems to have absorbed here. Even the swooping, gliding crane shots have a theatrical feel, the sensation you get when you're so riveted by something on stage that it's as if you've been physically transported from your balcony seat into the middle of the action.

Do the Right Thing was shot on a real Brooklyn street, and the buildings have a solidity no set could provide. On the other hand, the action is choreographed as if the street were a stage. Performers zip on and off as they would in a vaudeville revue. Lee juxtaposes fragments of scenes, isolating the revealing glance, gesture, word. Differing wildly in tone and style, the fragments are hung on a single thread of mounting tension. A trio of characters—one black, one white, one Asian—look straight into the camera as they read off a list of ethnic and racial slurs, enunciating every syllable as in a spelling contest. Mookie and Pino, Sal's overtly racist son, watch the ever so slightly flirtatious interplay between Sal and Mookie's sister from opposite angles and with mirrored emotions.

Had the space not been so theatricalized, the conceit that this one street is a microcosm of the social order (and specifically of race relations) would have frayed. We would have wondered why no one ventured outside its confines or how a dozen brownstones could house enough hungry pizza eaters to keep Mookie on the run for an entire day. The fusion of realism and theatricality not only generates aesthetic sparks, it suggests the complicated interplay between race as the bedrock of everyday life and race as a spectacle (the passing parade). As Mister See or Love Daddy is wont to say: "And that's the triple truth, Ruth."

CONSIDER

1. What are your thoughts on political messages and entertainment in films? Should films be political? Must they entertain? What happens when they try to do both?

2. How accurately must a film represent the social issues it comments on? Does limiting the scope of the action in *Do the Right Thing* to a single block affect the film's ability to represent race relations?

COMPOSE

3. Watch *Do the Right Thing*; then answer the question asked of Spike Lee: Does Mookie do the right thing at the end of the movie? Consider alternative perspectives as you develop an answer, and then develop a list of reasons that might be used to support your position. Report your stance in a brief presentation to a group of classmates.

The Big Lebowski

The Coen brothers, Joel and Ethan, make it into many discussions about contemporary films. Their movies avoid big production formulas, depicting instead eccentric characters in engaging comic situations. Films such as *Fargo* (1996) and *O Brother Where Art Thou?* (2000) have met both commercial and critical acclaim. Later films such as *Intolerable Cruelty* (2003) and *The Ladykillers* (2004) feature mainstream actors but maintain their sense of something out of the ordinary. As David Edelstein notes, *The Big Lebowski* (1998) has a smaller but heavily committed group of followers who admire the layers of meaning and critical commentary to be found in Coen brothers' films.

FYI David Edelstein is the film critic for Slate.com and reviews movies for *Fresh Air* on National Public Radio.

You're Entering a World of Lebowski

David Edelstein
(2004)

A cult gives its members license to feel superior to the rest of the universe, and so does a cult movie: it confers hipness on those who grok [understand, accept] what the mainstream audience can't. Joel and Ethan Coen's 1998 hyperintellectual stoner noir bowling comedy *The Big Lebowski*, starring Jeff Bridges as Jeff (The Dude) Lebowski, has the requisite exclusivity of a cult classic: it bombed at the box office; it was met with shrugs by many critics who had arguably overpraised the Coen brothers' Academy Award–winning *Fargo* (1996); and it has amassed an obsessive following on cable and video and by word of mouth. Nowadays, quoting its intricate, absurdist, often riotously profane dialogue earns you coolness points in widely disparate circles. Some would even say that the cult of *The Big Lebowski* is going mainstream.

It has a rolling national convention, for starters: the Lebowski Fest, which in June attracted 4,000 followers in Louisville, Ky., and on Friday arrives in

New York City. For two days, Lebowski fans (referred to as Achievers) will dress up as their favorite character (or prop, like a severed toe), dig some far-out rock bands at the Knitting Factory, bowl in far-out Queens, imbibe White Russians (and maybe less licit substances) and spend a lot of time shouting lines at one another like:

"This aggression will not stand, man."

"You're entering a world of pain."

"You want a toe? I can get you a toe. Believe me, there are ways, Dude. You don't want to know about it, believe me. Hell, I can get you a toe by 3 o'clock this afternoon, with nail polish."

And, of course, the Zen-like sign-off, "The Dude abides."

I suspect this will all grow old pretty quickly and I plan to be at home those nights with my pet marmot. But the festival offers a superb opportunity to celebrate *The Big Lebowski* for being not *Fargo* but one of filmdom's most inspired farragos—a monumentally disjunctive text that is much more fun to savor a second, third and tenth time, when all one's petit-bourgeois narrative concerns have dissipated like so much marijuana smoke.

Jeff Bridges in *The Big Lebowski* (1998), directed by Joel and Ethan Coen

The central joke—the raison d'être—of *The Big Lebowski* is a disjunction. The Coens take a disheveled stoner layabout, the former '60s activist the Dude—seen mostly in baggy shorts, sandals, an oversize T-shirt through which his gut is visible, often sucking a joint, mixing a White Russian or lying on his rug with headphones listening to bowling competitions or whale songs—and make him the gumshoe protagonist of a convoluted Raymond Chandler–style Los Angeles mystery-thriller in the tradition of *The Big Sleep*.

Robert Altman took steps in this direction in his masterly version of *The Long Goodbye* (1973), but he stuck to the outlines of Chandler's story. The joke of *The Big Lebowski* is that the kidnapping mystery, such as it is, turns out to be a nonstarter.

And so, of course, is the hero, which is why the Coens have paired him with Walter (John Goodman), a hothead Vietnam vet paranoiac with a tendency to wave his gun around over small slights, explaining that he did not watch his buddies "die facedown in the muck" to be, for example, asked to keep his voice down in a diner. It is Walter's sense of outrage that compels the Dude to seek payment for a rug that has been urinated on by goons who seek another Lebowski, the big one, a disabled rich Republican whose ex-porn-actress hottie wife owes money to a smut king, and whose daughter, an arty feminist splatter painter—you see: it's exhausting just getting a handle on the dramatis personae, and I haven't even mentioned the band of German nihilists and their savage marmot, or the purring cowboy narrator who inexplicably shows up in an L.A. bowling alley to order sarsaparilla and tell the Dude, "I like yer style, Dude." As the Dude himself puts it: "This is a complicated case, Maude. A lot of ins, a lot of outs, a lot of what-have-yous, a lot of strands to keep in my head, man. Lot of strands in old Duder's head."

But if *The Big Lebowski* is in the tradition of scattershot druggy comedies (represented in theaters at the moment by *Harold and Kumar Go to White Castle*), it is also the work of disciplined—not to mention show-offy—aesthetes. In virtuoso sequences, the Coens eroticize the sport of fat men, the only sport in which one gains weight, with pins that do sultry, slow-motion sambas and a hooded ball return that's like a mysterious feminine canal. They stage a surreal Freudian Busby Berkeleyish dream sequence in which the Dude wraps his manly arms around a helmeted Valkyrie (Julianne Moore, with golden bowling-ball breastplates) and thrusts his bowling ball heavenward, the Mighty Thor of Brunswick Lanes.

The Coens turned down requests to be interviewed about the cult of *The Big Lebowski*, which is frankly infuriating: I did not watch my buddies die facedown in the muck to be blown off by too-cool, insular, press-shunning elitists.

Steve Buscemi, John Goodman, and Jeff Bridges in *The Big Lebowski* (1998)

Fortunately, Jeff Dowd will talk. He's a 54-year-old producer, writer and producer's representative who was the inspiration for the Dude, and who actually goes by the name the Dude, showing up at Lebowski festivals (he is scheduled to be in New York) and signing autographs with "The Dude Abides." The festival's co-organizer Will Russell said that the Dude can drink people a third of his age under the table. "The guy, man, is a party machine," Mr. Russell said.

"Jeff Bridges only hung out with me once," said the Dude, by phone from Los Angeles. "But the body language is, like, 110 percent real, the slouch, all the physicality. My daughter said, 'Daddy, where did they get your clothes?'" The Dude is thrilled to have had his fictional counterpart named the 53rd best movie character ever by *Premiere* magazine—ahead, he pointed out, of Stanley Kowalski, Rocky, Sam Spade, Tony Manero of *Saturday Night Fever* and even George Bailey of *It's a Wonderful Life*.

But he wanted to add that the Dude of *The Big Lebowski* was short-lived. Although the movie is set in the '90s—when George H. W. Bush was telling Saddam Hussein, "This aggression will not stand"—the Dude depicted is the Dude of the late '70s and '80s, when the ideals of his beloved counter-culture seemed dead. Nowadays, the real Dude is back in the saddle. He's registering Lebowski Fest attendees to vote, and vowed to deliver a gift basket to the Republican National Convention containing (according to his news release) "symbolic gifts including an oversize pair of glasses to help the Republicans see what's going on in our country, a copy of the Constitution to remind them of our rights as free citizens and a bowling ball so they will have something to do for the next four years."

He added: "The Lebowski festival is the tip of the iceberg. It's remarkable how many people from different walks of life see this movie again and again. Not just potheads. There was a Wall Street guy I met who'd drop a 'Lebowski' line into job interviews and if the person didn't pick up on it he wouldn't be hired. I met this commander of a military base. He said they watch the movie down there in the missile silo two or three times a week."

It makes one feel safer already.

Mr. Dude—er, Dowd—likened the Coens to Jonathan Swift and Mark Twain. They are, he said, social satirists for the age. "People like that the Dude is a guy who is not allowing himself to become a corporate cog," he said. "So even if they are corporate cogs, they can live vicariously."

Like I said: mainstream.

CONSIDER

View *The Big Lebowski,* then answer the following questions.

1. Is it fair to characterize the film as a social satire? What messages does the movie offer about society?

2. How does the filmmaking contribute to the story told in the film? What techniques stand out, and what insights do they offer?

3. Why do some movies develop cult followings? Would you say that *The Big Lebowski* merits such attention? What other movies deserve cult status, in your opinion?

COMPOSE

4. View two films by the Coens, then write an essay explaining what constitutes their style of filmmaking. Consider the stories and messages in the film, the characters and acting, and the filmmaking as you discuss the films.

ANALYZING AND EVALUATING FILMS

Judging by the number of top ten lists you can find and the range of films critics consider to be exceptional, the criteria for what makes a great movie must be somewhat subjective. Some critics favor art films or foreign cinema, while others champion blockbuster epics. Still, there must be something about a film that allows it to stand the test of time and take its place among the best. In general, films may excel in three ways:

1. They may be technical masterpieces, incorporating innovative effects or cinematography that sets them apart.
2. Films might stand out for the stories they tell, offering a narrative that compels and grabs our attention more strongly than others.
3. Films may stand out for the acting and emotional intensity they deliver.

Of course, these are not the only ways we might judge movies, and a number of subcategories can be developed within these three categories. For instance, filmmaking techniques might include aspects of sound, computer-generated graphics, or dynamic uses of cameras or lighting. Storytelling might prompt us to consider the editing techniques or musical elements in a film. The characters in a film can be looked at as either central or supporting to the story. The real point when thinking about what makes a film outstanding is that you develop some criteria you can use more or less objectively to argue why a film should be considered one of the best.

CHALLENGE

5. Think about the films you have seen in the last five or so years, and select the movie that you feel deserves to be counted as one of the best of all time. Begin with your gut reactions, and then think about criteria that might underlie your judgment. You must move past opinion and toward arguing a position that others can agree or disagree with based on a rationale related to aspects of the filmmaking or the story told by the movie. Compose a paper in which you argue for your selection.

Learning from Graphic Novels

G raphic novels draw on elements of both cinema and comic books, combining high art and popular culture into a hybrid form of visual narrative. Graphic novelists report a process of composition that moves fluidly between images and words with the ultimate purpose of telling an engaging story. While not yet regarded as seriously as films, graphic novels may be poised to become, as Charles McGrath argues, "the new literary form."

FYI Charles McGrath is a writer at large for the *New York Times.* He has also written for *The New Yorker* and worked as editor for the *New York Times Book Review. Not Funnies* was originally published in the *New York Times Magazine.*

Not Funnies

Charles McGrath
(July 11, 2004)

You can't pinpoint it exactly, but there was a moment when people more or less stopped reading poetry and turned instead to novels, which just a few generations earlier had been considered entertainment suitable only for idle ladies of uncertain morals. The change had surely taken hold by the heyday of Dickens and Tennyson, which was the last time a poet and a novelist went head to head on the best-seller list. Someday the novel, too, will go into decline—if it hasn't already—and will become, like poetry, a genre treasured and created by just a relative few. This won't happen in our lifetime, but it's not too soon to wonder what the next new thing, the new literary form, might be.

It might be comic books. Seriously. Comic books are what novels used to be—an accessible, vernacular form with mass appeal—and if the highbrows are right, they're a form perfectly suited to our dumbed-down culture and collective attention deficit. Comics are also enjoying a renaissance and a newfound respectability right now. In fact, the fastest-growing section of your local bookstore these days is apt to be the one devoted to comics and so-called graphic novels. It is the overcrowded space way in the back—next to sci-fi probably, or between New Age and hobbies—and unless your store is staffed by someone unusually devoted, this section is likely to be a mess. "Peanuts" anthologies, and fat, catalog-size collections of "Garfield" and "Broom Hilda." Shelf loads of manga—those Japanese comic books that feature slender, wide-eyed teenage girls who seem to have a special fondness for sailor suits. Superheroes, of course, still churned out in installments by the busy factories at Marvel and D.C. Also, newer sci-fi and fantasy series like "Y: The Last Man," about literally the last man on earth (the rest died in a plague), who is now pursued by a band of killer lesbians.

You can ignore all this stuff—though it's worth noting that manga sells like crazy, especially among women. What you're looking for is shelved upside down and sideways sometimes—comic books of another sort, substantial single volumes (as opposed to the slender series installments), often in hard cover, with titles that sound just like the titles of "real" books: *Palestine, Persepolis, Blankets* (this one tips in at 582 pages, which must make it the longest single-volume comic book ever), *David Chelsea in Love, Summer Blonde, The Beauty Supply District, The Boulevard of Broken Dreams.* Some of these books have titles that have become familiar from recent movies: *Ghost World, American Splendor, Road to Perdition.* Others, like Chris Ware's *Jimmy Corrigan: The Smartest Kid on Earth* (unpaged, but a good inch and a quarter thick) and Daniel Clowes's *David Boring,* have achieved cult status on many campuses.

These are the graphic novels—the equivalent of "literary novels" in the mainstream publishing world—and they are beginning to be taken seriously by the critical establishment. *Jimmy Corrigan* even won the 2001 Guardian Prize for best first book, a prize that in other years has gone to authors like Zadie Smith, Jonathan Safran Foer and Philip Gourevitch.

The notion of telling stories with pictures goes back to the cavemen. Comic-book scholars make a big deal of Rodolphe Töpffer, a 19th-century Swiss artist who drew stories in the form of satiric pictures with captions underneath. You could also make a case that Hogarth's *Harlot's Progress* and its sequel, *A Rake's Progress,* were graphic novels of a sort—stories narrated in sequential panels. But despite these lofty antecedents, the comic-book form until recently has been unable to shed a certain aura of pulpiness, cheesiness and semi-literacy. In fact, that is what a lot of cartoon artists most love about their genre.

There was a minor flowering of serious comic books in the mid-'80s, with the almost simultaneous appearance of Art Spiegelman's groundbreaking *Maus*; of the "Love and Rockets" series, by two California brothers, Gilbert and Jaime Hernandez; and of two exceptionally smart and ambitious super-hero-based books, *Watchmen*, by Alan Moore and Dave Gibbons, and *Batman: The Dark Knight Returns*, by Frank Miller. Newspapers and magazines ran articles with virtually the same headline: "Crash! Zap! Pow! Comics Aren't Just for Kids Anymore!" But the movement failed to take hold, in large part because there weren't enough other books on the same level.

The difference this time is that there is something like a critical mass of artists, young and old, uncovering new possibilities in this once-marginal form, and a new generation of readers, perhaps, who have grown up staring at cartoon images on their computer screens and in their video games, not to mention the savvy librarians and teachers who now cater to their interests and short attention spans. The publicity that has spilled over from movies like *Ghost World*, originally a graphic novel by Dan Clowes, has certainly not hurt. And there is much better distribution of high-end comics now, thanks in part to two enterprising publishers, Drawn and Quarterly in Montreal and Fantagraphics Books in Seattle, which have managed to get their wares into traditional bookstores, not just the comics specialty shops. Some of the better-known graphic novels are published not by comics companies at all but by mainstream publishing houses—by Pantheon, in particular—and have put up mainstream sales numbers. *Persepolis*, for example, Marjane Satrapi's charming, poignant story, drawn in small black-and-white panels that evoke Persian miniatures, about a young girl growing up in Iran and her family's suffering following the 1979 Islamic revolution, has sold 450,000 copies worldwide so far; *Jimmy Corrigan* sold 100,000 in hardback, and the newly released paperback is also moving briskly.

These are not top best-seller figures, exactly, but they are sales that any publisher would be happy with, and several are now trying to hop on the graphic-novel bandwagon. Meanwhile, *McSweeney's Quarterly*, a key barometer of the literary climate, especially among the young and hip, has devoted its entire new issue to comics and graphic novels, and the contents are virtually a state-of-the-art anthology, edited and designed by Chris Ware. Dave Eggers, the editor of *McSweeney's*, told me, "I'm just trying to show how hard it is to do this stuff well and to give it a little dignity."

The term *graphic novel* is actually a misnomer. Satrapi's *Persepolis* books (another installment is due this summer) are nonfiction, and so, for that matter, is *Maus*, once you accept the conceit that human beings are played, so to speak, by cats, dogs, mice and frogs. The newest book by Chester Brown

. . . is a full-scale, 200-plus-page comic-book biography (which took five years to research and draw) of Louis Riel, who in Brown's native Canada occupies roughly the position that John Brown does here. Nor are all these books necessarily "graphic" in the sense of being realistic or explicit. (When I mentioned to a friend that I was working on an article about graphic novels, he said, hopefully, "You mean porn?")

Many practitioners of the form prefer the term *comix*, with that nostalgic *x* referring to the age of the underground comics, which were sold in head shops along with bongs and cigarette papers. Scott McLoud, the author of a very helpful guide (in comic-book form) called *Understanding Comics*, prefers the slightly pretentious term *sequential art*. Alan Moore, creator of *The League of Extraordinary Gentlemen*, likes "big expensive comic book"; Spiegelman is partial to "comic book that needs a bookmark."

But for want of a universally agreed-on alternative, the graphic-novel tag has stuck, and it received something like official sanction a year and a half ago when Spiegelman and Chris Oliveros, the publisher of *Drawn and Quarterly*, persuaded the book-industry committee that decides on subject headings to adopt a graphic-novel category with several subsections: graphic novel/literature, graphic novel/humor, graphic novel/science fiction and so on. Afterward, Spiegelman turned to Oliveros and said, "I think we've just created the state of Israel—one great big boundary dispute in one little corner of the bookshop globe."

The center of this dispute—the comic book with a brain—is a somewhat arbitrary and subjective place, not unlike pornography in Justice Stewart's famous formulation (you recognize it when you see it). But a few generalities may be hazarded. First of all, the graphic novel is not just like the old Classics Illustrated series, an illustrated version of something else. It is its own thing: an integrated whole, of words and images both, where the pictures don't just depict the story; they're part of the telling.

In certain ways, graphic novels are an almost primitive medium and require a huge amount of manual labor: drawing, inking, coloring and lettering, most of it done by hand (though a few artists have begun to experiment with computer drawing). It's as if a traditional novelist took his printout and then had to copy it over, word by word, like a quill-wielding monk in a medieval monastery. For some graphic novelists, just four or five panels is a good day's work, and even a modest-size book can take years to complete.

Like a lot of graphic novelists, Marjane Satrapi begins with a prose script and then begins to sketch it out, lightly and loosely, in pencil. "When I've done that, then in my brain my book is finished," she said from Paris, where she lives now. "The problem is that only I know what it looks like. For you to see it, then I have to drudge. It's a very, very long process."

Such labor demands a certain obsessional personality and sometimes results in obsessional storytelling. What all graphic novelists aspire to, however—whether they start with words or with an image or two—is a sense of motion, of action unfolding in the blank spaces between their stop-action frames. They spend a lot of time thinking about how the panels are arranged and the number of panels it takes (or doesn't) to depict a given amount of narrative. Most of these effects are meant to work on us, the readers, almost subconsciously, but they require a certain effort nonetheless. You have to be able to read and look at the same time, a trick not easily mastered, especially if you're someone who is used to reading fast. Graphic novels, or the good ones anyway, are virtually unskimmable. And until you get the hang of their particular rhythm and way of storytelling, they may require more, not less, concentration than traditional books.

The graphic novel—unlike the more traditional part of the comic-book universe now being celebrated by fiction writers like Michael Chabon and Jonathan Lethem—is a place where superheroes have for the most part been banished or where, as in *Jimmy Corrigan* and *David Boring*, they exist only as wistful emblems of a lost childhood. There is also little of that in-your-face, cinematic drawing style developed by Stan Lee, Jack Kirby and other pioneers of the action comic. Most of the better graphic novelists consciously strive for a simple, pared-down style and avoid tricky angles and perspectives.

The graphic novel is a man's world, by and large, though there are several important female artists (not just Satrapi, but also Lynda Barry, Julie Doucet and Debbie Drechsler). And to a considerable extent it is a place of longing, loss, sexual frustration, loneliness and alienation—a landscape very similar, in other words, to that of so much prose fiction.

A number of graphic novels are set in a kind of nostalgialand, like Ben Katchor's mythic, time-warped Lower East Side or the mid-'50s small-town Canada of the artist who goes by the name Seth (his real name is Gregory Gallant). Many more are set in the slacker world—the skanky Washington Heights neighborhood of Doucet's *My New York Diary*, the coffee-shop Portland and East Village sublet of *David Chelsea in Love*, the diners, card shops and apartment complexes of Adrian Tomine's West Coast—where people are always hooking up and breaking up and feeling both shy and lousy. It's the pictorial equivalent of Nick Hornby's *High Fidelity*.

A considerable percentage of the new graphic novels are frankly autobiographical. They are about people who are, or who are trying to be, graphic novelists, and they all follow, or implicitly refer to, a kind of ur-narrative, which upon examination proves to be, with small variations, the real-life story of almost everyone who goes into this line of work.

As most graphic novelists themselves will gladly tell you, you have to be a bit of a weirdo to want to pursue this odd and solitary art form. Julie Doucet, one of the most promising of the younger graphic novelists, found the life so hard that she flat out quit. "It was killing me," she said over the phone from her studio in Montreal. "Trying to make a living from it—I could never stop, never have a break. I was doing it all the time."

For those who do stick with it, the career of the graphic novelist can seem less a choice than a compulsion. The process of becoming one goes something like this: First there's a conversion moment, which happens at a remarkably young age, usually when the artist is still in grammar school. To put it simply, he falls in love with a comic strip—fairly often it's "Peanuts"—and then with comics in general. Soon he's copying them, and then he's generating his own. In high school, where this artist, a nerd, most likely, and an outcast, is unrecognized for the talent he is, cartooning becomes a refuge, a way to work out revenge fantasies and occasionally even a modest claim to fame.

More of the same in college or art school—if he even bothers with formal training. Cartooning is now an obsession, a visual diary in which the artist records every detail of his personal life, with a special emphasis on his sexual fantasies and his usually excessive masturbation, and then at some point, if he is lucky, he figures out how to turn all this rage and depression and thwarted energy, all those pages and pages of sketches and drawings, into story-telling, into a portrait of the artist as a young man. The benign version of this progress is Chester Brown's sweet and innocent-seeming novels *Playboy* and *I Never Liked You;* the dark, self-loathing, porn-addicted and parodic version is Joe Matt's *Poor Bastard,* which was recently optioned by HBO.

If some of this sounds familiar, it is because it is also the story of R. Crumb, so memorably laid out in Terry Zwigoff's 1994 documentary, wherein we learn that Crumb grew up not just in your basic unhappy family but in a spectacularly dysfunctional one, and that as a child he was sexually aroused by Bugs Bunny. Crumb dominates the brief history of the graphic novel the way Cimabue dominates Vasari's first volume of *Lives of the Artists*—as both an inescapable stylistic influence and a kind of moral exemplar. (Crumb is now 60 and lives in the south of France.) Almost every aspiring graphic novelist now goes through a Crumb period, and some never entirely outgrow it:

the cross-hatched line and bare light bulbs; the big feet, knobby knees, hairy legs and whiskery faces; the big breasts and even bigger behinds; the flying drops of perspiration (and other bodily fluids). It's a style as recognizable in its way, and as powerful, as Goya's or Brueghel's. Equally powerful is Crumb's example as someone who takes comics seriously as a form of self-expression and is unafraid to pour everything of himself into them. "Without Crumb, I really, honestly, think comics would have come to an end," Chris Ware says. "I think we all have his voice in our minds: 'You really want to do that? Are you sure you really want to do that?'"

The other overwhelming figure is Art Spiegelman, who to the comics world is a Michelangelo and a Medici both, an influential artist who is also an impresario and an enabler of others. As one publisher told me, "Art is just as important as he thinks he is." He, too, fits the Crumb paradigm: childhood fascination with comics (in his case with *Inside Mad*, a paperback *Mad* magazine anthology that he persuaded his mother to buy for him when he was 7), precocious development (as a teenager he was drawing for his weekly paper in Rego Park, Queens, and publishing his own magazine, *Blasé*) and deep immersion in the history and lore of comics. He had another asset: a case of uncorrectable ambylopia, or lazy eye, that makes it difficult for him to see in three dimensions. ("So cartoons really did seem real to me," he says. "Maybe more real.") After dropping out of SUNY Binghamton, he went to work for the Topps bubble-gum company, of all places, which had a small art and design department. If you are a parent of a certain age—or the offspring of such a parent—you have Art Spiegelman to thank for Wacky Packs and the Garbage Pail Kids.

Off and on, Spiegelman was with Topps for 20 years, but all the while he was working on his own comics. He went through the obligatory Crumb phase and then, under the influence of some obscure experimental filmmakers, found himself more and more interested in formal and technical issues. His strip "Ace Hole, Midget Detective" was a noir detective parody deliberately designed to unravel; "Don't Get Around Much Anymore" was a one-page piece in which almost nothing happens. At this point, Spiegelman says, he was on a path that led to becoming a gallery artist. Instead, he changed direction and set about trying to tell a story.

The result was the Pulitzer Prize-winning *Maus*, originally a three-page strip in a comics anthology called *Funny Aminals* (sic) but ultimately a two-volume story about Spiegelman's relationship with his father and his father's experiences at Auschwitz. *Maus* draws on a lot of Spiegelman's structural experiments and incorporates a number of subtle design elements, like having the shadow of a swastika fall almost undetectably across a page, but its great innovation—unmatched and possibly unmatchable—was in its combination of style and subject. Somehow the old cartoon vocabulary—the familiar imagery of cats and mice—made the Holocaust bearable and approachable, strange and yet familiar. It would be almost impossible to overstate the influence of *Maus* among other artists. Marjane Satrapi, for example, says that it was *Maus* that opened her eyes to the possibilities of the graphic novel—that in effect created her as an artist—and the same is true for many others.

Installments of *Maus* began appearing in the early '80s in a magazine owned and published by Spiegelman. This was *Raw*, which he founded in 1980 with his wife, Françoise Mouly (who is now the art editor of the *New Yorker*), and which is his other great gift to graphic novelists. *Raw* was originally meant to be a one-timer, a showcase for all the art that, with the collapse of underground comics a few years earlier (owing mostly to a legal crackdown on stores selling drug paraphernalia), had no other outlet. The first issue sold out, and subsequent issues kept rising "phoenixlike," Spiegelman says. "We finally decided to make it a biannual, because we weren't sure whether that meant twice a year or every other year."

Raw came out until 1991, published from Spiegelman's studio, a loft in SoHo that is also a kind of haphazard museum of comic-strip history and memorabilia, and it helped revive the careers of some older artists, veterans of the underground period, and showcased the work of many more new ones, most of whom found their calling and their inspiration from studying its pages.

Spiegelman, 56, has been such an ambassador for comics over the years—lecturing, promoting, writing articles—that to some extent his own productivity has suffered. His first solo comic book since *Maus*, called *In the Shadow of No Towers*, comes out in September, and for much of the spring he was happily working on the proofs in his cluttered and smoke-hazed studio. (Like the old-time comic-strip artists, Spiegelman is an unapologetic chain smoker, a genuine two-pack-a-day man.)

In the Shadow is a collection of broadsides he began publishing after the attack on the World Trade Center, just blocks away from where he lives. The broadsides are designed in the fashion of old newspaper funny pages, and they incorporate some of that old funny-page storytelling. (When Spiegelman wants to show himself and Françoise quarreling, for example, he draws it in the style of a Maggie and Jiggs strip; there are also allusions to the Katzenjammer Kids, Krazy Kat and Happy Hooligan.) An unhinged Spiegelman is a major character—paranoid, unshaven, a butt always in his mouth—and eventually he suffers a kind of nervous breakdown, convinced that the world is about to end any minute.

Many of these broadsides were so politically charged and so stridently opposed to the Bush administration that mainstream American papers were reluctant to print them; they appeared mostly in England and in Germany. Spiegelman has put them all together now in a big album-size book, along with several full-size reproductions of old comic-supplement pages, and the result, he says he hopes, is a kind of palimpsest in which the layers reflect and comment on each other, in which world history and personal history collide.

The book is also, inevitably, a working diagram of Spiegelman's own feverish, hyperactive imagination—a place in which comics and reality, present and past, are all but indistinguishable. He works on two desks, side by side, one 19th-century, as he likes to say, and one 21st. The first is an old-fashioned drafting table, and the second is a computer; in between, there is a scanner. He can sketch something by hand and then refine it on the screen, or do it the other way around. By the time he is finished with a piece, he says, he can no longer tell the difference between what is computerized and what has been done by hand.

By general agreement, Chris Ware, 36, and Daniel Clowes, 43, are Spiegelman's two most important discoveries. Clowes, who fits the classic profile (broken home, comics obsession, friendless, dateless adolescence), is the author of, among other works, *David Boring*, an unsummarizable novel in which a dweebish guy's fetish for big-bottomed women leads to his being shot twice, and the better-known *Ghost World*, about two punkish high-school girls trying to cling to friendship even as the onset of sex and adult responsibility seems to drive them apart. *Ghost World* the graphic novel is even better than *Ghost World* the movie. The dialogue (the best parts of which are unprintable here) has a Salingeresque poignancy, and the artwork is washed in a bluish-green tint that suggests a TV on the blink—exactly right for these lives in which much of the color has been drained by a crippling irony and hyper self-awareness.

Ware (abandoned by father, snubbed by classmates, discovered comics in grandmother's basement) is best known for *Jimmy Corrigan*, easily the most beautiful and most complicated of all the new graphic novels. The story of a sad-sack 36-year-old Chicagoan ("a lonely, emotionally impaired human castaway," as he calls himself) who is briefly reunited with a father he has never seen before, *Jimmy Corrigan* is laid out in wide, delicately colored pages in which the panels are sometimes large and painterly and sometimes resemble circuit diagrams. There are dream sequences, flashbacks (especially to the Chicago 1893 Columbian Exposition and the domed pavilions), and even home-assembly projects—models of a farmhouse and an

Page from *Ghost World*, by Dan Clowes (1998)

old-fashioned zoetrope to be cut out and pasted together. Some pages are crammed with information; in others, nothing happens except the passage of time, quietly punctuated by a little cough or a sigh.

Ware lives with his wife, a teacher, just outside Chicago in a small stucco house that is itself a little Corriganesque. There is a tiny upstairs studio overlooking the yard; in other rooms, there are a piano, some banjos, an old-fashioned Victrola and a collection of Edison cylinder recordings. (Ware is an old-music enthusiast, and in his spare time he edits and produces a magazine called the *Rag-Time Ephemeralist*.) I went there to see him recently, and as it happens, the artist known as Seth was visiting for the weekend from Guelph, Ontario.

They both resembled their characters a little. Ware is a taller, handsomer version of the bullet-headed Jimmy Corrigan. Seth, 41, looks like a zootier version of the fedora-wearing protagonist of his novel *It's a Good Life, If You Don't Weaken*, about a young man obsessed with old *New Yorker* cartoons. His hair is brilliantined and swept back; his glasses are old-fashioned black horn rims. Even though it was a warm Saturday in May, he was wearing a suit and tie, and when we went out for a late lunch, he put on a topcoat, fedora and a pair of leather gloves.

They were spending the day doing what graphic novelists apparently always do whenever they get together—talking about graphic novels. Ware, even though he is more successful and esteemed than just about any of his peers (his work has been shown at the Whitney Biennial, and he is the subject of a scholarly monograph coming from Yale University Press this fall), occasionally sounded like Samuel Beckett's idea of a graphic novelist. "This is just an incredibly inefficient way to tell a story," he said, and he explained that earlier in the week he had been working on a strip in which he had decided there could be no narration. "It involved maybe 8 to 10 seconds of actual narrative time," he said. "But it took me three days to do it, of 12 hours a day. And I'm thinking any writer would go through this passage in eight minutes of work. And I think: Why am I doing this? Is the payoff to have the illusion of something actually happening before your eyes really worth it? I find it's a constant struggle and a source of great pain for me, especially the last day when I'm inking the strip. I think, Why, why am I doing this? Whole years go by now that I can barely account for. I'm not even being facetious."

Seth nodded and returned to an earlier theme of his—the idea that cartooning is something the artist gets "tricked" into. "I think the impulse to cartooning comes as a compensation when you're young for the fact that you're unhappy," he explained. "So you start cartooning to create a fantasy world. That impulse is what makes you draw, and for me it made me draw enough that by the time I was in my 20s, I was tricked into being a cartoon-ist. It was too late then to start anything else."

But maybe because they were only talking, not working, they didn't seem all that glum, and they went on enthusiastically about the subject that seems to preoccupy all graphic novelists—their "rhythm," or the way their panels work on the page.

"It's like music," Ware said. He explained that when he is working, he first does quick sketches of what each panel should be like. "I never think of it as words," he said. "It's individual pictures, and it feels like a memory. When I think about it, it replays itself in my mind over and over, almost like a little melody or something. As I'm working on it, I'll read through the strip hun-dreds of times. It's like I'm writing a piece of music, and I'll keep playing it over and over in my head. And I'll realize that that didn't sound right or that didn't feel right or that's insincere or that movement seems staged or acted somehow. So I'll have to add or subdivide or do something. And then all of a sudden, it will click, and it will seem like a real thing happening."

"It's the medium we're stuck with," Seth said, "even if it seems a completely inappropriate medium to have chosen to tell a serious story." He thought for a second and added, "Though it's probably a less wildly inappropriate medium than it was 10 years ago"—by which he meant that now, at least, it's possible for a graphic novelist to make a living.

Joe Sacco's name came up while I was in Chicago, and Seth said: "He's defi-nitely an oddball cartoonist, because he has very excellent social skills. He goes out into the world and deals with people. In fact, of all the cartoonists I know, when I'm around Joe I get the least impression that he read all this junk as a kid. He seems relatively free from all that genre material."

This is only partly true. Sacco, who is now 43 and in person much better looking than the geeky guy with the big lips and the blank eyes who is his comic-book stand-in, was born on Malta and spent the early part of his childhood in Australia. He wallowed in plenty of comics there, and when he moved to this country at the age of 12, he became an instant convert to *Mad* magazine. Later, he went through a serious Crumb phase, drawing strips like *Oliver Limpdingle's Search for Love*, which is pretty much summed up by its title. For a while, Sacco even drew romance comics.

But in high school and again in college (the University of Oregon at Eugene), he was popular, well adjusted and a good student. His passion in those days was journalism, and he settled on cartooning only after failing to find a decent job doing anything else. In the mid-'80s, he worked briefly as a reporter for the *Comics Journal*, a magazine that covers the comics world, and that experience emboldened him to show the editor, Gary Groth, an epic Vietnam comic he had been working on. "Gary pretty much destroyed my hopes for it," Sacco says now. "At that point, I decided I should learn how to write a one-page story." Eventually he had enough of them for a comic book, and they were published by Fantagraphics in a six-installment series called "Yahoo."

Sacco's real breakthrough came in 1988, when he accompanied some friends of his, a rock band called the Miracle Workers, on a European tour. "In some ways, I started behaving journalistically again," he recalls. "I began taking notes and writing down every word people said." *In the Company of Long Hair*, a journal of the trip in comics form that appeared as part of the "Yahoo" series in 1989, marked the first appearance of the familiar big-lipped Sacco figure (though in this version he still has shoulder-length locks, not the buzz cut that turns up later), who is sometimes taking part in the action but more often just observing it, and of the familiar Sacco method, which is to use a cartoon style to document something that actually happened.

He refined this technique with *More Women, More Children, More Quickly*, a story told from his mother's point of view about the Italian and German bombing raids on Malta during World War II that required him to interview her and to re-create historical settings and events. *Palestine*, Sacco's account of several trips he made to Palestinian towns and refugee camps in the West Bank, was what first brought him a wider audience and serious attention in 1995. But his masterpiece is *Safe Area Gorazde*, which came out in 2000 and recounts four trips Sacco made to Gorazde, a U.N.-designated safe area during the Bosnian war, where the mainly Muslim population endured three and a half years of siege by the Bosnian Serbs.

Sacco . . . claims not to have a conscious style; his work, he says, is a "combination of knowledge and limitation." But his pages have become less and less cartoonish over the years—to the point where they now verge on a kind of realism, especially when depicting interiors and street scenes. This is partly accidental (Sacco studied mechanical drawing in school and says that he draws buildings and vehicles more easily than people) and partly the result of a reportorial passion for accuracy. Most graphic novelists keep sketchbooks; Sacco takes photographs and tape-records his interviews. His work subtly employs certain comic-book conventions—for example, in showing emotion (facial expressions are often slightly exaggerated) or in structuring a narrative. (In a chapter of *Safe Area Gorazde* describing a character's arduous trek through a forest, he deliberately draws the figure walking left—against the traditional flow of a comics page—to create a sense of slowness and difficulty.) At the same time, there's a documentary quality to

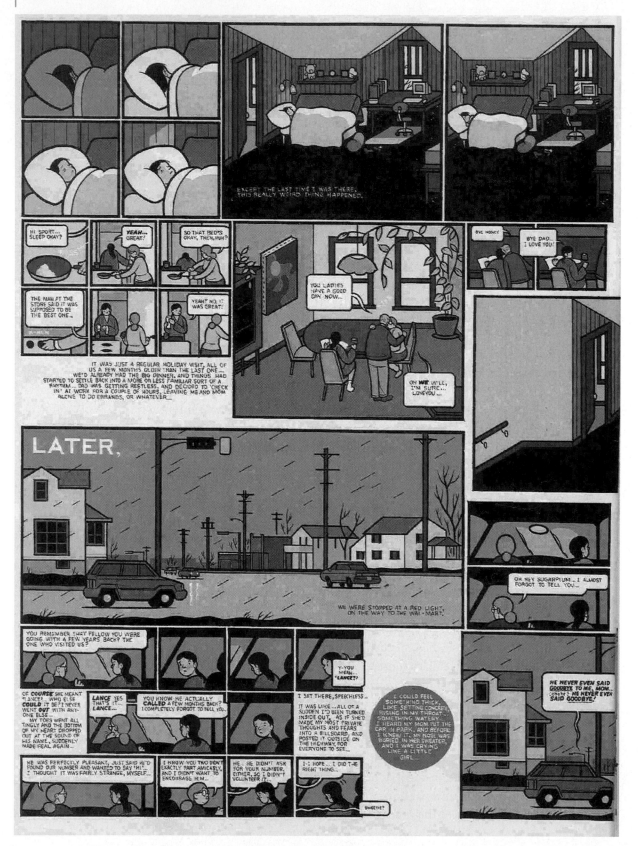

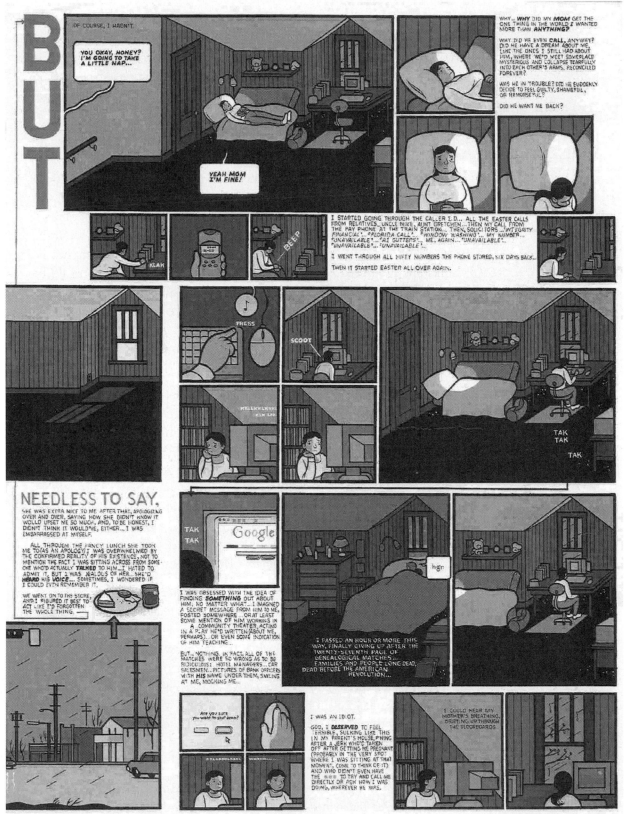

books like *Palestine* and *Safe Area Gorazde* that is often more effective and affecting than "real" documentary. His scenes never seem stagy, the way filmed "re-creations" so often do, and his people, verging ever so slightly on caricature, have an immediacy that talking heads on a screen seldom achieve.

Sacco typically spends weeks indexing and cross-referencing his notes and then writes out an entire story before starting to draw. "I think you have to do it that way for nonfiction," he says. "You have to be systematic. You can have a fictional character grow on the page and kind of lead you around, but that won't work for what I'm doing. I want to be a window on something." Sacco is currently working on another Palestinian project, a book about the town of Rafah, which he expects will take several years to finish, but he thinks about someday returning to made-up stories. "I'm not sure I'll be able to keep doing this," he said. "All the traveling, all that extra work. There was a point a couple of years ago, just after *Gorazde* came out, when if it hadn't done well, I think I might have folded. You can't eat on just good reviews. And now I sometimes ask myself, When I'm 60, do I still want to be traipsing around refugee camps?"

One solution to the drudgery of cartooning is to get others to do it for you. Companies like Marvel and D.C. essentially produce comics on an assembly line: one person thinks up the story, someone else draws it, another inks it, yet another colors it and so on. Most graphic novelists tend to be dismissive of such products, but a couple of people have emerged from the factory system and attained something like auteur status—as writers whose comics are worth paying attention to no matter who draws them. Neil Gaiman, creator of the enormously successful "Sandman" series, is one such figure; another is Alan Moore, creator of *Watchmen, From Hell* (a story about Jack the Ripper) and *The League of Extraordinary Gentlemen.*

Moore, who is 50, looks like a comic-book character. He has a long beard, shoulder-length hair and likes to dress in black. He also dabbles a little in the occult. Moore lives alone in Northampton, England, where he was born and grew up, and is a famous recluse. "I'm a stranger to the other end of the living room," he likes to say. Moore actually draws perfectly well. (His early strips, like "Roscoe Moscow," a detective parody, are more than passable Crumb knockoffs.) But in the early '80s, when he was a young man struggling to support himself, a wife and a baby, he realized that he couldn't draw fast enough to keep up with his deadlines. He decided to become a writer instead and began sending out scripts on spec.

From the beginning, Moore's scripts were extraordinarily detailed, not just plot summaries but panel-by-panel blueprints, and this made the artist's job much easier. Here, for example, is the script for just a single panel from an unpublished work called *Belly of Cloud*:

> IN THIS FIRST SMALL PANEL ON THE BOTTOM TIER WE CHANGE ANGLES SO THAT WE HAVE PART OF THE HEAD AND SHOULDERS OF THE ANGEL IN THE BOTTOM RIGHT FOREGROUND, FACING SLIGHTLY AWAY FROM US TOWARDS THE NEAR LEFT BACKGROUND AS SHE TAKES THE CIGARETTE FROM HER MOUTH AND EXHALES BLUE SMOKE . . . . LOOKING BEYOND HER WE CAN SEE THE YOUNG MAN AS HE SITS THERE IN HIS POST-COITALLY OPEN SHIRT, SMOKING HIS OWN CIGARETTE AND JUST GAZING AT HER WITH A LOOK OF STRICKEN PITY DAWNING IN HIS EYES.

Moore is a tireless researcher; when he took over the moribund "Swamp Thing" series from D.C. in the early '80s, he read botany books, listened to Cajun music and studied the geography and ecology of the Louisiana bayous. Of all the graphic novelists, in fact, Moore may have the purest and most inventive literary imagination. He also writes poetry and has published a novel (the old-fashioned kind, without pictures). His *League of Extraordinary Gentlemen*, which is far more interesting than you would ever guess from the movie, is an extremely clever literary pastiche of Victorian England in which all the characters (even the prime minister, Plantagenet Palliser) are taken from other Victorian novels—Bram Stoker's *Dracula*, H. G. Wells's *Invisible Man*, Stevenson's *Dr. Jekyll and Mr. Hyde* and Jules Verne's *20,000 Leagues Under the Sea*, to name just the most obvious. Right now, he is working on a pornographic graphic novel, *Lost Girls*, in which the main characters are the Alice of *Through the Looking Glass*, now known as Lady Fairchild and a laudanum-addicted lesbian; the slightly repressed Mrs. Harold Potter, nee Wendy Darling, from *Peter Pan*; and the randy Dorothy Gale, from *The Wizard of Oz*.

Moore was kicked out of school at 17 for using and selling LSD. "It was a fair cop," he says now, meaning that he deserved to be expelled. "The headmaster called me a moral health hazard, and he was probably right." But the headmaster also took steps to make sure he couldn't get into any other school, and Moore, who says he is still "embittered by the entire educational system," became a fierce and ambitious autodidact.

Part of his education was comic books, at first black-and-white English ones (which he says "were just something we had, like rickets") until, in the early '60s, at an open-air market, he came across full-color American comics. "I related to them very strongly," he says. "They were about America, which seemed to me to be like the future, like science fiction. Even without those fantastic characters, the whole country seemed to me an exotic landscape, like the Emerald City, and those comics lifted me right out of the streets I grew up in."

He added: "We all live, you know, on a kind of fictional planet—the place we have with us ever since we started listening to stories. We spend a lot of time in these imaginary worlds, and we get to know them better than the real locations we pass on the street every day. I think they play a more important part in our shaping of the world than we realize. Hitler, for example—we know he read a lot of Bulwer-Lytton. Osama bin Laden used to read quite a lot of Western science fiction. That's why comics feel important to me. They're immense fun as a game, but there's also something more serious going on."

How good are graphic novels, really? Are these truly what our great-grandchildren will be reading, instead of books without pictures? Hard to say. Some of them are much better than others, obviously, but this is true of books of any kind. And the form is better suited to certain themes and kinds of expression than others. One thing the graphic novel can do particularly well, for example, is depict the passage of time, slow or fast or both at once—something the traditional novel can approximate only with empty space. The graphic novel can make the familiar look new. The autobiographical hero of Craig Thompson's *Blankets*, a guilt-ridden teenager falling in love for the first time, would be insufferably predictable in a prose narrative; here, he has an innocent sweetness.

The graphic novel is also good at depicting blankness and anomie. This is a strength of Daniel Clowes's, and also of 30-year-old Adrian Tomine, who may, incidentally, be the best prose writer of the bunch. (He became an English major at the University of California, Berkeley, because the art department had no use for representation, let alone comics.) His young people, falling in and out of relationships, paralyzed by shyness and self-consciousness, might be unendurable if depicted in prose alone. Why would we care? But in Tomine's precisely rendered drawings (which owe something to Clowes, something to the Hernandez brothers and maybe even a tiny debt to the painter Alex Katz) they take on a certain dignity and individuality.

The graphic novel is great for stories of spookiness and paranoia, as in David Mazzucchelli's graphic adaptation of Paul Auster's novella, *City of Glass*, where the panels themselves become confining and claustrophobic, or in Charles Burns's creepy *Black Hole*, a story about a plague spread by sexually active teenagers. (*Black Hole* is still unfinished, and some graphic artists talk about it the way people talked about *Ulysses* back when it was appearing in installments.) And of course, drawing as it does on the long tradition of comic and satiric art, the graphic novel can be very funny.

In fact, the genre's greatest strength and greatest weakness is that no matter how far the graphic novel verges toward realism, its basic idiom is always a little, well, cartoonish. Sacco's example notwithstanding, this is a medium probably not well suited to lyricism or strong emotion, and (again, Sacco excepted) the very best graphic novels don't take themselves entirely seriously. They appeal to that childish part of ourselves that delights in caricature, and they rely on the magic, familiar but always a little startling, that reliably turns some lines, dots and squiggles into a face or a figure. It's a trick of sorts, but one that never wears out.

CONSIDER

1. In the opening paragraphs of "Not Funnies," McGrath describes a transitional moment when novels displaced poetry as the favored form of serious literature. He speculates that the comic book or graphic novel might eventually oust the novel as the literary form with the greatest mass appeal. What other forms of "literature" might compete with comics for that distinction in "our dumbed-down culture"? (You might want to expand the definition of literature to include movies, TV shows, video productions, hypertexts, and other electronic and multimedia genres.)

2. Is it fair for McGrath to stereotype the development of a typical graphic artist as one who begins with an obsession with cartoons, is a nerd in high school, lives out sexual fantasies in drawings, goes through a "Crumb" period, and so on? Or do people in other professions—engineers, teachers, clergy—also go through comparably distinctive stages in their lives as they move toward careers? Could you create such a narrative for people in your academic major (if you have one at this point)?

3. Do you agree with McGrath's closing assessment of what graphic novels can and cannot achieve? Given the elements of the cartoon form, why would a graphic novel likely be most successful depicting blankness, spookiness, and paranoia? Can you imagine a graphic novel aspiring to light romance? To epic or tragedy? Why or why not?

COMPOSE

4. McGrath suggests that the "thematic landscape" of graphic novels is similar to what can be found in prose fiction. Do you agree? Write an analysis in which you explore the influence of the form of a graphic novel on its thematic elements.

CHALLENGE

5. McGrath makes a point of distinguishing between true graphic novels and "the old Classics Illustrated series," which used the comic book form to introduce young readers to classics of literature. But imagine that you will turn a novel you know well or particularly like into a graphic novel for adults. How might you have to modify the original story to make it work as a graphic novel? What parts of the work would be easiest to turn into panels of images? What parts would be harder to illustrate? What would you gain or lose in making the transition from one narrative medium to another? In a short prospectus for your graphic novel, make an argument to a publisher for your graphic novel project. If you have the talent, offer a few panels to illustrate the story.

Assignments
and Projects

Project 1

Reviewing a Film

When you talk about movies informally with friends, you may discuss your immediate reactions ("That chase scene scared me to death") or personal tastes ("I loved the special effects" or "Tobey McGuire makes a great superhero"). But professional writers who review films must provide detailed descriptions of the technical aspects of the movie, discuss the film in terms of similar films, comment on the key concerns raised by the film, and offer recommendations for potential viewers. This assignment asks you to develop a similarly detailed assessment of a film you've recently seen by writing a two- to three-page review essay.

As you begin, you may find it helpful to review the composing questions introduced in Chapter 2 of this book:

WHAT'S IT TO YOU?

- Begin by selecting a film you would like to view. You might consider some of the suggestions listed earlier in the chapter or on our Web site, or you might select a film you have always wanted to see. Perhaps your roommate thinks that *The Manchurian Candidate* (2004) is the best film remake ever made; or maybe you're intrigued by the controversies ignited by *Fahrenheit 9/11* (2004) or *The Passion of the Christ* (2004) and want to judge the movie for yourself.

WHAT DO YOU WANT TO SAY ABOUT IT?

- Once you have a film in mind, prepare to view the movie by thinking about the larger **purpose** of the review you will write. The goal will be to describe the film to readers and then to offer some judgments about its technical aspects and any themes or issues the film treats.

WHO WILL LISTEN?

- As a reviewer, you must assume that your **audience** has not seen the movie. You'll need to introduce the film and its director and major actors and then very briefly summarize what takes place in the movie—without providing so much information that you'll spoil the experience if your readers decide to watch it themselves. Next, provide detailed descriptions that will help readers visualize the aspects of the film you find most significant. If, for instance, you think the use of lighting is exceptional, describe key scenes using details that demonstrate how lighting is used in the film. Also consider such aspects as sound, music, acting, editing, and camera use.

WHAT DO YOU NEED TO KNOW?

■ You'll gather the most important material for your review by carefully **analyzing what you see** in the film. When you view the film, then, concentrate on how exactly the film tells its story. What is distinctive about the director's technique or the work of actors? How do you react to the issues or themes explored in the movie? If possible, watch the film several times—or at the very least, carefully review key scenes that you plan to discuss in your draft. **Take good notes** so that details and insights don't fade.

In addition to these technical aspects, you'll need to understand the film in the context of similar movies. Conduct **research** in the library or on the Internet, looking both for texts and commentary and for other films that place your chosen film within larger contexts: You might relate the film to others made by the same director or starring the same actors. Or you could trace the film back toward earlier movies in the same genre.

HOW WILL YOU DO IT?

■ Consult magazines that regularly publish extended film reviews, such as the *New Yorker* or *Atlantic Monthly*, to get a sense of how these writers typically **structure** their commentary. Many reviews follow a general pattern, which can serve as an informal template as you begin your draft: Start with background information and a summary; then move on to evaluate technical and artistic elements and the major concerns treated in the movie. If the film touches on controversies, spell them out and explain for your readers how the film addresses these issues. For major themes developed by the film, consider how sophisticated the film is in treating these motifs, and comment on the strengths or weaknesses of the thematic elements. Finally, offer an overall judgment about the movie. What one or two things should readers thinking about viewing the film know? Is there a particular group who would appreciate the film more than others? Would you recommend the movie? How strongly?

HOW WELL DOES IT WORK?

■ If your review works, it will inspire readers to take your final recommendation—to watch the film if it's good or to avoid it if it's not. Check whether your draft is successful by asking a friend or classmate to read it and then say whether he or she is persuaded by your recommendation. This feedback may identify possible areas for **revision**.

STUDENT SAMPLE

Katie Doyle, "Mean Girls: High School Uncut"

Katie Doyle

Professor Anderson

English 3.1

18 October 2004

Mean Girls: High School Uncut

Mean Girls, directed by Mark Waters and starring Lindsay Lohan, Rachel McAdams, and Tina Fey, is a uniquely true and hilarious look at social life in high school today and more specifically "Girl World." When Cady (Lindsay Lohan) moves to the United States with her parents after a life of home schooling in Africa, she must quickly find a place to fit in at her suburban high school. Cady is immediately intimidated by the cliquey atmosphere and realizes that making friends (and keeping them) is going to be tougher than she thought. With a clever screenplay by Saturday Night Live star and writer Tina Fey, Mean Girls portrays how the evolutionary principle of survival of the fittest rules the social structure of high school. The film explores many facets of teen life including not only finding a place to belong among the cliques but also the role of adults in teenagers' lives.

When Cady (ironically mispronounced "catty" in the film) first arrives at her public high school, she has no friends and no idea how to make any. She is gradually taken in by two social outcasts, one a Gothic-looking girl and the other a gay boy, who explain to Cady the social caste system in place. However, much to her new friends' dismay, Cady also sparks the interest of "the Plastics," a group of three beautiful, white upper-class girls-- or mean girls, as they happen to be. These three are at the top of the social hierarchy in the school and manipulate almost everyone with their fake charm, popularity, and petty and often fictional gossip. Nearly everyone in the school envies the Plastics, and this gives them a unique position of being both feared and glorified in the school. When Regina (Rachel

McAdams) steals the boy Cady has her eye on, the gloves come off and Cady joins up with her two original outcast friends to systematically destroy the Plastics and more specifically Regina, the meanest of the mean girls, from inside of their close-knit group. However, talking, dressing, and acting like a Plastic all the time starts to seep into Cady's true self, and she is faced with the sad reality of what it is like to be a mean girl.

At times Mean Girls feels like a documentary due to the use of several editing and film techniques. First of all, Cady narrates much of the film, and the audience gets a sense of her own personal struggle to fit in and fight the influence of the Plastics. Her narrations are often contrary to her actions and thereby inform the viewer that she knows she is doing right or wrong in a given situation. Likewise, the incorporation of quickly edited flashbacks, montages, and fantasies conveys not only Cady's thoughts but also the thoughts of the rest of the school. There are several montages that highlight the responses of less popular people in the school and help place the Plastics in the social context of the school. The montages are responses or comments about Regina and eventually Cady that parallel those used in documentaries when different people are being asked the same question. The quick editing in these montages makes them feel like real interviews intended to prove a solidified point, as if the director is saying to the audience, "See, I told you so." The documentary feel to the film speaks to how successfully Fey has adapted the original source for the movie, Rosalind Wiseman's book Queen Bees and Wannabees, which examines the phenomenon of the cliques and "queen bees" in teen girl social groups. Mean Girls offers the social science of adolescent behavior in an entertaining package, as the montages and Cady's narrations make clear.

Although Mean Girls is a comedy, it is also rife with dramatic elements and topics. Almost every girl in this society knows about the cliques in high school and knows deep down within herself where she is on the social ranking. Although the film does overdramatize at times to add comic relief to the situation, the fact remains that teenage girls today are not unified. They make life hard on each other and can be petty, mean, and exclusive.

Cady personifies a feeling that most teenage girls have experienced at one time in their lives, a desire to belong in a structured society that does not accept anyone without some backhanded maneuvering.

Mean Girls also deals with the alienation of parents from their teens. For example, at one point Cady's parents ask her the usual parental questions ("How was school today? Were the people nice?") and are met with quick one-word responses from their daughter. On the other hand, Regina's mom is a "cool mom" who dresses like her daughter, talks to her daughter's friends, and maintains an open attitude about drinking and sex, among other things. However, despite her mom's coolness, Regina still gives her the same shut-out attitude. The fear of teen pregnancy is also a reality in this movie, in which the health teacher continually talks about abstinence and warns the students against having sex. These scenes and others emphasize the reality of sexually active teens today and at the same time the uncertainty adults feel regarding how to deal with it.

Overall, Mean Girls is an interestingly realistic dramatization of teenage girl culture in America today. The use of montages and fantasies gives the film a documentary-like interactive feel that speaks directly to the audience. This film might be considered the Clueless of the next generation in that it highlights the petty reality of being a teenage girl today but also outlines the transformation of one teen who overcomes the social hierarchy of high school. At least some aspect of this film will ring true for everyone who has ever gone to high school or who is in high school and certainly for all women who have experienced how petty and mean girls can be. This film contains an empowering message with a comedic twist and speaks directly to the audience. Due in large part to Lohan's down-to-earth performance and Fey's Saturday Night Live sense of humor, Mean Girls is a joy to watch.

Additional Student Work
www.ablongman.com/beyondwords22

Composing a Photo Essay

Earlier in this chapter, we discussed the ways in which multimedia genres like photo essays and Web pages are creating new kinds of narratives. In this project, we invite you to create a photo essay designed to instruct an audience about a moment in history or about an aspect of contemporary culture. Inform your essay with research conducted using the Internet, the library, or interviews. Select at least eight images that allow you to convey important information about your topic, and then incorporate those images into Web pages and add captions and explanations that allow you to tell a story about your topic.

OPTION 1: RESEARCH A HISTORICAL MOMENT OR EVENT

Select a time in the past that will provide ample opportunities for locating images. You might research the Vietnam War, the Great Depression, World War II, the civil rights movement, or some other major episode in history.

OPTION 2: RESEARCH AN ASPECT OF CULTURE

Consider some element of contemporary culture. You might look at a group or activity, like NASCAR fans or disc golf. You might explore a cultural issue such as teen pregnancy. You might look at a cultural phenomenon such as vacations or exercise.

WHAT'S IT TO YOU?

- You'll feel more invested in your photo essay if you choose a **subject** that you're curious about or have a strong personal connection to. Ask yourself, for example, what historical and cultural phenomena have affected your family—perhaps your grandfather was injured while fighting in Vietnam, or your older sister worked as an aide in the Clinton White House. Or you may be involved in an organization or hobby that you'd like to tell readers about.

WHAT DO YOU WANT TO SAY ABOUT IT?

- Because the **purpose** of your photo essay is to provide information about the topic, research should drive the process of developing your essay. To begin, you must gravitate toward a topic and then focus your thinking into a **research question**. For instance, you might ask "What was the role of music in the lives of soldiers in Vietnam?" or "What beliefs do NASCAR fans share about political issues?" Developing a research question often requires that you conduct some initial investigation to get a feel for a topic.

WHAT DO YOU NEED TO KNOW?

■ Next, conduct more extensive research. You have three options:

1. **Library research.** Begin by exploring the indexes and abstracts of the library, conducting keyword searches to locate information. Download articles or locate materials on the shelves. Explore your materials, selecting the most relevant sources and taking notes. (Be sure to keep track of the publication information.)

2. **Internet research.** Conduct keyword searches on the Net. Be sure to let your research question guide you so that you can focus your keyword searches to locate relevant materials. Evaluate the sources you discover. Keep track of valuable materials, reading and taking notes to develop information.

3. **Personal interviews.** Identify individuals who can inform your exploration of your topic. Divide your research question into a number of subquestions to pose to an interview subject. Phrase questions so that they let subjects respond in open-ended terms—for example, instead of saying, "Why are disc golfers always sloppy dressers?" say, "What are your thoughts on the way disc golfers dress?" Take careful notes, and be sure to tell the subject that you will be using the interview for your essay. You may want to take a digital picture or videotape your subject as well.

You may use any or all of these three options. Just be sure to have a wide array of research sources to support your project.

HOW WILL YOU DO IT?

■ Because its components combine elements of different media, you may find that your composing process for this project is more complicated than for a traditional essay. Here are some tips to get you started. First, locate **images** that will allow you to inform readers about your topic and your research. Images should not be selected randomly. Rather, each image should allow you to make points about your topic. Select at least eight images for the project. (See our Web tutorials for more on locating images.)

Next, compose a Web project that has an opening page, pages for each of the images, and a page for a conclusion. Create a **navigational and design scheme** for the pages.

Next, develop an **essay page** for each image. The page should have three components:

1. **The image.** Think about the order in which you arrange the images in your essay. Be sure to crop or size the images for maximum effect.

2. **A caption.** Compose a caption of not more than one sentence that emphasizes the key concerns of the image and situates the image within the structure of the essay.

3. **An explanation.** Compose at least four sentences explaining the significance of the image. Your explanation might discuss aspects of the image in more detail. It should also integrate your research information whenever possible. The explanation should make your topic meaningful to readers.

Next, compose an introduction and a conclusion. You may wish to use images on these pages as well. Be sure to include a properly formatted list of sources in your conclusion.

HOW WELL DOES IT WORK?

■ Proofread the text you have written, sharpening the language. Check that the order of the images makes sense. Revise the project, updating the Web pages as needed. As you refine and polish your project, look at some sample photo essays on our Web site or at Michael Lee's essay, which was composed in response to this assignment.

STUDENT SAMPLE

Michael Lee, "Images of History: The Hmong"

Michael composed this photo essay, excerpts of which follow, partly as a way of exploring his own heritage as a Hmong American. His family immigrated to the United States shortly after the Vietnam War, and, as Michael reports, the Hmong culture native to Vietnam has since been dispersed as communists in Laos have retaliated for the Hmong's assistance of U.S. troops during the war. Michael worries that "the Hmong traditions and the Hmong language itself are quickly diminishing and may be even inevitably dying off." He hopes that the essay will serve to preserve some of his personal and cultural history.

In the photo essay, Michael does a good job of surrounding his photographs with explanatory text that relates the history of the Hmong people and lays out the issues inherent in their treatment during and after the war. In addition to textual explanations and captions, Michael incorporates a brief quotation or catch-phrase into each page of the essay. The structure of his essay includes both *next* and *previous* links on every page and a standardized menu on the left that places the images in a chronological sequence.

All Work and No Play – Mozilla

photoessay | Search | Print

Michael's Photo Essay

Pre-Vietnam War

Picture #1: Hmong village

Picture #2: Hmong life

Picture #3: Hmong New Years

Picture #4: Hmong pastime and culture

Vietnam War Era

Picture #5: Hmong Quilt

Picture #6: The Secret Army

Picture #7: The Refugee Camps

Post-Vietnam

Picture #8: Hmong in the world

Picture #9: Hmong in America, New Year

Picture #10: Hmong Tar Heel

Works Cited

Images of History: The Hmong

PREVIOUS | NEXT

Picture #2:

Hmong farmers working on rice paddies.

"All work and no play"

For the Hmong, farming was a way of life and survival; the staple food was white rice and supplemented by vegetables like cucumbers and yams, among other things, and fish meat and a variety of spices and seasonings (Betancourt). Livestock was housed close to the home, if not in extensions of the houses themselves, and commonly included cattle and ox, pigs and chickens and sometimes horses (Quincy 70). Oxen, in particular, were very useful and few families could afford to own one. Oxen were very important for two reasons, the first for the role as draft animals and the second for sacrifices at funerals (Quincy 79). The farm fields were located a good distance from the villages, just far enough to keep the livestock from getting to them and close enough to cut down on travel time (Quincy 72). Most of the Hmong practiced "slash and burn" farming and demanded few tools to work the land: Axes, hoes, planting sticks, although hard work and determination were required. Although the slash and burn practice was an effective short term farming method, it depleted the soil so the families had to migrate often (Quincy 74).

"The pictures helped me pinpoint a starting point, but I had to narrow my topic to be able to clarify my goals and the steps I needed to take to achieve them. I tried my best to briefly describe the background of the Hmong, and I hope that is useful. Second, I had a huge problem identifying everything I would use to support the photo and how to effectively include the necessary information. Once again, narrowing my topic really helped me on this."

—MICHAEL LEE

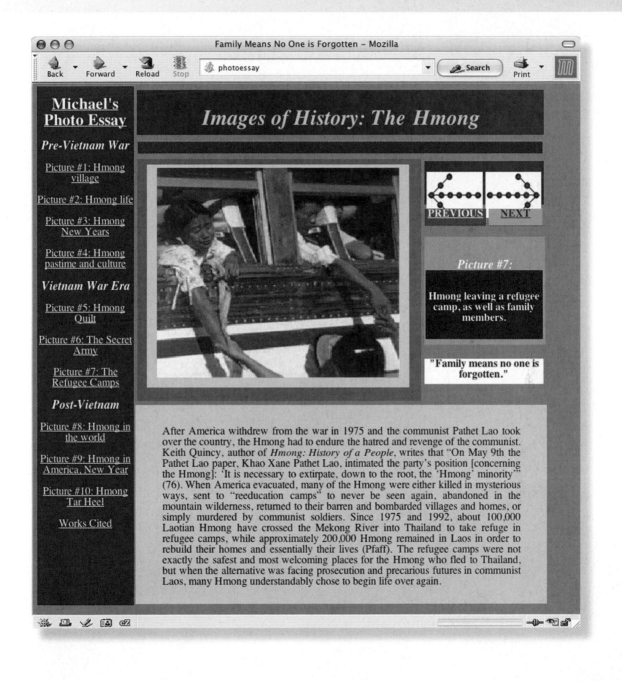

Michael's Photo Essay

Pre-Vietnam War

Picture #1: Hmong village

Picture #2: Hmong life

Picture #3: Hmong New Years

Picture #4: Hmong pastime and culture

Vietnam War Era

Picture #5: Hmong Quilt

Picture #6: The Secret Army

Picture #7: The Refugee Camps

Post-Vietnam

Picture #8: Hmong in the world

Picture #9: Hmong in America, New Year

Picture #10: Hmong Tar Heel

Works Cited

Images of History: The Hmong

PREVIOUS NEXT

Picture #7:

Hmong leaving a refugee camp, as well as family members.

"Family means no one is forgotten."

After America withdrew from the war in 1975 and the communist Pathet Lao took over the country, the Hmong had to endure the hatred and revenge of the communist. Keith Quincy, author of *Hmong: History of a People*, writes that "On May 9th the Pathet Lao paper, Khao Xane Pathet Lao, intimated the party's position [concerning the Hmong]: 'It is necessary to extirpate, down to the root, the 'Hmong' minority'" (76). When America evacuated, many of the Hmong were either killed in mysterious ways, sent to "reeducation camps" to never be seen again, abandoned in the mountain wilderness, returned to their barren and bombarded villages and homes, or simply murdered by communist soldiers. Since 1975 and 1992, about 100,000 Laotian Hmong have crossed the Mekong River into Thailand to take refuge in refugee camps, while approximately 200,000 Hmong remained in Laos in order to rebuild their homes and essentially their lives (Pfaff). The refugee camps were not exactly the safest and most welcoming places for the Hmong who fled to Thailand, but when the alternative was facing prosecution and precarious futures in communist Laos, many Hmong understandably chose to begin life over again.

On a hot and jazzy night the word HOT-CHA was invented.

③ Interlude

MAIRA KALMAN

a conversation about creating an illustrated book

Fireboat: The Heroic Adventures of the John J. Harvey recounts the events of September 11, 2001 through the story of the fireboat *John J. Harvey*. Originally launched in 1931 and decommissioned in 1995, the Harvey was refurbished by a group of friends in 2000 and was called back into service to help fight the fires at the World Trade Center.

What led you to write *Fireboat*, and what did you hope to achieve with it?

The idea was given to me by one of the owners of the fireboat. At first I did not want to do it. But then I was overwhelmed by how wonderful the people on the Harvey were. I love New York and I saw this as a love song to New York.

How does the Harvey's story allow you to tell the story of September 11 to children? What do you think it adds to the overall conversation about the event and its aftermath?

September 11 was a tragedy. Tragedies cannot be avoided—they are personal and epic. It is what you do with the information, how you rebuild that is important. One of the most important lessons in life is not to lose hope—to be optimistic and believe in the basic goodness of the people around you.

What do you hope children take away from it? And adults?

I always want children and adults to take away the same feelings—that there is always hope, no matter how horrible the situation seems, and that small acts are huge. A child can make a sandwich for someone, and that is as important as putting out a fire.

In my research for the book, I discovered that the word *hot-cha* was coined by Cab Calloway in the Cotton Club, the famous Harlem nightspot. That's Cab Calloway in the center of the painting. I always use lots of references and things that are, basically, non sequiturs in my books and in the imagery. So in addition to Cab Calloway, Weegee, the great photojournalist, is captured here, and that's Josephine Baker dancing in the pink dress.

How do you go about deciding what level of language to use when writing for young readers?

I don't decide anything. I follow my instinct. That is why there is no difference in writing for children or for adults. There are no considerations of marketing or suitability. I write from the heart with humor and intelligence.

What was the most difficult part of creating this book?

Painting the two planes flying into the buildings and the explosion. I was looking at the photos and just crying all the time. Painting and crying. But I thought that if I could show this kind of horror without it looking horrible in a way, then I could show the truth and keep on going. They are very important images for me, because they are looking at the devil right in the eye as opposed to being afraid. But it was very, very sad work.

What comes first, the pictures or the words? What process do you follow?

The process is a flow from one to the other. I go back and forth for a while, and then I write the book. Then I sketch and see how it works. Then I rewrite. Then I resketch and rewrite until I have cut it down to the bare, lyrical essentials. Things keep changing until the last minute.

Do you go through many drafts?

Absolutely. It's usually terrible the first time it's written, so I go through many, many rewrites. I wish that the first things I put down were wonderful. I don't even know if the last thing I end up with is wonderful, but I'm finally done. You usually have to go through many stages of confusion, overexplaining, unnecessary detours, and boring sections to finally edit yourself down and to understand what it is that you really want to say.

The book opens with a series of pages illustrating various events that happened in New York City in 1931, the year the Harvey was launched. So, for instance, you note that the Snickers bar was introduced that year, that the Empire State Building was completed, and that the word *hot-cha* became popular. None of these events really has anything to do with the Harvey or the events of September 11.

That's right. They are all irrelevant to the Harvey. This, to me, is a very important way of thinking: that you are allowed to go off the point. What I was really thinking here was, "What was New York about when the Harvey first appeared, and what was a particular, odd thing that happened then? What would be charming and funny and crazy for me to know?" I think if I had started straight off with the Harvey, it wouldn't have been as good as starting with New York and the atmosphere of the wonderful major *and* minute things that were going on.

Could you talk a little about the visual and verbal pacing of the pages concerned with the attack itself?

Once I knew where the story would begin—with the city itself—the pace just came naturally. Big image. Little text. The power of the combination.

On the spread where the planes are approaching the buildings, you wrote "crash, crash, crash," but there were only two crashes.

That would be too literal. I was just saying that this unbelievable, unfathomable event kept going on and on and on, and you couldn't believe that something else happened, then something else happened.

And on the next spread you filled the pages with the explosion and then you switch to the passive voice.

I probably wanted to be gentler. I'm unconscious of that kind of decision making other than that I probably wanted to be a little more poetic and less immediate and less violent after the violence of that image.

Were there any paintings you had that you didn't include in the end?

There were more paintings of people who were around the story but not directly involved. I often go through a bunch of sketches and a bunch of dummies before I get to my final, "OK, this is the book." I work on note cards and shuffle the ideas around. So usually by the time I get to painting, I really know what I'm going to paint. I'm designing it in my head and kind of loosely on the page. And then, since I have already written the words and I am also the designer, I paint knowing where the typography is going to go.

And on a sunny fresh day, the John J. Harvey fireboat was launched.

There were 12 fireboats in New York City. The Harvey was the largest, fastest and shiniest fireboat of them all.

◄ The Harvey was the premier boat of its time. There was fanfare and general festivities when it was launched. It was obviously a beautiful boat that was important to the history of firefighting in New York.

▼ This page precedes the spread showing the attack on the towers. We are in a kind of obvious graphic here—this is a black moment in our time, for the city, for the world. And it was a serious, deeply tragic moment, so it made sense to stop the kind of colorful festivities of the book and say, "OK, now something really deep and dark is about to happen."

But then on September 11, 2001
something so huge and horrible
happened that the whole world
shook.

It was 8:45 in the morning,
another beautiful and sunny day.

Milton Glaser talks about how computers have changed design. Do you think they have?

The idea of designing or painting on a computer is very unpleasant to me because I think that the mistakes that you make and the surprises that you have when you have a pencil in your hand are very, very different than when you're sitting in front of a computer that has a limited ability to do any number of things. I don't want to sound as if people can't be creative with a computer because that's not fair. But I think for most people, their creativity is diminished with a computer. Anybody can have the expertise. It's not hard to do typefaces and all that, but to have an idea, a creative idea, a new idea, is something that comes from a different place and certainly not from the computer.

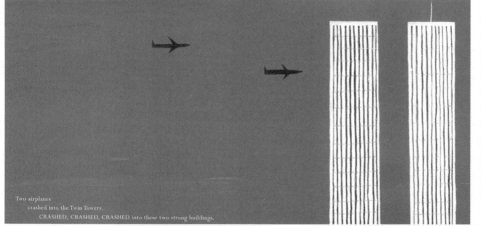

Two airplanes
crashed into the Twin Towers.
CRASHED, CRASHED, CRASHED into these two strong buildings.

◀ This was the first image that I knew I was going to put in the book. Originally, I had said that doing this book was absolutely not for me. When I decided that I *would* do it, this image just came to me, and that was the beginning. In a graphic sense, those two black planes coming into our world, destroying our world in a sense, was something that I just knew.

► This painting is based on an image that was in many papers and in the few books that were quickly put together after the event. I had hundreds of photographs, but this one felt right. It felt important. It felt like I could tell the story without it being horrific but yet show this thing that happened.

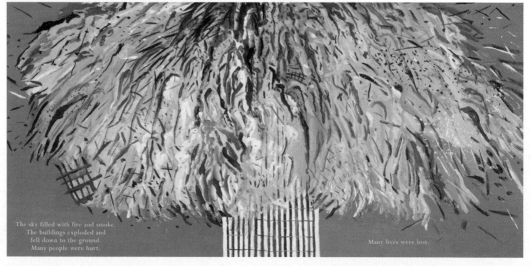

The sky filled with fire and smoke.
The buildings exploded and
fell down to the ground.
Many people were hurt.

Many lives were lost.

For four days and nights the Harvey pumped water. The crew took turns sleeping. People brought supplies: fuel, sweaters, gloves, pizza, sandwiches and coffee. They worked and cried. They fought the fire until it was under control.

◀ I interviewed every owner of the Harvey and every person who had anything to do with the Harvey, and I listened to their stories. One of the things that was very moving for all of them was the days and the nights they spent working, and the help and the hope and the despair, so showing a nighttime scene of everybody was important.

▶ This is the final spread in the book. I went onto the Staten Island Ferry a number of times to see the light and to see the city. Although it seems like an incredibly abstract painting, it is based on my photographs of the city and the sunset. The next day has come, and the world goes on.

Now the Twin Towers are gone. Something new will be built. The heroes who died will be remembered forever. The Harvey is back to being a very happy boat. NOT scrapped. NOT useless. NOT forgotten.

A proud and plucky friend. And all that's left to say is HOT-CHA (and thank you!)

Wait a minute. There is something more to say. The friends of the Harvey have found a little tugboat to adopt. Doesn't everyone need a tugboat?

CHALLENGE

1. What do you think of Kalman's comment that "a creative idea, a new idea, is something that comes from a different place and certainly not from the computer"? Do you agree that computers hinder creative thought? Write an essay that argues your position on this issue, discussing specific examples from your reading or personal experience to support your ideas.

2. Kalman emphasizes that words and images are thoroughly interwoven in *Fireboat*. Select an illustrated book that you really like—for example, a children's picture book, a graphic novel, or a how-to manual or illustrated encyclopedia. Write a two-page review evaluating how effectively the text and illustrations work together to present information, tell a story, or appeal to readers.

3. Try your hand at creating your own illustrated children's book. Select a recent event from the news and retell it in picture book form, tailoring your presentation to appeal to a young audience. In designing and composing your book, use whatever media best suit your purpose and skills—from pencil drawings and handwritten text to image-editing software.

For additional writing projects related to this Interlude see www.ablongman.com/beyondwords23

CHAPTER 6

MAPPING IDEAS

writing to inform and explain

The Hobo-Dyer Equal Area Projection

This new map belongs to the family of Cylindrical Equal Area projections in which the latitude and longitude lines form a rectangular grid. Other projections in this family include the Lambert, Gall, Behrmann, Edwards, and Peters projections. In the present case the "cylinder" is assumed to wrap round the globe and cut through it at 37½° north and south. In order to preserve the equal area property the shapes of the landmasses become progressively flattened towards the poles, but shapes between 45° north and south are well preserved.

The Hobo-Dyer Equal Area Projection Map of the World

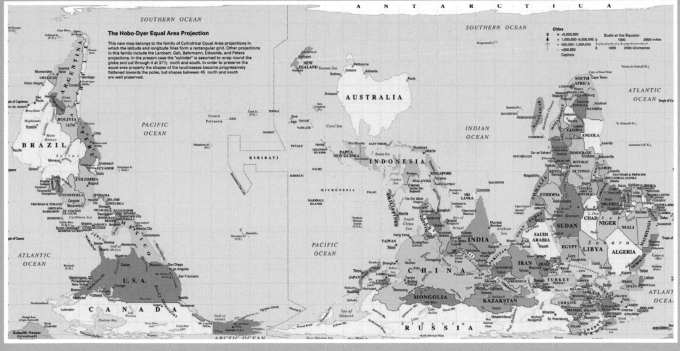

The Hobo-Dyer Equal Area Projection Map of the World, inverted

What grabs your attention in each of these maps? How do the different focal points change the way we read these mirror images?

How does flipping the orientation of a map change your views of the world?

Introduction

When we first look at the two views of the world that open this chapter, it might appear that someone has simply rotated a map 180 degrees in order to see the world from "upside down." If we look more carefully, however, we will see that the labels on the upside-down map are oriented up, printed left to right across the top as we would expect. A map key illustrates scale and points toward the geographical direction at the top of the map, in this case, south. The map shows countries, population centers, and bodies of water. The real change is that the image of the world has been flipped to orient the Southern Hemisphere toward the top.

But what might be the intent behind flipping the image? Shouldn't north appear at the top of any map? Well, maybe not if you live in Australia. In fact, if we use the equator as a dividing line for creating maps, any map of the Southern Hemisphere should probably be geared toward the South Pole. When we look at the upside-down map, the focal point is Australia, followed by South America and Africa. As a way of explaining the geographical makeup of the world, then, the two maps provide startlingly different views as they prompt us to consider who gets to be on top.

Choosing to emphasize the Northern or Southern Hemisphere changes the way information is presented in maps. And these choices help us think about how we write to inform and explain. More so than in expressive or persuasive writing, we make the appearance of objectivity a goal as we write to inform others. Both maps allow readers to locate land masses and countries—they each explain the world and aim for accuracy. Still, even our clearest explanations will be colored by our own perspectives. Both maps also offer information from a particular perspective; they reflect decisions about how their creators wish to present information to an audience.

Clearly, aims and agendas can color informative writing. But challenges also arise when we need to translate complex concepts and information into texts. Flat maps are doomed to fail when it comes to representing the three-dimensional, spheroid-shaped world. Buckminster Fuller's "dymaxion projection" map, shown on page 333, is designed to be folded and spliced into a globe shape to better capture the reality of our world. Fuller's model responds in part to the distortions that result from projecting a spherical shape onto a flat surface—think of the way Antarctica covers an entire edge of most maps. Fuller's Antarctica is more accurate in scale and placement.

INTRODUCTION

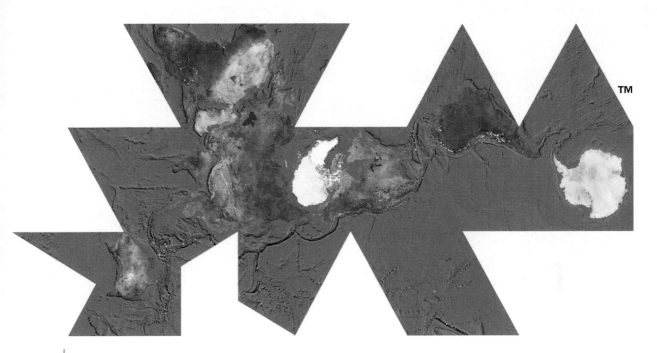

™

World Map Using the Dymaxion Projection

What's in This Chapter?

In this chapter, we look at some of the ways that information gets explained, especially those that rely on technology to inform us about our world. Some of this information helps us make sense of what is happening around us. We first look at transformations wrought by information in the natural sciences—the convergences among computers, satellites, and geography illuminate clearly how the digitization of data is changing scientific knowledge, and developments in medical imaging reveal how new sources of information affect our bodies and our behaviors. Then we turn to the virtual worlds of online experience to explore how the concepts of self and place are being transformed in a new kind of environment.

As you explore these images and texts, think about the ways in which writing to explain calls for you to make similar decisions about how best to present information.

Reading Images
That Explain

Even the most simple informational images must be read with care. A bar graph depicting statistics can seem straightforward enough, but by massaging the statistical data, the creator of the graph can distort the information to emphasize one category over another or to play up similarities or differences between categories. Other images must struggle with the challenges that come from presenting information clearly—think of illustrations for technical manuals that must rely on a single image to provide instructions for users who speak multiple languages.

It's up to you to investigate critically every text you encounter, especially those that might seem initially simply to share information. In some cases you must look for deliberate manipulation in the images you examine. In other instances you must uncover the design decisions that have gone into the creation of informational texts to appreciate them fully. And, at times, you will need to identify when images veer away from simple explanation and toward self-expression or argument. As you weigh these considerations, refer to our questions for understanding images that explain.

What do you see?

What is it about?

To what does it relate?

How is it composed?

What details matter?

What do you see?

When it is presented well, information should be clear and readily under-standable. *Graphs and charts* can facilitate this process. In a report on the impact of file sharing on music sales, Felix Oberholzer and Koleman Strumpf use a simple map (see below) to show where music downloads in the year 2003 took place. The top downloaders and countries where no file sharing occurs are clearly demonstrated by the sharp black and white contrasts of the chart, which focuses our attention on the United States.

But information, even when presented clearly, usually conveys meaning beyond its surface appearance. To understand the distribution of downloads by country shown in the accompanying chart, we must temper the initial visual impression that most downloading takes place in the United States with a careful evaluation of the information itself. The chart indicates that in 2003, 15–35% of the total number of downloads occurred in the United States. If we look only at the map without noting the percentages listed on the chart, we might assume that nearly all downloading took place in the United States. But a careful look at the num-bers reveals that in fact, less than half of all downloads took place in the United States and that parts of Europe fall into the same percentage range.

As this example illustrates, we need to maintain a sense of skepticism about displays of information. The accompanying *statistics* can be the key to criti-cally evaluating just how realistically information has been charted. Take a look at the two sample bar graphs representing music downloads on page 336. They both convey the same information, but one presents the change from one

File Sharing by Country, 2003

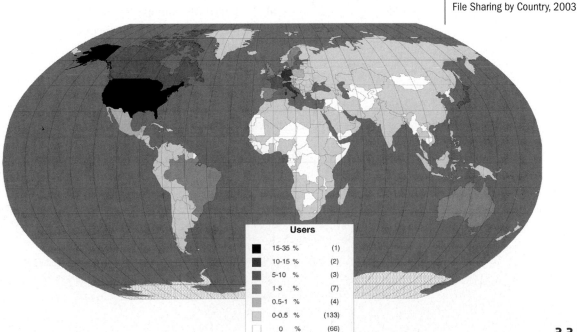

Users		
15-35 %		(1)
10-15 %		(2)
5-10 %		(3)
1-5 %		(7)
0.5-1 %		(4)
0-0.5 %		(133)
0 %		(66)

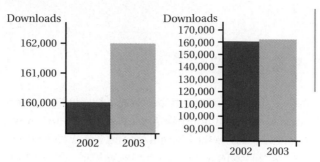

The same data can be represented visually in ways that exaggerate or minimize the increase in file downloads from 2002 to 2003.

Tables represent numerical data designed to provide detail rather than a concise visual explanation.

Table 1 – The Geography of File Sharing (numbers in %)

Country	Share of users	Share of downloads	Share World Population	Share World GDP	Share World Internet Users	Software Piracy Rate
United States	30.9	35.7	4.6	21.2	27.4	23
Germany	13.5	14.1	1.3	4.5	5.3	32
Italy	11.1	9.9	0.9	2.9	3.2	47
Japan	8.4	2.8	2.0	7.2	9.3	35
France	6.9	6.9	1.0	3.1	2.8	43
Canada	5.4	6.1	0.5	1.9	2.8	39
United Kingdom	4.1	4.0	1.0	3.1	5.7	26
Spain	2.5	2.6	0.6	1.7	1.3	47
Netherlands	2.1	2.1	0.3	0.9	1.6	36
Australia	1.6	1.9	0.3	1.1	1.8	32
Sweden	1.5	1.7	0.1	0.5	1.0	29
Switzerland	1.4	1.5	0.1	0.5	0.6	32
Brazil	1.3	1.4	2.9	2.7	2.3	55
Belgium	0.9	1.2	0.2	0.6	0.6	31
Austria	0.8	0.6	0.1	0.5	0.6	30
Poland	0.5	0.7	0.6	0.8	1.1	54

Notes on country covariates:
Shares of users and downloads is from the file sharing dataset described in the text. All other statistics are from *The CIA World Factbook* (2002, 2003), except the software piracy rates which are from the *Eighth Annual BSA Global Software Piracy Study* (2003). All values are world shares, except the piracy rates are the fractions of business application software installed without a license in the country. All non-file sharing data are for 2002 except population which is for 2003.

"There's no minimizing the impact of illegal file sharing. It robs songwriters and recording artists of their livelihoods, and it ultimately undermines the future of music itself, not to mention threatening the jobs of tens of thousands."

—CARY SHERMAN
president of the Recording Industry Association of America

year to the next as drastic, while the other suggests almost no change at all. It's tempting to see the red bar and react to the visual information; in reality, though, the figures themselves provide a better explanation of the changes.

Similarly, you must look at the **genre** of explanatory materials, considering any conventions used for presenting information and recognizing what elements to focus on. Compare Oberholzer and Strumpf's simple map with the above explanatory table from the music download study. The table is printed at the end of the report, aimed at statisticians interested in the data of the study. It is meant to help scholars interpret the findings of the report in detail rather than to provide a concise explanation.

CONSIDER

1. How carefully do you consider the statistics behind the graphs that you see in publications or ads? In what circumstances might the creators of graphs deliberately manipulate their presentations? Cite some examples.

2. What kinds of information do you expect to be most honestly presented? For example, are genres like technical documentation manuals or cookbooks subject to manipulation? Why or why not? Are weather maps skewed? Baseball statistics? Poll numbers?

What is it about?

The **subject** of a piece of informative writing should be clear and straightforward. When it isn't, readers get frustrated quickly—that's one reason we resent poorly written technical documentation. We just want to know how our new printer works, not every detail about its features and options. Even a picture doesn't always help. Many tasks involve a number of steps, and with each step comes an opportunity for doing the wrong thing. Most technical manuals also try to convey instructions through both words and images, and many offer variations of instructions in multiple languages. With technical descriptions, such as those in the printing manual excerpted below, writers must think carefully about the sequencing of steps, provide clear iconic images that show how to perform the individual tasks that make up the process being explained, and offer concise written text that complements the visual instructions—no small matter.

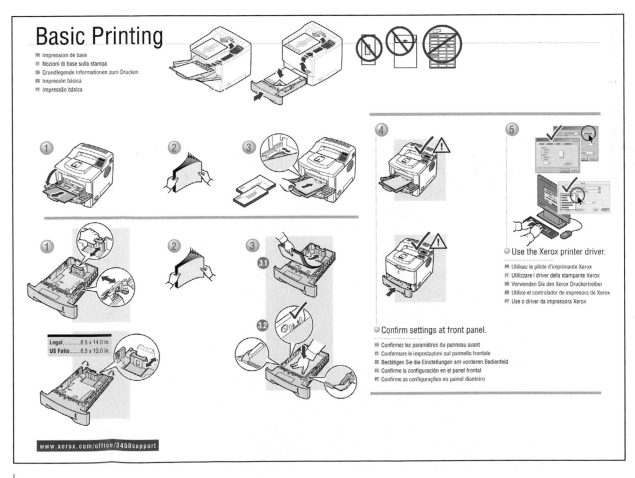

Basic printing instructions from the quick reference guide for a Xerox laser printer

Still using condoms, AIDS hasn't gone away, can't tell by looks, new treatments – but still no cure, best be careful, keep sex safer.

Phone for the facts.

Phone the National AIDS Helpline on **0800 567 123** for the facts about AIDS or for help about safer sex.
Welsh and minority ethnic language services are also available.
For an information leaflet call free on **0500 500 695**.

Yet even simple, informative messages may be doing more than just providing basic information. They may carry deeper messages. For example, an AIDS awareness poster like the one shown here might provide lots of facts. But behind the facts might be warnings about behavior that wouldn't be quite so powerful if stated directly. Readers get the message by reading between the lines. How much information can you cull from the "Phone for the facts" poster? What broader messages can you find in the poster? Is it easier to see the information or the subsequent messages the poster offers about sex and AIDS?

Other sources of scientific information rely on images both to convey and create knowledge. Medical imaging, for instance, now relies heavily on visual explanations that reveal microscopic, genetic, or internal parts of the body never before visible to the naked eye. In these cases, the subject may be the body, but the visual mapping of information of particular processes within it is often what the images and explanations are about.

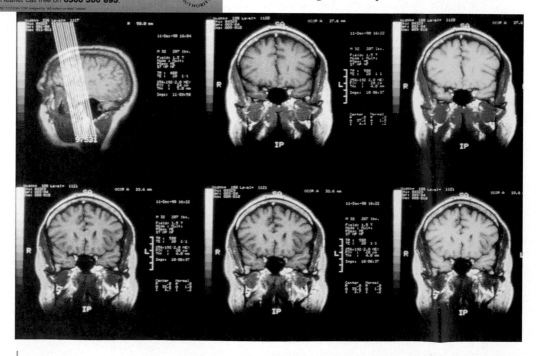

| MRI Scans

Missing persons flyers posted on a mailbox after the September 11, 2001 terrorist attack on the World Trade Center

Writing to explain also covers numerous other ways of sharing information with readers. In addition to how, we often need to know *who, what, when, where,* and *why*. These many forms of explaining are exemplified in what we think of as news. News tells stories but does so with the overall aim of informing the public about what is happening in the world. For example, following the September 11, 2001, terror attacks, people craved almost any source of information. Activity immediately spiked in online news sites, chat rooms, and message forums. Makeshift bulletin boards even appeared on mailboxes. In contemporary culture, such ad hoc sources of information and the status of the "stories" they provide are increasingly complex as twenty-four-hour news cycles, blogs, cable news, and online sources of information proliferate.

CONSIDER

1. In many fields today, scientists create knowledge using images that often provide digital models. Is it fair to say that scientists are still observing and explaining nature if they are relying on simulations?

2. The excerpt from the setup guide on page 337 for "Basic Printing" was a finalist in a technical communication contest. What do you think the judges might have liked about the documentation? How easily can you understand the instructions?

Petroglyphs of unknown meaning created by the Nootka Culture, Sproat Lake, British Columbia, Canada

To what does it relate?

You might be tempted to believe that because explanatory writing merely represents information, you need not worry about who wrote it or under what circumstances it was produced. But nothing could be farther from the truth. Asking "Who made it?" "When was it created?" "What **historical contexts** relate to it?" and "Who was it written for?" illuminates even the most basic explanatory writing. Petroglyphs, for example, have been characterized as both sacred and descriptive. Examples from British Columbia have been found in areas near the ocean inhabited by aboriginal people dating back tens of thousands of years. And yet these images seem strikingly informational. What knowledge might be conveyed by the inverted figures in the rock carving? How might the images in the petroglyph relate to native people's understanding of the natural world?

Clearly, informational writing also responds to specific needs or **situational contexts**. Consider the much-maligned ready.gov informational images meant to offer guidance in the event of a terrorist attack. The ready.gov

4. If you become aware of an unusual or suspicious release of an unknown substance nearby, it doesn't hurt to protect yourself.

5. Get away from the substance as quickly as possible.

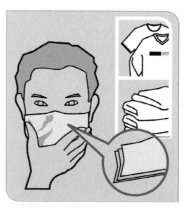

6. Cover your mouth and nose with layers of fabric that can filter the air but still allow breathing.

Informational images from Ready.gov, showing steps 4 through 6 of the visual guide to biological threats

images are carefully designed to convey pure information, information that can be understood in multiple situations and that responds directly to the fear associated with terrorist threats.

Without knowing this context, however, readers might be hard pressed to discern exactly what kind of information the images convey. Not surprisingly, the wordless government images have prompted parodists to offer humorous captions. The spoofs are funny in part because they both ignore and tap into our concerns about safety and terrorism. The sequence of images represented by panels #4-6 on page 340 certainly offers reasonable advice in context: We should probably run away from a noxious substance or odor that might pose a threat. But take away the original captions, and we're tempted to offer wholly different explanations for the odd items in the graphics. Yet our funny captions might also tap into the original terror context, as is the case with "Don't get so preoccupied with biological weapons that you forget to put on deodorant." (Try your hand with the pile of fish.) The point in attaching such a caption might then be to wonder whether responding to potential catastrophes with bureaucratic signs might be a gesture as futile as anticipating disasters with worries about body odor.

Of course, there is nothing frivolous about safety concerns, and if we look at the ready.gov images in the context of the entire precautionary Web site, the information becomes more useful and easier to understand. In this case, the explanatory text goes furthest in clarifying the instructions.

Ready.gov images, one with a parody caption.

1. Don't get so preoccupied with biological weapons that you forget to put on deodorant.

CONSIDER

1. Look back at the petroglyph on page 340 and think about other petroglyphs you have seen. Would you characterize these images as informational? What other functions might such images serve?

2. How seriously do you take government warnings about safety or other concerns? What kinds of communication problems arise when it comes to distributing safety information? How might ready.gov messages be improved?

CHALLENGE

3. Log on to the ready.gov Web site and explore the warning information. Also explore some of the parodies of ready.gov (do a Google search on "ready.gov parody"). Most of the parodies fail to recognize the sequencing in the ready.gov images. Select three images from the Web site, and create a spoof sequence that more closely mirrors the presentation of the information in its original context.

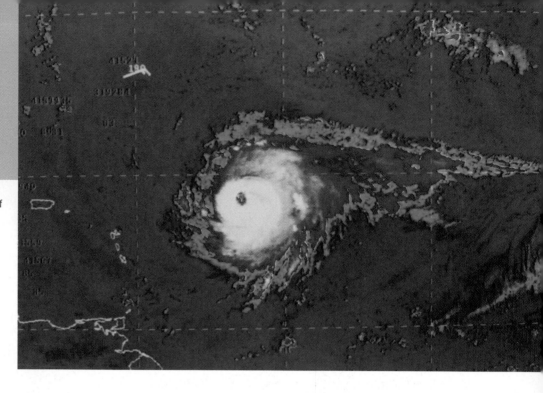

Satellite Image of
Hurricane Floyd

How is it composed?

Images can effectively explain concepts by emphasizing *contrasts*, *unity*, *repetition*, and other **structural elements** that help convey information. In most cases, the display of information corresponds to the purposes of its creator or the needs of the audience. Weather information, for instance, can be mapped in various ways, each tailored to different purposes and technologies. Instruments collect information about moisture and atmospheric conditions and map areas using a number scale. The information is essentially composed through a combination of data-gathering devices and computer programs. These programs will translate the raw data using patterns, contrasts, and maps to create images that are easier for a lay audience to comprehend. The example at the top of this page uses patterns and contrasts of color to create emphasis and demonstrate the location of severe weather.

Other examples of writing to inform more readily reveal the human hand behind their composition. The Weather Channel's Web site, for instance, uses similar images but situates them in a frame that also offers information about conditions for gardening or playing golf. The Web site uses repetition (maps are lined up across the bottom of the page), and white space to create appealing arrangements, and it combines images, animations, and text to provide a unified explanation of weather-related concerns.

Of course, there are numerous other ways of informing people about weather conditions and other situations. A scientific report might use print conventions such as headers and figure captions, combined with graphs, tables, and charts to detail weather-related concepts. A photo essay might emphasize sequencing, arranging images and captions in order to reveal the process through which a storm develops. A documentary might weave together weather imagery, video footage, interviews, and scientific research to provide a comprehensive picture of a weather event. A newspaper report might emphasize eyewitness accounts and photographs while relying on conventions of newspaper design such as headline size and the use of columns to convey information about a storm.

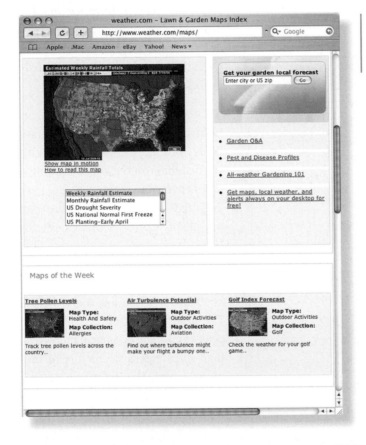

Weather Channel Web Site
Source: weather.com®.
Courtesy of Weather Channel.

CONSIDER

1. How important do you think design strategies are to informative writing? Is it fair to say that design is more important when it comes to informative writing than in other kinds of writing?

2. In addition to repetition and arrangement, what other structural elements can you recognize in the Weather Channel Web site? How many of these strategies could be applied to other forms of writing?

What details matter?

Often our understanding of informative material comes only after we move past our first impressions and look more closely and more critically at what elements are really the most significant. Consider a chart mapping the mean temperature of Angola, Indiana, over the past seventy years created by *CO$_2$ Science Magazine*. We might initially look at the many temperature peaks and valleys plotted in the chart and throw up our hands trying to make sense of it all—what might explain the huge dip in temperature in the late 1970s or the huge spike in 1998? The chart makers, however, have simplified our task in reading the chart by using a linear progression line to plot one aspect of the data. The linear progression line tells us that overall the mean temperatures fell in Angola during the past seventy years.

Graphs
Representing
Climate Change

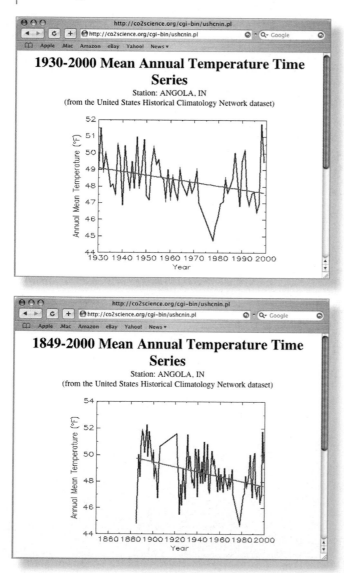

But there are more details, and some of the most important pieces of information are not likely to jump off the page as clearly as the colored lines on the chart. For one, look at the dates covered in the survey. Somewhat like the distorted bar graph demonstrating music downloads earlier in this chapter, the conclusions drawn from the data about mean temperatures may be misleading. Were we to adjust the graph generator to consider the years 1849–2000, we might see a different picture. The progression line is still present, but the peaks and valleys appear more regular, and a high spike enters the picture at the beginning of the record. The expanded plot might lead us to wonder what the data would look like if we went back even further and how we might project temperature change forward more accurately based on a longer record. In this light, we might conclude that even using 150 or so years, it is probably difficult to develop accurate explanations of climate change.

We might consider another detail in the image—the URL of the *CO$_2$ Science Magazine* Web site. We could send our Web browser to the *CO$_2$* home page and look for more information that could inform our reading. How might we read the prominent call for contributions at the top of the page? We might explore the site further, arriving at an editorial suggesting that there has been no global warming in the past seventy years. We could now reflect on any questions about the graph in light of details we have uncovered about the producers of the Web site. With informational writing, especially scientific explanations, we assume a certain amount of objectivity. We could now temper that assumption with the knowledge that the *CO₂ Science Magazine* may be operating from a position that does not adhere to claims of recent global warming.

The point is not that *CO₂ Science Magazine* is wrong or that there is inconclusive proof of global warming. What matters is that an issue such as global climate change is likely to be fraught with complexities, that there is scientific disagreement about issues of climate change, and that we must consider any information in light of these debates. The data plotted by *CO₂ Science Magazine* are probably accurate, but in all likelihood there is more to be explained before we draw conclusions about what we are seeing.

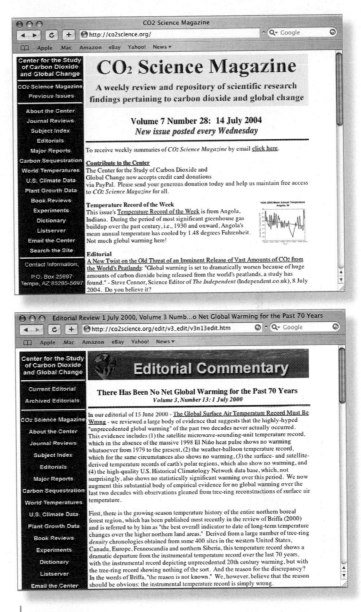

CO₂ Science Web Site

CONSIDER

1. How difficult is it to look beneath the surface of information presented in specialized fields such as global climate studies? Must we study deeply in those disciplines before we can understand and critique these kinds of explanations?

2. Just how objective is information in the sciences? Is it fair to say that the sciences are more objective than other fields such as law or the humanities?

Mapping Knowledge

Many people consider themselves lucky if they've managed to avoid the dreaded dissection lab in their high school biology class. For others, the experience of staring at and then beginning to cut open a well-preserved frog or earthworm is linked with their conception of what it means to study science. Others remember dropping agents in beakers or swirling liquids to test pH balance. Thoughts of science often evoke physical acts of experimentation—the lowering of the slide cover, the lifting of the dissection scalpel, even the smell of formaldehyde.

But today much scientific work bears little resemblance to what we might remember from biology lab. In disciplines ranging from the earth sciences to neurobiology, scientists are more likely to spend hours testing data models on their office PC than measuring rock formations or mixing chemicals in test tubes. In fact, the sciences, like most disciplines, are witnessing groundbreaking changes in the ways knowledge is created and shared.

Many of these changes can be attributed to larger transformations in society wrought by technology. The maturation of computing and the growth of digitized information has strongly affected the sciences—researchers now collect and process data at rates that would have been impossible even ten years ago. Similarly, networks now facilitate the sharing of both information and computing power, helping scientists to collaborate and build on one another's work. Finally, innovative modes of representing information have opened new fields and transformed others by harnessing scientific data and mapping them through two- or three-dimensional images.

All of these developments invite us to revisit what it means to work with information in the sciences. They also ask that we think carefully about how disciplines themselves take shape—disciplines like medicine, computing, statistics, and even the arts are contributing to the creation of new knowledge as technology and images transform the study of our world. The texts and images in this cluster emphasize these changes. They consider how the study of mapping is itself undergoing revolutionary change as geographers grapple with the impact of technology on their field. The selections also look at ways that medicine is creating maps of the human body, images constructed from data that promise new approaches to health and raise new questions about the role of the sciences in society.

We'll Never Fold This Map

The first astronauts to see the earth from space remarked at how the view utterly changed their perspectives on the political maps we have come to think of as a natural part of our geographical landscape—from space, no colors or borders divide the planet. Today, viewing the world from numerous global and mapped perspectives is fast becoming an everyday activity, thanks to technological transformations in the fields of geography and cartography (mapmaking).

"Before I flew, I was already aware of how small and vulnerable our planet is; but only when I saw it from space, in all its ineffable beauty and fragility, did I realize that humankind's most urgent task is to cherish and preserve it for future generations."

—SIGMUND JÄHN
German astronaut

Making the Ultimate Map

Steven Levy
(2004)

FYI

Steven Levy writes about cyberculture and information technology for *Newsweek*. He is the author of five books, including *Hackers* (1984) and *Crypto* (2001).

There it is, that good old pale blue clot in all its earthly glory, right there on your computer screen. It's a familiar sight, even from a skyhigh perspective experienced only by astronauts and angels. But hold on. By mousing around and clicking, you swoop like Superman, down, down, down, to a location on terra firma. Coastlines and rivers come into view, then cities, houses and even cars. And then, with another mouseclick, you can see the roads labeled, highlight the high-crime areas and locate the nearest Chinese restaurant. (The photography is provided by a combination of satellite images and pictures from aircraft flyovers.) If an alien flying-saucer jockey ever had an urge for chicken in black-bean sauce, this software would come in handy.

This particular Web-based program is called Keyhole and costs under $100. (Spy agencies used to spend millions for this, and they didn't even get the restaurant overlay!) But it's just one impressive product of many in an area marked by furious innovation. Digital mapping is about to change our world by documenting the real world, then integrating that information into our computers, phones and lifestyles. Roll over, Mason and Dixon: spurred by space photography, global satellite positioning, mobile phones, search engines and new ways of marking information for the World Wide Web, the ancient art of cartography is now on the cutting edge.

"The whole area of mapping is exploding in a lot of different directions," says Tom Bailey, an exec at Microsoft's MapPoint division. Millions of road-trippers download custom maps from Web ventures like MapQuest and Yahoo Maps. You can now Google things by location: type in a ZIP code and "laser surgery," and you'll find the closest places that can fix your vision. Carmakers offer GPS navigation systems as a built-in option; cell-phone and PDA users can find the nearest lavatory or pool hall; and a mobile application called Dodgeball lets you know if any friends—or friends of your friends—are within 10 blocks.

But just over the azimuth is the holy grail of mapping, where every imaginable form of location-based information is layered onto an aggregate construct that mirrors the whole world. "I call it the Virtual Globe," says Jack Dangermond, founder of Environmental Systems Research Institute (ESRI), a Redlands, Calif., company that pioneered what's known as Geographical Information Systems. "It combines the World Wide Web with geographical information like satellite images, roads, demographic information, sensors . . . and then you're modeling the planet as a living system."

Dangermond knows this turf well. When he started ESRI in 1969, geography was an uncool academic pursuit, and using computers for mapping was, well, uncharted territory. But at Harvard years before, he had been among the first to experiment in creating virtual maps that "layered" quantitative information from databases onto them. Though sometimes complicated to use, these efforts in "digital geography" were incredibly powerful and were invaluable to customers in corporations (notably energy companies looking for an edge in exploration) and the government. ESRI's products were used, for instance, to find the best location for a new mining town in Venezuela and the placement of ski runs in Utah. But in the 1990s, Dangermond understood that ESRI's original model of a closed, proprietary system wasn't going to work when geographical information became widely distributed on the Web and routinely integrated into thousands of applications and services. The company spent $340 million to change its system to conform to open standards, to make ESRI's software open to developers who write what Dangermond calls "maps for your apps."

Of course, now that the mapping field is expanding from the traditional players to the mass market, Jack Dangermond's strategy pits him against Bill Gates. Microsoft's MapPoint division has 150 engineers, including many cartographers, creating simple ways for developers to put mapping information into their software applications. And, of course, Microsoft isn't the only competitor: a slew of major tech companies, from IBM to AOL to Oracle, "are all involved in a big way," says David Schell of Open GIS, a nonprofit consortium that promotes open geographical-information standards. "It's now one of the key components of the Net."

Adding a geographical dimension to an existing application not only increases its utility but sometimes produces a level of information that's downright scary. For instance, the Federal Election Commission's requirement for digitally logged campaign contributions hadn't really caused much controversy—until Michael Frumin, a researcher for a nonprofit arts-based technology firm called Eyebeam, decided to "geocode" the information—assigning the precise latitude and longitude to the addresses. This allowed users of the Web site he set up, called Fundrace, to type in an address and see which candidates their

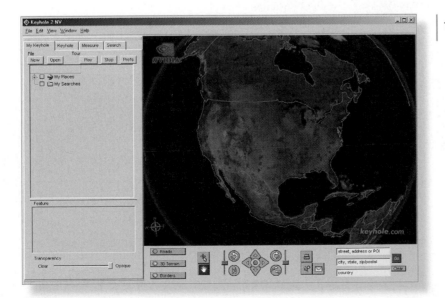

The Keyhole GIS Browser

neighbors were supporting, and how much they gave—you could virtually canvass the neighborhood to see who gave what. An extra bonus was that the contributions came with addresses that were sometimes otherwise unlisted. (There's Ben Affleck! And he gave to Dennis Kucinich?) The consternation of suddenly exposed donors may be a harbinger of complications to come when innovative mapping pegs hitherto obscure information to a specific location. In short, we're at the beginning of the age of geo-voyeurism.

We can soon expect even more powerful ways of extracting location data from everyday information. John Frank, the 27-year-old founder of a company called MetaCarta, has a method to "geo-parse" documents and files, extracting any mention of a place. (What's more, Frank says a location need not be an address or population center but "anything that's bolted down"— a physical landmark or even a fire alarm box.) When the word "media" appears in a document, for instance, his software uses the context to determine whether it refers to the news business or one of the nine U.S. localities that go by that name—and if it's the latter, which one. Then it tags the information with the geographical coordinates. So when someone does a MetaCarta search for a town in Iraq, a stretch of roadway or an area rich in crude oil, it searches its hundreds of geo-parsed databases (including research papers, news articles and 800 million Web pages) to come up with every document that refers to that location. Right now MetaCarta's customers are mostly in government (it's funded in part by the CIA), but similar technology will probably wind up being common on the Web.

Keyhole views of North America, California, the Golden Gate Bridge, and Cavillo Point, California

Clearly, we're headed toward the day when any reference to a place gets tied to the actual location—and vice versa, as GPS-equipped voyagers enhance their travels by accessing the secret history of the ground beneath their feet, as well as discovering what's on the road ahead. Because commercial databases only go so far in supplying that information, a number of independent, open-source-style projects are encouraging a participatory approach in providing digital annotations to the physical world. For instance, one project collects and maps interesting examples of graffiti in the streets of San Francisco. A scheme called GeoURL encourages bloggers to tag location information to their Web-log entries. (This allows people to keep track of what's going on in their area.) Eventually, between the databases, the parsing and the geo-hackers, millions of places will be digitally annotated, and the experience of traveling the world will be akin to visiting a museum with an exquisitely informed guide.

Products like Keyhole hope to become the substratum upon which all this information is layered—fighting Microsoft, ESRI and others for the honor. (Keyhole product general manager John Hanke boasts that it already has a program to allow amateurs to post their own layers to the maps.) Ideally, they'll all coexist: think of these supermaps as the equivalent of Web browsers yielding the world's knowledge through the lens of location. They'll spur companies and governments to make better-informed decisions and enrich the experience of just plain people as they take a walk through the city, hook up with their friends and hunt for Chinese food. These will be maps that change the territory.

Research GIS and other maps that change the territory.
www.ablongman.com/beyondwords24

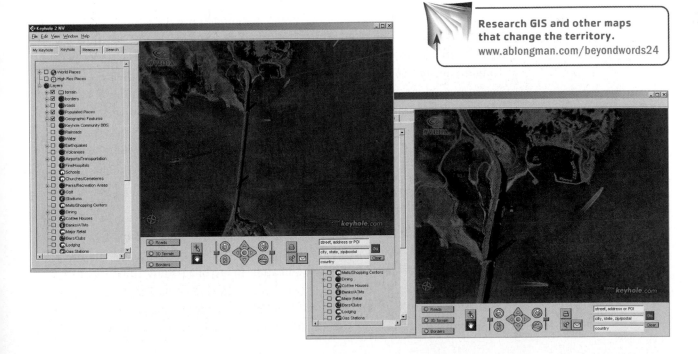

1. Astronauts who view the earth from space remark on the absence of visible political dividing lines and on how fragile the planet looks when viewed from a vast distance. What are your thoughts on the ability of a computer program to replicate this experience?

2. What limits should be placed on companies' ability to capture and market images of the earth? When these images contain private homes or other structures, should companies be required to obtain permission to use them? Who should have access to and be responsible for controlling such information?

CHALLENGE

3. Download the free trial version of the Keyhole mapping program at keyhole.com. Using the *Locate* program, find several places that interest you. Experiment with some of the overlays showing these locations. Write a page or more reporting on your experience.

Manhattan Timeformations

Maps often create a fixed representation of a place. A paper map seems final, like a static snapshot that captures and details a geographical location. But most maps capture far more than the physical dimensions of a place at a particular time. If you've ever used a map on a long drive, for instance, you've probably thought about the cities arrayed along the interstates—can I make it to Oklahoma City by nightfall? Can there possibly be a Holiday Inn in Tucumcari? We think about our human constructions as we evaluate most maps. Further, these human creations change over time. If you drove from Wyoming to New Mexico but forgot to buy a new road atlas, you might not know about the bypass around Denver and would probably spend an extra hour sitting in traffic. Because maps represent human culture, they lend themselves to studies ranging from environmental politics to archaeology, allowing us to consider the impacts humans have on places and on one another, especially over time.

The Skyscraper Museum brings the expertise of Caroll Willis, its founder, together with the latest GIS and Web delivery innovations to create an online site that allows readers to explore Manhattan today or to study the development of New York City over the last two centuries. Using computer animations and historical overlays, the museum's Manhattan Timeformations (http://www. skyscraper.org/timeformations/intro.html) exhibit enables readers to witness

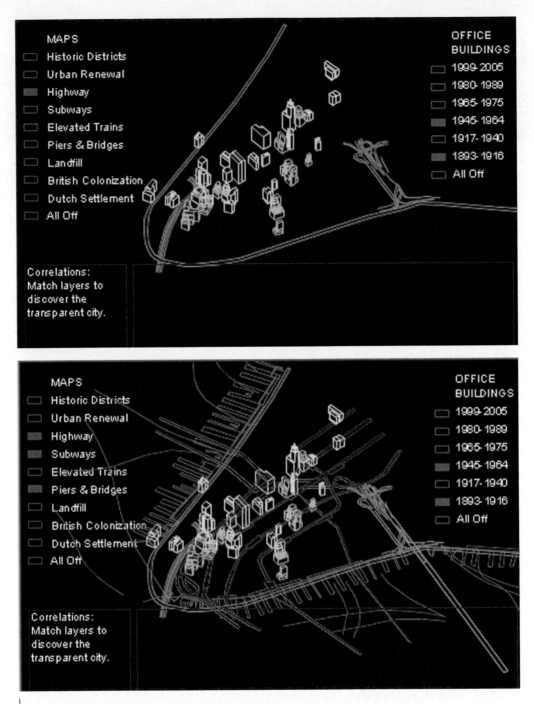

| Changes in Manhattan Over Time

changes that have taken place as landfill has been added to create more space in Manhattan, and as bridges, roads, settlements, and eventually skyscrapers have evolved. The images on this page show two snapshots of human activity on lower Manhattan during the periods 1893–1916 and 1945–1964; the first depicts only office buildings and highways, whereas the second also shows subway lines and bridges constructed during these periods.

Elizabeth Bishop (1911–1979) wrote numerous poems concerned with travel and places. She was known for the meticulous methods she used in composing and revising her poems. She would often work on a poem for months, even years, polishing the language until it conveyed the ideas exactly as she wished. "The Map" first appeared in her collection *North and South* in 1946.

The Map

Elizabeth Bishop
(1946)

Land lies in water; it is shadowed green.
Shadows, or are they shallows, at its edges
showing the line of long sea-weeded ledges
where weeds hang to the simple blue from green.
Or does the land lean down to lift the sea from under,
drawing it unperturbed around itself?
Along the fine tan sandy shelf
is the land tugging at the sea from under?

The shadow of Newfoundland lies flat and still.
Labrador's yellow, where the moony Eskimo
has oiled it. We can stroke these lovely bays,
under a glass as if they were expected to blossom,
or as if to provide a clean cage for invisible fish.
The names of seashore towns run out to sea,
the names of cities cross the neighboring mountains
—the printer here experiencing the same excitement
as when emotion too far exceeds its cause.
These peninsulas take the water between thumb and finger
like women feeling for the smoothness of yard-goods.

Mapped waters are more quiet than the land is,
lending the land their waves' own conformation:
and Norway's hare runs south in agitation,
profiles investigate the sea, where land is.
Are they assigned, or can the countries pick their colors?
—What suits the character or the native waters best.
Topography displays no favorites; North's as near as West.
More delicate than the historian's are the map-maker's colors.

Explore Bishop's poem in depth.
www.ablongman.com/beyondwords25

CONSIDER

1. Manhattan Timeformations allows viewers to see developments unfold in Manhattan over time. In what sense is it fair to say that all maps show the influence of humans on a geographical space?

2. What details matter in Elizabeth Bishop's poem "The Map"? Do these details tell us more about geography or about human activities?

3. How do you interpret the claim in "The Map" that "more delicate than the historian's are the map-maker's colors"? What can be said about thinking of maps as history?

COMPOSE

4. Find a map of an area that you have an interest in, and compose either a poem or a one- or two-paragraph explication detailing what the map expresses about its subject. Consider the geographical features covered by the map as well as design elements used by the mapmakers as you explain how the map can be regarded as an interpretation of the space.

FYI Geographer Alex Philip directs the Geospatial Research Group at the University of Montana. "A Spatial Exploration of Lewis and Clark" was published by *Geospatial Solutions*, a Web magazine devoted to exploring intersections among geography, global information systems, and technology.

A Spatial Exploration of Lewis and Clark

Alex Philip and the Geospatial Research Group
(2003)

Nearly 200 years after Lewis and Clark launched the Corps of Discovery, their daring journey continues to offer lessons about America. Today, thanks to a five-year effort to amass a definitive Lewis and Clark geodatabase, various Web-based spatial tools are helping us explore this epic geographical story.

On May 14, 1804, William Clark, Meriwether Lewis, and a crew of 46 men launched their Corps of Discovery expedition on the Missouri River to begin a multifaceted exploration of the American West. Pushing and pulling against the river's powerful current, the explorers chronicled their daily observations in their respective journals and, slowly, a highly descriptive narrative emerged of the surrounding geography.

The Lewis and Clark 200th Anniversary Mosaic provides a visual voyage of discovery through the cartographic history of the expedition. From the center, the mosaic moves from the 1814 Samuel Lewis map of the expedition based on Clark's original drawing to the General Land Office's first complete land survey of the late 1870s to a 1970 USGS National Atlas and then finally to Landsat imagery.

Guided by Thomas Jefferson's vision, this expedition was first and foremost a reconnaissance of the massive and newly acquired Louisiana Purchase, defined by the continental hydrography of the Missouri River watershed. Specifically, Jefferson instructed Lewis to find the fabled Northwest Passage, a navigable waterway connecting the headwaters of the Missouri with the great rivers of the far west and the Pacific Ocean. Simultaneously, it was a commercial venture wherein the Corps was to establish trade relations with the diverse Native American nations of this vast terra incognita. It was also a military expedition, to be sure, regimented with full exactitude and order as the Corps probed established territorial claims of the French, Spanish, British, and Russians. Explicit in Jefferson's instructions, the Corps of Discovery was also a scientific exploration of a geography barely conceived by western minds, yet inhabited by diverse aboriginal cultures for millennia.

By the expedition's conclusion on September 23, 1806, outside St. Louis, Missouri, the Corps of Discovery had marched roughly 8,000 miles. Lewis and Clark had crossed the Continental Divide, navigated the great Missouri and Columbia Rivers, encountered more than 50 distinct native peoples, and ultimately recorded their geographical observations in a manner unique to American history. Their naturalist observations, faithfully recorded in their journals, interwove the ecology and cultures of place into an unprecedented spatio-temporal transect across a continent.

A LEWIS AND CLARK
COMMUNITY EVOLVES

Almost 200 years later, as our nation begins to observe the Bicentennial Commemoration of the Lewis and Clark Expedition, we look back and interpret the meaning of the Corps of Discovery. As a historigraphical exercise, the complexity that typified the expedition remains, magnified by 200 years of change across the lands and peoples encountered by Lewis and Clark. Surveying the hundreds of organizations, thousands of events, endless publications, exponentially expanding Web sites, and incessant media narratives, the Lewis and Clark Expedition is clearly as significant today as it was in 1806. And for the geospatial community—with its drive to explore geography and culture and its ability to integrate vast amounts of information into a common picture—it seems particularly relevant.

So it's not surprising that, five years ago, with the commemoration rapidly approaching, a conversation developed among geographers interested in the Corps of Discovery. For geographers and others consumed with geospatial technologies (GIS, GPS, remote sensing, animation, and visualization), the expedition seemed the ideal case study, replete with things geographical—land, water, people, animals, plants, sky, navigation, observation, investigation, description, cartography, and journals. During the next several years, an organic network of organizations emerged and embarked on a grand experiment in geospatial data democracy. The core goal of this loosely knit community was to find and amass the definitive geodatabase of usable, accessible, standardized, documented, and profoundly unique spatial data coincident with the scope of the expedition's extent.

Being geographers, this involved, of course, concerns and questions of scale (macro, meso, and micro), projections and datums, and metadata, and ancillary desires to spatially enable that which was not. This included the Journals of the Lewis and Clark Expedition, the Academy of the Natural Sciences' Lewis and Clark Herbarium, the American Philosophical Society's primary-source Lewis and Clark Journals (high-resolution digital copies), the Library of Congress' Lewis and Clark cartography collection, Smithsonian artifacts, and so on. Questions regarding existing and future geospatial technologies loomed large given the fact that we were planning for an event five years before its commencement and, considering the cycle of development, we had to conceive of solutions before they existed. The community shared what they could, offered their geographical contributions, and formed a campaign.

Parallel convergence. Meanwhile, as the Lewis and Clark Bicentennial approached, a significant technological convergence began to shape the na-

E. S. Paxson, *Lewis and Clark at Three Forks* (1912)

ture of how the Lewis and Clark community would communicate with vast audiences. Most significantly, spatial technologies merged with the Web, making it possible to share geographical information via Internet protocols. Contrary to our initial designs of creating centralized data warehouses and clearinghouses—and moving beyond paper cartographic products—various organizations embarked on Internet strategies. This created an opportunity to share vast amounts of relevant spatial data regarding the Lewis and Clark Expedition. The resulting growth of activity was explosive, unprecedented, somewhat overwhelming, and continues to this day.

Though it's impossible to report on all the individual initiatives, it is feasible to highlight significant contributions and outline the future development of this evolving network.

THE GEOGRAPHY OF CHANGE

One of the more extensive and profoundly sublime efforts must be attributed to the work of David Rumsey, his Cartography Associates company, and their inspired collaboration with Telemorphic Inc. Having amassed a private historical cartographic library of original works, Rumsey has launched an impressive Web site (www.davidrumsey.com) sharing his valuable resources with the rest of the world. An awe-inspiring collection of digital images captures varying impressions of the North American continent, the Trans-Mississippi West, the manifest movement across the Continental Divide, and the eventual survey and settlement of the lands Lewis and Clark experienced. Presented as a geospatial portal, Rumsey's contributions include, among many more pieces, Nicholas King's famous map of 1803, used by the expedition to plan their route; Samuel Lewis' 1814 reproduction of Clark's classic postexpeditionary map; mid-19th-century assessments detailing the geography of the American West; General Land Office survey maps of the late 19th century; and modern USGS efforts associated with National Atlas of 1970. Thanks to Rumsey's efforts, all this and much more is now available as georeferenced image layers.

But Rumsey has not stopped there. Understanding the dialectical value of comparing the past and the present, Rumsey has combined his historical montage with relatively modern, remotely sensed impressions provided by Landsat TM. Dr. Robert Bergantino's rigorously detailed Lewis and Clark campsite and trail-line geodatabase has been added to the montage, making it possible to dynamically fuse these perspectives of change. For the first time, scholars, researchers, teachers, students—literally anyone—can examine, for free, a wealth of geographical information through a single, spatially enabled Web site. Rumsey and his colleagues have set the bar, delivering a most impressive Lewis and Clark geographical exhibit.

K–12 outreach. Simultaneously, similar efforts have emerged across the nation. At the University of Montana-Missoula, a NASA-funded K–12 earth system science education program, EOSEP, has spawned the National Lewis and Clark Education Center. The center provides teachers and students with the geospatial tools and spatial data to assess the concept of landscape change along the Lewis and Clark trail. Combining various geospatial technologies with technical leadership and support from the Lewis and Clark Congressional Caucus, the Lewis and Clark Information System has been launched.

The LCIS combines excerpts from Moulton's Journals of the Lewis and Clark Expedition, solicits the natural history narrative of Dr. Daniel Botkin, incorporates specialized spatial data of the trail, and introduces remotely sensed resources to the American classroom vis-à-vis Lewis and Clark. As a Web-based resource, the LCIS provides a virtual educational experience bolstered by the opportunity for educators to work at the University of Montana and explore the physical geography of the trail.

An educational climate. The Missouri Botanical Garden, under the leadership of Dr. Bob Coulter, shares a passion for K–12 geographical education as well, and has developed a Web-based biogeographical resource for America's classrooms. Through the financial support of NPS' Challenge Cost Share program, Coulter and his colleagues combine NOAA climatic data (precipitation and temperature), Robert Bailey's ecoregions, USGS National Land Cover, and Bergantino's campsite and trail-line data into an interactive, Web-based mapping system. Again, this resource provides both a vehicle for distance learning and a hands-on GIS educational program at the garden's headquarters in St. Louis.

According to Coulter, "When you get down to it, education is about engaging the mind and capturing the imagination. The adventures of the Corps of Discovery enable teachers to do just that—students can learn important science, math, history, and geography concepts in the context of a captivating story."

Coulter is currently working to include Lewis and Clark's plant and animal observations and georeference these historical observations with modern biogeographical information for key species along the trail. Coulter's efforts represent a fundamental educational process of comparing and contrasting basic environmental phenomena across landscapes. Coulter adds, "An abstract textbook concept like biotic-abiotic interaction comes alive as students see which plant and animal species Lewis and Clark found at certain points along the trail, and come to understand how climate and landforms brought that about."

FEDERAL CORPS OF REDISCOVERY

Various federal agencies are dedicating significant resources to the interpretation, understanding, and use of the Lewis and Clark story for the advancement of natural resource science and management. NFS' Corps of Discovery II program leads the national commemoration. USGS focuses on detailed scientific analysis of the trail's lands and waters. The U.S. Fish and Wildlife Service explores the coincidental relationship between landscape observation (1803), conservation via the refuge system (1903), and restoration (2003) of our modern ecosystems. The Army Corps of Engineers provides a unique institutional history of the major waterways used by the Corps of Discovery and a vast data repository quantifying riparian changes. NASA's various centers bring their geospatial and remote sensing expertise to the examination of trail archaeology, significant trends in landscape change, and national applications to be derived from their multifaceted earth system science missions. Permeating each of these, and many other significant efforts, is a core use of geospatial technologies to further comprehend the complexity of the lands through which the expedition passed.

In particular, NASA's John C. Stennis Space Center and the Johnson Space Center have active, ongoing programs devoted to particular aspects of the Lewis and Clark experience. Recently, through a project proposed by Don Scott and others of the NASA Aerospace Education Services program and facilitated by a frenetic exchange of e-mails coordinated by Cindy McArthur and Susan Runco at Johnson, program managers have asked Science Officer Astronaut Ed Lu and Commander Cosmonaut Yuri Malenchenko—currently on board the International Space Station (Mission 007)—to capture high-resolution digital images of key areas along the trail. Pointing their massive digital cameras down from orbit, the astronauts provide a metaphorical juxtaposition between our modern exploration of Earth and the Corps of Discovery's historical observations.

Teachers, students, scientists, and scholars are collaborating in an unprecedented way, sending requests to Johnson program officers, who in turn relay the requests via e-mail to the astronauts. As the space station orbit crosses a campsite coordinate, an image is acquired and downloaded to earth. Within a matter of days, these images are processed, catalogued, and disseminated around the world.

Finding campsites. At the Stennis Space Center, Earth Science Applications Directorate, remote sensing and GIS specialists are supporting active archaeological investigations of key campsite locations such as Fort Clatsop in Oregon and the Upper Portage Camp in Great Falls, Montana. These efforts involve the use of NASA remote sensing data from various satellite systems, including ASTER, MODIS, Landsat 5 TM, Eandsat 7 ETM+, SRTM, and commercial imagery from Ikonos and QuickBird sensors. For the project, NASA has enhanced these data using advanced georeferencing, data merging, and data visualization techniques.

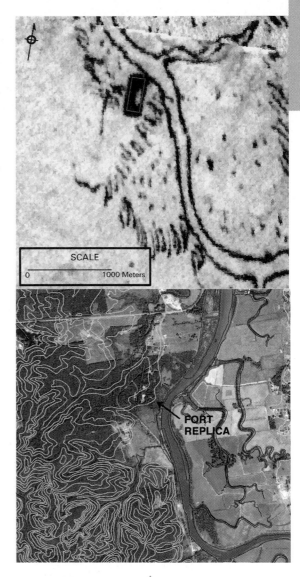

A map drawn by explorer William Clark (*top*) shows the location of Fort Clatsop during the winter of 1805–1806. A commercial satellite image of the area (*bottom*), with elevation lines superimposed, shows where the fort site might be if Clark's map is followed. The images suggest that the original fort site may be one-third of a mile from the fort replica that is part of the Fort Clatsop National Memorial near Astoria, Oregon.

"The data can be used to examine how the ecosystem has changed in the last 200 years," said Dr. Marco Giardino, NASA's Project Director. "This includes changes to the Missouri and Columbia River systems to mapping the spread of invasive species and even how population and migration have changed the face of the West."

Through a combination of archaeological data, incorporation of georegistered historical maps (including maps from the journals), historical aerial photography, and high-resolution satellite and aerial sensor imagery, archaeologists such as Dr. Ken Karsmizki of the Columbia Gorge Discovery Center and NASA scientists are pioneering advanced geospatial analyses of the trail in ways never before attained. Though these studies help conduct archaeological surveys of expedition encampments, they also have great potential for assessing landscape change along the trail.

Karsmizki uses satellite images and historical maps to try to pinpoint where the Lewis and Clark expedition bedded down. Instead of sifting through dirt for traces of their campsites, he scrutinizes satellite and aerial images to determine the most likely places to hunt for 200-year-old campsites. Once he's narrowed down the search, he and his colleagues use traditional—and pioneering—techniques to survey the sites.

At one site in Montana, for example, a U.S. Air Force Unexploded Ordnance team from Tyndall Air Force Base helped Karsmizki search a 3.5-acre site using robotic vehicles and GPS. The Air Force team remotely controlled the robotic units—which carried magnetometers and ground-penetrating radar integrated with GPS—to find and map the position of 24 campfires and other remnants of the centuries-old campsites.

ON THE HORIZON: A GEOSPATIAL NETWORK

Looking ahead, the Stennis Space Center has expanded its research objectives involving Lewis and Clark and through a Space Act Agreement with GCS Research endeavors to build the Lewis and Clark Geosystem. Conceived as a distributed, interconnected geospatial network, NASA and GCS are developing a Web-based interactive mapping and geoimagery system that connects researchers, scholars, teachers, and the interested public with vast amounts of geospatial information regarding the trail environment. Developing in phases and in parallel with advances in technology, the Lewis and Clark Geosystem seeks to link various geospatial systems dedicated to Lewis and Clark geography into an organic interchange of geospatial resources.

Leveraging the vast raster geospatial data resources of Stennis and the myriad Web-based geopublications, the Geosystem runs counter to earlier, core conceptualizations regarding technological explorations of the Lewis and Clark Bicentennial. In the place of a centralized, master repository of geodata, the Geosystem seeks to build functional connectivity among a multitude of data nodes and provide a seamless exploration of the vast geospatial resources detailing the Lewis and Clark trail.

For the Lewis and Clark Geosystem, GCS Research recently acquired submeter satellite imagery of key campsites and combined it with innovations in geodatabase design, raster storage and compression, metadata engines, SD-global animations, and Internet protocols to build a geospatial toolkit for this expanding effort. GCS and NASA continue to explore the benefits of this system to support collective investigations of the geography of change along the Lewis and Clark trail and, by extension, develop meaningful applications focusing on changes in vegetative patterns, riparian corridors, urban growth, invasive species, and more.

Although a variety of technical, as well as logistical, challenges remain, a fundamental insight has been achieved in the totality of this process. It is now possible to build global geospatial networks allowing us to explore our world in unimaginable ways. These geospatial networks are forming and growing exponentially, and the Lewis and Clark geospatial experience serves as a prime example.

Two hundreds years after Lewis and Clark and their party walked across a continent, a human network has been catalyzed to continue the process of discovery. Using a variety of geospatial tools, the world is engaged in the exploration for meaning inherent in this grand geographical story. As the Lewis and Clark Bicentennial unfolds and interest grows, it is hoped that others will join in the process of discovery, share what is found, and reflect on our collective experience.

This 60-centimeter spatial resolution satellite image shows the Lewis and Clark Travelers' Rest encampment area in Lolo, Montana. The pan-sharpened, multispectral image was acquired January 9, 2003, and purchased through NASA's Scientific Data Purchase Program. The overview image is displayed at a 1:40,000-foot scale and the inset is at 1:8,000.

CONSIDER

1. What do you think about explaining current developments in mapping and geography using metaphors of exploration? What benefits might such metaphors offer? What drawbacks?

2. To what degree is technology responsible for the collaborations fostered by projects like the Lewis and Clark Bicentennial? Would it be possible to conduct research like that done for the bicentennial without collaboration?

3. How relevant do you think activities conducted by K–12 students are to the study of science? Must we be experts to conduct scientific research? Are such activities a good use of our scientific resources?

COMPOSE

4. Write a one-page analysis of "A Spatial Exploration of Lewis and Clark." What strategies does the article use to convey information? Can you recognize instances of explaining processes in the article? Does the article ever veer toward offering an argument or perhaps toward other modes of writing? Are there any design strategies used in the article? How do the images in the article relate to its explanations? Discuss the strengths and weaknesses of the piece in terms of how it conveys information.

The Doctor Will
See You Now

We sometimes view the practice of medicine in inconsent ways. We consider the study of health and the body as one of the most advanced fields of science. At the same time, the human body remains something of a mystery and the practice of medicine is at times surprisingly low-tech—think of the perennial question "Where does it hurt?" It's no wonder that many people face their annual physical with some trepidation—when doctors break out the cold stethoscope or wield the rubber reflex hammer, we recognize the difficulty inherent in discovering just what might be wrong *inside* the human body.

But medicine is a highly advanced field of knowledge, and accordingly, changes wrought by technology and imaging have had a tremendous impact. Simple technologies like sonograms have moved beyond the examining room and into the mainstream. And advances like those in mircroscopy, genomics, magnetic imaging, and molecular chemistry are fundamentally altering the study of health. Researchers are rapidly learning to see what is taking place inside the human body and they are developing responses to human health concerns that will likely make contemporary medicine seem like low-tech child's play in the years to come.

FYI Joan O'C. Hamilton has covered the biotechnology and health care industry since 1983. Her work has included articles on Genentech, AIDS, cancer research, the 1992 biotech IPO phenomenon, and other science and business developments. She writes for *Business Week* as well as for *The Stanford Magazine*, *The San Jose Mercury*, and other publications. Hamilton is also author of "A Sharper Picture of Health," which begins on page 370.

Journey to the Center of the Mind

Joan O'C. Hamilton
(2004)

The clanking from within the giant white magnetic resonance imaging (MRI) scanner sounds like somebody banging a wrench on a radiator. "Tommy," a healthy 8-year-old, is halfway inside the machine's round chamber, and his little white-sweat-socked feet keep time with the noise. A mirror on a plastic cage around his head will allow him to see images and video. During the next 45 minutes, Dr. Golijeh Golarai, a researcher at Stanford University, will ask Tommy to hold his feet still as she directs a computer to flash pictures at him, including faces of African American men, landscapes, faces of white men, then scrambled faces in a cubist redux. When the boy thinks he sees the same image twice, he pushes a button. The machine is tracking the blood in his brain as it flows to the neurons he is using to perform the assigned task.

When Golarai's software is done analyzing the data, she'll have nothing less than a set of snapshots of the boy's thoughts, pinpointing exactly what part of his brain recognizes faces. "There go those feet again," chuckles Tommy's father, watching from the control room.

There was a time not long ago when an MRI scan of a child's brain would not be a lighthearted affair. The technology has been used since the 1980s to detect injury or disease in patients suffering from symptoms such as seizures, paralysis, or severe headaches. But in just the past few years, manufacturers have developed stronger MRI magnets and more sophisticated software that can sort through a flood of subtle signals the scans collect.

The upshot is that this imaging technology has leaped far beyond its roots looking for lumps and shadows. Psychiatrists are now studying the mental activities of patients suffering from depression and other emotional ills. Basic researchers are rolling thousands of healthy subjects like Tommy into MRI machines in order to explore the very essence of mind, asking them to think, decide, feel, and learn inside the scanners. Pharma companies hope the new "functional" MRI (fMRI) technology will enhance drug development. Law enforcement experts hope it could become a more accurate lie detector. Even our most private tastes and impulses are under scrutiny as so-called neuromarketing takes off.

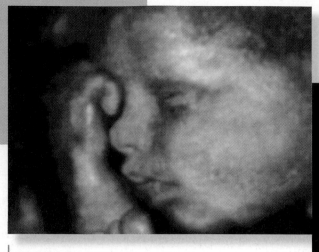
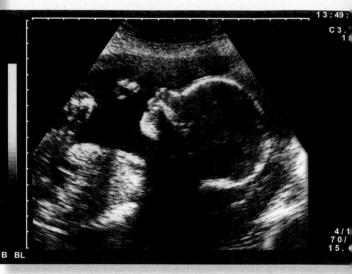

3-D (left) and 2-D (right) ultrasound images

PICK-ME-UP

The benefits in psychiatric diagnosis and treatment alone may be revolutionary. Psychiatrist Ned H. Kalin, director of HealthEmotions Research Institute at the University of Wisconsin at Madison, has been imaging the brains of depressed patients who are taking the antidepressant Effexor. Kalin and his colleagues have found that the drug works specifically on the anterior cingulate, a region of the brain involved in focused attention and conflict. They also found that depressed patients whose anterior cingulates were more active before taking the drug responded better to it.

That's powerful information, since it can take weeks for antidepressants to show an effect and about 30% of patients never benefit. "Physicians in the future will be able to predict which patients will be the best candidates for antidepressants simply by looking at brain scans," says Kalin. Adds Lindsey Carver, Global Manager of MR at General Electric Co.: "There is an opportunity for fMRI to play a major role in diagnosing psychiatric disorders and monitoring drug treatments." GE, along with Siemens and Philips Medical Systems, make the multimillion-dollar scanners that make fMRI possible.

The same kind of excitement is palpable in the field of developmental neuroscience. Unlike other brain-scanning technologies, such as positron emission tomography (PET), which exposes patients to radiation, fMRI simply tracks the response of brain tissue to magnetic fields. It's noninvasive and believed to be harmless. That means even very young children can be scanned—and scanned repeatedly as they grow older.

In her current study, Golarai is scanning kids 8 to 18 to examine what part of the brain they use to recognize faces and whether this changes over time. Golarai is also trying to determine if children, like adults, recognize faces of their own race more accurately. For the first time, it's possible for researchers to examine biological evidence about whether humans are hard-wired to recognize their own racial characteristics or whether they learn to do it. "It's at the heart of the nature-nurture debate," she says.

Teasing apart the mechanics of learning will be another important contribution of fMRI. Last year, researchers in Stanford psychologist John D. E. Gabrieli's lab showed that dyslexic children have different brain patterns from kids who read normally. But their brains can be rewired to perform better with training. It costs more than $500 to do a scan in the research setting, but "if imaging could really predict who would struggle at reading, it might not be so extravagant" for children to be scanned at very young ages, observes Gabrieli.

Almost weekly, scientific journals trumpet new findings across a wide swath of brain-related turf. In February, Columbia University psychologist Tor D. Wager produced imaging evidence of mind over matter in the journal *Science*. Researchers have long been divided over the "placebo effect" and whether some patients just report feeling better when they really don't. Wager says when subjects in his imaging trial were given a placebo but believed they had been given a pain-relieving cream, there was less activity in the pain-perceiving areas of their brains after a small electric shock and more in the subjects' lateral prefrontal cortex, a region associated with self-control. That region could represent a target for researchers trying to develop therapies that "engage our own willpower," he explains.

As the technology is applied more broadly, the business of peering into the intricacies of thought and emotion raises ethical concerns. One intriguing yet controversial use of fMRI is probing consumer preferences—a technique sometimes called neuromarketing. At the California Institute of Technology, researcher Steven R. Quartz is using fMRI to explore how the brain perceives a cool product vs. an uncool one. Among portable MP3 players, "the [Apple] iPod is by far the market leader. What about that gives us a different kind of signal in the brain?" he asks. Quartz also has formed a company that will offer a service to Hollywood studios, imaging the brains of test audiences as they view movie trailers to see which generate the most brain buzz.

BrightHouse is an "ideation consultancy" in Atlanta that used fMRI facilities at Emory University's neuroscience labs to conduct a study on how consumer preferences for different kinds of products—ranging from broccoli to trucks—track with activity in different parts of the brain. CEO Joey Reiman insists the company never scanned people reacting to client products.

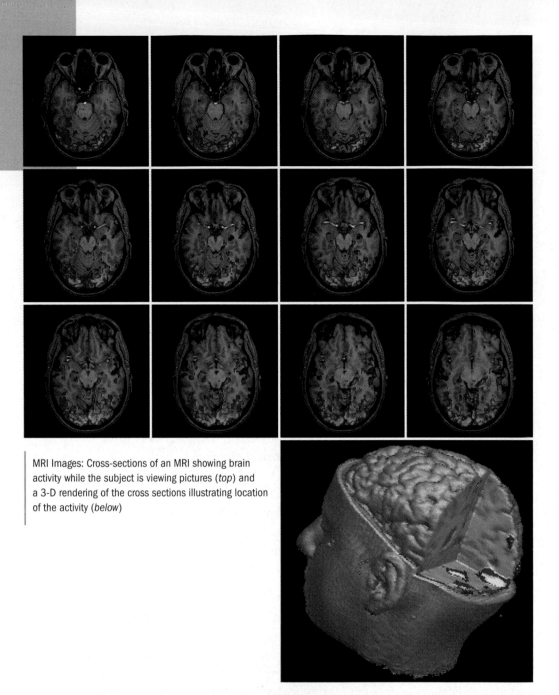

MRI Images: Cross-sections of an MRI showing brain activity while the subject is viewing pictures (*top*) and a 3-D rendering of the cross sections illustrating location of the activity (*below*)

Nevertheless, consumer watchdog Gary Ruskin, executive director of Commercial Alert, complained to Emory that "it's wrong to use a medical technology for marketing, not healing." Emory officials responded that the research would be made public and was of "fundamental scientific interest."

TREAD CAREFULLY

There are other ethical concerns—chief among them privacy. Stanford neurobiologist Donald Kennedy, former head of the Food & Drug

Administration and current editor of *Science*, has urged researchers to tread carefully in collecting brain data. "Far more than our genomes," Kennedy told the Society for Neuroscience last fall, "our brains are us, marking out the special character of our personal capacities, emotions, and convictions. . . . As to my brainome, I don't want anyone to know it for any purpose whatsoever."

Inevitably, insurers and employers will want access to scan data. And so may law enforcement. At the University of Pennsylvania, psychiatrist Daniel D. Langleben has found that specific areas in the front of the brain light up when subjects knowingly tell falsehoods. It's too soon to know how reliable fMRI would be as a truth machine.

One limitation of fMRI today is that most studies are based on small numbers of patients whose results are averaged. That's because there isn't enough of a data repository on how most "normal" brains behave to say definitively what any individual scan means. In other words, instant diagnoses—not to mention mind-reading—is many years in the future.

Still, it's thrilling to consider what will become of the scanning information provided by the healthy little boy in the white sweat socks. Researchers believe the data are contributing to a knowledge base that someday will help doctors diagnose and treat a child who is not so healthy. Or it may yield fundamental insights into such phenomena as racism. That potential is what's driving these reconnaissance missions deep inside the human mind.

CONSIDER

1. Is "Journey to the Center of the Mind" more about technology or about human psychology? What information might you cite to explain the article's focus?

2. What is your response to learning that corporations now use brain research to develop and market products? Is this new information for you? Does it change your sense of the field of medicine?

3. How much credence can you give to studies that try to explain human thinking? Do you believe that emotions and ideas can (or should) ultimately be explained using technology?

COMPOSE

4. Consider some of the ethical concerns raised by Hamilton in "Journey to the Center of the Mind." Using library databases and the Internet, conduct research into fMRI and areas related to the ethical concerns. Inform your class or a small group about the concerns in a five-minute oral report.

For more than sixty years, scientists have known that a strip of neural tissue that runs from ear to ear along the brain's surface orchestrates most voluntary movement, from raising a fork to kicking a ball. A new brain-imaging study has revealed that parts of this so-called motor cortex also respond vigorously as people do nothing more than silently read words.

Not just any words get those neurons going, however. They have to be action words—active verbs.

As volunteers read a verb referring to a face, arm, or leg action—such as *lick, pick,* or *kick*—the motor cortex areas that control the specified action exhibit higher blood flow, a sign of intense neural activity, say neuroscientist Friedemann Pulvermuller of the Medical Research Council in Cambridge, England, and his colleagues. For instance, reading the word *lick* triggers pronounced blood flow in sites of the motor cortex associated with tongue and mouth movements.

—BRUCE BOWER
"The Brain's Word Act"

A Sharper Picture of Health

Joan O'C. Hamilton
(2003)

Northwestern University chemist Thomas J. Meade means no disrespect to his medical colleagues, but when he looks at the state of the art in diagnostics, he suggests that for some procedures, physicians might as well use "stone knives." Take, for example, mammography. "You know going in that there's a one in five chance of a false positive or a false negative. You have an X-ray that's not even smart enough to differentiate a shadow cast by a calcium spot from a tumor. After reading the film and seeing a shadow, they do the prudent thing and stick a 16-gauge needle in you for a biopsy. Then you have to spend the next five days freaking out that you've got breast cancer until you get the results," he says.

Some of Meade's annoyance stems from the fact that his wife endured just such a false alarm—as will an estimated quarter to half of all women who undergo annual mammogram screening over the course of 10 years. But

Meade's criticisms go well beyond the specific failings of mammography and breast biopsies; to him and a growing number of other medical researchers, today's diagnostic tools are too uncertain and invasive—just too primitive. Working at select academic centers and industrial labs around the world, these researchers are developing a suite of new tools that will enable doctors to spot disease instantly and accurately, without ever taking a scalpel or biopsy needle to their patients' skin.

The new discipline is called "molecular imaging," and it is fundamentally altering physicians' ability to view the body and its processes. Most conventional imaging tools, from X-ray to magnetic-resonance imaging, provide anatomical or structural information: is there a lump in the breast or a shadow in the lung? Molecular imaging goes beyond anatomical information to reveal functional data—the cellular activities that characterize tumor growth or inflammation, for example.

This is important because cancer and other diseases often begin with subtle cellular changes, well before a structural abnormality, such as a tumor, is detectable. What's more, the new advanced imaging methods can help distinguish between diseases that look similar but actually involve different molecular malfunctions—and thus require different treatments. "Disease is being redefined in terms of its molecular signature," explains Daniel Sullivan, associate director of the National Cancer Institute and head of the institute's biomedical-imaging program. "In the future, people will talk about cancer by the molecular abnormality, not by the organ of origin."

And in the future, molecular imaging could be integral to every step of health care. Exquisitely sensitive periodic scans could flag any worrisome changes—the presence of a particular protein associated with the beginning of a cancer, for instance. Should doctors eventually spot a lesion, the imaging process itself would yield enough information about the biochemical malfunction, not only to make the diagnosis without a biopsy, but also to help determine the best therapeutic option. Still more noninvasive imaging would closely track the treatment's progress and the course of the disease.

It might take 20 years or more for this complete picture to emerge. But the first generation of technologies to make it possible is already appearing. Thanks to advances in a range of disciplines, from molecular biology to optics to computation, researchers have begun to design chemicals that, once injected into the body, swarm to particular molecules associated with certain diseases and light them up, allowing physicians to easily spot problem areas.

More than half a dozen such molecular-imaging agents are now on the market, most of them for cancer diagnosis; another handful are in clinical trials, and even more are in the development pipeline. Targets for these new diagnostic tools include not only cancers but cardiovascular disease and ills of the central nervous system. "All these technologies are growing incredibly rapidly," says Harvard Medical School radiologist Umar Mahmood, a principal investigator at Massachusetts General Hospital's Center for Molecular Imaging and Research. "We're not doing incremental work. These are leapfrog advances."

Indeed, it's a big enough jump forward that government, the established diagnostics industry, and a few venture capitalists are making substantial investments in the field. The National Cancer Institute has designated molecular imaging an "extraordinary opportunity," spending more than $100 million on it in recent years and asking for $78 million in 2004. To keep up, companies like General Electric—which already has a $9 billion business in conventional medical imaging machines and systems—are venturing further into molecular biology and chemistry and inking deals with major pharmaceutical companies and startups to develop new imaging agents. For the industry and patients alike, says Eric Stahre, general manager for genomics and molecular imaging at GE Medical, "molecular imaging has the potential to change the game."

THE NEXT BLOCKBUSTERS

Take Apomate, a molecular-imaging agent made by Boston-based Theseus Imaging (a subsidiary of North American Scientific) that gives physicians a novel view of a biological drama that plays out in the body all the time. The complex chain of events that leads to a cell's death, a process that biologists call apoptosis, is central to everything from embryonic development to aging; Apomate allows researchers to directly observe these events. By imaging cells' death throes, doctors might be able to see if a particular chemotherapy is successfully killing tumor cells, say, or more accurately assess damage caused by a heart attack.

Like many of the other new imaging agents in development, Apomate draws on the recent explosion in biologists' understanding of the details of the body's molecular processes. Among other findings, scientists have begun to unravel the precise details of apoptosis. It turns out that dying cells expose a binding site that's normally concealed. A naturally occurring protein then binds to that site, marking the cells for destruction by the immune system. Theseus created Apomate by engineering a synthetic version of the protein and linking it to a radioactive isotope that shows up under a scanner. When a patient is injected with Apomate, areas of the body where many cells are dying light up.

Apomate's potential market is large because of the myriad roles apoptosis plays in the body and the many ways doctors could use the agent. In human trials—ongoing in Europe now and likely to begin shortly in the United States—doctors are giving Apomate to lung cancer patients shortly after their first injections of chemotherapy. The aim is to determine within a day or two of the injections whether the drug is actually killing tumor cells. Patients who aren't helped by a particular chemotherapy drug can then be spared the wasted time and often debilitating side effects of the treatment—and can more quickly move on to explore other options. "Only 20 percent of these patients respond to the therapies, but 90 percent have side effects," explains Allan M. Green, chief technology officer at North American Scientific and Theseus. "To recognize early responses patient by patient is the most important near-term contribution we can make."

Theseus has also tested Apomate in more than 50 heart attack patients. Green says investigators have discovered a small subset of patients in whom apoptosis continues to take place in heart tissue even months after an attack. And researchers suspect these patients may be the most likely candidates for subsequent heart failure. If Apomate could help identify these patients, whose heart cells are continuing to die off, it could provide valuable clues as to who should be treated most aggressively—before their hearts begin to fail.

Researchers have also been using Apomate to try and identify unstable plaques in coronary blood vessels. It appears that the plaques most likely to rupture and cause heart attacks demonstrate a measurable amount of apoptosis as they crack and chip. If this work on imaging vulnerable plaques pays off, it could help doctors identify ahead of time some of the hundreds of thousands of people each year whose first indications of heart disease might otherwise be lethal heart attacks.

Doctors currently have ways of looking at structural changes in coronary arteries, but to find earlier danger signs "you need to know the biology," says Stanford University radiologist Francis G. Blankenberg, a consultant to Theseus. Blankenberg says he envisions imaging schemes that look for apoptosis becoming part of a standard battery of tests for patients showing any kind of chest pain.

NOISE REDUCTION

Despite its potential, however, molecular imaging is not without its technical challenges. For one thing, researchers are working hard to ensure that the images it produces are clear. Imaging agents are always on—always emitting radioactivity, like Apomate, or always glowing, in the case of some others. That works fine when there is an abundance of target molecules for the agents to bind to. The trouble is, sometimes the molecules characterizing a problem are so scarce that the few imaging agents that do reach and bind to them are lost in a haze generated by unbound agents floating nearby. That makes it hard to pick out a few precancerous cells in an otherwise healthy organ, for instance. And other times the agents collect in locations such as the liver, where they give off a bright but meaningless glow.

To address these problems, Northwestern's Meade and other researchers are inventing chemistry designed to keep the imaging agents invisible until they find their target molecules. "We're making molecular beacons that respond to physiological conditions," explains Meade. "They're off when injected, and only turned on by the presence of an enzyme target." That simple-sounding goal will nonetheless demand considerable basic research and complex chemistry.

Meade, for one, has come up with a novel scheme in which a target enzyme chews off the equivalent of a cap on the imaging agent, allowing it to beam out its signal. He hopes the approach will allow diagnosticians to use high-resolution MRI and computed-tomography scanners to probe ailments such as stroke, schizophrenia, and Alzheimer's disease.

Researchers at Massachusetts General Hospital are putting some of these same principles to work to improve the diagnosis of colon cancer—the second most common cause of cancer death in the United States, with more than 50,000 fatalities each year. Colonoscopy has helped physicians find colon cancer earlier. However, it can have difficulty differentiating between dangerous and more benign polyps. In a lab at Mass. General headed by Ralph Weissleder, scientists have found that an enzyme called cathepsin-B appears in higher concentrations in the most dangerous polyps than it does in nearby tissue and in other polyps.

Armed with this biological insight, the researchers designed a clever new imaging agent, taking advantage of the fact that cathepsin-B is an enzyme that cuts up specific proteins. They constructed the agent out of a fluorescent protein fragment attached to another molecule that keeps the fluorescence quenched. When the imaging agent finds cathepsin-B, the enzyme cleaves off the quenching arm, freeing up the probe to glow brightly. Since targets like cathepsin-B exist in very small quantities, turning off extraneous unbound agent molecules is like darkening the stars in a night sky to better spot a passing comet.

Because light scatters as it penetrates deep into tissues, it would be difficult to scan a human patient's colon optically from outside the body. But the

Molecular Colonoscopy

To distinguish between dangerous and benign polyps, doctors might inject a molecular imaging agent targeting an enzyme that's concentrated in dangerous polyps. The enzyme itself would activate the agent by cutting it up and releasing particles that glow when light from a fiber-optic scope shines on the colon wall.

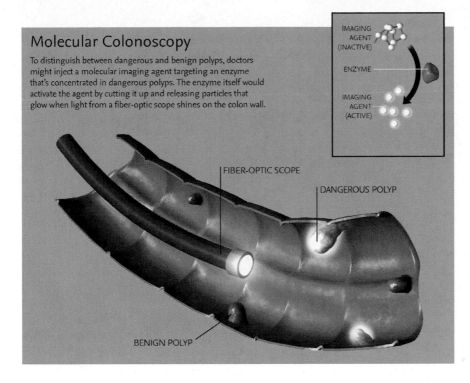

IMAGING AGENT (INACTIVE)

ENZYME

IMAGING AGENT (ACTIVE)

FIBER-OPTIC SCOPE

DANGEROUS POLYP

BENIGN POLYP

technology could be paired with conventional colonoscopy. In the future, doctors may inject a patient with a fluorescent imaging probe designed to find the enzyme, and then examine the colon using a fiber-optic scope that picks up the fluorescence. This will allow doctors to distinguish between the different kinds of polyps in real time, with a minimally invasive approach, instead of having to cut out sample tissue and send it to a pathology lab, then wait days or weeks for the results.

As a next step, says Mass. General's Mahmood, the researchers are now performing test colonoscopies on lab mice using the new imaging agent. According to Mahmood, the technique could make it possible to avoid many colon biopsies in five to ten years.

In the near term, optical imaging could also help improve the accuracy of breast biopsies. These procedures now can miss malignant cells because it's difficult for physicians working off of two-dimensional mammograms to know exactly where in the breast to place their needles. Experts estimate that in the United States alone, some 50,000 to 100,000 breast biopsies each year don't find existing cancer cells—and so do not properly diagnose the women's cancers.

To address the problem, University of Wisconsin-Madison biomedical engineer Nimmi Ramanujam is exploiting the fact that biological tissues naturally fluoresce in response to stimulation by certain wavelengths of light—and that healthy and cancerous tissues fluoresce differently. Ramanujam scaled down optical imaging technology to create a tiny fiber-optic sensor that can be threaded right through a biopsy needle. When the doctor inserts the needle into the breast, the device sends light into the tissue and collects the fluorescence emitted by cells at the needle's tip; algorithms developed by Ramanujam analyze this fluorescence in real time to distinguish between the telltale optical signatures of healthy and cancerous tissues.

Ramanujam and her colleagues at the University of Wisconsin Medical School are already testing the technology on women undergoing breast cancer surgery and plan trials with women undergoing breast biopsy within the next year.

BLURRED BOUNDARIES

These rapid advances in molecular imaging are helping to blur medicine's traditional boundary between diagnosis and treatment. That's because the potential to pinpoint molecular events involved in a disease, which is at the core of new imaging methods, raises an even more tantalizing possibility: in addition to diagnosing the problem, why not actively disrupt the process while you're at it?

Indeed, at Philips Medical Systems, a maker of traditional imaging devices, executives are increasingly excited about what they call the "see and treat" era. Says Josh Gurewitz, vice president of marketing in the nuclear-medicine division at Philips, "What sets molecular imaging apart is that we can not only identify and localize disease, we can now take this specific molecule and add a toxic payload."

Last year, just such a dual-purpose product won U.S. Food and Drug Administration approval for patients suffering from non-Hodgkin's lymphoma who have not responded to other treatments. Made by San Diego–based IDEC Pharmaceuticals (which will soon be called Biogen IDEC if a merger goes through as planned), Zevalin is a radioactively tagged antibody that ferrets out and binds directly to a specific protein on the rogue white blood cells that cause lymphoma.

Doctors inject the antibody, loaded with a harmless radioisotope, into a patient's body and monitor exactly where it goes, to make sure the tumor cells are safely treatable. Then they attach a different, more powerful isotope to the same antibody; once injected, it finds the cancer cells again and emits radiation to kill them.

Biotechnology companies have been dreaming about these sorts of two-pronged approaches for at least two decades. But it's taken progress in several disciplines, especially the chemistry required to snap the imaging and therapy components onto the same targeting molecules, to allow products like Zevalin to reach fruition. Now, however, the value of such new agents is becoming clear. "It's the treating that's so exciting," explains F. David Rollo, chief medical officer for Philips Medical Systems.

Indeed, IDEC is not the only pharmaceutical company bringing imaging technology into its product pipeline: both Amersham and GlaxoSmithKline are working with GE to develop improved imaging agents. But researchers say that while pharmaceutical companies seem to be intensely interested in molecular imaging, few are yet willing to fully embrace it. In the past, many drug companies avoided the imaging arena because markets—and profit margins—were perceived to be limited. Thanks in part to agents like Zevalin and Apomate, however, that perception is finally changing. And that could mean the boundaries between diagnosis and treatment will start to blur in the business arena, just as they have in the clinic.

Companies "have realized that this is the future," says Washington University biomedical engineer Samuel Wickline, a cofounder of Saint Louis–based startup Kereos, which is developing molecular-imaging agents for cancer and heart disease. "It takes advantage of all we've learned in basic science, all we've learned in imaging, and all clinicians have learned. There is a quantum leap around the corner."

And as the traditional distinctions and business models are challenged, says Rollo, "You have to build new core competencies. In general, we've focused on imaging, not on blood tests and therapies. So we're partnering with a number of companies. We are evolving to change the way we do business to meet this technology." The hope for patients is that evolution will do for biopsy needles what it did for stone knives.

> Learn more about the ethics and technologies of medical imaging.
> www.ablongman.com/beyondwords26

CONSIDER

1. How much of the information in "A Sharper Picture of Health" seems aimed at medical professionals? What other audiences can you imagine for the article?

2. What points does "A Sharper Picture of Health" make about different fields of knowledge and molecular imaging?

COMPOSE

3. Reread "A Sharper Picture of Health," looking for information related to the blurring between diagnosis and treatment. Write one or two paragraphs that explain the concept of blurring these two aspects of medicine.

Gene(sis): Contemporary Art Explores Human Genomics

Edourdo Kac, *GFP Bunny*

Edourdo Kac, *GFP Bunny*
"*GFP Bunny* comprises the creation of a green fluorescent rabbit, the public dialogue generated by the project, and the social integration of the rabbit. GFP stands for green fluorescent protein. . . . Transgenic art . . . is a new art form based on the use of genetic engineering to transfer natural or synthetic genes to an organism, to create unique living beings."

—Edourdo Kac

In 2002, the Henry Art Gallery at the University of Washington opened an exhibition featuring art created in response to human genetics research. Twenty-six artists submitted work ranging from organic creations constructed from Play-Doh to digital manipulations of photographs expressing the potential future of genetic research. We reproduce four of the submissions here: Edourdo Kac's *GFP Bunny*, a genetically altered rabbit created in collaboration with geneticists; one of Bill Scanga's series *Eighteen Frogs with Pants*

Bill Scanga, from the series *Eighteen Frogs with Pants Categorized by Color*

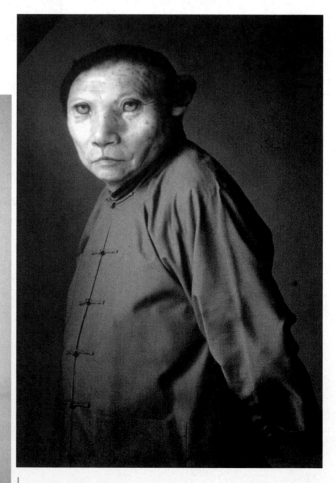

Daniel Lee, *Juror No. 6*

Categorized by Color, a comic critique that uses taxidermy to look at human attempts to manipulate animals; Daniel Lee's *Juror No. 6*, a digitally manipulated photograph exploring the combination of human and animal forms; and Susan Robb's *Eggspore 20*, created using Play-Doh, fibers, and spit.

Susan Robb, *Eggspore 20*
"By using common objects found in my studio . . . I create tissue samples, spores, germs, and genes. I then photograph these sculptures creating something that speaks in the 'style' of science and thus to the authority of science. I am interested in the consensual notion that things scientific look a particular way and that this look carries with it a certain supremacy of truth."

—Susan Robb

CONSIDER

1. Which of the images from the Gene(sis) exposition makes the strongest statement about transformation in medicine? How does the composition of the image help make that statement?

2. What point does Susan Robb make about images with a "scientific look"? What details in her image *Eggspore 20* could you talk about in terms of her point?

3. The four submissions from the exposition reproduced here all use different media to create art. How would you relate the different media to the topic of genetics? How does each piece's media relate to its message?

CHALLENGE

4. Would you say that it is ethical to genetically alter an animal for the purpose of art? How would you explain the difference between altering an animal for art versus for science? What might make one more ethical than the other? Hold an online discussion with classmates, and debate these questions.

Living in Virtual Worlds

The Brittanian lands pictured on this map exist only in the collective imagination of the online inhabitants of Electronic Arts' online role-playing game, Ultima Online. Massively multiplayer online role-playing games (MMORPGs), which enable thousands of gamers to participate simultaneously in a living virtual world through the Internet, are no longer the exclusive realms of the technological elite and the socially inept. Ultima Online, the most popular of these MMORPGs, boasts a player membership of over 225,000 and has been continuously "inhabited" since late 1997. These

Ultima Online Web Site

online communities have become a second life for many users, a virtual world that exists only in cyberspace.

Science fiction writer William Gibson popularized the concept of "cyberspace" in his 1984 novel *Neuromancer*. For Gibson, the virtual world of cyberspace could best be understood as a "consensual hallucination." As the readings in this section show, however, the effects of cyberspace on the psychology, economics, ethics, and laws of humans in the "real world" can be quite profound. How might our concepts of self and identity change in an environment where participants are encouraged to create fictional selves? How are attachments to virtual selves different from real-life relationships? What economic and legal principles govern trade and exchange in a virtual world?

FYI Stephen Totilo writes about video games. His articles have appeared in the *New York Times*, *Time* magazine, and on Slate.com. He has recently argued that video games ought to be funnier.

Do-It-Yourselfers Buy into This Virtual World

Stephen Totilo
(November 11, 2004)

In late summer, an armed airborne mechanical moose patrolled the skies of the online virtual world of Second Life. Its intended foe was a gold-armored man who would eventually set ablaze the moose owner's virtual headquarters, a replica of the German Reichstag. This was unconventional warfare even by the standards of massively multiplayer online games, where conflict is common.

What stood out was the ingenuity of the tools and the tactics, all designed and put in place not by a game programmer but by the players themselves. It is just one example of the creative freedom in Second Life, the most unpredictable of online worlds.

Second Life is the scrappy frontier of online games. It is a program of unusual freedoms and such undefined goals that many users call it a video game only for lack of a better term. And since its launch in mid-2003, it has tested the possibilities and limits of unfettered creative freedom.

There are no inherent goals, no monsters to kill, no skills to learn; there is essentially no grand design. The developers on the 25-person team at Linden Lab, based in San Francisco, create the game's virtual terrain and provide basic programming for users to walk or fly their humanoid avatars through this world.

Everything else—the buildings, the clothes, the animation that lets people dance the tango and the 48-acre replica of Peter Pan's London and Neverland, opening this week—is the handiwork of the users, who manipulate in-game design tools to build, animate and otherwise give purpose to the world.

It is also the only online game that officially supports third-party services that convert game money to dollars, encouraging its users to try to turn a profit.

"The only limit to the game is your own imagination," said Karen Huffman, a Georgia native who is one of Second Life's premier clothing designers. She created the costumes for the Peter Pan project.

But the no-limits nature of Second Life has raised some questions for its founders and citizens regarding the allure of unrestrained freedom.

Discussing the Reichstag conflict, a veteran creator of several online worlds, Randy Farmer, who last year consulted for Second Life and is still a fan of the project, said, "Do we want people to be able to firebomb Disneyland?"

The question has an obvious answer in real life. But in Second Life, even antisocial behavior (with a few limits) can advertise the potential of unlimited creativity. Now the question is whether a world defined by such freedom can go mainstream.

A tour through the game's ever growing landmass is a testament to the ingenuity of its mostly peaceful users. Some have built shops and casinos. In one sector someone constructed an extravagant airport where users can purchase the ability to skydive. In another, a series of rooms designed by James Cook, a physician affiliated with the University of California, Davis, lets visitors experience the visual and aural sensations of schizophrenia.

Philip Rosedale, Second Life's founder and a former chief technical officer for RealNetworks, said he had not foreseen most of this. But that lack of design was the design.

He had wanted to build a world of collaborative construction. He had been taken with the idea that many small variables could create a nuanced entity. He and Cory Ondrejka, Linden Lab's vice president for product development, prepared to build their world by studying the growth of a forest fire.

Mr. Rosedale said he was heartened by the 20 percent monthly growth in the game's population. Still, at 15,000 users, Second Life is tiny compared with City of Heroes, this year's most eagerly received massively multiplayer online game, which has more than 150,000 users, according to the game's publisher, NCsoft.

Mr. Rosedale predicts that Second Life can attract a million users in three years, pointing not just to the enthusiasm of his current users but to the $8 million of financing secured last month from the venture firm Benchmark Capital and the founder of eBay, Pierre Omidyar.

One concern, however, is that the program's ballyhooed freedom has proved more effective in drawing customers with an appetite for construction rather than those who—conditioned by video games, TV programs and movies made for them—simply like to consume.

"We don't think the message for a million people is to come and build your own world starting from bricks," Mr. Rosedale said.

So when Nanci Schenkein, 51, of West Orange, N.J., approached Linden Lab with an idea to re-create parts of early-20th-century London and Neverland in the game, Mr. Rosedale agreed to waive the standard rental fee for her

temporary use of 48 virtual acres. The hope was that large-scale attractions, which the uncreative masses could simply experience, would draw interest.

The free rent was a significant offer. Second Life (whose game software, available for the PC and the Macintosh, is available as a download at lindenlab. com) charges a one-time fee of $10 for those who enter its virtual borders and want to explore the lively world regularly. Linden Lab generates monthly fees from visitors who rent land, a necessity for builders, whose in-game materials are free but whose creations remain permanent only on land they rent.

The Neverland project's 48 acres would have cost $3,000 at the start and $600 a month after that. As part of the deal, Ms. Schenkein agreed to forgo any profit from the project.

In early October Ms. Schenkein enlisted a far-flung group of 25 people, including a charity worker from Idaho and a night clerk at a hotel in France, to assemble a replica of parts of London and Peter Pan's Neverland. They have created what Mr. Rosedale called a movie on rails.

Neverland represents a growing effort to balance the freedom of the world with some reliably structured experiences. For some Second Life citizens, the motivation to strike that balance stems not so much from attracting visitors as from a frustration with the shape the virtual world has taken.

Michael Parchomenko, 38, of Chicago, was dismayed that so much of Second Life simply emulated reality. So he enlisted two fellow citizens, Nick Brittain and Hugh Perkins, to help create something impossible on earth: a volcano that launches people into a field engineered for treasure hunting and medieval armed combat. In other words, on 32 acres of Second Life land, which costs $400 a month to rent, they built a video game.

Mr. Parchomenko said he planned to open his game, SimCast, to the general Second Life public in a few weeks. He is optimistic. But he, too, has discovered that creative freedom can snap back like a rubber band.

The fact that his game must technically allow its users to build objects on his plot of land has led him to worry that spoilsports can invade with virtual jumbo jets or a flood of boxes. "That's not fun when you're trying to keep a tight ship on a medieval theme setting," he said.

Freedom isn't simple. But Mr. Rosedale can't help but be enthusiastic. "If you take human beings and give them [fewer] ways to express themselves, generally their behavior becomes more base," he said.

He then considered the opposite. "Second Life almost unquestionably has more opportunity for self-expression," he said. "And, indeed, this is why we think it's competitive with and in many ways better than real life."

CONSIDER

1. What examples does Totilo use to support his claims about the "creative freedom" made possible by Second Life? What questions does this freedom raise for the "citizens" of Second Life? Why? What value might there be in the kinds of "antisocial behavior" reported by Totilo?

2. How does Second Life differ from "mainstream" videogames and online worlds? Would you be interested in participating in, and building, a world like Second Life? Why or why not? What values and behaviors do you think it promotes?

3. Constructed worlds like those created by the users of Second Life rely on detailed descriptions of virtual environments. In your opinion, is this writing more imaginative or informational? What examples would you cite to support your position?

COMPOSE

4. Visit the Second Life Web site at secondlife.com, and analyze the way Second Life presents itself to potential "citizens." Are you interested enough in the site's presentation to want to join? Why or why not? Write a brief analysis of the rhetorical strategies used by the Second Life site in its attempt to generate visitors and entice new members to join.

Virtual Selves, Real People

Sherry Turkle
(1996)

FYI Sherry Turkle is professor of the social studies of science and technology and director of the Initiative on Technology and Self at the Massachusetts Institute of Technology. She is perhaps the best-known scholar today in the area of psychology and cyberculture. Her book *Life on the Screen: Identity in the Age of the Internet* (1995) has influenced many writers and thinkers interested in the psychology of computer-mediated interactions and virtual worlds.

One of the things that happens on the Internet is that you can be who you say you are. It's one of the appeals. It's one of the things that I argue gives it a kind of excitement as a place to live out your fantasies and experiment with aspects of yourself. But it also means that when you meet people online they're not necessarily who they say they are.

I'd been interviewing, over two years in Boston, a 43-year-old man who was of interest to me as a subject because he was having an online relationship that had become very important to him. And he was having it with a woman. He was married, and he was having this online flirtation with a woman, who he thought was 23 and from Memphis, whose online name was something like "Fabulous Hot Babe." Now in fact it wasn't Fabulous Hot Babe, it was something else. But it was just like Fabulous Hot Babe. And our conversations really were about how to think about what was happening there in terms of other relationships and whether this was infidelity. We were discussing how to think about that, what it had done to him, and what he had discovered about himself in the course of the relationship. And for me, it was kind of case study of somebody who was taking seriously an online romance.

At one of our sessions he came in ashen-faced, and I said, "What's the matter?" Actually the first thing that had gone through my mind was that his wife had found out about the relationship, which was something we had been discussing for a year. But that was not the case. He had discovered, actually because the person finally confessed to him, that Fabulous Hot Babe wasn't a 23-year-old woman in Memphis, but an 80-year-old man in a nursing home in Miami. The thrust of our conversation now was how he was going to deal with this and how he felt about this.

I was very struck by the story because when you tell the story, people laugh. And of course they laugh because this was the most exciting thing that had happened to the 80-year-old and everybody on his floor in the nursing home in Miami; there was kind of a group participation in Fabulous Hot Babe's adventures. But it wouldn't be so funny if it was a 12-year-old boy or a 12-year-old girl who had been playing Fabulous Hot Babe and had somehow been able to fool this 43-year-old. Not only wouldn't it have been funny, but we would have been concerned for the 12-year-old. I also want to put in my vote for a great deal of concern for the 43-year-old, who would have been bereft had he thought that he was having a relationship with a child.

So where this story leads me is to both want to respect and make sure there's lots of space for adults to experiment and play (and with the widest possible experiments in multiplicity since I believe they can be very productive for many people), but to also try to protect people in some way so that they need not be afraid that they're dealing with children in these explorations.

Now, do I think that sometimes children will get into these environments in the same way that underage people regularly get their hands on *Penthouse* and *Playboy*, even though you have it behind Plexiglas or behind counters in convenience stores? I think that some children will get in, but I think that what you need to have is a sense that that is a transgression, just as kids know that somehow getting their hands on that stuff beyond the Plexiglas is a transgression.

And, you know, our society works because some things are transgressions, and they don't happen that often. Sometimes they happen, and we know how to think about that.

I don't think there has to be a sort of total barrier. I think there's more a sense of dividing the world of the Internet into places where children should be and children shouldn't be.

It's funny, we're talking here at a conference where I told that story. And a woman came up to me after I told it and said, "Would it have been as funny if an 80-year-old woman had been impersonating a 25-year-old man and having an affair with a woman?"

And I thought the question was very interesting because it's exactly the sort of question that cyberspace provokes. It allows us to do these thought experiments in which people really learn more about our construction of gender. And we learn what others think is acceptable and funny and how we think about men's and women's roles.

CONSIDER

1. What kinds of stories does Turkle focus on in this brief account of life on the Internet? What questions and issues do they allow Turkle to raise?

2. Turkle muses that cyberspace allows for a kind of experimentation with gender. Do you think she would claim that cyberspace allows people to escape gender? Or are gender roles reinforced? Do you agree with her insights?

COMPOSE

3. Conduct research online or in the library about gender issues in cyberspace. Compose a brief paper explaining the allure of online gender-switching, outlining the ethical and safety concerns raised by this practice.

The Unreal
Estate Boom

Julian Dibbell has written essays on hackers, computer viruses, online communities, encryption technologies, music pirates, and the cultural and philosophical questions concerning life in a digital age. Currently a contributing editor for *Wired* magazine, he is also author of *My Tiny Life: Crime and Passion in a Virtual World* (1999).

Julian Dibbell
(January 2003)

Not long ago, a 43-year-old Wonder Bread deliveryman named John Dugger logged on to eBay and, as people sometimes do these days, bought himself a house. Not a shabby one, either. Nine rooms, three stories, rooftop patio, walls of solid stonework—it wasn't quite a castle, but it put to shame the modest redbrick ranch house Dugger came home to every weeknight after a long day stocking the supermarket shelves of Stillwater, Oklahoma. Excellent location, too; nestled at the foot of a quiet coastal hillside, the house was just a hike away from a quaint seaside village and a quick commute from two bustling cosmopolitan cities. It was perfect, in short, except for one detail: The house was imaginary.

Equally unreal were the grounds the house stood on, the ocean it overlooked, the neighboring cities, and just about everything else associated with it—except Dugger himself, the man he bought it from, and the money he shelled out. At $750, Dugger's winning bid on the property set him back more than a week's wages and was, on the face of it, an astonishing amount for what he actually bought: one very small piece of Britannia, the fantasy world in which the networked role-playing game Ultima Online unfolds.

Yet there was nothing particularly unusual about the transaction. On any day you choose, dozens of Britannian houses can be found for sale online at comparable prices. And houses are just the start of it. Swords, suits of armor; iron ingots, lumber, piles of hay; tables, chairs, potted plants, magic scrolls; or any other little cartoon item the little cartoon characters of Britannia might desire can be had at auction, priced from $5 for a pair of sandals to $150 for an exceptionally badass battle-ax to $1,200 for a well-located fortress. A simple, back-of-the-envelope calculation puts the estimated sum of these transactions at $3 million per year.

Which in turn is just a fraction of the total wealth created annually by the residents of Britannia. For every item or character sold on eBay and other Web sites, many more are traded within the game itself—some bartered, most bought with Britannian gold pieces (a currency readily convertible into U.S. legal tender at about 40,000 to the dollar, a rate that puts it on par with the Romanian lei). The goods exchanged number in the millions, nearly every one of them brought into existence by the sweat of some player's virtual brow. Magic weapons won in arduous quests, furniture built with tediously acquired carpentry skills, characters made powerful through years of obsessive play—taken as a whole, they are the GNP of Britannia.

Literally. Last year—in an academic paper analyzing the circulation of goods in Sony Online's 430,000-player EverQuest—an economist calculated a full set of macro- and microeconomic statistics for the game's fantasy world, Norrath. Taking the prices fetched in the $5 million EverQuest auctions market as a reflection of in-game property values, Professor Edward Castronova of Cal State Fullerton multiplied those dollar amounts by the rate at which players pile up imaginary inventory and came up with an average hourly income of $3.42. He calculated Norrath's GNP at $135 million— or about the same, per capita, as Bulgaria's.

In other words, assuming roughly proportional numbers for Electronic Arts' 225,000-player Ultima and other major online role-playing games— Mythic's Dark Age of Camelot, Microsoft's Asheron's Call, Funcom's Anarchy Online—the workforce toiling away in these imaginary worlds generates more than $300 million in real wealth each year. That's about double what the game companies themselves make in subscription revenue, a fact that poses them a single, nettlesome question: How—and whether—to grab a piece of the action?

For the rest of us, though, the questions are a little more philosophical. The traffic in virtual goods, after all, isn't just another new market. It's a whole new species of economy—perhaps the only really new economy that, when all has boomed and crashed, the Internet has yet given rise to. And how poetic is that? For years, the world's economy has drifted further and further from the solid ground of the tangible: Industry has given way to postindustry, the selling of products has given way to the selling of brands, gold bricks in steel vaults have given way to financial derivatives half a dozen levels of abstraction removed from physical reality. This was all supposed to culminate in what's been called the virtual economy—a realm of atomless digital products traded in frictionless digital environments for paperless digital cash. And so it has. But who would have guessed that this culmination would so literally consist of the buying and selling of castles in the air?

These little economies raise big questions, therefore, and by no coincidence, they tend to be the big questions of the economic age. How, for instance, do we assign value to immaterial goods? What defines ownership when property becomes as fluid as thought? What defines productivity

Ken Brown, *Castle: $2,053*
(eBay resale price)

when work becomes a game and games become work?

And, of course, the question of questions—the one that in a sense asks them all: How, exactly, did a 7-[kilobyte] piece of digital make-believe become John Dugger's $750 piece of upmarket real estate?

At a construction site in Indianapolis, Troy Stolle sits with a hard hat in his lap and a Big Mac in his hands. Outside, the air is thick with dust and the rumble of bulldozers. A hundred yards away, the outline of a future Costco megastore shimmers in the heat, slowly taking shape as workers set rebar and pour concrete. Stolle's job, as a form carpenter, is to build the wooden molds the concrete gets poured into. His arms and hands are flecked with cuts and bruises, and at the moment he's got a pounding headache from the early stages of dehydration. Or maybe from the two-by-four that smacked him in the head earlier this morning. He's not certain which.

There's one thing he's sure of. Asked how this job compares to the work of building a virtual tower in Britannia two years ago, he answers like it's obvious: "That was a lot more stressful."

A lanky, bespectacled 30-year-old, Stolle looks less like the third-generation construction worker he is than like the second-generation sword-and-sorcery geek he also is. When Stolle was 10, his father, a union electrician, died of a heart attack, leaving behind a cherished 1967 paperback edition of *The Lord of the Rings* and a copy of the Dungeons & Dragons rule set.

It all started there. Through high school, on through his four-year union apprenticeship, and well into his first years as a carpenter, Stolle spent vast stretches of his free time immersed in the intricacies of D&D, Warhammer, BattleTech, and other tabletop role-playing and strategy games.

Then came Ultima Online. The first true massively multiplayer online role-playing game, UO went live in September 1997, and by December, Stolle had a character: a blacksmith he called Nils Hansen. The business of bettering Nils' lot in life quickly came to absorb him more intensely than any game ever had. In short order, he added two other characters: an archer, who went out hunting when Nils needed hides, and a mage, who cooked up potions to make the archer a better hunter. "I had everybody interlocked so that they totally supported one another," Stolle says. And to give this little team a base of operations—a place to store equipment, basically—he paid about 40,000 gold coins for a deed permitting him to build a small house. He found a nice, secluded spot in northern Britannia, placed his cursor there, and double-clicked the building into existence.

The house worked out fine for a while, but in a game about accumulation, no house stays big enough for long. Stolle's trio needed new digs, and soon. By now, though, real estate was acutely hard to come by. Deeds were still available, but there was nowhere left to build. The number of homeless was rising, and the prices of existing houses were rising even faster. At last, EA announced a solution that could work only in a make-believe world—a whole new continent was being added to the map.

Stolle started preparing for the inevitable land rush months before it happened. He scrimped and saved, sold his house for 180,000 gold, and finally had enough to buy a deed for the third-largest class of house in the game, the so-called Large Tower.

On the night the new continent's housing market was set to open, Stolle showed up early at a spot he had scouted out previously, and found 12 players already there. No one knew exactly when the zero hour was, so Stolle and the others just kept clicking on the site, each hoping to be the first to hit it when the time came.

"It was *so* stressful," Stolle recalls. "You're sitting there, you double-click the deed once and then click on the spot. And I did this for four hours." Finally, at about 1 in the morning, the housing option switched on, and as a couple of thousand "Build" commands went through at once, the machine that was processing it all swooned under the load. "The server message pops up, and everything just freezes. And I'm still clicking. Even though nothing's happening, I'm still clicking—boom, boom, boom. For like 10 minutes, everything's frozen. You see people kind of disappearing here and there. And then it starts to let up. And a tower appears! Nobody knows for sure whose it is. Guys are like, Whose is it? Did I get it? I double-clicked on it, and I couldn't tell. And so then I double-clicked again—and there was my key to the tower."

Just like that. In a single clock cycle and a double mouseclick, Stolle had built himself a real nice spread.

But of course there was more to it than that. In addition to the four hours of clicking, Stolle had had to come up with the money for the deed. To get the money, he had to sell his old house. To get that house in the first place, he had to spend hours crafting virtual swords and plate mail to sell to a steady clientele of about three dozen fellow players. To attract and keep that clientele, he had to bring Nils Hansen's blacksmithing skills up to Grandmaster.

To reach that level, Stolle spent six months doing nothing but smithing: He clicked on hillsides to mine ore, headed to a forge to click the ore into ingots, clicked again to turn the ingots into weapons and armor, and then headed back to the hills to start all over again, each time raising Nils' skill level some tiny fraction of a percentage point, inching him closer to the distant goal of 100 points and the illustrious title of Grandmaster Blacksmith.

Take a moment now to pause, step back, and consider just what was going on here: Every day, month after month, a man was coming home from a full day of bone-jarringly repetitive work with hammer and nails to put in a full night of finger-numbingly repetitive work with "hammer" and "anvil"—and paying $9.95 per month for the privilege. Ask Stolle to make sense of this, and he has a ready answer: "Well, it's not work if you enjoy it." Which, of course, begs the question: Why would anyone enjoy it?

But people do. And that's a curious thing. Throughout history, whenever human beings have tried to imagine the best of all possible worlds, they've pictured some version of paradise: a place of abundance and ease. Not too long ago, people insisted the Internet was just such an environment, with its effortlessly reproducible wealth of data and light-speed transcendence of geography and time. In the emerging online universe, it was said, scarcity had no place. And what's not to like about that?

Yet scarcity has turned out to be a feature, not a bug. Sure, people like the big, graphics-based chat arenas such as the Palace, where talk was the only real commodity, and that commodity was, as usual, cheap. But the worlds they actually want to be in—bad enough to pay an entrance fee—are the ones that make the digital goods hard to get to and even harder to copy. The addictive appeal of online role-playing games suggests that people will choose the constraining and challenging world over the one that sets them free.

Which in turn makes the fact that you can log on to eBay this minute and buy 10,000 imaginary iron ingots for $4.50 seem not only a little less improbable but in fact inevitable. Scarcity, after all, breeds markets, and markets will seep like gas through any boundary that gives them the slightest opening—never mind a line as porous as the one between real and make-believe.

"The minute you hardwire constraints into a virtual world, an economy emerges," explains Castronova, the Adam Smith of EverQuest. "One-trillionth of a second later, that economy starts interacting with ours."

On the border between Britannia's economy and ours sits Bob Kiblinger's downstairs den—part of a nice split-level house located in quiet Beckley, West Virginia. In the den sits a sofa, and on the sofa, most workdays, sits Kiblinger. As sole proprietor of UOTreasures.com, Kiblinger trades Ultima items for a living, scanning eBay listings on his laptop in search of assets undervalued and overlooked. One particularly lucky day, he caught sight of a diamond in the rough: UO account, 52 months old, Grandmaster Blacksmith, Large Tower. Not a single bid, he noticed.

Troy Stolle's account was definitely an opportunity. Kiblinger sized it up at about $1,500 worth of stuff, possibly $2,000. He fired off an e-mail asking Stolle how much money he wanted to close the deal and hand over the account. Stolle emailed back: $500. Minutes later, Kiblinger was on the phone to Indiana, making arrangements to finalize the transaction. Before he hung up, the two men chitchatted a bit: Stolle got to talking about the unfortunate reasons he'd sold the account—about how he'd been out of work since 9/11 and the bills were piling up. Kiblinger could hear an infant crying in the background, and he hoped the carpenter would never find out just how much stood to be made on the deal.

But business is business. Kiblinger knew that to keep his income up to speed he needed at least three or four fat, high-margin trades like this each week, and they weren't getting any easier to come by. Once upon a time, back when Ultima was young and most players still hadn't gotten wind of the auction markets, his percentage on a deal often hit quadruple digits. Players sold him thousand-dollar accounts for a hundred, and Kiblinger just kept his mouth shut, knowing full well that in their eyes he was the crazy one. Not long before, he might even have agreed with them.

"I would have done the same thing," he says. "If I had an account I was giving up, and you said you were going to give me a hundred dollars for it—for something that's not real—I would have said, 'Here, take it.'"

That was four years ago. Kiblinger was 28 years old, married, working for Procter & Gamble in Cincinnati as a chemist (he shares two patents on the odor-busting fabric spray Febreze), and feeding his Ultima jones at night and on weekends. Within a year, his marriage was over ("Yes, it's true, an Ultima widow"), he had moved back home to Beckley, and he was brokering make-believe products full-time. Asked how much he was earning by then, Kiblinger smiles affably and declines to answer, except to say that it was—and remains—a lot more than he made at Procter & Gamble.

Kiblinger's caginess is par for the course. There are dozens of people out there making a real living selling virtual goods, and none are particularly eager to disclose their profits. A few will talk off the record, and none of those claim to be netting less than six-figure incomes or 15 percent margins. But those are fragile numbers, threatened on all sides.

Hackers are among the biggest threats. To stay ahead of the latest tricks for stealing players' hard-won property—and to safeguard his own inventory—Kiblinger checks the Ultima cheat sites regularly. Even worse are the dupers—counterfeiters who look for software bugs that let them double and redouble their gold on command, turning a single piece into billions with just a few dozen mouseclicks. Not a bad deal for the dupers but deadly for

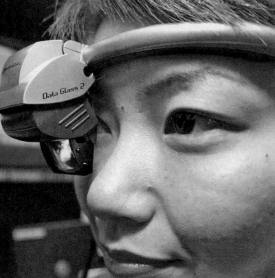

the Britannian economy: Some of Ultima's earliest duping schemes inflated the currency to the brink of worthlessness. Even today, the resulting monetary surplus keeps the game designers busy thinking up gold sinks—expensive luxury items that can be bought only from non-player merchant bots (neon-colored hair dye is an especially big seller), thus taking large sums of money out of circulation.

Ultimately, though, the spookiest threat to the dealers is the game companies themselves.

Well aware that his income exists at the sufferance of Ultima's corporate overseer, Electronic Arts, Kiblinger keeps his inventory as low as possible—even so, it often swells to tens of thousands of dollars' worth of goods.

"It's scary to have that much cash tied up in the business," he says, "when Ultima could just say, 'We deem this outside the rules. You're done.'"

Sony did this very thing last year when it announced a ban on the EverQuest auction market and got eBay to enforce it. But even seemingly market-friendly moves can play havoc with the traders' livelihoods. Recently EA announced that Ultima players could now, for a mere $29.95, order their own custom-built, high-level characters straight from the company.

At the far end of this line of thinking lie concepts like MindArk's Project Entropia, a game still in beta in which every item will be available for sale direct from the company—a move that could finally make corporate peace with the auction markets by rendering them completely superfluous.

Until then, though, Kiblinger remains relatively safe from competition. To watch him in action once he finally gets his hands on an account like Stolle's is to understand, a little, the uncommon expertise it takes to make this business pay. As he logs on for the first time and starts taking inventory, the casual once-over of his initial appraisal sharpens to a laser focus. Wandering through the newly auctioned house in the onscreen body Stolle previously inhabited, Kiblinger becomes a value-sifting machine. He's equipped with a massive mental database and can cross-reference the most obscure imaginary item with its latest market price.

Houses are invariably the most valuable items, and the easiest to judge. But almost as much money can lie hidden in a far subtler class of objects known as rares—curiosities whose value consists entirely, as the name suggests, in their scarcity. The original rares were accidents, pieces of scenery that the game designers misprogrammed or otherwise forgot to lock down—rocks, piles of horse dung, patches of waterfall, even portable error messages. By the time Kiblinger got into the market, these freaks of virtual nature were hundred-dollar collectibles, and for a long time they were his bread and butter. Eventually, the designers caught on to their popularity and introduced semi-rares: decorative fruit baskets and other knickknacks that pop into existence every month or so in some remote backwater of the land. This took a lot of the economic steam out of the rares scene, and Kiblinger shifted his focus to the tight housing market.

But the true rares remain big-ticket items, and so he is obliged to keep in mind, as he sorts through a new account, that an innocuous-looking piece of horse crap still sells for as much as $400. Such arcana make the job of sweeping out a typical account a two- or three-hour affair.

In Stolle's case, with nearly 2,000 items locked up in the tower, the job took even longer. But by the end of the night, the account was stripped: Ownership of the house was transferred to one of Kiblinger's characters, assorted rares were relocated to storage and cataloged, and the rest was warehoused for future sorting. The messy complex of characters and possessions that had been Troy Stolle's virtual identity was broken down into parts far more valuable than the whole. The priciest items were listed on eBay within a day or two, and one by one they went off to the highest bidder.

But the most valuable of all was the last to go. Not that Kiblinger lacked for house buyers in the month that Stolle's tower stood at auction. He sold one property to a single mom in Colorado, another to a manager for a database company in California. Yet another went to a woman in Virginia, who bought the house for her mother, an Alzheimer's sufferer whose last link to reality was her Ultima sessions with her daughter. Any of these bidders might have wound up with the tower that Troy Stolle built.

In the end, of course, it went to John Dugger, a Wonder Bread deliveryman in Stillwater, Oklahoma.

"A wage of $3.42 an hour is sufficient to sustain Earth existence for many people," writes Castronova, in his report about the economy of EverQuest. "Many users spend upward of 80 hours per week in Norrath, hours of time input that are not unheard of in Earth professions. In 80 hours, at the average wage, the typical user generates Norrathian cash and goods worth $273.60. In a month, that would be over $1,000, in a year over $12,000. The poverty line for a single person in the United States is $8,794." Do the math, Castronova suggests, and the bottom line is this: "Economically speaking, there is little reason to question, on feasibility grounds at least, that those who claim to be living and working in Norrath, and not on Earth, may actually be doing just that."

Troy Stolle stopped living in Britannia months ago. And Bob Kiblinger rarely logs on anymore except to inventory the remains of somebody else's existence there. But John Dugger is another story.

Separated from his wife for the last four years, Dugger lives alone. Most of the time, when he isn't working, he can be found in what he calls his dungeon, a section of the garage walled off to make a small, barely ventilated room, where he sits five hours a night, eyes fixed on his computer screen and on the tiny, make-believe self he maneuvers through Britannia's cartoon landscape.

"People have told me I need to get a life," Dugger says.

And seeing him here in his dungeon, you might agree with them. Follow him into Britannia, though, and you might think again. Watch, for instance, as he shows a visitor around the tower he bought just a few months ago. Note, as Dugger and his guest walk their characters from room to room, just how thoroughly he's made the place his own.

The first floor, once the austere workshop of a hardcore craftsman, has become a bright, busy public gallery for Dugger's collection of rares and semi-rares. "That bucket of water you see on the floor there is a true rare," he says proudly, narrating the tour by telephone. "It cost me 600,000 gold." Nothing much had been done with the second floor, so Dugger turned it into an armory. Likewise the roof, which came furnished as a kind of game room, complete with playable chess and backgammon sets, has been buried beneath the lush foliage of a rooftop garden designed by Dugger's in-game girlfriend, the Lady Lickeretta.

"I did pretty much leave the master bedroom alone, though. I liked the way they did it," says Dugger. As it happens, he has no idea who "they" are. At first he thought the previous owner was a character named Blossom. She handed off the deed. But Blossom turned out to be one of Kiblinger's avatars—and not even Kiblinger at the keyboard but his cousin Eugene, who gets $10 an hour to run around Britannia doing the deliveries that used to take up most of Kiblinger's workday.

So now Dugger can only guess. "There's some stuff in the house that the label says was made by a Lord Nils something or other, so that might have been one of the characters on that account," he surmises. "And to be a lord, that means he hasn't died in a very long time, so that means he was pretty good at what he did."

Dugger excuses himself to run his character upstairs. In a minute, he says over the phone: "Here it is. 'Nils Hansen.' N-I-L-S H-A-N-S-E-N."

There's a further pause as Dugger seems to lose himself in contemplation of whatever piece of Troy Stolle's handiwork he's found. An "exceptional wooden armoire," perhaps, clicked into being years ago with virtual saw and lathe. Or maybe a full suit of agapite plate mail, hammered out at the forge downstairs.

Whatever it is, it's the same kind of puzzle the tower itself is. No more or less than any chess castle or Monopoly hotel, John Dugger's tower is a gamepiece, and yet it's also something more meaningful than any gamepiece has a right to be. For if it's true that economies are in many ways like games, and that the world's economy is getting more gamelike everyday, there remains one defining difference between the two: Games attract us with their very lack of consequence, whereas economies confront us with the least trivial pursuit of all, the pursuit of happiness. And while not even Dugger himself can say precisely how much happiness he bought when he bought that imaginary house, one thing was certain from the moment Troy Stolle put it up for auction. The game was over, and something as real as life was suddenly in play.

Investigate the possibilities and perils of a "second life" online.
www.ablongman.com/beyondwords27

CONSIDER

1. Dibbell ends with this sentence: "The game was over, and something as real as life was suddenly in play." What does he mean by this? How does he come to this conclusion? Retrace the steps of Dibbell's essay to show how he arrives at his final point.

2. What consequences and implications does Dibbell want readers to see in the collision of "games" and real "economies"? What does Dibbell want us to understand about this "whole new species of economy"? What are "the big questions of the economic age" that Dibbell raises in this essay?

3. Do you think that Dibbell's essay seeks to inform people about virtual worlds, or is he primarily offering an argument? What aspects of the piece (tone, descriptions, assumptions, evidence, etc.) would you cite to support your opinion?

COMPOSE

4. Find and interview some friends who play or have played online games like Ultima Online. Develop a list of questions based on Dibbell's analysis, and explore those questions with your interviewees. Write a brief essay that confirms or challenges Dibbell's claims based on your own interviews and observations.

CHALLENGE

5. Do some research (perhaps read more of Sherry Turkle and other authors appearing in this section) on the issues of online identity and the psychology of online role-playing games. Do you think online gamers (and gamers in general) are stereotyped? In what ways? Write a reflective essay presenting your views on the gaming world and its inhabitants. You may want to cast your essay as a narrative or a profile essay.

Assignments and Projects

Mapping a Project Visually

We all know that prewriting, drafting, and then revising an essay leads to stronger work—it helps us think our ideas through and refine our focus in ways that are just not possible if we compose the night before an assignment is due. But visual mapping of ideas can do more than simply help us get a head start on a project. For many people, visual representations allow ideas to develop organically and help to pinpoint key areas of knowledge that must be developed for a project.

This assignment asks you to create three visual maps—a brainstorming map, a strategy map, and a reflection map—as part of a research writing assignment. Your maps will be created as you develop an essay that presents your findings about your topic. Your research project will be an inquiry-based exploration of an issue in a university discipline, such as history, the fine arts, chemistry, biology, philosophy, or some other field.

Your inquiry should begin with a research question. First, you will need to conduct initial research to get a feel for the field. Then home in on a specific topic that you would like to learn more about. For example, for an exploration of molecular imaging, you might ask, "What impact might molecular imaging have on the relationship between diagnosis and treatment?" Brainstorm until you have a question that can be articulated in a sentence and that opens an area of inquiry.

Note that for this project, you will need mapping materials; you can simply use blank paper and colored pens or pencils, or you can download a trial version of idea-mapping software (*Inspiration* software can be downloaded at www.inspiration.com).

Before you start, ask yourself these questions:

WHAT'S IT TO YOU?

- An inquiry research project will not have much appeal if you choose a topic about which you have little interest. Starting with broad disciplines of knowledge will allow you to focus in on a subtopic that engages you—if you know a friend or family member with a disease or you've enjoyed a topic in another class, gravitate toward those concerns and find something you can put your heart into.

WHAT DO YOU WANT TO SAY ABOUT IT?

- Your purpose in this research essay will center around providing information about your topic. You will need to make decisions about what information matters the most—and about how to best arrange that information. Concentrate on distilling the **key points** that you discover and selecting the best information you can find to inform readers about your topic.

WHO WILL LISTEN?

- As you work on your project, you are likely to become much better informed about your topic than your **audience** is. Think, then, about ways of explaining information to make it clear to readers who may be less knowledgeable—define key terms; use images, charts, and graphs when helpful; and translate specialized concepts or jargon so that others can grasp what you are telling them.

WHAT DO YOU NEED TO KNOW?

- Your project will evolve as you respond to this question. First of all, be sure that your **research question** addresses a genuine concern related to your field—if your question is too broad or has an obvious answer ("Is medical imaging changing society?"), you need to refine your initial approach so you can investigate with more **focus** ("How is fMRI influencing consumerism?"). Once you know you have an engaging topic and a worthy question, you can uncover relevant information through your research.

HOW WILL YOU DO IT?

- For the mapping aspects of this assignment, consider your technical skills—if you feel comfortable with new technologies, download and use mapping **software** like *Inspiration*; if you prefer, use low-tech materials but obtain large sheets of paper and enough drawing tools to really differentiate between ideas as you map them. Be sure also that you understand the intricacies of conducting research. You will need to know how to use online databases as well as the Internet. If necessary, get help from our Web site, your instructor, or your librarian as you conduct your **research.** Finally, think about the form your essay will take. You may simply write it out on your word processor. If your topic is likely to lead you to rich information sources online (animations, graphics, reports), consider composing a Web essay. Whatever form your essay takes, its structure should be reasonably straightforward. Use headings when needed to point out major areas of information. Incorporate images and other visual information that will help you explain your topic. Format the essay in an understated way so that the information is the focus. And be sure to document your sources.

HOW WELL DOES IT WORK?

■ This assignment includes a reflection map, but don't wait until it is all over to start assessing your work. As you research, think about how your topic or research question might be adjusted. Solicit feedback about your draft, and think about your writing in progress in terms of how well it conveys your information to your readers. When you have finished, think about your reflection map and about your writing process during the project, and consider any ways you might **revise.**

Additional Instructions:

Here are some steps to follow as you compose your project:

1. **Once you have conducted some initial research and developed a research question, develop a brainstorming map.** Begin by drawing or creating a bubble in the center of your map with your broad topic or your research question written in it. Surround this center bubble with other bubbles containing as many ideas, hypotheses, facts, and questions as you can. Record everything that comes to mind without necessarily trying to impose any order on the bubbles. When you are satisfied with the variety, range, and quantity of the surrounding bubbles, stop. Spend some more time conducting research and thinking about your topic before moving on to step 2.

2. **Return to your brainstorming map and look it over. Then begin a new map—a "strategy map."** You may maintain some of the items in the brainstorming map (if you are using *Inspiration*, simply save the brainstorming map with a new name and begin revising the map). Cluster bubbles you wish to keep, and develop a hierarchy of research priorities either with new clusters or in connection with your original ideas. Be wary of deleting bubbles because you are still in the early stages of research. Once your map has distinct clusters that articulate feasible research goals, stop and move on to step 3.

3. **Following your mapped priorities, use library sources, online databases, or the Internet to find information that will help you meet your research goals.** (See our Web site for more instructions on conducting

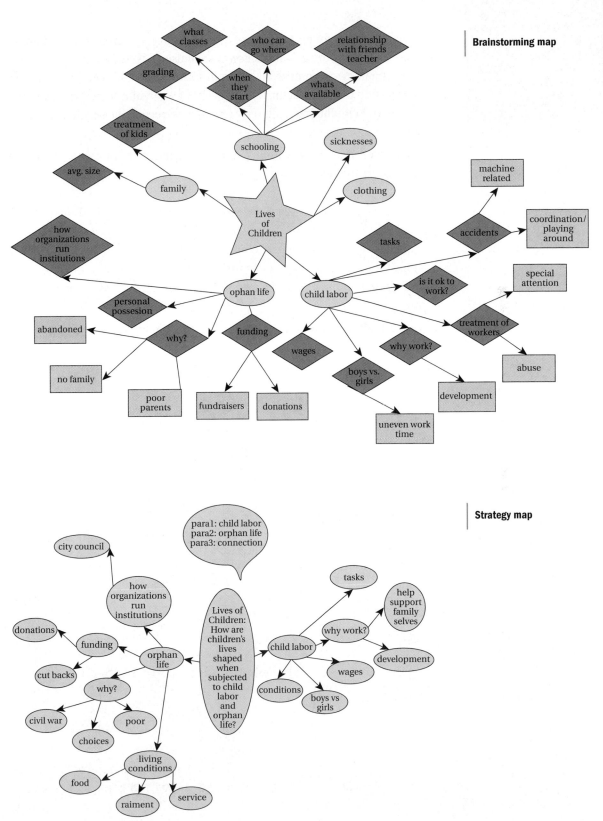

Brainstorming map

Strategy map

research.) Draft an essay that explains all that you have discovered about your topic. If your topic lends itself to the use of images, incorporate relevant graphics. Document all of your sources, and submit your draft to partners or your instructor for feedback. Revise your work, changing priorities and conducting additional research as needed, before polishing and creating a final copy and moving on to step 4.

4. **Look over your brainstorming and strategy maps, and then create a third map for reflection.** For the reflection map, identify all of the areas you have addressed in the completed project, especially areas that have been added or that might have evolved since you composed the strategy map. Use this map to show what you have learned about this topic. Consider how your understanding of the broad inquiry topic changed over time, think about strategies you used to convey information in your essay, and reflect on the role of the mapping exercises in the development of the project.

5. **Submit all three of your maps and your final essay to complete the project.**

Reflection map

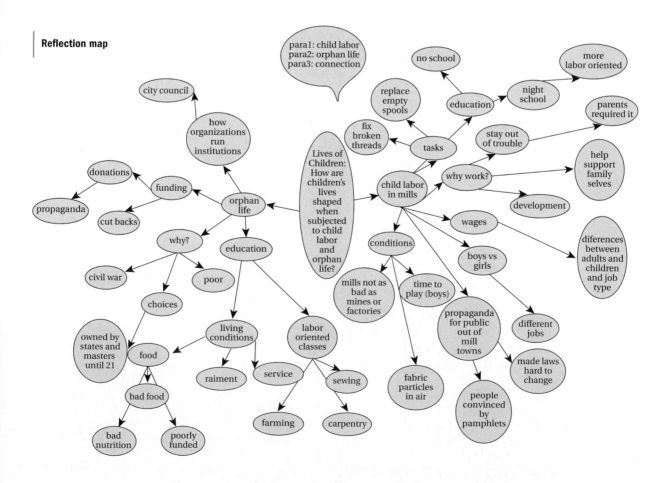

STUDENT PROJECT

Lindsay Carattini and Karen Lancaster, "The Lives of Children in the Old South"

This project was created by two students in response to the research inquiry assignment outlined on pages 398–402. The group began by combing through archives of documents related to the American South. They collaborated to select historical documents that would help them better understand issues of child labor around the turn of the twentieth century. We have used their three idea maps to illustrate steps 1, 2, and 4; we reproduce their final essay here.

Carattini and Lancaster 1

Lindsay Carattini

Karen Lancaster

English 101

4 May 2005

The Lives of Children in the Old South

Child labor was once a widely accepted institution. Today, many people envision it as a cruel and unusual punishment forced on children who did not know any better. But in the time period between the end of America's Civil War and World War I, child labor in the South was widely accepted yet highly debated as a moral issue.

In the 1832 case of Williams v. Barnes, Judge Daniel, who tried the case, determined that parents had the right to demand "services" from their children from "the time during which the child shall be considered an infant to the period of twenty-one years" (Thompson 256). This idea carried on as the motto of southern households for years after it was established by the courts. It was also one of the reasons why child labor remained commonplace even after laws were passed saying that children under twelve were not to be employed. Often younger children were put to work by their parents within their homes. For example, according to Guion Griffis Johnson, a burden children often had to bear was the care of their younger siblings.

If children had a job outside the home, their fathers would receive the wages earned. According to the first-hand experience of child laborer James Pharis, "You could go to work when you got big enough to talk" (Tullos 1). The reasons parents had for sending their children off to work at young ages were countless. One reason was that they simply wanted to keep their children out of trouble. It was not uncommon for children to skip school and get into trouble or spend their whole day playing with friends. Since this was not a productive use of their time, their parents would take them to factories or mills and plead with employers to allow their children to work. Parents knew that children were less likely to skip work because they might be fired and lose their income and then face harsh consequences at home. Other parents wanted their children to work so they did not have to work themselves; they simply lived off of their children's wages. Some fathers would fake illness or disability to avoid working: "Some frankly [said] that they worked to bring up their children during their early years, and now they expect the children to support them" (Thompson 238). However, the most common reason children were employed full time was that their family actually needed the income to survive. Often poor families would not have been able to survive if their children were not working.

CHILDREN IN MILLS

The most common places to see child labor were on farms and in mills (see fig.1). In the mills, many children worked in spinning rooms. The girls were constantly watching anywhere from 200 to 800 spindles at a time for broken threads to repair. Boys had a variety of jobs that in-cluded replacing empty spools with full ones. One advantage they had over the girls was the opportunity to go outside to play. Though all chil-dren worked sporadically, boys had more free time while on duty.

Workdays in the mill went on for eleven hours or more. This schedule prevented children from attending school, so they had to attend night school if they wanted to further their education. For example, one mill-workers' magazine from 1920 reports on a community night school estab-

Fig.1. Employees in a southern cotton mill in the late 1890s (Thompkins 110). Notice that a majority are children.

lished by the welfare department, which offered textiles courses for work-ers of all ages ("Mill News" 65). However, most children did not take this option because it made them tired and less efficient at both work and school. As for the children working on farms, they only attended school a few months out of the year when crops were out of season and their help was not needed. Also, the schools were often several miles away, making it even more difficult for children to attend. When answering the question "Did you go to any kind of school at all?" Pharis replied, "I graduated from third grade with honors" (Tullos 7). There were conflicting opinions on the value of work versus school for children during this time. According to Holland Thompson, "Some declare that children who have worked in the mill are more eager to utilize their opportunities and accomplish more than other children" (230). Others emphasized that child workers took more "pride in being wage earners" than they would in going to school (Thompson 232). In reality, working children's learning varied greatly, depending on their upbringing, their age when starting at the mill, and on the length of time and type of work they did (Thompson 230).

However, many parents and policy makers valued education more highly than earning a living at a young age. Alexander Jeffrey McKelway, the southern secretary of the National Child Labor Committee, agreed that education was more important than learning the responsibility of a job. He stated, "Abolish child labor and the child can go to school. We shall never have compulsory education in the cotton manufacturing states of the South until we abolish child labor first. Then the wage-scale will rise to the point where a man or woman can support the family. . . . This is not theory, but history" (11).

McKelway believed that working children were the cause of low wages. The children were able to do the same work and sometimes even do it better than their adult colleagues for very little pay. The employers argued that they were morally obligated to give equal pay for equal work. This is how they justified lowering adult wages below the level of those given to children. An example of unfair wages comes from a South Carolina mill: Doffers there that were 12 years old received $3.54 per week while those 20 years old and above received $2.52 per week. Also, spinners earned $4.54 a week, while scrubbers and sweepers earned $2.96. Clearly, the difference in wages not only depended on age but also on tasks performed.

It is possible that wages also depended on the dangers involved. Although no children worked continuously throughout the day and the work was not very physically demanding, their backs would be sore at the end of the day from bending over the machines. In addition, "the noise of the machinery. . . [had] its effect upon the nerves and indirectly upon bodily well-being" (Thompson 227). Finally, sometimes the poor-quality textiles being produced would fill the air with a certain amount of lint.

As these sources show, the problem of child labor in the South was difficult to resolve. Laws regulating it were difficult to pass because child labor was widely accepted by older generations. Many older people had worked as children themselves and survived the experience, so they did not see any need to abolish child labor.

Fig.2. A typical orphanage in the South (Johnson 703)

CHILDREN IN ORPHANAGES

Child labor had many forms, which added to the complexity of the situation when trying to pass laws against children working. For example, another side to the issue of child labor that was disguised and camouflaged was the use of child labor in orphanages (see fig. 2). By law, "boys were bound to their masters until they were twenty-one and girls until they were eighteen, sometimes until twenty-one." (Johnson 703). For children who had no family, in many cases, orphanages became their "masters," using them where they could or having them sold by the courts to public masters. The children would be assigned to their masters and expected to work for them, regardless of the fact that often expectations were too high for their age.

According to Guion Griffis Johnson, "The law has fixed the time during which the child shall be considered an infant, to the period of twenty-one years. The parent, during this period, has a right to the services of

6 | MAPPING IDEAS

the child to enable him to fulfill his obligation" (Johnson 256). This statement gave the orphanages full right to use the children as a labor workforce. One need only consider a typical day in the life of an orphan child to see the atrocious conditions to which many were subjected. One particular orphan, William Robertson, was brought before the court for misbehavior (Johnson 257). William was probably awakened early in the morning. He then trudged to the washroom, where he shared the communal wash basins and buckets while fighting over towels and soap. As soon as the festivities rose to a playful banter, the boys would be interrupted by a booming voice ordering them out of the room. The boys then had the luxury of being led into a big hall, filled with tables and chairs arranged like feeding troughs. They were then served up a breakfast made of grist, molasses, milk, bread, salt, and sugar (Moultrie 8). Leaving the table with their stomachs still grumbling, they would move on to their daily chores.

After the chores, William would work in the garden, tending to the vegetables. Perhaps just before midday, William and his companions would be allowed to engage in a game or a form of free play. After this they would work until lunchtime, when they were served their most extravagant meal of the day, a dish composed of beef, veal, bacon, rice, and vegetables (Moultrie 8).

If William were to step out of line, discipline would be enforced. "There [was] one male officer for the entire supervision, discipline and provisioning of the whole; and one matron for general management and direction; these [were], of course, essential" (Moultrie 6). If the boys did not adhere to the strict rules and laws of the orphanage there were harsh ramifications. They were under the state's care, so the matter could be sent directly to state authorities such as the courts. The record that we do have of William is in fact minutes from a court case where he was charged for disciplinary violations.

> The Orphans' Court of Edgecombe County . . . has on its record
> for 1800 the following entry: "William Robertson being brought
> before the Court for misbehavior—it is the sentence of the

Court that he be committed to jail, there to remain til tomorrow morning 12 o'clock—Ordered that the Sheriff execute the said sentence." (Johnson 257)

One can merely speculate about the ramifications that spending the night in jail would have on a young boy. The added concern comes in when we consider that this punishment was merely for "misbehavior" and not an actual crime.

Even though this extreme punishment suggests disregard for the well-being of the boys, the orphanage did make some attempts to care for their future. There was some schooling, although unfortunately it was a meager, underfunded enterprise. According to one source "There are in the school one principal, and eight teachers and assistants, for three hundred and thirty pupils; being one teacher to about forty children" (Moultrie 6). The orphanages also used schooling to train children to keep the orphanage running, using the children as their own private labor force.

The trades that were taught started the boys on the road to hard labor (see fig. 3). Some of the trades included farmer, brick mason,

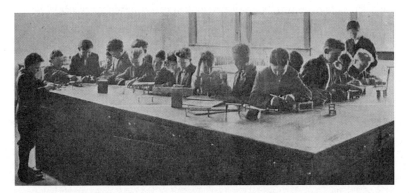

Fig.3. Children were often put into classes that taught labor skills rather than academic subjects. Such classes were found in both mill towns and orphanages ("Mill News" 63)

carpenter, blacksmith, butcher, fisherman, and machinist (Johnson 704). Some trades were favored over others. Most orphanages focused on farming and carpentry. These were the trades that would likely lead to an apprenticeship and were most transferable to working for the orphanage. For example, in learning to farm, the boys would need to practice by growing their own vegetables, which would help sustain the orphanage.

CONCLUSION

These accounts of child laborers in mills and orphanages raise complicated questions. Who was responsible for these children, and what arrangement was most likely to keep the child's best interest in mind? The parents of the child labor force consisted of biological parents, masters, and the state, all of whom cared for the children in various ways. The varying impacts are a point for closer examination. In some ways, all scenarios seemed to have the same outcome: The children all faced low income, hard work, and dangerous jobs. They had no rights, and they were seen as a valuable resource rather than human beings. That was the commonly accepted view.

Another commonality between the lives of orphans and those of working children was their lack of schooling. As mentioned before, many working children went to night school where courses were often based on labor skills. In orphanages, selling the children off to masters was seen as appropriate, and forcing them to churn out goods to support the orphanage was seen as accepted. The question remains: Which of these was the better life?

Works Cited

Johnson, Guion Griffis. "Ante-Bellum North Carolina: A Social History."
    1937. 4 Feb. 2003 <http://docsouth.unc.edu/nc/johnson/
    chapter8.html#n914>.

McKelway, Alexander Jeffrey. "Child Wages in the Cotton Mills: Our
    Modern Feudalism." 1913. 27 Jan. 2003 <http://docsouth.unc.edu/
    nc/mckelway/mckelway.html>.

"Mill News: The Great Southern Weekly for Textile Workers. Devoted to the
    Textile Industries." 1920. 13 Feb. 2003 <http://docsouth.unc.edu/
    nc/millnews/millnews.html>.

Moultrie, Jas. "Circular of the City Council on Retrenchment, and Report of
    the Commissioners of the Orphan House." 1861. 26 Jan. 2003
    <http://docsouth.unc.edu/circular/circular.html>.

Thompson, Holland A. M. "From the Cotton Field to the Cotton Mill: A
    Study of the Industrial Transition in North Carolina." 1906. 27 Jan.
    2003 <http://docsouth.unc.edu/nc/thompson/
    thompson.html#p219>.

Tompkins, Daniel Augustus. "Cotton Mill, Commercial Features. A Text-
    Book for the Use of Textile Schools and Investors. With Tables
    Showing Cost of Machinery and Equipments for Mills Making Cotton
    Yarns and Plain Cotton Cloths." 1899. 13 Feb. 2003 <http://
    docsouth.unc.edu/nc/tompkins/tompkins.html>.

Tullos, Allen. "Oral History Interview with James and Nannie Pharis, 1978
    December 5, 1979 January 8 and 30. Interview H-39. Southern Oral
    History Program Collection (#4007)." 1978–79. 13 Feb. 2003
    <http://docsouth.unc.edu/nc/pharisjn/pharisjn.html>.

Reporting on Research in the Sciences

This assignment requires you to bridge the distance between the ways in which information is conveyed in specialized disciplines and the ways in which the general public learns about issues in the natural or social sciences. You will conduct research using sources written for a specific field as well as sources aimed at nonexperts. You will then develop a photo essay for the general public that provides information about the issue in an easy-to-understand format.

As you begin working, answer these questions:

WHAT'S IT TO YOU?

■ For this assignment, pick a **topic** related to a field you can imagine yourself working in someday. Ask an expert about his or her work, and the person may or may not be able to explain what exactly the occupation entails. If you see yourself going into counseling or medicine, consider what the general public knows about those fields and how you might help make connections for people outside of the field. As a translator between specialized knowledge and the general public, you will be preparing yourself to answer a question like "What do you do?" in the future.

WHAT DO YOU WANT TO SAY ABOUT IT?

■ Here you will need to choose carefully which kinds of **information** you will convey to your readers. It may not be necessary for the general public to know, for instance, which enzyme helps researchers know whether cancer drugs might be effective; a general audience might be better served with information about changing rates of effectiveness for cancer treatment.

WHO WILL LISTEN?

■ The **audience** for this assignment is somewhat fixed, but you still need to think about your public's needs and characteristics. Consider how your readers, who may not have had any experience with your topic, will respond to the types of information you supply. It may be necessary to include some specialized images or discuss abstract concepts—think about when the communication of these materials is likely to trip readers up and how you can adjust your writing to help the audience get through key concepts.

WHAT DO YOU NEED TO KNOW?

- In this project, you will be learning primarily two things: (1) You will learn about a trend or issue in the field you select. You will need to locate **academic journal articles** to get up to speed on the topic. (2) You will also need to know something about the way specialists concerned with your topic and nonspecialists writing about your topic communicate—if **statistics** are cited or information is plotted or graphed, you will need to study these presentation approaches to understand just how people write in the field you have chosen. You will also need to examine how materials related to your topic are written for nonexperts You don't need to write like an expert, but you must get a sense of how the topic is written about for experts and for nonexperts so that you can develop your photo essay at an appropriate level for your audience.

HOW WILL YOU DO IT?

- The elements of a photo essay are actually straightforward and simple to create—you will need an image, a caption, and an explanation on each screen. More important will be thinking about the amounts of information your readers can handle and how you will present it to them. Design your screens using a **layout** that helps readers move through your information logically. Standardize the layout of your screens to keep readers focused on your images and information rather than on navigating the essay. Select **images** that help readers understand key concepts and then compose **explanations** succinctly so that they can take in the most crucial information.

HOW DID IT WORK?

- Photo essays require early work to develop the structure of the project. Set up the pages and create the navigation links right off the bat so that you can be sure that all of the pages function. It can also be easy to overlook mechanical problems or confusing language when working with Web pages. If possible, print out the text of the explanations you have written and read them as you would any other composition to polish and strengthen the language. Build in a draft date for the project that allows you to have the majority of the screens completed. **Solicit feedback** from peers or your instructor, and **revise** the pages accordingly. Since you will be creating a Web photo essay, you can also get feedback from a live audience—include keywords in the title to help readers find your work once you post it.

Your assignment is to create a photo essay designed to inform an audience about a trend or an issue in the natural or social sciences. Inform your essay with research conducted using the Internet, the library, or interviews. Select at least eight images that allow you to convey important information about your topic, and then incorporate those images into Web pages and add captions and explanations that allow you to tell a story about your topic. Proceed through the following seven steps.

1. **Begin by thinking about a field that you have an interest in or that you might see yourself pursuing one day.** Conduct initial research to see what issues or trends currently occupy the field—you might find that astronomers are interested in the privatization of space or geologists are occupied with climatology. You can explore postings to the Google groups archives to see what kinds of questions are debated informally, you can look through the contents of key journals in the field, and you can conduct research using library databases. Once you have identified some of the hot topics for the field, select one that strikes your interest.

2. **Next, conduct research either in the library or using online library databases to find academic journals.** (If you go to the physical library, ask a librarian for help—you might also check with a librarian if you have trouble finding a hot topic in the field.) Use your research to locate articles in academic journals related to your topic. Find at least three journal articles.

3. **Next, search general-interest databases (Proquest, EBSCO, LexisNexis, and the like) to look for articles that have been written for more general audiences.** You can also conduct searches of the Internet at this point, looking for general resources or specialized sources related to your topic. Collect at least three general-interest sources.

4. **Now take a day or two to carefully read the sources you have selected.** You may find that a general-interest source makes a good starting place before diving into the academic pieces. If you encounter obscure concepts or jargon in academic articles, try to make sense of them, but don't get discouraged if you don't understand every nuance—pay attention to the main ideas and the way the articles convey information. As you read, also watch for images you might be able to use in your photo essay.

5. **Next, gather your materials.** Collect all of your sources. Take notes about any quotations you want to use and key points you might draw from. Also, begin tracking down images you can use. You may be able to download images from online journal articles. You can also search for images on the Internet now that you have a sense of what your topic entails. You will need at least eight images, but you might wish to collect additional ones for possible use as the project evolves. Keep track of any im-

ages that you use, making note of where you found them and any other citation information.

6. **Next, compose the photo essay.** Develop a page for each image and concept you wish to explain to readers. The page should have three components: the image, a caption, and an explanation. Think about the order in which to arrange the images in your essay. Make sure that the first image introduces your topic and the last image adds closure to the project. The caption should consist of not more than one sentence that emphasizes the key concerns of the image and situates the image within the structure of the essay. The caption should also indicate the source of the image. For the explanation, compose four or more sentences discussing the significance of the image. Your explanation might explore aspects of the image in more detail. It should also incorporate your research information whenever possible. The explanation should do the work of making what you have learned about your topic meaningful to nonexpert readers.

7. **Proofread the text you have written, sharpening the language.** Check that the order of the images makes sense. Revise and polish the project, updating the Web pages as needed.

STUDENT SAMPLE

Erik Williams, "Genetic Research in 2004 and Beyond"

Eric Williams developed this Web photo essay, excerpts of which we've included here, as a way of exploring his interest in the field of medicine. He initially wanted to discuss much of the science behind genetic engineering. As his project progressed, however, he realized that the social issues related to genetics would be of more interest to his audience. His essay eventually evolved into an explanation of both the social and the scientific dimensions of current genetic research.

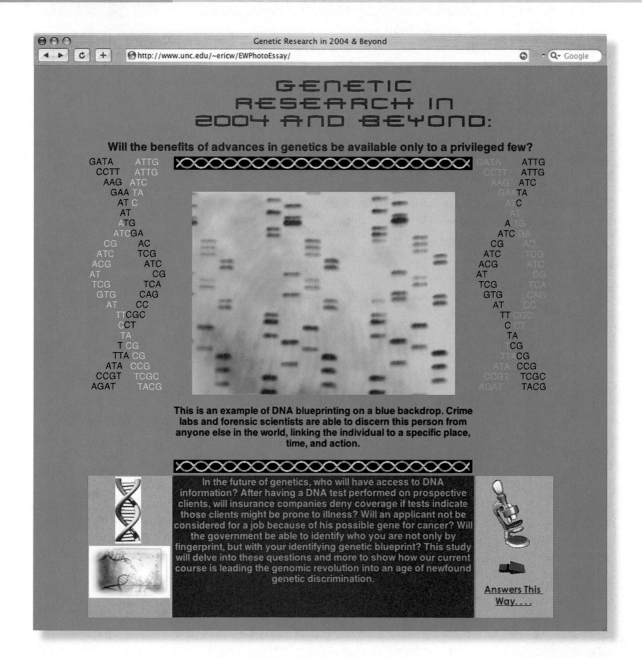

GENETIC RESEARCH IN 2004 AND BEYOND:

Will the benefits of advances in genetics be available only to a privileged few?

This is an example of DNA blueprinting on a blue backdrop. Crime labs and forensic scientists are able to discern this person from anyone else in the world, linking the individual to a specific place, time, and action.

In the future of genetics, who will have access to DNA information? After having a DNA test performed on prospective clients, will insurance companies deny coverage if tests indicate those clients might be prone to illness? Will an applicant not be considered for a job because of his possible gene for cancer? Will the government be able to identify who you are not only by fingerprint, but with your identifying genetic blueprint? This study will delve into these questions and more to show how our current course is leading the genomic revolution into an age of newfound genetic discrimination.

Answers This Way....

"My essay works by providing a captivating image along with an informative caption describing the message about genetic research. My color and animations further expand the point described in the explanation and help keep the Web site from becoming bogged down in scientific information. I think that the first slide is effective, announcing the path I took with this research. It is also the most creative, with the mirror X helixes on either side of the image made up of the genetic chemicals ATCG, which represent adenine, thymine, cytosine, and guanine, which make up the deoxyribonucleic acid (DNA) helix."

—ERIK WILLIAMS

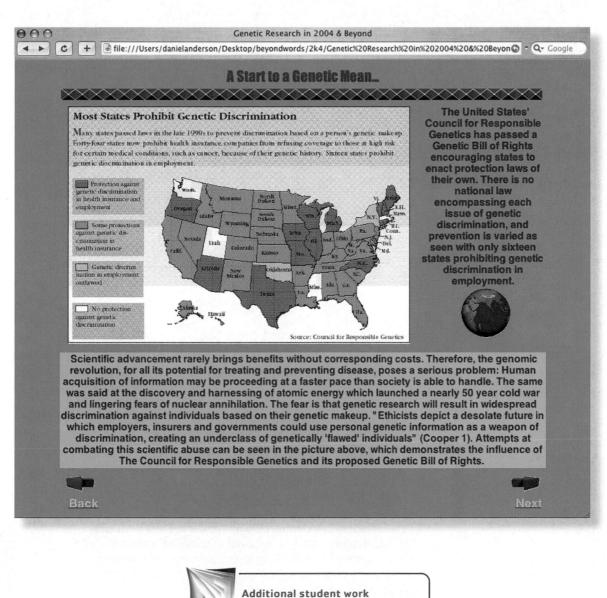

Additional student work
www.ablongman.com/beyondwords28

Url's Internet Cafe Coffee Bar

Address: http://www.urlsinternetcafe.com/coffeebar/coffeebar.html go

Live Home Page   Apple   Apple Support   Apple Store   .Mac   Mac OS X   Microsoft MacTopia   Office for Macintosh

Index   Coffee Bar   Books   Classroom   Basement   Cafe Staff   Contact Us   Attic

The **Coffee Bar** is where Url spills his guts about his adventures, his loves, and his pathetic life.

Adjoining Rooms:
Sportz Bar
Luddite Lounge
Art Gallery
Rest Roomz

On a recent trip to Kentucky for a **Robert Burns Supper**, cafe executive Robin W. and Url stopped by radio station WUKY in Lexington to be guests on the *Curtains@8!* show. Url wasn't allowed to talk, but he had his digital camera with him as DJ Nick Lawrence conducted **Robin's Radio Interview**.

Url tagged along with Robin to Las Vegas, Nevada, and reports on the **Las Vegas Cab Line Incident**.

In his quest to bring original content to the Cafe web site, Url has outdone himself by stowing away on a cruise ship. If you've been thinking about a cruise, click over to **Url's Carribbean Cruise Photo Album**. You just don't get stuff like this on other web sites.

Internet zone

▲ **Url's Internet Cafe** A Web site we designed and maintain.

④ Interlude

ROBIN WILLIAMS

AND JOHN TOLLETT

evaluating a web site

The World Wide Web is so amazingly new in this old world of ours, yet it has become such an important and integral part of communication that we are already evaluating how well a Web site works, how design works on Web pages, what makes a site usable, and what sorts of things hinder communication. Standards have already been set up, and users expect certain features to exist.

When we design a new site or when we visit a site we haven't been to before, we consciously evaluate a large number of features. Whether designing the site or visiting it, our evaluation criteria are pretty much the same. Here is a rundown of the sorts of things we look at.

STYLE

Does the theme or graphic style fit the goals of the site and appeal to the target audience?

Animation and Flash and lots of large images can be perfectly appropriate on a site designed for a tech-savvy target audience, an audience you assume has a fast computer and the latest software. If the target audience is seniors who have inherited older machines from their kids, the site should probably have fewer flashy gizmos that require up-to-the-minute hardware and software.

ORGANIZATION

Web sites can contain huge amounts of information. Organization is the critical element that makes the information accessible, and this can make or break a site. Organizing information on a large Web site requires serious thought and planning and testing and more thought and planning and testing.

Last year Robin needed to buy a new carafe for her coffee pot. She went to the Web site the local store recommended, and in THREE SECONDS she found exactly the carafe she needed. The site wasn't beautiful, but she didn't need beautiful—she needed a carafe. This site (which sold hundreds of coffee-related products) was so well organized that she could scan and find the first topic she needed in about one second; she clicked the button and saw the second level of information; she clicked the button, and there was exactly the carafe she needed. Amazing.

PRESENTATION

A very simple, well-organized page is more pleasing than an overdesigned, busy page that is badly organized. When Google.com first appeared, long before we recognized what a superior search engine it used, we loved it because it was simple. All of the other existing search pages were horrendously busy and cluttered and obnoxious; Google was white and clean with almost nothing on the page except the field in which to type the search topic. It was so comforting that since we found that site, we have never used another search engine.

Following are some of the features we see on poorly presented sites. These are easily fixable.

- Busy, distracting backgrounds
- Underlined text that is not a link
- Giant link buttons
- Anything that blinks
- Too many focal points on the page
- Long lines of text that stretch out across the page
- Anything that makes users scroll sideways (unless it is a specific and conscious design element)
- Bold type, especially when there is a lot of it, and especially when it is in color on a colored background
- Lots of text in all caps or italic
- Meaningless graphics
- Borders turned on in tables
- Clutter

LOGICAL AND CONSISTENT ARRANGEMENT

We don't like sites that are a puzzle we're expected to solve. Every page must be as intuitive and logical as possible and consistent with other pages in the site. You never know where visitors are going to drop into a site; they might find an obscure page through a search tool and pop into the archives. This means that no matter where visitors enter your site, they should instantly know whose site it is, have a rough idea of what the site is about, and how to get to the home page.

The entire site should feel familiar so that the visitor feels comfortable and confident. Don't invent a new way of navigating from page to page. Don't arbitrarily change the color scheme or layout.

FORGIVING FORMAT

Site visitors often make mistakes—they go to the wrong page or click a wrong button. If a site design is forgiving, no mistake is a big problem. Every page should have a familiar navigation that makes it easy to return to any part of the site.

We hate orphan pages, dead ends without links to return to previous pages or to the home page. Visitors often bookmark pages and return by choosing that bookmark; if they go to a bookmarked orphan page, they may not be able to find the rest of the site.

NO CHAIN YANKS

A chain yank sets you up with expectations and then abruptly disappoints you. For example, you click a link next to a graphic that says "Click here for a larger image." You click, expecting a larger image and perhaps some addi-

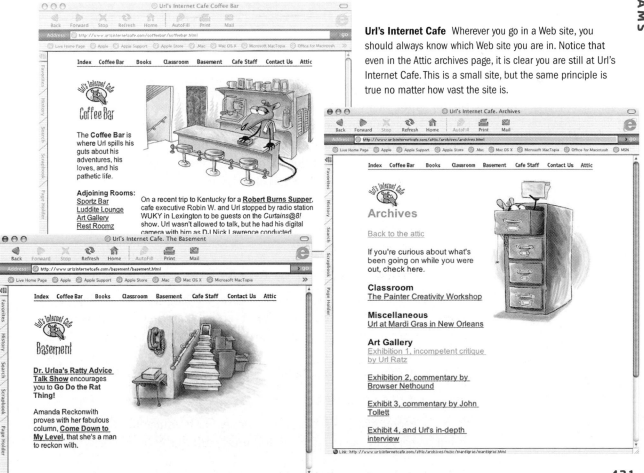

Url's Internet Cafe Wherever you go in a Web site, you should always know which Web site you are in. Notice that even in the Attic archives page, it is clear you are still at Url's Internet Cafe. This is a small site, but the same principle is true no matter how vast the site is.

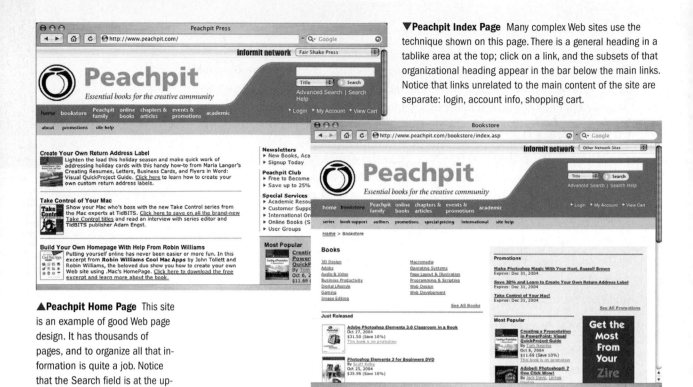

tional information, but you get a page with the same image on a bare page or an image that is a quarter-inch larger. This makes you feel stupid. Worse, it makes you think the Web site is stupid. If there is a link to another page, it must be worth the trip.

LINK VISIBILITY

The underline below text is a clue that indicates a link. We agree that it's an ugly look. Designers sometimes remove the underline and use colored text to indicate the links. The problem with removing the underline is that if the designer uses more than one color on the Web page, it's difficult to tell which text is a link and which is just in color. Users are forced to run the mouse over any text in any color on the page to see whether or not it's a link.

It's better to make links obvious and easy with an underline than to have a prettier page that's harder to use.

COMMUNICATION, NOT DECORATION

Visuals should enhance the content or repeat a design theme, making pages seem familiar, friendly, consistent, and useful. When photos or illustrations merely decorate a page, they have little effect other than slowing the download time. Now, I'm not discouraging visual elements—it's just that every element should have a purpose. Nothing should be on the page arbitrarily.

JUST A LITTLE DAZZLE

There are many dazzling techniques, such as Flash animation, that advanced Web designers can add to a site. Flash is great stuff. It can be entertaining, dramatic, and compelling. It can also be annoying, especially when it's so dazzling that you can't figure out how to get to another page. Most of us have grown tired of circles and squares that get bigger and then smaller and then fade out. The sites that use Flash effectively use it sparingly. Visit the Macromedia Web site and notice that even the creators of Flash use it in small doses. If we have to wait for a site to load before we can even see the first link, we're gone.

POP-UP WINDOWS

Pop-up windows can be wonderful when used appropriately. They are great for giving visitors extra bits of information without making them go to an entirely different page. (Pop-up ads are always hateful and annoying.)

HELP

Any good, large site will have a site map, a site outline with links to all pages, or a search feature that a visitor can use to locate information.

These are just some of the things that one can evaluate on any Web site in just a few minutes. It's a good exercise to spend an hour or so with a complex Web site and really see what makes it work or not work. Try to accomplish a task, such as find a particular item, buy a product, search for information, dig down deep in the structure and see if you can get out easily, contact someone, print a page. Is the design consistent so that you always know where you are in the site? Can you easily find what you need via the navigation bar? Is the search feature useful or cumbersome? Can you scan the page and know what the major topics of the site are? Is it so cluttered that it's difficult to find what you need? Once you spend the time to really evaluate a large site, you will feel more confident in appraising and using any Web site.

For additional writing projects related to this Interlude see
www.ablongman.com/beyondwords29

CHALLENGE

1. Evaluate a complex Web site you visit frequently, giving it the hour-long examination that Williams and Tollett recommend. Look at the site carefully, visiting places you don't ordinarily read and testing its features. When you are done with your study, design a one-page form for evaluating this site, using criteria developed by Williams and Tollett (for example, style, organization, presentation). Look for ways to present your evaluation both graphically and verbally. For example, you might use stars (★, ★★, ★★★, ★★★★) or bar graphs to express your judgment of various features; then add supporting reasons and details in an accompanying paragraph. Try to come up with a form or instrument you could use to evaluate and compare various other Web sites.

2. "We don't like sites that are a puzzle we're expected to solve," write Williams and Tollett. Do they put a crimp on creativity by championing Web sites that seem to put a premium on clarity, efficiency, and ease of use? Read their interlude carefully, looking for the principles or premises that underlie their basic recommendations. Then write your own reaction to these principles, while thinking about the Web sites you use and value. Would they meet the standards the authors favor? Would your own principles for evaluating Web sites be different?

EXPLORING DESIGN

writing to analyze

Hummer H2

Toyota Prius

How would you describe the differences between the Toyota Prius and the Hummer H2?

Is the design of one of these vehicles "better" than the other? What criteria would you use to argue for one or the other?

Introduction

Y ou don't have to be an engineer to figure out that the Hummer H2 and Toyota Prius are about as different as passenger vehicles in the U.S. market get. Every element of their designs sends strong signals about their missions and potential customers. The only buyers who might cross-shop the 6,400-pound H2 and the 2,855-pound Prius are people who must own the *latest* thing. Marketers do recognize such consumers, and both vehicles certainly have a touch of "cool." But other than four wheels, cool may be all they have in common.

The Hummer H2 (like its smaller, younger sibling, the H3) is based on the Humvee, a military truck made famous by its role in the first Iraq War (1991). With its squat stance and blunt, no-nonsense profile, the $100,000 street version of this military transport, now called the H1, became the preferred ride of action film stars (including a future governor of California).

General Motors figured—rightly, it turns out—that it could make a fortune if it could transfer the original Hummer look—slotted grill, squared contours, huge tires, and exposed mechanical bits—onto a more civilized chassis. And so it created the H2, a vehicle whose every surface detail said "Hummer" but under which beats the heart of a Chevy Tahoe—just like the soccer mom's down the street.

The Toyota Prius has a wholly different design language. The current model, already a second-generation hybrid car that runs on both gasoline and batteries, produces outstanding fuel economy and low emissions, especially in city driving. And the Prius design generates its own set of adjectives: sleek, efficient, lean, eco-friendly, smart, responsible. Long waiting lists suggest that Toyota has found the right design for hybrids—edgy enough to comple-

| Hummer H1

ment their technical sophistication, different enough to identify their drivers as concerned about the environment, and yet sufficiently handsome to make social responsibility painless.

The Prius and Hummer, like the other thousands of objects we encounter every day, from the computers on our laps to the toilet brushes in our bathrooms, all represent choices about design. We might not notice these decisions unless we pause to think about them and consider the ways they call to us and why.

CONSIDER

1. If you don't know much about the Prius or the H2, you can find out more at the Toyota and Hummer Web sites. When you've become more familiar with the vehicles, try your hand at describing the different "audiences" to whom they might appeal, regardless of whether they could afford one.

2. Hummer made a special effort to advertise the H2 to women. Why might that have been necessary? Would Toyota need to make a comparable appeal to men to sell the Prius? Are these vehicles gendered?

3. Try to identify several other objects or products that reflect the same sort of cultural divide as the Prius and the Hummer. Describe those differences in a paragraph.

What's in This Chapter?

In this chapter, we'll challenge you to examine patterns of design in written texts, in advertisements, in buildings, and even in your cell phone or MP3 player. We'll look at objects as familiar as Toyotas and TV commercials to see how designs work, both on their own terms and in wider cultural contexts. The readings in the chapter explore specific designs—for chairs, for the iPod, and for sneakers. We also broaden our focus to explore how the vehicles we drive express our values and desires. Finally, we ask you to consider some political dimensions of design. Much here will be familiar because you live in a world where designers try to please and influence you. This is your turn to do a little designing of your own.

Reading
Designs

The biggest challenge of learning to analyze design languages may be finding design in places you don't expect it. We all become art critics when we walk into a museum, and we may have a similar sensitivity to style when we go to a movie or buy clothes for a special occasion. But we may not immediately recognize the elements that make up the style of the restaurants we patronize, the newspapers we read daily, the papers we write, or even the people we work with. Of course, we meet so much design every day that it's not reasonable to expect that we'd be critiquing the use of white space or choice of fonts in every advertisement we encounter. Nor are we likely to have much of an opinion about objects or artifacts we don't know much about. But the world becomes far more compelling when we start attending to the stories even the most common objects can tell. It takes a little practice to see such objects with fresh eyes, but we can ask probing questions that will help us to critically analyze what we see and to explore what design choices tell us about who we are.

- **What do you see?**
- **What is it about?**
- **To what does it relate?**
- **How is it composed?**
- **What details matter?**

What do you see?

We analyze design constantly in our daily lives. We think about the **style** of a movie when we buy a ticket for a James Bond film or the latest Jack Black comedy. We might expect state-of-the-art special effects in the Bond film. In Black's movie, we'd look for comic situations, clever wordplay, or humorous cultural references. We might say these devices make up the design language for comedies. A good comedic film, however, will take these conventions and modify them to express a unique message.

The trick with analyzing design is learning to recognize the distinctions that give something its style. For example, our personal sense of style is often directly linked to the groups we inhabit—the nerds, the geeks, the freaks, the Goths, the preppies, the jocks—whose members define styles that can seem almost natural to the people who adopt them. Products and pieces of written communication will have their own characteristics, patterns, and details that convey a message and create a style—we can call these patterns and characteristics a **design language.**

Jack Black in *The School of Rock* (2003)

Artwork used on the poster promoting the film *Clueless* (1995)

When thinking about a design language, try placing related items side by side and then observing what changes from one to the other. For example, the U.S. $20 bill has been recently revised to discourage counterfeiting. The challenge for bill designers was to create something with the recognizable style of the old bill while incorporating changes to thwart potential copying. Consider the two bills. Can you recognize a common design language? How would you describe the design of the revised bill (on the left)? What might the intent of the designers have been as they instituted changes? If you have a twenty on you, take it out and consider its design.

Design is everywhere. Successful companies establish a recognizable design language, one they can maintain for decades, cultivating an identity that often represents a lifestyle or an idea as much as a particular product. Ben & Jerry's and The Body Shop are known for their support of social issues. Diesel sells not only clothes but also a carefree and exciting way of life. Even a mass marketer like Target works hard to sell designer goods that appeal to shoppers who see themselves as money-conscious but interested in products with an upmarket design.

Because companies work hard at designing their image, knock-offs remain the highest form of commercial flattery, whether the product imitated is a purse, a cocktail dress, or a remedy for an aching head. For an introduction to design language, spend a half hour in a local drugstore, comparing the designs of branded over-the-counter drugs to the packages of their generic counterparts. Do customers see this sharing of design languages and assume that the cheap aspirin are just as good as the name brand? That assumption may not make sense, but then the biggest difference between the products may in fact be the box.

To appreciate how designs influence you, make a conscious effort to identify their features—look for patterns expressed by design and compare items, thinking about their characteristics and their design languages.

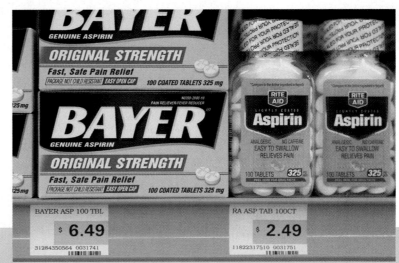

CONSIDER

1. Review the poster art used for *Clueless*. Then Google "teen movie" to jog your memory about the many films in this genre. Using the resources of the Web, write a detailed description of the design language associated with a particular stereotypical teen depicted in such films: the jock, the cheerleader, the nerd, the Goth, the stereotyped minority student, the preppie, and so on.

2. Conduct online research about a type of product—flat-screen TVs, low-cut hiking boots, disposable razors. How would you describe the design language of the product itself? What do you notice about design in materials promoting the product?

COMPOSE

3. Compare the style of two very different kinds of writing. For example, you might compare a newspaper story on a political event with commentary on the same event in a political blog such as Instapundit.com. Choose an interesting pairing, and then write one to two pages relating their styles and design languages. (The Writing Tip on p. 432 offers some guidelines for approaching this kind of analysis.)

ANALYZING VERBAL STYLE

Everything you read has a style you can describe and analyze, though it may take some practice to recognize the elements that give writing its character. Here are some features to look for in a document:

- Voice. How individual is the voice you *hear* as you read? Some writing is very cordial, other writing has a manufactured personality, and much academic work is deliberately impersonal, purged of character. You can point to features such as pronouns (*I, you, we, us, it*), contractions (*we're, you'll, won't*), or dialogue to indicate voice.

- Tone. Words can express both emotions and emotional distance. Look for specific words or phrases in writing that makes a piece warm or cold, friendly or intimidating, and so on.

- Word choice. Words send many signals, and the level and choice of vocabulary items reveal much about a piece of writing. Vocabulary items may indicate the age or experience of the writers, the social groups to which they belong, the audiences they wish to reach, and their sensitivity to difference. A word like *underprivileged* has a denotative meaning; it comes across as objective, and we can agree on its meaning. A word like *downtrodden* has a more connotative meaning; it strikes us as more opinionated and emotional.

- Sentence length and structure. The length and variety of sentence structures contribute to their style. Using sentences all of the same length or in the same structure comes across as boring. Short sentences are not necessarily easier to read or clearer than long ones, nor are they always more appropriate.

- Paragraph length. Like sentences, paragraphs are shaped by purpose. In newspaper columns, paragraphs may run only a sentence or two; in serious academic articles, paragraphs may require a full page to make a point.

- Level of formality. Formality in writing is related to tone and voice. You might characterize writing as casual and easy (as in a personal letter); direct and professional (as in business writing and journalism); or serious and formal (as in academic writing, legal writing, or writing for special occasions).

- Level of technicality. Some writing tries to explain every detail, some works hard to accommodate the needs of generally educated readers, and some is written specifically for experts.

- Figures of speech. Writing of all kinds relies on metaphors, analogies, and other figures of speech to convey thoughts, ideas, and emotions. You can learn much about a given piece by identifying its most characteristic devices of language. Fiction, for example, is usually thick with metaphors and similes. PowerPoint presentations rely heavily on lists and parallel phrases.

What is it about?

If your hometown includes Victorian-style houses in its older neighborhoods, you might have noticed what critics in later times have disparaged as "gingerbread," the highly decorated, though largely nonfunctional, balusters, porch

A **Victorian home** (left) and a **geodesic dome house** (below)

rails, gables, and cornices that make the exteriors of such houses a riot of surfaces. If you've ever driven past a geodesic dome, you've seen a completely
different approach to home design.

The Victorian home and the dome house say something about the eternal tension between form (what something looks like) and function (what something
does). Twentieth-century designers frequently fell back on the mantra "Form
follows function," believing that design should primarily fulfill a purpose—to
them, decoration like that found on the nineteenth-century gingerbread
house seemed distracting and unnecessary.

Function helps us consider what design is about. For instance, an instruction
manual for a digital camera should efficiently provide information. A table of
contents directs you to the pages you need. Diagrams should help you iden-

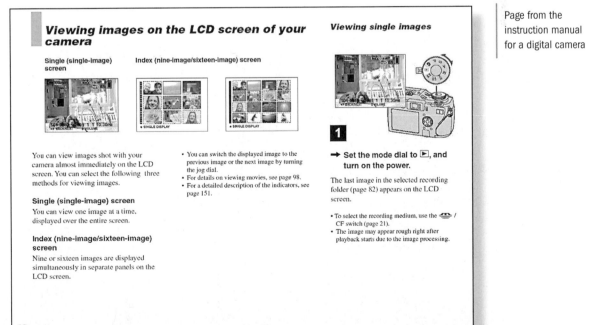

Page from the
instruction manual
for a digital camera

tify the features of the camera. Page design can help distinguish critical information from more incidental facts.

But designs are also about the aesthetic qualities they project and the experience they provide for users. Consider the dilemma of the designer of the camera itself. There are only so many dials and buttons you can fit on a camera, so designers have come up with multifunction controls. A single thumbpad and an LCD screen may provide an elegant-looking means of controlling the camera, but many users find the computer-style menus confusing and never use the advanced features of the camera.

The challenge for designers is to make things both attractive and functional. For instance, your DVD remote control may look stylish, but how well can you operate it in the dark? Design must anticipate the difficulties users may encounter, particularly those who cannot see, hear, or move as easily as others. A home, a staircase, a remote control, a manual, or a Web site should be made as accessible as possible, and that challenge raises important questions for all who think about function in design.

Finally, designs also express messages in the ways they employ **form** to fulfill their purpose. The gingerbread style of the Victorian house says something about the people who could afford to construct homes for themselves in the latter half of the nineteenth century–they had plenty of money and time to spend considering the intricacies of decorations. The dome house, on the other hand, came into its own during the 1960s amid calls to live simply and overlook divisions of wealth and class. The dome house design is not just about a place to live; it expresses ideas about *how* to live.

CONSIDER

1. Choose a building you pass by daily to which you have never paid much attention. Describe its "language," analyzing elements in terms of form, function, and any messages expressed by the structure.

2. Designer or branded fashions are now routinely available at stores such as Kmart and Target. What is the appeal of these high-profile (in some circles) names on relatively low-budget products?

CHALLENGE

3. Write a short paper in which you both diagnose and attempt to solve a design problem you find somewhere in your environment, perhaps by looking at something familiar from the perspective of someone with a physical or other disability. Or consider how something familiar can be made easier or safer to use. Try to solve such a problem while still paying attention to good form. (The writing tip on page 435 offers some guidelines for approaching this kind of paper.)

WRITING A PROBLEM/SOLUTION PAPER

You can follow certain steps in writing a paper that analyzes a problem and explores its solution. Not every problem/solution paper you write will have all of the elements listed here.

- **Describe a problem you want to address.** Be precise about the problem you want to solve. Play the journalist here, answering factual questions such as *who, what, where, when, how,* and *why.*

- **Explain why the problem needs to be solved.** Readers need to know why a problem deserves their attention. Don't take it for granted that they will be concerned about handicapped access problems at your school's football stadium. Explain why they should be concerned.

- **Explain how the problem has been addressed before.** If a problem has been around for a long time, review the history of attempts to solve it. For example, designers have puzzled for decades over the need to make complex audio equipment in cars easier to use. Solutions have ranged from lots of tiny square buttons to touch-screen interfaces. Readers not only need to know what's been tried in the past but also that you are aware of these unsuccessful efforts.

- **Explain why previous solutions have failed.** What's wrong with a radio with dozens of buttons or a touch-screen interface? Don't assume that readers will know.

- **Describe your solution.** Provide a detailed explanation of what you propose as a solution to the problem. Don't get argumentative yet. Play the journalist again, answering *who, what, where, when, how,* and *why.*

- **Explain the advantages of your solution.** Once you have made it very clear what you are proposing, provide good reasons for adopting your solution. You should also anticipate objections others may have to your ideas.

- **Defend the feasibility of your solution.** Your solution may sound plausible, but can it be implemented? Will people go along with it? Is it legal? Is it cost-effective? Does form get in the way of function, or vice versa?

- **Explain how your solution might be implemented.** Once you've persuaded readers that your solution is both sensible and feasible, explain how it will be implemented. Who has to approve, fund, and administer it? Over what period of time will the solution play out?

To what does it relate?

We can only guess at the significance of statues, carvings, or cave paintings archaeologists discover, although we do immediately speculate, attempting to connect these objects with other artifacts from the same periods and peoples. We create meaning by discovering all we can about where an object or design comes from—its **context.**

Kong atop the Empire State Building in the classic film *King Kong* (1933)

It's no different with more contemporary designs. You don't have to know much about architecture or cultural contexts to appreciate the designs of New York City's famous skyscraper, the Empire State Building (1930–1931). The building represents an enduring expression of a common design style called Art Deco as well as a strong statement about its cultural context. America may have been in a deepening depression in the early 1930s, but people still believed in progress and technology—which the Empire State Building came to represent. It is no accident that a giant ape chose to climb the Empire State Building in the first version of *King Kong* (1933). Even Kong appreciated the building's significance: It embodied the very spirit of modernity that threatened his way of life.

In some cases, designs become so associated with their **historical contexts** that we don't even recognize the influence a generation's tastes and beliefs have had. Consider the difference between the NBA uniforms worn by Larry Bird and Allen Iverson. Were Iverson to walk onto the court during Bird's 1986 game, the coach might well have sent him to the locker room in search of a proper uniform. Were Bird to enter a game today wearing his skimpy shorts and high-rise

Larry Bird, of the Boston Celtics (1986) (left)
Allen Iverson, of the Philadelphia 76ers (2004) (right)

socks from the late 1980s, what might be the reaction? These objects are so entwined with their historical moments that when they are removed from their culture, they seem comical and almost incomprehensible.

Design not only reflects its historical circumstances but also often draws from its **cultural surroundings** to create appealing products and pitches. Consider all the contexts cleverly evoked by a now famous television spot for the Hummer H2 sport utility vehicle called "Big Race." The ad—in 30- and 60-second versions—was so popular that the company created a Web site to chronicle its making.

The site (www.hummer.com/bigrace) offers a defense for a young man who wins a soapbox derby–like race by taking his homemade Hummer off road: "The rules . . . don't say anything about what route you have to take."

What aspects of culture does the ad tap into? Does it appeal to some and not other groups? Could the ad have an impact on attitudes and actions? Asking these kinds of questions helps us recognize the close relationship between design and society.

A sequence of frames from "The Big Race," a television commercial for the Hummer H2.

1. If you have access to an attic, basement, closet, storeroom, or even a museum, find an object whose design makes better sense when you place it in its historical and cultural context. Briefly, provide as much of that context as you can. Begin by locating the object in time and place. Then explain why it may look the way it does.

2. Do as much library research as necessary to provide the context for the style of a written text or musical composition. The text could be anything from a poem to an advertisement. A particular piece of music—from "The Star-Spangled Banner" to "Cry Me a River" (the Justin Timberlake version)—might take a great deal of cultural explanation. Write two or three paragraphs describing your findings.

COMPOSE

3. Select a video clip of an ad on the Web or analyze an ad currently running on TV. Write a short paper that places the ad in its cultural context, explaining what knowledge a viewer might need to appreciate it fully. You might use a screen capture to reproduce (with appropriate documentation and credit) frames that illustrate points you wish to make.

CHALLENGE

4. Try to identify a human-made object that requires little context to understand. Compare your object with others found by classmates to see which object (if any) seems to be least connected to time, culture, or societal knowledge. (You can try the opposite exercise as well, identifying objects that make no sense stripped of their contexts.)

How is it composed?

When analyzing design, recall the elements explored in Chapter 1 of this book: arrangement, emphasis, repetition, patterns, balance, contrasts, and hierarchies. Any design that competes for your attention will employ these and other strategies to create a compelling product or message. You can recognize these principles by practicing critical reading. Look initially for the **focus**, thesis, or center of gravity of the piece—where your mind or eye is first drawn or directed. In a visual item, focus can be signaled by the size, shape, mass, placement, lighting, or color of elements, or any combination of these devices.

Other designs will emphasize balance, patterns, or repetitions rather than hierarchy. Take the commuter rail bench developed by Antenna Designs. Created to function as seating for passengers awaiting the thirty-minute commute to and from New York City each day, the bench employs **balance** and **repetition** to embody the sense of the daily routine of its users. The symmetry creates seating space for passengers heading both directions with a cen-

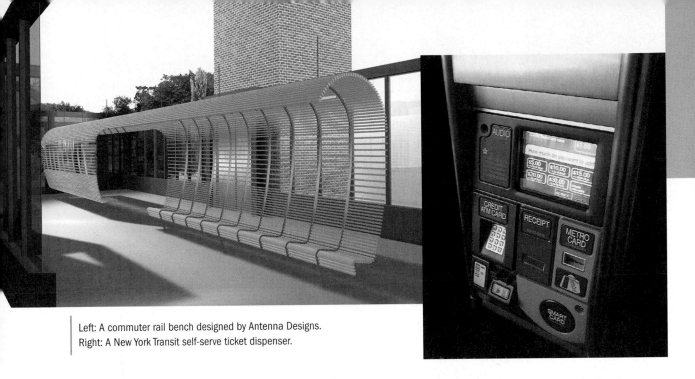

Left: A commuter rail bench designed by Antenna Designs.
Right: A New York Transit self-serve ticket dispenser.

tered pass-through that connects the ideas of coming and going. Here we see a clear structure in the composition of the design, but one that relies less on hierarchy and more on balance.

Finally, **patterns** and **contrasts** enable designs to both convey information and fulfill their functions. The even spacing of the aluminum dividers set into the rail bench serve both to differentiate the seats for potential passengers and discourage sleeping on the benches. A self-serve ticket dispenser designed for the station uses contrasting colors to differentiate between functions of the machine. These patterns and contrasts create relationships that convey meaning and constitute the design of the objects.

CONSIDER

1. If you could attach only one word to the commuter rail bench shown above, which would it be—form or function? How would you defend your decision?

2. How necessary is it that people understand something of the elements of design in order to use objects like the self-serve ticket dispenser shown above? Must we understand the principle of contrast and differentiation to get the most out of these products?

COMPOSE

3. Choose an ad or poster, and write a brief analysis of its basic structure: focus, hierarchy balance, contrasts, patterns. Remember that designs work in many different ways, and some may resist expectations or meet them with strategies you may not anticipate. Don't assume, for example, that symmetry is the norm. But do look for an interesting interplay of elements.

439

What details matter?

It's usually the details that betray the difference between the real thing and a knockoff, the Gucci bag and its box-store parody. Most of us have a practiced appreciation for the details when it comes to the things we know and care about. And it is such details that we need to appreciate when we look at and assess designs.

In printed documents, we've all become more attentive to **fonts** and **typefaces** since computer technologies have given us control over such details. In the old days of IBM typewriters, writers usually could produce nothing fancier than a traditional Courier font, in which every letter and element took up the same amount of space.

`This is a sentence set in Courier type.`

But we can now routinely choose from dozens of fonts from a menu, each of which gives a different style and grace to a text. Who knew? Printers certainly did, as well as book designers, commercial artists, and people who loved books. They cherished the clarity, elegance, or style of their favorite fonts. Now more people notice them and can usually tell the difference between unadorned *sans serif* fonts so striking for headings and titles, *serif* fonts so comforting to the eye in blocks of prose, and display fonts intended for special uses.

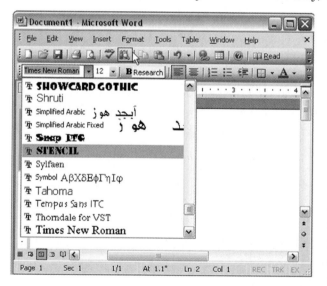

Helvetica is a popular *sans serif* font.

Times New Roman is a familiar *serif* font.

STENCIL IS A *DISPLAY* FONT.

And the choice of fonts is but one detail giving shape and emotion to printed texts. Other factors include **type size, letter spacing, line spacing, alignment, color,** and **variations** including all caps, italics, boldface, and outline. Even the paper that books and documents are printed on influences the reader through **weight, texture, color, gloss,** and other tangible qualities. Consider how much time goes into perfecting wedding invitations, and you have some sense of how much details of this kind matter.

The same can be said for anything that has had conscious effort put into its design. Consider the interface for your word processor. Countless design cues are incorporated into modern software to help users stay oriented and more easily accomplish their tasks. Subtle highlighting, for instance, will colorize a toolbar item that has been selected. Placing your cursor over a toolbar icon will display a tool tip providing a textual description of the function controlled by the icon.

You can also analyze the ways that **choices of materials** create subtle or significant additions to a design. Building materials, from woods to marble to plastics to cardboard, each have a character of their own that helps give a design its distinctive quality. What appeals do wood and stone add to the design of an interior? How does using plastic to design a portable shelter create a space for sleeping but also send a message about homelessness and contemporary culture?

A sleeping shelter made of lightweight plastic and a wooden home use materials to send very different messages about housing.

CONSIDER

1. How often do you adjust the fonts when you compose a document? When you make decisions about fonts, how conscious are you of the needs of readers as they encounter sections of prose, headings, or display fonts?

2. Open your word processor or another piece of software, and develop a list of six or more design strategies employed to make using the application easier. Which of these features seem especially helpful? What other features might be added to improve the software?

3. Visit a favorite building, and consider the materials used to create the structure. You might look at construction materials or at design materials used for the interior of the building. How do these materials contribute to your appreciation of the structure?

COMPOSE

4. Explain the design details of some object or item you know well enough to consider yourself an expert—a tennis racquet, a pair of dress shoes, a hunting rifle. In a few paragraphs, share some of your expertise with others by analyzing the details of that object.

The Design of
Everyday Things

The most difficult things to design may be the simplest, such as the items in this cluster of readings, which examine the not-so-rudimentary principles behind objects as familiar as chairs and MP3 players. Considering the diverse challenges designers face, principles such as those offered by the Center for Universal Design provide a starting point for discussions of design, form, function, and practicality.

Questions for
Niels Diffrient

A Machine for Sitting

Interview by Pilar Viladas
(2003)

In your 50 years as a designer, what have you wanted to accomplish?

It's my intent to make design a more consequential endeavor, not a decorative endeavor. I decided the best field to work in would be commercial furniture. [Industrial designer] Henry Dreyfuss introduced me to "human-factors engineering" in 1955—it's now called ergonomics. We worked on making the machines fit people. I had worked in [architect] Eero Saarinen's office on furniture. I learned a lot from Eero. We didn't know a lot about ergonomics then. We learned it, pardon the pun, by the seat of our pants.

For something as technical as ergonomics, where does the inspiration come from?

The nature of inspiration includes the understanding of all the factors necessary to design. It's like a physicist trying to bring together a comprehensive theory of the universe. You can't leave anything out. Academics in human-factors engineering are only interested in the data. I'm looking to find out how the data may be used to improve a situation. Why would you design something if it didn't improve the human condition?

How does this apply to the Freedom Chair, one of the designs you're most known for?

The problem with many ergonomically designed office chairs is they have all these knobs and levers—to adjust the seat height, recline of the backrest, height of the armrests, the headrest and so on. But most people never use them. The things that this chair does to address that problem are: When you recline, you don't have to adjust the chair—it adapts to your body weight. When you decide that the armrests are not where you want them to be, you grab one or both arms and move them up or down. They're coordinated, so if you pull one up, the other follows.

What's an example of an everyday object that you think is well designed?

One of my favorites is the umbrella. I also like the titanium-and-carbon-fiber tennis rackets. They're light, strong and never warp. The umbrella, the bicycle, the pencil, the tennis racket—these are immensely efficient. The Post-it note—most of us take it for granted, but it's a design. The F-16 fighter jet—it's a beautiful object that does its job.

What about things that don't work?

The New York City taxicab is one of the worst-adapted products for its purpose. Also, those entrancing, simple chairs that people love to look at. A good deal of the Bauhaus falls into that category of what I call functional style. I'm a sucker

The Freedom Chair, designed by Niels Diffrient.

The Bauhaus (1919–1933) was a highly influential German school of design and architecture. Embodying what it regarded as the principles of modernism, its basic premise was that form should follow function in the design of products for the mass market. Bauhaus designs were admired for their simplicity and purity; they were faulted for their unornamented starkness and impracticality.

for this stuff, too, like everyone else—I have Breuer and Mies bent-tube furniture in my living room, but I hardly ever sit in them. I sit in a comfortable chair and look at them. I saw a photo of Ettore Sottsass, who designs all this way-out stuff, in his studio. That's not design to be used. I have tremendous respect for Ettore because his competence at form-giving is extraordinary. So is Michael Graves's, and so is Philippe Starck's. That's their strength. You can't blame them—they look upon themselves as poets and artists. Sottsass did things for Olivetti—typewriters, adding machines. When someone of his caliber moves into accepting constraints of performance and function, he does extraordinary design.

Do you agree with the notion that people are more savvy about design these days?

Yes, with qualifiers. There is a class of person who is educated enough and sensitive to elements of aesthetic refinement. You could almost directly design for these people because they're discriminating. But the whole nature of my profession is design for the masses. They're [attuned] to certain things—price, availability, distribution, functionality. If it does something obviously better, they'll buy it. You want to use function as a door-opener. After that, it would be nice if the product were well styled.

Is there anything you haven't designed but would like to?

Clothing. I carry a pocketknife, and when I sit down, it slides out of my pocket. If men's trousers had just a little "step" in the pocket, things wouldn't slide out. It could be a major marketing advantage to address functional issues in clothing.

CONSIDER

1. Diffrient describes designs that he particularly admires: umbrellas, pencils, tennis rackets, and bicycles. Consider these objects closely, and then try to list the design qualities they might have in common. Why might a designer like Diffrient admire a pencil? What do you see when you look at a pencil?

2. Do a Google search for "Marcel Breuer furniture" to see what kind of chairs Diffrient looks at in his living room. What might the rationale be for either designing or owning such furniture?

CHALLENGE

3. Diffrient points out that an object as ordinary as a Post-it® note can embody great design. Working in a group, try to come up with an alternative design for the Post-it note or, perhaps, the umbrella. What effect does an existing design have on our ability to imagine alternatives?

At first glance, an iPod seems too simple to warrant all the fuss it has generated. But that simplicity is the key to its success as just about the most elegant interface imaginable between people and the music they crave. The iPod is pricey and has cheaper competitors. But at least for a while, it is enjoying the status of a product good enough to stand for an entire genre—like Xerox, Kleenex, and the original Ford Mustang. Rob Walker explores the iPod in extraordinary detail in "The Guts of a New Machine" to show that good design is about more than just looks.

 FYI Rob Walker is a contributing writer for *The New York Times Magazine* and *Inc.* He is co-author of *Titans of Finance*, a graphic novel featuring "true tales from the world of big money, wittily translated through America's most populist medium." Other examples of his work are available on his personal Web site at http://robwalker.net.

The Guts of a New Machine

Rob Walker
(2003)

Two years ago this month, Apple Computer released a small, sleek-looking device it called the iPod. A digital music player, it weighed just 6.5 ounces and held about 1,000 songs. There were small MP3 players around at the time, and there were players that could hold a lot of music. But if the crucial equation is "largest number of songs" divided by "smallest physical space," the iPod seemed untouchable. And yet the initial reaction was mixed: The thing cost $400, so much more than existing digital players that it prompted one online skeptic to suggest that the name might be an acronym for "Idiots Price Our Devices." This line of complaint called to mind the Newton, Apple's pen-based personal organizer that was ahead of its time but carried a bloated price tag to its doom.

Since then, however, about 1.4 million iPods have been sold. (It has been updated twice and now comes in three versions, all of which improved on the original's songs-per-space ratio, and are priced at $300, $400 and $500, the most expensive holding 10,000 songs.) For the months of July and August, the iPod claimed the No. 1 spot in the MP3 player market both in terms of unit share (31 percent) and revenue share (56 percent), by Apple's reckoning. It is now Apple's highest-volume product. "It's something that's as big a brand to Apple as the Mac," is how Philip Schiller, Apple's senior vice president of worldwide product marketing, puts it. "And that's a pretty big deal."

Of course, as anyone who knows the basic outline of Apple's history is aware, there is no guarantee that today's innovation leader will not be copy-catted and undersold into tomorrow's niche player. Apple's recent and highly publicized move to make the iPod and its related software, iTunes, available to users of Windows-based computers is widely seen as a sign that the company is trying to avoid that fate this time around. But it may happen anyway. The history of innovation is the history of innovation being imitated, iterated and often overtaken.

Whether the iPod achieves truly mass scale—like, say, the cassette-tape Walkman, which sold an astonishing 186 million units in its first 20 years of existence—it certainly qualifies as a hit and as a genuine breakthrough. It has popped up on *Saturday Night Live*, in a 50 Cent video, on Oprah Winfrey's list of her "favorite things," and in recurring "what's on your iPod" gimmicks in several magazines. It is, in short, an icon. A handful of familiar clichés have made the rounds to explain this—it's about ease of use, it's about Apple's great sense of design. But what does that really mean? "Most people make the mistake of thinking design is what it looks like," says Steve Jobs, Apple's C.E.O. "People think it's this veneer—that the designers are handed this box and told, 'Make it look good!' That's not what we think design is. It's not just what it looks like and feels like. Design is how it works."

So you can say that the iPod is innovative, but it's harder to nail down whether the key is what's inside it, the external appearance or even the way these work together. One approach is to peel your way through the thing, layer by layer.

THE AURA

If you want to understand why a product has become an icon, you of course want to talk to the people who dreamed it up and made it. And you want to talk to the design experts and the technology pros and the professors and the gurus. But what you really want to do is talk to Andrew Andrew. Andrew Andrew is a "highly diversified company" made up of two personable young men, each named Andrew. They dress identically and seem to agree on everything; they say, among other things, that they have traveled from the future "to set things on the right course for tomorrow." They require interviewers to sign a form agreeing not to reveal any differences between Andrew and Andrew, because to do so might undermine the Andrew Andrew brand—and since this request is more interesting than whatever those differences might be, interviewers sign it.

Among other things, they do some fashion design and they are DJs who "spin" on iPods, setting up participatory events called iParties. Thus they've probably seen more people interact with the player than anyone who doesn't work for Apple. More important, they put an incredible amount of thought into what they buy, and why: In a world where, for better or worse, aesthetics is a business, they are not just consumers but consumption artists. So Andrew remembers exactly where he was when he first encountered the iPod: 14th Street near Ninth Avenue in New York City. He was with Andrew, of course. A friend showed it to them. Andrew held the device in his hand. The main control on the iPod is a scroll wheel: You spin it with your thumb to navigate the long list of songs (or artists or genres), touch a button to pick a track and use the wheel again to adjust the volume. The other Andrew also tried it out. "When you do the volume for the first time, that's the key moment," says Andrew. "We knew: We had to have one." (Well, two.)

Before you even get to the surface of the iPod, you encounter what could be called its aura. The commercial version of an aura is a brand, and while Apple may be a niche player in the computer market, the fanatical brand loyalty of its customers is legendary. A journalist, Leander Kahney, has even written a book about it, *The Cult of Mac*, to be published in the spring. As he points out, that base has supported the company with a faith in its will to innovate—even during stretches when it hasn't. Apple is also a giant in the world of industrial design. The candy-colored look of the iMac has been so widely copied that it's now a visual cliché.

But the iPod is making an even bigger impression. Bruce Claxton, who is the current president of the Industrial Designers Society of America and a senior designer at Motorola, calls the device emblematic of a shift toward products that are "an antidote to the hyper lifestyle," which might be symbolized by hand-held devices that bristle with buttons and controls that seem to promise a million functions if you only had time to figure them all out. "People are seeking out products that are not just simple to use but a joy to use." Moby, the recording artist, has been a high-profile iPod booster since the product's debut. "The kind of insidious revolutionary quality of the iPod," he says, "is that it's so elegant and logical, it becomes part of your life so quickly that you can't remember what it was like beforehand."

Tuesday nights, Andrew Andrew's iParty happens at a club called APT on the spooky, far western end of 13th Street. They show up at about 10 in matching sweat jackets and sneakers, matching eyeglasses, matching haircuts. They connect their matching iPods to a modest Gemini mixer that they've fitted with a white front panel to make it look more iPodish. The iPods sit on either side of the mixer, on their backs, so they look like tiny turntables. Andrew Andrew change into matching lab coats and ties. They hand out long song lists to patrons, who take a number and, when called, are invited up to program a seven-minute set. At around midnight, the actor Elijah Wood (Frodo) has turned up and is permitted to plug his own iPod into Andrew Andrew's system. His set includes a Squarepusher song.

Between songs at APT, each Andrew analyzed the iPod. In talking about how hard it was, at first, to believe that so much music could be stuffed into such a tiny object, they came back to the scroll wheel as the key to the product's initial seductiveness. "It really bridged the gap," Andrew observed, "between fantasy and reality."

The idea of innovation, particularly technological innovation, has a kind of aura around it, too. Imagine the lone genius, sheltered from the storm of short-term commercial demands in a research lab somewhere, whose tinkering produces a sudden and momentous breakthrough. Or maybe we think innovation begins with an epiphany, a sudden vision of the future. Either way, we think of that one thing, the lightning bolt that jolted all the other pieces into place. The Walkman came about because a Sony executive wanted a high-quality but small stereo tape player to listen to on long flights. A small recorder was modified, with the recording pieces removed and stereo circuitry added. That was February 1979, and within six months the product was on the market.

The iPod's history is comparatively free of lightning-bolt moments. Apple was not ahead of the curve in recognizing the power of music in digital form. It was practically the last computer maker to equip its machines with CD burners. It trailed others in creating jukebox software for storing and organizing music collections on computers. And various portable digital music players were already on the market before the iPod was even an idea. Back when Napster was inspiring a million self-styled visionaries to predict the end of music as we know it, Apple was focused on the relationship between computers and video. The company had, back in the 1990s, invented a technology called FireWire, which is basically a tool for moving data between digital devices—in large quantities, very quickly. Apple licensed this technology to various Japanese consumer electronics companies (which used it in digital camcorders and players) and eventually started adding FireWire ports to iMacs and creating video editing software. This led to programs called iMovie, then iPhoto and then a conceptual view of the home computer as a "digital hub" that would complement a range of devices. Finally, in January 2001, iTunes was added to the mix.

And although the next step sounds prosaic—we make software that lets you organize the music on your computer, so maybe we should make one of those things that lets you take it with you—it was also something new. There were companies that made jukebox software and companies that made portable players, but nobody made both. What this meant is not that the iPod could do more, but that it would do less. This is what led to what Jonathan Ive, Apple's vice president of industrial design, calls the iPod's "overt simplicity." And this, perversely, is the most exciting thing about it.

THE SURFACE

Ive introduces himself as Jony, but really he seems like more of a Jonathan: friendly and soft-spoken, almost sheepish at times, but also, with his shaved head and English accent and carefully chosen words, an extremely precise man. We spoke in a generic conference room in Apple's Cupertino, Calif., headquarters, decorated mostly with the company's products.

Before I really had a chance to ask a question, Ive spent about 10 minutes talking about the iPod's packaging—the way the box opens, how the foam is cut. He talked about the unusually thin and flexible FireWire cable, about the "taut, crisp" cradle that the iPod rests in, about the white headphones. "I remember there was a discussion: 'Headphones can't be white; headphones are black, or dark gray.'" But uniform whiteness seemed too important to the product to break the pattern, and indeed the white headphones have become a kind of secondary, unplanned icon—as Apple's current ads

"The Dells of the world don't spend money [on design innovation]. They don't think about these things."
—STEVE JOBS

featuring white-headphoned silhouettes now underscore. It's those details, he said, that make the iPod special: "We are surrounded by so many things that are flippant and trivial. This could have been just another self-important plastic thing."

When it came to pinning Ive down on questions of how specific aspects of the product came to be, he stressed not epiphanies but process. Asked about

the scroll wheel, he did not mention the Bang & Olufsen BeoCom phones that use a similar radial dial; rather, he talked about the way that his design group collaborates constantly with engineers and manufacturers. "It's not serial," he insisted. "It's not one person passing something on to the next." I'd push for a lightning-bolt moment, and he'd trail off. Finally, at one point, he interrupted himself and said, with sudden energy, "It's almost easier to talk about it as what it's not."

The surface of the iPod, white on front and stainless steel behind, is perfectly seamless. It's close to impenetrable. You hook it up to a computer with iTunes, and whatever music you have collected there flows (incredibly fast, thanks to that FireWire cable) into the iPod—again, seamless. Once it's in there, the surface of the iPod is not likely to cause problems for the user, because there's almost nothing on it. Just that wheel, one button in the center, and four beneath the device's LCD screen. (The look, with the big circle at the bottom, is reminiscent of a tiny stereo speaker.)

"Steve"—that would be Steve Jobs—"made some very interesting observations very early on about how this was about navigating content," Ive says. "It was about being very focused and not trying to do too much with the device—which would have been its complication and, therefore, its demise. The enabling features aren't obvious and evident, because the key was getting rid of stuff."

Later he said: "What's interesting is that out of that simplicity, and almost that unashamed sense of simplicity, and expressing it, came a very different product. But difference wasn't the goal. It's actually very easy to create a different thing. What was exciting is starting to realize that its difference was really a consequence of this quest to make it a very simple thing."

Before Ive came to Apple, he worked independently, often on projects that never got out of the prototype phase; one working model would be made, and then it would sit on a shelf in his office. You can think of innovation as a continuum, and this phase is one end of it. The dreams and experiments that happen outside of—and in a state of indifference toward—the marketplace. At the other end of the continuum are the fast followers, those who are very attuned to the marketplace, but are not particularly innovative. They let someone else do the risky business of wild leaps, then swoop in behind with an offering that funnels some aspect of the innovation into a more marketable (cheaper? watered down? easier to obtain?) package—and dominate. Fairly or not, the shorthand version of this in the technology world would have at one end of the continuum Xerox PARC, the famous R&D lab where all manner of leading-edge innovations (including some of the "look and feel" of the Mac) were researched but never developed into marketable products. And at the other end you'd have companies like Microsoft and Dell.

Apple presents itself as a company whose place on this continuum is unique. Its headquarters in Cupertino is a series of connected buildings arranged in a circle. Behind this surface is a kind of enclosed park. It looks like public space, but of course it isn't: You can't get to it unless you're an Apple employee or are accompanied by one. Along one side of this hermetic oasis are a bunch of tables, set just outside the company cafeteria, and a sign that says Cafe Macs. Here I sat with my P.R. minder and watched Steve Jobs approach in long, energetic strides. It was a perfect day, and he wore shorts with his black turtleneck, and sneakers.

He was very much on message, and the message was that only Apple could have developed the iPod. Like the device itself, Apple appears seamless: It has the hardware engineers, the software engineers, the industrial designers, all under one roof and working together. "As technology becomes more complex, Apple's core strength of knowing how to make very sophisticated technology comprehensible to mere mortals is in even greater demand." This is why, he said, the barrage of devices made by everyone from Philips to Samsung to Dell that are imitating and will imitate the iPod do not make him nervous. "The Dells of the world don't spend money" on design innovation, he said. "They don't think about these things."

As he described it, the iPod did not begin with a specific technological breakthrough, but with a sense, in early 2001, that Apple could give this market something better than any rival could. So the starting point wasn't a chip or a design; the starting point was the question, What's the user experience? "Correct," Jobs said. "And the pieces come together. If you start to work on something, and the time is right, pieces come in from the periphery. It just comes together."

THE GUTS

What, then, are the pieces? What are the technical innards of the seamless iPod? What's underneath the surface? "Esoterica," says Schiller, an Apple V.P., waving away any and all questions about the iPod's innards. Consumers, he said, don't care about technical specs; they care about how many songs it holds, how quickly they can transfer them, how good the sound quality is.

Perhaps. But some people are interested in esoterica, and a lot of people were interested in knowing what was inside the iPod when it made its debut. One of them was David Carey, who for the past three years has run a business in Austin, Tex., called Portelligent, which tears apart electronic devices and does what might be called guts checks. He tore up his first iPod in early 2002.

Inside was a neat stack of core components. First, the power source: a slim, squarish rechargeable battery made by Sony. Atop that was the hard disk—the thing that holds all the music files. At the time, small hard disks were mostly used in laptops, or as removable data-storage cards for laptops. So-called 2.5-inch hard disks, which are protected by a casing that actually measures about 2 3/4 inches by 4 inches, were fairly commonplace, but Toshiba had come up with an even smaller one. With a protective cover measuring just over 2 inches by 3 inches, 0.2 inches thick and weighing less than two ounces, its 1.8-inch disk could hold five gigabytes of data—or, in practical terms, about a thousand songs. This is what Apple used.

On top of this hard disk was the circuit board. This included components to turn a digitally encoded music file into a conventional audio file, the chip that enables the device to use FireWire both as a pipe for digital data and battery charging and the central processing unit that acts as the sort of taskmaster for the various components. Also here was the ball-bearing construction underlying the scroll wheel. (The newer iPod models got slimmer by replacing that wheel with a solid-state version and by using a smaller battery.) It is, as Carey notes, an admirable arrangement.

Exactly how all the pieces came together—there were parts from at least a half-dozen companies in the original iPod—is not something Apple talks about. But one clue can be found in the device itself. Under the Settings menu is a selection called Legal, and there you find not just Apple's copyright but also a note that "portions" of the device are copyrighted by something called PortalPlayer Inc. That taskmaster central processing unit is a PortalPlayer chip. The Silicon Valley company, which describes itself as a "supplier of digital media infrastructure solutions for the consumer marketplace," has never publicly discussed its role in the iPod. Its vice president for sales and marketing, Michael Maia, would talk to me only in general terms.

PortalPlayer was founded a little more than four years ago with an eye toward creating basic designs for digital computer peripherals, music players in particular. Specifically, the company wanted to build an architecture around tiny hard disks. Most early MP3 players did not use hard disks because they were physically too large. Rather, they used another type of storage technology (referred to as a "flash" chip) that took up little space but held less data—that is, fewer songs. PortalPlayer's setup includes both a hard disk and a smaller memory chip, which is actually the thing that's active when you're listening to music; songs are cleverly parceled into this from the hard disk in small groups, a scheme that keeps the energy-hog hard disk from wearing down the battery. More recently, PortalPlayer's work has formed the guts of new players released by Samsung and Philips. A trade journal called *Electronics Design Chain* described PortalPlayer as having developed a "base platform" that Apple at least used as a starting point and indicated that PortalPlayer picked other members of the iPod "design chain" and helped manage the process.

Interestingly, the legal section in the first version of the iPod used to include another copyright notice on behalf of a company called Pixo, which is reported to have created the original operating system for the iPod. Pixo has since been bought by Sun Microsystems, and the credit has disappeared from both newer iPods and even more recent software upgrades for the original model.

> "The iPod came together in somewhere between six and nine months, from concept to market, and its coherence as a product given the time frame and the number of variables is astonishing."

Apple won't comment on any of this, and the nondisclosure agreements it has in place with its suppliers and collaborators are described as unusually restrictive. Presumably this is because the company prefers the image of a product that sprang forth whole from the corporate godhead—which was certainly the impression the iPod created when it seemed to appear out of nowhere two years ago. But the point here is not to undercut Apple's role: The iPod came together in somewhere between six and nine months, from concept to market, and its coherence as a product given the time frame and the number of variables is astonishing. Jobs and company are still correct when they point to that coherence as key to the iPod's appeal; and the reality of technical innovation today is that assembling the right specialists is critical to speed, and speed is critical to success.

Still, in the world of technology products, guts have traditionally mattered quite a bit; the PC boom viewed from one angle was nothing but an endless series of announcements about bits and megahertz and RAM. That 1.8-inch hard disk, and the amount of data storage it offered in such a small space, isn't the only key to the iPod, but it's a big deal. Apple apparently cornered the market for the Toshiba disks for a while. But now there is, inevitably, an alternative. Hitachi now makes a disk that size, and it has at least one major buyer: Dell.

THE SYSTEM

My visit to Cupertino happened to coincide with the publication of a pessimistic installment of the *Wall Street Journal*'s Heard on the Street column pointing out that Apple's famous online music store generates little profit. The more interesting point, noted in the back half of the column, is that Apple doesn't expect it to generate much profit—it's a "Trojan horse" whose real function is to help sell more iPods. Given that the store was widely seen as a pivotal moment in the tortuous process of creating a legitimate digital music source that at least some paying consumers are willing to use, this is an amazing notion: Apple, in a sense, was willing to try and reinvent the entire music business in order to move iPods.

The column also noted that some on Wall Street were waiting to see what would happen to the iPod once Dell came out with its combination of music store and music player. (The Dell DJ is slightly bigger than the iPod but claims a longer battery life, which the company says is what its consumer research indicated people wanted; it costs $250 for a 15-gigabyte version, $300 for 20 gigabytes, or nearly 5,000 songs.) Napster's name has been bought by another company that has launched a pay service with a hardware partner, Samsung. But it was Dell that one investor quoted in the *Journal* article held out as the rival with the greatest chance of success: "No one markets as well as Dell does." This was causing some eye-rolling in Cupertino; Dell is not a marketer at all. Dell has no aura; there is no Cult of Dell. Dell is a merchandiser, a shiller of gigs-per-dollar. A follower. Dell had not released its product when I met Jobs, but he still dismissed it as "not any good."

About a week later Jobs played host to one of the "launch" events for which the company is notorious, announcing the availability of iTunes and access to the company's music store for Windows users. (In what seemed an odd crack in Apple's usually seamless aura maintenance, he did his demo on what was clearly a Dell computer.) The announcement included a deal with AOL and a huge promotion with Pepsi. The message was obvious: Apple is aiming squarely at the mainstream.

This sounded like a sea change. But while you can run iTunes on Windows and hook it up to an iPod, that iPod does not play songs in the formats used by any other seller of digital music, like Napster or Rhapsody.

MP3 Players and design
www.ablongman.com/beyondwords30

Nor will music bought through Apple's store play on any rival device. (The iPod does, of course, work easily with the MP3 format that's common on free file-swapping services, like KaZaA, that the music industry wants to shut down but that are still much more popular than anything requiring money.) This means Apple is, again, competing against a huge number of players across multiple business segments, who by and large will support one another's products and services. In light of this, says one of those competitors, Rob Glaser, founder and C.E.O. of RealNetworks, "It's absolutely clear now why five years from now, Apple will have 3 to 5 percent of the player market."

Glaser says he admires Apple and likes Jobs, but contends that this is simply the latest instance of the company's tendency, once again, to sacrifice commercial logic in the name of "ideology." Not that Apple can't maintain a business by catering to the high end and operating in a closed world. But maintaining market leadership, while easy when the field of competitors is small, will become impossible as rivals flood the market with their own innovations and an agnostic attitude about what works with what. "The history of the world," he says, "is that hybridization yields better results." With Dell and others aiming a big push at the Christmas season, it's even possible that Apple's market share has peaked.

Jobs, of course, has heard the predictions and has no patience for any of it. Various contenders have come at the iPod for two years, and none have measured up. Nothing has come close to Apple's interface. Even the look-alike products are frauds. "They're all putting their dumb controls in the shape of a circle, to fool the consumer into thinking it's a wheel like ours," he says. "We've sort of set the vernacular. They're trying to copy the vernacular without understanding it." (The one company that did plan a wheel-driven product, Samsung, changed course after Apple reportedly threatened to sue.)

"We don't underestimate people," Jobs said later in the interview. "We really did believe that people would want something this good, that they'd see the value in it. And that rather than making a far inferior product for a hundred dollars less, giving people the product that they want and that will serve them for years, even though it's a little pricier. People are smart; they figure these things out."

The point that companies—like Dell—that have no great reputation as innovators but a track record of winning by playing a price-driven, low-margin volume game was dismissed. The iPod has already been improved several times, Jobs said, and will keep improving in ways that keep it ahead of the pack. (He wouldn't get specific.) "For whatever reason," he said with finality, "the superior product has the largest share. Sometimes the best product does win. This may be one of those times."

THE CORE

Actually, Jobs seemed a little annoyed. Looking back at my notes, I found it remarkable how many of his answers begin with some variation of "No," as if my questions were out of sync with what he wanted to say. (Before I could finish a question about the significance of Apple's pitching a product to Windows users, for instance, he corrected me: "We're not pitching the Windows user. We're pitching the music lover.") After half an hour of this, my inquiries really did start to fall apart, so I didn't expect much when I resorted to asking, in so many words, whether he thinks consciously about innovation.

"No," he said, peevishly. "We consciously think about making great products. We don't think, 'Let's be innovative!'" He waved his hands for effect. "Let's take a class! Here are the five rules of innovation, let's put them up all over the company!'"

Well, I said defensively, there are people who do just that.

"Of course they do." I felt his annoyance shift elsewhere. "And it's like . . . somebody who's not cool trying to be cool. It's painful to watch. You know what I mean?" He looked at me for a while, and I started to think he was trying to tell me something. Then he said, "It's like . . . watching Michael Dell try to dance." The P.R. minder guffawed. "Painful," Jobs summarized.

What I had been hoping to do was catch a glimpse of what's there when you pull back all those layers—when you penetrate the aura, strip off the surface, clear away the guts. What's under there is innovation, but where does it come from? I had given up on getting an answer to this question when I made a jokey observation that before long somebody would probably start making white headphones so that people carrying knockoffs and tape players could fool the world into thinking they had trendy iPods.

Jobs shook his head. "But then you meet the girl, and she says, 'Let me see what's on your iPod.' You pull out a tape player, and she walks away." This was an unanticipated, and surprisingly persuasive, response. That's thinking long-term, I said. "No," said Steve Jobs. "That's being an optimist."

CONSIDER

1. Review Walker's lengthy essay, looking for different ways that people define good design. Are those various definitions contradictory, or do they describe different dimensions of the same basic principles? Try to summarize those principles in a paragraph of your own.

2. An Apple executive suggests that the key to the iPod's success as a design was "getting rid of stuff" that distracted from its main task, making music available. In what other areas might "getting rid of stuff" be a useful design principle? Would it work for writers?

3. How much is the cachet of a designer product like the iPod worth to you as a consumer? Explore this question with a group of classmates, thinking about when and why you would pony up the premium price that signature products command. Generic blades or Mach II? Kmart undies or Calvin Klein? Generic Kibble or Science Diet for Rover?

COMPOSE

4. Write a narrative about a manufactured object you have coveted, explaining what made you notice it, what made it desirable, and whether you actually acquired it. If you did eventually own the product, did it live up to your expectations? Why or why not? Could it? Use your essay to explore the way design works in our society to create needs or desires.

We're accustomed to movie, restaurant, and product reviews, so why not reviews of commercials? Slate.com runs a regular feature called "Ad Report Card" analyzing some of the more popular or controversial television advertisements. Seth Stevenson examines the classy spots Apple created for its iPod and found them maybe a bit too good.

FYI
Seth Stevenson writes a regular feature called "Ad Report Card" for Slate.com, in which he analyzes some of the most popular and controversial television advertisements.

You and Your Shadow

The iPod ads are mesmerizing. But does your iPod think it's better than you?

Seth Stevenson

(2004)

The Spot: *Silhouetted shadow-people dance in a strenuous manner. Behind them is a wall of solid color that flashes in neon shades of orange, pink, blue, and green. In each shadow-person's hand is an Apple iPod.*

I myself own an iPod, but rarely dance around with it. In part because the earbuds would fall out (Does this happen to you? I think I may have narrow auditory canals) and in part because I'm just not all that prone to solitary rump-shaking. It's a failing on my part. Maybe if I were a silhouette I might dance more.

All that said, these are very catchy ads. I don't get sick of watching them. And yet I also sort of resent them, as I'll later explain.

First, let's talk about what the ads get right. For one, the songs (from groups like Jet and Black Eyed Peas) are extremely well-chosen. Just indie enough so that not everybody knows them; just mainstream enough so that almost everybody likes them. But as good as the music is, the visual concept is even better. It's incredibly simple: never more than three distinct colors on the screen at any one time, and black and white are two of them. What makes it so bold are those vast swaths of neon monochrome.

This simplicity highlights the dance moves, but also—and more importantly—it highlights the iPod. The key to it all is the silhouettes. What a brilliant way to showcase a product. Almost everything that might distract us—not just background scenery, but even the actors' faces and clothes—

Apple CEO Steve Jobs watches an iPod television ad during his keynote address at the Macworld Conference and Expo in San Francisco, January 2004.

has been eliminated. All we're left to focus on is that iconic gizmo. What's more, the dark black silhouettes of the dancers perfectly offset the iPod's gleaming white cord, earbuds, and body.

This all sounds great, so far. So what's not to like?

For the longest time, I couldn't put my finger on it. And then I realized where I'd seen this trick before. It's the mid-1990s campaign for DeBeers diamonds—the one where the people are shadows, but the jewelry is real. In them, a shadow-man would slip a diamond ring over a shadow-finger, or clasp a pendant necklace around a ghostly throat. These ads used to be on television all the time. You may recall the stirring string music of their soundtrack, or the still-running tagline: "A Diamond Is Forever."

Like the iPod ads, these DeBeers ads used shadow-people to perfect effect. The product—in this case, diamonds—sparkles and shines on a dusky background. But what bothered me about the spots was the underlying message. They seem to say that we are all just transient shadows, not long for this world—it's our diamonds that are forever. In the end, that necklace is no overpriced bauble. It's a ticket to immortality!

My distaste for these ads stems in part from the fact that, with both the iPod and the diamonds, the marketing gives me a sneaking sense that the product thinks it's better than me. More attractive, far more timeless, and frankly more interesting, too. I feel I'm being told that, without this particular merchandise, I will have no tangible presence in the world. And that hurts. I'm a person, dammit, not a featureless shadow-being! If you prick me, do I not write resentful columns?

Like diamond jewelry, the iPod is designed and marketed to draw attention to itself, and I think (I realize I'm in a minority here) I prefer my consumer goods to know their place. If I did it over, I might opt for an equally functional but slightly more anonymous MP3 player. One that deflects attention instead of attracting it. Because I'm the one with the eternal soul here—it's my stuff that's just transient junk.

Grade: B−. Perfectly executed. Mildly insulting message.

Source: "You and Your Shadow: The iPod ads are mesmerizing. But does your iPod think it's better than you?" by Seth Stevenson from Slate.com, March 2, 2004. SLATE ARTICLE © reprinted by permission of United Feature Syndicate, Inc.

CONSIDER

1. Stevenson's analysis of the iPod ad is highly subjective and personal. What are the advantages and risks of this strategy?

2. The iPod is widely praised for its appealing simplicity and clever functionality (see Rob Walker's "Guts of a New Machine" on page 445). Does the iPod TV spot match the style of the product it represents? Why or why not?

3. Can you determine specific criteria by which Stevenson is evaluating the iPod ad? What do they seem to be?

COMPOSE

4. Pick a television commercial and analyze it, modeling your evaluation directly on the formula "Ad Report Card" uses. Be sure that you describe the ad briefly ("The Spot") and conclude the analysis with a grade for the ad and a few pithy remarks.

WRITING AN AD ANALYSIS

You have seen so many ads, whether on TV or in print, that you likely feel qualified to judge them. You are the target audience, in most cases, aren't you? But when you write about one, you still need to make a point, present evidence for any claims you make, and show an appreciation for detail.

- **Describe the ad as if the reader has not seen it.** Taking the time to summarize the spot will also sharpen your appreciation of its structure and strategies. A short description near the opening of the analysis usually helps orient readers, and brief sketches of details throughout the piece will demonstrate your command of all aspects of the ad.

- **Make a point.** Whether evaluating an advertisement or just describing how it works, be sure you develop a coherent and stimulating claim. Does the ad succeed, fail, insult, obfuscate, confuse, celebrate, persuade? Make a specific claim, and then prove it.

- **Understand the point of the ad.** Look for any strategies that bring together the separate elements of design in the spot—verbal, visual, and auditory. Assume that there is a deliberate strategy in the ad, even if you don't initially detect it.

- **Understand the audience of the ad.** How specifically does the spot signal its demographic boundaries, and how well does it appeal to the targeted group? Consider that you might not be the target audience of the commercial. Don't assume you should be.

- **Don't underestimate the savvy of a professional ad.** Not all ads work, and even professional efforts fail spectacularly at times. But you will do a sharper analysis if you assume, at least at the outset, that the creators of the spot weren't stupid.

- **Understand the persuasive tools used.** Does the spot rely on facts, on emotions, or on an appeal to the reputation or authority of its sponsor? What does the choice of tactics say about the ad?

- **Understand the visual tools used.** How is the spot arranged or narrated? How are images and words connected? How are key ideas highlighted? How is color employed? What fonts are selected and why?

- **Understand the way sound is used.** For a TV or radio spot, consider what the soundtrack or dialogue contributes to the ad. How are silences used? What type of music is offered and why?

- **Present evidence for the points you make.** Show precisely how any claim you make is supported by describable elements of the ad. Don't hurry through your presentation of evidence or assume that it is obvious to your readers.

Local iPod sick of playing Avril Lavigne

by Chris Rose, Staff Writer

CAMPUS — A local iPod declared on Sunday that it was "absolutely sick" of always having to play Avril Lavigne.

"Every time my owner puts on my headphones, it's that freaking 'Complicated' song," stated the iPod in exasperation to a sympathetic USB scanner. "And really, I don't even mind 'Complicated' too much, but 'Ska8er Boi' is absolutely horrible. I usually have to play that one like four times a day. I mean, what kind of artist rhymes 'skater boy' with 'see ya later boy?' It's absolutely ridiculous."

The iPod went on to say that it fears the Avril trend may be long lasting, especially because of multiple Grammy nominations for the punk princess.

"I thought it would have gone away by now, but every day it's just more and more and more," continued the iPod. "Now I'm not saying that my owner only listens to stuff like that. I mean, every once in a while she'll blast out some good old Red Hot Chili Peppers or that new Missy Elliott jam."

The owner of the iPod, who is currently shopping for a new punk tie at Hot Topic, could not be reached for comment, but is believed to be unaware of the iPod's distaste with her music selection.

"One more Avril song and I'll slit my wiring."
[illustration: Aaron Stanush]

An iPod parody story by Chris Rose, from *Texas Travesty* (2003), a humor publication created by students at the University of Texas at Austin.

Do the people who create child-proof caps and packages understand that their designs can make taking medications extraordinarily difficult for the infirm or aged? One wouldn't think so when even a healthy adult sometimes struggles to disengage the tabs on a bottle of aspirin. But if one creates objects to meet a single goal, or using no specific standards at all, it's easy to lose sight of larger consequences and other audiences. During the frenzied early years of the Internet, for example, few Web designers worried whether their sites would be accessible by the visually impaired. Today, Web access for the disabled has become a national concern. The Center for Universal Design at North Carolina State University is working to address the consequences of thoughtless design, wherever it occurs. A set of principles to guide designers in their work has been compiled at the Center by Bettye Rose Connell, Mike Jones, Ron Mace, Jim Mueller, Abir Mullick, Elaine Ostroff, Jon Sanford, Ed Steinfeld, Molly Story, and Gregg Vanderheiden.

Universal Design Principles

Center for Universal Design

(1997)

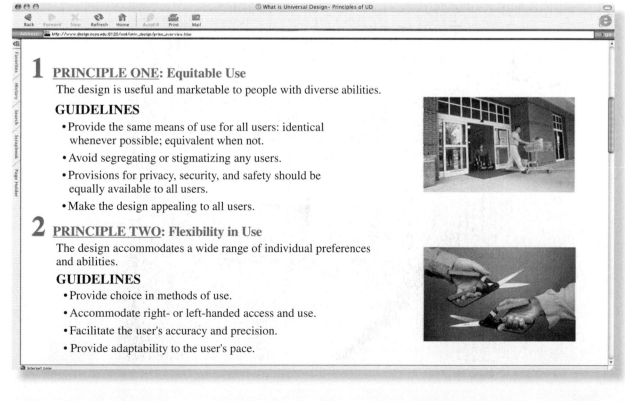

What is Universal Design- Principles of UD

Address: http://www.design.ncsu.edu:8120/cud/univ_design/princ_overview.htm

1 PRINCIPLE ONE: Equitable Use

The design is useful and marketable to people with diverse abilities.

GUIDELINES

- Provide the same means of use for all users: identical whenever possible; equivalent when not.
- Avoid segregating or stigmatizing any users.
- Provisions for privacy, security, and safety should be equally available to all users.
- Make the design appealing to all users.

2 PRINCIPLE TWO: Flexibility in Use

The design accommodates a wide range of individual preferences and abilities.

GUIDELINES

- Provide choice in methods of use.
- Accommodate right- or left-handed access and use.
- Facilitate the user's accuracy and precision.
- Provide adaptability to the user's pace.

3 PRINCIPLE THREE: Simple and Intuitive

Use of the design is easy to understand, regardless of the user's experience, knowledge, language skills, or current concentration level.

GUIDELINES

- Eliminate unnecessary complexity.
- Be consistent with user expectations and intuition.
- Accommodate a wide range of literacy and language skills.
- Arrange information consistent with its importance.
- Provide effective prompting and feedback during and after task completion.

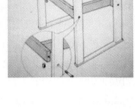

4 PRINCIPLE FOUR: Perceptible Information

The design communicates necessary information effectively to the user, regardless of ambient conditions or the user's sensory abilities.

GUIDELINES

- Use different modes (pictorial, verbal, tactile) for redundant presentation of essential information.
- Provide adequate contrast between essential information and its surroundings.
- Maximize "legibility" of essential information.
- Differentiate elements in ways that can be described (i.e., make it easy to give instructions or directions).
- Provide compatibility with a variety of techniques or devices used by people with sensory limitations.

5 PRINCIPLE FIVE: Tolerance for Error

The design minimizes hazards and the adverse consequences of accidental or unintended actions.

GUIDELINES

- Arrange elements to minimize hazards and errors: most used elements, most accessible; hazardous elements eliminated, isolated, or shielded.
- Provide warnings of hazards and errors.
- Provide fail safe features.
- Discourage unconscious action in tasks that require vigilance.

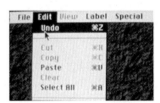

6 PRINCIPLE SIX: Low Physical Effort

The design can be used efficiently and comfortably and with a minimum of fatigue.

GUIDELINES

- Allow user to maintain a neutral body position.
- Use reasonable operating forces.
- Minimize repetitive actions.
- Minimize sustained physical effort.

7 PRINCIPLE SEVEN: Size and Space for Approach and Use

Appropriate size and space is provided for approach, reach, manipulation, and use regardless of user's body size, posture, or mobility.

GUIDELINES

- Make reach to all components comfortable for any seated or standing user.
- Provide a clear line of sight to important elements for any seated or standing user.
- Accommodate variations in hand and grip size.
- Provide adequate space for the use of assistive devices or personal assistance.

7 | EXPLORING DESIGN

CONSIDER

1. Many of the principles and guidelines of Universal Design may at first seem self-evident. If so, why do the principles need to be spelled out?

2. Working with a group, apply the principles to your own classroom and the objects there, including the desks, fixtures, and audiovisual equipment. Which principles are violated most often in the classroom? Could they be satisfied with reasonable modifications?

3. How many of the principles of universal design might be adapted to assess the effectiveness of a piece of writing?

CHALLENGE

4. Imagine objections to the principles of universal design, or express any reservations you yourself may have. Do the principles imagine a world that is too safe or too neutral or demand designs stripped of all character and physical challenge? If you object, express your dissent in a reasoned essay, a photo essay, or a parody of the principles.

DESIGNING A SYMBOLIC LANGUAGE

"A few years ago, the U.S. Congress gave a scientific commission the task of developing a symbolic language that would make clear the danger posed by the U.S. storage site for atomic waste. The problem to be solved was the following: How should the concepts and symbols be constituted in order to communicate to those living 10,000 years from now?

"The commission was made up of physicists, anthropologists, linguists, brain researchers, psychologists, molecular biologists, gerontologists, artists, etc. The commission looked for examples from the oldest symbols of humanity, studied the ruins of Stonehenge (1500 BC) and the pyramids, researched the reception of Homer and the Bible, and heard explanations of the life cycle of documents. These, however, only reached a few thousand, not 10,000 years into the past. The anthropologists recommended the symbol of the skull and crossbones. A historian, however, remembered that the skull and crossbones meant resurrection to the alchemist. And a psychologist carried out experiments with three-year-olds: If the skull and crossbones is stuck on a bottle, they cry in fear, 'poison'; if it is stuck on a wall, they enthusiastically call out, 'pirates!'"

—ULRICH BECK, *Security Dialogue*

CHALLENGE

Working in a group, try your hand at the puzzle presented by the U.S. Congress to the scientific commission. How would you transmit a warning about nuclear waste over a period of ten thousand years? Be creative, and be sure to consider what media might be the most enduring.

Car Culture

As objects of design and desire, cars and trucks have wide appeal in American culture. Youngsters in California spend small fortunes customizing Japanese coupes, while Hispanic neighborhoods celebrate the cool designs of the lowriders cruising their streets. Texans dress up pickups, and hip-hop artists compete for the coolest Escalade. While cars are just a means of transportation to some people, to others they are reflections of their style, their personality, and even their politics. The readings and images that follow explore some of these issues. First, Sharon Waxman argues that the 2004 Academy Award ceremonies played out on a battleground in the automotive culture wars, cutting many different ways—politically, economically, and socially—and the combatants were the Hummer H2 and the Toyota Prius. Warren Brown and Dana White report on some ways in which gender differences now influence car design. And Martin Wolk speculates about why some people—surprisingly—want cars that are deliberately odd or out of the mainstream. Yet the impulse makes sense if product design, in part, reflects how we choose to see ourselves.

FYI Sharon Waxman is a Hollywood reporter for the *New York Times*. She has also worked as a Middle East correspondent and a style reporter for the *Washington Post*.

A Prius-Hummer War Divides Oscarville

Sharon Waxman
(2004)

It was very early Monday morning by the time Tim Robbins lurched out of the *Vanity Fair* Oscar party at Mortons restaurant and toward the valet line, with his [partner] Susan Sarandon, two children and his golden statue for best supporting actor, in *Mystic River*.

The driver pulled up, not in a limousine, but in the diminutive Prius, the hybrid gas-electric car that Hollywood—part of it, anyway—so adores.

Meanwhile, down the street a stretch Hummer limousine was parked at the corner of Melrose and San Vicente, having deposited a group of younger, less famous, *après nous le déluge* type partygoers to the very same *Vanity Fair* bacchanal.

As Mr. Robbins folded his six-foot-five frame into the front passenger seat, and the rest of his family curled themselves into the back seat, Ms. Sarandon was heard to remark that the fans behind the barriers were screaming in their direction "because they're trying to figure out why we're in this crazy little car," a loaner.

Why, indeed? The culture wars roll on in Hollywood, this time on wheels, and nothing divides people like that nine-mile-a-gallon former military truck or the tiny Japanese-made sedan with dual engines under the hood. It's Hummer versus hybrid, Hollywood hedonism versus holier-than-thou Hollywood political correctness.

Both cars have been on the streets for some time, in the Hummer's case more than a decade. But with the Hummer's most ardent celebrity fan, Arnold Schwarzenegger (he owns seven), elected governor last year, just in time for a large-scale H2 promotional campaign, the car-culture wars have been reignited with a vengeance.

The environmental campaigner Laurie David, the wife of Larry David of the HBO series *Curb Your Enthusiasm*, worked herself into a lather not long ago over a Hummer-driving mother in the parking lot of the Crossroads School in Los Angeles. She rolled down her Prius window to share her displeasure. "I said," Mrs. David recalled, "'Are you crazy to bring this car into this parking lot? Do you understand how dangerous it is to the kids you can't see?' She stared at me blankly."

Nowadays the divide is more than cultural. It is also political. It is class- and age-oriented, too. Really.

New money is very Hummer.

Old money (dating, say, from the 1980s), very Prius.

Entertainment industry executives like Jim Wiatt, the president of the William Morris Agency, who used to be seen in a big fancy Mercedes-Benz, drove to the *Vanity Fair* party in a hybrid. Tom Hanks just bought the re-designed 2004 Prius, the second generation of the car Toyota first introduced in 2000. It is the movie people who can afford mansions who are driving the $20,000 hybrids. And it is the rappers who just made their first couple of million dollars who are buying the $50,000 Hummer. It is the kids of entertainment industry executives who rent Hummer limos for their proms and big nights out.

In the rap world, Tupac Shakur helped popularize the Hummer. His H1, unused since his death in 1996, was offered on eBay for a starting bid of $500,000, but did not sell.

Celebrity Hummer owners include the actor Adrien Brody and the director James Cameron, who made the macho *Titanic*. Hugh Hefner has been seen in a Hummer. And Steven Soderbergh's agent, Pat Dollard, says he loves the "sheer excess" of the truck, which he owns.

"It's a high-profile vehicle — it's what you want to be seen in," said Richard Sterman, a Hummer salesman at a dealership in the San Fernando Valley.

But not on Oscar night. "The Catherine Zeta-Joneses— they don't fall out of Hummer limos," said De André Armstrong, president of A Total Success, a Hollywood limousine rental company. "They come out of regular stretch limousines." Indeed, Mr. Brody, who bought his Hummer H2 last year, left it in the garage on Oscar night and arrived by limo.

Patrick Quinn, the director of special events at Z Valet, who parked Mr. Robbins's hybrid, observed about a dozen Priuses at the *Vanity Fair* party. Many were there because an environmental group, Global Green USA, had recruited celebrities, including Mr. Robbins, to attend the Oscars in Priuses. Among the other recruits were Charlize Theron (the best-actress Oscar winner), Robin Williams and Sting.

So some Oscar-night hybrid flaunters were merely driving loaners. Evidently, they had not put their money where their green principles are. It is a good bet that more than one flies by private studio jet, burning hydrocarbons as wastefully as the Daytona 500.

Lately, however, the Hummer seems to be losing ground in the culture wars. Mr. Quinn of Z Valet said he saw fewer than he used to. Roseanne Barr used to drive a Hummer, but she gave it to her former husband, Ben Thomas, in a divorce settlement. He sold it. The rap star Coolio got one from his record company but gave it up because of the poor mileage (about 11 to 12 miles a gallon, according to General Motors). Nationally, sales for the H2 fell 21 percent in February, Reuters reported, the sixth straight month of falling sales compared with the previous year. G.M. is offering dealers incentives to help spur sales.

Howard Drake, an owner of the Hummer dealership in Sherman Oaks in the San Fernando Valley, said his sales were down in January and February, only because he did not have enough supply.

Every once in a while, he acknowledged, the culture wars seep onto the lots of the dealerships. Mr. Drake said he was approached by a well-known actress, whose name he declined to share.

"She told me she wanted to buy a hybrid, and she was concerned about the Hummer and its effect on the environment," Mr. Drake recalled. "I asked where she lived. She said Beverly Hills. I said, 'Out of curiosity: How big is your house?'

"She said: 'What does that matter? It's 20,000 square feet.'"

He said he replied: "I don't know what's less correct. Having three people live in a 20,000-square-foot house, with a pool and heaters and air-conditioners. Or me driving my Hummer 500 miles a month."

Mr. Drake's house, he said, is 3,000 square feet.

> **Design and politics in America's car culture**
> www.ablongman.com/beyondwords31

CONSIDER

1. Reread "A Prius-Hummer War Divides Oscarville," making a two-column list that separates the Prius advocates and their values from the Hummer fans and all they hold dear. What do the lists reveal about the designs of the cars and the people who drive them? After you have drawn up your lists based solely on details from Waxman's story, extend each column by five to ten items (including people) that might belong to the set. What cultural differences do these products mark?

COMPOSE

2. Write an essay modeled on Waxman's in which you describe two other products that mark a similar design and cultural divide. One obvious split, for example, might be the chasm between PC computers and Apple Macintoshes or, more important, the people who use them. But be more original if you can, perhaps explaining a design and cultural divide that most people might not think of.

FYI Warren Brown is automotive columnist for www.washingtonpost.com and *The Washington Post*. His "On Wheels" column is carried in 167 newspapers, including the *Los Angeles Times*, *Detroit Free Press*, and *New York Post*.

Women Giving the Directions: Now, It's Time for Female Designers

Warren Brown
(2004)

Women consumers rule the U.S. auto market. But men remain in control of the design, development and retailing of most of the cars and trucks women buy.

It is a curious development on the road to gender equality that has thrown the auto industry into a tizzy.

Women are directly responsible for the purchase of 50 percent of all new cars and trucks sold in the United States—8.5 million of the 17 million new vehicles sold in this country last year, according to studies by J. D. Power and Associates, a consumer marketing research firm based in Agoura Hills, Calif.

"Directly responsible" means that women selected, financed or otherwise arranged for the financing (through parental or other personal loans) of the vehicles purchased.

Overall, according to research by Power analysts and by *American Woman Road and Travel* and *Good Housekeeping* magazines, women influence the purchases of 85 percent of the new vehicles annually sold in the United States.

Influence translates as, "If the woman of the house does not want a certain vehicle in the family driveway, it is not likely to wind up there," said Courtney Caldwell, president and chief executive of Caldwell Communications Inc., a firm in Troy, Mich., that produces *American Woman Road and Travel* and other publications and programs related to women in the automotive and travel markets.

In terms of dollars, women in America "are worth" $85 billion to automotive and related businesses, according to research done by the Caldwell and Power groups.

That's purchasing clout—the kind that has a male-dominated car and truck industry scratching its head about what to do to make and keep women buyers happy.

Some of those efforts, going back as far as the 1950s, were as comical as they were condescending. General Motors, for example, got the idea that husbands in gray flannel suits could better woo their wives by buying them cars in pink or "exclusively for women" salmon. There was the 1956 salmon-and-white Buick Roadmaster and the "factory pink" 1958 Cadillac Sedan DeVille. Ford Motor Co. offered limited editions of "salmon pink" Thunderbirds.

Some car dealers, eager to capitalize on what they believed a good idea, also offered pink parasols and purses to go along with the pink cars.

The late Mary Kay Ash, founder of Mary Kay Cosmetics, eventually got some attention for pink by awarding pink Cadillac cars to the company's top salespeople. But pink was a loser among women in the retail market.

No one in the auto industry would dare approach women in such a brazenly stereotypical fashion today. But therein lies a problem, according to many car-industry executives and women such as automotive journalist and former racecar driver Denise McCluggage, now in her seventies, who in 2001 was inducted into the Automotive Hall of Fame.

"The industry now knows what it shouldn't do to women, but it's having some problems trying to figure out what it should do for them," McCluggage told me during a recent test drive in California.

"Diversity" is one answer, said Ed Welburn, 52, who last year became the sixth GM design chief in that company's 95-year history. No woman has ever held that position at GM or any other major car company.

Welburn, a graduate of Howard University, is the first black man to hold the GM design leader's job. He said he has launched a campaign to bring more women into vehicle design and development. "But the idea is not to put them in some sort of a female ghetto."

Welburn said he wants women involved in all aspects of vehicle design—exterior, interior and overall ergonomics, the last of which speaks to ease of use of gauges, gears and other devices. To the extent that they have been admitted to automotive design studios at all, women have traditionally been restricted to working on the soft features of interiors—seats, panels, that sort of thing.

"The thing is that there just aren't many women in vehicle design, or in the design schools," Welburn said. "It's mostly men—good, talented, creative men. But we clearly need more women," he said.

The Volvo YCC concept car

Volvo Cars, Ford Motor Co.'s Swedish subsidiary, has taken a unique and controversial approach in this regard. The company created the first mostly female vehicle design and development team to create a concept car primarily aimed at meeting the motoring needs and wants of affluent women.

According to Volvo's sales statistics, 53 percent of its primary buyers (the people who actually pay for the cars) in the United States are women, but only 14 percent of its European buyers are women. So, at an October 2001 meeting at Volvo headquarters in Gothenburg, Sweden, company officials, both men and women, decided Volvo could be more successful with women buyers on the Continent if it developed a car for women by women.

In the United States, women buy Volvo primarily because of the brand's reputation for safety. But in Europe, Volvo is often seen, by men and women, as being a nanny's car—a reputation the company has been trying to erase with increasingly sexy offerings such as the Volvo C70 convertible and the S60-R sedan.

But how can Volvo combine sex with safety in a bid to increase sales to women in Europe, while continuing to increase its already healthy market share among women in America?

The company's tentative answer is the YCC, otherwise known as Your Concept Car, which was introduced earlier this year at the Geneva Motor Show.

The YCC's target buyer is an affluent Everywoman whom Volvo calls Eve. Eve wants everything a man wants in a car, plus a whole lot more, said YCC communications manager Tatjana Butovitsch Temm.

Eve wants constant, easy access to her umbrella, which can be stored in a tubular portal in the driver's-side door. She wants safe yet convenient storage spaces for her handbag and cell phone.

Eve wants to get in and out of the car without kneeling or bending. Thus, the gull-winged YCC kneels for her. Eve uses a remote control device to open the driver's door. As it rises, the car automatically lowers, allowing Eve to walk in and sit down.

And because Eve often wears high-heeled shoes, she wants the pedals and the driver's-side floor designed so she can wear them while driving.

Also, the YCC's seats can be given different looks for spring, summer, fall and winter.

Ah, and the YCC's rear seats can be flipped and folded and put out of the way, thus allowing Eve, who prefers not to use a trunk, to put groceries and other cargo in the rear of the car's cabin.

There is no hood on the YCC. For maintenance, the car must be taken to a garage where the front section can be lifted and the car serviced. The thinking here is that most women, especially affluent businesswomen, don't want to be bothered with poking their heads beneath the hood to check oil and other fluids.

When the YCC needs maintenance (every 31,000 miles, according to the concept), the car automatically contacts the dealership electronically. In turn, the dealership calls the YCC's owner to make a service appointment.

But is all of this YCC stuff just a different form of pink, or is it a credible attempt to satisfy the needs of women in the automotive marketplace?

"Well, let me ask you," said Paul Eisenstein, publisher of www.thecarconnection.com and one of the country's most vocal industry critics. "If a man designed a car like that for women, with all of the business about taking into consideration the kinds of shoes a woman might wear while driving, don't you think he would be accused of sexism?"

I chose not to answer. Instead, I called a good friend, Paula Hayden, a Washington area software developer who describes herself as "a fortyish, single, independent woman of means."

"It all sounds nice," Hayden said of the YCC. "But none of it will make or break a deal for me in buying a car."

Hayden currently owns a 2003 Mercedes-Benz E500 sedan, for which she paid $62,000. That car was a replacement for a 1998 Mercedes-Benz SL500, for which she paid $84,000. She's shopping for another car, possibly a Jaguar S-Type R, "because everybody seems to have a Mercedes-Benz E-Class."

"I don't want to be a part of somebody's everybody's-got-one parade," Hayden said. "I want something different, something that looks good on me, something exclusive."

Goodness! That sounds a lot like a man talking.

"Yeah, so what?" Hayden said. "I want the same thing any guy wants in a car, a house, a boat or anything else. The only difference is that I have the money and I can afford it, and a lot of men can't."

And then there is Elaine Jesmer, who runs her own public relations company in Los Angeles.

In matters automotive, Jesmer sees herself as the practical sort, the kind of person who would rather rent than buy a car. "It's transportation," she says.

I am tempted to believe her. Jesmer, after all, usually rents small cars, such as the Dodge Neon or Ford Focus. But on closer examination, her "It's transportation" claim comes off as being a ruse.

Why? Because Jesmer, whenever possible, rents the fastest, highest-horsepower cars she can find. Yes, she'll get a Neon. But it will be the sporty Neon SRT-4.

"I like to drive fast," she said. "I want the car to be small, but it has to be fast."

She hates SUVs. "Too big, too selfish, totally unnecessary," she said.

But if she ever weakened and entered a showroom to buy a car, she said she'd buy "my dream"—the super-high-horsepower V-10 Dodge Viper coupe.

But, hey, Elaine, isn't that a tad hypocritical?

"No," she said. "Because I'm never going to buy it. It's just a fantasy; and fantasies can be fabulous."

Car Makers Aim for the "Love It Or Hate It" Category

Why We'll See More Ugly Cars

Martin Wolk
(2003)

FYI Martin Wolk is chief economics correspondent for MSNBC and msnbc.com.

There is a very good reason the nation's auto showrooms are filling up with models that strike a lot of would-be buyers as just plain ugly. As it turns out, ugly sells.

Vehicles that make a mark with "extreme" styling — like the Chrysler PT Cruiser and Chevrolet Avalanche— move off the lot faster and generate a significantly higher profit margin than their plain-vanilla brethren, according to a study from J. D. Power and Associates.

Chrysler PT Cruiser (*left*)
Chevrolet Avalanche (*right*)

Of course, quirky looks are hardly any guarantee of success. Just think of the Edsel, a car so widely reviled for its looks that Ford halted production in just three years. More recently Saturn's new Ion sedan has struggled for sales at least in part because of its unusual appearance.

But some designers clearly are going out of their way to create bizarre-looking vehicles they know will instantly repulse many consumers, betting that others will be drawn in by the chance to own a vehicle that fits no traditional mold.

Just take a look at the box-on-wheels Scion xB from Toyota, which is being promoted to young would-be buyers in a promotional campaign that urges them to "rage against beige."

According to the [J. D. Power] study . . . , many quirkily styled cars like the Scion fall into the "love it or hate it" category. And while not all designers are actively trying to chase away part of the car-buying public, a bit of negative energy is not necessarily a bad thing, said Chris Denove, a partner at J. D. Power.

"It's OK to have a large group of people who hate the styling of your vehicle, as long as the same styling causes another group of people to say, 'I want that,'" he said.

J. D. Power surveyed 27,000 owners of new cars and trucks to find out why they avoided certain models when they were shopping. The No. 1 reason was styling, followed by concerns about reliability and cost.

Edsel (*top*)
Scion xB (*middle*)
Pontiac Aztek (*bottom*)

But considering that some smaller-brand models are never even considered by 90 percent or more of shoppers, a controversial style may be just what is needed to draw the curious into the showroom.

"It's better to polarize some shoppers than to generate mass apathy," Denove said.

It may not always be immediately apparent which vehicles fall into the love-it-or-hate-it category.

Some vehicles are almost universally beloved for their appearance. The Mini Cooper somewhat surprisingly falls into this category, as do luxury models like the Jaguar S-Type, Infiniti G-35 and Mercedes-Benz CLK.

Other cars have an appearance that is displeasing to just about everybody, such as the Pontiac Aztek, a classic ugly car that attracts buyers for other reasons, such as its versatility. According to results of the survey, "almost nobody bought [the Aztek] because of its styling," said Denove.

And of course there is a vast middle ground of cars styled so blandly they will offend almost nobody, while also inspiring little passion. The best-selling Honda Accord and Toyota Camry are standouts of the genre.

"Very few people either purchase or avoid those two vehicles because of styling," Denove said. "Because they are benchmarks in quality and reliability, the styling is far less important for the sales volume."

Cars that tend to polarize people include the PT Cruiser, the Avalanche and its sister Cadillac Escalade EXT, the Infiniti FX, and even the car Denove was driving as he answered questions about his survey, the retro-looking Ford Thunderbird convertible.

On average, such love-it-or-hate it models moved off the lot four days faster and carried a profit margin that was $609 higher than cars that ignited little passion over styling, according to the J. D. Power survey.

"Extreme styling, when it is successful, will allow the manufacturer to charge a price premium and more importantly avoid costly incentives," Denove said. The finding "not only helps explain the growth of extreme styling vehicles, it suggests we've only just seen the tip of the iceberg," he said.

Of course, manufacturers also run the risk of creating the next Edsel.

"There is a risk-reward when pushing the envelope in styling," Denove said.

CONSIDER

1. As a design cue, "love it or hate it" would seem to work better in some areas than in others. Identify some design efforts to which it might apply and others for which the strategy might be risky. You might consider clothing, shoes, hardware, electronic appliances, furniture, campaigns for political candidates, public buildings, museums, or monuments.

2. Even though vehicles are expensive items with practical purposes, the J. D. Power survey suggests that style is the primary reason some buyers avoid certain models, trumping reliability and cost. Would you cite this survey as evidence of the power of design, or might other factors explain why the style of a vehicle might matter more than other seemingly more important matters?

Periodically, the *New York Times* runs "My Life, My Car" features, exploring the connections between vehicles and their owners. It is no surprise that the profiles sometimes divulge a great deal about American culture.

My Life, My Cadillac Escalade EXT

Courtney Leigh Hyan, as told to Dana White
(2004)

WHO: Courtney Leigh Hyan, 16, high school sophomore, Yorba Linda, Calif.
WHAT: 2004 Cadillac Escalade EXT

I was expecting to get a watch for my 16th birthday, but I got a Cadillac pickup instead. All my friends drive trucks. My dad says, "I don't know what it is with girls today; they want pickups." I think it's the feminism factor. Usually guys are the ones who have pickups, but now girls are like, "Hey, we can have them, too." We get one, and the guys think it's cool. So it's a win-win.

The Escalade EXT is a luxury version of another G.M. pickup, the Chevy Avalanche. It has satellite radio, leather seats and a navigation system. I haven't used the G.P.S. yet, but I will—I get lost easily. I'm going to get custom chrome wheels and rims for it. My favorite brand is Lexani. They're so nice looking.

I'm a car nut, just like my dad. I'm also an only child, so I guess I'm a little like a son in that way. My dad and I used to buy car magazines at the grocery store and circle the cars we liked.

When I was 13, I started to think about what kind of car I wanted when I started to drive. I saw an EXT in a music video and thought, "Hey, having a pickup truck is way cuter than having a car." I started babysitting every week to save money for one. Then I went on the Cadillac Web site and saw how much it cost, and I thought that's a lot of babysitting. Finally, my parents told me if I got a 3.0 G.P.A. or higher on my report card, they'd buy me any car I wanted, within reason.

I started working on my dad. I kept telling him, "Have you seen the new Cadillac pickup trucks, Dad? They're really cool." After school I'd drag him down to the dealership in Fullerton to look at them. About three months ago, my dad bought a ranch in Park City, Utah, and I made him go to Jerry Seiner Cadillac, the dealership in Salt Lake City, to check out their EXTs. Dad kept asking me, "Do you really like this car?" I told him I loved it.

My birthday was Jan. 3. I wanted to spend it with my friends in Orange County, but my dad urged me to come to Park City. He said he was throwing me a party and inviting my favorite snowboarder, J. P. Walker, so I agreed. The party was at a restaurant called Easy Street, which has a big picture window that looks out on the street. I was waiting at the table thinking, where is this guy? So my parents suggested I open my presents. The last one looked like a watch box, but when I opened it, there were car keys inside. I looked out the window and saw a brand new EXT parked in front of the restaurant. It was the color I wanted: "Out of the Blue." I couldn't believe it. I was like, "Oh my God, are you serious?" I ran outside in the falling snow, climbed into the truck and sat there for a bit. Then I called my friends back in California on my cell. The whole thing was like a car commercial.

Driving my EXT makes me feel powerful, safe and very high. I feel as if everybody is looking at it, maybe because the color is so vibrant. You can make the cargo bed longer by folding down the rear seat, lowering a panel and removing the window. My dad said, "Now you can carry hay to the horses," and I was like, "I don't think so."

Some people may think my dad spoils me, but he knows how happy it makes me to drive. Cars are my thing. I'm never ungrateful for anything my parents give me. I feel totally blessed.

My dad drove my Escalade out to California last week. The first time I drove up to the school, about 25 girls came running out to look at it. "That is so cool," they cried. "We hate you!" It was like a dream come true. I felt like, "Wow, I'm a princess."

Explore this article in depth.
www.ablongman.com/beyondwords32

CONSIDER

1. Courtney suggests that feminism has made trucks more attractive to young women: "Usually guys are the ones who have pickups, but now girls are like, 'Hey, we can have them, too!'" Can you think of additional explanations for the appeal of the trucks? In what ways do pickups and large SUVs appeal to women?

2. Courtney describes her birthday as "like a car commercial." What elements of the story might work in a commercial? What elements might you have to modify? Why?

COMPOSE

3. The Avalanche is a real truck designed for hauling and towing. With no interest in such activities, Courtney Hyan—like many other Americans—now owns and drives a vehicle that is likely more trendy than practical. What responsibilities, if any, do designers bear for leading people, including sixteen-year-olds, into making choices driven more by passion ("That is so cool," they cried. "We hate you!") than good sense? Do designers have other choices?

Reading the Politics of Design

I f design reflects the values of a society, it must also be engaged with its politics. Indeed, "reading" the design patterns in our society is one way of appreciating its values. And creating a design—of a sneaker, for example—is a way of expressing or resisting those values.

Just how seriously designers take their work is evident in the texts in this section. We begin with a manifesto by a group of designers seeking to distance their profession from the hype and exploitation that surrounds it. But it may be impossible to separate the art of designers from the activities that earn them a living, especially advertising. That's the thesis of Jeffery Keedy's "Hysteria," a direct response to the manifesto. And it's even possible to read displays of commercialism optimistically, as Virginia Postrel's essay on trends in Christmas decorating illustrates. The section ends with a discussion of the nonprofit magazine *Adbusters*' Black Spot sneaker campaign. As you read, ask yourself: Is the design of this sneaker an act of political resistance, or is it ultimately just a different kind of sales pitch?

First Things First Manifesto 2000

Thirty-Three Designers
(1999)

W e, the undersigned, are graphic designers, art directors and visual communicators who have been raised in a world in which the techniques and apparatus of advertising have persistently been presented to us as the most lucrative, effective and desirable use of our talents. Many designs teachers and mentors promote this belief; the market rewards it; a tide of books and publications reinforces it.

Encouraged in this direction, designers then apply their skill and imagination to sell dog biscuits, designer coffee, diamonds, detergents, hair gel, cigarettes, credit cards, sneakers, butt toners, light beer and heavy-duty recre-

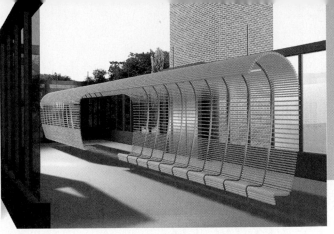

ational vehicles. Commercial work has always paid the bills, but many graphic designers have now let it become, in large measure, what graphic designers do. This, in turn, is how the world perceives design. The profession's time and energy [are] used up manufacturing demand for things that are inessential at best.

Many of us have grown increasingly uncomfortable with this view of design. Designers who devote their efforts primarily to advertising, marketing and brand development are supporting, and implicitly endorsing, a mental environment so saturated with commercial messages that it is changing the very way citizen-consumers speak, think, feel, respond and interact. To some extent we are all helping draft a reductive and immeasurably harmful code of public discourse.

There are pursuits more worthy of our problem-solving skills. Unprecedented environmental, social and cultural crises demand our attention. Many cultural interventions, social marketing campaigns, books, magazines, exhibitions, educational tools, television programs, films, charitable causes and other information design projects urgently require our expertise and help.

We propose a reversal of priorities in favor of more useful, lasting and democratic forms of communication—a mindshift away from product marketing and toward the exploration and production of a new kind of meaning. The scope of debate is shrinking; it must expand. Consumerism is running uncontested; it must be challenged by other perspectives expressed, in part, through the visual languages and resources of design.

In 1964, 22 visual communicators signed the original call for our skills to be put to worthwhile use. With the explosive growth of global commercial culture, their message has only grown more urgent. Today, we renew their manifesto in expectation that no more decades will pass before it is taken to heart.

(Signed)
Jonathan Barnbrook, Nick Bell, Andrew Blauvelt, Hans Bockting,
Irma Boom, Sheila Levrant de Bretteville, Max Bruinsma,
Siân Cook, Linda van Deursen, Chris Dixon, William Drenttel,
Gert Dumbar, Simon Esterson, Vince Frost, Ken Garland,
Milton Glaser, Jessica Helfand, Steven Heller, Andrew Howard,
Tibor Kalman, Jeffery Keedy, Zuzana Licko, Ellen Lupton,
Katherine McCoy, Armand Mevis, J. Abbott Miller, Rick Poynor,
Lucienne Roberts, Erik Spiekermann, Jan von Toorn, Teal Triggs,
Rudy Vanderlans, Bob Wilkinson

FYI Jeffery Keedy has been teaching in the Graphic Design Program at California Institute of the Arts since 1985. His design and essays have been published widely in design periodicals and books.

Hysteria

Jeffery Keedy
(2001)

To many, the word "design" is practically synonymous with commercial hype. You can't expect people to see a line between advertising and design when designers don't bother to draw one. But they had better draw one soon, because people are getting hysterical, and they're not after witches in Salem or commies in Hollywood. This time, they're after corporate tools like you.

In an era of inscrutable complexity, corporate marketing has become the one-cause-fits-all scapegoat for almost everything wrong with the world. Ecological chaos, racism, sexism, class warfare—you name it, you'll find it represented in corporate consumerism, because virtually everything today is connected to commerce. Best of all, marketing is an enemy that won't fight back; it needs you. No wonder designers are getting their Calvins in a knot. Who wants to be on the receiving end of all that rage?

As problem solvers, many designers would no doubt like to be a part of the solution to the problems created in the wake of global capitalism. But can they honestly be part of the solution when they remain a large part of the problem? This September, a guerrilla army in Prada shoes, toting Titanium PowerBooks, will be checking their Tumi luggage in at the Marriott Hotel in Washington, DC, to strategize their social and political engagement with capitalism. This revolution will not be televised, but it will have corporate sponsorship. At the annual AIGA [American Institute of Graphic Arts] conference, the designer-activists will no doubt accessorize their dissent with *Adbusters* magazine and a copy of Naomi Klein's *No Logo*, this fall's coolest anti-consumer consumables. At best, this designer insurrection is an honest attempt to "fight fire with fire;" at worst, it confirms social conscience and anti-consumerism as the test cultural fad (next year: yoga).

In the context of graphic design, anti-consumerism is a radical idea precisely because it doesn't make much sense. The graphic designer as anti-consumerist is a lot like the liquor company promoting responsible drinking, or the tobacco company discouraging underage smoking—maybe they're sincere, but it's hard to believe. Perhaps the bursting of the e-commerce bubble and the sudden interest in anti-consumerist design is more than just a coincidence. Are the designers who lost their jobs designing websites for the home delivery of butt toners now designing websites about the butt toner industry's use of sweatshop labor?

Design as a practice doesn't have much of a conscience, even if individual designers do. Design organizations have rules of ethical practice, but is anyone ever busted for breaking them? For the most part, the pseudo-profession of graphic design does not require a license because it is satisfactorily regulated by the marketplace. Designers can draft codes of behavior, make proclamations, sign manifestoes and offer up ideas and solutions to any number of problems. In the end, somebody has to buy what they create, or none of it is going anywhere.

Some designers believe they have found a liberating alternative to commercial servitude in culture jamming and subvertising. The idea is to topple existing power structures by subverting their messages, pulling pranks and being a pain in the corporate ass. In the ensuing chaos and anarchy, artists and designers start running the show, which needless to say, results in Utopia. Wow! A world run by artists and designers. That's pretty close to my idea of hell, but that may just be me.

A typical example of this type of intervention is to sneak around at night and illegally paste your clever one-liner on top of an existing clever one-liner on an advertisement nobody likes. This demonstrates to the world (for free) that you are equally clever and morally superior to those advertising hacks, and you're not buying what it is they're selling, so they had better listen to you . . . I mean, us! It's a strategy that transforms the artist's or designer's personally motivated aesthetic self-indulgence into a selfless act of civic duty. It's a trick the art world invented in the late '80s so that artists' self-importance could compete on a corporate and institutional scale.

No doubt culture jamming is fun—it's like being a good terrorist, how cool is that? But is being even more obnoxious than the enemy really the best answer? Forget about trying to one-up the ad hacks (you can't). The question is, why are you playing the same creepy game? The idea that a design intervention can drive consumer reform is putting the designer cart in front of the horse—it looks good but it doesn't work. And design, unlike art, is supposed to work.

So when I signed First Things First 2000, it wasn't because the world needs an anti-consumerist declaration of independence to encourage design

Technically, this is "doing something around the house."

shenanigans. If that was all I had read into the manifesto, I wouldn't have added my John Hancock.

Back in 1987, I gave a lecture entitled "Greasing the Wheels of Capitalism with Style and Taste," which I expanded into an essay for *Emigré* magazine in 1997. For the past 15 years I have watched advertising-oriented values infiltrate the culture of design. With the arrival of FTF2000, I could see that others had concerns along similar lines and that they wanted to open up the issue to a more general discussion. I have hoped that designers would establish their own ethics, free from commercial duplicity and without imitating art-world politics or pop-star platitudes. Maybe not a "new kind of meaning," but at least a new way of thinking. It was a good start to revisit the ideas behind the original, 1964 First Things First manifesto, but I would add to that the ideas of other designers and critics like Christopher Jones, George Nelson, Otl Aicher, Eva Zelsel and W. A. Dwiggins.

Ironically, designers can make their biggest social and political impact by not designing. After all, someone designs most of our ecological, social and cultural nightmares before they are unleashed on the world. Yes, it's helpful to make a pretty poster for the Save the Kittens Coalition, but it's hardly essential—a less fashionable choice of typeface or color won't jeopardize the cause. It's much more important to not stretch a magazine article into a 500-page hardbound book, or design a hot website-of-the-week that makes corporate jackals look like giggling pro-teens.

In the past decade, advertising has gotten a lot hipper and cooler, due in large part to a handful of talented graphic designers handpicked from design annuals and magazines. They get to make a ton of money and work on big projects that otherwise would never come to them, while the ad agencies get the best talent and make more money still. This exchange has created a handful of design superstars, while turning the profession into an art ghetto where advertising "creatives" shop for cheap, disposable talent. Now there is an endless supply of young designers trying to get noticed— "Pick me, pick me next!"—because design conferences and magazines celebrate opportunist sellouts, as if they were doing us all a big favor. Gee, thanks!

Designers think of themselves as good people whose clients make them do bad things—the "I was only following orders" defense. This is usually followed by the "a person's got to make a living" defense, as if the only way a designer can make ends meet is by crafting insipid propaganda for multinational corporations. The debate about the designer's responsibility in society tends to get polarized between powerless complicity and social actualization. The vast majority of designers work somewhere in the middle, within subtle gradations, and it is in these gray areas that distinctions need to be made. That is, in the real world, not the theoretical extremities.

If you are a corporate tool, at least be a good one. Everyone knows the difference between engaging and deceptive messages. If you are doing work that you feel conflicted about, however, don't kid yourself that some pro bono work or anonymous culture jamming will even the score. It doesn't, and stop pretending you're an artist, because you're not.

Try to make less, and make it better; brands should be memorable because they are good, not because they are omnipresent. The difference between design and advertising used to be that design was informative, not persuasive; compelling, not intrusive; and intelligent, not just clever. What's the difference now? Truth in advertising is an oxymoron, but does it have to be in design as well? The increasingly personal and invasive presence of marketing and corporate control in people's lives has provoked global hysteria. Design has played a part in the problem, but, unlike advertising, design can also help offer an alternative—and this time, a real alternative.

CONSIDER

1. What role would designers have in a society without a consumer culture? Would such a culture support the kinds of products that Jeffery Keedy chides the designers for owning themselves, such as Prada shoes, Titanium PowerBooks, and Tumi luggage? Is such a criticism fair? Why or why not?

2. Keedy suggests that a worthy cause won't be sunk by an inept poster. Do you agree? Can you point to public service or political advertising that did change the way you look at things?

COMPOSE

3. Using Keedy's essay and the Web, explore the notion of "culture jamming." Define the concept, and look for particular examples of the phenomenon in your town or on your campus. Sources might include the graffiti on buses, articles in alternative newspapers or magazines, or riffs on radio talk shows or late-night TV programs. In a brief essay, assess the impact, if any, of culture jamming.

CHALLENGE

4. Use the following sentence from Keedy's "Hysteria" as the starting point for a project in which you explore his claim: "The difference between design and advertising used to be that design was informative, not persuasive; compelling, not intrusive; and intelligent, not just clever." You can write a paper with Keedy's sentence as the lead-in, create a montage examining or challenging his thesis, or assemble a photo essay or Web site to explore its implications.

FYI Virginia Postrel is a cultural critic and author of *The Substance of Style: How the Rise of Aesthetic Value is Remaking Commerce, Culture, and Consciousness.*

Light unto the Wealth of Nations

Virginia Postrel
(2003)

As Christmas lights go up on homes around the country, you've probably noticed that the displays seem to get more elaborate every year. No longer does decorating a single evergreen in the front yard suffice. Every tree demands its own ropes of light, wrapping trunks as well as branches. Ubiquitous icicle lights drape even the most generic tract home in sparkling abundance.

Arbiters of taste may clash over the merits of white versus colored bulbs, and energy Puritans may denounce the inessential use of electricity. But even stylistic snobs can't entirely deny the appeal of a thousand points of holiday light.

Today's lavish displays do more than brighten the night. They tell a story of economic progress. Like the electronic gadgets aimed at gift buyers, the tiny lights outlining rooflines and tree limbs illustrate new sources of growth, productivity, and prosperity. Aesthetic pleasure, they tell us, is an increasingly important source of economic value and hence of new jobs and business opportunities. And the same trends that boost living standards in other areas also make Christmas lights more abundant.

A holiday-lighting dollar simply goes further than it used to. Homeowners buying Christmas lights benefit from the same intense retail and manufacturing competition that have driven down prices and improved reliability in so many other industries, raising the American standard of living.

As a teenager in the mid-1980s, David VanderMolen's job was to buy and install holiday lights for his family's Charlotte, Michigan, home. Each year his parents would give him $10, enough for two 35-light strings, each 20 feet long, from Kmart. If the weather wasn't too bad, a string of lights would last

about three years. VanderMolen eventually built up a collection of 350 miniature lights, enough to make his house the most elaborately decorated in the neighborhood.

Today, that display would be nothing special. You can buy a 100-light string, nearly 50 feet long, for $2.44 at Wal-Mart. Even without adjusting for inflation, VanderMolen's old $10 annual budget would cover more lights in a single year than he could accumulate over seven years in the 1980s. Today's cheaper lights, mostly made in China, also last longer.

"The stuff now is so well made that you can put it up in November before it gets too cold or wet, and leave it up until a January thaw, and it doesn't all fall apart," says VanderMolen.

As a result, today's homeowners can put on light shows that would have made theme park news a generation ago. Says VanderMolen, "It is easy and inexpensive to put up a tasteful display, and not much more cost or effort to try and humiliate your weak-willed neighbors."

Not everyone wants to climb around on the roof, however, and not everyone has the skills to put together an attractive display. More and more homeowners are contracting out the lighting work, creating satisfying jobs that never existed before. It's part of the long-term trend toward greater and greater specialization. The business also illustrates just how experience improves productivity even in service industries.

Christmas Décor, based in Lubbock, Texas, has more than 350 franchise locations throughout the U.S. and Canada. The company estimates that its franchisees do more than $32 million in holiday light business a year. (At least four other national companies offer similar franchises.) Most franchisees are landscaping companies looking for ways to keep working through the slow winter months. Like the inventory controls that have improved efficiency in manufacturing, adding a holiday lighting service allows landscapers to avoid the boom and bust of hiring and laying off employees.

Franchisers like Christmas Décor give local contractors the benefits of scale—not only buying lights by the container load but learning from experience. Christmas Décor franchisees serve about 300,000 customers each year. "The information you receive from that kind of volume is scientific," says Brandon Stephens, the company's director of marketing. "If there's a problem, it's going to repeat."

If one local contractor figures out a way to save labor, the company incorporates the technique nationwide, changing its vendor specifications if necessary. To make wrapping tree branches more efficient, for instance, Christmas Décor has suppliers deliver lights in balls rather than lined up on cards, the way homeowners shopping at Wal-Mart find them.

Hiring a lighting contractor saves homeowners trouble and raises quality expectations, creating a ratchet effect that in turn generates more demand for specialists.

People who do the same job over and over again get better and better at it. They hang lights in more consistently attractive patterns. The more people see professional displays, the more they expect to be wowed. Although lighting contractors do some direct marketing, their most effective advertising is the impressively decorated house down the block. Exposure creates demand.

"The more lights that go up, the more lights that go up," says Tom Tolkacz, president of Swingle Tree Co., a Christmas Décor franchisee in Denver. His business has about 70 employees during the holiday season, 20 to 30 more than before Swingle added the lighting franchise. (At its seasonal peak, the landscaping company employs about 200 people.) Its lighting business continued to grow right through the recession, posting some of its greatest gains ever in 2001 and 2002.

Most customers are two-income couples with homes valued at $400,000 or more, says Tolkacz, a "middle market" of people who would not have hired professionals in the past. Some less affluent single parents also hire the company because they "don't want to get on the roof." The service appeals more to baby boomers than to the over-60 crowd, who tend to believe that hiring someone to install holiday lights is frivolous.

That disparaging attitude toward aesthetics affects us not only as consumers deciding where to spend our money but as citizens trying to understand the sources of future economic growth. We mourn the loss of manufacturing jobs—"real jobs"—and ignore growing aesthetic professions, from installing holiday lights and landscaping lawns to giving manicures and facials, from designing brochures to crafting granite countertops.

Yet in an advanced economy, in which competition is pushing the prices of goods ever lower and their quality ever higher, enhancing the look and feel of people, places, and things will become more and more important over time. Just as surely as the horsepower of a car engine or the warmth of a blanket, the pleasure of twinkling Christmas lights offers real value.

CONSIDER

1. Postrel attributes the elaboration of holiday displays to lowered costs, which enable more people to exercise their design and aesthetic sensibilities. Can you suggest other motives for these conspicuous displays?

2. Is the aesthetic pleasure consumers get from their lighting displays lessened if they are created by professionals? Postrel suggests otherwise, pointing to other areas where a sense of style is driving new industries in developed countries. Can you offer additional examples, or do you find her argument unconvincing?

COMPOSE

3. Working in a group, make a list of design or consumer trends that seem insignificant. (Remember, too, that a trend may indicate the disappearance of objects or phenomena, such as pay phones in public places.) Then choose one trend and write an essay like Postrel's, studying the implications of the design trend.

Linda Baker is a freelance journalist based in Portland, Oregon. Her work focuses on the changing status of the American family, land use and transportation planning and the environment. Baker's essays have appeared in *Sierra, E, The Progressive, Utne Reader*, and many other publications.

For years, the non-profit magazine *Adbusters* has published parodies and articles that use the design language of commercial images to critique U.S. consumer culture and corporate practices. Its Black Spot sneaker campaign, described in the images and texts that follow, ventures into new design territory—the actual creation and production of a product.

Salon.com asks "Are you ready for some 'unswooshing'"?

Linda Baker
(October, 2003)

Kalle Lasn isn't scared of the U.S. PATRIOT Act. "America has become a bit of a monster," says the punchy, 60-something founder of Adbusters, the anti-consumption magazine based in Vancouver, B.C. "Some of the things the U.S. is doing, in Israel, in Cancún with the WTO, I just can't take it any longer. It's gotten to the point where I almost think I've become a terrorist."

But Lasn is no Osama bin Laden. The author of "Culture Jam: How to Reverse America's Suicidal Binge," Lasn is one of the leading figures in the "culture jamming" movement, an international grassroots effort that uses the logic of commercial images to critique corporate hegemony and rampant consumerism. Under his leadership, Adbusters' preferred method of culture jamming has been to publish ad parodies, such as "Absolute Impotence," a photo of the familiar bottle drifting in spilled vodka, or a Nike satire that morphs Tiger Woods' smile into a Swoosh.

Last month, Adbusters announced a new phase in state-of-the-art meme warfare. ("Memes" refer to the core images, slogans or ideas that culture

Adbuster's home page for the Blackspot Sneaker, designed to market an anti-corporate shoe

jammers manipulate: e.g., a swoosh, or "Just Do It.") Although the campaign's targets, Nike and CEO Phil Knight, appear frequently in the magazine's culture jams, the latest strategy moves Adbusters out of the realm of parody and into the competitive world of global marketing and production.

More specifically, the Adbusters Media Foundation, the nonprofit that brought the world Buy Nothing Day and TV Turnoff Week, has decided to go into the sneaker manufacturing business. According to Lasn, the plan is to market a "Black Spot sneaker, a shoe that will resemble the retro-style Converse but with one crucial difference." In place of the ubiquitous Nike swoosh, the Adbusters shoe will display a prominent anti-logo "black spot," the magazine's anti-corporate trademark.

"Phil Knight had a dream," reads the, well, ad for the "Unswoosher," located on the back cover of Adbusters' October issue. "He'd sell shoes. He'd sell dreams. He'd get rich. He'd use sweatshops if he had to. Then along came a new shoe. Plain. Simple. Cheap. Fair. Designed for only one thing: kicking Phil's ass."

By January, the magazine plans to manufacture an initial line of 10,000 sneakers, which will retail globally for about $65 a pair. The release will follow a $500,000 marketing campaign, hyping the sneakers on CNN, in the *New York Times*, and on the major networks. "One of the many reasons I really love this campaign," said Lasn. "Is that we are selling a product, not an idea or advocacy. We are selling a sneaker. So those stations that have systematically refused to sell us air time over the past 10 years for our ideas will now have no choice but to sell us air time."

Since the nonprofit broke the news of the Black Spot late last August, Nike hasn't exactly been shaking in its shoes. "As a global leader, it doesn't surprise us that we occasionally get targeted by groups who use the strength of our brand to leverage their agenda," said Caitlin Morris, senior manager of Nike corporate communications.

Reaction on the anti-corporate-globalization front has been mixed. Some question the wisdom of an anti-advertising magazine going into the advertising business, while others think Lasn would be better off targeting clothing manufacturers that don't receive as much international scrutiny. But for some heavy hitters in the no-sweatshop movement, the Black Spot couldn't have come at a more propitious time—just days after the Converse brand sold out the "Chuck Taylor" shoe to Nike. For years, that was the sneaker of choice for millions opposed to megabrands churning out sneakers in Third World factories.

"The anti-sweatshop forces need a few alternatives in the marketplace," says Jeff Ballinger, author of the original *Harpers' Magazine* 1993 exposé on Nike's labor practices, and now vice president for policy and sourcing at No Sweat. "Kalle's right to see that. I've given 'sweatshop' talks to a wide variety of groups for over a decade and one of the first questions is: 'What can we buy?'"

Lasn admits the "ethical sneaker" may not succeed. Still, employing what appears to be a signature combination of brashness and nostalgia, Lasn said the time has come for a change in how activists deal with "rogue companies."

"We got tired of all the lefty whining and the boycotting. It wasn't making any difference," he said. "Quite apart from how many percentage points in market share the Black Spot sneaker can take away from Phil Knight—that's of course the ultimate goal but may be a long time coming—in the meantime, we can go a long way toward uncooling the Swoosh, which is losing momentum fast." "I have a grandiose plan," Lasn said. "My dream as a culture jammer is that a small group of people with a limited budget could have the power to choose a megabrand we don't like for valid reasons and uncool that brand, to show that we the people as a civil society have the power to keep a corporation honest. Now that would be something that would actually redefine capitalism."

Adbusters, which has a circulation of 120,000, bills itself as the "Journal of the Mental Environment." The magazine's philosophy is that advertising encourages people to see themselves primarily as consumers, and its parodies reveal the "truth" behind slick corporate logos: the environmental and human costs of consumption, the abuses of corporate power, and private monopolization of public airwaves.

Lasn, whose descriptions of Knight [. . .] bear a certain resemblance to the "axis of evil" rhetoric coming out of Washington, D.C., is the former head of a market research company in Tokyo. As a culture critic, his diatribes against Nike don't focus on the athletic footwear corporation's labor practices per se, but on the notion of branding in general and the "pseudo-empowerment" brand that Nike attaches to its products in particular. Citing research on the 3000 marketing images most people consume every day, as well as studies linking advertising to an increase in mood disorders, Lasn said rage against the toxic cultural clutter epitomized by Nike ads is going to launch a new kind of revolution.

"Twenty-five years ago we woke up to the fact that the chemicals in our food, water and air, even a few parts of a billion, actually will give you cancer," he said. "That was when the modern environmental movement was born. Once people make that connection between advertising and their own mental health, that could be the birth of the modern mental health environmental movement."

When that moment happens, said Lasn, "we will suddenly see the $400 billion worldwide industry collapse to half its size." But for some, Lasn's railing against the Orwellian force of advertising is exactly what makes his decision to market a Black Spot sneaker a bit curious. After all, we live in a world where AIDS, crime and all sorts of global unrest have been turned into fodder for Benetton ads. The medium, as they say, is the message.

This is why people like Naomi Klein, Canadian author of the landmark text "No Logo," aren't quite so enthusiastic about the revolutionary potential of the Unswoosher. "Publications that analyze the commercialization of our lives have a responsibility to work to protect spaces where we aren't constantly being pitched to," she told the *Toronto Globe & Mail*. "This can be undermined if they are seen as simply shilling for a different 'anti-corporate' brand." Lasn disagrees.

"Nike's empowerment is pseudo-empowerment," he says. "But if we are actually able to launch an anti-brand, then the empowerment around the black spot is actually a real kind of empowerment: the power of us the people to have a business climate that is to our liking. It's the most beautiful kind of empowerment I can think of."

Adbusters launched Buy Nothing Day, says Lasn. "But we never said it's bad to buy something, just bad to buy too much." What's more, promoting the Black Spot sneaker will not be Adbusters' first foray into "real" advertising. The magazine has been raising money to get a Black Spot ad, a series of anti-corporate, anti-U.S. phrases set to Jimi Hendrix's rendition of "The Star Spangled Banner," on television. Although all the major networks have rejected the ad, CNN has aired the Black Spot promo—during the *Crossfire* political debate program.

At Adbusters' offices, located in a Vancouver residential district, the Unswoosher enterprise has something of a Mouse That Roared quality to it. A newly hired business manager is working on locating investors and distributors for the Black Spot. The magazine has already taken preorders for 1,000 pairs, and will use its nest egg of $250,000 to bankroll the initial 10,000 sneakers. According to Lasn, people are "coming out of the woodwork" to offer advice about where the Black Spot should be manufactured—and what kind of labor to use.

Industry watchers are skeptical. "[Adbusters] has absolutely no idea how complicated global production and marketing is," says John Horan, pub-

lisher of *Sporting Goods Intelligence.* The magazine could save time and money, he suggested, by selling T-shirts emblazoned with "We want to kick Phil Knight's butt" for $10 each.

Ignoring the naysayers, Adbusters has generated a final list of three possible factories: a factory in Missouri, referred by a former Nike employee who has inspected more than 70 factories worldwide, and two union factories in Asia: one in South Korea, and another in Indonesia. The latter were recommended by Ballinger, whom Lasn has retained to help Adbusters source a union factory for the Unswoosher.

Lasn obviously relishes the idea of manufacturing the sneaker in Missouri. But just as he rejects the argument that there is something problematic about Adbusters advertising shoes, so he has contrarian things to say about some of the anti-sweatshop rhetoric governing the international workers' rights debate. In particular, he says, the "go local" movement is overrated, propelled more by trade unions than activists.

"I have a huge amount of disdain for all those people who are trying to keep all the jobs in North America," he said. "Here we are, the richest part of the world, we're only 5 percent of people in the world, and all of a sudden we're losing a few doldrums in our economy. Let's give the jobs to the Koreans and Indonesians. They need it more, and if we can find a good factory and if we could promote workers' rights worldwide, all the better."

The Estonian-born Lasn recalled a seminal trip he took around the Third World when he was in his 20s. "I know from personal experience that many of those factories that campus people dismiss as sweatshop labor are actually very good factories," he says, "and that the people who live near those factories are just yearning to work in those factories. A good part of those sweatshop people are seriously misguided."

If Lasn's idea of pulling Third World workers up by their bootstraps mimics the language of liberal capitalism—not to mention Phil Knight—it's also an idea that reverberates across segments of the no-sweatshop apparel movement.

"Globalization is an opportunity to globalize the labor movement," says Ballinger. "Today, the only way to protect a worker's job anywhere is to defend worker's rights everywhere." The Black Spot sneaker represents a clear step forward in the anti-sweatshop movement, says Ballinger. "If the union-made Black Spot sneaker can kick Phil Knight where he feels it—in the pocketbook, we won't get more window dressing from Nike and Reebok; we'll get a real change in policy."

But Marsha Dickson, director of Educators for Socially Responsible Apparel Business, says the Black Spot campaign is naïve in light of efforts that have been made by Nike and other members of the Fair Labor Association, a coalition of industry, university and nongovernmental organizations that issued its first public report in June.

"While the tracking charts clearly show that much work remains to be done," said Dickson via e-mail, "the bottom line is that Nike, Reebok and Adidas are really acting as leaders. If a campaign such as [the Black Spot sneaker] is needed, it should focus attention to the thousands of clothing manufacturers and retailers that are not participating in the FLA. We know nothing or very little about how these companies treat the workers that make their products." The FLA was the recipient of the $1.5 million Kasky vs. Nike settlement in June. In 1998, Marc Kasky, a California anti-globalization activist, sued Nike for allegedly stretching the truth in its statements regarding contract factory labor practices in Asia. The California Supreme Court agreed with Kasky in a 4-3 ruling. Nike then appealed to the U.S. Supreme Court. Corporate interests had paid close attention to the case, in which Nike claimed that what it said—whether or not it was true—was non-commercial speech protected under the First Amendment.

At its Sept. 22 shareholders' meeting in Portland, Ore., Nike stockholders celebrated their first protester-free gathering in several years. The footwear company registered a record $10.7 billion in revenue in its 2003 fiscal year, and its stock price increased 40 percent, to a high of $62.50 in late September.

Lasn, about to fly off to Indonesia in his newly minted role as factory inspector, is undeterred. The Black Spot sneaker, he says, is part of a larger goal to "tweak the genetic code of corporations": an anti-corporate-globalization process that ranges from rewriting the rules under which corporate charters are reviewed and revoked, to a general "crusade against bigness."

"I grew up in a time when cynicism didn't exist," says Lasn, "that hidden assumption that nothing can change, that you better get used to capitalism, and that cultural revolution is not even possible."

"I don't quite see it that way. I am old enough to have seen a number of cultural revolutions. I believe another one is coming up."

Explore the politics of design in consumer culture.
www.ablongman.com/beyondwords33

CONSIDER

1. Visit the Black Spot Sneaker Web site (http://adbusters.org/metas/corpo/ blackspotsneaker/ home.html) and look closely at how the site is composed. How would you characterize this site's design language? How does the design of the site reinforce or work against the magazine's goal of creating an "anti-brand" product?

2. In your opinion, would buying a pair of Black Spot Sneakers be a politically meaningful act? Why or why not?

3. How would you characterize the tone and word choices Lasn uses in Linda Baker's article to express his disdain for Nike and for Nike CEO Phil Knight? How do these choices influence your impression of Lasn? Do you find his comments persuasive? Credible?

CHALLENGE

4. Choose a consumer product or organization and examine its brand logo or advertising campaign. Then create a parody ad for that product or organization, using the company's own design language to subvert or criticize the product. Use an image editor to dummy up an actual ad. Lacking the technical expertise, you might sketch the parody you would create and briefly annotate it.

Assignments and Projects

Project 1

Analyzing the Design of an Everyday Text

For this assignment, we'd like you to look closely at the design of a text or object that you use in your everyday life—a box of cereal, your favorite CD, or a pair of jeans, for example. Then write a 3–5 page analysis that carefully describes its design and speculates about what messages about identity, values, or culture that the design suggests.

What does an analysis of this kind look like? See "Girl Power Gone Wrong" by Elizabeth Catanese (pages 500-502), which was written in response to this assignment. Also consider the following questions, first introduced in Chapter 1, as you plan and draft your project.

WHAT'S IT TO YOU?

■ This assignment offers you a chance to take a second look at items in your daily life that you might otherwise take for granted. So choose as your **topic** an object or text that's familiar, but which sparks your curiosity. Suppose you stop at a coffee shop for an extra-large iced latte every morning on your way to class. What does your latte say about you? What does it suggest about university life, or about our culture in general? For instance, why do so many Americans drink nearly a quart of coffee in one sitting, when in other parts of the world, a standard coffee cup holds about 8 ounces?

WHAT DO YOU WANT TO SAY ABOUT IT?

■ Your **purpose** in analyzing the text or object you've chosen is to carefully describe and analyze the design choices that went into its creation. Don't feel obligated, however, to stop here. Take the next step and offer some conclusions about how the design elements work together to affect behavior or to suggest particular values or meanings.

WHO WILL LISTEN?

- Since you will be writing about everyday items, your **audience** will likely be familiar with the general kind of object or text you're discussing: almost everyone has been to a coffee shop, owned a pair of jeans, or read the back of a cereal box. But you'll need to provide detailed descriptions of the particular subject of your analysis: the extra-large iced latte, the Calvin Klein low-rise jeans, or the box of Honey-Nut Cheerios. Incorporate images into the paper, if possible, to help readers see what you're talking about.

WHAT DO YOU NEED TO KNOW?

- Begin with a close examination of the object or text you're discussing; take notes on how it's put together and keep your eyes open for interesting or unexpected patterns. Although most of your material for the project will come from direct **observation**, you should do **background research** in the library or online, if needed, to find out basic facts about the text or object you're studying and its creator.

HOW WILL YOU DO IT?

- Many of the **analytical skills** required for this assignment you already possess—you've developed and practiced them throughout this chapter. After studying the text or object carefully and taking notes, identify key design features and come to some conclusions about the messages these features suggest. Then consider the best **structure** for this project. Many analysis essays begin with a careful description of the text or object at hand, move on to identify patterns of meaning, and then end with conclusions about the larger implications of those patterns.

HOW WELL DOES IT WORK?

- Check that the logistical elements of the paper work smoothly: If you've incorporated images, are they clear and readable? Have you documented any outside source materials? Does the structure and content of your analysis make sense—can readers move easily from idea to idea as you develop your analysis? Solicit **feedback** about the project and make necessary **revisions.**

STUDENT SAMPLE

Elizabeth Catanese, "Girl Power Gone Wrong"

Catanese 1

Elizabeth Catanese

Professor Friend

Introduction to Rhetoric

14 May 2005

Girl Power Gone Wrong

"Girl Power," a pop-culture movement centering on female empower-ment, arrived on the American culture scene in the mid-1990s, riding a tide propelled by The Spice Girls' Wannabe and the American soccer vic-tory in the women's World Cup. Its manifestations included the PowerPuff Girls cartoon series, Britney Spears, and "girls rule!" buttons on elemen-tary school backpacks. The popularity of "girl power" has influenced not only the entertainment industry, but also fashion. In 2003, I purchased a grey T-shirt reading "Queen of the Universe" at a South Carolina branch of the Marshall's chain. The shirt's message seems empowering. However, when its design is closely analyzed, the shirt as a whole is anything but empowering. Even in the midst of "girl power," evidence of a male-centered power structure remains.

Manufactured by One, the 100% cotton shirt is designed to be worn in a classic eighties fashion. With an oversized neck and token sleeves, it hangs off one shoulder, revealing both of the wearer's collarbones. The neckline plunges halfway between the wearer's breasts and neck; the bottom hem reaches only to mid-belly, and it sports two long edges, which tie together to form a knot on the wearer's left side.

The selling point of the shirt, however, is the bold, black letters cen-tered in the middle, dotted with silver glitter. QUEEN OF THE UNIVERSE, the shirt proclaims. Below the word QUEEN is a large circle, fashioned to look like a royal seal. OF and THE flank the seal in a smaller font, and UNIVERSE curves along the bottom. The top of the seal, curving around with the circle, reads GOT A PROBLEM?, and the bottom proclaims

GENUINE ARTICLE.

  The middle of the seal is a stylized representation of a crown, reminiscent of the type worn for state occasions by the Queen of England. The jewels lowest on the crown resemble lipstick kisses, and the middle jewel is a cross-like emblem, flanked by two fleurs-de-lis. Sitting vertically in the middle of the design, the crowning jewel reminds the viewer of nothing so much as a screw.

  And what does the wearer have to be, to be QUEEN OF THE UNIVERSE? First and foremost, small. The shirt is sized as an extra large, yet perfectly fit to a size five frame. Second, the queen has to be skinny; the shirt style popularized in the eighties coincided with a glamorization of the supermodels' anorexic frame: this is a shirt designed to showcase poking collarbones. The shirt is also too short to wear without displaying a line of bare belly. No one carrying excess weight would dare wear a shirt this small; to do so would risk displaying "unsightly" abdominal rolls ("Showing skin is a privilege, not a right," I've often heard male friends gripe).

  This queen also has to be daring: the shirt is almost impossible to wear with a standard bra, and only marginally easier with a strapless. The wearer either resigns herself to showing her bra straps, or does without-- and doing without, in this shirt, means taking the utmost care in leaning over. The queen has to be something of an exhibitionist.

  What kind of royal treatment does this QUEEN OF THE UNIVERSE receive from her subjects? The center of her crown is a screw, a common slang term for a sexual encounter. This euphemism sits at the pinnacle of her crown, as the focal point of her symbol of power. This queen of the universe, then, gets and keeps her power through sex. She may be a queen, but the center of her power is the ubiquitous phallic symbol. The empowerment of the statement is undercut by this image. This queen has a title, but she earns the title through her ability to please the eye of the man.

  You GOT A PROBLEM? This queen expects problems with her rule-- the shirt anticipates them--and answers them not in a statement, but a question. The question mark invites disagreement, begs for an answer, and further undercuts the queen's authority. Underneath GOT A PROBLEM? are the words GENUINE ARTICLE, which add a hint of desperation to the claim, a need to proclaim oneself genuine to those who might question the shirt's (and the wearer's) authenticity.

This shirt seems to empower, but the power is an illusion--not only is the queen subject to patriarchal ideals of the female body (small and thin), but she is also on display to them. The queen gets her authority from the sexualized symbol in the center of her crown. The message that seems to validate her power is still dependent on men, and her reign as queen depends not on her worth, but on whether or not her subjects (presumably male) enjoy her body. Even in the midst of "girl power," this T-shirt shows us a woman still dependent on men.

Project 2
Studying Design and Its Contexts

For this assignment, you will conduct research to explore the relationships between design and its historical and cultural contexts. The more specific your topic the better, though some big questions might intrigue you: for example, how did the great pyramids of ancient Egypt reflect the political power of the Pharaohs who created them? How did murals produced during the Great Depression depict the realities of class conflict? You can conduct some of your research on the Internet, but you should also locate sources using library databases.

Before beginning, look at Sean Nixon's paper on pages 504–509 for an example of how one student writer responded to this assignment. Also consider these questions, first presented in Chapter 2:

WHAT'S IT TO YOU?

- Thinking about the cultural dimensions of design should afford numerous opportunities to choose a **topic** that speaks to your interests. Issues of gender, for instance, can be addressed as you look at a variety of designs. Consider other human concerns—economics, relationships, communities, politics, social movements—anything that will help you emphasize the connections between design and culture.

WHAT DO YOU WANT TO SAY ABOUT IT?

■ You may be able to make a point about a design simply by placing it in a context: big fins on cars during the booming 1950s, for example. Or you may want to study a subject that requires you to connect the dots because the connection between the product and its context may not be obvious.

WHO WILL LISTEN?

■ Be careful about how you frame the connections you discover between design and culture. It may seem clear to you that a design, for instance, capitalizes on concerns for the environment, but not every one of your **readers** is likely to agree that the strategy is admirable. Different readers bring their perspectives and biases to bear on what you have written. With historical designs and their issues you may need to create more informational compositions to bring readers up to date.

WHAT DO YOU NEED TO KNOW?

■ **Research** will allow you to create a project that ties together design with culture. Some of this research may involve learning more about the evolution of designs—for instance, you might track down information on aircraft design to understand its influence on other, seemingly unrelated products. Or you may need to look deeper into issues of culture—for instance, examining family structures from the 1950s to analyze an advertisement. Spell out in detail the connections you find.

HOW WILL YOU DO IT?

■ Begin by finding the right **topic.** You might start with some designs that simply call out to you. Or you may start with a cultural concern. Use the Internet and some library databases to collect information about your topic. Also locate **images** that you can analyze.

HOW WELL DOES IT WORK?

■ Check that you make connections between the designs you discuss and social issues. Be sure as well that you consider how your readers will react to any positions inherent in your discussion of culture and design. Make sure that a process of analysis shows up in your composition—discuss characteristics of what you analyze, make comparisons, explain patterns, and show the details that matter. Solicit **feedback**, and **revise** your work to make it stronger.

Once you have considered these questions, compose a four- to five-page essay in which you discuss design in terms of historical and cultural contexts. (You may compose for the Web if you wish.)

STUDENT SAMPLE

Sean Nixon, "The Transformation of American Architecture during the 1920s and 1930s"

Sean Nixon

Professor Nardgne

English 201

November 22, 2004

The Transformation of American

Architecture during the 1920s and 1930s

A combination of structure, function, and aesthetics, architecture tangibly illustrates the society of which it is a part. Society dictates which qualities of architecture it most values, and in this way society molds the look, feel, and mood of its buildings. Not only does society affect architecture, but architecture also influences society in a symbiotic relationship. Society "defines the uses of its buildings" and "sets the price it is willing to pay for architecture in competition with other things." In return architecture "acts as a catalyst" in that it "provides symbols, reinforces conservatism or encourages a people to be adventurous" (Burchard and Bush-Brown 4). Architecture can provide a historical snapshot, for often designs can "divulge what the men in power were like who built them, when they were built, and why" (4). An investigation of American architecture during the 1920s and 1930s reveals how architecture relates to the culture that creates it. From the big business internalization of Coolidge to the New Deal progressivism of Roosevelt, this period was marked by severe jolts in the history of America, and architecture responded to changes accordingly.

By the end of World War I in 1918, the world had witnessed a terrible and violent spectacle the likes of which it had never seen. In America, citizens were disillusioned and their fundamental beliefs disrupted.

Despite the irreversible changes the Great War inflicted on American principles, American citizens "tried desperately to pretend that nothing had changed at all, that there had been no entanglement, that the world was just as wide and Europe was just as far away as ever" (Gowans 421). The war gave Americans a vision of a "sick" and "corrupt" Europe, and in the early 1920s a move toward pure Americanism ensued. However, this push was superficial and short-lived. Socially, President Coolidge unsuccessfully attempted Prohibition to purify the soul. In dealing with foreign affairs the government tried isolation through high tariffs and anti-immigration laws. Politically the idea of "normalcy" prevailed (Gowans 422).

Architecture followed suit in an attempt to revert to a Victorian style of design. The result borrowed an eclectic mix of historical styles that falsely boasted of "modernism" and "Americanism." This form of design was no more than a simplified "colonial" style. The clearest example of this superficial attempt at a unique cultural design is exemplified in the "period house" (see fig. 1). This type of house, resembling a colonial cottage, borrows obvious details from historic styles and presents them in a simplified manner. For many people, these forms portrayed "the concept of American life as somehow distinctly plainer and purer than that of degenerate Europeans" (Gowans 424). Such provincial and insular ideas

Fig. 1. Period house, 1926 (Gowans 423)

7 | EXPLORING DESIGN

"made the [early] 1920s a dark [period] of modern architecture in America" (424). Even the "wholly American bred" concept of the sky-scraper suffered from this narrowmindedness (Koeper and Whiffen 320). Despite the technologically advanced principles behind these massive new structures, they still derived their design "not from present or future, but from the past" (Gowans 424).

When the time came to take nominations for a skyscraper design for the Chicago Tribune Building (1922), the majority of entries came from European architects. One of the most acclaimed designs was submitted by the Finnish architect Eliel Saarinen, whose plan came in second in the contest. Interestingly, though, Saarinen did not introduce any radical ideas or philosophies, which is the key reason his design was so widely accepted (see fig. 2). Only because his "modern architecture" was "so far from radical . . . and so close in spirit to the period house" (Gowans 428) were plans for his buildings approved. The "radical character found in other foreign architects' submissions" would not have an impact on sky-scraper design until decades later (Koeper and Whiffen 329).

The Chicago Tribune skyscraper provides a clear example of architec-ture clinging to the past. The idea of a skyscraper, a monumental and technologically advanced structure, is contradicted here by the eclectic Victorian columns and ornamental decoration employed in the design. Thus, even in the face of new inno-vations such as the skyscraper, American architecture in the early 1920s was stagnant and unimagina-tive. The mood of the Coolidge era seemed as if it would be prolonged indefinitely until the economic crash in 1929. Americans were shaken by the "realization that their society . . . had failed to solve its

Fig. 2. Chicago Tribune Building, 1922 (Koeper and Whiffen 322)

own internal problems" (Burchard and Bush-Brown 390). They were forced to accept that their ideas were not perfect and that in every society, no matter how strong, there are flaws. In architecture, the year 1929 served as a hinge to close the door on the old eclectic Victorian style and open the door to an age of modernism and imagination.

Architecture was not totally revolutionized during the 1930s, for a revolution of that scale takes time, but the 1930s does mark the initial stages of change toward a truly "American" stylistic form. Architecture in the 1930s diverged in two directions. Roosevelt's New Deal administration, which focused on rebuilding the economy and restoring faith in government, served a very functional purpose; architecture of the New Deal perfectly reflected this theme. From the "alphabet soup" of Roosevelt's public programs emerged housing and building projects such as the Federal Housing Administration (FHA), the Public Works Administration (PWA), and the United States Housing Association (USHA). Each of these organizations established by Roosevelt's Works Progress Administration did its best to benefit the general public but did little to further the progress of architecture in the United States. The architecture of the New Deal was aesthetically uninspired and focused mainly on the function of the buildings being built.

During the 1930s Roosevelt and the New Dealers had no incentive to concentrate their efforts on new forms of design, and architecture's "aesthetic aspirations were muffled in the social ideals" of the time (Burchard and Bush-Brown 402).

New Deal architecture served a purely functional purpose on a large scale and contributed little to new styles. However, another simultaneous movement made great progress in terms of public acceptance of radical ideas during the 1930s. During that decade, "European ideas flooded into the United States as they never had since the 1860s" (Gowans 421). Ironically, "it was Europe that supplied answers to the aesthetic problem of American" design (Koeper and Whiffen 320). Streamline Moderne was a major stylistic development with European origins. Streamline Moderne differed greatly from the eclectic style of the 1920s in that "it was stripped of ornament" and was "symbolic of the dynamic twentieth

Fig. 3. Johnson Wax Administration Building, exterior, 1936–1939 (Koeper and Whiffen 333)

century" (331). The sleek, smooth look of this futuristic style celebrated the use of metal and glass and implied that the age of the machine was here to stay. Frank Lloyd Wright, the most famous of American architects, gave Streamline Moderne an American identity during the 1930s. In his design for the Johnson Wax Company's administration building (see fig. 3), Wright created a harmony between technology and humanism. In an age when many people feared rapid technological development and the use of machines, Wright managed to bring people and machines together in a cohesive unit, thus setting the tone for architecture in the coming decades.

Although the two paths of architecture during the 1930s seem drastically different, by the end of the decade it was clear that they shared a common goal: to eliminate the enclaves of eclecticism and create an architectural style unique to American ideals and principles. The New Deal architecture overcame eclecticism through mass production, and many observers believe that modern architecture was "born in the study of structure" and functional necessity (Burchard and Bush-Brown 393). From another perspective, styles such as Streamline Moderne defeated eclecticism by introducing radical new designs manufactured with new technology. The combination of these two approaches eventually phased out eclectic Victorianism altogether by the end of the 1930s.

Americans realized that buildings were a direct representation of themselves, and they chose to have their structures reflect their power and advancement. Just as Roosevelt's progressive administration saved America from Coolidge's big business conservatism, the progressive designs of the 1930s saved architecture from the stagnant, uninspired styles of the 1920s.

Works Cited

Burchard, John E., and Albert Bush-Brown. <u>The Architecture of America: A Social and Cultural History</u>. Boston: Little, 1961.

Gowans, Alan. <u>Images of American Living</u>. Philadelphia: Lippincott, 1964.

Koeper, Frederick, and Marcus Whiffen. <u>American Architecture 1607–1976</u>. Cambridge: MIT, 1981.

Additional Student Work
www.ablongman.com/beyondwords34

7 | EXPLORING DESIGN

FYI Kurtis Harris, Detective First Grade (Retired), managed approximately 1,900 homicides, suspicious deaths, and other major crime investigations during his thirteen-year career with the New York City Police Department. He is a board certified Senior Crime Scene Analyst and a former faculty member of the NYPD Detective Bureau's Advanced Training Unit.

5 Interlude

KURTIS HARRIS

crime scene photography

When a violent crime occurs in a small city or town, it is often possible to close streets and thoroughfares for extended periods of time, allowing a variety of forensic specialists and scientists to respond. When, for instance, the Federal Bureau of Investigation's Evidence Response Team is called to a town to respond to a major crime scene, it sends a team of personnel specializing in narrowly defined categories of forensic science, such as photographers, ballistic examiners, cartographers, serologists (blood spatter and DNA specialists), and fingerprint examiners. The group is coordinated by a team leader who is responsible for deciding which forensic discipline should be applied to the scene first. Thus, for example, if the team leader should see in his or her initial walk-through of the scene that there is both dry, flaking blood present on the sill of an open window and a patent fingerprint in a candle on a table in the dining room, the leader will call for the serologist first to collect the blood, which could be lost if not recorded and collected expeditiously. The candle, which is not in danger of degrading, would be addressed later.

This approach to crime scene analysis, while effective, requires uninterrupted access for an extended period of time to allow the various forensic specialists and scientists to perform their examinations. However, in large municipalities, open-ended crime scene examinations are simply not feasible, and much smaller teams of investigators are dispatched to collect and document evidence to be sent to the lab, where scientists and specialists can analyze it. In New York City, for example, the New York City Crime Scene Unit assigns a team of two investigators to each homicide or other major crime. Being extensively trained in recognizing the significance of various types of evidence, the detectives will use methods prescribed by specialists to retrieve, package, and disseminate these materials for analysis.

A key step in the evidence-gathering process is crime scene, or forensic, photography. Forensic photography is the documentation and memorialization of anything that will later be used in courts of law and considered by triers of fact (the jury) during the trial process. Photographs of a crime scene not only record the overall condition of the scene to familiarize juries and refresh the memories of witnesses but also provide a means to subsequently extract additional information for analyses. Thus the worthiness of a forensic photograph is based not on its artistic content but on its accuracy.

To properly document a crime scene, photographs must be taken from a minimum of three perspectives: long range (overall), intermediate, and close up. Overall views are necessary to establish where an item of evidence is located within the context of the scene. Intermediate views show the item in its immediate surroundings and its position relative to other items of evidence. Close-up, detailed photographs are used for identification or analyses. Close-up photographs must be taken first with the object exactly as found and only later with an acceptable scale to determine its actual size.

Ultimately, decisions about which photographic technique to apply to which piece of evidence depend on the needs of the scientist who will be examining the image. Shoe print analysis, for instance, is a specialized area of forensic science. To be useful for analysis, photographs of shoewear impressions in soft dirt have to be taken from four separate angles (north, east, south, west) using a side flash. This technique allows for the reproduction of the class and individual characteristics of the impression by eliminating the shadows that would result from using a perpendicular flash.

The investigator must also be aware of how his or her evidence will be used in a courtroom. Competent investigators are able to anticipate what an aggressive defense attorney will ask them about in court. This understanding of the judicial process, along with knowledge of the principles of a wide variety of forensic specialties, contributes to effective decision making while investigating scenes of violent events.

The photographs shown here offer an example of forensic protocol in crime scene photography. On December 9, 1997, at 10:45 p.m., I was called to the southeast corner of Bergen Street and Kingston Avenue in Brooklyn, New

York, to assist in a shooting investigation. Upon arrival, I learned that a 31-year-old male had been shot in the abdomen, groin, and back by another male during a dispute in front of a neighborhood supermarket. The victim had been removed from the scene to King's County Hospital prior to my arrival, and the officers on site had cordoned off the area. The assailant had fled soon after the attack. Information about the crime was scant, and possible witnesses had yet to be identified. Little physical evidence was present at the scene. However, as blood spatter expert Herbert McDonnell has noted, an "absence of evidence is not evidence of absence."

▲ I began documenting the scene by taking four overall photographs. I initially recorded the scene using only available light (without a flash) to assist the trier of facts in assessing the actual, unaided lighting conditions. As lighting conditions are key to what people can see, recording the conditions at the time of the crime is important to verify the credibility of witnesses' observations. This photograph depicts an overall view of the southeast corner of Bergen Street and Kingston Avenue from the northwest corner of the intersection. This photograph allows the viewer to plainly see the supermarket where the shooting occurred (at the center of the photograph); it shows the south sidewalk of Bergen Street (left of photo) and the east sidewalk of Kingston Avenue (right of photo). Adjacent to the crime scene, you can see entrances to attached apartment buildings. This is an important part of the photograph, as it was later learned that an enclosed entrance allowed the assailant to successfully ambush the victim prior to the confrontation. Notice also the numerous apartment windows above the scene of the shooting. This part of the photograph allowed the jury to see how close witnesses might have been and to therefore credit or discredit their testimony.

► This photograph depicts the same corner at approximately the same distance but from a different angle. Again, the photograph was taken with consideration of possible witnesses entering or exiting not only the supermarket at the crime scene but also the small deli-grocery at the northeast corner of the intersection (left of photo). It is very likely that observers from the vantage point of the small deli-grocery would have had a sense of curiosity and may have lingered there because they felt they were far enough from the crime to be safe. A photograph such as this is crucial in providing investigators with leads to witnesses who can provide accounts of what happened from eye level.

◄ This is an overall view of the east sidewalk of Kingston Avenue. I took it from the sidewalk facing north toward the intersection and the scene of the event. I wanted a photograph from this vantage point to show the sources of light. As you can see, there were two streetlights illuminating the area: one on the northeast corner of the intersection (middle of photo) and one on the southwest corner (top left of photo). Also apparent in this photograph is a third grocery diagonally across the street from the location of the shooting. (Do you think additional witnesses may be found?)

► This photo, taken from the entrance of the deli-grocery across from the crime scene, is an opposite view of the previous photograph. This photograph allows the jury to stand where a witness may have stood and permits a critical assessment of a witness's credibility. Had I used artificial illumination to light the scene, the illumination provided by the fluorescent lights beneath the supermarket's awning would not be apparent.

► This photograph is one of several intermediate views I took of the shooting scene that show the context in which evidence was discovered and its relative proximity to various structures (the supermarket's entrance, the red emergency call box, the public telephone). Here, I began to use artificial lighting to better reproduce individual elements of the shooting event. The emphasis has shifted, in other words, from recording possible witness observations to showing a portion of the scene and event artifacts in context with each other. Note that the green refuse bin and the milk crate to its left were introduced to the scene by zealous officers in order to establish a crime scene perimeter—doing so is absolutely not recommended.

◄ This close-up view of the east curb of Kingston Avenue in front of the crime scene shows key evidence in detail: bloodstains at the base of the red emergency call box, a gray knit hat, and a brown paper bag (containing an alcoholic beverage). Emergency medical artifacts are also visible. By looking at this photograph in the context of the others, and with an understanding of the wounds sustained by the victim, a crime scene analyst can learn much about what happened during and just after the assault. For instance, the absence of pooled blood on the sidewalk and the presence of blood stains on the base of the emergency call box suggest that someone propped the victim up against the box soon after the shooting—the extent of the injuries the victim sustained would have resulted in his lying on the ground, not propping himself up on the call box. The absence of "defensive bullet wounds" in the hands, arms, and legs of the victim also suggest that the victim did not perceive the threat until the first shot was fired. In this particular case, it was shown at trial that the victim had been ambushed. The victim survived, and the person tried for the crime was found guilty.

For additional writing projects related to this Interlude see
www.ablongman.com/beyondwords35

CHALLENGE

1. Which form of evidence do you believe is generally more credible: forensic evidence from the scene or eyewitness testimony? What can photographs reveal that eyewitness testimony cannot, and vice versa? Design and conduct an experiment to test your hypothesis: take several photographs of a place or an event on your campus or community, and compare them to information provided by firsthand eyewitnesses you interview. Compose an informative essay, including several of your photographs, to report your findings and conclusions.

2. One function of crime-scene photography, Harris says, is to refresh the memories of witnesses whose recollections of the events might otherwise fade. Choose a place where something important in your life has happened and create several "snapshots" in words or images that help you or others to remember what happened there.

DEBATING CULTURE
writing to advocate and persuade

Poster created by *Modern Humorist* magazine

Both of these posters are directed to the same audience—young adults who use the Internet to download music and movies. Which poster do you think is more likely to influence members of that group? Why?

What do you find persuasive? Think of some instances when words or images have changed your opinions, feelings, or behavior. What convinces you? What changes you? Why?

Introduction

YOU CAN CLICK BUT YOU CAN'T HIDE

I | **ILLEGAL DOWNLOADING**
Inappropriate for All Ages

If you think you can get away with illegally swapping movies, you're wrong. Illegally trafficking in movies is not just a dirty little secret between you and your computer. You leave a trail. The message is simpler if you are downloading copyrighted movies without proper authorization, you are breaking the law. You face serious consequences if you illegally swap movies. The only way not to get caught is to stop.

Pursuant to the Copyright Act (17 U.S.C. Section 504(c)), statutory damages can be as much as $30,000 per motion picture, and up to $150,000 per motion picture if the infringement is willful.

WHEN YOU PAY FOR MP3s, You're Rockin' Out with The Man!

A REMINDER FROM
Gnutella, Freenet & Geeks Everywhere

I magine you're at home on a rainy Friday night, trying to decide whether to venture out to the movie theater to see the new *Pirates of the Carribean* sequel, when your roommate offers to show you how to download a free—but illegal—copy of the film onto your laptop. Which version of the movie would you choose? What issues, values, or information would you consider in making your decision? To whose advice would you be willing to listen? What words or images might sway you?

The two posters that open this chapter take positions—albeit opposing ones—on whether people should use the Internet to obtain copyrighted material without paying for it. Both direct their appeals to young adults, the demographic group most likely to engage in this practice. Both want to influence attitudes and behavior.

The first poster on the left, created by the Motion Picture Association of America (MPAA) as part of its "respect copyrights" ad campaign, uses scare tactics and a blunt, "in your face" approach to make its point. A dramatic image in the middle of the poster catches our attention; ominous block letters warn, "You Can Click but You Can't Hide;" and small print describes in lurid language the criminal consequences of illegal file sharing. The message is clear: This is serious business. Don't do it.

Created by the online magazine *Modern Humorist*, the second poster on the left pokes fun at ad campaigns like the MPAA's and invites us in on the joke. No ominous warnings or threats of jail time here. Instead, an innocent-looking young man stares trancelike into a coin-operated computer screen, which he has apparently paid to use. Looming above, possessively gripping his shoulder, is "the Man"—a tuxedoed corporate tycoon who looks like he's been imported straight from a Monopoly board game. The final line of text attributes the poster's message to Gnutella and Freenet—two Internet sites that distribute free downloading software and advocate unregulated file sharing. Better visit those sites, we might conclude. After all, who wants to "be rockin' out with the Man"?

Whether you respond better to the MPAA's ponderous directives or *Modern Humorist*'s playful challenge, there's no doubt that both these posters make **arguments**.

■ **Arguments stake out claims** on issues about which people disagree or need to make choices. Arguments provide a method for expressing and resolving differences and for discovering the best course of action in complex situations.

- **Arguments use strategic arrangements of** words, data, images, sounds, design features, and other elements to present a convincing case.

- **Arguments reach out to audiences,** appealing to shared concerns and values in order to create common ground.

- **Arguments spark responses** and promote ongoing discussion. The *Modern Humorist* poster was created in response to recording industry ad campaigns. The MPAA poster was designed to improve on previous efforts to influence consumers' behavior. These posters have in turn sparked new responses and proposals, and debate on the issue continues to evolve.

- Finally, **arguments can take many forms**. Arguments today often combine visual and verbal elements. Political campaigns, for instance, sell their candidates using devices as different as yard signs, thirty-second TV spots, bumper stickers, white papers, and Web sites. That's nothing new, but technology has certainly made it easier for almost everyone to *compose* these different kinds of arguments rather than just analyze them.

What's in This Chapter?

This chapter discusses the key elements of argument, from clear claims to responsible use of evidence, illustrating these principles through arguments ranging from advertisements and posters to formal essays and bumper stickers.

We then explore some controversial topics and present them through different media. Some may cause you to cringe ("Not gender roles again!"). But precisely because the topics are familiar, we ask you to move beyond simple, pro or con choices and ask how more nuanced claims might be supported. Other topics are a little offbeat. We ask you to consider a controversial Urban Outfitters T-shirt ("Voting Is for Old People"), the ways in which fast-food outlets influence Americans' dietary choices, and what is sure to be a controversial subject for many years to come—the shape of New York City's memorials to the victims of the 9/11 terror attacks.

Some of the topics you'll see in this chapter are hotly controversial, even difficult to discuss—and that's OK. We think it is important for you to consider how civil arguments about tough issues should be made in a democratic society. We offer our opinions on this matter as we invite you to explore the following words and images.

Reading
Arguments

Simply reacting to arguments differs from understanding how they work—or ought to work. In reacting to arguments, you might simply agree or disagree with the claims, evidence, and assumptions offered (*Stem cell research should be outlawed!*). Or you might blow off the whole issue (*Who cares about stem cell research?*) or be confused by the appeal (*What's a stem cell?*) or want more information (*How does stem cell research potentially affect me?*) or see related issues that merit attention (*Who profits from stem cell research?*).

Understanding arguments means paying close attention to how different elements of an argument work together and to the responses they evoke: *How did the writer get me to care about stem cell research, when an hour ago I wasn't even sure what it was?* Good arguments engage you and then, ideally, educate you to make thoughtful choices. But not all arguments are responsible or transparent in their methods. Why exactly *did* you react a certain way to an editorial cartoon or a *Daily Show* skit? Was it because an important claim was defended powerfully—or just cleverly? Or maybe you didn't like its verbal or visual style. Too whiny. Too heavy-handed. Not cool. How might you explain those reactions? You can get started by asking these questions, first discussed in Chapter 1:

- What do you see?
- What is it about?
- To what does it relate?
- How is it composed?
- What details matter?

What do you see?

Serious arguments can be made in just about any **medium** of communication: *words, images, music, sound, sculpture, space*, and so on. Naturally, these media can be combined. But every medium of argument seems to have its own way of stating a case or sending a message.

Words, for example, entirely on their own, have full-bodied power to present claims. Slogans such as "Just say no" or "Just do it" make simple points that people remember, and yet words can also swell into book-length arguments, complex and subtle. Words have unique authority in our culture. We cite them, quote them, memorize them, declare our independence with them, and affix our signatures to them. Even in the age of the Internet, serious journals of public opinion still print lengthy arguments, and newspaper editorials retain considerable clout. Words can express nuances that images can only hint at, and—like the books from which movies are adapted—they can be richer in detail than their visual equivalents and far better at acknowledging differing opinions and rebuttals. But let's be frank, words can also be dull, and unless managed skillfully, they may be better at getting people to think than to act.

World War I U.S. Army recruiting poster.

Images deliver an emotional punch quickly and more easily than words—like a direct injection into a vein. Perhaps they also require less mental processing and offer more immediate rewards. (Most people today prefer watching the movie to reading the book.) But who can deny the power of a truly persuasive image? Pictures and images have changed behavior, politics, and people. They can also be shaped, manipulated, and arranged in startling ways. And they stick in the memory, even—maybe especially—the simple ones.

When those pictures start to move or show live action, they become yet another potential medium of persuasion. Television news and film documentaries can make convincing and responsible arguments, combining the emotional power of images with the sustained analysis possible through language. Of course, arguments presented on video can become overly cinematic, driven more by clever editing, dramatic music, and sonorous voice-overs than by serious evidence. (Think of pseudo-documentaries about the Bermuda Triangle, Atlantis, and the other-worldly origins of the Egyptian Pyramids.)

As a reader or viewer, you should consider the medium of an argument, recognizing both its limitations and the opportunities it presents. Think about the humble political bumper sticker. You might not consider it a mode of argument at all: It's just a small piece of polyester backed by acrylic glue.

But there's strength in numbers and mobility. When you're stuck behind a car with a bumper sticker, you read it, don't you? Does it make you want to vote for a candidate or save the whales? Not likely, but the little decal may help you recognize a name or recall an issue. And it identifies a candidate or cause with a community member concerned enough to post a message. A bumper sticker can express civic commitment and extend political community wherever the vehicle goes—or it may give voice to an attitude of defiance or even contempt for civic culture.

Of course, bumper stickers (like all media) have limitations. Though the stickers come in different shapes and sizes, they are physically constrained by the shape and size of the bumpers or windows on which they'll appear. There's no room to provide background information or explain the nuances of an issue, so unless readers already know something about the context of the argument, a bumper sticker may confuse rather than persuade.

Bumper stickers advocate causes and present concise arguments but rarely have room for nuance or ambiguity.

MANIPULATING MEDIA

In the 1960s, pop artist Andy Warhol (1928–1987) attracted public attention by doing paintings of the same red-and-white Campbell's soup cans that lined grocery shelves everywhere in America. In the process, he crossed media, transforming the labels of commercial products into what would become gallery art. Warhol may also have been making an argument about the influence of consumer culture on twentieth-century art. Or maybe the Pittsburgh native was suggesting that there was no line between commercial and so-called high art. In any case, his controversial paintings certainly made people look at both paintings and soup cans differently.

This same manipulation of media can occur in other kinds of arguments. Look at what happens when a familiar box becomes a political poster. In 1982, activist Ester Hernández created *Sun Mad Raisins* to protest the dangerous working conditions in California faced by Chicano farmworkers. The poster works especially well precisely because the product it parodies seems to glow with contrasting vitality and health.

1. List as many examples as you can of moments when spoken words have a special power to commit, even compel, people to do things of consequence. Are such words arguments? Why or why not?

2. Identify as many kinds of visual arguments as you can other than advertisements. Are items such as stop signs or warning symbols arguments? Why or why not?

3. Identify several minor forms of argument—comparable to the bumper sticker—and then explore how they work: the messages they can convey, the audiences they would reach, the social connections they can make or suggest. Consider engraved pens, T-shirts, Web site pop-ups, and similar items.

COMPOSE

4. Make the same political claim in two distinctly different media. You might imagine, for example, that you are running for a student government seat or campaigning for a local political initiative. Mock up the arguments as fully as you can, or simply describe them in words.

What is it about?

Arguments seek to move people to specific viewpoints or actions. That's another way of saying that arguments aren't accidental; they have intentions and motives, expressed in a **claim** or statement, a caption, or maybe just a word or two.

You probably have plenty of experience with **thesis statements** as they typically work in written arguments. In academic and journalistic writing, thesis statements often combine a claim with a supporting reason or reasons: *College students receiving state-funded financial aid should be required to do community service because they owe a debt to the community paying for their education.* To support this claim, the writer would then assemble evidence and other supporting materials: *In the past three years, taxpayers have funded more than $50 million in student grants. Yet after-school programs and services for the homeless have suffered sharp budget cuts, increasing their need for volunteers.* But what you've learned about traditional written arguments may not apply directly to visual and multimedia arguments. These arguments often make claims in ways that are indirect, more visceral, and open to interpretation.

Occasionally an image does make an argument entirely on its own by its sheer power. That may be the case with an image by Pulitzer Prize–winning photographer Charles Porter IV taken moments after the 1995 bombing of the Murrah

Federal Office Building in Oklahoma City. The photograph of a dead child cradled in the arms of a fireman spoke eloquently against domestic political terrorism. The Vietnam War similarly produced several memorable and self-evidently persuasive images—two unforgettable images showed a naked child burned in a napalm bombing and a suspected Viet Cong rebel executed, gun to his head, in a street. The pictures suggested strongly to American audiences that *This war may be wrong.*

But it's not unusual for argumentative claims in visual media to be implicit, left for viewers to infer. Is Prince's controversial music video "Cinnamon Girl" making a passionate case for tolerance or promoting terrorism when it shows us a young Arab American woman who fantasizes about setting off a bomb after a lifetime of ethnic discrimination? Viewers have interpreted it both ways. Yet implied claims may also be intriguing and effective. For instance, Pulitzer Prize–winning cartoonist Dick Locher doesn't take after the critics of illegal immigrants directly in a Thanksgiving-season spoof that appeared in the *Chicago Tribune*, but his sentiments are clear, leavened by both humor and irony.

Photo by Charles Porter IV, Oklahoma City, April 19, 1995.

WHAT DO YOU THINK—COULD WE USE A PROPOSITION AGAINST ILLEGAL IMMIGRATION?

Editorial cartoon by Dick Locher (2003).

1. Pick up a newspaper or a newsmagazine such as *Time* or *Newsweek*, and examine the captions that accompany the news photos. Do the captions usually make claims that make the image argumentative, or do they tend to be more neutral? Point to specific examples that support your answer.

2. Come up with a caption for Charles Porter IV's photograph of the fireman and child. Do you think the photo is more persuasive with or without the caption? Why?

3. Choose several news photos without argumentative captions, and turn them into more aggressive claims in any way you find effective. You might create a new caption, try juxtaposing contrasting images, or add some copy of your own.

4. Find an advertisement, poster, or other visual argument that uses very few words—or none at all—to make its point. Write a paragraph that explicitly spells out its claim and supporting reasons. Is it difficult to do so? Does your paragraph adequately capture the argument? Why or why not?

Think small.

In the 1960s, this print ad for the VW Beetle urged readers to "think small."

To what does it relate?

No argument exists in a vacuum. Debates unfold within complex personal, historical, social, and cultural **contexts.** More than two millennia ago, Aristotle argued that persuasive arguments work by responding to these contexts in three basic ways: by appeals to *logos*—appeals involving subject matter, including facts, good reasons, and logic; to *pathos*—appeals to the emotions and values of the audience; and to *ethos*—appeals to the good character, reputation, authority, and honesty of the person or institution making the claim.

Appeals to *facts* and *logic* are easy to spot in most media. In written arguments, you may find information carefully culled from reliable sources or field evidence. Pie charts, tables, and graphs offering visual testimony for or against a claim may also assist the case. Even

1990 Census poster designed by Choctaw artist Jerry Ingram

advertisements can be logical when they make reasonable claims based on evidence. Volkswagen of America successfully marketed the original Beetle in the 1960s to Americans through a series of classic magazine ads that challenged everything that postwar Americans (and many today) believed about vehicles. The ads succeeded because they gave the appearance of being perfectly reasonable with their claims of efficiency that encouraged consumers to "think small."

Emotions affect people in different ways, and appeals to them are often risky because they rely on precisely what makes human actions so unpredictable. Yet making people feel happy, fearful, proud, patriotic, embarrassed, selfish, superior, angry, or contented certainly directs them in different ways to specific claims. For instance, the U.S. Bureau of the Census commissioned Native American artists to create posters to urge reluctant Native Americans to participate in the 1990 census. Choctaw artist Jerry Ingram designed the poster shown above that placed the census process within tribal traditions, a powerful image evoking native pride while supporting the poster's claim.

Still another way to support a claim is through *ethos*, appeals to the *good character*, *authority*, and *reputation* of the party or parties making a claim. In arguments that are mainly verbal, ethos can be established when writers cite reliable sources, seem sensitive to the opinions of others, or speak in reasonable or cordial ways. Writers with a reputation as honest, knowledgeable, or plain-dealing people often find that their claims receive a fair hearing, even when readers are initially skeptical.

Ziyi Zhang is one of many celebrities featured in the well-known "Got Milk?" ad campaign.

9 essential nutrients in every easy-to-open bottle.

got milk?

Ethos is also at work when famous people endorse an idea or a product. (What exactly these spokespersons are renowned for may vary.)

For several years, for example, the National Association of Dairy Farmers has used the ethos of celebrities—including supermodels, actors, Olympic athletes, rock stars, and teen idols—to counteract the widespread impression that drinking milk is strictly for small children. Consider the ad on page 528 featuring actress Ziyi Zhang. What qualities and talents does the ad associate with milk? How are these connections suggested in the image and accompanying text? To what audience(s) do you think this ad is directed? Why would the choice of Zhang as spokesperson appeal to this audience?

Ethos appeals can be powerful and immediate; accordingly, it is quite easy to manipulate ethos—to make something seem more reputable than it is. (Consider all the unlucky people who buy what they think are Rolex watches or Prada handbags for $75.) But the very same kind of manipulation of ethos is what makes some parodies work, and they can be powerful and legitimate forms of argument. The mock ads at www.adbusters.org or articles in *The Onion* routinely manipulate ethos to make serious points.

FYI Many of the posters in this chapter are featured in "Posters American Style," an online exhibit of the Smithsonian American Art Museum. You can find more posters at the site (americanart.si.edu/collections/exhibits/posters).

CONSIDER

1. Examine the ads and posters in this section. How does each make use of appeals to *logos, pathos,* and *ethos*? Which appeals do you find most compelling? Do any of these texts employ appeals that seem ineffective, irresponsible, or unethical? Explain.

COMPOSE

2. Visit www.adbusters.org or theonion.com, and find a parody that you think is effectively constructed. Write a few paragraphs explaining how the parody makes use of appeals to *ethos, logos,* or *pathos.* How does the text use these strategies differently than they would be used in a serious argument about the topic? How are the strategies used in ways similar to how they'd be used in a serious argument?

3. Try your hand at composing an ad that expresses your views on a current issue—or, alternatively, create a parody of one of the ads presented in this chapter.

How is it composed?

Whatever form they take, most arguments—either explicitly or implicitly—incorporate certain **basic elements**. As we've already mentioned, an argument stakes out one or more *claims* and presents *reasons* and *evidence* that support them. These elements are grounded in *assumptions*—values or beliefs that the writer or designer assumes the audience shares. Often arguments may include *rebuttals* that acknowledge and respond to opposing viewpoints. They may also build in *qualifiers* that clarify the argument's limitations in order to avoid overstating the claim.

However, despite these common elements, the larger **structure** of an argument can vary greatly depending on its purpose—on what *kind of claim* it makes:

- An argument that develops a **factual claim**—for instance, insisting that something is true or not or that something happened or didn't happen—must present information in a logical sequence. Maybe the information can be presented along a timeline, as used in some criminal cases. Or perhaps the argument will borrow the structure of a lab report, police report, research paper, or even newspaper story: who, what, where, when, how, and why?

- An argument over the **definition** of a term—*Is a particular crime manslaughter or murder?*—might require a totally different structure, one that begins by listing the properties or qualities that make something what it is. Those properties themselves might be debatable, but then controversy is the lifeblood of arguments.

- An argument might make a claim about **causes and effects.** (Think about all you've read in recent years about global warming or unemployment.) Such an argument will have to explore the connections between particular phenomena and their origins—sometimes quite complex and multifaceted relationships.

- Arguments that present **evaluations** contain certain features: a movie review should comment on the plot and characters of a film. A *Consumer Reports* article on toaster ovens might rely on comparison charts or checklists heavy on visual signals and numbers. Arguments that evaluate should present criteria or standards, either implied or spelled out.

- A **proposal** argument offers ideas for fixing a problem. Such an argument would define a problem (*students on your campus can't find convenient parking*), look at alternative solutions (*build a monorail to parking lots on the campus periphery*), come up with a better one (*build parking garages*), and explain why it works (*parking fees can finance the garages*). All these parts would have to follow in logical sequence before readers pay attention to the solution offered.

The point is that arguments do different things and so will have different structures. When arguments are mainly verbal, the structures may be easy to see, marked by titles or headings or helpful transitional phrases. But when an argument is mainly visual, aural, or some combination, the relationships among claims, reasons, and evidence may be structured in an entirely different way. Back in 1967, when the Sierra Club was trying to save redwood groves, it created a simple but effective poster in which three key statements, each in a different font, provided the links between two images. A larger image, covering two-thirds of the argument space, depicts the aftermath of logging a forest of redwoods, a few surviving trees standing forlornly on the horizon. "Beautiful, weren't they?" the poster asks in an italic red font. A much smaller image—a photograph of a redwood grove by James D. Rose—stands above the main caption, which is in all caps, signaling a critical possibility: THE LAST REDWOODS.

How did we get from the beautiful trees in the Rose photo to the devastation that dominates the argument? The key bit of evidence lies in a callous, handwritten remark scrawled beneath the larger image: "When you've seen one redwood *stump*, you've seen them all." If that kind of thinking isn't enough to set you foraging in the small print at the bottom of the page to learn what you can do, nothing will. Like many posters for political causes, the structure is that of a proposal argument: problem, cause, solution.

CONSIDER

1. Summarize the argument made in the Sierra Club poster. How might you make such an argument using only words?

2. Think of several arguments you've composed recently—papers, essays, or exams in your courses, flyers or other promotional materials for an organization you belong to, or messages to friends or online forums, for example. How did you go about organizing these arguments? Did you construct outlines or sketches beforehand, or did you arrange materials as you composed? What factors did you consider as you decided how to arrange and order your argument?

What details matter?

The details in arguments can be just as important as the claims. In verbal arguments, you expect claims and reasons to be supported by **evidence:** *examples, analogies, facts, statistics, testimony,* and so on. Evidence has to be sufficient to make a point. It also needs to be powerfully phrased and presented. Consider how Andrea Lewis in "A 'Return' of the White Patriarchy?"—an essay from Tolerance.com—supports a claim that *The Return of the King* is a less racially and sexually progressive film than *The Matrix Revolutions*:

> The *Rings* films are like promotional ads for those tired old race and gender paradigms that were all the rage back in author J.R.R. Tolkien's day.
>
> Almost all of the heroes of the series are manly men who are whiter than white. They are frequently framed in halos of blinding bright light and exude a heavenly aura of all that is Eurocentric and good. Who but these courageous Anglo-Saxon souls can save Middle Earth from the dark and evil forces of the world?
>
> On the good side, even the mighty wizard Gandalf the Grey (Ian McKellen) is sanitized and transformed from the weed-smoking, rather dingy figure we first meet in the *The Fellowship of the Ring* into Gandalf the White, who, by the time of *Return of the King,* has become a powerful military leader complete with pure white hair and an Eisenhower attitude.

... where every boy can dream of being President. Where free schools, free opportunity, free enterprise, have built the most decent nation on earth. A nation built upon the rights of all men ★ *This is your America*

... Keep it Free!

No one who has seen the film can deny that everyone in the fellowship, from Frodo to Legolas, is pretty darn white. The Gandalf example is especially acute—precisely the detail to drive home Lewis's point.

You might not have noticed the absence of gender and racial diversity in the film version of *The Lord of the Rings.* But chances are you would immediately sense something missing in "Where Every Boy Can Dream of Being President," a 1942 poster from the "This Is America" series. Very few public school classrooms now look like the one envisioned in the World War II poster, and one might wonder if many ever did, even in the 1940s. Today we'd probably read that image ironically, especially given its concluding claim that "This is your America."

Often key details can be found in the **design elements** in any visual argument—details representing choices made by the artist or institution creating the image. Consider the difference design elements make in these two covers, created to sell the same book to two different audiences. *The Great Unraveling*, a collection of *New York Times* columns by economist Paul Krugman, arrived in American bookstores with an almost scholarly face. But the British publisher took a startlingly different tack with Krugman's work, previewing its content with a brash collage of political images that's hard to ignore.

W. W. Norton, the book's American publisher, takes a low-key approach to marketing this product to its readers, perhaps because its author is a respected economist well known to influential segments of the American reading public. At the bottom, the subtitle leaves much to the imagination: "Losing Our Way in the New Century." What exactly is it that's unraveling, and how did we get lost in it? Clearly, knowing Krugman's work is key to understanding what's going on between these covers. But Norton must be confident that its target American audience—and you may not be included—will.

Not so the British publisher, Penguin. Krugman's name—far less recognizable in London—is unlikely to inspire many sales, so a different line of argument is in order, one supported with different details. In a cluttered collage, Bush is drawn to resemble Frankenstein and Vice President Cheney to echo Hitler. Sandwiched between them is a cartoon version of Enron CEO Kenneth Lay. Bush clutches greenbacks while oil oozes down Cheney's chin. In case readers miss the point, the subtitle at the bottom screams in all caps "From BOOM to BUST in three scandalous years." So although both covers encourage readers to buy Krugman's book, the British cover makes a far bolder political statement.

Covers of the U.S. (top) and British (bottom) editions of Paul Krugman's 2003 book *The Great Unraveling*

CONSIDER

1. Do you find persuasive the evidence presented in the excerpt from Andrea Lewis's critique of *The Return of the King*? Why or why not? Can you think of other kinds of information she might have presented to support her claim?

2. Some Americans were offended by the cover of Krugman's British edition of *The Great Unraveling*. Do you think any elements of the cover go "over the line"? Try to explain what that line is. Which cover would be more likely to catch your eye? Which would be more likely to encourage you to buy the book? Why?

CHALLENGE

3. Imagine how you might redesign the cover (within reason) of some book you own to make it more salable, honest, or sensational. It might be a work like Eric Schlosser's *Fast Food Nation* or a book by a political pundit such as Michael Moore or Ann Coulter. It might even be your calculus book—though a work that makes an argument would likely offer more interesting possibilities. Sketch your design for the new dust jacket, or use appropriate software to mock up your proposal.

Rocking the Vote

Demographers have branded people born after 1980 as Generation Y, the first Americans immersed from birth in an information culture typified by a glut of round-the-clock news, infotainment, and multimedia of all kinds, including the Internet. This information overload has made Generation Y perhaps the most media-savvy in history, with a healthy skepticism of corporations, big media conglomerates, and politicians. Research suggests that people in this group can't be easily persuaded.

Contrary to their predecessors in Generation X or the still earlier baby boomers, kids from Generation Y are more likely (it has been suggested) to share their parents' values about life, career, and politics. There's less of a "generation gap" now than there has been in decades. People in the Y group reach decisions in their own ways—and not necessarily in opposition to what came before. Also, as a group, Generation Y is less likely than previous generations to vote or be involved in political campaigns.

In fact, young people vote in far fewer numbers than just about any demographic group except convicted felons. In practical terms, that means that politicians in Washington or city hall don't pay much attention to the complaints or needs of college-aged voters. For several election cycles, student activists, political parties, and MTV veejays have done what they can to persuade more 18- to 25-year olds to punch their chads on Election Day. But they've had so little impact that someone at Urban Outfitters briefly saw a marketing opportunity in producing a $28 T-shirt that said what many young people must be thinking.

This section presents some of the controversy sparked by that T-shirt and then goes on to consider some of the broader issues related to college students' orientations toward political and civic involvement. Whatever your views on these topic (or your age), if you own a "Voting is for old people" T, hold on to it. It could become a collector's item.

"This shirt's real intention is to sum up the current state of political affairs, pointing a finger at all of us."

— T-SHIRT DESIGNER
JOHN FOSTER-KEDDIE

Punkvoter's Letter to Urban Outfitters

Al Jourgensen

Urban Outfitters T-shirt (2004)

Mr. Richard A. Hayne
Chairman of the Board of Directors and President
February 25, 2004

Dear Mr. Hayne:

How can you possibly rationalize that selling a T-Shirt stating: "Voting is for Old People" is not a political agenda? As an artist, I appreciate expressions of outrage. I understand rebellion, and respect the use of irony and sarcasm to prove a point in public speech. But as a board member of Punkvoter.com, I find your T-shirt "Voting is for Old People" to be an anti-American abomination. Mr. Hayne, I am sure I don't have to give you a history lesson regarding the incredible amount of lives lost fighting for the Right to Vote in America alone. I am shocked and appalled at your recklessness, especially given the historical roots of your company, Urban Outfitters. What has happened to you?

Voting is the right and obligation of all voting age citizens. Your company markets to a young clientele and a voting demographic that are severely under-represented and need to be encouraged to exercise their Constitutional Rights as Americans. In 2000, the US Statistical Abstract and Census Bureau's research reported 36 percent of 64 million voters aged 18–34 voted in the last election. These young voters represent three times the voters aged 65–75. If voting were only for our senior citizens, America's youth would be completely marginalized from our country's democratic process.

535

Your T-shirt design is knowingly irresponsible. It is a disgusting effort to reap profit from cynicism while suppressing civic involvement, and encouraging apathy, not to mention referring to our senior citizens as "old people." I see your actions as a blatant attempt to quash the efforts of Punkvoter.com, Music for America and Rock the Vote, and other pro-youth vote organizations. It is public knowledge that you contribute to the Republican Party. Could this be the motivation behind your anti-vote strategy to suppress the youth vote you have so much influence over? Shame on you, Mr. Hayne. I know you know better.

The same kid who saves up and spends 28 bucks on this type of merchandise has real decisions that he/she will be facing in the near future. Life decisions, such as how are they going to get a decent paying job when unemployment rates are ever increasing. How can they get a job if our job creation is hitting this younger generation the hardest (youth unemployment rates have been as high as 12.8 percent). How many McJobs do they need to get to cover their increasing prices of healthcare and increasing tuition costs, never mind having to pay to join the football teams at their high schools? What is the average age of the kids fighting the war in Iraq and dying? What about the 375,000 low income college students that lost their higher education funding or the over 1.5 million kids that had their Pell Grants reduced because of our current Administration's fiscal policies? And you purport voting is for old people?

For Urban Outfitters, it is damage control time. In an ideal world, I would love to have your product removed from your stores, but this is a Free Country and you have a right to sell the product that you want. But to sell it under the guise of not having a political agenda is hypocritical and underhanded. In a next to ideal world, you could sell "Voting Matters" shirts to your clientele, preferably T-shirts that do not come from Third World sweatshops, but I won't get into THAT now—that's another letter. If you are a real American, a true business leader, and if you have an ounce of the 60s activist you once were left in you, you will consider my letter. Punkvoter.com, and the thousands of fans that have joined our ranks know not only how to vote with our ballots, we know how to vote with our wallets, and we know how to boycott. No joke.

Sincerely,
Al Jourgensen
Ministry, Lard, RevCo

Explore the controversy surrounding Urban Outfitters and its products.
www.ablongman.com/beyondwords36

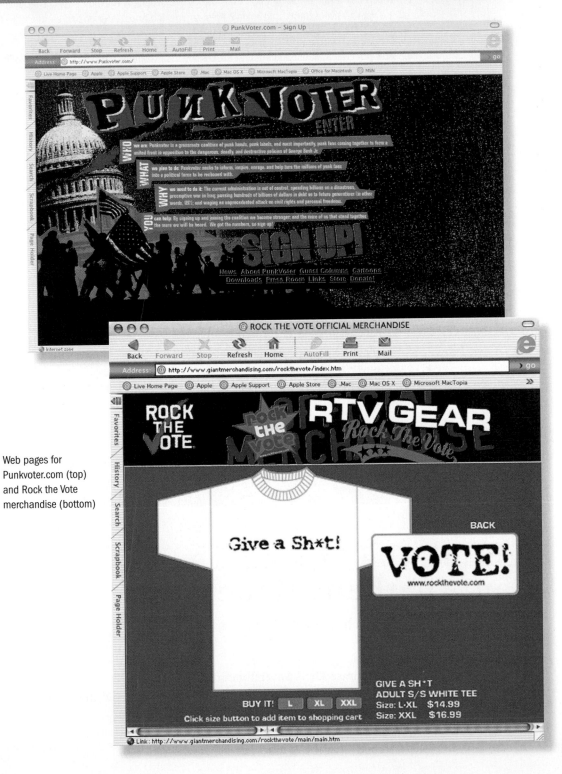

Al Jourgensen (b. 1959), also known as Hypo Luxa and Buck Satan, is a Grammy-nominated singer and musician who founded the band Ministry in 1980 and has worked with other groups in a long career. He is now active in Punkvoter.com, a group dedicated to making punk fans politically active.

Web pages for Punkvoter.com (top) and Rock the Vote merchandise (bottom)

1. T-shirt designer John Foster-Keddie seems to blame everyone for the political environment that makes "Voting is for Old People" possible. Is that sweeping indictment fair? Explain your response.

2. Which T-shirt would you be more likely to buy, the "Voting is for Old People" shirt or Rock the Vote's "Give a Sh*t" shirt? Why? Point to specific appeals or design elements in the shirts to explain your preference.

3. How powerful a medium is a T-shirt for making claims and advancing arguments? Within what groups, if any, might it have special appeal?

COMPOSE

4. Describe or design a get-out-the-vote T-shirt that might appeal to a young person inclined to buy the "Voting is for Old People" item.

5. Write a paragraph or two evaluating the arguments made in Al Jourgensen's letter to Urban Outfitters' chairman of the board, focusing especially on the effectiveness of his use of logical, emotional, and ethical appeals.

6. Visit the Web sites of several organizations that aim to encourage young people to get politically involved. What strategies do they use to motivate and convince viewers? What kinds of information and arguments do they offer? How are the Web sites arranged and designed? Write an essay reporting on the patterns of similarity you find as well as the differences.

CHALLENGE

7. Efforts like Rock the Vote and Punkvoter.com are grounded in the assumption that the best way to encourage civic participation and voting is to make it seem "cool," by associating these activities with celebrities and youth culture. Is this a valid assumption? Or are there other reasons and appeals that could more effectively motivate young voters? If so, what are they? Write an essay that explores your views on this question.

Fighting the Stigma of an Apathetic Generation

Elisabeth Kwak-Hefferan
(2003)

To paraphrase Alicia Silverstone in *Clueless,* I don't want to be a traitor to my generation and all . . . but I just don't understand the way the youth of America has settled into political apathy.

Until last week's State of the Union address, I held the naïve fantasy that all kids at [my university] and beyond looked forward to such events with excitement characteristic of the good little citizens we are. My proverbial bubble was burst the very next day, though, when I asked some friends what they thought about Dubya's latest proposals. They hadn't watched—in itself, forgivable—but to my chagrin, they told me they weren't even registered to vote.

To someone who marks her ballots for even the local primary elections in a state of glee, that came as a shock. But to be fair to my friends, it's not just them. In a nation that barely gets half its citizens to the polls for the presidential elections, we (18- to 24-year-olds) make up the worst offenders. Ever since 1972, the first presidential election in which those 18 and up could vote, our turnout has regularly declined—making us, my friends, the lowest of the low.

It's unbelievable, really, how little some of us seem to care about the affairs of our great nation, especially now when the issues at hand are so critical. I know there's still some truth to the notion that young people are idealistic, socially active crusaders, but I wouldn't call those people a majority. It's fine that it's not everyone's cup of tea to write petitions and attend rallies, but we've got to raise the bar. At the very least, we've got to vote.

For those who slept through civics class in high school, this democracy is supposed to be "of the people." Let's put aside our cynicism and wave the flag for a bit. While I'm under no illusions that this government is perfect, I still realize how lucky we all are to live in a truly free country. It's an amazing thing to have a voice in the way this nation is run—an ability we should hold dear.

Consider for a moment: women did not win the right to vote in this country until 1920, meaning that some of our grandmothers were born into a world where their political opinions were invisible. African Americans were effectively denied the same right until as recently as the passage of the 1965 Voting Rights Act. Think of the years of struggle that it took to finally reclaim this foundation of American democracy—people have literally died in pursuit of it.

Could we have forgotten it all, and so quickly too?

So what's our problem? Despite what the old guard may say, we're not just spoiled, ungrateful, sorry people—rather, we just put too much faith in a few stock excuses. Allow me to address the most popular ones (it helps if you read them out loud in a whiny voice).

"But my one vote won't make a difference." Ah, the granddaddy of them all. Unfortunately, this one just doesn't hold water anymore. There are numerous counterexamples scattered throughout history, the most obvious one being our last presidential election.

"But politicians don't really care about what's important to me." Well, if that's true, it's because we won't vote. Given our age demographic's dismal turnout, politicians don't want to waste their time trying to appeal to us. If we'd rise up and become the powerful voting bloc we could be, suddenly they'd be falling all over themselves making promises about student loans and free beer.

"But I don't know anything about the candidates." True, an uneducated vote is no service to our country. So educate yourself. There's a world of information out there for those who take the initiative to find it—read the newspaper, watch the news, look up the party platform. Sorry, but ignorance is no excuse for shirking your civic duty.

"But I don't know how to register." Contact your local elections office—a Google search should do it. Or keep your eyes out for the groups that set up on [campus] around election time to register students. Or go to the Federal Election Commission's Web site and download a mail registration form. Local offices should be able to set you up with an absentee ballot as well.

"But I'm too busy to vote." Come on now, that's the lamest of them all. Simply rearranging the day to omit the 45 minutes spent online reading rumors about the Olsen twins can work wonders.

No matter what our excuses are, we all know deep down that we should be heading to the polls whenever we can. So if you're still not registered, go do it—you're making the rest of us look bad.

College students at Kenyon College in Ohio lined up to vote in the 2004 presidential election. Some waited more than ten hours.

ROCKING THE VOTE

FYI

The Onion, billing itself as "America's Finest News Source," is a satirical newspaper featuring world, national, and community news. *The Onion*'s scathing commentary on world events attracts over three million readers each week to its print and online editions. Like the essay reprinted here, some of its articles appear as unsigned editorials, mimicking the journalistic conventions of many major newspapers.

American People Ruled Unfit to Govern

The Onion
(1999)

The controversial decision, the first of its kind in the 210-year history of US representative government, was, according to Justice David Souter, "a response to the clear, demonstrable incompetence and indifference of the current US citizenry in matters concerning the operation of this nation's government."

As a result of the ruling, the American people will no longer retain the power to choose their own federal, state and local officials or vote on matters of concern to the public.

"This decision was by no means easy, but it unfortunately had to be done," said Justice Antonin Scalia, who penned the majority decision in the case. "The US Constitution is very clear: In the event that the voting public becomes incapacitated or otherwise unfit to carry out its duties of self-governance, there is a danger posed to the republic, and the judicial branch is empowered to remove said public and replace it with a populace more qualified to lead.

"In light of their unmitigated apathy toward issues of import to the nation's welfare and their inability to grasp even the most basic principles upon which participatory democracy is built, we found no choice but to rule the American people unfit to govern at this time," Scalia concluded.

The controversial ruling, court members stressed, is not intended as a slight against the character of the American people, but merely a necessary measure for the public good.

"The public's right to the best possible representation is a founding principle of our nation," Justice Sandra Day O'Connor told reporters. "If you were on a jet airliner, you wouldn't want an untrained, incompetent pilot at the controls, and this is the same thing. As federal justices, we have taken a solemn oath to uphold every citizen's constitutional rights, and if we were to permit an irresponsible, disinterested public to continue to helm the ship of state, we would be remiss in our duties and putting the entire nation at risk."

The ruling brings to an end a grueling 10-month process, during which more than 100 Supreme Court hearings were held to determine the public's capacity for self-governance. Despite the fact that these hearings were aired on C-SPAN, a majority of US citizens were unaware of them because coverage was largely eclipsed by the Clinton-Lewinsky scandal, the retirement of NBA legend Michael Jordan, and the release of *Titanic* on home video.

The Supreme Court found that, though 78 percent of US citizens have seen the much-anticipated *Star Wars* prequel trailer, only one in 200,000 was aware that the multibillion-dollar "Star Wars" missile-defense system had been approved by Congress. Additionally, while 62 percent of citizens correctly identified the cast of *Suddenly Susan*, only .01 percent were able to identify Attorney General Janet Reno beyond "some woman Jay Leno always says looks like a man." Further, only .0003 percent could correctly identify the ancient Greek city-state of Athens as the birthplace of the concept of an educated citizenry participating in democratic self-rule.

But the final straw, Supreme Court justices said, came last week, when none of the 500,000 random citizens polled were aware that Russian President Boris Yeltsin had threatened global thermonuclear war in response to NATO air attacks in Yugoslavia.

"I mean, come on," Justice William Rehnquist said. "Global thermonuclear war? It's just ridiculous. There was just no way we could trust such a populace to keep running things after that."

Populations currently being considered to fill the leadership void until the American people can be rehabilitated and returned to self-governance include those of Switzerland, Sweden and Canada.

"I'm willing to do what I can to help out in this time of crisis and make sure that my vote counts," said Stockholm resident Per Johannesen. "I've been reading up on America a bit, just to get a general idea of what needs to be done, and from what I can tell, they really need some sort of broad-based health-care reform over there right away."

In a provisional test of the new system, the Canadian province of Saskatchewan will hold primaries next Tuesday to re-evaluate last fall's gubernatorial election in Minnesota.

The lone dissenting vote came from Justice Anthony Kennedy, who, in his minority opinion wrote, "Although the American people are clearly unable to make responsible decisions at this time, it is not their fault that they are so uninformed. Rather, the blame lies with the media interests and corporate powers that intentionally keep them in the dark on crucial issues."

Kennedy concluded his opinion by tendering his immediate resignation and announcing his intent "to move to a small island somewhere."

Thus far, reaction to the ruling has been largely indifferent.

"The people ruled unfit to govern? Yeah, I think I might've heard something about that," said Covington, Kentucky, sales representative Neil Chester. "I think I saw it on the news or something, when I was flipping past trying to find that show about the lady sheriff."

"If you ask me, voting was a big pain anyway," agreed mother of four Sally Heim of Augusta, Maine. "At least now I'm free to do my soap-opera-trivia crossword puzzles in peace without all that distraction about who's running for Second District Alderperson and what-not."

Despite the enormous impact the ruling would seem to have, many political experts are downplaying its significance.

"It doesn't really change anything, to be honest," said Duke Univesity political-science professor Benjamin St. James. "The public hasn't made any real contributions to the governance of the country in decades, so I don't see how this ruling affects all that much.

"I wouldn't worry about it," St. James added. "It's not that important."

> Are college students really apathetic? Research the arguments at www.ablongman.com/beyondwords37

CONSIDER

1. Do you think that characterizations of college students as politically apathetic and reluctant to engage in rigorous debate are accurate? If so, why? If not, is your disagreement based on personal experience, on evidence you have discovered, or a combination of both?

2. Kwak-Hefferan's essay offers rebuttals of several excuses young people might make for not voting. Do you find these rebuttals convincing? Why or why not? Do you think the tone of her essay affects the argument?

3. Summarize the argument implicit in *The Onion*'s parody. Do you think this piece suggests that young people aren't the only ones to blame for political apathy in the United States?

COMPOSE

4. Most of the readings and images in this section start from the assumption that apathy among college students is a problem. But are college students really as uninvolved as these pieces would have you believe? Do research in the library or on the Web to find data about young adults' civic attitudes and behavior. Then write a paper arguing whether or not college students as a group are politically irresponsible.

CHALLENGE

5. Choose one of the arguments in this section, study the way it makes its claims and supports them, and then construct a counterargument in some form—another poster, an editorial, a print ad, a letter to the editor, a parody.

Pushing the Hot Buttons

All debates about human concerns push us to examine issues and ultimately choose the best course of action. But when arguments focus on our status as people, our interactions with each other, or even our physical bodies, they become personal and often heated. That may be because they touch on the choices we make in our lives. And ultimately, if they are successful, they may change the way we behave or help us defend our actions.

This section examines arguments that touch on such querulous concerns. We begin by looking at how attitudes toward women's roles and health evolved in the twentieth century. We also look at how women (and in some ways men) interact with one another, examining the "queen bee" phenomenon and considering the shape of attitudes about popularity. Finally, we look at specific concerns related to health and behavior that are associated with fast-food consumption in America.

The "F" Word

No question about it. Arguments about the role women should play in American society have changed people's lives dramatically over the years. Until women finally gained the right to vote in 1920, feminist arguments focused mainly on gaining the right to vote. In the 1960s, a so-called second wave of feminism was launched. Many credit this second wave to arguments voiced by feminists like Betty Friedan, who observed in her book *The Feminine Mystique* that women in the late 1950s and early 1960s suffered heavily from a "problem that has no name" but that ultimately derived from a cultural attitude that dictated that personal fulfillment for women was to be found almost exclusively in the roles of dutiful housewife and mother.

It would be misleading to credit *The Feminine Mystique* with changes in women's roles in the past half century. But Friedan's book certainly exposed dominant attitudes that limited what women could expect to accomplish in America and inspired a much larger debate about feminism. As we will see, the extent and the implications of that change are still open to debate.

"For over fifteen years there was no word of this yearning in the millions of words written about women, for women, in all the columns, books and articles by experts telling women their role was to seek fulfillment as wives and mothers. Over and over women heard in voices of tradition and of Freudian sophistication that they could desire no greater destiny than to glory in their own femininity. Experts told them how to catch a man and keep him, how to breastfeed children and handle their toilet training, how to cope with sibling rivalry and adolescent rebellion; how to buy a dishwasher, bake bread, cook gourmet snails, and build a swimming pool with their own hands; how to dress, look, and act more feminine and make marriage more exciting; how to keep their husbands from dying young and their sons from growing into delinquents. They were taught to pity the neurotic, unfeminine, unhappy women who wanted to be poets or physicists or presidents. They learned that truly feminine women do not want careers, higher education, political rights—the independence and the opportunities that the old-fashioned feminists fought for. Some women, in their forties and fifties, still remembered painfully giving up those dreams, but most of the younger women no longer even thought about them."

—BETTY FRIEDAN
The Feminine Mystique (1963)

Print advertisements from the 1960s (above) and 1950s (right) offer visual representations of the cultural attitudes of their times.

1. How would you characterize your understanding of women's roles from the 1950s and '60s? Do you have clear sense of prior attitudes toward women? Where did your understanding come from?

2. Do you think the advertising and magazine cover images from the '50s and '60s provide an accurate representation of cultural attitudes?

3. Could you argue that images of women in contemporary advertising limit the roles women may play today as much as or more than they were limited during the 1950s and 1960s? For instance, might advertising today discourage the choice to seek fulfillment as housewives and full-time mothers? Write a paper that supports or argues against this possibility.

COMPOSE

4. Research Betty Friedan, Gloria Steinem, or other figures related to 1960s feminism. Write a paper in which you argue whether the work of such activists resulted in tangible positive change.

FYI Anna Quindlen is a bestselling author of four novels (*Blessings, Black and Blue, One True Thing,* and *Object Lessons*) and four nonfiction books (*A Short Guide to a Happy Life, Living Out Loud, Thinking Out Loud,* and *How Reading Changed My Life*). She has also written two children's books. Her *New York Times* column, "Public and Private" won the Pulitzer Prize in 1992. Her column now appears every other week in *Newsweek*.

Still Needing the *F* Word

Anna Quindlen
(2003)

Let's use the *f* word here. People say it's inappropriate, offensive, that it puts people off. But it seems to me it's the best way to begin, when it's simultaneously devalued and invaluable.

Feminist. Feminist, feminist, feminist.

Conventional wisdom has it that we've moved on to a postfeminist era, which is meant to suggest that the issues have been settled, the inequities addressed, and all is right with the world. And then suddenly from out of the South like Hurricane Everywoman, a level '03 storm, comes something like the new study on the status of women at Duke University, and the notion that we're post-anything seems absurd. Time to use the *f* word again, no matter how uncomfortable people may find it.

Fem-i-nism *n.* 1. Belief in the social, political and economic equality of the sexes.

That wasn't so hard, was it? Certainly not as hard as being a female undergraduate at Duke, where apparently the operative ruling principle is something described as "effortless perfection," in which young women report expending an enormous amount of effort on clothes, shoes, workout programs and diet. And here's a blast from the past: They're expected "to hide their intelligence in order to succeed with their male peers." "Being 'cute' trumps being smart for women in the social environment," the report concludes.

That's not postfeminist. That's prefeminist. Betty Friedan wrote *The Feminine Mystique* exactly 40 years ago, and yet segments of the Duke report could have come right out of her book. One 17-year-old girl told Friedan, "I used to write poetry. The guidance office says I have this creative ability and I should be at the top of the class and have a great future. But things like that aren't what you need to be popular. The important thing for a girl is to be popular."

Of course, things have changed. Now young women find themselves facing not one, but two societal, and self-imposed, straitjackets. Once they obsessed about being the perfect homemaker and meeting the standards of their male counterparts. Now they also obsess about being the perfect professional and meeting the standards of their male counterparts. In the decades since Friedan's book became a best seller, women have won the right to do as much as men do. They just haven't won the right to do as little as men do. Hence, effortless perfection.

While young women are given the impression that all doors are open, all boundaries down, empirical evidence is to the contrary. A study from Princeton issued at the same time as the Duke study showed that faculty women in the sciences reported less satisfaction in their jobs and less of a sense of belonging than their male counterparts. Maybe that's because they made up only 14 percent of the faculty in those disciplines, or because one out of four reported their male colleagues occasionally or frequently engaged in unprofessional conduct focusing on gender issues.

Californians were willing to ignore Arnold Schwarzenegger's alleged career as a serial sexual bigot, despite a total of 16 women coming forward to say he thought nothing of reaching up your skirt or into your blouse. (Sure, they're only allegations. But it was Arnold himself who said that where there's smoke, there's fire. In this case, there was a conflagration.) The fact that one of the actor's defenses was that he didn't realize this was objectionable—and that voters were OK with that—speaks volumes about enduring assumptions about women. What if he'd habitually publicly humiliated black men, or Latinos, or Jews? Yet the revelation that the guy often demeaned women with his hands was written off as partisan politics and even personal behavior. Personal behavior is when you have a girlfriend. When you touch someone intimately without her consent, it's sexual battery.

The point is not that the world has not changed for women since Friedan's book lobbed a hand grenade into the homes of pseudohappy housewives who couldn't understand the malaise that accompanied sparkling Formica and good-looking kids. Hundreds of arenas, from government office to the construction trades, have opened to working women. Of course, when it leaks out that the Vatican is proposing to scale back on the use of altar girls, it shows that the forces of reaction are always waiting, whether beneath hard hats or miters.

But the world hasn't changed as much as we like to tell ourselves. Otherwise *The Feminine Mystique* wouldn't feel so contemporary. Otherwise Duke University wouldn't find itself concentrating on eating disorders and the recruitment of female faculty. Otherwise the governor-elect of California wouldn't be a guy who thinks it's "playful" to grab and grope, and the voters wouldn't ratify that attitude. Part fair game, part perfection: that's a tough standard for 51 percent of everyone. The first women's rights activists a century ago set out to prove, in Friedan's words, "that woman was not a passive empty mirror." How dispiriting it would be to those long-ago heroines to read of the women at Duke focused on their "cute" reflections in the eyes of others. The *f* word is not an expletive, but an ideal—one that still has a way to go.

CONSIDER

1. How would you describe Quindlen's tone in her article? How does her tone influence your reception of her argument?

2. Do you believe we have entered a postfeminist era? How might we be able to recognize such an era?

3. What is the main point that Quindlen makes in her argument? Do you find her claims convincing?

Girl Culture

Attitudes toward women can often seem abstract when discussed in terms of media representations or cultural critiques. In reality, however, these attitudes have lasting effects on our day-to-day lives and our interactions with others. Recently, writers like Rosalind Wiseman have begun examining these daily interactions and the attitudes that support them. Wiseman specifically looks at the social behavior of teenage girls. Her book *Queen Bees and Wannabes* examines high school cliques and the phenomenon of "alpha" groups and individuals. The 2004 film *Mean Girls* was based on Wiseman's work.

8 | DEBATING CULTURE

FYI

Rosalind Wiseman stepped on a media land mine when an article about her work with cliques was featured in the *New York Times Magazine*. Titled "Mean Girls and the New Movement to Tame Them," it discussed Wiseman's work with the Empower Program, which teaches middle school girls about nasty social behaviors and how to stop them. "It was an extraordinary, mind-blowing experience," Wiseman says of the media fallout that followed the article. "I got responses from all over the world—from England, Ireland, Australia, multiple requests from movie companies, and the *Times* got hundreds of letters. The emotional response has been unbelievable—we're finally acknowledging what we do to each other."

Cliques No Worse than Ever

Rosalind Wiseman
(2002)

We like to think that girls' cliques are worse today than they used to be, but I know that's not true. While writing the book [*Queen Bees and Wannabes*] I was struck by how universal an experience this seems to be, but it's a universal experience that no one talked about. I had 60- and 30-year-old women follow me around at parties to tell me about clique incidents as if they had just happened yesterday—all the girls' names are still right there. They told me about situations identical to the ones I'm working with right now. So yes, I think this kind of behavior has always been around. It may start a little younger than it used to. Girls are sexualized at a younger age and will deal with these friendship issues at a younger age too. I see 8-year-old girls, even 4-year-old girls, anointing certain friends and excluding others.

There are always going to be Queen Bees, even in the poorest schools. But typically the wealthier a community is, the more of a problem this is.

One thing that is worse today is how parents behave. I think that today's parents are either micromanaging their kids' lives or they are out of the picture, which is equally problematic. These kids will do anything to create space or get the appropriate attention.

But I disagree with some critics, who say worrying about clique behavior is micromanaging kids' social lives. Instead, I think every time you deal with one of these friendship issues it's a teaching moment about ethics. It's at these moments that your kids realize what you stand for.

HOW TO HANDLE GIRLS' CRUELTY

The whole issue of mean girls touches a nerve with parents, especially with mothers. Women are in such turmoil about how to raise assertive, strong women. Yet in our efforts to raise girls with high self-esteem, we sometimes lose sight of the importance of kindness. In schools I've worked in, I've seen girls with very high self-esteem who are really, really nasty.

As a parent, one of the hardest things to do is to decide how to handle these situations. Should you wade in, do nothing, or stand there and cheerlead, but let her fight for herself?

I think that unless a child is in a very serious situation, you should encourage her to stand up for herself, with her skills in place. By that I mean that parents should affirm their daughter and her courage, and then help her think through how to deal with the situation. Have her write it down, and decide what the most important issue is. The best strategy is usually for a girl to get the bully away from the other girls, describe to her what's happening, what she needs to happen differently, and have the bully affirm her.

In other words, parents should be their daughter's cheerleaders, but not take care of her business. If she can face this, she can face anything. Dealing with a girl bully will give her practice for someday having to deal with an inappropriate boss.

SETTING THE STAGE
FOR TALKING WITH HER

To let her know it's okay to tell you about clique problems, say something like, "Hey look, lots of times it's normal to have problems with friendships. If you ever have a problem with that, I'll help you or we can get you an ally, like an aunt or an older friend, to help you." Then you run away. Plant the seed and run away.

When do kids tell me they will reach out to their parents? The number one time is in the car while the parent is driving. Girls also tell me that if they try to get alone with their mom, it's usually because they need to talk. Even if they say it isn't a big deal, it is. They need at that moment to check in with her.

One final point about talking with girls. Sometimes parents ask questions that are actually springboards to asserting what they think or feel. They say, "How's it going with Amy?" because they want to say they don't like her. In cases like these, your daughter will shut down. Keep in mind that talking with her is not an opportunity to force-feed her your opinions.

HOLDING YOUR DAUGHTER ACCOUNTABLE

Unfortunately, it's really the exceptional parent who holds his or her child responsible for bad clique behavior. Recently I heard of a woman who [was informed by the school principal] that her daughter was behind all the nastiness going on in the girl's fifth grade class—the girl was totally the Queen Bee—and this mom believed the principal even though she was shocked. She talked to her kid and withdrew her privileges, which mostly meant taking away her means of communication—instant messaging and e-mail. And that really hurts a girl that age. But sadly, I've found that it's rare for most parents to hold their kids accountable for these unacceptable behaviors.

The hardest work for me is dealing with a Queen Bee girl and a Queen Bee mom. Those operating from a position of privilege don't like to be told they should change, nor do they believe there really is a problem. It's the kids on the outside who know the most about a school's social hierarchy.

Over and over again I have been struck by parents' unwillingness to apologize to other parents for their kids' behavior. It really hurts parents' relationships with each other at the worst possible time. Kids may start lying to you when they're teens, and if those parent friendships dry up, you'll be cut off from knowing what's going on, making it harder for you to keep your own girl safe.

The bottom line? Affirm her and hold her accountable. If your girl does something mean, she's not necessarily a mean person and you're not a bad parent.

QUEEN BEES DON'T HAVE IT MADE

One thing to remind your daughter is that lots of girls in the Alpha group don't want to be there; it's very confining. Most people look at the "it girl" and think she's got it all. I see her as stuck in solitary confinement, so tied to stereotypical femininity that she has no choices.

What's especially sad is that those girls in the Alpha clique are so vulnerable to early sex, drinking, drugs, and even abuse. That's because they need to keep the Alpha boy for status, even if he's abusive. Often these girls know their lives are a house of cards, which makes them anxious, and so they self-medicate.

Girls who are on the outside of the box are much more likely to be successful and authentic. They are not frauds, not always pleasing others. Remind your girl that there are true costs to being popular.

WHEN ALL ELSE FAILS, TRY THIS

Outside activities, such as theater or sports, can be an excellent way to help girls remember that there's life outside junior high or high school. On the other hand, some of the worst cliques I've seen have been in regional soccer teams—the girls and parents both. In fact, any time you have parents inappropriately involved in kids' social status, bad stuff happens.

Changing schools should be the last resort. You want your daughter to know that she can figure this out, and that you're not fighting her battles for her. But if the school turns a blind eye, or even seems to be helping create a bad social environment, you may have to pull her out of school.

If she's unable to get her work done, if she's so distracted she can't focus—or if your gut tells you she's really in trouble, trust it, and intercede.

The bottom line is to remember that parents do matter. You might feel rejected over the next few years, but you are essential to your daughter navigating adolescence safely.

CONSIDER

1. How does Wiseman's article square with your own sense of how cliques operate, whether among girls or boys? Does she provide sufficient evidence to support her proposed argument?

2. Wiseman makes a number of claims about the prevalence of the Queen Bee syndrome. Do you find the assertions to be well supported? What additional evidence might make the argument stronger?

3. Do you agree that Queen Bees are rarely held accountable for their actions? What about the suggestion that popularity has costs? Would you argue against any of these assertions?

CHALLENGE

4. Wiseman's piece is written as advice for parents. Using your own experience, what you have learned from Wiseman, and perhaps some additional research, write your own article about the Queen Bee syndrome with teen boys as your target audience.

One "Mean" Teen Satire

Michael O'Sullivan
(2004)

FYI Michael O'Sullivan is the film critic for the *Washington Post*. An archive of his recent reviews can be found online at washingtonpost.com.

If you've ever taken an anthropology class, you may remember watching one of those documentary films about some tribe somewhere whose members rub seeds under their eyelids or perform ritual scarification. Watching *Mean Girls* can feel a little like that, which is to say, disturbing and fascinating at the same time. Welcome to Girl World. Better get your shots because the natives bite.

Based on author Rosalind Wiseman's pop ethnography, *Queen Bees and Wannabes: Helping Your Daughter Survive Cliques, Gossip, Boyfriends and Other Realities of Adolescence*—and set in the natural habitat of the adolescent female, genus Americanus—the comedy is also funny as hell.

And yes, I mean hell, not heck. Adapted by caustic *Saturday Night Live* head writer and *Weekend Update* co-anchor Tina Fey (who also plays a small part as a high school math teacher), *Mean Girls* burns. If its satire leaves a mark, and it does, it does so because *Mean Girls* understands exactly where the tenderest flesh of its victims lies. Like its titular subject—the casually cruel cliques of the popular girls—the film itself is more than a little nasty. Ultimately, though, its nastiness is there in the service of something rather nice, for its message is one about what it really means to grow up.

Like *Heathers* and *Election*, its comedy is an exaggeration of high school life, but without the fundamental dishonesty so rampant in teen comedy. Its adolescent heroes and villains are not children—no, not exactly—but neither are they merely smaller, cooler, better-looking versions of their parents. Yes, they cuss and drink when the folks aren't around, and some of them even mess around sexually, but they're far from adults and still need a life lesson or two.

Set in an upscale suburban high school, *Mean Girls* tracks the progress of one Cady Heron (Lindsay Lohan), a 16-year-old newbie who is just making the transition from years of home schooling in Africa to the jungles of North Shore High in Evanston, Ill.

Initially rejected by all but a pair of outsiders—a vaguely Goth art freak with the ironic name of Janis Ian (Lizzy Caplan), and her overweight, gay best friend, Damian (Daniel Franzese)—Cady soon finds herself recruited somewhat reluctantly into the ranks of the "Plastics," a trio of catty It Girls ruled by the iron, if impeccably manicured, fist of Regina (Rachel McAdams). What begins as an exercise in espionage, essentially, with Cady expected to report back

PUSHING THE HOT BUTTONS

to Janis and Damian on the back-stabbing machinations of the alpha females, backfires when Cady herself gets caught up in the mean behavior of her new social circle.

Contrary to what the film's trailers may have led you to believe, *Mean Girls* is not a movie about revenge. Okay, it is, sort of, but only superficially. With the assistance of Janis and Damian, Cady does set out to methodically punish Regina after Regina sabotages Cady's chances with a boy Cady likes (Jonathan Bennett)—a boy, it just so happens, Regina used to date. In the process of payback, however, Cady threatens to become what she destroys, losing not only her moral bearings but her real friends, too.

It sounds as though it could become preachy, but *Mean Girls* is no *ABC Afterschool Special*, despite some third-act moralizing. Nor is it filled with dumb yuks. Although rated PG-13 and contain-

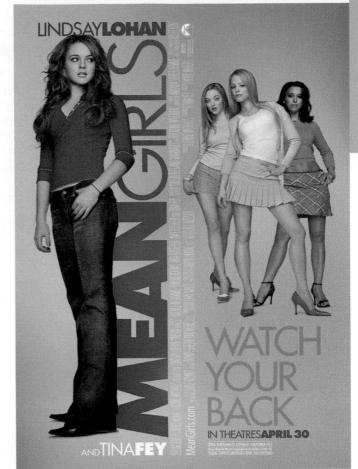

ing a joke here and there about flatulence, *Mean Girls* has a sharp, grown-up sensibility that belies its marketing as airhead comedy. That doesn't mean it's a movie exclusively for adults, either, although they'll probably enjoy it, too. Its target audience? All the mean girls in the world. But because the movie doesn't talk down to them while making them laugh at themselves, the ones who will really get the joke are the smart girls.

CONSIDER

1. "One 'Mean' Teen Satire" takes the form of a film review. Can you recognize any aspects of argument in the review—claims made or evidence used, for instance?

2. Consider the publicity poster for *Mean Girls*. Does the poster make a statement about the behavior of Queen Bees? How might you read the poster as an argument?

COMPOSE

3. View the film *Mean Girls*, and write your own review of the movie. In your review, concentrate on aspects of the film—moviemaking techniques, thematic concerns, acting, and so on. Rather than offer your opinion, give readers clear descriptions that help them visualize these aspects, and then develop an argument about the possible significance of the details in terms of the Queen Bee phenomenon.

FYI Lauren Greenfield is widely recognized for her collections bringing together interviews and photographs that document teen life in America. Her collection *Fast Forward* (1997) documented growing up in Los Angeles by comparing the experiences of well-to-do Hollywood High School students with those of teens from South Central and East Los Angeles. In *Girl Culture*, Greenfield focuses on teen girls, looking especially at the ways that culture affects attitudes toward popularity and self worth.

Images from Girl Culture

Lauren Greenfield
(2002)

"Britney's a role model. She's fashionable, and she has movements that I like. Britney, Christina Aguilera, Destiny's Child: They're role models 'cause they like action and movement so much." —LILY

Lily, then 5, shops at Rachel London's Garden, where Britney Spears has some of her clothes designed. Los Angeles, California.

"Our group tends to wear a lot more makeup than other people. I don't want to look trashy. I try to look natural. [When I was getting ready, I was wondering] if I should spend a long time worrying about my hair or if I should just put it up and bring a pony-tail holder and not care, because I knew by the end of the night it wouldn't matter. And with my makeup, it was the same deal. Should I spend a long time on it? Would it be all blended in by the end of the night? Would it really matter?" —HANNAH, 13 YEARS OLD

Allie, Annie, Hannah, and Berit, all 13, before the first big party of the seventh grade, Edina, Minnesota

CONSIDER

1. Is it possible to argue that one of Lauren Greenfield's photographs better captures issues of girl culture than an essay might? If not, why not? If so, which image would you choose and why?

CHALLENGE

2. Visit the Lauren Greenfield resources at www.girlculture.com, and explore *Girl Culture* in more detail. Select two of the photographs and interviews, and discuss them in terms of one of the readings from this chapter. Develop an argument that explores whether the images adequately capture the concerns in the article.

3. Has the media's focus on girl culture and feminism made boys disappear? By many measures, they are doing less well than girls in American society: for instance, they have lower academic achievements than girls and higher suicide, drug, and crime rates. Do you believe that arguments involving the condition of boys should get more media attention? Do some research on the subject and then write an argument exploring the validity of the question.

More images and commentary on Lauren Greenfield's Girl Culture
www.ablongman.com/beyondwords38

Fast Food Fights

A recent advertisement for Subway in Europe caused a stir with its depiction of a bloated Statue of Liberty holding, instead of a torch, a large order of fries. The ad featured the caption, "Why are Americans so fat?" The controversy even reached the level of political leadership with Congressman Tom DeLay calling the ad un-American. Perhaps associating fast food with the Statue of Liberty does poke fun at America, but in all likelihood the reaction was strong not only for its political dimensions but also because it touched a nerve. In fact, the debate over fast food, health, and American culture has been developing for years, as the film *Super Size Me* and a number of commentators make clear.

Filmmaker Offers Food for Thought

FYI

Jim Keogh's review of Morgan Spurlock's documentary, *Super Size Me*, first appeared on June 10, 2004, in the Worcester (Massachusetts) *Telegram & Gazette*.

Jim Keogh
(2004)

A few years ago I read a book called *Fast Food Nation*, which described in graphic detail the process by which those delicious burgers and fries wind up in the gut of millions of Americans daily. The book was an exceptional piece of muckraking by investigative journalist Eric Schlosser, diving into everything from how beef cows are treated to the dangerous working conditions within the meat-packing industry. When I'd finished, I was sufficiently disgusted to swear off fast food, and recommended to my co-workers they do the same.

My boycott lasted about a week, maybe two. I don't remember how I slipped back into old habits, but it probably had something to do with needing a quick meal while racing between the job and my kids' games. Schlosser's warnings were replaced by the drive-up menu that promised flavor and convenience at a reasonable price. While I'm no junk-food junkie, in my weaker moments I'm a sucker for its greasy charms.

Now comes Morgan Spurlock's entertaining documentary *Super Size Me*, chronicling America's love affair with McDonald's. By now you've probably heard about the central gimmick to Spurlock's movie: He ate nothing but McDonald's food three meals a day for 30 days. He had to sample everything on the menu, and if asked by the cashier if he wanted to "supersize" his meal, he was obligated to do so.

The ramifications to his health were astounding: Spurlock gained 25 pounds, his cholesterol shot up from 168 to 230, and his liver became so larded with fatty deposits one doctor compared it to pâté. Spurlock grew increasingly depressed, and his sexual performance noticeably declined (according to his girlfriend).

Twenty-six days into his experiment, Spurlock's physician was urging him to cut the cord to the Golden Arches. "You're sick," he tells Spurlock. We assume he's referring only to the filmmaker's physical condition, but the horrified look on the doc's face leaves the statement open to interpretation.

Spurlock's methods have been called into question, most notably, understandably, by McDonald's corporation officials, who argue that people simply don't eat the way Spurlock eats—essentially trying to commit hara-kiri via cheeseburgers—during the course of his movie.

Indeed, Spurlock glories in his excesses. When he vomits while trying to make his way through a double Quarter Pounder with cheese and supersized fries, he turns the camera on the scarcely digested splatter on the pavement like it was a newly discovered Jackson Pollock masterpiece.

But Spurlock is obviously using his binge as a launching pad to make larger points about the fast-food culture in America and the increasing incidence of obesity that it fosters. I love the scene where he asks a group of tourists in Washington, D.C., to recite the Pledge of Allegiance. They fumble for the words, never quite getting them correct. When he asks if they know the slogan for the Big Mac, a woman steps forward and whips it off the way a believer delivers a favorite Bible verse: "Twoallbeefpattiesspecialsaucelettuce cheesepicklesoniononasesameseedbun."

Spurlock, a New Yorker, traveled across the country to dine at McDonald's and actually made a pit stop in Worcester, where he interviewed first-graders at the Francis J. McGrath Elementary School. The kids he spoke with could more rapidly identify a picture of Ronald McDonald than they could one of Jesus Christ. Yes, Spurlock should have accounted for the separation of church and state, though I believe his point is that RM has reached the status of secular saint. (Taxpayers will be happy to know the students batted 1.000 when picking out George Washington.)

There is something ineffably strange about a country that can claim overeating as a health crisis when so much of the rest of the world is worried about having enough to eat. In 1990, independent filmmaker Henry Jaglom made a movie simply titled *Eating*, in which a group of women sat around and talked about their often unhealthy relationship with food. Where else could such a film be made and viewed with a straight face?

Spurlock seems to be trying to tread the middle ground when it comes to where corporate responsibility must cede to personal responsibility. He elicits convincing arguments from professor John F. Banzhaf III that the fast-food industry has used the same marketing tactics as Big Tobacco to hook their customers at a young age and should be held legally responsible when they get fat on their products. Then when Spurlock asks lawyer Samuel Hirsch why he's brought suit against the fast-food giants, Hirsch smirks, and responds, "You want to hear a noble cause?"

Ugh.

The lawsuits are specious. A more effective weapon to curb people's obsession with fast food may be for school systems to show Spurlock's documentary—even in an edited form—as part of the health curriculum. Spurlock presents his information with a Michael Moore-ish comic bite and plenty of illustrative graphics to hold middle and high school attention spans. *Super Size Me* would be a painless way to get at least some kids thinking about the ramifications of the stuff they're cramming into their mouths.

Of course, after seeing the film, I'm newly soured on fast food. I will try to be strong for as long as possible, but I'm unsure. When Ronald McDonald calls my name, can I resist?

FYI

- Each day, one out of every four Americans visits a fast-food restaurant.
- In 1972, we spent $3 billion a year on fast food; today, we spend more than $110 billion.
- McDonald's feeds more than 46 million people a day—more than the entire population of Spain.
- French fries are the most eaten vegetable in America.
- You would have to walk for seven hours straight to burn off a supersized Coke, fries, and Big Mac.
- In the United States, we eat more than one million animals an hour.
- 60 percent of all Americans are overweight or obese.

—from www.supersizeme.com

CONSIDER

1. What are your thoughts on lawsuits against fast-food sellers? Is it fair to say fast food is like tobacco? Would you support such lawsuits? Defend your position in a brief paper or create a poster that expresses your opinion.

2. Do you regard Spurlock's thirty-day binge as making a significant point or more of a publicity stunt? How else might assertions about the dangers of fast food be effectively made?

3. How should we approach the relationships between documentaries and arguments? Is it fair for a documentary filmmaker to take a stance? Write two or three paragraphs supporting your opinion.

CHALLENGE

4. View *Super Size Me* or another controversial documentary, and take note of argumentative strategies that you notice. Compose a summary that captures the main argument advanced by the film, and then develop a response that either supports or refutes that argument.

Downsize This! Americans Escalate Their War on Fat

Daniel B. Wood
(2004)

FYI Daniel B. Wood is a reporter for the *Christian Science Monitor*.

B obo "Refrigerator" Simon says his days with a 48-inch waistline are numbered—whether he likes it or not.

"McDonald's cutting back its supersize menu is the last straw," says the appliance salesman, chomping into a carton of fries in the cold shadow of some Golden Arches here. "You know when the dieting craze hits one of America's biggest fast-food outlets, there's no place left for us fatties to hide."

That isn't literally true, of course, not in the land of the Big Gulp. But America has a fresh fixation on a problem that, apparently, has become extra, extra large. The nation's war on fat is escalating on several fronts, from exercise to fast-food-bashing to the carb-consciousness in which "Atkins" is in, starch is out.

On one level, it's all too familiar. The "battle of the bulge" has gone from dieting catchphrase to cliché and back to a piece of World War II history. But there's now an undercurrent of urgency that makes this time different.

Tuesday the government said smoking may soon be overtaken by poor diet and lack of exercise as the leading cause of preventable deaths.

"America is in the midst of a sea change in shifts of how we look at food and dieting," says Amy Lanou, nutrition director for the Physicians Committee for Responsible Medicine, a Washington research group that emphasizes preventive approaches.

The comment echoes that of other health experts and culture watchers who see McDonald's announcement last week that it will no longer offer the famous portion upgrade known as "supersize"—larger fries and drinks for pennies extra—as part of a new consciousness in the United States.

Recent studies indicate that one-third of Americans are overweight and one-fifth are obese.

The responses are becoming widespread:

- With obesity surging in children, school districts increasingly are saying no to sugary food and sodas.
- State legislatures doubled the number of bills and resolutions this year targeting what is now perceived as a crisis, especially among children— taxing movie tickets to pay for fat-fighting programs, beefing up phys-ed

in schools, and requiring restaurants to offer healthier options on children's menus. And a number are considering exempting restaurants from being sued for weight-related health issues.

- Whether liable or not, businesses are adapting, too. Southwest Airlines now asks some larger passengers to purchase two seats on crowded flights—to prevent discomfort for other fliers. Grocery aisles offer smaller soda cans and "low-carb" foods.

Where the view in the mirror has long driven the diet-conscious, today more and more parents are noticing how many of their kids are dimpled, dumpy, paunchy and plump, and are concerned.

The move by McDonald's is about more than just portion size. After decades of dieting focused on low-fat foods, the battleground has shifted to carbohydrates as the primary culprit in the nation's overeating habits. Ads for the "Atkins" and "South Beach" low-carb diets are virtually inescapable. Newer methods ("Beyond Atkins") are already refining the concept.

Besides nutritional scrutiny, experts say the last quarter century has highlighted other American predilections that are as close under our noses as the sneeze guard at your local buffet. One is the need for exercise, especially as sedentary commutes grow longer. Another is for a healthy mental outlook. Then there's the fact that Americans like their products on the big side—from SUVs to big-screen TVs. Put food in that equation, and it helps explain why the American body has been getting larger.

Mix the two trends together and you get a fat sandwich with a side of corpulence.

"For all kinds of reasons, Americans have become completely conditioned to see basic serving sizes as something much larger than 30 to 40 years ago, and that is our biggest problem," says Ms. Lanou. American meal portions have grown, along with markings on packages which say what a "normal" helping is.

The trend separates America from the practices of Europeans, experts say, with smaller portions typical from France to Italy to Spain and even Germany.

"From candy bars to soda to bagels, the portions are out of control," says Madelyn Fernstrom, director of the Weight Management Center at the University of Pittsburgh. She chronicles the rise of all-you-can-eat restaurants where consumers learn to overeat because they want the most for their money.

The obesity challenge may run up against another American penchant—the habit of suing to hold others accountable. The prospects of endless litigation about such food is becoming of more than passing concern.

"Psychologically in America in the past 10 years, we have become so lawsuit driven that it has seeped into the mind-set of an entire generation that anything can be made the problem of anyone else except yourself," says Terra Wellington, host of a Phoenix-based national TV series on balanced living. "We are becoming a nation of blaming, rejecting personal responsibility and lacking common sense."

But the U.S. Congress is considering a so-called cheeseburger bill, which would prevent Americans from suing fast-food giants such as McDonald's for making them overweight.

Indeed, even in a blame-game society, there is evidence that Americans are learning lessons and moving forward.

Grocery and restaurant associations report that the growth of healthier cuisines has never been stronger since the early days of nouvelle cuisine in the mid-'70s, to spa and California cuisines in the '80s and "fusion" in the '90s—all food movements which focused on lighter, less caloric food and sauces and more diverse menus, balanced by fish, vegetables and fruits.

"It is taking time, but we are wising up, somewhat," says Susan Johnson, owner of Susan's Healthy Gourmet, a southern California firm that delivers fresh, calorie-counted gourmet meals. Nine years ago, she says her firm was considered a niche market, now her fare is mainstream.

"People are . . . telling waiters to hold the butter, put the dressing on the side, and hold the bun."

CONSIDER

1. What would you say is responsible for the incorporation of healthier fare into fast-food menus? Is it fair to say that films like *Super Size Me* or articles arguing for better fare are responsible for menu changes?

2. If you were restricted to using one strategy to persuade people to eat better, which appeal would you choose: logical, ethical, or emotional? Explain and defend your choice in a brief paper that also hints at how you would use these strategies or, perhaps, which successful campaigns you might imitate. (For example, the famous "Got milk?" ads might give you ideas for a campaign based on ethos.)

CHALLENGE

3. Visit a fast-food restaurant, and examine its menu. Consider the food offered by the restaurant, the presentation of the menu items, the pricing, the packaging of the actual food, and any other details that seem relevant to your experience. Write an argument exploring the degree to which the restaurant promotes healthy eating.

Making Our Place
in History

Memorials and monuments are one of our most important ways of making arguments to future generations. They embody our best visions of our community—what we think matters and what we've accomplished. They constitute what classical rhetoricians called *epideictic arguments*—arguments of praise that are grounded in shared values. Obviously, in our culture, arguably the most diverse in human history, finding those shared values can be difficult. As you read this section, think about the memorials you've seen and the controversial memorials we discuss. What claims do they make about who we are?

Remembering MLK

Martin Luther King Jr.'s call for an end to judging people on the basis of their skin color is too familiar to repeat—it recalls for most Americans the proud achievements of the civil rights movement of the 1950s and 1960s. It's not surprising that King has become a national icon, a symbol of the cultural diversity and tolerance for difference that we value as part of our nation's ethos. Yet precisely because of the central place he holds in our national consciousness, the issue of how best to remember King's legacy has sometimes sparked disagreement. This section features a sampling of artists' renditions of King and describes a small controversy that exploded in Rocky Mount, North Carolina, when some townspeople rejected a sculpture of King commissioned from a white artist, Erik Blome.

A Tale of Two Cities and Two Kings

Eugene Kane
(2004)

In just six years, the statue of Dr. Martin Luther King Jr. that looks out over King Drive with an upraised arm has become one of the north side's most prominent landmarks.

Most consider the sculpture by Illinois artist Erik Blome a fitting tribute to the legacy of the slain civil rights leader.

But not so in Rocky Mount, N.C., where another Blome statue of King erected last summer has divided opinions across racial and political lines in the city of 56,000 people.

Some Rocky Mount blacks believe the commissioned work of art just doesn't do King justice.

Others have been so blunt as to suggest the statue doesn't even look like the man. Which can be enough to break a sculptor's heart.

"When people say something like that, it cuts really deep," said Blome, who has done sculptures of prominent African-American figures for years.

In a telephone interview from his home in Crystal Lake, Ill., Blome said the controversy over his statue caught him by surprise last summer because he had worked with a committee of civic leaders during the project.

Throughout the process, he presented sketches of his intended vision of King step by step to the committee. Nobody ever said he was on the wrong track.

But once the statue was up, some residents began to grumble. One amateur critic—a member of the most vocal opposition—described the statue to a *Washington Post* reporter as looking like "a slave" and being "an insult" to King's memory.

Part of the grumbling had to do with the color of the artist, too.

Blome, who describes himself as a liberal who supports affirmative action, said he was baffled when some black residents used his race against him.

"Can a white guy relate to King? Absolutely," he said. "I feel very connected to King.

"To me as a white person, King was so important, I think to limit him to only artists of a certain race or color diminishes him."

It was the first time Blome had faced such critical examination of his work. In the past, he's done sculptures of black figures such as Rosa Parks, Duke Ellington and Thurgood Marshall. He even did a statue of Michael Jordan's late father.

Nobody ever complained before.

Particularly not in Milwaukee, where Blome's statue on King Drive has become an integral part of the landscape.

"I've never seen a memorial dedicated to a pessimist."

—PAUL HARVEY
radio commentator

In fact, he said the success of the King Drive statue was one of the reasons he was chosen for the work in Rocky Mount. But it's not a duplication; as an artist, Blome said, "I didn't want to repeat what I did in Milwaukee."

Looking beyond the racial implications, Blome said he suspected the flap over the King statue in Rocky Mount was more about political shenanigans in a small southern town than any real aesthetic concerns.

Last year, the statue became a hot issue during the mayoral race, with a black candidate who opposed the white incumbent leading the charge.

As a result, Blome thinks the controversy isn't about his work at all.

"This is about way more than art," he said.

He remembered his Milwaukee experience as a relatively pain-free process, even though he wasn't a unanimous choice.

"Milwaukee did it professionally," said Blome, describing the process used by the YWCA to form a diverse committee to pick the final sculpture.

"I suspect, in a small town, it must be harder to get a committee like that," Blome said.

Currently, plans are for Rocky Mount to remove his statue and let Blome try to produce another version.

He's trying hard not to be offended by the rejection.

Sculptor Erik Blome (bottom) and the statue (above) of Martin Luther King, Jr., he created for Rocky Mount, North Carolina.

"Art cuts so close to your heart, it's like a religion," he said.

He is now at work on another Wisconsin project, a statue for the state firefighters association that will become part of a memorial in Wisconsin Rapids.

But he regrets the decision to remove the statue in Rocky Mount.

"A piece of artwork needs to be looked at for a long time before you make up your mind," he said.

Or, as in the case of Milwaukee's Dr. King on King Drive, it can be love at first sight.

Lev T. Mills, *Out-Loud Silent* (1969) (above)
Elijah Pierce, *Martin Luther King,* (Love), (1968) (right)

CONSIDER

1. Is Eugene Kane's essay an argument? Why or why not? Consider his claims, reasons, and evidence. Does he use particular lines of argument?

2. How important are the images of Blome and his statue to your understanding of the controversy? Might one object to the MLK statue on its own merits without raising a racial issue?

3. Is Blome's statue itself an argument? If so, how would you summarize its claim or claims? What do you think critics of the statue mean when they say that the statue depicts King as "slavelike"?

4. The two works of art shown above are part of the Smithsonian Institution's traveling exhibit "In the Spirit of Martin." What arguments do you think each work suggests about King and his legacy? Which of the three works of art honoring King (Blome's statue, Pierce's wood carving, or Mills's print) appeals to you most? Why?

COMPOSE

6. Using the Kane essay as a starting point, construct a series of argumentative claims that might follow from it, ones that explore different elements and issues potentially raised by the controversy in North Carolina. Then develop one of those claims into a convincing argument presented as a letter to the editor of the local newspaper.

7. In an argument of your own, explore an issue that involves racial boundaries. Perhaps a local sports team carries a name that some groups find offensive. Or maybe your campus has culture rooms for ethnic and racial groups or separate graduate ceremonies or job fairs for different groups. Research the controversy thoroughly, explore various sides of the issue, and then offer a claim you can defend.

Remembering September 11, 2001

Late in 2003, proposals for a monument on the site where the World Trade Center towers stood generated a flurry of news and editorial activity in New York City and around the country. In recent decades, Americans have debated the shape and placement of several important museums and memorials—the Vietnam Veterans Memorial, the United States Holocaust Memorial Museum, the National World War II Memorial, and the Oklahoma City National Memorial. But the scale and location of the September 11 monument will likely provoke questions and arguments for many years to come. The following essays—the first a news story, the latter two opinion pieces—and images raise some of those issues and demonstrate how arguments can provoke thought, learning, and public awareness.

FYI The Lower Manhattan Development Corporation (LMDC) administered the World Trade Center Site Memorial Competition. Through this competition, the jury selected a design for a single memorial that remembers and honors all loss of life on September 11, 2001, and February 26, 1993. The LMDC received an enormous outpouring of ideas from across the globe, with 13,683 registrants and 5,201 memorial submissions from sixty-three nations. After a two-stage judging process that included substantial public feedback, the design shown on page 572 by Michael Arad and Peter Walker, was selected as the winner. This memorial will be incorporated into the larger plans for reconstructing the site. For more information about the memorial competition and plans for rebuilding on the site, visit <www.wtcsitememorial.org>

Are Memorial Designs Too Complex to Last?

Julie V. Iovine
(2003)

Julie Iovine writes on architecture and design for the *New York Times.*

Apart from Daniel Libeskind standing in a swarm of camera lights, there were relatively few architects present on Wednesday when the eight finalist designs in the World Trade Center Site Memorial Competition officially went on view downtown at the Winter Garden.

But they were paying close attention elsewhere. They were logging onto a Lower Manhattan Development Corporation Web site (www.wtcsitememorial.org) from home and office, from airports and hotels around the world, and looking with practiced eyes at the plans. Shimmering pools of eternal reflected light, cathedral-size expanses underground: the details prompted both professional responses and emotional reactions among two dozen American architects reached for comment. They discussed aesthetics and the relative youth of the finalists and wondered how the memorials would endure over time.

Margaret Helfand, the 2001 president of the American Institute of Architects, considered the designs too timid, saying they bore only a fragile connection to the rest of the site, the neighborhood and city. "This memorial cannot be cordoned off," she said in a telephone interview from Amsterdam, adding that she had expected to see more design features at street level rather than below ground. "This will be a piece of New York that has to be knitted into the fabric of the city, not just on a profound level but at the street level."

Wendy Evans Joseph, president of the Architectural League, who worked with James Ingo Freed on the United States Holocaust Memorial Museum in Washington and who recently designed a Holocaust garden in Salt Lake City, said the program requirement to recognize the two footprints of the original trade towers had led to overly complicated memorial concepts.

"Most of the designers used one footprint for one thing and the second for another and then joining the two becomes a third event," Ms. Joseph said. "Treating each as separate is hurting the designs."

No one was surprised, given the ages of the finalists, that minimalism was the universal vocabulary of the submissions. It is a post–Maya Lin [designer of the Vietnam war memorial in Washington DC] generation, noted Michael Manfredi, whose firm Weiss/Manfredi designed the women's memorial at Arlington Cemetery and was a finalist for the World War II memorial competition in Washington.

"A reductive minimalist sensibility is very much what we see in memorials at this cultural moment," Mr. Manfredi said. Society today, he said, is too diverse as well as too inclusive to allow for a more figurative or symbolic language for memorials. "You just can't do the statues of 30 years ago, because who are you going to show?" The burden of conveying the weight of reality now falls on lists of names, which in its own way undermines the ability to create resonant simplicity, he said.

Too much depends on language, rather than the shaping of space, said Annabelle Selldorf, a Manhattan architect. "Everything is about language and conceptual thinking these days," she said. "Sculpture and architecture are physical. They provide an experience of space that should let you think as you may."

Many of the architects had practical questions: What happens to all those water features in case of drought? Can such vast spaces underground be free of columns? How many people can cross a narrow bridge at one time?

"I always worry about programs dependent on technology. LMDC can't exist forever, so who is going to maintain it all for all the ages?" said Hugh Hardy, the architect who oversaw the restoration of Radio City Music Hall. "When light bulbs don't work and the water gets scuzzy, what have you got?"

Mr. Hardy attended the Winter Garden opening and, that afternoon, convened with 25 architects, landscape designers, engineers and lawyers to review the plans for New York New Visions, a group that also prepared a 20-page document last spring analyzing the submissions for the master plan of the site. They intend to submit a similar analysis of the memorial plans to the development corporation by Tuesday.

There was no euphoria in the room where the design professionals met, Mr. Hardy said. "There was no sense of 'You've done it!,'" he added. The reaction was more "even-tempered, like the nature of the designs themselves." A key issue that emerged was maintenance. Several designs rely on high-tech solutions. The fuel that would light "Votives in Suspension" drips down cords cut to lengths that vary according to the victims' ages. Keeping them all lighted could require constant vigilance. "Look at the poor Irish potato famine memorial," Mr. Hardy said. "It's so successful after one year, it started falling apart, and they already have had to put it back together."

The dependence on artificial light and large underground spaces will call for sophisticated climate control and the most advanced engineering. "It's all going to be phenomenally expensive," said Alex Gorlin, a Manhattan architect who is now designing a mausoleum for 2,000 in an Olmsted-designed cemetery in Oakland, Calif. "They are all loaded with a ton of intricate programmatic elements.

"All the designs treated 200-foot open spaces as if that's all in a day's work. Where are the support columns? Cathedrals of space under tilted planes of earth make a great image, but there doesn't seem to be an understanding of structural practicality and cost. Even water is expensive."

Complicated as the designs appear to be, the architects interviewed saw no reason to think that any were too difficult to build, although at a cost. They

warned, however, that the seductive images of renewal and peace now on display in videos, models and renderings at the Winter Garden would be hard to translate into the reality of a heavily trafficked space. They asked how the memorial would hold up as a ruin.

"I yearn for something simple with no moving parts, like a Mayan pyramid," Ms. Helfand said. "What did they understand that somehow we don't?"

Placing the cornerstone for the Freedom Tower reconstruction project, July 4, 2004

Memorial Proposal: Reflecting Absence

Michael Arad and Peter Walker

(2004)

This memorial proposes a space that resonates with the feelings of loss and absence that were generated by the destruction of the World Trade Center and the taking of thousands of lives on September 11, 2001, and February 26, 1993. It is located in a field of trees that is interrupted by two large voids containing recessed pools. The pools and the ramps that surround them encompass the footprints of the twin towers. A cascade of water that describes the perimeter of each square feeds the pools with a continuous stream. They are large voids, open and visible reminders of the absence.

A computer rendering of the site design for the Freedom Tower and the memorial plaza.

The surface of the memorial plaza is punctuated by the linear rhythms of rows of deciduous trees, forming informal clusters, clearings, and groves. This surface consists of a composition of stone pavers, plantings, and low ground cover. Through its annual cycle of rebirth, the living park extends and deepens the experience of the memorial.

Bordering each pool is a pair of ramps that lead down to the memorial spaces. Descending into the memorial, visitors are removed from the sights and sounds of the city and immersed in a cool darkness. As they proceed, the sound of water falling grows louder, and more daylight filters in from below. At the bottom of their descent, they find themselves behind a thin curtain of water, staring out at an enormous pool. Surrounding this pool is a continuous ribbon of names. The [great size] of this space and the multitude of names that form this endless ribbon underscore the vast scope of the destruction. Standing there at the water's edge, looking at a pool of water that is flowing away into an abyss, a visitor to the site can sense that what is beyond this curtain of water and ribbon of names is inaccessible.

The names of the deceased will be arranged in no particular order around the pools. After carefully considering different arrangements, [we] have found that any arrangement that tries to impose meaning through physical adjacency will cause grief and anguish to people who might be excluded from that process, furthering the sense of loss that they are already suffering.

The haphazard brutality of the attacks is reflected in the arrangement of names, and no attempt is made to impose order upon this suffering. The selfless sacrifices of rescue workers could be acknowledged with their agency's insignia next to their names. Visitors to the site, including family members and friends of the deceased, would be guided by on-site staff or a printed directory to the specific location of each name. For those whose deceased were never physically identified, the location of the name marks a spot that is their own.

In between the two pools is a short passageway that links them at this lower level. A single alcove is located along this passageway, containing a small dais where visitors can light a candle or leave an artifact in memory of loved ones. Across from it, in a small chamber, visitors might pause and contemplate. This space provides for gatherings, quiet reflection, and memorial services.

Along the western edge of the site, a deep fissure exposes the slurry wall from plaza level to bedrock and provides access via a stairway. Descending alongside its battered surfaces, visitors will witness the massive expanse of the original foundations. The entrance to the underground interpretive center is located at bedrock. Here visitors could view many preserved artifacts from the twin towers: twisted steel beams, a crushed fire truck, and personal effects. The underground interpretive center would contain exhibition areas as well as lecture halls and a research library.

In contrast with the public mandate of the underground interpretive center is the very private nature of the room for unidentified remains. It is situated at bedrock at the north tower footprint. Here a large stone vessel forms a centerpiece for the unidentified remains. A large opening in the ceiling connects this space to the sky above, and the sound of water shelters the space from the city. Family members can gather here for moments of private contemplation. It is a personal space for remembrance.

The memorial plaza is designed to be a mediating space; it belongs both to the city and to the memorial. Located at street level to allow for its integration into the fabric of the city, the plaza encourages the use of this space by New Yorkers on a daily basis. The memorial grounds will not be isolated from the rest of the city; they will be a living part of it.

FYI Daniel Henninger is deputy editor of *The Wall Street Journal*'s editorial page. His column appears Fridays in the *Journal* and on OpinionJournal.com.

Wonder Land: Build It and They Won't Come

Daniel Henninger
(2003)

Looking out my office window in lower Manhattan, across the 16 acres that have become an excavation site, I can see a steel mesh fence on the far side, and from one end to the other people are standing at the fence, looking into the September 11 space. This is Christmas week, and you could say these are just holiday tourists who've come to gawk at "Ground Zero." But these people are always at the fence, and have been at all hours for more than two years, looking in.

Now we have arrived at the end of 2003, the year of the war in Iraq, and the people who are rebuilding the 16 acres where the towers were have released a modified construction plan for the site, as imagined by architects Daniel Libeskind and David Childs, working on behalf of the site's developer and leaseholder, Larry Silverstein.

At the northwest corner of the site, they would build a 1,776-foot-high Freedom Tower, and inside the current footprint would be four or five new buildings, restoring the 10 million square feet of lost office space, plus new cultural venues. At the southwest corner there would be space for a memorial.

If they build this plan, they won't come.

Oh, they'll come for a while, out of curiosity. But 20 years from now? 15? I don't think so. The Civil War has hallowed ground, as at Gettysburg. World War II has Pearl Harbor and the Arizona memorial. September 11 will have . . . an office complex and a shopping mall.

The high-minded argument for doing this (the low one comes in a moment) is that we have to replace everything, which I guess means the aggregate square footage, to "show the terrorists"; otherwise "they will win." They're not winning. American GIs are fighting and dying for us at this hour to ensure that the terrorists don't win, and they won't. This site in downtown Manhattan is what it is: the remains of an attack on the American landmass and the murder of several thousand innocent civilians. It should be remembered for what happened that day—a violation, a bloody trespass. But it won't be if the site is choked with buildings and a memorial off in a corner. The crowdedness of this plan's buildings, stores and people means this will be a denser urban space than even Times Square. New York's foot traffic is a rough force, which in time will erode and erase September 11.

Remembrance in our time has become difficult. We are becoming a culture of short-term memory, with mass media creating inexhaustibly new experiences for us to have, discard and forget. The practice of deep memory, much less common memory, is becoming harder to maintain.

There is also our politics. Everyone was impressed with the nation's sense of common purpose after September 11 and hoped it would last. But it didn't. Though the Bush administration's decision to go to war against Saddam Hussein was controversial, it is remarkable how quickly partisanship returned and how deep and bitter that partisanship became in a time of war. There is little talk of September 11 in New York City, an irrepressibly partisan place. The act of remembrance is now done by the visitors at the fence, looking in.

The low reason for building the current plan is that the site is owned by the Port Authority of New York and New Jersey, and the Port Authority, the landlord-owner of the real estate, wants its rent flow back (some $120 million annually). There is as well New York City's desire for property-tax flows. As such, it's an odds-on bet that all the planned buildings will go up, with New York State bureaucracies as the first and primary tenants. Inside the politics of Ground Zero, memory is merely a piece of the deal.

I wrote sometime back that I believe the former World Trade Center site should not be rebuilt. That is an extreme position, which isn't going to happen. They will rebuild. So I propose a middle way that would serve the needs of commerce and New York's tax flows, and the larger goal of national remembrance.

Go ahead and build the torqued Freedom Tower in the corner. Let it soar 1,776 feet into the New York skyline, carrying up its glassy flue all the site's burning emotions. And let it stand alone. It should be the only big building inside the 16-acre space. Look at the drawing nearby and imagine the Freedom Tower standing alone and you will understand the difference between pride of place and what's mostly just an overbuilt office mall.

As to the offices, the politicians should help Mr. Silverstein move the rest of the commercial space to other downtown sites. The largeness of the place should remain large. This grand, austere space is the vision that captures, fixes and silences those who come to look. Remake the land into a beautiful place, to be sure, but let those stark gray foundation walls of the fallen buildings remain. That is the only sight that will ensure the remembrance that day deserves.

Historical memory matters. It carries in it the nation's longest-surviving traditions. September 11 is tied forever to this line. Or should be. Give those people staring through the steel fence the chance to walk freely on that ground. They won't forget it.

Firehouse on 14th Street between 1st and 2nd Avenues, September 13, 2001; Sue Luftschein, photographer

FYI The events of September 11, 2001 inspired the construction of hundreds, perhaps thousands, of informal memorials. The photographs presented on pages 576, 579, and 580 are part of the September 11 Digital Archive (911digitalarchive.org/), a project co-sponsored by the Alfred P. Sloan Foundation, the City University of New York Graduate Center, George Mason University, and the Library of Congress. This project aims to collect and preserve firsthand accounts of the attacks and their aftermath.

9/11: Commemorative Art, Ritual, and Story

Steve Zeitlin and Ilana Harlow

(2001)

On September 11, New York City filled with such overwhelming sorrow that personal rituals of grief spilled out of private lives and homes into public spaces. Feelings of loss were inscribed on the city itself. People used every available medium to express themselves; some even scrawled messages in the dust from the explosions that coated vehicles and windows. Public surfaces were plastered with "Missing" posters. Parks, firehouses, subway stations, traffic islands, and even curbsides became sites of continually evolving shrines of flowers, candles, poems, and art.

In the great public gathering places of Washington Square Park and Union Square Park, New Yorkers re-created the towers in miniature using tin, papier-mâché, and paint. Red, white, and blue candles flickered alongside Christian votives, Jewish memorial *yahrtzeit,* and offertory candles petitioning intercessors from St. Anthony to the Virgin of Guadalupe to the Siete Potencias de Africa. The wax from the candles dripped and flowed together as our differences seemed to melt away. Representing prayers for peaceful repose of the dead, prayers for the welfare of the injured, and prayers for peace, these candles also symbolized solidarity. New Yorkers came together in a public ritual that in its transcendence of any single belief system represented all of them. The magnitude of the expression of grief approached the enormity of the loss.

Two years ago we began writing a book about creative responses to death and mourning. As folklorists, we were struck by the way people are increasingly expressing their grief by telling stories, crafting commemorative art, and creating personal rituals. Such creative projects counter the destructiveness of death and give mourners a focus that allows them to work through their grief. Expressive responses serve not only to give shape to sorrow, but also to keep the dead present in the lives of the living. [Our book,] *Giving a Voice to Sorrow: Personal Responses to Death and Mourning,* both documents and advocates outward expressions of inner struggles, expressed in storytelling, ritual, and commemorative art.

All three forms of expression became public in dramatic ways following the tragedy. Again and again on September 11, the networks broadcast footage of United Airlines flight 175 slicing diagonally into the South Tower and erupting in a fireball. Again and again, we heard the details of flight numbers and moment of impact. Yet this wasn't just the sensationalism of the media. This was the beginning of telling the story of our loss. In our personal lives, when a loved one dies, his or her last days, hours, and moments are recounted again and again. The recurring broadcasts addressed our need to hear and retell the story of any death—to help make it real. Undertaker and poet Thomas Lynch has noted that such images and details are the first step in assimilating the unfathomable, "the round and witless horror of someone who / one dry night in perfect humor ceases measurably to be."

There are no set rituals for dealing with the deaths of 3,000 people in a terrorist attack. They are being created as we go along. Many New Yorkers have participated in the public ritual of making pilgrimages to sites where "Missing" posters hang. Although Union Square Park was not an officially designated site for public grieving, it was the farthest south most people could go once the city below Fourteenth Street was closed off. Just as after the crash of TWA Flight 800, people brought flowers to the seaside, to get as close as possible to the place where the plane went down and the place where, it seems, the souls of the dead must hover, after September 11, mourners walked to the edge to make their shrines and utter their prayers.

In many neighborhoods of the city, memorial murals were already a familiar part of the urban landscape. These vibrant splashes of color in the gray of the city generally include portraits of the deceased, their dates of birth and death, and images that convey something about who they were. They celebrate the lives of those who used to enliven the streets with their presence. The walls, often memorializing those who died young, sometimes violently, keep the dead in the community and are constant reminders of community loss. Drawing on this familiar idiom, on the afternoon of September 11, graffiti artist Chico painted a memorial wall on the corner of Fourteenth and Avenue A dominated by images of the smoking towers and

Chico's mural, Avenue A at 14th Street, September 13, 2001, Sue Luftschein, photographer

the words, "In memory of families and friends RIP Sept. 11, 2001." In the tradition of memorial walls, this became a site of community gathering. "Missing" posters were affixed to the wall; candles, flowers, and teddy bears accumulated on the sidewalk below.

About three weeks after the attack on the World Trade Center, we were distraught to see that the shrines of candles, flowers, and art had been removed from the public parks, cleared out by well-meaning officials who plan to preserve the memorials for posterity. But memorials need to stay on the site where they mark grief. The process of public mourning needs to play itself out, even if our public spaces lose their tidiness. As a society, we are learning how to grieve publicly as well as privately, and the arts of ordinary people have a role to play. Yes, future generations must see the outpouring of humanity that followed the tyrannical assault on our city. Yet at this moment, it is equally important for the memorials to serve their intended function in their intended settings.

When we began writing *Giving a Voice to Sorrow*, we could not have imagined the current devastation. But we do hope that some of the art projects and rituals featured in it will inspire and help individuals and communities who have been affected by the tragedy to cope with their losses by becoming involved in projects that express their grief in personal and creative ways. Our conversations with the bereaved confirmed our initial feelings about the importance of storytelling, ritual, and commemorative art. Tragically, this is also being borne out in the wake of the events of September 11.

Makeshift memorial in Union Square, New York City, September 13, 2001, Sue Luftschein, photographer

**Discover the famous and
not-so-famous memorial designs.**
www.ablongman.com/beyondwords39

CONSIDER

1. Arad and Walker provide a detailed description of their design and of the associations and responses they believe it will evoke among visitors. What do you think of the design? Would you have been able to infer the architects' purposes without the accompanying description?

2. Iovine and Henninger are critical of the plans for the Freedom Tower site and memorial. What goals or purposes does each believe the reconstruction should serve? How do these differ from the goals expressed by the architects? Which do you agree with?

3. Compare and contrast the official memorial with the informal memorials pictured in this section and discussed by Zeitlin and Harlow. What similarities and differences do you see in their purposes, audiences, and designs? Which of the memorials do you find most powerful or effective?

COMPOSE

4. Write an argument about an important project in your hometown or on your college campus, modeling it on the kinds of issues and questions raised in these essays on the 9/11 memorial.

5. Do research in the library or on the Web on informal memorials associated with another event or phenomenon—for example, roadside memorials for the victims of auto accidents, murals dedicated to community heroes, commemorative Web sites, or pet cemeteries. Compose a written essay or a photo essay reporting what you find.

6. Describe a space in your own home or neighborhood that you or someone else has made into a remembrance: an altar, a mantel or shelf that's reserved for particular photographs or mementos, or a graffiti wall, for example. Does this space share any features or purposes in common with the informal memorials Zeitlin and Harlow discuss? Explain.

CHALLENGE

7. How do you think official and informal memorials differ as arguments? For example, to what audiences do they speak? What purposes do they serve? Who should have a say about the design, location, and maintenance of each—the people personally affected by them? Community officials? Artists? Tourists?

8. Choose a public event that you think is important, and imagine that you've been asked to propose a design for a monument or memorial. Prepare a proposal similar to Arad and Walker's. Include in your proposal both a visual and a written description of your design.

Assignments and Projects

Project 1

Reading Visual Arguments

The readings and images in this chapter demonstrate how closely tied arguments are to particular audiences and contexts. Recall the starkly different approaches taken by the issue posters produced in the 1940s–1960s and those created today.

This project asks you to select two or more visual arguments—either texts consisting entirely of visual images or texts that combine words and images—that address the same issue but are designed to appeal to different audiences. Write a three- to five-page rhetorical analysis comparing and contrasting the persuasive strategies these texts use. Your analysis should draw readers' attention to the patterns of similarity and difference you find most interesting: their use of rhetorical appeals to *ethos, pathos,* and *logos*; the ways in which the arguments are structured; the kinds of claims made; the use of evidence or design elements; or any combination of these factors.

Before you begin this project, take a look at Jonathan Butler's "Visual Images of National Identity as Rhetoric: Propaganda Posters of the Great War" (pages 585–588) to see how one student writer approached this assignment. As you develop your draft, keep in mind the composing questions introduced in Chapter 2:

WHAT'S IT TO YOU?

■ A rhetorical analysis requires substantial time and thought, so it's best to find a **topic** that you feel passionate about. Perhaps you're a staunch advocate of gun control or you've been following a campus debate over whether to use student fees to build a campus child care center. If you know a topic well, you'll already have a sense of what arguments are being made about it, and you'll likely be eager to undertake sustained research and analysis.

WHAT DO YOU WANT TO SAY ABOUT IT?

■ Your primary **medium** for this project is print; however, since you'll be analyzing visual texts, you'll probably need to incorporate images—either representations of entire visual texts or of portions relevant to your discussion—as supporting examples and illustrations. (Be sure to cite the source of any images you include in your paper.)

Also consider **purpose** as you explore what you want to say in this project. A rhetorical analysis looks at the way an argument works and may evaluate its effectiveness. You might think of your analysis as an argument about an argument. Accordingly, rather than simply listing every rhetorical detail you see in the texts, you should focus on some specific **thesis**, or **claim**. *After* examining the arguments closely, generate a claim with supporting reasons that describe or assess the way the texts work: "Whereas the City Ballet's mailing to season ticket holders and their print ad in last Sunday's newspaper both emphasize the quality and entertainment value of their upcoming *Nutcracker* production, the visual styles and emotional appeals used in the two publications couldn't be more different."

WHO WILL LISTEN?

■ If you've chosen arguments that interest you, readers will sense your enthusiasm and want to learn more. But remember that they won't necessarily be familiar with the texts you're analyzing. You'll need to provide **background information** and enough **examples**—quotations or images—to show them how the arguments work. Notice, for example, that Jonathan Butler combines thumbnail images of World War I posters with detailed descriptions in words in his paper. The images re-create the posters' overall effects, while the accompanying explanations draw attention to particular rhetorical details.

WHAT DO YOU NEED TO KNOW?

■ When you write a rhetorical analysis, it's obviously important to study your chosen texts carefully to identify key patterns. It's also important to lay out for each text the basic facts of what is called the rhetorical situation: *who* is writing about *what* for which *audience* (or audiences). Conduct **research** in the library or on the Internet so that you can accurately identify the argument, where and when it appears, in what medium, and so on. You may need to provide a paragraph or more of background information early in your paper to set the context for the argument: "In a letter published online at Punkvoter.com on February 25, 2004, rock musician and political activist Al Jourgensen addressed himself to Urban Outfitters' chairman of the board."

HOW WILL YOU DO IT?

■ This assignment requires that you compare and contrast several texts. To do that, you should decide on a variety of argumentative features to examine systematically in each text, point by point. One strategy might be to discuss how each text uses the three basic rhetorical appeals discussed on pages 526–529.

> **Examine the logical appeals.** Look carefully at how well the claims made in a piece are stated, qualified, and supported. Be specific in identifying these appeals, quoting from verbal arguments and describing visual arguments.

> **Examine the emotional appeals.** Is the argument enhanced by legitimate emotional appeals? Identify those emotions, explain how they are generated, and evaluate their relevance to the claim offered. Again, be specific, quoting or describing the emotional details clearly enough for readers to understand them.

> **Examine *ethos*.** Assess the credibility of the writer, artist, or sponsoring institution. Is the argument presented by someone you are moved to trust? Is the appeal honest? Do you find yourself identifying with the argument? Explain precisely why, using specific evidence from the argument you are analyzing.

> **Also consider how each text treats rebuttals or alternative perspectives.** Does the argument show an awareness of alternative perspectives or points of view? How well does the argument answer obvious objections?

These analyses make up the core, or the **body**, of your essay. You'll then need to frame this discussion with an **introduction**, perhaps outlining your thesis and providing relevant background information, and a **conclusion** that summarizes and comments on the main points you've made.

HOW WELL DOES IT WORK?

■ Once you've completed a draft, **review** your analysis to see that you've identified and demonstrated clear similarities and differences in the arguments and that your discussion is clearly organized, engaging, and persuasive. As with any writing project, be sure that you've accurately **cited** and **documented** all outside sources. The five preceding questions can help you assess your draft and identify possible areas for **revision**. If possible, also ask a classmate or friend to read the draft and offer suggestions.

STUDENT SAMPLE

Jonathan Butler, "Visual Images of National Identity: British and French Propaganda Posters of the Great War"

"I'm very interested in visual arguments, and propaganda posters in particular, so when the university exhibited its collection of World War I posters, I seized the opportunity to write about the documents, hoping to develop a better understanding of how visual rhetoric interacts with and reinforces national identity."

—JONATHAN BUTLER

Butler 1

Jonathan Butler

Professor Friend

English 387

Dec. 8, 2004

Visual Images of National Identity:

Propaganda Posters of the Great War

Although rhetoric has traditionally been thought of as being confined to the realm of language, the art takes other forms as well. As the exhibit of World War I propaganda posters currently on display at the University of South Carolina's McKissick Museum demonstrates, rhetoric happens not just through speech and the written word, but may also work through visuals, or through a combination of words and images that persuade. The dramatic propaganda posters of the Great War seek to evoke emotional and financial civilian support for the war through a variety of persuasive strategies. The posters created in each of the Allied nations were all crafted with the same basic goals; however, each nation employs a distinct style in appealing to its citizens. These different styles in large part reflect the ethos, or preexisting identity, that each nation brought to the table. As the following examples from British and French posters show, each nation's histories and values played a large role in shaping its propaganda.

British posters usually rely on traditional British concepts of honor and the empire to instill nationalism and promote military enlistment. One poster,

Fig. 2. <u>Lord Kitchener Says: Enlist To-Day</u>, 1915 ("Posters")

Fig. 1. Arthur Wardle, <u>The Empire Needs Men</u>, 1919 ("Posters")

for instance, shows a male lion, an image traditionally associated with patri-archal royalty, standing on a rock above his pride, his mane flowing, his chest swollen with pride (see fig. 1). The poster associates Britain with the Old Lion who defies his foes with the help of the young lions, presumably the United States and France. Drawing on the sentiments raised by words and images of the empire, United Kingdom posters often also rely on a feeling of honor-bound obligation--one might even say feelings of guilt--for their rhetorical power. Another typical poster features a portrait of field marshal Lord Kitchener, and the following quote, which scolds young men who do not vol-unteer for military service: "Does the call of duty find no response in you until reinforced--let us rather say superseded--by the call of compulsion?" (see fig. 2). While it's never explicitly stated, one gets the feeling looking at British posters that civilians are being asked to support the war for the Crown, to preserve the history and values of their empire.

The French posters in this exhibit, on the other hand, rely instead on their traditional values expressed in France's motto: "Liberty, Equality, Fraternity." More dramatically symbolic than British posters, French posters create a sense of camaraderie between the Allies, often depicting soldiers representing France, Britain, and the United States collectively defeating a symbolic representation of German forces, usually the black eagle. In one poster, Allied troops in the uniforms of their nations scale a mountain, on top of which the black eagle is perched, its claws red with blood. The inscription reads, "One final effort and we'll have it" (see fig.3). Even the few French posters that deviate from this "Allies triumphing together" theme still maintain the romanticized style of the others, usually depicting images symbolic of French victory over German forces. Not only are the traditional French values of equality and fraternity represented on the posters, but liberty plays a large role as well. Since Liberty has been personified in French culture since the Revolution, it is not surprising that her image was frequently used on French posters. Images of Liberty, resembling a Greek goddess, complete with laurels, abound on posters with and without representations of the other Allied nations. Liberty is often shown posing, huge and specterlike, above a group of soldiers, as in this exhortation to buy liberty bonds (see fig. 4).

Fig. 3. <u>Un Dernier effort et on l'aura</u>, 1917, ("Posers")

Fig. 4. Lucien Jonas <u>Emprunt de la Celebration</u>, 1918 ("Posers")

Butler 4

While the styles of each nation's posters differ as a result of each country's individual ethos and the stylistic choices of the nation's artists, the posters all have the rhetorical use of imagery and text in common. While French poster illustrators use very dramatic imagery to catch the eyes and stir the emotions of their audiences, for example, British posters tend towards a more realistic, reserved style that reflects their traditional notions of duty and honor. By examining these posters and the various rhetorical strategies their creators employed to reach their audience, we can gain a better understanding of the ways in which both image and text can be manipulated for persuasion--as well as some notion of how a society's cultural features shape the development of its texts.

Butler 5

Work Cited

"Posters of the Great War." Exhibit of posters from the Joseph Bruccoli
    Collection. McKissick Museum, University of South Carolina,
    Columbia. Fall 2003 <http://www.sc.edu/library/spcoll/hist/
    gwposters/posterintro.html>.

Read the full text of a longer research project Jonathan Butler composed on this topic.
www.ablongman.com/beyondwords40

Project 2

Composing a Visual Argument

As a college student, you've probably had plenty of opportunities to write persuasive essays and to present argumentative speeches or debates in your academic courses. But you may have had little chance to express your views through visual or multimedia texts. As we've emphasized throughout this book, visual texts are the products of sophisticated rhetorical and design choices—choices at least as complex as those involved in producing a traditional paper or speech. This project invites you to grapple with these choices as you produce a visual argument about an issue of your choice. You may choose what form your argument will take, as long as it uses visual elements as a significant component of the argument. Possibilities include a poster, flyer, Web page, brochure, advertisement, or short film. (Check with your instructor for additional guidelines and suggestions.) Before you begin to compose your visual text, research your topic thoroughly so that you'll have comprehensive, current information at hand, and identify the target audience you want your text to reach.

The composing questions discussed in Chapter 2 provide useful starting points for planning, drafting, and revising your project:

WHAT'S IT TO YOU?

- Arguments, by definition, grow from disagreements. As you consider possible **topics** for this project, focus on issues that spark genuine controversy or that raise awareness about current problems.

WHAT DO YOU WANT TO SAY ABOUT IT?

- Decide early on the **medium** and **genre** of your visual argument. Will you create a Web site with several pages? A flyer that could be photocopied and posted around campus? A glossy advertisement suitable for publication in a printed magazine? A filmed public service announcement to be broadcast on a local cable TV station? Your choices will to a large degree determine what materials, technology, and rhetorical conventions you'll draw on as you produce your argument. Be realistic when you plan your argument: If you've never used video-recording equipment and aren't sure where to procure it, save your documentary film idea for a longer-term project.

Once you've identified the form your argument will take, think about what **claim** you want to make and whether you'll state it directly or implicitly. Remember that *implicit claims* often work best with resistant or opposing audiences, whereas readers who already agree with your view respond well to *direct arguments*. A campus religious organization, for instance, may be less receptive to a poster that screams "Get prayer out of our public schools!" than to a photo advertisement that raises issues of church-state separation by depicting an elementary classroom in which one child sits isolated as the teacher leads the rest of the class in prayer. When you make implicit arguments, however, be sure that they are absolutely clear—you don't want your audience to miss your point.

WHO WILL LISTEN?

■ In determining your target **audience,** ask yourself, Who cares about this issue? Who should care? What kind of text is most likely to reach this group? The answers to these questions should help you make the initial choices of medium, genre, and claim. Once you've begun drafting, keep in mind the characteristics of your audience as you develop your ideas: How much background information will your readers need to understand your claim? What opinions do they likely have about this subject? What values and emotions do they bring to the issue? Most important of all, what do you want them to believe or do as a result of your argument?

WHAT DO YOU NEED TO KNOW?

■ Before you take a position on any issue, **research** it thoroughly. You'll need to understand its complexities and have accurate information at hand to present a **credible** claim. Of course, few—perhaps none—of the facts, figures, and testimony you encounter in your research will actually appear in your visual text; such material, however, helps you make informed choices about how to present your argument. For example, Melissa Johnson reviewed a number of statistics related to child abuse in the United States before she created "Are You Licensed?"; of these, only one shows up in the visual text. However, these data shaped her opinion that many parents are poorly suited to raise children—a conclusion that directly influenced her claim.

HOW WELL DOES IT WORK?

■ Once you've generated a draft of your text, assess its effectiveness and identify areas that need **revision.** If possible, show the draft to several members of your target audience and ask them to comment on the clarity and effectiveness of your argument. Don't forget to **cite** any outside sources you use in your argument. Edit the text and fine-tune the design and format before submitting the final version. For advice on revision and editing, consult Chapter 2.

Additional Student Work
www.ablongman.com/beyondwords41

STUDENT SAMPLE

Melissa Johnson, "Are You Licensed?" A Public Service Advertisement to Prevent Child Abuse

"The first thing a viewer's eyes are drawn to is the bold lettering in the center of the picture: 'Are you licensed?' The lettering is red to draw attention and connect with the word *help* at the top. It is asking a rhetorical question; the viewer most likely does have some kind of license. But underneath . . . is another line: 'to be a parent.' Then the viewer needs to stop and think, 'You don't need a license to be a parent. Do you?'"

■ ■ ■

"[I chose the] black-and-white photo to give the feeling of sadness. The older girl is looking right into the viewer's eyes. She has a slight smile that looks forced. She is clinging to her sister as if they have . . . no one else. The younger girl is looking off to the side. Her longing look makes you wonder what she's looking for and want to reach out and help."

—MELISSA JOHNSON

81% of child abuse victims were abused by a parent.
The facts are startling.
Problems this gigantic don't fix themselves.
Get educated and find out what you can do to
HELP.

Are you licensed?
to be a parent

1-800-2HELP-NOW   www.childabuseinfo.org

FYI Jon Foster has been shooting action sports, most notably surfing, windsurfing, and snowboarding, for more than twenty-five years. His photographs have appeared in publications around the world. He was an associate photo editor of *Breakout Surf* magazine in the late 1980s and the photo editor, chief photographer, and editor-in-chief of *TransWorld Snowboarding* magazine from 1990 to 2002. He also was the executive producer of *TransWorld Snowboarding Video* magazine. Foster is currently the publisher and creative director of a new snowboarding magazine, *The Snowboard Journal*.

6 Interlude

JON FOSTER

snowboard and surf photography

Snowboard photography has some very specific and demanding challenges. Knowledge of the sport is absolutely essential to getting great shots of snowboarding. You must know what the riders are doing, when they are doing it right, and what the peak of that particular action or move is. The lighting, angle, composition, and exposure can all be perfect. But unless the image captures the perfect moment in the maneuver, the photo will not be considered any good.

For the photograph of the road gap jump on page 592, I had an easy time moving around on this small road in Norway, although watching out for cars was a concern. A nearby resort was closed, and I had five of the top snowboarders in the world with me ready to shoot. The weather was getting worse by the minute. It looked like it would be bad for days and that the trip would be over and I would be returning with no photos. Some of the riders decided that it might be fun to jump across this road gap. After much discussion of the speed needed from the hill and the snow conditions, which dictate the speed of the board on the snow, a few test runs were made to the edge of the road. The athletes decided that it was possible and they were going to jump it, landing on the other side of the road.

I had to decide quickly how I was going to shoot the photo. There were two directions of the road to choose from. I chose this point of view because the sky looked slightly lighter than in the other direction, which I knew would show off the snowboarder better. I also had to decide whether to stay down on the road or shoot from the snowbank edge, where I would be able to see the approach and landing and possibly get sequences of the whole jump. I

593

knew that once they started I wouldn't have time to move—maybe only one or two jumps would happen, or maybe the first guy would fall to the street below. I chose the angle from the street because I liked seeing the height of the cut snowbank and the added danger of cars coming toward the camera.

I quickly loaded the camera with high-speed black-and-white film, as the available light was still dropping. The first rider was on his way. I would not be able to see him until he was in the air. I composed the frame for what I could see and where I imagined he would be in the air. I left room at the top of the frame because I didn't know high he would be and I didn't want to lose the view of the road. This is Jamie Lynn's second jump, and he spun 540 degrees with a perfect board grab while clearing the gap. His style is perfect.

The black-and-white film and the somewhat ominous sky add to the sense of danger. The assorted cars, driving and parked, with one driver having jumped from his car to see what was going on, add to the spontaneous, slightly chaotic feeling on the ground juxtaposed against a snowboarder in complete control, spinning above it all.

■ ■ ■

For the photo below, I wanted to get the mountains in the background. Besides being beautiful, large peaks, they were slightly shadowed in a blue cast, which I knew would allow the snowboarder, who was brightly lit in full sunlight, to pop from the background. The snowboarder's red pants helped with this also. To accentuate the contrast between the rider and the back-

ground, I used a telephoto lens to slightly blur the background and make it appear closer. I shot the photo vertically to get the tall mountain peak in the background. Then I shot some horizontal photos with a wide angle to get more of the takeoff and landing for reference. I chose this one partly because a full-page vertical was needed for a magazine and video box cover. I think it is a good photo, mainly due to the position and skill of the snowboarder, who is mid-spin with perfect style. The lighting is great and there are huge mountain peaks in the background, a combination that is not easy to find.

For the photo on page 595, taken during a photo shoot with a few professional snowboarders, we took a snowcat into the backcountry of Colorado looking for pristine, uncrowded conditions. We found this band of rocky cliffs as we rode down the backside of one of the mountain peaks. There were three or four good places to jump from with good steep landings.

After seeing Joe Curtes in the air a few times, I was able to move in closer to the rocks, which placed him against the sky instead of the trees. It also helped make him stand out from the background and accented the white trail of snow coming from his board. I chose a wide-angle lens to enlarge the rocks in the foreground. The sticks and tree limb sticking out are other interesting elements that almost seem to frame the rider. He is grabbing the tail of his board at the peak of his air with seemingly effortless style. This is the essential ingredient of a good action shot. The color and lighting are as good as they could possibly be.

The composition of the original photograph (on the left) is good, but I found that when I cropped it a little at the top of the frame (right), it was better.

■ ■ ■

Surf photography has its own set of challenges and difficulties. You are at the mercy of the weather and the problems of getting around, jockeying for the best angle to shoot from, but with surfing, you also have the waves to deal with. Surf photography has two means of approach. The first is standing on the beach with huge telephoto lenses and a sturdy tripod. The pluses to this approach are that you have visual contact with the surfers and can shoot most of the action happening in front of you. The disadvantages are that you are stationary and your angle of shooting stays pretty much the same; long lenses are affected by haze and dirt in the air, which degrades the image; and there are mosquitoes, intense heat, or cold and rain.

The second approach is from the water. If you are in the water, you need a waterproof housing protecting your camera and lenses. You need to be an experienced surfer and have a knowledge of waves and what the surfers are doing. An option is to shoot in the water from a boat which is ideal if you have deep channels of ocean near shallow reefs where waves are breaking.

I took the photo below halfway into a two-week boat trip in some islands off Sumatra, and the waves were not cooperating. I had prepared for every eventuality I could think of, including every lens I might need, and had various waterproof containers to keep the photography equipment and film safe, and here we were sitting for days waiting for waves.

Todd Chesser, the surfer in this photo, decided to paddle out and wait for a wave even though there were no signs of any on the horizon. After a considerable amount of time, he paddled for and caught a very small wave. I kept my eye on him, as every once in a while he would catch another. Then I noticed three young local boys paddling from the other direction in their dugout canoe. If somehow I could get the canoe in the foreground, while Todd was surfing a wave, I knew I would have something. I could see a slight swell on the horizon making its way toward Todd. This could be it.

The swell was forming into a wave as it met the resistance of the shallow reef. Todd caught the wave and made his first turn. He is flying out to the shoulder of the wave, putting him as close to the canoe as he is going to get. He leans into a hard cutback (a turn back into the wave). I'm waiting and fire two or three shots at seven frames a second to catch the peak of the action. And there is the photo. After much waiting and preparing and thinking and planning, it comes down to brief seconds, or one one-thousandth of a second, of the shutter fired on instinct that comes from years of shooting and waiting.

I like this photo for a couple of reasons. It is a good surf photo because an excellent surfer is at the peak action of a great cutback. Then there is also the old, handmade dugout canoe in the foreground contrasting against the modern fiberglass surfboard slicing through

the water. The inclusion of the canoe also gives a sense of place that would be lacking if only a surfer were on the wave.

Todd Chesser died in the surf on the north shore of Oahu three years after I took this photo. The original picture was in color. I printed the black-and-white version for a memorial page in a national surf magazine. I think I prefer it that way.

■ ■ ■

The photo at right is a good example of how things can just happen in front of your camera and you have to be able to react quickly on instinct.

We had just finished a day of shooting snowboarding. I was standing on a slope, just kind of watching as the riders headed down toward the cabin. One rider had made opposing S turns, creating a nice figure eight in the snow on his way down the slope. Jason Brown rode up to me and without really stopping yelled that he was "going to dot the *I*'s on those eights all the way down and you should shoot it," his voice trailing off as he passed me by. I quickly swung around my camera with an attached zoom lens—a lens I keep on that camera for just these kind of surprises—zoomed in slightly, and squeezed off three shots with the motor drive before he got too far away.

This photo works because it tells a story. It is composed to show the figure eights all the way down, continuing out of the frame. This photo captures the fun and playfulness of snowboarding and illustrates that sometimes decisions have to be made in split seconds when shooting sports like snowboarding.

CHALLENGE

1. Jon Foster provides detailed accounts of how he created the photographs in this interlude. Read these narratives closely, then prepare a short essay that summarizes the principles of successful action photography you can deduce from these stories. What skills, elements, and circumstances need to converge to produce memorable shots? In preparing this summary, you might also consider how widely these principles apply to other kinds of photography. For example, would the skills that make a photographer of athletes successful also work for a landscape or wedding photographer?

2. In a few hundred words, tell the story of an intriguing or arresting photograph you have taken yourself. It can be a carefully crafted shot or one you took with your cell phone. Give readers both any photographic details you remember and the full story behind the shot: where you were, what or whom the photograph captures, what it expresses. Unless you are, in fact, an experienced photographer, the people or events in the image will likely interest readers more than the techniques that produced it. Feel free to pair up photographs or even discuss a related series of images you created.

For additional writing projects related to this Interlude see www.ablongman.com/beyondwords42

IMAGE CREDITS

P. xi, Sean Gallup/Getty Images; 20th Century Fox/The Kobal Collection/Tursi, Mario; p. 1, Warner Universal Pictures/Zuma Press; p. 6, Scala/Art Resource, NY; p. 7, top, Bildarchiv Steffens/Bridgeman Art Library; bottom, HIP/Art Resource, NY; p. 9, left, Muzammil Pasha/Reuters; right, Sayed Salahuddin/Reuters; pp. iii, 11, 15, 16, 28, 44, Pere Borrell del Caso/Banco de España Biblioteca; p. 12, top, Courtesy David Nutley, www.nutleys.com; p. 12, center right, Copyright The Frick Collection, New York; center left, Agi Orsi Productions/Vans Off The Wall/The Kobal Collection/Pat Darrin; bottom, American Illustrators Gallery, NYC/www.asapworldwide.com;/www.bridgeman.co.uk; p. 13, top, © 2002, 2004 www.odt.org; center, Toyota/AP/Wide World Photos; bottom, Motion Picture Association of America (MPAA), 2004; p. 17, David Muench/Muench Photography Inc.; p. 19, Brand X Pictures/Alamy Images; p. 20, The Advertising Archives; p. 21, Bettmann/CORBIS; p. 22, Bettmann/CORBIS; p. 24, bottom, Liz Boyd/Alamy Images; top, Bizuayehu Tesfaye/AP/Wide World Photos; p. 25, top, *Woman Holding a Balance*, Widner Collection, Image © 2004 Board of Trustees, National Gallery of Art, Washington; bottom, Copyright Daimler Chrysler Corporation. Used with permission; p. 26, left, *The Examiner*, San Francisco, California; right, *The Hartford Courant*, A Tribune Publishing Company; center, © *The Arizona Republic*, September 12, 2001. Used with permission. Permission does not imply endorsement. p. 27, top, *Albuquerque Journal*, Albuquerque Publishing Company; bottom, *The Calgary Sun*; p. 28, top, Courtesy MIT Museum; p. 29, top, Bizuayehu Tesfaye/AP/Wide World Photos; p. 30, Stephen Breen/Copley News Service; p. 31, Photofest; p. 32, right, DECLA-BIOSCOP/The Kobal Collection; left, Bizuayehu Tesfaye/AP/Wide World Photos; p. 35, SCALA/Art Resource, NY; p. 39, Rick Friedman/CORBIS; p. 41, left, Mark Ulriksen for *The New Yorker*; right Mark Ulriksen; p. 42, top, Bill Greene/*The Boston Globe*; p. 43, top, Bonnie Gayle Morrill; p. 45, left and right, Gehry Partners, LLP; pp. iii, 47, Courtesy David Nutley, www.nutleys.com; p. 52,, Rob Elliott/AFP/Getty Images; p. 55, Dorothea Lange/Library of Congress; p. 56, top, Courtesy The Dorothea Lange Collection, Oakland Museum of California; p. 58, Howard Sochurek/TimeLife Pictures/Getty Images; p. 60, bottom, 20th Century Fox/The Kobal Collection; p. 61, Tim Sloan/AFP/Getty Images; p. 62, Tim Sloan/AFP/Getty Images; p. 64, Tony Garcia/Getty Images; p. 65, top, Henrick Sorensen/Getty Images; bottom, Paul Franz/AP/Wide World Photos; p. 66, center, Lewis W. Hine/New York Public Library/Art Resource, NY; bottom, 20th Century/Fox/Dreamworks/The Kobal Collection/Francois Duhamel; p. 69, Getty Images; p. 70, Grant Wood, *American Gothic*, 1930, Friends of American Art Collection, 1930.934. Reproduction, The Art Institute of Chicago; p. 72, Photofest; p. iv, 74, Copyright The Frick Collection, New York; p. v, 75, Cover Illustration by Roberto Prada From *Rolling Stone*, July 24, 2003. © Rolling Stone LLC 2003. All Rights Reserved. Reprinted by Permission; p. 79, Bettmann/CORBIS; p. 81, Bettmann/CORBIS; p. 82, right, Walker Evans/Library of Congress; left, Photo courtesy International Museum of Photography and Film, George Eastman House. Reprinted with permission of Joanna T. Steichen; p. 84, Harry Benson/Express/Getty Images; p. 85, left, Erich Lessing/Art Resource, NY; center, Scala/Art Resource, NY; right, Giraudon/Art Resource, NY; p. 86, 87, 88, Dorothea Lange/Library of Congress; p. 90, Ian White/*WIRED*, Conde Nast Publications Inc.; p. 91 © Man Ray Trust/ADAGP-ARS/Telimage-2004; p. 93, right, Northwestern University Library, Edward S. Curtis's 'The North American Indian': the Photographic Images, 2001. http://memory.loc.gov/ammem/award98/ienhtml/curthome.html; center, Gertrude Käsebier/ The National Museum of American History, Smithsonian Institution; left, Northwestern University Library, Edward S. Curtis's 'The North American Indian': the Photographic Images, 2001 http://memory.loc.gov/ammem/award98/ienhtmlcurthome.html; p. 95, Bettmann/CORBIS; p. 98, right, Richard Ray Whitman; p. 99, right, Hulleah J. Tsinhnahjinnie; p. 100, William Albert Allard/National Geographic Society p. 101, Coles Hairston; p.

103, Bernard Williams; p. 105, Courtesy Zoe Leonard. Photo: Mark Woods; pp. 109, 112, 142–143, Covers Courtesy of *Rolling Stone*, 2004 © Rolling Stone LLC 2005 All Rights Reserved. Reprinted by Permission; p. 110, Robert Laberge/Getty Images; p. 116, Jose Azel/Aurora Photos; p. 118, Chris Hondros/Getty Images; pp. 137, 138, 139, Hulton Archive/Getty Images; p. 123, top and bottom, Jim Goldberg/Magnum Photos, Inc.; p. 128, Steve McCurry/Magnum Photos, Inc.; p. 130, top, Bruce Davidson/Magnum Photos, Inc.; bottom, Steve McCurry/Magnum Photos, Inc.; p. 132, Denis O'Regan/CORBIS; p. 134, Francesco Mastalia; p. 140, Metronome/Getty Images; p. v, 160, 163, ©David Hockney. Photo courtesy of Tate Gallery, London/Art Resource, NY; pp. v, 161, Agi Orsi Productions/Vans Off The Wall/The Kobal Collection/ Pat Darrin; p. 165, top, David Muench/Muench Photography Inc.; bottom, Retrofile; p. 166, Photograph: Jack MacDonough/Milwaukee Art Museum; p. 167, Melissa Ann Pinney/Catherine Edelman Gallery; 169, right, left, bottom, Alice Attie; p. 171, Van Gogh Museum, Amsterdam, The Netherlands/Art Resource, NY; p. 172, top, Acquired through the Lillie P. Bliss Bequest. (472.1941) The Museum of Modern Art, New York, NY. Digital Image © The Museum of Modern Art/Licensed by SCALA/Art Resource, NY; p. 173, Library of Congress; p. 174, Susan Meiselas/Magnum Photos, Inc.; p. 175, Marc Riboud/Magnum Photos, Inc.; p. 176, Stephen Shore; p. 177, Gueorgui Pinkhassov/Magnum Photos, Inc.; p. 179, right, Hulton|Archive Photos/Getty Images; p. 180, right, The Advertising Archives; left, San Francisco Museum of Modern Art, Accessions Committee Fund: gift of Barbara and Gerson Bakar. ©William Eggleston. Photography: Ben Blackwell; p. 181, top, Bill Owens/www.billowens.com; bottom, New Line/The Kobal Collection-Ralph Nelson Jr.; p. 182, The Advertising Archives; pp. 183, 184, Wes Thompson/CORBIS; pp. 187, 190, 194, Steve Dunwell/Index Stock Imagery, Inc.; p. 188, Paul Conrath/Getty Images; p. 192, Dana Hoff/Beateworks/Getty Images; p. 196, bottom, Agi Orsi Productions/Vans Off the Wall/The Kobal Collection/Glen E. Friedman; top, Mark J. Terrill/AP/Wide World Photos; p. 197, Agi Orsi Productions/Vans Off The Wall/The Kobal Collection/Pat Darrin; p. 199, Mark J. Terrill/AP/Wide World Photos; p. 202, Courtesy The City of Santa Clara, CA Skate Park; pp. 205 top, 209 top, Private Collection; bottom, Grayce Roessler/Index Stock Imagery, Inc.; p. 206, right, left, Photo courtesy Food for the Poor, www.foodforthepoor.org; p. 212, Frank Micelotta/Getty Images; p. 215, bottom, Grayce Roessler/Index Stock Imagery, Inc.; p. 217, Marc A. Williams; p. 218, right, Ralph Barker; p. 218, left, Morgan Foehl; p. 224, The Advertising Archives; p. 227, Retrofile; pp. vi, 246, American Illustrators Gallery, NYC/ www.asapworldwide.com;/www.bridgeman.co.uk; pp. 249, 262top, Archer Street/Delux/Lion's Gate/The Kobal Collection/Jaap Buitendijk; p. 250, Courtesy Pixel Press, www.pixelpress.org; p. 254, Dave Mirra ©2004 America's Dairy Farmers and Milk Processors. Courtesy Lowe New York; p. 255, Martin Parr/Magnum Photos, Inc.; p. 256, Vince Paolo Gerace/CORBIS; p. 257, ©Harold and Esther Edgerton Foundation, 2005, courtesy of Palm Press, Inc.; p. 258, Lewis Hine/Library of Congress; p. 260, top, M. Eliason/*Santa Barbara News*/Zuma Press/CORBIS; center, Phil Klein/CORBIS; bottom, Armando Arorizo/Zuma Press/CORBIS; p. 262, bottom, Dreamworks/Universal/The Kobal Collection; p. 263, left, Dreamworks/Jinks/Cohen/The Kobal Collection/Lorey Sebastian; right, Dreamworks/Jinks/Cohen/The Kobal Collection/Lorey Sebastian; 265, top, bottom, Library of Congress; p. 268, Scott Peterson/Getty Images; p. 273, Hulton Archive/Getty Images; p. 274, George Strock/Hulton Archive/Getty Images; p. 278, right, Paramount/The Kobal Collection; left, Warner Bros./The Kobal Collection; p. 279, left, Warner Bros./The Kobal Collection; right, Zuma Press; pp. 280, 281, MGM/The Kobal Collection; pp. 283, 285, Universal/The Kobal Collection; pp. 289, 291, Polygram/Working Title/The Kobal Collection; p. 299, Courtesy Drawn and Quarterly; p. 304, Courtesy Dan Clowes; pp. 308–309, First published in *McSweeny's Quarterly* and *McSweeny's Quarterly Concern* and reprinted by permis-

598   IMAGE CREDITS

sion of Chris Ware and Aragi Inc.; pp. vii, 330, 331, © 2002, 2004 www.odt.org; p. 333, The Fuller Projection Map design is a trademark of the Buckminster Fuller Institute ©1938, 1967 & 1992. All rights reserved. www.bfi.org; p. 338, top, The Advertising Archives; bottom, Mike Agliolo/Photo Researchers, Inc.; p. 339, Kathy Willens/AP/Wide World Photos; p. 340, top, Werner Forman/Art Resource, NY; p. 342, top, Chris Sattlberger/Photo Researchers, Inc.; p. 347, NASA; p. 356, Copyright 2002 Cartography Associates and Telemorphic, Inc. All rights reserved.; p. 358, *Lewis and Clark at Three Forks,* E.S. Paxson, 1912. Courtesy of the Montana Historical Society. Don Beatty photographer 10/1999; p. 361, top, Image provided through NASA's Stennis Space Center Earth Science Enterprise Scientific Data Purchase Program; Procured, under NASA contract from Space Imaging. Original maps courtesy the William Robertson Coe Collection, Yale University; bottom, Image provided through NASA's Stennis Space Center Earth Science Enterprise Scientific Data Purchase Program; Procured, under NASA contract from Space Imaging; p. 363, Image provided through NASA's Stennis Space Center Earth Science Enterprise Scientific Data Purchase Program; Procured, under NASA contract from Digital Globe; p. 366, right, LADA/Photo Researchers, Inc.; left, GE Medical Systems/Photo Researchers, Inc.; p. 368, top, bottom, Image courtesy of Dr. Stephen Smith, Oxford University Centre for Functional MRI of the Brain; p. 375, Illustration by John MacNeill; p. 378, top, Eduardo Kac, *GFP Bunny, 2000. Alba, the fluorescent rabbit.* Courtesy the artist and Julia Friedman Gallery; bottom left, Bill Scanga; bottom right, Courtesy Daniel Lee and OK Harris Works of Art; p. 379, right, Susan Robb; p. 390, Kenn Brown/Mondolithic Studios; p. 394, Yoshikazu Tsuno/AFP/Getty Images; pp. 405, 407, 409, Documenting the American South (http://docsouth.unc.edu), The University of North Carolina at Chapel Hill Libraries, North Carolina Collection; pp. viii, 424, General Motors Corporation/AP/Wide World Photos; pp. viii, 425, Toyota/AP/Wide World Photos; p. 426, AP/Wide World Photos; p. 427, Orlin Wagner/AP/Wide World Photos; p. 429, Paramount/Andrew Schwartz/The Kobal Collection; p. 430, top, Everett Collection; bottom left, Zuma Press; p. 431, Rachel Epstein/PhotoEdit Inc.; p. 433, left, Chuck Pefley/Alamy Images; right, Joseph Sohm/Chromosohm, Inc./CORBIS; p. 435, Nevada Wier/CORBIS; p. 436, top, RKO/The Kobal Collection; bottom left, Andrew D. Bernstein/NBAE/Getty Images; bottom right, Jason Szenes/EPA/Landov; p. 437, 2005 General Motors Corporation. Used with permission of HUMMER and General Motors.; p. 439, left, right, Courtesy Antenna Designs; p. 441, left, Michael Rakowitz; right, Brad Simmons/Beateworks Inc./Alamy; p. 443, www.humanscale.com; p. 446, Olivier Pojzman/Zuma Press/NewsCom; p. 450, Justin Sullivan/Getty Images; p. 458, Richard B. Levine/NewsCom; p. 459, Norbert von der Groeben/The Image Works; p. 467, General Motors Corporation/AP/Wide World Photos; p. 468, Toyota/AP/Wide World Photos; pp. 472, top, bottom,, 474, top, bottom, Pascal Le Segretain/Getty Images; p. 475, right, Courtesy of General Motors Corporation/Zuma Press; p. 475, left, Getty Images; p. 476, bottom, Pontiac/Zuma Press; p. 476, top, SSPL/The Image Works; center, Stan Honda/AFP/Getty Images; p. 479, Tom Smart; p. 481, Courtesy Antenna Designs; p. 505, Philip Wegener/Index Stock Imagery, Inc.; p. 484, Scott Gries/Getty Images; p. 487 Nick Gunderson/Corbis; p. 506, Robert Harding World Imagery/Getty Images; p. 508, Library of Congress; pp. ix, 516, Modern Humorist, Inc.; pp. ix, 517, Motion Picture Association of America (MPAA), 2004; p. 521, Library of Congress; p. 522, Mark Gibson/Index Stock Imagery, Inc.; p. 523, bottom, ©1981 Ester Hernandez; p. 525, top, Charles Porter/Zuma Press; bottom, Copyright, Tribune Media Services, Inc. All Rights Reserved. Reprinted with Permission.; p. 526, The Advertising Archives; p. 527, US Bureau of the Census. Reprinted by permission of the artist, Jerry Ingram.; p. 528, Zhang Ziyi ©2002 America's Dairy Farmers and Milk Processors. Courtesy Lowe New York; p. 531, Photo courtesy of The Oakland Museum of California; p. 532, National Museum of American History, Smithsonian Institution, Behring Center; p. 533, top, From *The Great Unravelling: Losing Our Way In The New Century* by Paul Krugman. Copyright ©2003 by Paul Krugman. Used by permission of W.W. Norton & Company, Inc.; bottom, Reproduced by permission of Penguin Books Ltd.; p. 535, Courtesy Vintage Vantage; p. 540, Beth Durbin/*Mount Vernon News*; p. 545, right, The Advertising Archives; p. 550, Getty Images; p. 551, left, The Advertising Archives; p. 553, Getty Images; p. 555, Paramount/The Kobal Collection; p. 556, bottom, top, 557, ©2004 Lauren Greenfield/VII; p. 566, top, Abigail Seymour; bottom, Kenneth Dickerman; p. 567, right, From the Collection of Ms. Janet Fleisher. Photo courtesy Fleisher Ollman Gallery; left, Gift of Donald M. Anderson. Collection of the Madison Museum of Contemporary Art, Wisconsin; p. 568, The Advertising Archives; p. 571, right, Mike Segar/Reuters/NewsCom; pp. 576, 579, 580, Susan Luftschein/http://911digitalarchive.org; pp. 586, left, right, 587 top, bottom, Library of Congress.

TEXT CREDITS

Chapter 1

p. 4, "Homepage"CNN, August 27, 2004. Copyright © 2004 by CNN. Usage of this CNN material does not constitute an implied or expressed endorsement by CNN. **p. 5,** From "The Fan Films Strike Back" by M.E. Russell from The Weekly Standard, May 14, 2004. Copyright © 2004. Reprinted by permission. / From THEFORCE.NET Theatre FanFilms.com, April 18, 2004. Copyright © 2004 by THEFORCE.NET. Used by permission. / Screen shots reprinted by permission from Apple Computer, Inc. **p. 23** "Clearances" from *The Haw Lantern* by Seamus Heaney. Copyright © 1998 by Seamus Heaney. Reprinted by permission of publishers Faber and Faber Ltd. **p. 25,** From "All American?" by Jamie Kitman from Automobile Magazine, June 2004. Reprinted by permission. **p. 26,** Front page, San Francisco Examiner, September,12, 2001. Copyright © 2001 The Examiner. Used by permission. / Front page, The Arizona Republic, September 12, 2001. Copyright © 2001 The Arizona Republic. Used by permission. **pp. 28–29,** From "Building for Science" by Robert Campbell from Boston Globe, April 18, 2004. Copyright © 2004. Reprinted with permission. **p. 29,** From "the 411" Found Magazine, October 14, 2004. Copyright © 2004 Found Magazine. Used by permission. **p. 35,** "The New Typography" by Jan Tschichold, translated by Ruari McLean, introduction by Robin Kinross. Copyright © 1995 Regents of the University of California, © 1987 Brinkmann & Bose. Reprinted with permission. **pp. 37, 43,** From "The Way Forward Making It Work" by Hamish McRae. Reprinted by permission of the author. **p. 39,** From "Dizzying Heights" by Robert Campbell from Boston Globe, April 25, 2004. Copyright © 2004. Reprinted with permission. **p. 44,** By William Carlos Williams, from COLLECTED POEMS: 1909-1939, VOLUME I, copyright © 1938 by New Directions Publishing Corp. Reprinted by permission of New Directions Publishing Corp.; **p. 45,** From "MIT Splices Whimsy Into Its Architectural DNA? by Lawrence Biemiller. The Chronicle of Higher Education, May 7, 2004. Reprinted by permission.

Chapter 2

p. 47, Nutley & Nutley, Ltd., "Dark Skies", September, 2004. Copyright © 2004. Reprinted with permission. **p. 48,** Nutley & Nutley, Ltd., "Lightsabre Rotoscoping Tutorial", September, 2004. Copyright © 2004. Reprinted with permission. **p. 49,** From "The Fan Films Strike Back" by M.E. Russell from The Weekly Standard, May 14, 2004. Copyright © 2004. Reprinted by permission. **p. 59,** From "The Ocean, The Bird, and The Scholar" by Helen Vendler. 2004 Jefferson Lecture. Reprinted by permission of the author.

p. **442,** "A Machine for Sitting" interview by Pilar Viladas, from New York Times Magazine, November 30, 2003. Copyright © 2003 by The New York Times Co. Reprinted with permission. **p. 445,** "The Guts of a New Machine" by Rob Walker, from The New York Times Magazine, November 30, 2003. Copyright © 2003 by The New York Times Co. Reprinted by permission. **p. 462,** "Local iPod sick of playing Avril Lavigne" by Chris Rose, Texas Travesty, March 2003. Copyright © 2003 Texas Travesty. Reprinted by permission. **p. 463,** From "The Principles of Universal Design". Copyright © 1997 NC State University. The Center for Universal Design. **p. 465,** "A Prius-Hummer War Divides Oscarville" by Sharon Waxman, March 7, 2004. Copyright © 2004 by The New York Times Co. Reprinted with permission. **p. 470,** "Women Giving the Directions: Now It's Time for Female Designers" by Warren Brown, April 29, 2004. Copyright © 2004, The Washington Post, reprinted with permission. **p. 475,** "Why We'll See More Ugly Cars" by Martin Wolk, from MSNBC, October 9, 2003. Copyright © 2003 MSNBC. Reprinted by permission. **p. 478,** "My Life, My Cadillac Escalade EXT" as told to Dana White from New York Times, March 5, 2004. Copyright © 2004 by The New York Times Co. Reprinted by permission. **p. 480,** "First Things First Manifesto 2000" from Émigré Magazine, No. 51, 1999. Copyright © 1999. Reprinted with permission. **p. 482,** "Hysteria" by J. Keedy from Adbusters Magazine, No. 37, 2001. Copyright © 2001. Reprinted with permission of the author. **p. 486,** "Light Unto the Wealth of Nations" by Virginia Postrel. Reprinted, with permission, from Reason Online. Copyright © 2004 by Reason Foundation, 3415 S. Sepulveda Blvd, Suite 400, Los Angeles, CA 90034. www.reason.com. **p. 490,** "Are you ready for some unswooshing?" by Linda Baker. This article first appeared in Salon.com, at http://www.Salon.com An online version remains in the Salon archives. Reprinted with permission. **p. 491,** Adbusters, "Blackspot Sneaker", Adbusters.org, March 22, 2005. Copyright © 2005 Adbusters.org. Used by permission.

Chapter 8

p. 532, From "A 'Return' of the White Patriarchy?" by Andrew Lewis from Tolerance.org, January 28, 2004. Copyright © 2004 Tolerance.org. Reprinted by permission. **p. 535,** "Punkvoter's Letter to Urban Outfitters" by Al Jourgensen from CNSNews.com, February 26, 2004. Copyright © 2004 CNSNews.com. Reprinted by permission. **p. 537,** PunkVoter, "Homepage" September, 2004. Copyright © 2004 PunkVoter. Reprinted by permission. / From Rockthevote, January 2005. Copyright © 2005 RocktheVote. Reprinted by permission. **p. 538,** "Fighting the Stigma of an Apathetic Generation" by Elizabeth Kwak-Hefferan, from Daily Pennsylvanian, February 5, 2003. Reprinted by permission. **p. 545,** From THE FEMININE MYSTIQUE by Betty Friedan. Copyright © 1983, 1974, 1973, 1963 by Betty Friedan. Used by permission of W.W. Norton & Company, Inc. **p. 546,** "Still Needing the F Word" by Anna Quindlen from Newsweek, October 30, 2003. Copyright © 2003 by Anna Quindlen. Reprinted by permission of International Creative Management, Inc. **p. 549,** "Rosalind Wiseman on Cliques" from *Daughters* (Sept/Oct. 2002), pp: 1, 6-7.Reprinted, with permission, from Daughters: for Parents of Girls; Copyright Dads and Daughters, Duluth, MN $24.95/1 year. 888-849-8476. www.daughters.com **p. 554,** "One 'Mean' Teen Satire" by Michael O'Sullivan from The Washington Post, April 30, 2004. Copyright © 2004, The Washington Post, reprinted with permission. **p. 558,** "Filmmaker offers food for thought" by Jim Keogh, from Telegram and Gazette Worcester, June 10, 2004. Copyright © 2004 Telegram and Gazette Worcester. Reprinted by permission. **p. 561,** "Downsize this! Americans escalate their war on fat" by Daniel B. Wood, from The Christian Science Monitor, March 10, 2004. Copyright © 2004 Christian Science Monitor. Reprinted by permission. **p. 565,** "A tale of two cities, and two Kings" by Eugene Kane from Milwaukee Sentinel, January 24, 2004. Copyright © 2004. Reprinted by permission. **p. 569,** "Are Memorial Designs Too Complex to Last?" by Julie V. Iovine, November 22, 2003. Copyright © 2003 by The New York Times Co. Reprinted by permission. **p. 572,** "Memorial Proposal: Reflecting Absence" by Michael Arad and Peter Walker. Copyright © LMDC 2004. Reprinted with permission of the Lower Manhattan Development Corporation. **p. 574,** "Wonder Land: Build It and They Won't Come" by Daniel Henninger from The Wall Street Journal, December 26, 2003. Copyright © 2003 Reprinted by permission. **p. 577,** "9/11: Commemorative Art, Ritual, and Story" by Steve Zeitlin and Ilana Harlow from Voices, Vol. 27, Fall-Winter, 2001. Copyright © 2001 New York Folklore Society. Reprinted by permission.

INDEX

GUIDE TO writing TIPS